Library of Congress Cataloging in Publication Data

ARYA, JAGDISH C
    Mathematical analysis for business and economics.

    Includes index.
    1. Mathematical analysis. 2. Business mathematics.
3. Economics, Mathematical. I. Lardner, Robin W.,
joint author. II. Title.
QA300.A75   515   80-23293
ISBN 0-13-561019-2

To Niki and Shanti

Printed in the United States of America

10 9 8 7 6 5 4 3

Editorial/production supervision:
    Eleanor Henshaw Hiatt
Interior design and cover design:
    Suzanne Behnke
Editorial assistant: Susan Pintner
Art production: Bob Verbeek, Amy Rosen,
    and Debra Watson
Manufacturing buyer: John Hall

Prentice-Hall International, Inc., *London*
Prentice-Hall of Australia Pty. Limited, *Sydney*
Prentice-Hall of Canada, Ltd., *Toronto*
Prentice-Hall of India Private Limited, *New Delhi*
Prentice-Hall of Japan, Inc., *Tokyo*
Prentice-Hall of Southeast Asia Pte. Ltd., *Singapore*
Whitehall Books Limited, *Wellington, New Zealand*

CONTENTS

iii

PREFACE

This book is designed to provide a two-semester course in basic mathematics at the college or university level for students whose major area is in business or economics or some related discipline. The main areas covered in the book are algebra, finite mathematics, and differential and integral calculus. The level of the book is such as to make it accessible to students in their first year of college.

The orientation of the book is toward the teaching of the applications and use of mathematics rather than toward pure mathematics for its own sake. Proofs of theorems are not stressed and are not given a prominent place in the development of the text. Typically, after stating a particular theorem we have first illustrated it and discussed its significance with a number of examples, and only then has a proof been given. The more difficult proofs are omitted entirely.

This de-emphasis of mathematical detail allows the students who are primarily interested in the applications of mathematics the time to improve their skills in using the various techniques. It is our experience that such students who learn to master the techniques usually develop reasonably sound intuition in the process, and the lack of complete mathematical rigor is not a serious deficiency.

The material in the book has been chosen to consist of those parts of basic mathematics that are of most interest to students majoring in business and economics and also, to a lesser extent, to students in the social sciences. The applications given in these areas have been completely integrated into the development: sometimes a particular application is used to motivate a certain piece of mathematics; elsewhere, a certain mathematical result might be applied either immediately or in a subsequent section, to a particular problem in, say, business analysis. Usually, the applications are given in close proximity to the particular piece of mathematics that is being applied. Having said this, however, it should be added that the mathematics in the book is usually developed "cleanly," that is, not in the context of any particular application. Only after establishing each result at a purely algebraic level is it applied to a practical problem. We believe that it is a mistake to teach a mathematical method within the limited context of one particular application, because then the student is not alerted to the possibly wider applications of the method in other problem areas.

The book is divided into three parts. Part I consists of pre-calculus algebra, Part II covers finite mathematics, and Part III covers calculus. Parts II and III are almost totally independent of each other and can be covered in either order.

The pre-calculus algebra comprises the first six chapters of the book. In the first three of these we have given a fairly detailed review of high-school algebra and of the solution of equations and inequalities in one variable. Students who are familiar with this material may prefer to begin directly with Chapter 4 in which linear equations and systems are discussed. The remainder of the first part consists of a chapter on functions and one on exponentials and logarithms.

The finite mathematics part of the book itself consists of three almost independent parts: Chapter 7 on the mathematics of finance, Chapter 8 on discrete probability, and Chapters 9–11 on matrices, determinants, and linear programming. Chapter 11 on linear programming requires some of the material in Chapter 9, but does not require Chapter 10.

Chapters 12–15 cover the differential calculus of one variable. The first two of these chapters are concerned with the definition and calculation of the derivative and with its significance from various points of view. The next chapter applies differential calculus to optimization and curve sketching, and the fourth of these chapters contains certain more advanced topics in differential calculus.

Chapter 16 and 17 concern integral calculus and its applications. In the first chapter, which covers antiderivatives, a choice is given as to how integration is to be approached. After discussing the substitution method, tables of integration are immediately introduced so that the instructor who wishes to proceed quickly to applications can do so. On the other hand, the instructor who wishes to spend more time on teaching techniques of integration can postpone the section of tables and cover first the final section of Chapter 16. The second of these chapters concerns the definite integral and its application to areas, business analysis, and differential equations.

The final chapter provides an introduction to the calculus of functions of several variables.

By selecting appropriate chapters and/or sections of chapters the book can be used for a variety of different types of courses, as long as the emphasis is toward applications in business and economics. For example, courses in college algebra, algebra and finite mathematics, algebra and calculus, or finite mathematics and calculus can all be taught by making use of selected chapters. The following diagram illustrates the pre-requisite structure of the book, and it will be clear from this diagram how these different types of courses can be put together by making the appropriate selections.

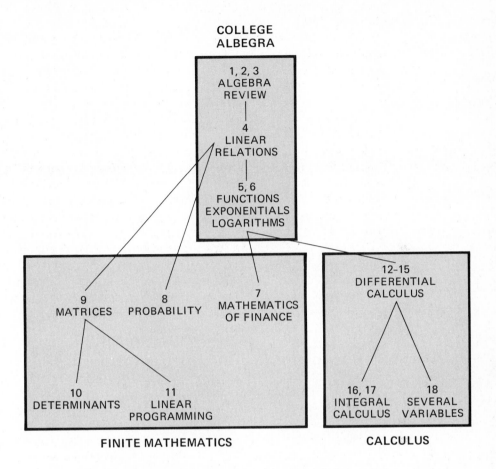

It is a pleasure to acknowledge our indebtedness to those colleagues and students who have made suggestions for improving the book. Our thanks go to Professors David Zerling, Philadelphia College of Textiles and Science; James F. Hurley, University of Connecticut; Terry D. Lenker, Central Michigan University; Frank Wattenberg, University of Massachusetts; Budmon Davis, University of Toledo; and Michael Kostreva, University of Maine at Orono. The reviewers' comments have had a substantial effect on the final form that the book has assumed.

J.C.A.
R.W.L.

ALGEBRA

PART

REVIEW
OF ALGEBRA

CHAPTER

1-1 THE REAL NUMBERS

We shall begin by giving a brief outline of the structure of the real numbers.

The numbers 1, 2, 3, and so on, are called **natural numbers**. If we add or multiply any two natural numbers, the result is always a natural number. For example, $8 + 5 = 13$ and $8 \times 5 = 40$; the sum, 13, and product, 40, are natural numbers. But if we subtract or divide two natural numbers, the result is *not* always a natural number. For example, $8 - 5 = 3$ and $8 \div 2 = 4$ are natural numbers, but $5 - 8$ and $2 \div 7$ are not natural numbers. Thus, within the system of natural numbers, we can always add and multiply but cannot always subtract or divide.

To overcome the limitation of subtraction, we extend the natural number system to the system of **integers**. The integers include the natural numbers, the negative of each natural number, and the number zero (0). Thus we may represent the system of integers by

$$\ldots, -3, -2, -1, 0, 1, 2, 3, \ldots.$$

Clearly, all the natural numbers are also integers. If we add, multiply, or subtract any two integers, the result is always an integer. For example, $-3 + 8 = 5, (-3)(5) = -15$, and $3 - 8 = -5$ are all integers. But we still cannot always divide one integer by another and get an integer as the result. For instance, we see that: $8 \div (-2) = -4$ is an integer, but $-8 \div 3$ is not. Thus, within the system of integers, we can add, multiply, and subtract, but we cannot always divide.

To overcome the limitation of division, we extend the system of integers to the system of **rational numbers**.

A number is a rational number if it can be expressed as a ratio of two integers with the denominator nonzero. Thus $\frac{8}{3}$, $-\frac{5}{7}$, $\frac{0}{3}$, and $6 = \frac{6}{1}$, are examples of rational numbers. We can add, multiply, subtract, and divide any two rational numbers (with division by zero excluded)* and the result is always a rational number. Thus all the four fundamental operations of arithmetic, addition, multiplication, subtraction, and division, are possible within the system of rational numbers.

When a rational number is expressed as a decimal, the decimal either terminates or develops a pattern that repeats indefinitely. For example, $\frac{1}{4} = 0.25$ and $\frac{93}{80} = 1.1625$ both correspond to decimals that terminate, whereas $\frac{1}{6} = 0.1616161\ldots$ and $\frac{4}{7} = 0.5714285714285\ldots$ correspond to decimals with repeating patterns.

*See the final paragraph of this section.

There also exist some numbers in common use that are not rational—that is, they cannot be expressed as the ratio of two integers. For example, $\sqrt{2}$, $\sqrt{3}$, and π are not rational numbers. Such numbers are called **irrational numbers**. The essential difference between rational and irrational numbers can be seen through their decimal expressions. When an irrational number is represented by a decimal, the decimal continues indefinitely without developing any recurrent pattern. For example, to ten decimal places, $\sqrt{2} = 1.4142135623\ldots$ and $\pi = 3.1415926535\ldots$. No matter to how many decimal places we express these numbers, they would never develop a repeating pattern, in contrast to the patterns that occur with rational numbers.

The term **real number** is used to mean a number that is either rational or irrational. The system of real numbers consists of all possible decimals. Those decimals that are terminating or repeating correspond to the rational numbers, while the rest correspond to the irrational numbers.

Geometrically, the real numbers can be represented by the points on a straight line called a **number line**. In order to do this, we select an arbitrary point O on the line to represent the number zero. The positive numbers are then represented by the points to the right of O and the negative numbers by the points to the left of O. If A_1 is a point to the right of O such that OA_1 is of unit length, then A_1 represents the number 1. The integers $2, 3, \ldots, n, \ldots$ are represented by the points $A_2, A_3, \ldots, A_n, \ldots$, which are on the right of O, such that

$$OA_2 = 2OA_1, \quad OA_3 = 3OA_1, \ldots, OA_n = nOA_n, \ldots.$$

Similarly, if $B_1, B_2, \ldots, B_n, \ldots$ are the points to the left of O such that the distances $OB_1, OB_2, OB_3, \ldots, OB_n, \ldots$ are equal to the distances $OA_1, OA_2, \ldots, OA_n, \ldots$, respectively, then the points $B_1, B_2, B_3, \ldots, B_n, \ldots$ represent the negative integers $-1, -2, -3, \ldots, -n, \ldots$. In this way, all the integers can be represented by points on a number line. (See Figure 1.)

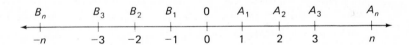

FIGURE 1

Rational numbers can be represented by points on a number line that lie an appropriate fractional number of units from O. For example, the number $\frac{9}{2}$ is represented by the point which lies four and one-half units to the right of O and $-\frac{7}{3}$ is represented by the point which lies two and one-third units to the left of O. In a similar manner, every rational number can be represented by a point on the line.

It turns out that every *irrational* number can also be represented by a point on a number line. Consequently, all the real numbers, both rational and irrational, can be represented by such points. Furthermore, each point on a number line corresponds to one and only one real number. Because of this, it is quite common to use the word *point* to mean *real number*.

Properties of Real Numbers

When two real numbers are added, the result is always a real number; similarly, when two real numbers are multiplied, the result is also always a real number. These two operations of addition and multiplication are fundamental to the system of real numbers, and they possess certain properties which we shall now briefly discuss. These properties by themselves may appear to be rather elementary, perhaps even obvious, but they are vital to understanding the various algebraic manipulations with which we shall later be involved.

COMMUTATIVE PROPERTIES If a and b are any two real numbers, then

$$a + b = b + a \quad \text{and} \quad ab = ba.$$

For example, $3 + 7 = 7 + 3$, $3 + (-7) = (-7) + 3$, $3 \cdot 7 = 7 \cdot 3$, and $(3)(-7) = (-7)(3)$. These properties state that it does not matter in which order two numbers are added or multiplied—we get the same answer whichever order we use. They are known as the **commutative properties of addition and multiplication**, respectively.

ASSOCIATIVE PROPERTIES If a, b, and c are any three real numbers, then

$$(a + b) + c = a + (b + c) \quad \text{and} \quad (ab)c = a(bc).$$

For example, $(2 + 3) + 7 = 2 + (3 + 7) = 12$ and $(2 \times 3) \times 7 = 2 \times (3 \times 7) = 42$. These properties are known as the **associative properties of addition and multiplication**, respectively. They state that if three numbers are being added (or multiplied) together then it does not matter which two of them are added (or multiplied) together first. We get the same answer in either case.

Because of these properties, it is not necessary to write the parentheses in the above expressions. We can write $a + b + c$ for the sum of a, b, and c and abc for their product without ambiguity.

DISTRIBUTIVE PROPERTIES If a, b, and c are real numbers, then

$$a(b + c) = ab + ac \quad \text{and} \quad (b + c)a = ba + ca.$$

For example, $2(3 + 7) = 2(3) + 2(7) = 6 + 14 = 20$. This is clearly true because $2(3 + 7) = 2 \times 10 = 20$. Also, $(-2)[3 + (-7)] = (-2)(3) + (-2)(-7) = -6 + 14 = 8$. We can evaluate the given expression directly, getting the same answer: $(-2)[3 + (-7)] = (-2)(-4) = 8$.

The second form of the distributive property actually follows from the first since, by the commutative property,

$$(b + c)a = a(b + c)$$

and
$$ba + ca = ab + ac$$

Since the two right sides are equal to one another by virtue of the first distributive property, the two left sides must also be equal.

The following examples illustrate some elementary uses of these properties of real numbers in simplifying algebraic expressions.

EXAMPLE 1

(a) $x(y + 2) = xy + x(2)$ (distributive property)
$ = xy + 2x$ (commutative property)

(b) $2x + 3x = (2 + 3)x$ (distributive property)
$ = 5x$

(c) $2(3x) = (2 \times 3)x$ (associative property)
$ = 6x$

(d) $(2x)(3x) = [(2x) \times 3]x$ (associative property)
$ = [(3 \times (2x)]x$ (commutative property)
$ = [(3 \times 2)x]x$ (associative property)
$ = (6x)x$
$ = 6(x \cdot x)$ (associative property)
$ = 6x^2$

where x^2 denotes $x \cdot x$.

This final answer could be obtained by collecting the similar terms in the original product: the numbers 2 and 3 multiplied together give 6 and the two x's multiplied together give x^2. The next part further illustrates this procedure.

(e) $[5(3ab)]2a = (5 \times 3 \times 2)(a \times a)b = 30a^2b$. This answer can be justified with a sequence of steps using the associative and commutative laws, as in the previous example.

(f) $2x + (3y + x) = 2x + (x + 3y)$ (commutative property)
$ = (2x + x) + 3y$ (associative property)
$ = (2x + 1x) + 3y$
$ = (2 + 1)x + 3y$ (distributive property)
$ = 3x + 3y$

The distributive property can be used in the case when more than two quantities are added within the parentheses. That is,

$$a(b + c + d) = ab + ac + ad$$

and so on.

EXAMPLE 2

$4(x + 3y + 4z) = 4x + 4(3y) + 4(4z)$ (distributive property)
$ = 4x + (4 \times 3)y + (4 \times 4)z$ (associative property)
$ = 4x + 12y + 16z$

IDENTITY ELEMENTS   If a is any real number, then

$$a + 0 = a \quad \text{and} \quad a \cdot 1 = a.$$

That is, if 0 is added to a, the result is still a and if a is multiplied by 1, the result is again a. For this reason, the numbers 0 and 1 are often called the **identity elements** for addition and multiplication, respectively, because they leave any number unchanged under their respective operations.

INVERSES If a is any real number, then there exists a unique real number called the **negative of** a (denoted by $-a$) such that

$$a + (-a) = 0.$$

If a is nonzero, there also exists a unique real number called the **reciprocal of** a (denoted by a^{-1}) such that

$$a \cdot a^{-1} = 1.$$

Observe the similarity between these two definitions: when $-a$ is added to a, the result is the additive identity element and when a^{-1} is multiplied by a, the result is the multiplicative identity element. We often refer to $-a$ as the **additive inverse of** a and to a^{-1} as the **multiplicative inverse of** a. (Sometimes a^{-1} is simply called **the inverse of** a.)

EXAMPLE 3   (a) The additive inverse of 3 is -3 since $3 + (-3) = 0$. The additive inverse of -3 is 3 since $(-3) + 3 = 0$. Since the additive inverse of -3 is denoted by $-(-3)$, it follows that $-(-3) = 3$. In fact, a corresponding result holds for any real number a:

$$-(-a) = a.$$

(b) The multiplicative inverse of 3 is 3^{-1} since $3 \cdot 3^{-1} = 1$. The multiplicative inverse of 3^{-1} would be denoted by $(3^{-1})^{-1}$ and would be defined by the requirement that $3^{-1} \cdot (3^{-1})^{-1} = 1$. But since $3^{-1} \cdot 3 = 1$, it follows that $(3^{-1})^{-1}$ is equal to 3.

Again this result generalizes for any nonzero real number a:

$$(a^{-1})^{-1} = a.$$

(The inverse of the inverse of a is equal to a.)

Having defined the additive and multiplicative inverses of a, we can define what we mean by the operations of *subtraction* and *division*. We define $a - b$ to mean the number $a + (-b)$, that is, a plus the negative of b. Similarly, we define $a \div b$ to mean the number ab^{-1}, that is, a multiplied by the reciprocal of b. The expression $a \div b$ is defined only when $b \neq 0$. It is also denoted by the fraction a/b, and we have

$$\frac{a}{b} = ab^{-1}. \tag{1}$$

Putting $a = 1$ in Equation (1), we have $1/b = 1 \cdot b^{-1} = b^{-1}$. Hence the fraction $1/b$ means the same as the multiplicative inverse b^{-1}. For example, $3^{-1} = \frac{1}{3}$. It therefore follows from Equation (1) that

$$\frac{a}{b} = a\left(\frac{1}{b}\right)$$

since $b^{-1} = 1/b$.

EXAMPLE 4   (a) $\dfrac{7}{(1/3)} = 7\left(\dfrac{1}{3}\right)^{-1}$ (Equation (1), with $a = 7$ and $b = \frac{1}{3}$)

$$= 7(3)$$
$$= 21$$

This result extends to any pair of real numbers a and b ($b \neq 0$):

$$\frac{a}{(1/b)} = ab.$$

(b) For any real number b, $(-1)b = -b$. This follows because

$$b + (-1)b = 1 \cdot b + (-1)b$$
$$= [1 + (-1)]b \qquad \text{(distributive property)}$$
$$= 0 \cdot b = 0$$

Therefore, $(-1)b$ must be the additive inverse of b, namely $-b$. Then

$$a(-b) = a[(-1)b]$$
$$= (-1)(ab) \qquad \begin{array}{l}\text{(using associative and} \\ \text{commutative properties)}\end{array}$$
$$= -(ab)$$

For example, $3(-7) = -(3 \cdot 7) = -21$.

(c) $3(x - 2y) = 3[x + (-2y)]$ (definition of subtraction)

$$= 3x + 3(-2y) \qquad \text{(distributive property)}$$
$$= 3x - [3(2y)] \qquad \text{(from part (b))}$$
$$= 3x - [(3 \cdot 2)y] \qquad \text{(associative property)}$$
$$= 3x - 6y$$

In general, the distributive property extends to expressions that involve negative signs. For example,

$$a(b - c) = ab - ac.$$

Thus, we can solve this example more directly.

$$3(x - 2y) = 3x - 3(2y) = 3x - 6y$$

Observe that when an expression inside parentheses is multiplied by a negative quantity, every term inside the parentheses must change sign.

$$-(a + b) = (-1)(a + b) = (-1)a + (-1)b$$
$$= -a - b$$

EXAMPLE 5 $-2(x - 3y) = (-2)x - (-2)(3y)$
$$= -2x + 6y$$

Note that both the x and $-3y$ inside the parentheses change signs, becoming $-2x$ and $+6y$, respectively.

The statement $a/b = c$ is true if and only if the inverse statement $a = b \cdot c$ is true. Consider a fraction in which the denominator b is zero, such as $\frac{3}{0}$. This cannot equal any real number c because the inverse statement $3 = 0 \cdot c$ cannot be true for any c. Therefore $\frac{3}{0}$ is not well defined. Also, $\frac{0}{0}$ is not a well-defined real number because the inverse statement $0 = 0 \cdot c$ is true for all real numbers c. Thus we conclude that any fraction with denominator zero is not a well-defined real unmber or, equivalently, *division by zero is a meaningless operation*.

EXERCISES 1

1. State whether each of the following is true or false. Replace each false statement by a corresponding true statement.

    a. $3x + 4x = 7x$ b. $(3x)(4x) = 7x$
    c. $2(5 - 4y) = 10 - 4y$ d. $-(x + y) = -x + y$
    e. $5x - (2 - 3x) = 2x - 2$ f. $5 - 2x = 3x$
    g. $-3(x - 2y) = -3x - 6y$ h. $(-a)(-b)(-c) \div (-d) = -(abc \div d)$
    i. $a \div (b \div c) = (ac) \div b$ j. $a - (b - c) = (a + c) - b$

    k. $(-x)(-y) = -xy$ l. $\dfrac{-a}{-b} = \dfrac{a}{b}$

(2–45)   Simplify the following expressions.

2. $5 - (-3)$ 3. $-7 - (-3)$ 4. $5(-3)$
5. $(-3)(-7)$ 6. $8 \div (-2)$ 7. $(-9) \div (-3)$
8. $-(2 - 6)$ 9. $-(-4 - 3)$ 10. $(3)(-2)(-4)$
11. $(-5)(-3)(-2)$ 12. $3(1 - 4)$ 13. $2(-2 - 3)$
14. $-2(-4 - 2)$ 15. $-4(3 - 6)$ 16. $-(x - 6)$
17. $-(-x - 3)$ 18. $3(x - 4)$ 19. $2(-x - 3)$
20. $-2(-x - 2)$ 21. $-4(x - 6)$ 22. $-x(y - 6)$
23. $-x(-y - 6)$ 24. $x(-y)(-z)$ 25. $(-x)(-y)(-z)$
26. $(-2)(-x)(x + 3)$ 27. $(-x)(-y)(2 - 3z)$ 28. $2(-a)(3 - a)$
29. $(-3p)(2q)(q - p)$ 30. $x(-2)(-x - 4)$
31. $(-2x)(-3)(-y - 4)$ 32. $2x + 5 - 2(x + 2)$
33. $3x - t - 2(x - t)$ 34. $2(x - y) - x$
35. $4x(x + y) - x^2$ 36. $4[2(x + 1) - 3]$
37. $x[3(x - 2) - 2x + 1]$ 38. $x[-3(-4 + 5) + 3]$
39. $4[x(2 - 5) - 2(1 - 2x)]$ 40. $x^{-1}(x + 2)$
41. $x^{-1}(2x - 1)$ 42. $(-2x)^{-1}(3x - 1)$ 43. $(-3x)^{-1}(6 + 2x)$
44. $(xy)^{-1}(x + y)$ 45. $(-xy)^{-1}(2x - 3y)$

1-2 FRACTIONS

In the previous section, we showed how the fraction a/b is defined as the product of a and the inverse of b:

$$\frac{a}{b} = ab^{-1} \qquad (b \neq 0).$$

In particular,

$$\frac{1}{b} = b^{-1}.$$

From this definition it is possible to derive all the properties which are commonly used in calculating with fractions. In this section, we shall briefly discuss such calculations.*

Multiplication of Fractions

The product of two fractions is obtained by first multiplying the two numerators and then the two denominators.

$$\left(\frac{a}{b}\right)\left(\frac{c}{d}\right) = \frac{ac}{bd}$$

EXAMPLE 1

(a) $\left(\dfrac{2}{3}\right)\left(\dfrac{5}{9}\right) = \dfrac{2\cdot5}{3\cdot9} = \dfrac{10}{27}$

(b) $\left(\dfrac{2x}{3}\right)\left(\dfrac{4}{y}\right) = \dfrac{(2x)4}{3\cdot y} = \dfrac{8x}{3y}$

(c) $3x\left(\dfrac{4}{5y}\right) = \left(\dfrac{3x}{1}\right)\left(\dfrac{4}{5y}\right) = \dfrac{(3x)\cdot4}{1\cdot(5y)} = \dfrac{12x}{5y}$

Division of Fractions

In order to divide one fraction by another, the second fraction is inverted and then multiplied by the first. In other words,

$$\left(\frac{a}{b}\right) \div \left(\frac{c}{d}\right) = \left(\frac{a}{b}\right)\left(\frac{d}{c}\right) = \frac{ad}{bc}.$$

EXAMPLE 2

(a) $\left(\dfrac{3}{5}\right) \div \left(\dfrac{7}{9}\right) = \left(\dfrac{3}{5}\right)\left(\dfrac{9}{7}\right) = \dfrac{27}{35}$

(b) $\left(\dfrac{3x}{2}\right) \div \left(\dfrac{4}{y}\right) = \left(\dfrac{3x}{2}\right)\left(\dfrac{y}{4}\right) = \dfrac{3xy}{8}$

(c) $5y \div \left(\dfrac{6}{5x}\right) = \left(\dfrac{5y}{1}\right)\left(\dfrac{5x}{6}\right) = \dfrac{25xy}{6}$

*Proofs of the quoted properties are given as a series of theorems at the end of this section.

(d) $\left(\dfrac{3}{2x}\right) \div (2y) = \left(\dfrac{3}{2x}\right) \div \left(\dfrac{2y}{1}\right) = \left(\dfrac{3}{2x}\right)\left(\dfrac{1}{2y}\right) = \dfrac{3}{4xy}$

(e) $\left(\dfrac{a}{b}\right)^{-1} = 1 \div \left(\dfrac{a}{b}\right) = 1 \cdot \dfrac{b}{a} = \dfrac{b}{a}$

(That is, the reciprocal of any fraction is obtained by exchanging the numerator and denominator of the fraction.)

Cancellation of Common Factors

The numerator and denominator of any fraction can be multiplied or divided by any *nonzero* number, without changing the value of the fraction.

$$\frac{a}{b} = \frac{ac}{bc} \qquad (c \neq 0)$$

EXAMPLE 3   (a) $\dfrac{a}{b} = \dfrac{2a}{2b}$

(b) $\dfrac{3}{5} = \dfrac{6}{10} = \dfrac{9}{15} = \dfrac{-12}{-20} = \cdots$

(c) $\dfrac{5x}{6} = \dfrac{10x^2}{12x}$ (provided that $x \neq 0$)

This property of fractions can be used in order to reduce a fraction to its **lowest terms**, which means dividing by all the common factors in the numerator and denominator. (This is also called **simplifying the fraction**.)

EXAMPLE 4   (a) $\dfrac{70}{84} = \dfrac{2 \cdot 5 \cdot 7}{2 \cdot 2 \cdot 3 \cdot 7} = \dfrac{\cancel{2} \cdot 5 \cdot \cancel{7}}{\cancel{2} \cdot 2 \cdot 3 \cdot \cancel{7}}$

$\qquad\qquad\quad = \dfrac{5}{2 \cdot 3} = \dfrac{5}{6}$

Observe that the numerator and denominator are first written in terms of their prime factors and then numerator and denominator are divided by those factors which are common to both numbers, namely 2 and 7. (This process is sometimes called *cancelling*.)

(b) $\dfrac{6x^2y}{8xy^2} = \dfrac{2 \cdot 3 \cdot x \cdot x \cdot y}{2 \cdot 2 \cdot 2 \cdot x \cdot y \cdot y} = \dfrac{\cancel{2} \cdot 3 \cdot \cancel{x} \cdot x \cdot \cancel{y}}{\cancel{2} \cdot 2 \cdot 2 \cdot \cancel{x} \cdot y \cdot \cancel{y}}$

$\qquad\qquad = \dfrac{3x}{4y}$

In this example, the numerator and denominator were divided by $2xy$ in the simplification.

(c) $\dfrac{2x(x + 1)}{4y(x + 1)} = \dfrac{x}{2y}$ $(x + 1 \neq 0)$

Here the common factor of $2(x + 1)$ is divided from numerator and denominator.

Addition and Subtraction of Fractions

When two fractions have a common denominator, they may be added by simply adding their numerators.

$$\frac{a}{c} + \frac{b}{c} = \frac{a+b}{c}$$

A similar rule applies for subtraction:

$$\frac{a}{c} - \frac{b}{c} = \frac{a-b}{c}.$$

EXAMPLE 5 (a) $\dfrac{5}{12} + \dfrac{11}{12} = \dfrac{5+11}{12} = \dfrac{16}{12} = \dfrac{4}{3}$

(b) $\dfrac{3}{2x} - \dfrac{5}{2x} = \dfrac{3-5}{2x} = \dfrac{-2}{2x} = -\dfrac{1}{x}$

(Note the cancellation of common factors in arriving at the final answers.)

When two fractions with unequal denominators are to be added or subtracted, the fractions must first be rewritten with the same denominator.

EXAMPLE 6 (a) Find $\dfrac{5}{6} + \dfrac{1}{2}$.

(b) Find $\dfrac{5}{6} - \dfrac{3}{4}$.

Solution (a) We can write $\dfrac{1}{2} = \dfrac{1 \times 3}{2 \times 3} = \dfrac{3}{6}$. Then both fractions have the same denominator, so we can add.

$$\frac{5}{6} + \frac{1}{2} = \frac{5}{6} + \frac{3}{6}$$
$$= \frac{5+3}{6} = \frac{8}{6} = \frac{4}{3}$$

(b) In part (a), we multiplied the numerator and denominator of $\frac{1}{2}$ by 3 to give it a denominator equal to that of the other fraction. In this part, both fractions must be changed to obtain a common denominator. We write

$$\frac{5}{6} = \frac{10}{12} \quad \text{and} \quad \frac{3}{4} = \frac{9}{12}.$$

Therefore

$$\frac{5}{6} - \frac{3}{4} = \frac{10}{12} - \frac{9}{12} = \frac{10-9}{12} = \frac{1}{12}.$$

In general, when adding or subtracting fractions with different denominators, we first replace each fraction by an equivalent fraction having some common denominator. To keep the numbers as small as possible, we choose the smallest possible common denominator, called the **least common denominator** (LCD). We would still get the right answer by using a larger common denominator, but it is preferable to use the smallest possible denominator. For example, in part (b) of Example 6, we could use 24 as a common denominator:

$$\frac{5}{6} - \frac{3}{4} = \frac{20}{24} - \frac{18}{24} = \frac{20 - 18}{24} = \frac{2}{24} = \frac{1}{12}.$$

The final answer is the same, but we had to work with bigger numbers.

In order to find the LCD of two or more fractions, the two denominators must first be written in terms of their prime factors. The LCD is then formed by taking all of the prime factors that occur in any of the denominators. Each such prime factor is included as many times as it occurs in any one denominator. For example, to find the LCD of $\frac{5}{6}$ and $\frac{3}{4}$, we write the denominators as $6 = 2 \cdot 3$ and $4 = 2 \cdot 2$. The prime factors that occur are 2 and 3, but 2 occurs twice in one denominator. So the LCD is $2 \cdot 2 \cdot 3 = 12$. As a second example, consider the LCD of $3/12x$ and $7/10x^2y$. We write

$$12x = 2 \cdot 2 \cdot 3 \cdot x \quad \text{and} \quad 10x^2y = 2 \cdot 5 \cdot x \cdot x \cdot y.$$

Taking each factor the greatest number of times it occurs, we have

$$\text{LCD} = 2 \cdot 2 \cdot 3 \cdot 5 \cdot x \cdot x \cdot y = 60x^2y.$$

EXAMPLE 7 Evaluate: (a) $\dfrac{x}{6} + \dfrac{3y}{4}$; (b) $\dfrac{1}{9x} - \dfrac{1}{6}$; (c) $\dfrac{a}{c} + \dfrac{b}{d}$.

Solution (a) The LCD is 12.

$$\frac{x}{6} = \frac{2x}{12} \quad \text{and} \quad \frac{3y}{4} = \frac{3(3y)}{12} = \frac{9y}{12}$$

Therefore

$$\frac{x}{6} + \frac{3y}{4} = \frac{2x}{12} + \frac{9y}{12}$$

$$= \frac{2x + 9y}{12}.$$

(b) The LCD in this case is $18x$, so

$$\frac{1}{9x} = \frac{2}{18x} \quad \text{and} \quad \frac{1}{6} = \frac{3x}{18x}.$$

Then

$$\frac{1}{9x} - \frac{1}{6} = \frac{2}{18x} - \frac{3x}{18x}$$

$$= \frac{2 - 3x}{18x}.$$

(c) The LCD in this case is cd.

$$\frac{a}{c} + \frac{b}{d} = \frac{ad}{cd} + \frac{bc}{cd}$$

$$= \frac{ad + bc}{cd}$$

We conclude this section by giving proofs of the basic properties of fractions which have been used in the above examples.

THEOREM 1

$$\left(\frac{1}{b}\right)\left(\frac{1}{d}\right) = \frac{1}{bd}$$

PROOF By definition, $\left(\frac{1}{b}\right) = b^{-1}$ and $\left(\frac{1}{d}\right) = d^{-1}$, so that

$$\left(\frac{1}{b}\right)\left(\frac{1}{d}\right) = b^{-1}d^{-1}.$$

But

$$(b^{-1}d^{-1})(bd) = (b^{-1}b)\cdot(d^{-1}d) \qquad \text{(using the associative and commutative properties)}$$
$$= 1\cdot1$$
$$= 1.$$

Therefore $b^{-1}d^{-1}$ must be the multiplicative inverse of bd, that is,

$$b^{-1}d^{-1} = \frac{1}{bd}.$$

Thus

$$\left(\frac{1}{b}\right)\left(\frac{1}{d}\right) = \frac{1}{bd}$$

as required.

Note: This result can be rewritten as $(bd)^{-1} = b^{-1}d^{-1}$.

THEOREM 2

$$\left(\frac{a}{b}\right)\left(\frac{c}{d}\right) = \frac{ac}{bd}$$

PROOF

$$\frac{a}{b} = ab^{-1} = a\left(\frac{1}{b}\right)$$

and

$$\frac{c}{d} = c\left(\frac{1}{d}\right).$$

Therefore, using the commutative and associative properties, we can write

$$\left(\frac{a}{b}\right)\left(\frac{c}{d}\right) = a\left(\frac{1}{b}\right)\cdot c\left(\frac{1}{d}\right)$$
$$= ac\cdot\left(\frac{1}{b}\cdot\frac{1}{d}\right)$$
$$= ac\left(\frac{1}{bd}\right) \qquad \text{(by Theorem 1)}$$
$$= \frac{ac}{bd}$$

as required.

THEOREM 3

$$\left(\frac{a}{b}\right)^{-1} = \frac{b}{a}$$

PROOF　By definition, $a/b = ab^{-1}$.
Therefore, by Theorem 1,

$$\left(\frac{a}{b}\right)^{-1} = (ab^{-1})^{-1} = a^{-1}(b^{-1})^{-1}.$$

But $(b^{-1})^{-1} = b$, so

$$\left(\frac{a}{b}\right)^{-1} = a^{-1}b = ba^{-1}$$

$$= \frac{b}{a}$$

as required.

THEOREM 4

$$\left(\frac{a}{b}\right) \div \left(\frac{c}{d}\right) = \left(\frac{a}{b}\right) \cdot \left(\frac{d}{c}\right)$$

PROOF　By definition, $x \div y = xy^{-1}$. Therefore we have the following.

$$\left(\frac{a}{b}\right) \div \left(\frac{c}{d}\right) = \left(\frac{a}{b}\right) \cdot \left(\frac{c}{d}\right)^{-1}$$

$$= \left(\frac{a}{b}\right) \cdot \left(\frac{d}{c}\right) \qquad \text{(by Theorem 3)}$$

THEOREM 5

$$\frac{a}{b} = \frac{ac}{bc} \qquad (c \neq 0)$$

PROOF　For any $c \neq 0$, the fraction $c/c = 1$, since, by definition $c/c = cc^{-1}$.
Therefore, by Theorem 2,

$$\frac{ac}{bc} = \left(\frac{a}{b}\right) \cdot \left(\frac{c}{c}\right) = \frac{a}{b} \cdot 1$$

$$= \frac{a}{b}$$

as required.

THEOREM 6

$$\frac{a}{c} + \frac{b}{c} = \frac{a+b}{c} \qquad (c \neq 0)$$

PROOF　By definition,

$$\frac{a}{c} = ac^{-1} \quad \text{and} \quad \frac{b}{c} = bc^{-1}.$$

Therefore

$$\frac{a}{c} + \frac{b}{c} = ac^{-1} + bc^{-1}$$

$$= (a + b)c^{-1} \qquad \text{(by the distributive property)}$$

$$= \frac{a + b}{c}$$

as required.

EXERCISES 2

1. State whether each of the following is true or false. Replace each false statement by a corresponding true statement.

    a. $\dfrac{3}{x} + \dfrac{4}{x} = \dfrac{7}{x}$ b. $\dfrac{x}{3} + \dfrac{x}{4} = \dfrac{x}{7}$

    c. $\dfrac{a}{b} + \dfrac{c}{d} = \dfrac{a + c}{b + d}$ d. $\dfrac{a}{b} \cdot \left(\dfrac{c}{d} \cdot \dfrac{e}{f}\right) = \dfrac{ace}{bdf}$

    e. $\left(\dfrac{a}{b} \div \dfrac{c}{d}\right) \div \dfrac{e}{f} = \dfrac{adf}{bce}$ f. $\dfrac{a}{b} \div \left(\dfrac{c}{d} \div \dfrac{e}{f}\right) = \dfrac{adf}{bce}$

    g. $\dfrac{1}{a} + \dfrac{1}{b} = \dfrac{1}{a + b}$ h. $\dfrac{\cancel{x}}{\cancel{x} + y} = \dfrac{1}{1 + y}$

    i. $\dfrac{6}{7} \cdot \dfrac{8}{9} = \dfrac{6 \cdot 9 + 7 \cdot 8}{7 \cdot 9}$ j. $\dfrac{1 + 2 + 3 + 4 + 5}{2 + 4 + 6 + 8 + 10} = \dfrac{1}{2}$

(2–31) Evaluate the following expressions. Write the answers in simplest terms.

2. $\dfrac{2}{9} \cdot \dfrac{6}{5}$ 3. $\left(\dfrac{8}{3}\right)\left(\dfrac{15}{4}\right)$ 4. $\dfrac{3}{4} \cdot \dfrac{8}{5} \cdot \dfrac{4}{9}$

5. $\dfrac{2}{5} \cdot \dfrac{3}{6} \cdot \dfrac{10}{7}$ 6. $\left(\dfrac{3x}{25}\right)\left(\dfrac{25}{9x}\right)$ 7. $\left(\dfrac{14x}{15y}\right)\left(\dfrac{25y}{24}\right)$

8. $7x^2\left(\dfrac{6y}{21x}\right)$ 9. $\left(-\dfrac{2x}{3y}\right)(-5xy)$ 10. $\left(\dfrac{18}{11}\right) \div \left(\dfrac{8}{33}\right)$

11. $\left(\dfrac{14}{3}\right) \div \left(\dfrac{6}{15}\right)$ 12. $\dfrac{4}{9} \div \left(\dfrac{2}{3} \cdot 8\right)$ 13. $\left(\dfrac{12}{25} \cdot \dfrac{15}{7}\right) \div \dfrac{20}{7}$

14. $\left(\dfrac{7x}{10}\right) \div \left(\dfrac{21x}{5}\right)$ 15. $(2x) \div \left(\dfrac{3xy}{5}\right)$ 16. $4 \div \left(\dfrac{8}{9x}\right)$

17. $\left(\dfrac{3}{8x}\right) \div \left(\dfrac{4x}{15}\right)$ 18. $\dfrac{1}{6} - \dfrac{1}{2}$ 19. $\dfrac{1}{10} + \dfrac{1}{15}$

20. $\dfrac{4x}{5} - \dfrac{x}{10}$ 21. $\dfrac{1}{x} + \dfrac{1}{2x}$ 22. $\dfrac{x}{2} + \dfrac{x}{3}$

23. $\dfrac{y}{2x} + \dfrac{1}{3x}$ 24. $\dfrac{a}{6b} - \dfrac{a}{2b}$ 25. $\dfrac{a}{6b} + \dfrac{2a}{9b}$

26. $\dfrac{7}{6x} + \dfrac{3}{4x^2}$ 27. $\dfrac{3y}{10x^2} - \dfrac{1}{6x}$ 28. $\dfrac{\frac{1}{2} - \frac{1}{3}}{\frac{1}{4} + \frac{1}{5}}$

29. $\dfrac{\frac{8}{5} + \frac{2}{3}}{2 + \frac{4}{7}}$ 30. $\dfrac{(7x - 2x/3)}{(15y - y/3)}$ 31. $\dfrac{(2a/3b)(4b/5) + a}{2b + b/15}$

1-3 EXPONENTS

If m is a *positive integer*, then a^m (read *a to the power m* or *the mth power of a*) is defined to be the product of m a's multiplied together. Thus

$$a^m = a \times a \times a \times \cdots \times a.$$

In this product, the factor a appears m times. For example,

$$2^4 = 2 \times 2 \times 2 \times 2 = 16 \quad \text{(four factors of 2)}$$

$$3^5 = 3 \times 3 \times 3 \times 3 \times 3 = 243 \quad \text{(five factors of 3)}.$$

In the expression a^m, m is called the **power** or **exponent** and a the **base**. Thus in 2^4 (the fourth power of 2), 2 is the base and 4 is the power or exponent; in 3^5, 3 is the base and 5 the exponent. This definition of a^m when the exponent is a positive integer holds for all real values of a.

Observe the pattern in Table 1, in which several powers of 5 are given in decreasing order. Let us try to complete the table. We notice that every time

TABLE 1

5^4	625
5^3	125
5^2	25
5^1	5
5^0	?
5^{-1}	?
5^{-2}	?
5^{-3}	?
5^{-4}	?

the exponent is decreased by 1, the number in the right column is *divided* by 5. This suggests that the table should be completed by continuing to divide by 5 with each reduction in the exponent. Thus we are led to the following:

$$5^1 = 5 \qquad\qquad 5^{-2} = \frac{1}{25} = \frac{1}{5^2}$$

$$5^0 = 1 \qquad\qquad 5^{-3} = \frac{1}{125} = \frac{1}{5^3}$$

$$5^{-1} = \frac{1}{5} = \frac{1}{5^1} \qquad\qquad 5^{-4} = \frac{1}{625} = \frac{1}{5^4}$$

This pattern naturally leads to the following definition of a^m when the exponent m is zero or a negative integer.

DEFINITION If $a \neq 0$, then $a^0 = 1$, and if m is any *positive* integer (so that $-m$ is a *negative* integer), then

$$a^{-m} = \frac{1}{a^m}.$$

For example, $4^0 = 1$, $(\frac{3}{7})^0 = 1$, $(-5)^0 = 1$, and so on. Also,

$$3^{-4} = \frac{1}{3^4} = \frac{1}{81} \quad \text{and} \quad 2^{-5} = \frac{1}{2^5} = \frac{1}{32}.$$

From these definitions, it is possible to establish a series of properties called the **laws of exponents**. These are as follows.

$$a^m \cdot a^n = a^{m+n} \tag{1}$$

That is, *when two powers of a common base are multiplied, the result is equal to the base raised to the sum of the two exponents.* This result holds for any real number a, except that if either m or n is negative, we require $a \neq 0$.

EXAMPLE 1   (a) $5^2 \cdot 5^3 = 5^{2+3} = 5^5$

We can verify that this is correct by expanding the two powers in the product.

$$5^2 \cdot 5^3 = (5 \cdot 5) \cdot (5 \cdot 5 \cdot 5) = 5 \cdot 5 \cdot 5 \cdot 5 \cdot 5 = 5^5$$

(b) $x^5 \cdot x^{-3} = x^{5+(-3)} = x^2$

Again, we can verify this result by expanding the two powers.

$$x^5 \cdot x^{-3} = (x \cdot x \cdot x \cdot x \cdot x)\left(\frac{1}{x \cdot x \cdot x}\right) = x \cdot x = x^2$$

$$\frac{a^m}{a^n} = a^{m-n} \qquad (a \neq 0) \tag{2}$$

That is, *when one power is divided by another with the same base, the result is equal to the base raised to an exponent which is the difference between the exponent in the numerator and the exponent in the denominator.*

EXAMPLE 2   (a) $\dfrac{5^7}{5^3} = 5^{7-3} = 5^4$

(b) $\dfrac{4^3}{4^{-2}} = 4^{3-(-2)} = 4^{3+2} = 4^5$

(c) $\dfrac{3^{-2}}{3} = \dfrac{3^{-2}}{3^1} = 3^{-2-1} = 3^{-3}$

$$(a^m)^n = a^{mn} \qquad (a \neq 0 \text{ if } m \text{ or } n \text{ is negative}) \tag{3}$$

That is, *a power raised to a power is equal to the base raised to the product of the two exponents.*

EXAMPLE 3   (a) $(3^3)^2 = 3^{3 \cdot 2} = 3^6$

We can see that this is correct, since

$$(3^3)^2 = 3^3 \cdot 3^3 = 3^{3+3} = 3^6.$$

(b) $(4^{-2})^{-4} = 4^{(-2)(-4)} = 4^8$

$$(ab)^m = a^m b^m \qquad (ab \neq 0 \text{ if } m < 0) \tag{4}$$

That is, *the product of two numbers all raised to the mth power is equal to the product of the mth powers of the two numbers.*

EXAMPLE 4
(a) $6^4 = (2 \cdot 3)^4 = 2^4 \cdot 3^4$
(b) $(x^2 y)^4 = (x^2)^4 y^4 = x^8 y^4$
(c) $(3a^2 b^{-3})^2 = 3^2 (a^2)^2 (b^{-3})^2 = 9a^4 b^{-6}$

$$\left(\frac{a}{b}\right)^m = \frac{a^m}{b^m} \qquad (b \neq 0 \text{ and } a \neq 0 \text{ if } m < 0) \tag{5}$$

That is, *the quotient of two numbers all raised to the mth power is equal to the quotient of the mth powers of the two numbers.*

EXAMPLE 5
(a) $\left(\dfrac{3}{2}\right)^4 = \dfrac{3^4}{2^4}$

(b) $\left(\dfrac{x}{y}\right)^5 = \dfrac{x^5}{y^5} = x^5 y^{-5}$

EXAMPLE 6 Simplify the following, eliminating parentheses and negative exponents.
(a) $\dfrac{(ax)^5}{x^{-7}}$ 　　　　　　　(b) $\dfrac{(x^{-2})^2}{(x^2 z^3)^3}$
(c) $x^4(2x - 3x^{-2})$ 　　　　　(d) $(x^{-1} + y^{-1})^{-1}$

Solution
(a) $\dfrac{(ax)^5}{x^{-7}} = \dfrac{a^5 x^5}{x^{-7}} = a^5 x^{5-(-7)} = a^5 x^{12}$

(b) $\dfrac{(x^{-2})^2}{(x^2 z^3)^3} = \dfrac{x^{(-2)(2)}}{(x^2)^3 (z^3)^3} = \dfrac{x^{-4}}{x^6 z^9} = \dfrac{1}{x^{10} z^9}$

Note that if we wish to avoid negative exponents, both factors must be left in the denominator.

(c) $x^4(2x - 3x^{-2}) = x^4(2x) - x^4(3x^{-2})$
$$= 2x^{4+1} - 3x^{4-2}$$
$$= 2x^5 - 3x^2$$

(d) It would be *completely incorrect* in this example if we were to write
$$(x^{-1} + y^{-1})^{-1} = (x^{-1})^{-1} + (y^{-1})^{-1} = x + y!$$

For example, suppose that $x = 2$ and $y = 4$. Then
$$(x^{-1} + y^{-1})^{-1} = (\tfrac{1}{2} + \tfrac{1}{4})^{-1} = (\tfrac{3}{4})^{-1} = \tfrac{4}{3}.$$

This is clearly not equal to $x + y$, which is 6. Instead we must first simplify the expression inside the parentheses.
$$x^{-1} + y^{-1} = \frac{1}{x} + \frac{1}{y} = \frac{y}{xy} + \frac{x}{xy} = \frac{y + x}{xy}$$

Observe that the common denominator is xy. Now recall that the reciprocal of a fraction is obtained by exchanging the numerator with the denominator.

$$(x^{-1} + y^{-1})^{-1} = \left(\frac{y + x}{xy}\right)^{-1} = \frac{xy}{y + x}$$

EXERCISES 3

(1–34) Simplify the following. Do not use parentheses or negative exponents in the final answer.

1. $(2^5)^2$
2. $(3^4)^3$
3. $(2x)^2(2x^{-1})^3$
4. $\left(\frac{x}{2}\right)^3(4x^{-1})^2$
5. $(x^2yz)^3(xy)^4$
6. $(3yz^2)^2(y^3z)^3$
7. $(x^{-2}y)^{-2}$
8. $(ab^{-3})^{-1}$
9. $(xy^2z^3)^{-1}(xyz)^3$
10. $(x^2pq^2)^2(xp^2)^{-1}$
11. $\frac{(2^4)^2}{4^2}$
12. $\frac{(3^3)^2}{3^5}$
13. $(\tfrac{1}{3})^{-2} \div 3^{-4}$
14. $(\tfrac{1}{5})^3 \div 5^{-2}$
15. $\frac{(x^2y)^{-3}}{(xy)^2}$
16. $\frac{(ab^{-2})^{-1}}{a^{-2}b^{-1}}$
17. $\frac{(-2xy)^3}{x^3y}$
18. $\frac{(-ab^2c)^{-1}}{a^{-2}bc^{-1}}$
19. $\frac{(-3x)^2}{-3x^2}$
20. $\frac{(2x^2y)^{-1}}{(-2x^2y^3)^2}$
21. $x^2(x^4 - 2x)$
22. $x^3(x^{-1} - x)$
23. $2x(x^5 + 3x^{-1})$
24. $3x^2(x^4 + 2x^{-3})$
25. $x^4(2x^2 - x - 3x^{-2})$
26. $2x^{-3}(x^5 - 3x^4 + x)$
27. $(2^{-1} + x^{-1})^{-1}$
28. $[(2x)^{-1} + (2y)^{-1}]^{-1}$
29. $(xy)^{-1}(x^{-1} + y^{-1})^{-1}$
30. $(a^{-2} + b^{-2})^{-1}$
31. $\left(\frac{7}{x}\right)\left(\frac{3}{14x}\right) + \left(\frac{3}{2x}\right)^2$
32. $x^{-3}\left(\frac{6}{5x}\right)^{-1} - \left(-\frac{1}{2x}\right)^2$
33. $\frac{3y}{10x^3} + \frac{2}{15xy}$
34. $\frac{5}{12x^{-3}} - \frac{2}{15x^{-2}}$

1-4 FRACTIONAL EXPONENTS

Having defined a^m when m is any integer, we shall now extend the definition to the case when m is any rational number. We should like to make this extension in such a way that Properties 1–5 of the last section continue to hold when m and n are no longer integers.

We shall first consider the definition of $a^{1/n}$ where n is a nonzero integer. If Property 3 is to remain true when $m = 1/n$, then it must be true that

$$(a^{1/n})^n = a^{(1/n)n} = a^1 = a.$$

So, if we set $b = a^{1/n}$, it is necessary that $b^n = a$.

EXAMPLE 1   (a) $8^{1/3} = 2$ since $2^3 = 8$.

(b) $(-243)^{1/5} = -3$ since $(-3)^5 = -243$.

When n is an even integer, two difficulties arise with this definition of $a^{1/n}$. For example, let $n = 2$ and $a = 4$. Then $b = 4^{1/2}$ if $b^2 = 4$. But there are *two* numbers whose square is equal to 4, namely $b = 2$ and $b = -2$. Thus we need to decide which we mean when we write $b = 4^{1/2}$. In fact, we shall *define* $4^{1/2}$ to mean $+2$.

Second, suppose that a is negative. Then $b = a^{1/2}$ if $b^2 = a$. But the square of any real number (positive, negative, or zero) is never negative. For example, $4^2 = 16$ and $(-3)^2 = 9$, both of which are positive numbers. Thus b^2 is never negative for any real number b, so when $a < 0$, $a^{1/2}$ does not exist in the real numbers. For example, $(-1)^{1/2}$ or $(-\frac{4}{3})^{1/2}$ have no meanings as real numbers. This leads us to adopt the following definition.

DEFINITION If n is a positive even integer (such as 2, 4, or 6) and if a is any *nonnegative* real number, then b is said to be the **principal nth root of a** if $b^n = a$ and $b \geq 0$. Thus the principal nth root of a is the *nonnegative* number which, when raised to the nth power, gives the number a. We denote the principal nth root by $b = a^{1/n}$.

If n is a positive *odd* integer (such as 1, 3, or 5) and if a is *any* real number, then b is the *nth root of a* if $b^n = a$, again denoted by $a^{1/n}$. Thus

$$b = a^{1/n} \text{ if } b^n = a; \qquad b \geq 0 \text{ if } n \text{ is even.}$$

The odd roots are defined for all real numbers a, but the even roots are defined only when a is nonnegative.

The symbol $\sqrt[n]{a}$ is also used instead of $a^{1/n}$. The symbol $\sqrt{}$ is called a **radical sign** and $\sqrt[n]{a}$ is often called a **radical**. When $n = 2$, $a^{1/2}$ is denoted simply by $\sqrt{a}$ rather than $\sqrt[2]{a}$: it is called the **square root** of a. Also, $\sqrt[3]{a} = a^{1/3}$ is the third root of a, usually called the **cube root**, $\sqrt[4]{a} = a^{1/4}$ is the fourth root of a, and so on.

Clearly every real number (positive, negative, or zero) has an nth root if n is a positive odd integer, but only the nonnegative real numbers have nth roots when n is a positive even integer.

EXAMPLE 2   (a) $32^{1/5} = 2$ because $2^5 = 32$.

(b) $(-216)^{1/3} = -6$ because $(-6)^3 = -216$.

(c) $16^{1/4} = 2$ because $2^4 = 16$ and $2 > 0$.

(d) $(729)^{1/6} = 3$ because $3^6 = 729$ and $3 > 0$.

(e) $1^{1/n} = 1$ for every positive integer n, because $1^n = 1$.

(f) $(-1)^{1/n} = -1$ for every positive odd integer n, because $(-1)^n = -1$ when n is odd.

(g) $(-81)^{1/4}$ does not exist, because negative numbers have nth roots only when n is odd.

Now we are in a position to define $a^{m/n}$ with a rational exponent m/n.

DEFINITION Let n be a positive integer, m be a nonzero integer, and a be a real number. Then

$$a^{m/n} = (a^{1/n})^m$$

That is, *the (m/n)th power of a is the mth power of the nth root of a.*

Note: If n is even, a must be nonnegative. If m is negative, a must be nonzero.

EXAMPLE 3 (a) $9^{3/2} = (9^{1/2})^3 = 3^3 = 27$

(b) $4^{-1/2} = (4^{1/2})^{-1} = 2^{-1} = \frac{1}{2}$

(c) $16^{-3/4} = (16^{1/4})^{-3} = 2^{-3} = \frac{1}{8}$

From part (b) of Example 3, we can generalize to the following result.

$$a^{-1/n} = \frac{1}{\sqrt[n]{a}}$$

This follows since

$$a^{-1/n} = (a^{1/n})^{-1} = \frac{1}{a^{1/n}}.$$

THEOREM 1

$$a^{m/n} = (a^m)^{1/n}$$

That is, *the (m/n)th power of a is equal to the nth root of the mth power of a.*

This theorem, which we shall not prove, offers an alternative method of calculating any fractional power.

EXAMPLE 4 (a) $16^{3/4} = (16^{1/4})^3 = 2^3 = 8$, or

$16^{3/4} = (16^3)^{1/4} = (4096)^{1/4} = 8$

(b) $36^{3/2} = (36^{1/2})^3 = 6^3 = 216$, or

$36^{3/2} = (36^3)^{1/2} = (46,656)^{1/2} = 216$

From Examples 3 and 4, it is clear that when evaluating $a^{m/n}$, it is easier to take the nth root first and then raise to the mth power; we then work with smaller numbers. In other words, in practice, to evaluate $a^{m/n}$ we use the definition $(a^{1/n})^m$ rather than $(a^m)^{1/n}$.

With these definitions, it is possible to show that the laws of exponents, which were stated in Section 3, remain valid for fractional exponents. Let us restate these laws and illustrate them with some examples.

1. $a^m \cdot a^n = a^{m+n}$	**2.** $\dfrac{a^m}{a^n} = a^{m-n}$
3. $(a^m)^n = a^{mn}$	**4.** $(ab)^m = a^m b^m$
5. $\left(\dfrac{a}{b}\right)^m = \dfrac{a^m}{b^m}$	

In writing these laws, we must keep in mind that certain restrictions apply: in any power, if the exponent is negative, the base must not be zero; and if the exponent involves an even root, the base must not be negative.

EXAMPLE 5
(a) $5^3 \cdot 5^{7/2} = 5^{3+7/2} = 5^{13/2}$

(b) $4^{-2} \cdot 4^{7/3} = 4^{-2+7/3} = 4^{1/3}$

(c) $\dfrac{(4)^{7/2}}{(4)^{3/2}} = 4^{7/2-3/2} = 4^2 = 16$

(d) $\dfrac{9^{1/2}}{9^{-2}} = 9^{1/2-(-2)} = 9^{5/2} = (9^{1/2})^5 = 3^5 = 243$

(e) $\dfrac{x^{9/4}}{x^4} = x^{9/4-4} = x^{-7/4}$

(f) $(5^3)^{7/6} = 5^{3(7/6)} = 5^{7/2}$

(g) $(3^{-4/3})^{-6/5} = 3^{(-4/3)(-6/5)} = 3^{8/5}$

(h) $a^{-m} = (a^m)^{-1} = \dfrac{1}{a^m}$ for any rational number m

(i) $(36)^{1/2} = (4 \cdot 9)^{1/2} = 4^{1/2} \cdot 9^{1/2} = 2 \cdot 3 = 6$

(j) $(x^2 y)^{1/2} = (x^2)^{1/2} y^{1/2} = x^{2(1/2)} y^{1/2} = xy^{1/2}$

(k) $(3a^{2/5}b^{-4})^{-1/2} = 3^{-1/2}(a^{2/5})^{-1/2}(b^{-4})^{-1/2} = 3^{-1/2} a^{-1/5} b^2$

(l) $\sqrt[4]{ab} = (ab)^{1/4} = a^{1/4} b^{1/4} = \sqrt[4]{a}\,\sqrt[4]{b}$

(m) $\sqrt{x/y} = (x/y)^{1/2} = x^{1/2}/y^{1/2} = \sqrt{x}/\sqrt{y}$

(n) $\left(\dfrac{8}{27}\right)^{-2/3} = \dfrac{8^{-2/3}}{27^{-2/3}} = \dfrac{(8^{1/3})^{-2}}{(27^{1/3})^{-2}} = \dfrac{2^{-2}}{3^{-2}} = \dfrac{1/4}{1/9} = \left(\dfrac{1}{4}\right)\left(\dfrac{9}{1}\right) = \dfrac{9}{4}$

EXAMPLE 6   Evaluate: (a) $\left(1\dfrac{64}{225}\right)^{1/2}$; (b) $\left(\dfrac{64x^3}{27}\right)^{-2/3}$

Solution
(a) $\left(1\dfrac{64}{225}\right)^{1/2} = \left(\dfrac{289}{225}\right)^{1/2} = \left(\dfrac{17^2}{15^2}\right)^{1/2}$

$= \left[\left(\dfrac{17}{15}\right)^2\right]^{1/2}$ (by Law 5)

$= \left(\dfrac{17}{15}\right)^{2 \cdot (1/2)}$ (by Law 3)

$= \left(\dfrac{17}{15}\right)^1 = 1\dfrac{2}{15}$

(b) $\left(\dfrac{64x^3}{27}\right)^{-2/3} = \left(\dfrac{4^3 x^3}{3^3}\right)^{-2/3} = \left[\left(\dfrac{4x}{3}\right)^3\right]^{-2/3}$ (by Law 5)

$= \left(\dfrac{4x}{3}\right)^{-2} = \dfrac{1}{(4x/3)^2}$ (by Law 3)

$= \dfrac{1}{16x^2/9} = \dfrac{9}{16x^2}$

EXAMPLE 7   Simplify the following expression.

$$\dfrac{4^p \cdot 27^{p/3} \cdot 125^p \cdot 6^{2p}}{8^{p/3} \cdot 9^{3p/2} \cdot 10^{3p}}$$

Solution   In expressions such as this, it is usually a good idea to express all the bases in terms of their prime factors.

$$\frac{4^p \cdot 27^{p/3} \cdot 125^p \cdot 6^{2p}}{8^{p/3} \cdot 9^{3p/2} \cdot 10^{3p}} = \frac{(2^2)^p \cdot (3^3)^{p/3} \cdot (5^3)^p \cdot (2 \cdot 3)^{2p}}{(2^3)^{p/3} \cdot (3^2)^{3p/2} \cdot (2 \cdot 5)^{3p}}$$

$$= \frac{2^{2p} \cdot 3^{3p/3} \cdot 5^{3p} \cdot 2^{2p} \cdot 3^{2p}}{2^{3 \cdot (p/3)} \cdot 3^{2 \cdot (3p/2)} \cdot 2^{3p} \cdot 5^{3p}} \qquad \text{(by Laws 3 and 5)}$$

$$= \frac{(2^{2p} \cdot 2^{2p})(3^p \cdot 3^{2p}) \cdot 5^{3p}}{(2^p \cdot 2^{3p})(3^{3p}) \cdot 5^{3p}} \qquad \begin{array}{l}\text{(combining terms}\\ \text{with like bases)}\end{array}$$

$$= \frac{2^{4p} \cdot 3^{3p} \cdot 5^{3p}}{2^{4p} \cdot 3^{3p} \cdot 5^{3p}} = 1$$

EXAMPLE 8   Simplify $(\sqrt{27} + \sqrt{75})/2\sqrt{12}$.

Solution   We observe that the three radicals in this expression can be simplified by factoring out a perfect square from each of the numbers.

$$\sqrt{27} = \sqrt{9 \times 3} = \sqrt{9} \cdot \sqrt{3} = 3\sqrt{3}$$

$$\sqrt{75} = \sqrt{25 \times 3} = \sqrt{25} \cdot \sqrt{3} = 5\sqrt{3}$$

$$\sqrt{12} = \sqrt{4 \times 3} = \sqrt{4} \cdot \sqrt{3} = 2\sqrt{3}$$

Therefore

$$\frac{\sqrt{27} + \sqrt{75}}{2\sqrt{12}} = \frac{3\sqrt{3} + 5\sqrt{3}}{2(2\sqrt{3})}$$

$$= \frac{8\sqrt{3}}{4\sqrt{3}} = \frac{8}{4} = 2.$$

EXERCISES 4

(1–6) Find m such that the following statements are true.

1. $8\sqrt[3]{2} = 2^m$
2. $\dfrac{\sqrt[3]{2}}{8} = 2^m$
3. $\sqrt[3]{\dfrac{2}{8}} = 2^m$

4. $3\sqrt{3} \cdot \sqrt[3]{3} = 3^m$
5. $\sqrt{\sqrt{\sqrt{2}}} = 4^m$
6. $\sqrt[4]{\sqrt[3]{\sqrt{2}}} = 2^m$

(7–21) Evaluate the following expressions.

7. $\sqrt{81}$
8. $\sqrt[3]{27}$
9. $\sqrt{1\frac{9}{16}}$

10. $\sqrt[3]{3\frac{3}{8}}$
11. $\sqrt[5]{-32}$
12. $\sqrt[3]{-0.125}$

13. $\sqrt{(-3)^2}$
14. $\sqrt{(-\frac{2}{3})^2}$
15. $(81)^{-3/4}$

16. $(\frac{8}{27})^{-4/3}$
17. $(0.16)^{-1/2}$
18. $(16x^4)^{3/4}$

19. $\left(\dfrac{27x^3}{64}\right)^{2/3}$
20. $(32x^5y^{-10})^{1/5}$
21. $\sqrt[3]{\dfrac{8a^3}{27b^3}}$

(22–34) Simplify the following expressions.

22. $(27)^{-2/3} \div (16)^{1/4}$
23. $(9^{-3} \times 16^{3/2})^{1/6}$

24. $a^{2/3} \times a^{-3/4} \times (a^2)^{-1/6} \times \dfrac{1}{(a^{1/12})^5}$
25. $a^{2/3} \times b^{-5/7} \times \left(\dfrac{a}{b}\right)^{7/8} \times \dfrac{a^{11/24}}{b^{23/56}}$

26. $\dfrac{2^{3m} \times 3^{2m} \times 5^m \times 6^m}{8^m \times 9^{3m/2} \times 10^m}$

27. $\dfrac{(x^{a+b})^2(y^{a+b})^2}{(xy)^{2a-b}}$

28. $\left(\dfrac{x^a}{x^b}\right)^c \cdot \left(\dfrac{x^b}{x^c}\right)^a \cdot \left(\dfrac{x^c}{x^a}\right)^b$

29. $\left(\dfrac{x^{a+b}}{x^{2b}}\right)\left(\dfrac{x^{b+c}}{x^{2c}}\right)\left(\dfrac{x^{c+a}}{x^{2a}}\right)$

30. $\dfrac{(27)^{2n/3} \times (8)^{-n/6}}{(18)^{-n/2}}$

31. $2\sqrt{18} - \sqrt{32}$

32. $\sqrt{63} - \sqrt{175} + 4\sqrt{112}$

33. $\dfrac{8\sqrt{2} - 4\sqrt{8}}{\sqrt{32}}$

34. $\sqrt{112} - \sqrt{63} + \dfrac{224}{\sqrt{28}}$

35. State whether the following statements are true or false.

a. $\sqrt{5} = \sqrt{2} + \sqrt{3}$ **b.** $\sqrt{8} = \sqrt{2} + \sqrt{2}$

c. $\sqrt{21} = \sqrt{7} \cdot \sqrt{3}$ **d.** $\sqrt{(-3)^2} = 3$

e. $\sqrt{-9} = -3$ **f.** $\sqrt{a^2} = a$ for all real a

g. $\sqrt{a^2 + b^2} = a + b$ if $a > 0$ and $b > 0$

h. $a^m \cdot a^n = a^{mn}$ **i.** $\dfrac{a^m}{a^n} = a^{m/n}$

j. $\sqrt[3]{\sqrt[3]{a}} = a^{1/6}$ **k.** $\sqrt{a^2} = a$ if $a > 0$

1-5   ALGEBRAIC OPERATIONS

Quantities of the type $2x^2 - 3x + 7$, $5y^3 - y^2 + 6y + 2$, and $2x - 3/y + 4$ are called **algebraic expressions**. The building blocks of an algebraic expression are called its **terms**. For example, the expression $2x^2 - 3x + 7$ has three terms, $2x^2$, $-3x$ and 7. The expression $x^2y/3 - y/x$ has two terms, $x^2y/3$ and $-y/x$.

In the term $2x^2$, the factor 2 is called the **numerical coefficient** (often the word *numerical* is dropped and we simply call such a number the **coefficient**). The factor x^2 is called the **literal part** of this term. In the term $-3x$, the coefficient is -3 and the literal part is x. In the term $x^2y/3$, the coefficient is $\frac{1}{3}$ and the literal part is x^2y. The term 7 has no literal part and is called a **constant term**. The coefficient is 7.

An algebraic expression containing only one term is called a **monomial**. An expression that contains exactly two terms is called a **binomial**, and one containing exactly three terms is called a **trinomial**. The following are a few examples of expressions of these types.

Monomials: $2x^3$, $-5y^2$, $7/t$,   3, $2xy/z$

Binomials: $2x + 3$, $3x^2 - 5/y$, $6x^2y - 5zt$

Trinomials: $5x^2 + 7x - 1$, $2x^3 + 4x - 3/x$, $6y^2 - 5x + t$

In general, an algebraic expression containing more than one term is called a **multinomial**.

Addition and Subtraction of Expressions

When 4 apples are added to 3 apples we get 7 apples. In the same way, $4x + 3x = 7x$. This is simply a consequence of the distributive property, since

$$4x + 3x = (4 + 3)x = 7x.$$

The distributive property enables us in an exactly similar way to add any two expressions whose literal parts are the same. We simply add together the two numerical coefficients.

EXAMPLE 1
(a) $2x + 9x = (2 + 9)x = 11x$

(b) $4ab + 3ab = (4 + 3)ab = 7ab$

(c) $\dfrac{2x}{y} + \dfrac{x}{2y} = 2 \cdot \dfrac{x}{y} + \dfrac{1}{2} \cdot \dfrac{x}{y} = \left(2 + \dfrac{1}{2}\right) \dfrac{x}{y}$

$$= \dfrac{5}{2} \cdot \dfrac{x}{y} = \dfrac{5x}{2y}$$

Two or more terms in an algebraic expression are said to be **like** if they have equal literal parts. For example, the two terms $2x^2y$ and $5yx^2$ are like terms since their literal parts, x^2y and yx^2, are equal. Similarly, the three terms $3x^2yz^3$, $-7x^2z^3y$ and $yz^3x^2/2$ are all like terms. In general, two like terms can differ only in their numerical coefficients or in the order in which the variables appear.

Two or more like terms can be added or subtracted by making use of the distributive property, as illustrated in Example 1.

EXAMPLE 2
(a) $2x^3 - 7x^3 = (2 - 7)x^3 = -5x^3$

(b) $5x^2y - 3x^2y + 2yx^2 = (5 - 3 + 2)x^2y = 4x^2y$

Terms that are not like cannot be combined in the above manner. Thus the terms in the expression $2x^2 + 5xy$ cannot be combined into a single term.

When adding or subtracting two or more algebraic expressions, we rearrange the terms in the two expressions so that like terms are grouped together.

EXAMPLE 3 Add $5x^2y^3 - 7xy^2 + 3x - 1$ and $6 - 2x + 4xy^2 + 3y^3x^2$.

Solution The required sum is

$$5x^2y^3 - 7xy^2 + 3x - 1 + (6 - 2x + 4xy^2 + 3y^3x^2)$$
$$= 5x^2y^3 - 7xy^2 + 3x - 1 + 6 - 2x + 4xy^2 + 3x^2y^3.$$

Rearranging the terms, so that like terms are grouped together, we obtain the sum in the following form.

$$\underline{5x^2y^3 + 3x^2y^3} \quad \underline{-7xy^2 + 4xy^2} + \underline{3x - 2x} - \underline{1 + 6}$$
$$= (5 + 3)x^2y^3 \quad + (-7 + 4)xy^2 + (3 - 2)x + (-1 + 6)$$
$$= \quad 8x^2y^3 \quad\quad + \quad (-3)xy^2 \quad + \quad 1x \quad + \quad 5$$
$$= \quad 8x^2y^3 \quad\quad - \quad 3xy^2 \quad\quad + \quad x \quad + \quad 5$$

EXAMPLE 4   Subtract $3x^2 - 5xy + 7y^2$ from $7x^2 - 2xy + 4y^2 + 6$.

Solution   In this case, we want

$$7x^2 - 2xy + 4y^2 + 6 - (3x^2 - 5xy + 7y^2).$$

Upon removal of the parentheses, each term inside the parentheses changes sign. Thus the above expression is equivalent to the following.

$$7x^2 - 2xy + 4y^2 + 6 - 3x^2 + 5xy - 7y^2$$
$$= 7x^2 - 3x^2 - 2xy + 5xy + 4y^2 - 7y^2 + 6$$
$$= (7 - 3)x^2 + (-2 + 5)xy + (4 - 7)y^2 + 6$$
$$= \quad 4x^2 \quad + \quad 3xy \quad + (-3)y^2 \quad + 6$$
$$= \quad 4x^2 \quad + \quad 3xy \quad - \quad 3y^2 \quad + 6$$

Multiplication of Expressions

The expression $a(x + y)$ denotes the product of a and $x + y$. To simplify this expression by removing the parentheses, we multiply each term within the parentheses by the number outside, in this case a:

$$a(x + y) = ax + ay.$$

This is simply the distributive property. Similarly,

$$-2(x - 3y + 7t^2) = (-2)x - (-2)(3y) + (-2)(7t^2)$$
$$= -2x + 6y - 14t^2.$$

This method works whenever a multinomial is multiplied by any monomial.

EXAMPLE 5 $x^2y(x^2 + 3x - 5y^3) = x^2y \cdot x^2 + x^2y \cdot 3x - x^2y \cdot 5y^3$
$$= x^4y + 3x^3y - 5x^2y^4$$

When multiplying two multinomial expressions together, the distributive property must be used more than once in order to remove the parentheses. Consider the product $(x + 2)(y + 3)$. We can use the distributive property to remove the first parentheses.

$$(x + 2)(y + 3) = x(y + 3) + 2(y + 3)$$

We now use this property again to remove the remaining parentheses.

$xy + 3x$

$2y + 2\cdot3$

FIGURE 2

$$x(y + 3) = xy + x\cdot3 = xy + 3x$$
and
$$2(y + 3) = 2y + 2\cdot3 = 2y + 6.$$

Therefore $(x + 2)(y + 3) = xy + 3x + 2y + 6.$

In Figure 2 the four terms (products) on the right can be obtained by multiplying each of the terms in the first parentheses in turn by each of the terms in the second parentheses. Each term in the first parentheses is connected by an arc to each term in the second parentheses and the corresponding product is written down. The four products then give the complete expansion of the given expression.

EXAMPLE 6   Expand the product $(3x - 4)(6x^2 - 5x + 2)$. (This means to remove the parentheses.)

Solution   We use the distributive property.

$$(3x - 4)(6x^2 - 5x + 2) = 3x(6x^2 - 5x + 2) - 4(6x^2 - 5x + 2)$$
$$= (3x)(6x^2) - (3x)(5x) + (3x)(2)$$
$$\quad + (-4)(6x^2) - (-4)(5x) + (-4)(2)$$
$$= 18x^3 - 15x^2 + 6x - 24x^2 + 20x - 8$$
$$= 18x^3 - 15x^2 - 24x^2 + 6x + 20x - 8$$
$$\qquad\qquad\qquad\text{(grouping like terms)}$$
$$= 18x^3 - (15 + 24)x^2 + (6 + 20)x - 8$$
$$= 18x^3 - 39x^2 + 26x - 8$$

Alternatively, we can obtain the answer by drawing arcs connecting each term in the first parentheses to each term in the second. In this case, there are six such arcs, giving six products in the expansion on the right. (See Figure 3.)

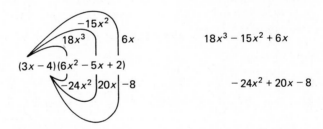

$$18x^3 - 15x^2 + 6x$$

$$- 24x^2 + 20x - 8$$

FIGURE 3

EXAMPLE 7   Simplify $3\{5x[2 - 3x] + 7[3 - 2(x - 4)]\}$.

Solution   To simplify an expression which involves more than one set of parentheses, we always start with the innermost parentheses.

$$3\{5x[2 - 3x] + 7[3 - 2(x - 4)]\} = 3\{5x[2 - 3x] + 7[3 - 2x + 8]\}$$
$$= 3\{10x - 15x^2 + 21 - 14x + 56\}$$
$$= 3\{-15x^2 + 10x - 14x + 21 + 56\}$$
$$= 3\{-15x^2 - 4x + 77\}$$
$$= -45x^2 - 12x + 231$$

There are certain special products that are encountered often and may be treated as standard formulas. First, we consider the product $(x + a)(x + b)$.

$$(x + a)(x + b) = x(x + b) + a(x + b)$$
$$= x^2 + bx + ax + ab$$
$$= x^2 + (b + a)x + ab$$

Therefore

$$(x + a)(x + b) = x^2 + (a + b)x + ab. \tag{1}$$

EXAMPLE 8   (a) Taking $a = 2$ and $b = 7$ in Equation (1), we have
$$(x + 2)(x + 7) = x^2 + (2 + 7)x + 2 \cdot 7 = x^2 + 9x + 14.$$
(b) $(x + 3)(x - 2) = (x + 3)(x + (-2))$
$$= x^2 + [3 + (-2)]x + 3(-2) = x^2 + x - 6$$

In Equation (1), if we replace b by a, we get
$$(x + a)(x + a) = x^2 + (a + a)x + a \cdot a$$
or

$$(x + a)^2 = x^2 + 2ax + a^2. \tag{2}$$

This result gives an expansion for the square of a binomial. *The square of the sum of two terms is equal to the sum of the squares of the two terms plus twice their product.*

EXAMPLE 9   (a) $(2x + 7)^2 = (2x)^2 + 2(2x)(7) + 7^2$
$$= 4x^2 + 28x + 49$$
(b) $\left(3x + \dfrac{4}{y}\right)^2 = (3x)^2 + 2(3x)\left(\dfrac{4}{y}\right) + \left(\dfrac{4}{y}\right)^2$
$$= 9x^2 + \frac{24x}{y} + \frac{16}{y^2}$$

If we replace a by $-a$ in Formula (2), we obtain another formula.

$$(x - a)^2 = x^2 - 2ax + a^2 \tag{3}$$

This expresses *the square of the difference of two terms as the sum of the squares of the two terms minus twice their product.*

Finally, if we replace b by $-a$ in Equation (1), we obtain
$$(x + a)(x - a) = x^2 + (a - a)x + a(-a) = x^2 + 0x - a^2.$$
Thus, we have

$$(x + a)(x - a) = x^2 - a^2. \tag{4}$$

This result states that the *product of the sum and difference of two terms is the difference of the squares of the two terms.*

EXAMPLE 10   (a) $(2x + 3)(2x - 3) = (2x)^2 - 3^2 = 4x^2 - 9$

        (b) $(\sqrt{3} + \sqrt{2})(\sqrt{3} - \sqrt{2}) = (\sqrt{3})^2 - (\sqrt{2})^2 = 3 - 2 = 1$

        (c) $(3x - 4y)(3x + 4y) = (3x)^2 - (4y)^2 = 9x^2 - 16y^2$

Division of Expressions

We saw in Theorem 6 of Section 1–2 that the distributive law extends to division, and we have the following general expression.

$$\frac{a + b}{c} = \frac{a}{c} + \frac{b}{c}$$

This property is useful when dividing an algebraic expression by a monomial, since it allows us to divide each term separately by the monomial.

EXAMPLE 11   (a) $\dfrac{2x^2 + 4x}{2x} = \dfrac{2x^2}{2x} + \dfrac{4x}{2x} = x + 2$

Observe that we divide each term by the common factor $2x$.

        (b) $\dfrac{2x^3 - 5x^2y + 7x + 3}{x^2} = \dfrac{2x^3}{x^2} - \dfrac{5x^2y}{x^2} + \dfrac{7x}{x^2} + \dfrac{3}{x^2}$

$$= 2x - 5y + \frac{7}{x} + \frac{3}{x^2}$$

        (c) $\dfrac{25t^3 + 12t^2 + 15t - 6}{3t} = \dfrac{25t^3}{3t} + \dfrac{12t^2}{3t} + \dfrac{15t}{3t} - \dfrac{6}{3t}$

$$= \frac{25t^2}{3} + 4t + 5 - \frac{2}{t}$$

In a fraction, the number or algebraic expression in the numerator is often called the **dividend** (which means the quantity which is being divided) and the number or expression by which it is divided is called the **divisor**. In Example 11(b) $2x^3 - 5x^2y + 7x + 3$ is the *dividend* and x^2 is the *divisor*, while in Example 11(c), $25t^3 + 12t^2 + 15t - 6$ is the *dividend* and $3t$ is the *divisor*.

When we want to divide an algebraic expression by a divisor that contains more than one term, we can often use a process called **long division**. We shall describe this process for expressions that contain only positive integral powers of a single variable. (Such expressions are called **polynomials**.)

EXAMPLE 12   Divide $23 - 11x^2 + 2x^3$ by $2x - 3$.

Solution   Here $23 - 11x^2 + 2x^3$ is the dividend and $2x - 3$ is the divisor. Before we start division, the terms in the dividend and divisor must be arranged in order of decreasing powers of x and any missing powers filled in with zero coefficients. Thus the dividend must be written as $2x^3 - 11x^2 + 0x + 23$.

$$
\begin{array}{r}
\;x^2 - 4x - 6 \quad\longleftarrow\ \textbf{QUOTIENT} \\
\textbf{DIVISOR}\ \longrightarrow\ 2x-3\,\overline{)\,2x^3 - 11x^2 + 0x + 23}\quad\longleftarrow\ \textbf{DIVIDEND} \\
\underline{2x^3 - 3x^2} \\
-8x^2 + 0x + 23 \\
\underline{-8x^2 + 12x} \\
-12x + 23 \\
\underline{-12x + 18} \\
5 \quad\longleftarrow\ \textbf{REMAINDER}
\end{array}
$$

The details of the long division are shown above and are explained as follows: First of all, we divide $2x^3$ (the first term in the dividend) by $2x$ (the first term in the divisor), obtaining $2x^3/2x = x^2$. This gives the first term in the quotient. We multiply the divisor, $2x - 3$, by the first term in the quotient, x^2, to obtain $2x^3 - 3x^2$. Subtracting this from the dividend, we have the difference $-8x^2 + 0x + 23$. To obtain the next term in the quotient, we divide the first term in this difference, $-8x^2$, by $2x$, the first term in the divisor. This gives $-8x^2/2x = -4x$, which becomes the second term in the quotient. We multiply the divisor again by this second term, $-4x$, obtaining $-8x^2 + 12x$; we then subtract this from $-8x^2 + 0x + 23$, which gives the next difference, $-12x + 23$. We continue this process until we obtain a difference whose highest power is less than that of the divisor. We call this last difference the **remainder**. The answer may be written as

$$
\frac{2x^3 - 11x + 23}{2x - 3} = x^2 - 4x - 6 + \frac{5}{2x - 3}.
$$

In general, we have

$$
\boxed{\ \frac{\text{Dividend}}{\text{Divisor}} = \text{Quotient} + \frac{\text{Remainder}}{\text{Divisor}}.\ }
$$

Remark: This form of writing the result of the long division is exactly the same as we use in arithmetic. For example, consider the fraction $627/23$, in which the dividend is 627 and the divisor is 23. By ordinary long division we find that the quotient is 27 and the remainder is 6.

$$
\begin{array}{r}
27 \quad\longleftarrow\ \textbf{QUOTIENT} \\
\textbf{DIVISOR}\ \longrightarrow\ 23\,\overline{)\,627}\quad\longleftarrow\ \textbf{DIVIDEND} \\
\underline{46} \\
167 \\
\underline{161} \\
6 \quad\longleftarrow\ \textbf{REMAINDER}
\end{array}
$$

We therefore write

$$
\frac{627}{23} = 27 + \frac{6}{23}.
$$

If we multiply both sides of this calculation by 23, we obtain the result

$$
627 = (27 \times 23) + 6.
$$

This is an example of the general result that

> Dividend = (Quotient)(Divisor) + Remainder.

This is a useful result, because it allows us to check the answer to any long division. We can use the result to verify Example 12.

$$2x^3 - 11x^2 + 23 = (x^2 - 4x - 6)(2x - 3) + 5$$

$$\text{Dividend} = \quad (\text{Quotient})(\text{Divisor}) + \text{Remainder}$$

EXERCISES 5

(1–38) In the following exercises, perform the indicated operation and simplify.

1. $(5a + 7b - 3) + (3b - 2a + 9)$
2. $(3x^2 - 5x + 7) + (-2 + 6x - 7x^2 + x^3)$
3. $(2\sqrt{a} + 5\sqrt{b}) + (3\sqrt{a} - 2\sqrt{b})$
4. $(4xy + 5x^2y - 6x^3) + (3y^3 - 6xy^2 + 7xy + x^3 - 2x^2y)$
5. $(7t^2 + 6t - 1) - (3t - 5t^2 + 4 - t^3)$
6. $(x^2 + 3xy + 4y^2) - (2x^2 - xy + 3y^2 - 5)$
7. $(2\sqrt{x} + \sqrt{2y}) - (\sqrt{x} - 2\sqrt{2y})$
8. $3(x^2 - 2xy + y^2) - (2xy - x^2 + 2y^2)$
9. $x(2x^2 + 3xy + y^2) - y(5x^2 - 2xy + y^2)$
10. $a^2b(a^3 + 5ab - b^3) + 2ab(a^4 - 2a^2b + b^3a)$

11. $(a + 2)(3a - 4)$
12. $(x + 3y)(2x + y)$
13. $(x + 3)(2x^2 - 5x + 7)$
14. $(a - 2b)(a^2 - 2ab + b^2)$
15. $(\sqrt{a} - \sqrt{b})(\sqrt{a} + \sqrt{b})$
16. $(\sqrt{x} + 3\sqrt{y})(\sqrt{x} - 3\sqrt{y})$
17. $(x + y - z)(x + y + z)$
18. $(x - 2y + z)(x + 2y + z)$
19. $(2x + 3y)^2$
20. $(3a - b)^2 + 3(a + b)^2$
21. $(\sqrt{2}x - \sqrt{3y})^2$
22. $(\sqrt{x} + 2\sqrt{y})^2$
23. $(x^2 - 1)(x^3 + 2)$
24. $(y^2 + 2y)(y^3 - 2y^2 + 1)$
25. $3\{x^2 - 5[x + 2(3 - 5x)]\}$
26. $2\{a^2 - 2a[3a - 5(a^2 - 2)]\} + 7a^2 - 3a + 6$
27. $2a\{(a + 2)(3a - 1) - [a + 2(a - 1)(a + 3)]\}$
28. $(a + 3b)(a^2 - 3ab + b^2) - (a + b)^2(a + 2b)$

29. $\dfrac{x^3 + 7x^2 - 5x + 4}{x^2}$
30. $\dfrac{y^4 + 6y^3 - 7y^2 + 9y - 3}{3y^2}$

31. $\dfrac{t^2 - 2t + 7}{\sqrt{t}}$
32. $\dfrac{t^3 + 2t^2 - 3t + 1}{t\sqrt{t}}$

33. $(x^2 - 5x + 6) \div (x - 2)$
34. $(6x^2 + x - 1) \div (3x - 1)$
35. $(t^2 + 1) \div (t - 1)$
36. $x^3 \div (x + 1)$
37. $(2x^3 - 3x^2 + 4x + 6) \div (2x + 1)$
38. $(6x^3 + 11x^2 - 19x + 5) \div (3x - 2)$

1-6 FACTORS

If the product of two integers a and b is c, that is, $c = a \cdot b$, then a and b are called **factors** of c. In other words, an integer a is a factor of another integer c if a divides c exactly with no remainder. For example, 2 and 3 are factors of 6; 2, 3, 4 and 6 are all factors of 12; and so on.

This terminology is also used for algebraic expressions. If two (or more) algebraic expressions are multiplied together, these expressions are said to be *factors* of the expression obtained as their product. For example, the expression $2xy$ is obtained by multiplying 2, x, and y, so 2, x, and y are the factors of $2xy$. Furthermore, for example, $2y$ is a factor of $2xy$ since $2xy$ can be obtained by multiplying $2y$ by x.

Similarly, x is a factor of the expression $2x^2 + 3x$ since we can write $2x^2 + 3x = x(2x + 3)$ and x^2 is a factor of $6x^2 + 9x^3$ since we can write $6x^2 + 9x^3 = x^2(6 + 9x)$.

The process of writing a given expression as the product of its factors is called **factoring** the expression. In this section, we shall discuss certain methods by which multinomial expressions can be factored.

The first step in factoring a multinomial expression is to extract all the monomial factors that are common to all of the terms. The following example illustrates this.

EXAMPLE 1   Factor all the common monomial factors from the following expressions.

(a) $x^2 + 2xy^2$ (b) $2x^2y + 6xy^2$ (c) $6ab^2c^3 + 6a^2b^2c^2 + 18a^3bc^2$

Solution   (a) Let us write each term in the given expression in terms of its basic factors.

$$x^2 = x \cdot x \qquad 2xy^2 = 2 \cdot x \cdot y \cdot y$$

Looking at the two lists of basic factors, we see that only the factor x is common to both terms. So we write

$$x^2 + 2xy^2 = x \cdot x + x \cdot 2y^2$$
$$= x(x + 2y^2).$$

Observe how the distributive property is used to extract the common factor, x.

(b) Expressing each term in terms of basic factors, we have:

$$2x^2y = 2 \cdot x \cdot x \cdot y \quad \text{and} \quad 6xy^2 = 2 \cdot 3 \cdot x \cdot y \cdot y.$$

The factors 2, x, and y occur in both lists, so the common factor is $2xy$. This gives

$$2x^2y + 6xy^2 = 2xy \cdot x + 2xy \cdot 3y$$
$$= 2xy(x + 3y)$$

again using the distributive property.

(c) We first factor the terms.

$$6ab^2c^3 = 2 \cdot 3 \cdot a \cdot b \cdot b \cdot c \cdot c \cdot c$$
$$6a^2b^2c^2 = 2 \cdot 3 \cdot a \cdot a \cdot b \cdot b \cdot c \cdot c$$
$$18a^3bc^2 = 2 \cdot 3 \cdot 3 \cdot a \cdot a \cdot a \cdot b \cdot c \cdot c$$

The common factor of these three terms is $2 \cdot 3 \cdot a \cdot b \cdot c \cdot c = 6abc^2$.

$$6ab^2c^3 + 6a^2b^2c^2 + 18a^3bc^2 = 6abc^2 \cdot bc + 6abc^2 \cdot ab + 6abc^2 \cdot 3a^2$$
$$= 6abc^2(bc + ab + 3a^2)$$

Now let us turn to the question of extracting factors that are themselves binomial expressions from multinomial expressions of various kinds. Some of the formulas established in Section 5 are useful for factoring, in particular the following formula.

$$a^2 - b^2 = (a - b)(a + b) \tag{1}$$

This formula can be used to factor any expression which is reducible to a *difference of two squares*.

EXAMPLE 2   Factor completely: (a) $x^2y^4 - 9$; (b) $5x^4 - 80y^4$.

Solution   (a) The given expression can be written as

$$(xy^2)^2 - 3^2$$

which is the difference of two squares. Using Formula 1 with $a = xy^2$ and $b = 3$, we have

$$x^2y^4 - 9 = (xy^2)^2 - 3^2 = (xy^2 - 3)(xy^2 + 3).$$

Neither of the expressions in parentheses on the right side can be factored any further.

(b) First of all, we check whether we can take out any common monomial factor in $5x^4 - 80y^4$. In this case, because each term is divisible by 5, we take out a common factor of 5.

$$5x^4 - 80y^4 = 5(x^4 - 16y^4)$$

The expression $x^4 - 16y^4$ is a difference of squares.

$$5x^4 - 80y^4 = 5[(x^2)^2 - (4y^2)^2]$$
$$= 5[(x^2 - 4y^2)(x^2 + 4y^2)]$$
$$= 5(x^2 - 4y^2)(x^2 + 4y^2)$$

The factoring is not complete, because $x^2 - 4y^2 = x^2 - (2y)^2$ can be factored further as $(x - 2y)(x + 2y)$. Thus we need one more step.

$$5x^4 - 80y^4 = 5(x^2 - 4y^2)(x^2 + 4y^2)$$
$$= 5(x - 2y)(x + 2y)(x^2 + 4y^2)$$

Notes: 1.   Formula 1 allows us to factor any expression which takes the form of the difference between two squares. There is no corresponding formula expressing the sum $a^2 + b^2$ as the product of two or more factors. An expression that involves the *sum* of two squares, such as $a^2 + b^2$ or $4x^2 + 9y^2$, cannot be factored.

Expressions such as $a^3 + b^3$, $a^4 + b^4$, and so on, that involve the sum of two higher powers can however be further factored. This is discussed below.

2. We can write

$$x^2 - 2 = x^2 - (\sqrt{2})^2 = (x - \sqrt{2})(x + \sqrt{2}).$$

It is usually acceptable to include irrational numbers (such as $\sqrt{2}$) in the factors. However, we would usually not wish to use expressions involving $\sqrt{x}$ as factors. For example, as a rule we would not write

$$x - 4 = (\sqrt{x})^2 - 2^2 = (\sqrt{x} - 2)(\sqrt{x} + 2).$$

A useful technique in factoring multinomial expressions involving an even number of terms is the **grouping method**. In this method, the terms are grouped in pairs and the common monomial factors are extracted from each pair of terms. This often reveals a binomial factor common to all the pairs. This method is particularly useful for expressions containing four terms.

EXAMPLE 3   Factor $ax^2 + by^2 + bx^2 + ay^2$.

Solution   We can group the terms in the given expression into those which have x^2 as a factor and those which have y^2 as a factor:

$$(ax^2 + bx^2) + (ay^2 + by^2).$$

Each term in the first parentheses is divisible by x^2, and each term in the second parentheses is divisible by y^2; therefore we can write this expression as

$$x^2(a + b) + y^2(a + b).$$

We notice that $(a + b)$ is common to both terms. Thus we have

$$x^2(a + b) + y^2(a + b) = (a + b)(x^2 + y^2).$$

Hence the given expression has as its factors $(a + b)$ and $(x^2 + y^2)$.

EXAMPLE 4   Factor the expression $2x^3y - 4x^2y^2 + 8xy - 16y^2$.

Solution   We first observe that the terms in this expression have a common monomial factor of $2y$ and we write

$$2x^3y - 4x^2y^2 + 8xy - 16y^2 = 2y(x^3 - 2x^2y + 4x - 8y).$$

Inside the parentheses, we group the first two terms together and take out the common factor x^2; we also group the last two terms and take out the common factor of 4.

$$\underbrace{x^3 - 2x^2y}_{x^2 \text{ common}} + \underbrace{4x - 8y}_{4 \text{ common}} = x^2(x - 2y) + 4(x - 2y)$$
$$= (x^2 + 4)(x - 2y)$$

Observe that this same result could also be obtained by grouping the first and third terms and the second and fourth terms together.

$$\underbrace{x^3 + 4x}_{x \text{ common}} - \underbrace{2x^2y - 8y}_{-2y \text{ common}} = x(x^2 + 4) - 2y(x^2 + 4)$$
$$= (x - 2y)(x^2 + 4)$$

Returning to the original expression, we have:

$$2x^3y - 4x^2y^2 + 8xy - 16y^2 = 2y(x - 2y)(x^2 + 4).$$

It is not possible to factor the expressions on the right any further, so the factoring is complete.

––––––––––––––

An important type of factoring which arises frequently involves finding the factors of expressions of the type

$$x^2 + px + q$$

where p and q are constants. Often such expressions can be written as the product of two factors $(x + a)$ and $(x + b)$, where a and b are two real numbers. For example, it is readily verified that the expression $x^2 + 3x + 2$ (in which $p = 3$ and $q = 2$) is equal to the product of $x + 1$ and $x + 2$:

$$x^2 + 3x + 2 = (x + 1)(x + 2).$$

In this case, $a = 1$ and $b = 2$.

In general, with p and q given, we wish to find a and b such that

$$x^2 + px + q = (x + a)(x + b).$$

But we saw in Section 1–5 that

$$(x + a)(x + b) = x^2 + (a + b)x + ab$$

and so

$$x^2 + px + q = x^2 + (a + b)x + ab.$$

These two expressions are the same provided that $a + b = p$ and $ab = q$. So, in order to determine a and b, we must find two numbers whose sum is equal to p and whose product is equal to q. In terms of the original expression $x^2 + px + q$, the sum $a + b$ is equal to the coefficient of x and the product ab is equal to the constant term.

The procedure for finding a and b is to examine all possible pairs of integers whose product is equal to q. We then select the pair (if one exists) whose sum is the given coefficient of x.

EXAMPLE 5   Factor $x^2 + 7x + 12$.

Solution   Here $p = 7$ and $q = 12$. We must find two numbers a and b whose product is 12 and whose sum is 7. Let us consider all the possible pairs of factors of 12.

$a = 1, \quad b = 12$	$a + b = 13$
$a = -1, b = -12$	$a + b = -13$
$a = 2, \quad b = 6$	$a + b = 8$
$a = -2, b = -6$	$a + b = -8$
$a = 3, \quad b = 4$	$a + b = 7$
$a = -3, b = -4$	$a + b = -7$

From the above list, we see that the appropriate choice is $a = 3$ and $b = 4$.

Therefore
$$x^2 + 7x + 12 = (x + 3)(x + 4).$$

(*Note*: The choice $a = 4$ and $b = 3$ gives exactly the same pair of factors.)

EXAMPLE 6   Factor: (a) $x^2 - 5x + 6$; (b) $3x^2 - 3x - 6$.

Solution   (a) In order to factor $x^2 - 5x + 6$, we have to find two factors of $+6$ (the constant term) whose sum is -5 (the coefficient of x). The possible factors of 6 are $(1)(6)$, $(-1)(-6)$, $(2)(3)$, and $(-2)(-3)$. The two factors of 6 that have the sum -5 are -2 and -3. Thus we let $a = -2$ and $b = -3$.
$$x^2 - 5x + 6 = (x + a)(x + b)$$
$$= [x + (-2)][x + (-3)]$$
$$= (x - 2)(x - 3)$$

(b) We first observe that there is a common monomial factor of 3:
$$3x^2 - 3x - 6 = 3(x^2 - x - 2).$$
To factor $x^2 - x - 2$, we have to find two factors of -2 (the constant term) whose sum is -1 (the coefficient of x). The possible factors of -2 are $1(-2)$ and $(-1)(2)$. Only the factors 1 and -2 have the sum -1, that is, $1 + (-2) = -1$. Thus
$$x^2 - x - 2 = (x + 1)[x + (-2)] = (x + 1)(x - 2).$$
Our original expression therefore factors as follows.
$$3x^2 - 3x - 6 = 3(x^2 - x - 2)$$
$$= 3(x + 1)(x - 2)$$

EXAMPLE 7   Factor $x^2 + 6x + 9$.

Solution   We have $p = 6$ and $q = 9$.
Clearly the two factors of 9 whose sum is 6 are 3 and 3. Thus the given expression has factors $x + 3$ and $x + 3$, so
$$x^2 + 6x + 9 = (x + 3)(x + 3) = (x + 3)^2.$$

Now let us turn to the problem of factoring an expression of the form
$$mx^2 + px + q$$
where m, p, q are nonzero constants with $m \neq 1$ or -1. In this case, the first step consists of finding two factors of the product mq that have a sum of p, the coefficient of x. Then we split p into the sum of these two factors. This changes the given expression into the sum of four terms. These four terms can be considered two by two and factored by the method of grouping. The method is illustrated by Examples 8 and 9 below.

EXAMPLE 8 Factor $3x^2 + 11x + 6$.

Solution In this expression, the coefficients are $m = 3$, $p = 11$, and $q = 6$. The product of the coefficient of x^2 and the constant term is $mq = 3(6) = 18$. We must find two factors of this product 18 that have a sum equal to 11, the coefficient of x. Clearly two such factors of 18 are 9 and 2. Thus, in the given expression, we split the coefficient of x, 11, into $9 + 2$ and write

$$3x^2 + 11x + 6 = 3x^2 + (9 + 2)x + 6$$
$$= 3x^2 + 9x + 2x + 6.$$

We can take $3x$ as a common factor from the first two terms and 2 as a common factor from the last two terms.

$$3x^2 + 11x + 6 = 3x(x + 3) + 2(x + 3)$$
$$= (x + 3)(3x + 2)$$

Observe that, in the last step, we have taken $x + 3$ as common factor from the two terms.

EXAMPLE 9 Factor $6x^2 - 5x - 4$.

Solution The product of the coefficient of x^2 and the constant term is $6(-4) = -24$. We must find two factors of -24 that add up to -5, the coefficient of x. Clearly the two factors of -24 that have the sum -5 are 3 and -8. Therefore we write -5 as $-8 + 3$ in the given expression. This gives the following factoring.

$$6x^2 - 5x - 4 = 6x^2 + (-8 + 3)x - 4$$
$$= 6x^2 - 8x + 3x - 4$$
$$= 2x(3x - 4) + 1(3x - 4)$$
$$= (3x - 4)(2x + 1)$$

The following two formulas are helpful in factoring an expression which can be expressed as either the sum or the difference of two cubes.

$$a^3 + b^3 = (a + b)(a^2 - ab + b^2) \qquad (2)$$
$$a^3 - b^3 = (a - b)(a^2 + ab + b^2) \qquad (3)$$

These formulas can be verified by multiplying out the two expressions on the right.

EXAMPLE 10 Factor $8x^3 + 27y^3$.

Solution We use Formula (2).

$$8x^3 + 27y^3 = (2x)^3 + (3y)^3$$
$$= (2x + 3y)[(2x)^2 - (2x)(3y) + (3y)^2]$$
$$= (2x + 3y)(4x^2 - 6xy + 9y^2)$$

Note that the expression $4x^2 - 6xy + 9y^2$ cannot be factored further because the product of the coefficient of x^2 and the constant term is $4(9y^2) = 36y^2$, which cannot be expressed as the product of two factors whose sum is $-6y$, the coefficient of x. In fact, if all common monomial factors have been removed earlier, this second factor can *never* be factored further in such examples.

Note: According to Formulas (2) and (3) above, the sum and difference of two cubes can always be factored. In fact, every expression of the type $a^n + b^n$ or $a^n - b^n$ can be factored for all integers $n \geq 2$ with the single exception of the sum of two squares, $a^2 + b^2$. For example,

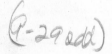

$$a^4 - b^4 = (a^2 - b^2)(a^2 + b^2) = (a - b)(a + b)(a^2 + b^2)$$
$$a^5 + b^5 = (a + b)(a^4 - a^3b + a^2b^2 - ab^3 + b^4)$$
$$a^4 + b^4 = (a^2 + \sqrt{2}\,ab + b^2)(a^2 - \sqrt{2}\,ab + b^2)$$

and so on.

Summary: We conclude this section with a summary of factoring for algebraic expressions.

1. The first step in factoring an algebraic expression should be to remove all common monomial factors.

2. If the remaining factor is the *difference of two squares*, the *difference of two cubes*, or the *sum of two cubes*, then use Formula (1), (2), or (3) in order to factor further.

3. In order to factor a multinomial expression consisting of four terms, the *grouping method* should be used.

4. A trinomial expression of the type $mx^2 + px + q$ can often be factored into the product of two factors of the type $(ax + b)(cx + d)$, as outlined above.

EXERCISES 6

(1–44) Factor the following expressions completely.

1. $3a + 6b$
2. $2x^2 - 10xy + 4x^3$
3. $4xy - 6yz$
4. $5x^2y + 10xy^2$
5. $2u + av - 2v - au$
6. $px - qy + py - qx$
7. $6xz - 16y - 24x + 4yz$
8. $15ac - 9ad - 30bc + 18bd$
9. $x^2 - 16$
10. $4y^2 - 25$
11. $3t^2 - 108a^2$
12. $5x^2 - 20y^2$
13. $x^2 + 5x + 6$
14. $2x^2 + 2x - 12$
15. $5y^4 + 25y^3 - 70y^2$
16. $12x - 7x^2 + x^3$
17. $2x^2 + 5x + 3$
18. $6x^2 + 10x - 4$
19. $6t^3 - 7t^2 - 20t$
20. $6t^4 + 15t^3 - 9t^2$
21. $x^3y - 25xy^3$
22. $9 + 12x + 4x^2$
23. $9t^2 - 12t + 4$
24. $(x^3 - 9x) + (45 - 5x^2)$
25. $x^3 - 27$
26. $8t^3 + 125$
27. $27u^3 + 8v^3$
28. $128x^3 - 54$
29. $6x^3y + 4x^2y - 10xy$
30. $x^2y^2 - a^2y^2 - b^2x^2 + a^2b^2$
31. $x^2y^2 - 9y^2 - 4x^2 + 36$
32. $5u^2v^2 - 20v^2 + 15u^2 - 60$
33. $x^2z^2 - 4z^2 + x^4 - 4x^2$
34. $ax^3 + by^3 + bx^3 + ay^3$

35. $a^3 + (b + 2)^3$ **36.** $x^6 + y^6$ **37.** $x^6 - 8y^6$

38. $x^3 + 1$ **39.** $xa + a + x + a^2$

40. $x^3 + y^3 + x^2y + xy^2$ **41.** $x^4 + 4y^4$

42. $16a^4 + b^4$ **43.** $x^4 - 16y^4$ **44.** $x^5 + y^5$

1-7 ALGEBRAIC FRACTIONS

The term **algebraic fraction** is used generally for the ratio of two expressions containing one or more variable, such as the following.

$$\frac{x^2 - 7x + 5}{2x + 3} \quad \text{and} \quad \frac{x^2y + xy^2}{x - y}$$

To make an algebraic fraction meaningful, it is understood that the variable or variables do not take values which make the denominator of the fraction zero. Thus, in the fraction on the left, $x \neq -\frac{3}{2}$, because if $x = -\frac{3}{2}$, $2x + 3 = 2(-\frac{3}{2}) + 3 = -3 + 3 = 0$, and the denominator is zero. Similarly, in the fraction on the right, $y \neq x$.

In this section, we shall study methods of simplifying algebraic fractions and of adding, subtracting, multiplying, and dividing two or more such fractions. Factoring plays an important role in such operations, as will be clear from the following examples. *The basic principles involved will be the same as those described for simplifying fractions in Section 1–2.*

Simplification of Fractions

EXAMPLE 1   Simplify $\dfrac{4x^2 - 20x + 24}{6 + 10x - 4x^2}$.

Solution   First of all, we completely factor the expressions that appear in the numerator and denominator. In this case, we have

$$4x^2 - 20x + 24 = 4(x^2 - 5x + 6)$$
$$= 2 \cdot 2(x - 2)(x - 3)$$

and

$$6 + 10x - 4x^2 = -2(2x^2 - 5x - 3)$$
$$= -2(2x + 1)(x - 3).$$

Note that in factoring the denominator, we first made the coefficient of x^2 positive, so that the x terms in the factors are positive both in the numerator and denominator. Therefore

$$\frac{4x^2 - 20x + 24}{6 + 10x - 4x^2} = \frac{2 \cdot 2(x - 2)(x - 3)}{-2(2x + 1)(x - 3)}$$
$$= \frac{2(x - 2)}{-(2x + 1)} = \frac{-2(x - 2)}{2x + 1}.$$

Observe that we have divided the numerator and denominator by the factors 2 and $x - 3$, which appear in both the numerator and denominator. This cancellation of factors was justified in Section 1–2 (see page 12 and Theorem 5). It can be done for binomial factors such as $(x - 3)$ in this example just as well as for monomial factors.

———————

We sometimes encounter fractions that involve radicals in the denominator, such as

$$\frac{2}{3 - \sqrt{2}} \quad \text{and} \quad \frac{x}{\sqrt{x + 2} - \sqrt{2}}.$$

The first fraction is purely arithmetical, whereas the second is algebraic. In such cases, since the denominator involves only two terms, we can simplify the fraction by transferring the radical to the numerator. Consider the first of the above two fractions as an example. We multiply numerator and denominator by $3 + \sqrt{2}$, which has the effect of putting the radical in the numerator:

$$\frac{2}{3 - \sqrt{2}} = \frac{2(3 + \sqrt{2})}{(3 - \sqrt{2})(3 + \sqrt{2})}.$$

This works since the denominator in this new fraction can be simplified using the formula for the difference of two squares,

$$(a - b)(a + b) = a^2 - b^2.$$

Taking $a = 3$ and $b = \sqrt{2}$, we have

$$(3 - \sqrt{2})(3 + \sqrt{2}) = 3^2 - (\sqrt{2})^2 = 9 - 2 = 7.$$

Therefore

$$\frac{2}{3 - \sqrt{2}} = \frac{2(3 + \sqrt{2})}{7}.$$

We say that the denominator has been *rationalized*.

In general, to rationalize a fraction involving an expression of the form $A + \sqrt{B}$ in the denominator, we multiply numerator and denominator by $A - \sqrt{B}$. If $A - \sqrt{B}$ occurs, we multiply numerator and denominator by $A + \sqrt{B}$. More generally, if a factor of the type $P\sqrt{A} \pm Q\sqrt{B}$ occurs in the denominator of a fraction, we multiply the numerator and denominator by $(P\sqrt{A} \mp Q\sqrt{B})$. (Note the change in sign of the second term.) This is illustrated in Example 2.

EXAMPLE 2   Rationalize the denominators of the following expressions.

(a) $\dfrac{2}{3 + \sqrt{5}}$ (b) $\dfrac{1}{2\sqrt{5} - 3\sqrt{3}}$

Solution   (a) Since the factor $3 + \sqrt{5}$ occurs, we multiply top and bottom by $3 - \sqrt{5}$.

$$\frac{2}{3 + \sqrt{5}} = \frac{2(3 - \sqrt{5})}{(3 + \sqrt{5})(3 - \sqrt{5})} = \frac{2(3 - \sqrt{5})}{3^2 - (\sqrt{5})^2}$$

$$= \frac{2(3 - \sqrt{5})}{9 - 5} = \frac{2(3 - \sqrt{5})}{4} = \frac{1}{2}(3 - \sqrt{5})$$

(b) The factor $2\sqrt{5} - 3\sqrt{3}$ occurs in the denominator, so we multiply by $2\sqrt{5} + 3\sqrt{3}$.

$$\frac{1}{2\sqrt{5} - 3\sqrt{3}} = \frac{1(2\sqrt{5} + 3\sqrt{3})}{(2\sqrt{5} - 3\sqrt{3})(2\sqrt{5} + 3\sqrt{3})}$$

$$= \frac{2\sqrt{5} + 3\sqrt{3}}{(2\sqrt{5})^2 - (3\sqrt{3})^2}$$

$$= \frac{2\sqrt{5} + 3\sqrt{3}}{4(5) - 9(3)} = \frac{2\sqrt{5} + 3\sqrt{3}}{20 - 27}$$

$$= -\frac{1}{7}(2\sqrt{5} + 3\sqrt{3})$$

Addition and Subtraction of Fractions

Two or more fractions that have a common denominator can be added or subtracted simply by adding or subtracting their numerator while keeping the denominator unchanged.

EXAMPLE 3

(a) $\dfrac{2x + 3}{x + 1} + \dfrac{x - 1}{x + 1} = \dfrac{(2x + 3) + (x - 1)}{x + 1} = \dfrac{2x + 3 + x - 1}{x + 1} = \dfrac{3x + 2}{x + 1}$

(b) $\dfrac{2x + 5}{x - 1} - \dfrac{7}{x - 1} = \dfrac{(2x + 5) - 7}{x - 1} = \dfrac{2x - 2}{x - 1} = \dfrac{2(x - 1)}{x - 1} = 2$

When the fractions to be added or subtracted do not have the same denominator, we first find their least common denominator (LCD) and then replace each of the given fractions by an equivalent fraction having this LCD as its denominator. The method is, in principle, no different from that described in Section 1–2.

To find the LCD of two or more fractions, we factor each denominator completely. The LCD is then obtained by multiplying all the distinct factors that appear in the denominators and raising each factor to the highest power to which it occurs in any one denominator. For example, the LCD of

$$\frac{2x + 1}{x - 3} \text{ and } \frac{3x - 1}{2x + 7} \text{ is } (x - 3)(2x + 7).$$

The LCD of $\dfrac{x + 1}{(x - 1)^2}$, $\dfrac{5}{(x - 1)(x + 2)}$, and $\dfrac{7}{(x + 2)^3(x + 3)}$ is

$$(x - 1)^2(x + 2)^3(x + 3).$$

EXAMPLE 4   Simplify $\dfrac{2x + 1}{x + 2} + \dfrac{x - 1}{3x - 2}$.

Solution   Here the denominators are already completely factored. The LCD in this case is $(x + 2)(3x - 2)$. To replace the first fraction, $(2x + 1)/(x + 2)$, by an equivalent fraction with the LCD $(x + 2)(3x - 2)$ as its denominator, we multiply the numerator and denominator of the fraction by $3x - 2$. Thus

$$\frac{2x + 1}{x + 2} = \frac{(2x + 1)(3x - 2)}{(x + 2)(3x - 2)}.$$

Similarly,

$$\frac{x - 1}{3x - 2} = \frac{(x - 1)(x + 2)}{(x + 2)(3x - 2)}.$$

Therefore we have the following sum.

$$\frac{2x + 1}{x + 2} + \frac{x - 1}{3x - 2} = \frac{(2x + 1)(3x - 2)}{(x + 2)(3x - 2)} + \frac{(x - 1)(x + 2)}{(x + 2)(3x - 2)}$$

$$= \frac{(2x + 1)(3x - 2) + (x - 1)(x + 2)}{(x + 2)(3x - 2)}$$

$$= \frac{(6x^2 - x - 2) + (x^2 + x - 2)}{(x + 2)(3x - 2)}$$

$$= \frac{7x^2 - 4}{(x + 2)(3x - 2)}$$

EXAMPLE 5 Simplify $\dfrac{5}{x^2 - 3x + 2} - \dfrac{1}{x + 2} + \dfrac{3}{x^2 - 4x + 4}$.

Solution The given expression, after factoring the denominators, is

$$\frac{5}{(x - 1)(x - 2)} - \frac{1}{x + 2} + \frac{3}{(x - 2)^2}.$$

Here the LCD is $(x - 1)(x - 2)^2(x + 2)$.

$$\frac{5}{(x - 1)(x - 2)} - \frac{1}{x + 2} + \frac{3}{(x - 2)^2}$$

$$= \frac{5(x - 2)(x + 2)}{(x - 1)(x - 2)^2(x + 2)} - \frac{(x - 1)(x - 2)^2}{(x + 2)(x - 1)(x - 2)^2}$$

$$+ \frac{3(x - 1)(x + 2)}{(x - 2)^2(x - 1)(x + 2)}$$

$$= \frac{5(x - 2)(x + 2) - (x - 1)(x - 2)^2 + 3(x - 1)(x + 2)}{(x - 1)(x + 2)(x - 2)^2}$$

$$= \frac{5(x^2 - 4) - (x - 1)(x^2 - 4x + 4) + 3(x^2 + x - 2)}{(x - 1)(x + 2)(x - 2)^2}$$

$$= \frac{5x^2 - 20 - (x^3 - 5x^2 + 8x - 4) + 3x^2 + 3x - 6}{(x - 1)(x + 2)(x - 2)^2}$$

$$= \frac{-x^3 + 13x^2 - 5x - 22}{(x - 1)(x + 2)(x - 2)^2}$$

EXAMPLE 6 Simplify $\sqrt{1 - x^2} + \dfrac{1 + x^2}{\sqrt{1 - x^2}}$.

Solution In this case, we write both terms as fractions with an LCD of $\sqrt{1 - x^2}$.

$$\sqrt{1 - x^2} = \frac{\sqrt{1 - x^2}\sqrt{1 - x^2}}{\sqrt{1 - x^2}} = \frac{1 - x^2}{\sqrt{1 - x^2}}$$

Thus we have the following sum.

$$\sqrt{1-x^2}+\frac{1+x^2}{\sqrt{1-x^2}}=\frac{1-x^2}{\sqrt{1-x^2}}+\frac{1+x^2}{\sqrt{1-x^2}}$$

$$=\frac{1-x^2+1+x^2}{\sqrt{1-x^2}}=\frac{2}{\sqrt{1-x^2}}$$

Multiplication of Fractions

Two or more fractions can be multiplied together simply by multiplying their numerators and denominators, as illustrated in Example 7.

EXAMPLE 7

(a) $\dfrac{2x+1}{x-2}\cdot\dfrac{3-x}{x+1}=\dfrac{(2x+1)(3-x)}{(x-2)(x+1)}$

(b) $\dfrac{x^2-5x+6}{6x^2+18x+12}\cdot\dfrac{4x^2-16}{2x^2-5x-3}=\dfrac{(x^2-5x+6)(4x^2-16)}{(6x^2+18x+12)(2x^2-5x-3)}$

This product can be simplified by factoring the numerator and denominator and dividing numerator and denominator by their common factors.

$$\frac{(x-2)(x-3)\cdot 2\cdot 2(x-2)(x+2)}{2\cdot 3(x+1)(x+2)(x-3)(2x+1)}=\frac{2(x-2)(x-2)}{3(x+1)(2x+1)}=\frac{2(x-2)^2}{3(x+1)(2x+1)}$$

Division of Fractions

To divide a fraction a/b by another fraction c/d, we invert c/d and multiply. (See page 11 and Theorem 4 of Section 1–2.)

$$\frac{a}{b}\div\frac{c}{d}=\frac{a/b}{c/d}=\frac{a}{b}\cdot\frac{d}{c}$$

The method is illustrated for algebraic fractions in Example 8.

EXAMPLE 8

(a) $\dfrac{2x+3}{x-1}\div\dfrac{x+3}{2x^2-2}=\dfrac{2x+3}{x-1}\cdot\dfrac{2x^2-2}{x+3}=\dfrac{(2x+3)\cdot 2(x-1)(x+1)}{(x-1)(x+3)}$

$$=\frac{2(x+1)(2x+3)}{(x+3)}$$

(b) $\dfrac{\dfrac{3x-1}{x-2}}{\dfrac{x+1}{1}}=\dfrac{\dfrac{3x-1}{x-2}}{\dfrac{x+1}{1}}$

$$=\frac{3x-1}{x-2}\cdot\frac{1}{x+1}=\frac{3x-1}{(x-2)(x+1)}$$

EXAMPLE 9

Simplify $\dfrac{x+2-\dfrac{4}{x-1}}{\dfrac{x^2-5x+6}{x^2-1}}$.

Solution   First of all, we simplify the numerator.

$$x + 2 - \frac{4}{x - 1} = \frac{x + 2}{1} - \frac{4}{x - 1}$$

$$= \frac{(x + 2)(x - 1)}{x - 1} - \frac{4}{x - 1}$$

$$= \frac{(x + 2)(x - 1) - 4}{x - 1}$$

$$= \frac{x^2 + x - 6}{x - 1}$$

Using this value for the numerator, we complete the division.

$$\frac{\dfrac{x^2 + x - 6}{x - 1}}{\dfrac{x^2 - 5x + 6}{x^2 - 1}} = \frac{x^2 + x - 6}{x - 1} \cdot \frac{x^2 - 1}{x^2 - 5x + 6}$$

$$= \frac{(x^2 + x - 6)(x^2 - 1)}{(x - 1)(x^2 - 5x + 6)}$$

$$= \frac{(x - 2)(x + 3)(x - 1)(x + 1)}{(x - 1)(x - 2)(x - 3)}$$

$$= \frac{(x + 3)(x + 1)}{x - 3}$$

EXERCISES 7

(1–24)   In the following questions, perform the indicated operations and simplify.

1. $\dfrac{4x}{2x + 3} + \dfrac{6}{2x + 3}$

2. $\dfrac{2x}{x - 2} - \dfrac{4}{x - 2}$

3. $\dfrac{x^2}{x - 3} - \dfrac{5x - 6}{x - 3}$

4. $\dfrac{2 - 3x}{x - 1} + \dfrac{x^2}{x - 1}$

5. $\dfrac{2x + 1}{x + 2} + 3$

6. $\dfrac{3x - 2}{x + 1} - 2$

7. $\dfrac{x}{x + 2} + \dfrac{3}{2x - 1}$

8. $\dfrac{x}{2x - 6} + \dfrac{x - 2}{x + 1}$

9. $\dfrac{1}{x^2 - 5x + 6} - \dfrac{1}{x^2 - 3x + 2}$

10. $\dfrac{x}{x^2 + 2x - 3} + \dfrac{1}{x^2 + x - 2}$

11. $\dfrac{x}{x^2 + 2x - 3} + \dfrac{1}{1 - 2x + x^2}$

12. $\dfrac{2}{9x^2 - 6x + 1} - \dfrac{3}{x + 1} + \dfrac{1}{3x^2 + 2x - 1}$

13. $\dfrac{1}{x^2 + 4x + 3} + \dfrac{3}{x^2 - 1} - \dfrac{2}{x + 3}$

14. $\dfrac{x}{2x^2 - x - 1} - \dfrac{3}{1 - 2x + x^2} + 2$

15. $\dfrac{2x + 4}{1 - x} \cdot \dfrac{x^2 - 1}{3x + 6}$

16. $\dfrac{x^2 - 7x + 12}{x^2 - x - 2} \cdot \dfrac{x^2 + 4x + 3}{2x^2 - 5x - 3}$

17. $\left(3 + \dfrac{1}{x - 1}\right)\left(1 - \dfrac{1}{3x - 2}\right)$

18. $\left(x - \dfrac{3}{x - 2}\right)\left(\dfrac{9}{x^2 - 9} - 1\right)$

19. $\dfrac{3x^2 - x - 2}{x^2 - x - 2} \div \dfrac{3x^2 + 5x + 2}{2x^2 - 5x + 2}$

20. $\dfrac{2x^2 + x - 1}{2x^2 + 10x + 12} \div \dfrac{1 - 4x^2}{4x^2 + 8x - 12}$

21. $\left(\dfrac{x^2 + x - 2}{2x + 3}\right)\Big/\left(\dfrac{x^2 - 4}{2x^2 + 5x + 3}\right)$

22. $\dfrac{1 - 1/t^2}{t + 1 - 2/t}$

23. $\dfrac{x + 2 + \dfrac{3}{x - 2}}{x - 6 + \dfrac{7}{x + 2}}$

24. $\left(p - \dfrac{2}{p + 1}\right)\Big/\left(1 - \dfrac{4p + 7}{p^2 + 4p + 3}\right)$

(25–30) Rationalize the denominators of the following expressions.

25. $\dfrac{1}{3 + \sqrt{7}}$

26. $\dfrac{3 + \sqrt{2}}{2 - \sqrt{3}}$

27. $\dfrac{1 + \sqrt{2}}{\sqrt{5} + \sqrt{3}}$

28. $\dfrac{6\sqrt{2}}{\sqrt{3} + \sqrt{6}}$

29. $\dfrac{3}{3 + \sqrt{3}}$

30. $\dfrac{1}{2\sqrt{3} - \sqrt{6}}$

REVIEW EXERCISES FOR CHAPTER 1

1. State whether each of the following is true or false. Replace each false statement by a corresponding true statement.

a. $a^m \cdot b^n = (ab)^{mn}$

b. $a^m + b^m = (a + b)^m$

c. $(2^0)^m = 1$

d. $(a - b)^2 = a^2 - b^2$

e. $-2(a + b) = -2a + b$

f. $(x + y)^2 = x^2 + y^2$

g. $\sqrt{a - b} = \sqrt{a} - \sqrt{b}$

h. $\dfrac{\cancel{a} + 2b}{\cancel{a}} = 2b$

i. $\sqrt[3]{a^2} = \sqrt[6]{a^4}$

j. $\dfrac{1}{a} - \dfrac{1}{b} = \dfrac{1}{a - b}$

k. $\dfrac{a/b}{c} = \dfrac{a}{b} \cdot \dfrac{c}{1}$

l. $(2a)^5 = 2a^5$

m. $\dfrac{a}{b} \div \dfrac{c}{d} = \dfrac{a \div c}{b \div d}$

n. $\dfrac{a}{b} \cdot \dfrac{c}{d} = \dfrac{a \cdot c}{b \cdot d}$

o. $(-1)^n = -1$ if n is an odd integer.

p. $\left(\dfrac{2}{3}\right)\left(\dfrac{3}{4}\right)\left(\dfrac{4}{5}\right)\left(\dfrac{5}{6}\right)\left(\dfrac{6}{7}\right) = \dfrac{2}{7}$

q. Every terminating decimal number represents a rational number.

r. Every rational number can be expressed as a terminating decimal.

(2–16) In the following expressions, perform the indicated operations and simplify the results.

2. $(125)^{2/3} \div (81)^{-3/4}$

3. $(32)^{-2} \times (243)^{1/5}$

4. $\left(\dfrac{x^a}{x^b}\right)^{a+b} \cdot \left(\dfrac{x^b}{x^c}\right)^{b+c} \cdot \left(\dfrac{x^c}{x^a}\right)^{c+a}$

5. $\left(\dfrac{x^a}{x^b}\right)^c \cdot \left(\dfrac{x^b}{x^c}\right)^a \cdot \left(\dfrac{x^a}{x^c}\right)^b$

6. $\dfrac{1}{x + 2} + \dfrac{2}{x - 3}$

7. $\dfrac{1}{x^2 + 1} + 2$

8. $\dfrac{1}{x-1} + \dfrac{1}{x^2-3x+2} - \dfrac{1}{x^2-2x+1}$

9. $\dfrac{2}{x^2+2x+1} - \dfrac{1}{x^2+4x+3} + \dfrac{3}{x^2-x-2}$

10. $\dfrac{x+y}{p^2-q^2} \div \dfrac{x^2-y^2}{p+q}$

11. $\dfrac{x^2+4x+4}{y^2-9} \div \dfrac{x^2+5x+6}{y^2-y-6}$

12. $\dfrac{a^2-b^2}{2a+4} \div \dfrac{a^2-3ab+2b^2}{a^2-4}$

13. $\dfrac{a^2+2ab+b^2}{x^2+5x+6} \cdot \dfrac{x^2-x-6}{a^2-b^2}$

14. $\left(x - \dfrac{2}{x+1}\right) \cdot \left(x + \dfrac{1}{x+2}\right)$

15. $\left(a + \dfrac{2}{a+3}\right) \cdot \left(a - \dfrac{9}{a}\right)$

16. $\dfrac{x+1}{x-2} + \dfrac{3x^2-27}{x+3} - \dfrac{2x+1}{2x-1}$

(17–26) Factor the following expressions completely.

17. $3x^2 - 75y^2$

18. $x^2 + 7x + 10$

19. $6x^2 - x - 15$

20. $2p^2 + p - 28$

21. $(a+4)(a-3) + (2a+3)(a+1)$

22. $(x+2)(x^2+x-1) + (2x-1)(x^2-3x-2)$

23. $4(x+1)^2 - (2x+5)^2$

24. $(p+q)^2 + 3(p+q) - 4$

25. $x^3 + \dfrac{8}{x^3}$

26. $(x-1)(x^2+1) + (x+1)(x^2-1)$

27. Prove that $\dfrac{1}{\sqrt{2}-1} + \dfrac{2}{\sqrt{3}+1} = \sqrt{2} + \sqrt{3}$.

28. Given $\sqrt{2} \doteq 1.414$ and $\sqrt{3} \doteq 1.732$, evaluate $\dfrac{1}{\sqrt{3}-\sqrt{2}}$ without using tables or long division.

EQUATIONS IN
ONE VARIABLE

CHAPTER

2-1 LINEAR EQUATIONS

An **equation** is a statement that expresses the equality of two algebraic expressions. It generally involves one or more variables and the equality symbol, $=$. The following are examples of equations.

$$2x - 3 = 9 - x \qquad (1)$$

$$y^2 - 5y = 6 - 4y \qquad (2)$$

$$2x + y = 7 \qquad (3)$$

$$\frac{a}{1 - r} = s \qquad (4)$$

In Equation (1), the variable is the letter x, while in Equation (2), it is y. In Equation (3), we have two variables, x and y. We do not allow the variable in any equation to take a value that would make an expression occurring in the equation undefined. For example, in Equation (4) above, r cannot be 1 because this would result in division by zero.

The two expressions separated by the equality symbol are called the two **sides** of the equation; individually they are called the *left side* and the *right side*.

Equations involving only constants and no variables are either true or false statements. For example,

$$3 + 2 = 5 \quad \text{and} \quad \tfrac{3}{15} = \tfrac{4}{20}$$

are true statements, while

$$2 + 5 = 6 \quad \text{and} \quad \tfrac{3}{2} = \tfrac{2}{3}$$

are false statements.

An equation containing a variable usually becomes a true statement for certain values of the variable, whereas it is a false statement for other values of the variable. For example, consider the equation

$$2x - 3 = x + 2.$$

If x takes the value 5, this equation becomes

$$2(5) - 3 = 5 + 2 \quad \text{or} \quad 10 - 3 = 5 + 2$$

which is a true statement. On the other hand, if x takes the value 4, we get

$$2(4) - 3 = 4 + 2 \quad \text{or} \quad 5 = 6$$

which is a false statement.

A value of the variable that makes an equation a true statement when substituted in the given equation is called a **root** or **solution** of the given equation. We say that the equation is *satisfied* by such a value of the variable.

Thus, for example, 5 is a root of the equation $2x - 3 = x + 2$. Similarly,

-2 is a root of the equation $y^2 + 3y = 6 + 4y$ because when we substitute -2 for y in the equation we obtain

$$(-2)^2 + 3(-2) = 6 + 4(-2)$$

or

$$4 - 6 = 6 - 8$$

which is a true statement.

Similarly, 5 is *not* a root of the equation $t^2 + 2t = 6 + 3t$ because when t is replaced by 5, we have

$$(5)^2 + 2(5) = 6 + 3(5)$$

or

$$25 + 10 = 6 + 15$$

which is *not* a true statement.

We are often interested in finding the roots of some given equation—that is, in determining all the values of the variable that make the equation a true statement. The process of finding the roots is called **solving the equation**. In carrying out this process, we usually perform certain operations on the equation which transform it into a new equation that is simpler to solve. Such simplifications must be made in such a way that the new equation has the same roots as the original equation. The following two operations give new equations, while at the same time satisfy this requirement of leaving the roots of the equation unchanged.

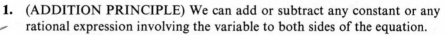

1. (ADDITION PRINCIPLE) We can add or subtract any constant or any rational expression involving the variable to both sides of the equation.

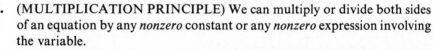

2. (MULTIPLICATION PRINCIPLE) We can multiply or divide both sides of an equation by any *nonzero* constant or any *nonzero* expression involving the variable.

(*Note:* Multiplication by an expression may produce an equation whose roots differ from those of the original equation if the expression becomes zero for certain values of the variable, as illustrated below.)

Consider, for example, the equation

$$x - 3 = 2 \tag{5}$$

Let us add 3 to both sides of this equation. By the addition principle, this operation will not change the roots of the equation.

$$x - 3 + 3 = 2 + 3$$

After simplification, this becomes

$$x = 5.$$

We conclude, therefore, that if x satisfies Equation (5) then $x = 5$: 5 is the one and only solution of Equation (5).

As a second example, consider the equation

$$5x = 15. \tag{6}$$

Let us divide both sides of this equation by 5. By the multiplication principle, this operation will not change the roots of the equation since the number by which we are dividing is nonzero. We get

$$\frac{5x}{5} = \frac{15}{5}$$

or

$$x = 3.$$

Thus the one and only solution of Equation (6) is $x = 3$.

Two equations with exactly the same solutions are said to be **equivalent** to one another. Operations 1 and 2 therefore transform a given equation into a new equation that is equivalent to the old one. In solving a given equation, we may have to use these operations several times in succession.

EXAMPLE 1   Solve the equation

$$5x - 3 = 2x + 9. \tag{7}$$

Solution   First let us subtract $2x$ from both sides of the equation and simplify.

$$5x - 3 - 2x = 2x + 9 - 2x$$
$$5x - 2x - 3 = 2x - 2x + 9 \tag{8}$$
$$3x - 3 = 9$$

Next we add 3 to both sides and simplify.

$$3x - 3 + 3 = 9 + 3$$
$$3x = 12 \tag{9}$$

Finally, we divide both sides by 3 (which is nonzero).

$$\frac{3x}{3} = \frac{12}{3}$$

$$x = 4$$

Thus the solution of Equation (7) is $x = 4$.

We observe that Equation (8) in Example 1 could be obtained from Equation (7) simply by moving the term $2x$ from the right side to the left side and changing its sign. We would get

$$5x - 3 - 2x = 9$$

or

$$3x - 3 = 9$$

which agrees with Equation (8). Again, we can obtain Equation (9) from Equation (8) by simply moving the term -3 from the left side to the right side and changing its sign. We would get

$$3x = 9 + 3$$

or

$$3x = 12.$$

Thus we can see that the addition principle stated earlier is equivalent to the following: *We can move any term from one side of an equation to the other side after changing its sign without affecting the roots of the equation.*

According to this principle, the equation $5x + 3 = 2x$ is equivalent to $5x - 2x + 3 = 0$, or $3 = 2x - 5x$.

According to the multiplication principle, any expression by which we multiply or divide must be nonzero, so care must be taken not to multiply or divide the equation by an expression that can be equal to zero. For example, consider the equation

$$x^2 = 5x.$$

Clearly $x = 0$ is a root of this equation. If we divide both sides by x, we obtain

$$x = 5.$$

We see that $x = 0$ is *not* a root of this resulting equation, although zero was a root of the original equation. The problem is that we have divided both sides by x, which can be zero, and this violates the multiplication principle. In dividing by x, we have lost one root of the equation. To avoid such pitfalls, care must be exercised not to divide by an expression that contains the variable unless we are sure that this expression is nonzero.

 An important class of equations consists of those called **polynomial equations**. In a polynomial equation, the two sides may consist of one or several terms added together, each term comprising a positive integral power of the variable multiplied by a constant coefficient. The **degree** of a polynomial equation is the highest power of the variable that occurs in the equation.

EXAMPLE 2 (a) $\frac{2}{3}x^2 - 1 = 3x + 2$ is a polynomial equation of degree 2.

(b) $x^4 - \frac{3}{2}x^2 - 5x = 4$ is a polynomial equation of degree 4.

(c) $(x^2 + 1)/(x + 1) = 2x$ is not a polynomial equation because of the fraction with x in its denominator.

A polynomial equation of degree 1 is called a **linear equation** and a polynomial equation of degree 2 is called a **quadratic equation**. Linear and quadratic equations will be studied in this and the next two sections of this chapter. We have the following definition.

 DEFINITION A *linear equation* in the variable x is an equation that can be expressed in the form

$$ax + b = 0 \qquad (a \neq 0)$$

where a and b are constants.

EXAMPLE 3 (a) $x - 4 = 0$ is a linear equation. Moving the 4 to the right side and changing its sign, we have $x = 4$. (*Note:* This is equivalent to adding 4 to both sides.) Thus the number 4 is the only solution of this equation.

(b) $2x + 3 = 0$ is a linear equation. Moving 3 to the right side, we have $2x = -3$; dividing by 2, we find $x = -\frac{3}{2}$. Thus $-\frac{3}{2}$ is the only solution of the given equation.

(c)   In the general case,

$$ax + b = 0$$

we can move the constant b to the right side, which gives

$$ax = -b.$$

Now if we divide by a, we get $x = -b/a$. Thus the linear equation $ax + b = 0$ has one and only one solution, namely $x = -b/a$.

Observe that in solving these equations, we kept the terms involving x on the left side of the equation and moved the constant terms to the right side. This is the general strategy for solving all linear equations. (We used it in solving Example 1 earlier.)

Often equations arise that do not appear at first glance to be linear, but which may be reduced to linear equations by appropriate simplification. In carrying out such a reduction, the following step-by-step procedure is often helpful.

Step 1   Remove any fractions which occur in the equation by multiplying both sides by the common denominator of the fractions involved.

Step 2   Expand any parentheses which occur. (Steps 1 and 2 may be interchanged.)

Step 3   Move all the terms containing the variable to the left side and all other terms to the right side; then simplify, if possible, by combining like terms.

This procedure is amplified in the following examples.

EXAMPLE 4   Solve the equation $3x - 4(6 - x) = 15 - 6x$.

Solution   *Step 1*   Since there are no fractions in the equation, we do not need step 1.

Step 2   Expanding the parentheses gives $3x - 24 + 4x = 15 - 6x$.

Step 3   Moving all the terms containing the variable to the left and the constant terms to the right, not forgetting to change their signs, we get

$$3x + 4x + 6x = 15 + 24$$

or

$$13x = 39.$$

We now obtain a solution by dividing both sides by 13, the coefficient of x.

$$x = \tfrac{39}{13} = 3$$

EXAMPLE 5   Solve the following equation.

$$\frac{5x}{3} - \frac{x - 2}{4} = \frac{9}{4} - \frac{1}{2}\left(x - \frac{2x - 1}{3}\right)$$

Solution   After removing the last parentheses, we can write the given equation as

$$\frac{5x}{3} - \frac{x - 2}{4} = \frac{9}{4} - \frac{x}{2} + \frac{2x - 1}{6}.$$

In order to remove the fractions, we multiply both sides by 12, the common denominator, and simplify.

$$12\left(\frac{5x}{3}\right) - 12\left(\frac{x-2}{4}\right) = 12\left(\frac{9}{4}\right) - 12\left(\frac{x}{2}\right) + 12\left(\frac{2x-1}{6}\right)$$

$$4(5x) - 3(x-2) = 3(9) - 6x + 2(2x-1)$$

$$20x - 3x + 6 = 27 - 6x + 4x - 2$$

Moving the x-terms all to the left and the constant terms to the right, we have

$$20x - 3x + 6x - 4x = 27 - 2 - 6$$

$$19x = 19.$$

Finally, dividing both sides by 19, we obtain $x = 1$, the required solution.

EXAMPLE 6   Solve the equation

$$\frac{x - 2t}{a} = \frac{3(x - y)}{z}$$

(a) for x;   (b) for t.

Solution   Here the common denominator is az. Multiplying both sides by az to clear the fractions, we have

$$z(x - 2t) = 3a(x - y)$$

$$xz - 2zt = 3ax - 3ay.$$ (∗)

(Note that neither a nor z can be zero, since otherwise the given equation would have a fraction with zero denominator. Hence we are allowed to multiply by az.)

(a) Since we are solving for x, all of the other letters involved in the equation are treated as constants. Moving all the terms containing the variable x to the left and all the terms without x to the right, we have

$$xz - 3ax = -3ay + 2zt$$

$$x(z - 3a) = 2zt - 3ay.$$

We divide both sides of the equation by $z - 3a$, assuming this factor to be nonzero.

$$x = \frac{2zt - 3ay}{z - 3a}$$

(b) Since we are solving for t, we shall keep only those terms which contain the variable t on the left and move all other terms to the right. Thus, from (∗) above, we have

$$-2zt = 3ax - 3ay - xz.$$

Dividing both sides by $-2z$, the coefficient of t, which, as noted above, cannot be zero, we have

$$t = \frac{3ax - 3ay - xz}{-2z}$$

$$= \frac{1}{2z}(-3ax + 3ay + xz)$$

which is the required solution for the variable t.

EXAMPLE 7   Solve the equation $(2x + 1)^2 = 4(x^2 - 1) + x - 1$.

Solution   At first glance, this equation does not appear to be linear because of the terms involving x^2. However, we shall see that it does reduce to a linear equation. Let us remove the parentheses and move all the terms involving x to the left side of the equation. We obtain

$$4x^2 + 4x + 1 = 4x^2 - 4 + x - 1$$
$$4x^2 + 4x - 4x^2 - x = -4 - 1 - 1.$$

We observe that the two terms involving $4x^2$ cancel one another out (that is, $4x^2 + 4x - 4x^2 - x = (4 - 4)x^2 + (4 - 1)x = 0x^2 + 3x$) and we are left with

$$3x = -6.$$

Hence the solution is $x = -2$.

___

EXERCISES 1

(1–10)   Check whether the given number(s) are solutions of the corresponding equations.

1. $3x + 7 = 12 - 2x$;   1

2. $5t - 3 = 18 + 3(1 - t)$;   3

3. $\dfrac{u + 2}{3u - 1} + 1 = \dfrac{6 - u}{u + 1}$;   2

4. $\dfrac{1 - 2y}{3 - y} + y = \dfrac{1}{y + 2}$; -2

5. $x^2 = 5x - 6$;   2, 5

6. $y^2 + 12 = 7y$;   4, -3

7. $\dfrac{5}{x} - \dfrac{3}{2x} = \dfrac{x}{2}$;   3

8. $\dfrac{7}{x + 1} + \dfrac{15}{3x - 1} = 8$; $-\frac{1}{2}, \frac{1}{3}$

9. $\dfrac{3}{x - 1} - \dfrac{5x}{x + 2} = \dfrac{1}{4}$;   1

10. $4x + \dfrac{7}{x} = 3$;   0

(11–14)   Reduce the following equations to polynomial equations and state the resulting degree.

11. $x^3 - 7x^2 + 5 = x(x^2 - 1) + 3x^2 - 2$

12. $(y - 2)(y + 5) = (2y - 1)(y + 1) + 7$

13. $y^2 + 7 = (y - 1)^2 + 3y$

14. $(u - 1)^2 = (u + 1)(u + 3) + 5$

(15–26)   Solve the following equations.

15. $4(x - 3) = 8 - x$

16. $2x - 5(1 - 3x) = 1 - 3(1 - 2x)$

17. $3 - 2(1 - x) = 5 + 7(x - 3)$

18. $6y - 5(1 + 2y) = 3 + 2(1 - y)$

19. $3z - 2 + 4(1 - z) = 5(1 - 2z) - 12$

20. $5[1 - 2(2z - 1)] = -3(3z - 1) + 1$

21. $\dfrac{3x + 7}{2} = \dfrac{1 + x}{3}$

22. $\dfrac{2x - 7}{3} = 5 - \dfrac{3x - 2}{4}$

23. $1 - \dfrac{2u - 3}{4} = \dfrac{2 - 5u}{3} - 3u$

24. $\dfrac{5y - 6}{2} = y - \dfrac{2 - y}{3}$

25. $\frac{1}{3}(2y + 1) + \frac{1}{2}y = \frac{2}{5}(1 - 2y) - 4$

26. $\dfrac{1}{2}\left[1 + \dfrac{1}{4}(3z - 1)\right] = \dfrac{2z}{3} - \dfrac{1}{2}$

(27–32) Reduce the following equations to linear equations and solve them.

27. $(x - 4)^2 = (x - 2)^2$

28. $(x - 1)(x + 3) = (x + 2)(x - 3) + 1$

29. $x^2 + (x + 1)^2 = (2x - 1)(x + 3)$

30. $(3x - 1)(x + 2) + 5x = (2x + 1)(x - 3) + x^2$

31. $(2x + 1)(x - 1) + x^2 = 3(x - 1)(x + 2) - 3$

32. $(3x + 1)(2x - 1) - 2x^2 = (2x - 3)^2 + 6x + 5$

2-2 QUADRATIC EQUATIONS

An equation of the type

$$ax^2 + bx + c = 0 \qquad (a \neq 0) \tag{1}$$

where a, b, and c are all constants, is called a **quadratic equation** in the variable x.

There are three methods of solving such an equation: factoring, use of the quadratic formula, and completing the square. Whichever of these methods is used, the first step in solving is to arrange the equation in the standard form of Equation (1). In this form, the right side of the equation is zero; on the left side, the x^2-terms, x-terms, and constant terms are collected together. The procedure in arriving at this standard form is therefore first to remove all fractions that occur by multiplying through by their common denominator, then to remove all parentheses, next to transfer all terms to the left side of the equation, and finally to group all like terms together.

The following examples illustrate this procedure, together with the factoring method.

EXAMPLE 1 Solve the equation $3(x^2 + 1) = 5(1 - x)$.

Solution There are no fractions in this equation. Removing the parentheses, we find

$$3x^2 + 3 = 5 - 5x.$$

After the terms on the right are moved across, the equation becomes

$$3x^2 + 3 - 5 + 5x = 0$$

or

$$3x^2 + 5x - 2 = 0.$$

Thus we have a quadratic equation in which the coefficients are $a = 3$, $b = 5$, and $c = -2$. When using the method of factors, we factor the expression on the left. In this example, we have

$$3x^2 + 5x - 2 = (3x - 1)(x + 2)$$

and so the equation takes the form

$$(3x - 1)(x + 2) = 0.$$

The product of the two factors $3x - 1$ and $x + 2$ is zero. The only way in which this can happen is if one of these two factors is itself zero.* Thus either $3x - 1 = 0$ or $x + 2 = 0$. In the first case, $3x = 1$ and so $x = \frac{1}{3}$. In the second case, $x + 2 = 0$ implies $x = -2$. Thus either $x = \frac{1}{3}$ or $x = -2$; these two numbers provide us with the two roots of the given equation.

We see then that the crux of the factoring method consists of writing the quadratic expression $ax^2 + bx + c$ that occurs in the standard form of the equation as the product of two linear factors. Since this product is given to be zero, it follows that one of the two factors must also be zero.*

EXAMPLE 2   Solve $(2x + 3)(3x - 1) = -4$.

Solution   We write the given equation with right side zero and simplify.

$$(2x + 3)(3x - 1) + 4 = 0$$
$$(6x^2 + 7x - 3) + 4 = 0$$
$$6x^2 + 7x + 1 = 0$$

Factoring, we have

$$(6x + 1)(x + 1) = 0.$$

Therefore we have the following.

$$6x + 1 = 0 \qquad \text{or} \qquad x + 1 = 0$$
$$6x = -1 \qquad\qquad\qquad x = -1$$
$$x = -\tfrac{1}{6}$$

The required roots are $-\frac{1}{6}$ and -1.

Quadratic Formula

You should recall from previous work in algebra that the roots of the quadratic equation

$$ax^2 + bx + c = 0 \qquad (a \neq 0)$$

are given by the **quadratic formula**

$$x = \frac{-b \pm \sqrt{b^2 - 4ac}}{2a}.$$

(This formula will be proved at the end of this section.)

To solve a quadratic equation, we can use this formula in the following way. First we reduce the equation to the standard form. Then we identify a, b, and c, the three coefficients that occur in that standard form, and simply substitute these coefficients into the quadratic formula.

EXAMPLE 3   Solve the equation $(2x + 3)(3x - 1) = -4$.

Solution   This equation was solved by the method of factors in Example 2; we shall now solve it by using the quadratic formula.

*The product of two factors cannot be zero unless one of the two factors is equal to zero.

The given equation when expressed in standard form (see Example 2) is

$$6x^2 + 7x + 1 = 0.$$

Comparing this with the general equation $ax^2 + bx + c = 0$, we have $a = 6$, $b = 7$, and $c = 1$. The quadratic formula gives the following.

$$
\begin{aligned}
x &= \frac{-b \pm \sqrt{b^2 - 4ac}}{2a} \\
&= \frac{-7 \pm \sqrt{49 - 4(6)(1)}}{2(6)} \\
&= \frac{-7 \pm \sqrt{49 - 24}}{12} \\
&= \frac{-7 \pm \sqrt{25}}{12} \\
&= \frac{-7 \pm 5}{12} \\
&= \frac{-7 + 5}{12} \quad \text{or} \quad \frac{-7 - 5}{12} \\
&= \frac{-2}{12} \quad \text{or} \quad \frac{-12}{12} \\
&= \frac{-1}{6} \quad \text{or} \quad -1
\end{aligned}
$$

Hence the roots are $-\frac{1}{6}$ and -1, exactly as we found in Example 2.

Remark: Every quadratic equation can be solved by using the quadratic formula. The method of factors is often a quicker method than the formula method, but on many occasions it is difficult to spot the factors of the quadratic expression. Furthermore, many quadratic expressions do not factor into rational factors; in such cases it is virtually impossible to factor by inspection.

EXAMPLE 4   Solve the equation $2x^2 - x - 2 = 0$.

Solution   Comparing the given equation with the standard equation $ax^2 + bx + c = 0$, we see that the coefficients are $a = 2$, $b = -1$, and $c = -2$. Thus we have the following.

$$
\begin{aligned}
x &= \frac{-b \pm \sqrt{b^2 - 4ac}}{2a} \\
&= \frac{-(-1) \pm \sqrt{(-1)^2 - 4(2)(-2)}}{2 \cdot 2} \\
&= \frac{1 \pm \sqrt{1 + 16}}{4} \\
&= \frac{1 \pm \sqrt{17}}{4}
\end{aligned}
$$

Hence the two roots are $\frac{1}{4}(1 + \sqrt{17}) \approx 1.281$ and $\frac{1}{4}(1 - \sqrt{17}) \approx -0.781$.

Completing the Square

The third method of solving quadratic equations is called **completing the square**. We shall explain this method with reference to a particular equation,

$$x^2 + 6x - 7 = 0. \tag{2}$$

Let us write this equation in the equivalent form

$$x^2 + 6x = 7. \tag{3}$$

We observe from the binomial square identity that

$$(x + 3)^2 = x^2 + 2 \cdot x \cdot 3 + 3^2$$
$$= x^2 + 6x + 9. \tag{4}$$

Comparing the right side of Equation (4) with the left side of Equation (3), we see that they differ only by the constant 9. So if we add 9 to both sides of Equation (3), we get

$$x^2 + 6x + 9 = 7 + 9 = 16$$

or, in other words,

$$(x + 3)^2 = 16.$$

This equation is now easily solved by taking the square root of both sides.

$$x + 3 = 4 \quad \text{or} \quad x + 3 = -4$$

Thus either $x = 4 - 3 = 1$ or $x = -4 - 3 = -7$. The two solutions are $x = 1$ and $x = -7$.

The question remains why we decided, following Equation (3), to look at the quantity $(x + 3)^2$. Why not consider $(x - 3)^2$ or $(x + 57)^2$ instead? The reason is that, after expanding this binomial square, we want the result to coincide with the left side of Equation (3) as far as the x^2- and x-terms are concerned. For example, if we took $(x - 3)^2$ instead, we would have $(x - 3)^2 = x^2 - 6x + 9$; although the x^2-term is the same as on the left side of Equation (3), the x-term is different. In order to get the same coefficient of x in Equation (3), we must have $(x + k)^2$, where k is half the coefficient of x in Equation (3)— that is, k equals half of 6, or 3.

The procedure in solving a quadratic equation by completing the square is outlined in these steps.

Step 1 Divide through by the coefficient of x^2.

Step 2 Move the constant term to the right side.

Step 3 Add k^2 to both sides of the equation, where k is half the coefficient of x occuring on the left side.

Step 4 The left side of the equation will now be the perfect square $(x + k)^2$, so the solution is found by taking the square root of both sides.

EXAMPLE 5   Solve the equation $2x^2 - x - 2 = 0$ by completing the square.

Solution   **Step 1**   Dividing through by 2, we get

$$x^2 - \tfrac{1}{2}x - 1 = 0.$$

Step 2 $x^2 - \tfrac{1}{2}x = 1$

Step 3   The coefficient of x is $-\frac{1}{2}$. We must take k equal to half of this, namely $-\frac{1}{4}$. So we must add $k^2 = (-\frac{1}{4})^2 = \frac{1}{16}$ to both sides.

$$x^2 - \tfrac{1}{2}x + \tfrac{1}{16} = 1 + \tfrac{1}{16} = \tfrac{17}{16}$$

Step 4   The left side of this equation is now $(x + k)^2$, that is, $[x + (-\frac{1}{4})]^2 = (x - \frac{1}{4})^2$. So

$$(x - \tfrac{1}{4})^2 = \tfrac{17}{16}.$$

Taking the square root of both sides, we find that

$$x - \frac{1}{4} = \pm\sqrt{\frac{17}{16}} = \pm\frac{\sqrt{17}}{4}$$

and therefore $x = \frac{1}{4} \pm \sqrt{17}/4$. (These agree with the roots found in Example 4.)

We close this section by deriving the quadratic formula from the quadratic equation $ax^2 + bx + c = 0$, with $a \neq 0$. The method of proof follows the method of completing the square. We begin by moving the constant term to the right:

$$ax^2 + bx = -c.$$

Dividing both sides by a (this is possible because $a \neq 0$), we get

$$x^2 + \frac{b}{a}x = -\frac{c}{a}. \tag{5}$$

According to the method of completing the square, we must divide the coefficient of x (which is b/a) by 2 (giving $b/2a$), square the result, and add this to both sides. We have the following:

$$x^2 + \frac{b}{a}x + \left(\frac{b}{2a}\right)^2 = -\frac{c}{a} + \left(\frac{b}{2a}\right)^2$$
$$= \frac{-4ac + b^2}{4a^2}.$$

But the left side here is $(x + b/2a)^2$, as can be seen from the binomial square formula. Therefore we obtain

$$\left(x + \frac{b}{2a}\right)^2 = \frac{b^2 - 4ac}{4a^2}.$$

After taking the square root of both sides, we get

$$x + \frac{b}{2a} = \pm\sqrt{\frac{b^2 - 4ac}{4a^2}} = \pm\frac{\sqrt{b^2 - 4ac}}{2a}.$$

Therefore

$$x = \frac{-b \pm \sqrt{b^2 - 4ac}}{2a}$$

as required.

One final remark: If the coefficients satisfy the condition $b^2 = 4ac$, the term involving square root in the quadratic formula becomes zero. In this case, the two roots of the equation coincide, so there are not two distinct roots. For example, an equation of this type is the quadratic equation $x^2 - 10x + 25 = 0$, which has just one root, $x = 5$.

If the coefficients are such that $b^2 < 4ac$, then the quantity under the square root in the quadratic formula is negative. In this case, the quadratic equation $ax^2 + bx + c = 0$ has no roots that are real numbers. For example, consider the equation $x^2 - 2x + 2 = 0$ (where $a = 1$, $b = -2$, and $c = 2$). From the quadratic formula, we have the following.

$$x = \frac{-b \pm \sqrt{b^2 - 4ac}}{2a}$$

$$= \frac{-(-2) \pm \sqrt{(-2)^2 - 4(1)(2)}}{2(1)}$$

$$= \frac{2 \pm \sqrt{-4}}{2}$$

But the expression $\sqrt{-4}$ has no meaning as a real number, so we must conclude that the given equation has no real roots.*

EXERCISES 2

(1–14) Solve the following equations by factoring.

1. $x^2 + 5x + 6 = 0$
2. $x^2 + 3x + 2 = 0$
3. $x^2 + 9x + 14 = 0$
4. $x^2 - 5x + 6 = 0$
5. $x^2 + 4x + 4 = 0$
6. $x^2 - 6x + 9 = 0$
7. $x^2 - 7x + 12 = 0$
8. $x^2 + 2x - 3 = 0$
9. $x^2 - 1 = 0$
10. $x^2 - 25 = 0$
11. $x^2 - 8x = 0$
12. $4x^2 - 5x = 0$
13. $6x^2 + \frac{5}{2}x + \frac{1}{4} = 0$
14. $\frac{x^2}{2} + \frac{10}{3}x + 2 = 0$

(15–24) Solve the following equations by the quadratic formula.

15. $x^2 + 3x + 1 = 0$
16. $x^2 - 4x + 2 = 0$
17. $2x^2 + 3x - 4 = 0$
18. $3x^2 + 6x - 2 = 0$
19. $x^2 + x - 3 = 0$
20. $4x^2 - 12x + 9 = 0$
21. $4x^2 + 20x + 25 = 0$
22. $2x^2 + 5x - 3 = 0$
23. $5x(x + 2) + 6 = 3$
24. $(4x - 1)(2x + 3) = 18x - 4$

---

*Quantities that are the square roots of negative numbers are called *imaginary* numbers. In particular, $\sqrt{-1}$ is called the imaginary unit and is denoted by i. Then, for example, we can write $\sqrt{-4} = \sqrt{(4)(-1)} = 2\sqrt{-1} = 2i$. In a similar way, every imaginary number can be written in the form iB, where B is some real number.

The solution of the last example can be written in the form

$$x = \tfrac{1}{2}(2 \pm \sqrt{-4}) = \tfrac{1}{2}(2 \pm 2i) = 1 \pm i.$$

We see that these solutions consist of two parts, a **real part**, which is 1, and an **imaginary part**, which is i or $-i$, depending on which root we take. Any number that can be written as the sum of a real number and an imaginary number is called a **complex number**. In general, a complex number has the form $A + iB$, where A and B are real numbers.

Thus when $b^2 - 4ac > 0$, the solutions of a quadratic equation consist of two different real numbers. When $b^2 - 4ac = 0$, there is only one solution and it is a real number. And when $b^2 - 4ac < 0$, there are two different solutions, both of which are complex numbers.

All of the standard operations can be carried out with complex numbers. One simply has to remember that $i^2 = -1$.

(25–32) Solve the following equations by completing the square.

25. $x^2 + 6x - 1 = 0$ **26.** $x^2 + 2x - 4 = 0$ **27.** $x^2 - 3x - 1 = 0$

28. $x^2 + 5x + 5 = 0$ **29.** $4x^2 - 8x - 3 = 0$ **30.** $2x^2 - 14x + 1 = 0$

31. $7x + 3(x^2 - 5) = x - 3$ **32.** $2x(4x - 1) = 4 + 2x$

(33–46) Solve the following equations by any appropriate method.

33. $6x^2 = 11$ **34.** $5x^2 + 7 = 0$ **35.** $6x^2 = 11x$

36. $2(x^2 + 1) = 5x$ **37.** $15x^2 = 40(x + 2)$

38. $(3x + 5)(2x - 3) = -8$ **39.** $3x(2x - 5) = -4x - 3$

40. $(x + 1)^2 = 2x^2$ **41.** $x^2 = 2(x - 1)(x + 2)$

42. $2x(x + 1) = x^2 - 1$ **43.** $\frac{2}{3}x^2 - \frac{5}{3}x = x - 1$

44. $\frac{x^2}{3} + 2x = 1 + x$ **45.** $\frac{x^2}{3} = \frac{11}{6}x + 1$

46. $5x^2 - \frac{7}{2}x = \frac{1}{2}x + 1$

2-3 APPLICATIONS OF EQUATIONS

Algebraic methods are very useful in solving applied problems in many different fields. Such problems are generally stated in verbal form; before we can make use of our algebraic tools, it is necessary to translate the verbal statements into corresponding algebraic statements. The following step-by-step procedure will very often be helpful in carrying out this process.

Step 1 Represent the unknown quantity—that is, the quantity to be determined—by an algebraic symbol, such as x. In some problems, two or more quantities must be determined; in such cases we choose only one of them to be x.

Step 2 Express all of the other quantities involved in the problem, if there are any, in terms of x.

Step 3 Translate verbal expressions occurring in the problem into algebraic expressions involving x. In this context, words such as *is* or *was* are translated into the algebraic symbol $=$.

Step 4 Solve the algebraic statement or statements according to the methods of algebra.

Step 5 Translate the algebraic solution back into verbal form.

In verbal problems, a number of typical expressions occur involving phrases such as some amount more than or less than a certain value or multiples such as twice or half of a certain quantity. The following examples illustrate how to translate such expressions into algebraic terms.

EXAMPLE 1   (a)   If Jack has x dollars and Jill has 5 more than Jack, then Jill has $(x + 5)$ dollars. If Sam has 3 less than Jack, then Sam has $(x - 3)$ dollars.

(b)   If Chuck is x years old and his father is 4 years more than twice Chuck's age, then Chuck's father is $(2x + 4)$ years old.

(c)   If a certain store sells x refrigerators per month and a second store sells 5 less than one-third as many, then the second store sells $(\frac{1}{3}x - 5)$ refrigerators.

We shall begin with some examples of an elementary nature to illustrate as simply as possible the translation between verbal and algebraic forms.

EXAMPLE 2   Determine two consecutive integers whose sum is 19.

Solution   **Step 1**   Since we must find two integers, we must decide which of them to call x. Let us denote the smaller integer by x.

Step 2   The second integer is then $x + 1$, since the two are consecutive.

Step 3   The expression *sum of the two integers* is translated into the algebraic expression $x + (x + 1)$. The statement that this sum is 19 translates into the equation

$$x + (x + 1) = 19.$$

Step 4   We solve for x.

$$2x + 1 = 19$$
$$2x = 19 - 1 = 18$$
$$x = \frac{18}{2} = 9$$

Step 5   The smaller of the integers is therefore 9. The larger, $x + 1$, is 10.

EXAMPLE 3   A man is 7 years older than his wife. Ten years ago he was twice her age. How old is he?

Solution   Let x denote the present age of the man in years. Since his wife is 7 years younger than he is, her present age must be $(x - 7)$ years.

Ten years ago, the age of the man was 10 years less than it is now, so his age then was $x - 10$. (For example, if his present age is $x = 38$, then 10 years ago he was $x - 10 = 38 - 10 = 28$ years old.) Similarly, 10 years ago his wife's age was 10 years less than it is now, so her age was $(x - 7) - 10$ or $x - 17$. We are told that at that time the man's age, $x - 10$, was twice his wife's age, $x - 17$. Thus we write

$$x - 10 = 2(x - 17).$$

We simplify and solve for x.

$$x - 10 = 2x - 34$$
$$x - 2x = -34 + 10$$
$$-x = -24$$
$$x = 24$$

The present age of the man is therefore 24 years. His wife is 17. Ten years ago they were 14 and 7, respectively.

EXAMPLE 4   A salesperson earns a basic salary of $600 per month plus a commission of 10% on the sales she makes. She finds that on average, she takes $1\frac{1}{2}$ hours to make $100 worth of sales. How many hours must she work on the average each month if her monthly earnings are to be $2000?

Solution   Suppose that she works x hours per month. Each $\frac{3}{2}$ hours, she makes $100 in sales, so each hour, she averages two-thirds of this, or $(200/3)$ in sales. Her commission is 10% or one-tenth of this, so her average commission per hour is $\frac{20}{3}$. In x hours, she will therefore earn a commission of $(\frac{20}{3})x$ dollars.

Adding on her basic salary, we obtain a total monthly income of $600 + (\frac{20}{3})x$. This must be equal to 2000, so we obtain the equation

$$600 + \tfrac{20}{3}x = 2000.$$

Solving gives the following equations.

$$\tfrac{20}{3}x = 2000 - 600 = 1400$$

$$x = \tfrac{3}{20}(1400) = 210$$

The salesperson must therefore work 210 hours per month, on the average, if she is to reach the desired income level.

EXAMPLE 5   A cattle dealer bought 1000 steers for $150 each. He sold 400 of them at a profit of 25%. At what price must he sell the remaining 600 if his average profit on the whole lot is to be 30%?

Solution   His profit on each steer in the 400 already sold is 25% of the cost price, which is 25% of $150, or $37.50. On 400 steers, his profit was therefore $37.50 × 400 = $15,000. Let his selling price on the remaining 600 steers be x dollars. Then his profit per steer is $x - 150$ and his profit on the remaining 600 is $600(x - 150)$ dollars. Therefore his total profit on the whole purchase is

$$15,000 + 600(x - 150) \text{ dollars.}$$

This profit should be 30% of the price he paid for the 1000 steers, that is, 30% of $150,000. This is equal to $[\frac{3}{10}(150,000)]$, or $45,000. Thus we arrive at the equation

$$15,000 + 600(x - 150) = 45,000.$$

We next solve.

$$15,000 + 600x - 90,000 = 45,000$$

$$600x = 45,000 - 15,000 + 90,000 = 120,000$$

$$x = \frac{120,000}{600} = 200$$

The dealer must sell the remaining steers at $200 each for a 30% average profit.

EXAMPLE 6   Ms. Cordero has $70,000 to invest. She wants to receive an annual income of $5000. She can invest her funds in 6% government bonds or, with a greater risk, in 8.5% mortgage bonds. How should she invest her money in order to minimize her risk and yet earn $5000?

Solution   Let the amount invested in government bonds be x dollars. Then the amount invested in mortgage bonds is $(70,000 - x)$ dollars. Income received from government bonds at 6% is $\frac{6}{100}x$ dollars. Income received from mortgage bonds at 8.5% is

$$\frac{8.5}{100}(70,000 - x) \text{ dollars} = \frac{85}{1000}(70,000 - x) \text{ dollars}.$$

Since the total income received from the two types of bonds must be $5000,

$$\tfrac{6}{100}x + \tfrac{85}{1000}(70,000 - x) = 5000.$$

We multiply both sides by 1000 and solve for x.

$$60x + 85(70,000 - x) = 5,000,000$$
$$60x + 5,950,000 - 85x = 5,000,000$$
$$-25x = 5,000,000 - 5,950,000$$
$$= -950,000$$
$$x = \frac{-950,000}{-25} = 38,000$$

Thus Ms. Cordero should invest $38,000 in government bonds and the remaining $32,000 in mortgage bonds. She could increase her income by investing a bigger proportion of her capital in mortgage bonds, but this would increase her risk.

EXAMPLE 7   A winery wishes to make 10,000 liters of sherry by fortifying white wine, which has an alcohol content of 10%, with brandy, which has an alcohol content of 35% by volume. The sherry is to have an alcohol content of 15%. Determine the quantities of wine and brandy which should be mixed together to produce the desired result.

Solution   Let x liters of brandy be used in making the 10,000 liters of sherry. Then the volume of white wine used will be $(10,000 - x)$ liters. Since brandy contains 35% alcohol, the amount of alcohol in x liters of brandy is $\frac{35}{100}x$. Similarly, the wine contains 10% alcohol, so $(10,000 - x)$ liters of wine contain $\frac{1}{10}(10,000 - x)$ liters of alcohol. Therefore the total amount of alcohol in the mixture will be

$$\tfrac{35}{100}x + \tfrac{1}{10}(10,000 - x) \text{ liters}.$$

The mixture is to contain 15% alcohol, so in the 10,000 liters there should be $\frac{15}{100}(10,000) = 1500$ liters of alcohol. Therefore we have the equation

$$\tfrac{35}{100}x + \tfrac{1}{10}(10,000 - x) = 1500.$$

Solving, we have the following.

$$\tfrac{35}{100}x + 1000 - \tfrac{1}{10}x = 1500$$
$$\tfrac{35}{100}x - \tfrac{1}{10}x = 1500 - 1000 = 500$$
$$35x - 10x = 50,000$$
$$25x = 50,000$$
$$x = \frac{50,000}{25} = 2000$$

So 2000 liters of brandy and 8000 liters of wine must be mixed together.

EXAMPLE 8   Steve owns an apartment building that has 60 suites. He can rent all the suites if he charges a rent of $180 per month. At a higher rent, some of the suites will remain empty; on the average, for each increase of $5 in rent, 1 suite becomes vacant with no possibility of renting it. Find the rent he should charge per suite in order to obtain a total income of $11,475.

Solution   Let n denote the number of 5-dollar increases. Then the increase in rent per suite is $5n$ dollars, which means that the rent per suite is $(180 + 5n)$ dollars. The number of units not rented will then be n, so that the number rented will be $60 - n$. The total rent he will receive equals

$$\text{(rent per suite)} \times \text{(number of suites rented)}.$$

Therefore

$$11,475 = (180 + 5n)(60 - n)$$

or

$$11,475 = 5(36 + n)(60 - n).$$

Dividing both sides by 5, we get

$$2295 = (36 + n)(60 - n)$$
$$= 2160 + 24n - n^2.$$

Therefore

$$n^2 - 24n + 135 = 0$$
$$(n - 9)(n - 15) = 0.$$

Thus $n = 9$ or 15. Hence the rent charged should be $180 + 5n$, which is $180 + 45 = \$225$ or $180 + 75 = \$255$. In the first case, 9 of the suites will be vacant and the 51 rented suites will produce an income of $225 each. In the second case, when the rent is $255, 15 suites will be vacant, and only 45 rented, but the total revenue will be the same.

EXAMPLE 9   The egg marketing board of British Columbia knows from past experience that if it charges p dollars per dozen eggs, the number sold per week will be x million dozens, where $p = 2 - x$. Its total weekly revenue would then be $R = xp = x(2 - x)$ million dollars. The cost to the industry of producing x million dozen eggs per week is given by $C = 0.25 + 0.5x$ million dollars. The weekly profit of the industry is $P = R - C$. What price should the marketing board set for eggs to ensure a weekly profit of 0.25 million dollars?

Solution   The profit is given by the following equation.

$$P = R - C$$
$$= x(2 - x) - (0.25 + 0.5x)$$
$$= -x^2 + 1.5x - 0.25$$

Setting this equal to 0.25, we obtain the equation

$$-x^2 + 1.5x - 0.25 = 0.25$$

or

$$x^2 - 1.5x + 0.5 = 0.$$

Using the quadratic formula, we find the roots for x.

$$x = \frac{-b \pm \sqrt{b^2 - 4ac}}{2a}$$

$$= \frac{-(-1.5) \pm \sqrt{(-1.5)^2 - 4(1)(0.5)}}{(2)(1)}$$

$$= \frac{1.5 \pm \sqrt{2.25 - 2}}{2}$$

$$= \tfrac{1}{2}(1.5 \pm 0.5)$$

$$= 1 \quad \text{or} \quad 0.5$$

Now $p = 2 - x$. So when $x = 1$, we have $p = 1$, and when $x = 0.5$, $p = 1.5$. Thus the marketing board has a choice of two policies: It can charge $1 per dozen, in which case the sales will be 1 million dozen, or it can charge $1.50 per dozen, when the sales will be 0.5 million dozen per week. In either case the profits to the industry will be $0.25 million per week.

EXAMPLE 10   A corporation wishes to set aside a sum of $1 million to be invested at interest and used at a later date to repay two bond issues that will become due. One year after the sum is first invested, $250,000 will be required for the first issue; 1 year later, $900,000 more will be required for the second issue. Determine the rate of interest necessary in order that the investment will be sufficient to cover both repayments.

Solution   Let the rate of interest be R percent per annum. When invested at this rate, a sum S gains interest during one year equal to $(R/100)S$. (For example at a 5% rate of interest, the interest per annum is $\frac{5}{100}S$ or $0.05S$.) So after the first year, the $1 million earns interest of $(R/100)(1$ million$)$. Adding this interest to the original sum, we see that the value of the investment after 1 year is

$$1 + \left(\frac{R}{100}\right)(1 \text{ million}) = \left(1 + \frac{R}{100}\right) \text{ million dollars.}$$

At this time, 0.25 million is withdrawn; at the beginning of the second year, the amount still invested is (in millions); therefore

$$S' = \left(1 + \frac{R}{100}\right) - 0.25 = 0.75 + \frac{R}{100}.$$

After a second year at interest, the value of the investment is

$$S' + \left(\frac{R}{100}\right)S' = S'\left(1 + \frac{R}{100}\right) = \left(0.75 + \frac{R}{100}\right)\left(1 + \frac{R}{100}\right).$$

This must be the amount (0.9 million) necessary to pay off the second bond issue. Therefore we arrive at the equation

$$\left(0.75 + \frac{R}{100}\right)\left(1 + \frac{R}{100}\right) = 0.9.$$

Thus

$$0.75 + 1.75\left(\frac{R}{100}\right) + \left(\frac{R}{100}\right)^2 = 0.9.$$

Multiplying both sides by 100^2 to remove the fractions, we arrive at the equation

$$7500 + 175R + R^2 = 9000$$

or

$$R^2 + 175R - 1500 = 0.$$

From the quadratic formula (with $a = 1$, $b = 175$, and $c = -1500$), we find the following value for R.

$$R = \frac{-175 \pm \sqrt{175^2 - 4(1)(-1500)}}{2(1)}$$

$$= \tfrac{1}{2}[-175 \pm \sqrt{30,625 + 6000}]$$

$$= \tfrac{1}{2}[-175 \pm \sqrt{36,625}]$$

$$= \tfrac{1}{2}[-175 \pm 191.4]$$

$$= 8.2 \quad \text{or} \quad -183.2$$

Clearly, the second solution does not make any practical sense—a rate of interest would hardly be negative. The meaningful solution is $R = 8.2$. So the investment must earn 8.2% per annum in order to provide sufficient funds to pay off the bond issues.

EXERCISES 3

(1–3) If Joe has x dollars, how many dollars does Judy have in each case?

1. She has $4 more than Joe.

2. She has $3 less than twice as much as Joe.

3. She has $2 more than half as much as Joe.

(4–7) If Joe is x years old and Judy is four years younger, how old is Fred in each case?

4. Fred is 3 years older than Judy.

5. Fred is 1 year more than the average age of Joe and Judy.

6. Fred is 10 years less than the sum of Joe's and Judy's ages.

7. Fred is 2 years less than five times the difference between Joe's and Judy's ages.

8. Bruce and Jack together have $75. If Jack has $5 more than Bruce, how much does Jack have?

9. In a business mathematics class, there are 52 students. If the number of boys is 7 more than twice the number of girls, determine the number of girls in the class.

10. A father is three times as old as his son. In 12 years, he will be twice the age of his son. How old are the father and the son now?

11. Five years ago, Marlene was twice as old as her brother. Find the present age of Marlene if the sum of their ages today is 40 years.

12. Sue has 3 more nickels than dimes and 5 more dimes than quarters. In all she has $2.10. How many of each coin does she have?

13. I have twice as many dimes in my pocket as I have quarters. If I had 4 fewer dimes and 3 more quarters, I would have $2.60. How many dimes and quarters do I have?

14. A man invests twice as much at 8% as he invests at 5%. His total annual income from the two investments is $840. How much is invested at each rate?

15. A college has $60,000 to invest in an endowment fund in order to have an annual income of $5000 for a scholarship. Part of this will be invested in government bonds at 8% and the remainder in long-term fixed deposits at 10.5%. How much should be invested in each to provide the required income?

16. The trustees of an endowment fund want to invest $18,000 in two kinds of securities paying 9% and 6% annual dividends, respectively. How much must be invested at each rate if the annual income is to be equivalent to a yield of 8% on the total investment?

17. It costs a manufacturer $2000 to buy the tools to manufacture a certain household item. If it costs 60¢ for the material and labor for each item produced and if the manufacturer can sell the items for 90¢ each, find how many items should be produced and sold to make a profit of $1000.

18. The cost of publishing each copy of a weekly magazine is 28¢. The revenue from the dealer sales is 24¢ per copy and from advertising is 20% of the revenue obtained from sales in excess of 3000 copies. How many copies must be published and sold each week to earn a weekly profit of $1000?

19. A used-car dealer bought two cars for $2900. He sold one at a gain of 10% and another at a loss of 5% and still made a gain of $185 on the whole transaction. Find the cost of each car.

20. A trader offers a 30% discount on the marked price of an article and yet makes a profit of 10%. If it costs $35 to the trader, what must be the marked price?

21. A dealer sold a watch for $75. His percentage profit was equal to the cost price in dollars. Find the cost price of the watch.

22. For every $100 invested in secured commercial loans, a bank receives $116.64 after two years. This amount represents capital and the interest compounded annually. What is the rate of interest?

23. In two years, the XYZ company will require $1,102,500 to retire some of its bonds. At what rate of interest compounded annually should $1,000,000 be invested over the two-year period to receive the required amount to retire the bonds?

24. Royal Realty has built a new rental unit of 60 apartments. It is known from past experience that if they charge a monthly rent of $150 per apartment, all the units will be occupied, but for each $3 increase in rent, one apartment unit is likely to remain vacant. What rent should be charged to generate the same $9000 total revenue as is obtained with a rent of $150 and at the same time to leave some vacant suites?

25. In Exercise 24, the maintenance, service, and other costs on the building amount to $5000 per month plus $50 per occupied suite and $20 per vacant suite. What rental should be charged if the profit is to be $1225 per month? (The profit is rental revenue minus all costs.)

26. If a publisher prices a book at $20, 20,000 copies will be sold. For every dollar by which the price is increased, sales will fall by 500 books. What should the book cost in order to generate a total revenue from sales of $425,000?

27. In Exercise 26, the cost of producing each copy is $16. What price should the publisher charge to have a profit of $200,000?

28. In Exercise 27, assume that in addition to the cost of $16 per copy, the publisher must pay a royalty to the author of the book equal to 10% of the selling price. What price should now be charged per copy in order to realize a profit of $200,000?

29. A sum of $100 is invested at interest for 1 year; then, together with the interest earned, it is invested for a second year at twice the first rate of interest. If the total sum realized is $112.32, what are the two rates of interest?

30. In Exercise 29, $25 is withdrawn after the first year and the remainder is invested at twice the rate of interest. If the value of the investment at the end of the second year is $88, what are the two rates of interest?

REVIEW EXERCISES FOR CHAPTER 2

1. State whether each of the following is true or false. Replace each false statement by a corresponding true statement.

    a. If both sides of an equation are multiplied by any constant, the roots of the equation remain unchanged.

    b. Any expression can be added to both sides of an equation and the roots will remain unchanged.

    c. The roots of an equation remain unchanged when both sides are multiplied by an expression containing the variable.

    d. It is possible to square both sides of an equation without altering its roots.

    e. If $px = q$, then $x = q - p$.

    f. A quadratic equation is an equation of the form $ax^2 + bx + c = 0$, where a, b, and c are any constants.

    g. The solution of the equation $x^2 = 4$ is given by $x = 2$.

    h. The roots of the quadratic equation $ax^2 + bx + c = 0$, $a \neq 0$, are given by

    $$x = -\frac{b}{2a} \pm \sqrt{b^2 - 4ac}.$$

    i. A linear equation always has exactly one root.

    j. A quadratic equation always has two different roots.

    k. It is possible for a linear equation to have no roots at all.

    l. It is possible for a quadratic equation to have no roots at all.

(2–21) Solve the following equations for x.

2. $3(2 - x) + x = 5(2x - 1) + 2$
3. $2(1 - 4x) - 1 = x - 2(2 - 3x)$
4. $x^2 + 13x + 40 = 0$
5. $3x^2 - 11x + 10 = 0$
6. $\dfrac{1}{x} + \dfrac{1}{a} = \dfrac{c}{b}$
7. $\dfrac{x}{bc} + \dfrac{x}{ca} + \dfrac{x}{ab} = a + b + c$
8. $(3x - 2)^2 = (3x + 1)^2$
9. $(2x - 1)^2 = 3x^2 + (x - 1)(x - 2)$
10. $(2x + 1)(x - 3) = (2x + 5)(x - 1)$
11. $(x + 2)(x - 3) = 2 + (x - 1)(x - 2)$
12. $(x + 1)(2x - 5) = (x + 2)(x - 3)$
13. $1 + (3x + 4)(x - 2) = (2x + 1)(x - 3)$
14. $(x + 2)(2x - 1) = 1 + (x + 3)(x + 1)$
15. $28 + (x - 5)(x + 7) = (3x - 1)(x - 2)$
*16. $\sqrt{2x + 5} = x + 1$
*17. $\sqrt{x + 5} = x - 1$
*18. $x + 3 = \sqrt{5x + 11}$
*19. $\sqrt{x - 2} = 2 - x$
*20. $2^{x^2} = \dfrac{8}{4^x}$
*21. $4^x = 8^{3-x}$

(22–24) Solve the following equations for the indicated variables.

22. $\dfrac{1}{x} + \dfrac{1}{y} = \dfrac{1}{z}$ **a.** for y **b.** for z

23. $S = \dfrac{a - rl}{1 - r}$ **a.** for r **b.** for l

24. $P = P_0(1 + R/100)^2$ **a.** for P_0 **b.** for R

25. The winner of Western Express Lottery wants to invest his prize money of $100,000 in two investments at 8% and 10%. How much should he invest in each if he wants to obtain an annual income of $8500?

26. The Western Furniture Mart received a shipment of 55 tables, some night tables and some coffee tables. They were billed for $645. If each night table costs $9 and each coffee table costs $15, how many tables of each type were received by the store?

27. The manufacturer of a certain product can sell all she can produce at a price of $20 each. It costs her $12.50 to produce each item in materials and labor, and she has additional overhead costs of $7000 per month in order to operate the plant. Find the number of units she should produce and sell to make a profit of $5000 per month.

28. A television manufacturer wants to decide whether to manufacture his own picture tubes that have been purchased from outside suppliers at $5.70 each. Manufacturing the picture tubes will increase overhead costs by $960 per month and the cost of labor and materials will be $4.20 for each picture tube. How many picture tubes would have to be used by the manufacturer each month to justify a decision to manufacture picture tubes?

29. The number of items of a product that a manufacturer can sell each week depends on the price charged for them. Assume that at a price of p dollars, x items per

week can be sold, where $x = 300(6 - p)$. Each item costs \$3 to manufacture. The profit per item is therefore $(p - 3)$ dollars and the weekly profit is $(p - 3)x$ dollars. Find the value of p that will produce a weekly profit of \$600.

30. A manufacturer can sell x units of a product each week at a price of p dollars per unit, where $x = 160(10 - p)$. It costs $(4x + 400)$ dollars to produce x units per week. How many units should be produced and sold to obtain a weekly profit of \$1000?

INEQUALITIES

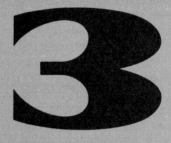

3-1 SETS AND INTERVALS

Let us begin by recalling the definitions of the symbols $<$, $\leq$, $>$, and $\geq$, called **inequality symbols**.

The real numbers other than zero are divided into the two classes, positive numbers and negative numbers. We write $a > 0$ (*a is greater than zero*) to mean that a is positive and $a < 0$ (*a is less than zero*) to mean that a is negative. The sum $a + b$ and the product $a \cdot b$ of any two positive real numbers a and b are both positive. If a is positive, then $-a$ is negative.

If a and b are two different real numbers, we write $a > b$ if the difference $a - b$ is positive and we write $a < b$ if $a - b$ is negative. For example, $5 > 2$ because $5 - 2 = 3$ is positive and $2 < 8$ because $2 - 8 = -6$ is negative. Geometrically, $a > b$ means that the point on the number line representing the number a lies to the right of the point representing the number b and $a < b$ means that the point representing a lies to the left of the point representing b. (See Figure 1.)

FIGURE 1

We define $a \geq b$ (*a is greater than or equal to b*) to mean that either $a > b$ or $a = b$. Similarly, $a \leq b$ (*a is less than or equal to b*) is used to denote that either $a < b$ or $a = b$. For example, $5 \leq 7$ because $5 < 7$ is true and $5 \geq 5$ because $5 = 5$ is true.

Statements like $a < b$, $a > b$, $a \geq b$, or $a \leq b$ are called **inequalities**. In particular, $a > b$ and $a < b$ are **strict inequalities**. The inequality $a > b$ can be equivalently written in the opposite direction as $b < a$. Thus $5 > 3$ is the same as $3 < 5$.

When a number b lies between two numbers a and c with $a < c$, we write $a < b < c$. The double inequality $a < b < c$ is used to mean that $a < b$ *and* $b < c$.

Sets

Knowledge of sets and operations on sets is basic to all modern mathematics. Many lengthy statements in mathematics can be written concisely and neatly in terms of sets and set operations.

DEFINITION Any well-defined collection of objects is referred to as a **set**. The objects constituting the set are called the **members** or **elements** of the set.

By a **well-defined** collection, we mean that given any object, we should be able to decide unambiguously whether or not it belongs to the collection.

A set may be specified in two ways, either by making a list of all of its members or else by stating a rule for membership in the set. Let us examine these two methods in turn.

LISTING METHOD   If it is possible to specify all of the elements of a set, the set can be described by listing all the elements and enclosing the list inside braces.

For example, $\{1, 2, 5\}$ denotes the set consisting of the three numbers 1, 2, and 5 and $\{p, q\}$ denotes the set whose only members are the two letters p and q.

In cases where the set contains a large number of elements, it is often possible to employ what is called a **partial listing**. For example, $\{2, 4, 6, \ldots, 100\}$ denotes the set of all the even integers from 2 up through 100. An ellipsis, $\ldots$, is used to show that the sequence of elements continues in a manner that is clear from the first few members listed. The sequence terminates with 100. By use of the ellipsis, the listing method can be employed in cases in which the set in question contains infinitely many members. For example, $\{1, 3, 5, \ldots\}$ denotes the set of *all* the odd natural numbers. The absence of any number following the ellipsis indicates that the sequence does not terminate, but continues indefinitely.

RULE METHOD   There are many cases in which it is not possible or in which it would be inconvenient to list all the members of a particular set. In such a case the set can be specified by stating a rule for membership.

For example, consider the set of all people living in Mexico at the present moment. To specify this set by listing all the members by name would clearly be a prodigious task. Instead we can denote it as follows.

$$\{x \,|\, x \text{ is a person currently living in Mexico}\}$$

The symbol $|$ stands for *such that*, so this expression is read *the set of all x such that x is a person currently living in Mexico*. The statement that follows the vertical bar inside the braces is the rule specifying the membership in the set.

As a second example, consider the set

$$\{x \,|\, x \text{ is a point on this page}\}$$

which denotes the set of all the points on this page. This is an example of a set that cannot be specified by the listing method even if we wanted to do so.

Many sets can be specified either by listing or by stating a rule, and we can choose whichever of the two methods we like. We shall give several examples of sets, some of which are specified using both methods.

EXAMPLE 1   (a) If N denotes the set of all natural numbers, then we can write
$$N = \{1, 2, 3, \ldots\}$$
$$= \{k \,|\, k \text{ is a natural number}\}.$$

(b) If P denotes the set of integers between -2 and $+3$ inclusive, then

$$P = \{-2, -1, 0, 1, 2, 3\}$$
$$= \{x \,|\, x \text{ is an integer}, -2 \leq x \leq 3\}.$$

Observe that the membership rule consists of two conditions separated by a comma. Both conditions must be satisfied by any member of the set.

(c) $Q = \{1, 4, 7, \ldots, 37\}$
$$= \{x \,|\, x = 3k + 1, k \text{ is an integer}, 0 \leq k \leq 12\}$$

(d) The set of all students currently enrolling at ABC Business College can be represented formally as

$$S = \{x \,|\, x \text{ is a student currently enrolled at ABC Business College}\}.$$

This set could also be specified by listing the names of all the students involved.

(e) The set of all real numbers greater than 1 and less than 2 can be specified by the rule method as

$$T = \{x \,|\, x \text{ is a real number}, 1 < x < 2\}.$$

A set is said to be **finite** if the number of elements belonging to it is finite, that is, if they can be counted. If the number of elements in a set is not finite, the set is called an **infinite** set.

In Example 1, the sets in parts (b), (c), and (d) are all finite, but those in parts (a) and (e) are infinite.

It is common to use capital letters to denote sets and lower-case letters to denote the elements in the sets. Observe that we followed this convention in Example 1. If A is any set and x any object, the notation $x \in A$ is used to denote the fact that x is a member of A. The statement $x \in A$ is read x *belongs to A* or x *is an element of A*. The negative statement x *is not an element of A* is denoted by writing $x \notin A$.

In part (b) of Example 1, $2 \in P$ but $6 \notin P$. For the set in part (e), $\sqrt{2} \in T$ and $\frac{3}{2} \in T$, but $2 \notin T$ and $\pi \notin T$.

DEFINITION   A set that contains no elements is called an **empty set**. (The terms **null set** and **void set** are also used.)

The symbol $\varnothing$ is used to denote a set that is empty, and the statement $A = \varnothing$ means that the set A contains no members. Examples of empty sets include the following.

$$\{x \,|\, x \text{ is an integer and } 3x = 2\}$$

$$\{x \,|\, x \text{ is a real number and } x^2 + 1 = 0\}$$

The set of all living dragons.

The set of all magnets having only one pole.

DEFINITION   A set A is said to be a **subset** of another set B if every element of A is also an element of B. In such a case, we write $A \subseteq B$.

The set A is said to be a **proper subset** of the set B if every element of A is in B but there is at least one element in B which is not in A. In this case, we write $A \subset B$.

EXAMPLE 2   (a) Let $A = \{2, 4, 6\}$ and $B = \{1, 2, 3, 4, 5, 6, 7, 8\}$. Then $A \subset B$.

(b) If N is the set of all natural numbers, I is the set of all integers, Q is the set of all rational numbers, and R is the set of all real numbers, then

$$N \subset I \subset Q \subset R.$$

(c) The set of all women students at **XYZ** University is a subset of the set of all students at that university.

(d) Every set is a subset of itself; that is,

$$A \subseteq A \text{ for any set.}$$

However, the statement $A \subset A$ is not true.

(e) An empty set $\varnothing$ is a subset of any set A:

$$\varnothing \subseteq A \text{ for any set } A.$$

In order to explain this last example more fully, let us rephrase the definition of a subset: B is a subset of A if and only if there is no object that belongs to B and does not belong to A. It is clear that there exists no object that belongs to $\varnothing$ and does not belong to A for the simple reason that there exists no object that belongs to $\varnothing$ at all. Hence $\varnothing \subseteq A$.

Two sets are equal to one another if they contain identical elements. More formally, we have the following definition.

DEFINITION   Two sets A and B are said to be **equal** if $A \subseteq B$ and $B \subseteq A$. In such a case, we write $A = B$.

Thus $A = B$ if there is no object that belongs to A and does not belong to B or that belongs to B and does not belong to A.

EXAMPLE 3   (a) If $A = \{x \mid x^2 = 1\}$ and $B = \{-1, +1\}$, then $A = B$.

(b) If $A = \{y \mid y^2 - 3y + 2 = 0\}$ and $B = \{1, 2\}$, then $A = B$.

DEFINITION   Let a and b be two real numbers with $a < b$. Then the **open interval** from a to b, denoted by (a, b), is the set of all real numbers x that lie between a and b. Thus

$$(a, b) = \{x \mid x \text{ is a real number and } a < x < b\}.$$

Similarly, the **closed interval** from a to b, denoted by $[a, b]$ is the set of all real numbers that lie between a and b, together with a and b themselves. Thus

$$[a, b] = \{x \mid x \text{ is a real number and } a \leq x \leq b\}.$$

Semiclosed or **semiopen** intervals are defined as follows.

$$(a, b] = \{x \,|\, a < x \leq b\}$$
$$[a, b) = \{x \,|\, a \leq x < b\}$$

Note: The statement that x is a real number has been omitted from the rules defining these sets. This is commonly done to avoid repetition when we are dealing with sets of real numbers.

For all these intervals, (a, b), $[a, b]$, $[a, b)$, and $(a, b]$, a and b are called the **endpoints** of the interval. An open interval does not contain its endpoints, whereas a closed interval contains both its endpoints. A semiclosed interval contains only one of its endpoints.

The geometric representation of these intervals is shown in Figure 2.

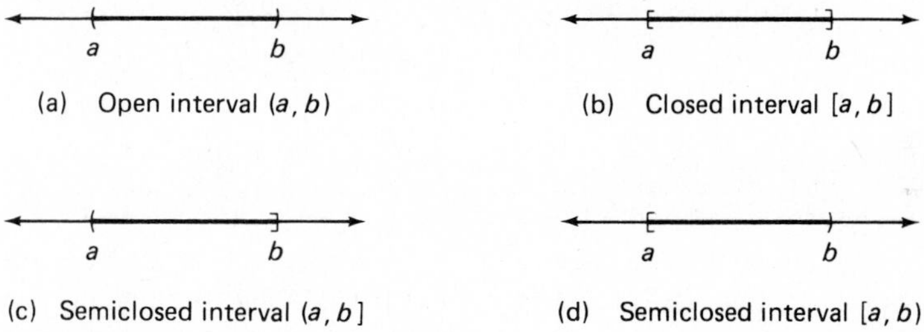

(a) Open interval (a, b) (b) Closed interval $[a, b]$

(c) Semiclosed interval $(a, b]$ (d) Semiclosed interval $[a, b)$

FIGURE 2

We use the symbols ∞ (*infinity*) and $-\infty$ (*negative infinity*) to describe unbounded intervals. (See Figure 3.)

(a) $(a, \infty) = \{x \,|\, x > a\}$

(b) $[a, \infty) = \{x \,|\, x \geq a\}$

(c) $(-\infty, a) = \{x \,|\, x < a\}$

(d) $(-\infty, a] = \{x \,|\, x \leq a\}$

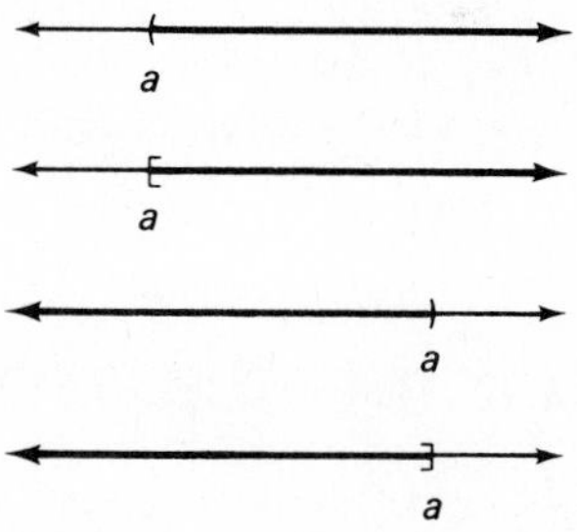

FIGURE 3

Note that ∞ and $-\infty$ are not real numbers.

EXERCISES 1

(**1–6**) Use the listing method to describe the following sets.

1. The set of all integers less than 5 and greater than -2.

2. The set of all natural numbers less than 50.

3. The set of all prime numbers less than 20.

4. $\left\{y \,\middle|\, y = \dfrac{1}{h+2}, h \text{ is a natural number}\right\}$

5. $\{x \mid x \text{ is a prime factor of } 36\}$

6. $\left\{p \,\middle|\, p = \dfrac{1}{n-1}, n \text{ is a prime number less than } 20\right\}$

(7–12) Use the rule method to describe the following sets.

7. The set of all even numbers less than 100.

8. The set of all prime numbers less than 30.

9. $\{1, 3, 5, 7, 9, \ldots, 19\}$ **10.** $\{\ldots, -4, -2, 0, 2, 4, 6, \ldots\}$

11. $\{3, 6, 9, \ldots\}$ **12.** $\{1, \frac{1}{2}, \frac{1}{3}, \frac{1}{4}, \ldots\}$

13. State whether the following statements are true or false. If false, explain why.

    a. $2 \in \{1, 2, 3\}$ **b.** $3 \subseteq \{1, 2, 3, 4\}$ **c.** $4 \in \{1, 2, 5, 7\}$

    d. $\{a, b\} \subseteq \{a, b, c\}$ **e.** $\varnothing = 0$ **f.** $\{0\} = \varnothing$

    g. $0 \in \varnothing$ **h.** $\varnothing \in \{0\}$ **i.** $\varnothing \subseteq \{0\}$

    j. $\{1, 2, 3, 4\} = \{4, 2, 1, 3\}$

    k. $\left\{x \,\middle|\, \dfrac{(x-2)^2}{x-2} = 0\right\} = \{x \mid x - 2 = 0\}$

    l. If $A \subseteq B$ and $B \subseteq C$, then $A \subseteq C$.

    m. If $A \subseteq B$ and $B \subseteq A$, then $A = B$.

    n. The set of all rectangles in a plane is a subset of the set of all squares in a plane.

    o. The set of all equilateral triangles is a subset of the set of all triangles.

    p. The open interval (a, b) is a subset of the closed interval $[a, b]$.

    q. $\{x \mid 2 \leq x \leq 3\} \in \{y \mid 1 \leq y \leq 5\}$

14. If A is the set of all squares in a plane, B is the set of all rectangles in a plane, and C is the set of all quadrilaterals in a plane, then which of these sets is a subset of one (or both) of the others?

3-2 LINEAR INEQUALITIES IN ONE VARIABLE

In this section, we shall consider certain inequalities that involve a single variable. The following example gives a simple business problem that results in such an inequality.

Suppose the total cost (in dollars) of production of x units of a certain commodity is given by $C = 3100 + 25x$ and each unit sells for $37. The manufacturer wants to know how many units should be produced and sold to gain a profit of at least $2000. Suppose x units are produced and sold. The revenue R obtained by selling x units at $37 each is $R = 37x$ dollars. The profit P (in dollars) obtained by producing and selling x units is then given by the following equations.

$$\text{Profit} = \text{Revenue} - \text{Cost}$$
$$P = 37x - (3100 + 25x)$$
$$= 12x - 3100$$

Since the profit is required to be at least \$2000, that is, it should be \$2000 or more, we must have

$$P \geq 2000$$

or

$$12x - 3100 \geq 2000. \tag{1}$$

This is an inequality involving the single variable x. We observe that the terms occurring in it are of two types, either constant terms or terms that are constant multiples of the variable x. Any inequality that has terms only of these two types is called a **linear inequality**. If the inequality symbol is either $>$ or $<$, the inequality is called a **strict** inequality; if the symbol is $\geq$ or $\leq$, the inequality is said to be a **weak** inequality.

EXAMPLE 1
(a) $3 - x \leq 2x + 4$ is a weak linear inequality in the variable x.
(b) $\frac{1}{4}z + 3 > 5 - \frac{1}{3}z$ is a strict linear inequality in the variable z.

DEFINITION The **solution** of an inequality in one variable is the set of all values of the variable for which the inequality is a true statement.

For example, the solution of Equation (1) is the set of all values of x (the number of units sold) that make the profit at least \$2000.

As with equations, the solution of an inequality is found by performing certain operations on the inequality to change it to some standard form. There are two basic operations that can be used to manipulate inequalities; we shall now state the rules that govern these operations.

RULE 1

> *When the same real number is added to or subtracted from both sides of an inequality, the direction of inequality remains unaltered.*

In symbols, if $a > b$ and c is any real number, then

$$a + c > b + c \quad \text{and} \quad a - c > b - c.$$

EXAMPLE 2
(a) We see that $8 > 5$ is a true statement. If we add 4 to both sides, we get $8 + 4 > 5 + 4$, or $12 > 9$, which is still true. If we subtract 7 from both sides we get $8 - 7 > 5 - 7$, or $1 > -2$, which is again true.
(b) Let $x - 1 > 3$. Adding 1 to both sides, we get

$$x - 1 + 1 > 3 + 1$$

or

$$x > 4.$$

The set of values of x for which $x - 1 > 3$ is the same set as that for which $x > 4$.

In the last example, we see that the inequality $x > 4$ can be obtained from the given inequality $x - 1 < 3$ by moving the term -1 from the left side to the right side and changing its sign. In general, the above rule allows us to do this kind of operation: *Any term can be moved from one side of the inequality to the other side after changing its sign without affecting the direction of inequality.* In symbols, if $a > b + c$, then $a - b > c$, and $a - c > b$.

EXAMPLE 3   (a) If $8 > 5 + 2$, then $8 - 2 > 5$.

(b) If $2x - 1 < x + 4$, then $2x - x < 4 + 1$, or $x < 5$. Both x and -1 were moved from one side to the other.

RULE 2

> *The direction of the inequality is preserved if both sides are multiplied (or divided) by the same positive number and is reversed when multiplied (or divided) by the same negative number.*

In symbols, if $a > b$ and c is any positive number, then

$$ac > bc \quad \text{and} \quad \frac{a}{c} > \frac{b}{c}$$

while if c is any negative number, then

$$ac < bc \quad \text{and} \quad \frac{a}{c} < \frac{b}{c}.$$

EXAMPLE 4   (a) We know that $4 > -1$ is a true statement. Multiplying both sides by 2, we obtain $8 > -2$, which is still true. If, however, we multiply by (-2), we must reverse the direction of inequality. We get

$$(-2)(4) < (-2)(-1) \quad \text{or} \quad -8 < 2$$

which is again true.

(b) If $2x \leq 4$, then we can divide both sides by 2 and obtain the equivalent inequality $2x/2 \leq 4/2$, or $x \leq 2$.

(c) If $-3x < 12$, then we divide by -3, which is negative, so we must reverse the inequality:

$$\frac{-3x}{-3} > \frac{12}{-3} \quad \text{or} \quad x > -4.$$

Before doing further examples, let us derive these two basic rules.

PROOF OF RULE 1   We suppose that $a > b$ and we let c be any real number. If $a > b$, then by definition $a - b > 0$. Now consider the difference between $(a + c)$ and $(b + c)$:

$$(a + c) - (b + c) = a + c - b - c = a - b > 0.$$

But since $(a + c) - (b + c)$ is positive, this means that

$$a + c > b + c$$

which is what we want to prove.

PROOF OF RULE 2 Again we suppose that $a > b$ and we let c be any positive real number. Then, as before, $a - b > 0$. Thus $a - b$ and c are both positive numbers, so their product is also positive:

$$(a - b)c > 0.$$

That is,

$$ac - bc > 0.$$

It follows, therefore, that $ac > bc$, as required. If, on the other hand, c were negative, the product $(a - b)c$ would be negative since one factor is positive and the other negative. It follows that

$$ac - bc < 0$$

and hence that $ac < bc$, as required.

EXAMPLE 5   Find all real numbers that satisfy the inequality

$$3x + 7 > 5x - 1.$$

Solution   We move all x-terms to one side of the inequality and all constant terms to the other side. Moving $5x$ to the left side and 7 to the right side, changing their signs, and simplifying gives the following.

$$3x - 5x > -1 - 7 \qquad \text{(Rule 1)}$$
$$-2x > -8$$

We next divide both sides by -2 and reverse the direction of inequality (because -2 is negative).

$$\frac{-2x}{-2} < \frac{-8}{-2} \qquad \text{(Rule 2)}$$
$$x < 4$$

0   4

FIGURE 4

Therefore the solution consists of the set of real numbers in the interval $(-\infty, 4)$. This is illustrated in Figure 4.

EXAMPLE 6   Solve the inequality

$$y + \frac{3}{4} \le \frac{5y - 2}{3} + 1.$$

Solution   First of all we must clear the inequality of fractions. Here the common denominator is 12, so we multiply both sides by 12.

$$12\left(y + \frac{3}{4}\right) \le 12\left(\frac{5y - 2}{3} + 1\right)$$
$$12y + 9 \le 4(5y - 2) + 12$$
$$12y + 9 \le 20y - 8 + 12$$
$$12y + 9 \le 20y + 4$$

Moving y-terms to the left and constant terms to the right, we get

$$12y - 20y \le 4 - 9$$
$$-8y \le -5.$$

We next divide both sides by -8 and reverse the direction of inequality (because -8 is negative).

$$y \geq \frac{-5}{-8} \quad \text{or} \quad y \geq \frac{5}{8}$$

FIGURE 5

Hence the solution consists of the set of all real numbers greater than or equal to $\frac{5}{8}$, that is, the numbers in the interval $[\frac{5}{8}, \infty)$. This set is illustrated in Figure 5.

EXAMPLE 7   Solve the double inequality for x.

$$8 - 3x \leq 2x - 7 < x - 13$$

Solution   The given double inequality is equivalent to the following two inequalities.

$$8 - 3x \leq 2x - 7 \quad \text{and} \quad 2x - 7 < x - 13$$

We solve these two inequalities separately by the methods described above. This gives

$$x \geq 3 \quad \text{and} \quad x < -6.$$

Both of these inequalities must be satisfied by x. But it is clearly impossible for both $x \geq 3$ and $x < -6$ to be satisfied. Thus there is *no solution*; there is no real number which satisfies the given double inequality.

EXAMPLE 8   The manufacturer of a certain item can sell all he can produce at the selling price of $60 each. It costs him $40 in materials and labor to produce each item, and he has additional costs (overhead) of $3000 per week in order to operate the plant. Find the number of units he should produce and sell to make a profit of at least $1000 per week.

Solution   Let x be the number of items produced and sold each week. Then the total cost of producing x units consists of $3000 plus $40 per item, which is

$$(40x + 3000) \text{ dollars.}$$

The revenue obtained by selling x units at $60 each will be $60x$ dollars. Therefore

$$\text{Profit} = \text{Revenue} - \text{Cost}$$
$$= 60x - (40x + 3000) = 20x - 3000.$$

Since we want a profit of at least $1000 each week, we have the following.

$$\text{Profit} \geq 1000$$
$$20x - 3000 \geq 1000$$
$$20x \geq 4000$$
$$x \geq 200$$

Thus the manufacturer should produce and sell at least 200 units each week.

EXAMPLE 9   The management of a manufacturing firm wants to decide whether they should manufacture their own gaskets, which the firm has been purchasing from outside suppliers at $1.10 each. Manufacturing the gaskets will increase the overhead costs of the firm by $800 per month, and the cost of materials and labor will be 60¢ for each gasket. How many gaskets would have to be used by the firm each month to justify a decision to manufacture their own gaskets?

Solution   Let x be the number of gaskets used by the firm each month. Then the cost of purchasing x gaskets at $1.10 each is $1.10x$ dollars. The cost of manufacturing x gaskets consists of $0.60 per gasket plus an overhead of $800 per month, so the total cost is

$$0.60x + 800.$$

To justify manufacturing gaskets by the firm itself, the following must be true.

$$\text{Cost of Purchasing} > \text{Cost of Manufacturing}$$
$$1.10x > 0.60x + 800$$
$$1.10x - 0.60x > 800$$
$$0.50x > 800$$
$$x > 1600$$

Thus the firm must use at least 1601 gaskets each month to justify manufacturing them.

EXERCISES 2

(1–14)   Solve the following inequalities.

1. $5 + 3x < 11$

2. $3 - 2y \geq 7$

3. $2u - 11 \leq 5u + 6$

4. $5x + 7 > 31 - 3x$

5. $3(2x - 1) > 4 + 5(x - 1)$

6. $x + \dfrac{4}{3} > \dfrac{2x - 3}{4} + 1$

7. $\dfrac{1}{4}(2x - 1) - x < \dfrac{x}{6} - \dfrac{1}{3}$

8. $\dfrac{3}{2}(x + 4) \geq 2 - \dfrac{1}{3}(1 - 4x)$

9. $2x + 1 < 3 - x < 2x + 5$

10. $4 - 2x < x - 2 < 2x - 4$

11. $3x + 7 > 5 - 2x \geq 13 - 6x$

12. $2x - 3 < 1 + x < 3x - 1$

13. $3x - 5 < 1 + x < 2x - 3$

14. $5x - 7 \geq 3x + 1 \geq 6x - 11$

15. A manufacturer can sell all units produced at $30 per unit. Fixed costs are $12,000 per month; in addition, it costs $22 to produce each unit. How many units must be produced and sold each month by the company to realize a profit?

16. A stereo manufacturer can sell all the units produced at a price of $150 each. Weekly fixed costs are $15,000 and the units cost $100 each in materials and labor. Find the number of stereos which must be manufactured and sold each week to obtain a weekly profit of at least $1000.

17. A firm manufacturing cars wants to know whether to manufacture their own fan belts, which the firm has been purchasing from outside suppliers at $2.50 for each unit. Manufacturing the belts by the firm will increase its fixed costs by $1500 each month, but it will cost only $1.70 to manufacture each belt. How many belts must be used by the firm each month to justify manufacturing the belts themselves?

18. A firm can hire a subcontractor to package each unit of its product at a cost of $2.75. On the other hand, the firm can package its own products by installing a packaging machine. Installing the machine will increase the fixed costs of the firm by $2000 each month, and the packaging itself costs $1.50 per unit. How many units would have to be made each month to make the installation of the packaging machine worthwhile?

19. The cost of publishing each copy of the weekly magazine *Buy and Sell* is 35¢. The revenue from the dealer sales is 30¢ per copy, and the revenue from advertising is 20% of the revenue obtained from sales in excess of 2000 copies. How many copies must be published and sold each week to earn a weekly profit of at least $1000?

20. The publisher of a monthly magazine has a publishing cost of 60.5¢ per copy. The revenue from dealer sales is 70¢ per copy, and the revenue from advertising is 15% of the revenue obtained from sales in excess of 20,000 copies. How many copies must be published and sold each month to earn a monthly profit in excess of $4000?

3-3 QUADRATIC INEQUALITIES IN ONE VARIABLE

A **quadratic inequality** in one variable, such as x, is an inequality of the form

$$ax^2 + bx + c > 0 \qquad \text{(or } < 0)$$

or

$$ax^2 + bx + c \geq 0 \qquad \text{(or } \leq 0)$$

where a, b, and c are certain constants ($a \neq 0$).

Again we are interested in solving a given inequality, that is, in finding the set of x for which the inequality is true. In the event that the quadratic expression in the inequality can be factored, a quadratic inequality can be solved by first resolving this quadratic expression into two linear factors and then examining the signs of these two factors. The method will be explained more fully in Example 1.

EXAMPLE 1　　Solve the inequality $x^2 + 3x < 4$.

Solution　　We must first make the right side of the inequality zero. We move the constant term to the left (and change its sign).

$$x^2 + 3x - 4 < 0.$$

Factoring the left side gives:

$$(x - 1)(x + 4) < 0.$$

The expression $(x - 1)(x + 4)$ is the product of two numbers, $x - 1$ and $x + 4$. The product is required to be negative, so one of these factors must be positive while the other must be negative. It is clear, therefore, that we should examine the signs of these two factors.

　　$x - 1$ is positive when $x > 1$ and negative when $x < 1$.
　　$x + 4$ is positive when $x > -4$ and negative when $x < -4$.

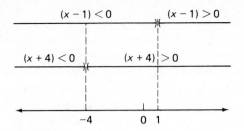

FIGURE 6

The two factors $x - 1$ and $x + 4$ change sign at $x = 1$ and $x = -4$, respectively. When plotted on a number line, as in Figure 6, it is obvious that they divide the line into three separate intervals, $x < -4$, $-4 < x < 1$, and $x > 1$.

In the interval $x < -4$, both $x - 1$ and $x + 4$ are negative. Hence their product is positive. In the interval $-4 < x < 1$, one factor $(x + 4)$ is positive, while the other factor $(x - 1)$ is negative. Hence their product is negative. Finally in the interval $x > 1$, both $x - 1$ and $x + 4$ are positive. Hence their product is positive. The signs of these two factors and their product are summarized in Table 1.

TABLE 1

Interval	$x < -4$	$-4 < x < 1$	$x > 1$
$x - 1$	$-$	$-$	$+$
$x + 4$	$-$	$+$	$+$
$(x - 1)(x + 4)$	$+$	$-$	$+$

We conclude therefore that the inequality
$$(x - 1)(x + 4) < 0$$
is satisfied when $-4 < x < 1$ and for no other values of x. The solution is illustrated in Figure 7. (We note that the end points $x = 1$ and $x = -4$ are not included in the interval since at these points $(x - 1)(x + 4)$ is zero, not negative.)

FIGURE 7

The basic method of treating quadratic inequalities is therefore to factor the quadratic expression that occurs into the product of linear factors. A product of two such factors is positive when both factors have the same sign, that is, both positive or both negative. The product is negative when one of the factors is positive and the other is negative.

EXAMPLE 2   Solve the inequality $5x \leq 2(x^2 - 6)$.

Solution   Moving all the terms to the left, the given inequality becomes
$$5x - 2x^2 + 12 \leq 0.$$
It is always convenient to have the square term positive, because then factoring is easier. Thus we multiply both sides of this inequality by -1 and reverse the direction of inequality.
$$-5x + 2x^2 - 12 \geq 0$$
$$2x^2 - 5x - 12 \geq 0$$

On factoring, this becomes

$$(2x + 3)(x - 4) \geq 0.$$

The expression $(2x + 3)(x - 4)$ is the product of two factors, $2x + 3$ and $x - 4$. This product is positive when both factors are positive or when both are negative. Now $x - 4$ is positive when $x > 4$ and negative when $x < 4$. Similarly, $2x + 3$ is positive when $2x > -3$, that is, when $x > -\frac{3}{2}$, and it is negative when $x < -\frac{3}{2}$.

These two factors divide the number line into the three intervals $x < -\frac{3}{2}$, $-\frac{3}{2} < x < 4$, and $x > 4$. (See Figure 8.) Examining the two factors in each interval, we construct Table 2.

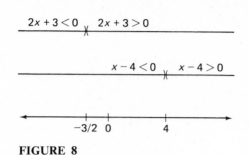

FIGURE 8

TABLE 2

Interval	$x < -\frac{3}{2}$	$-\frac{3}{2} < x < 4$	$x > 4$
$x - 4$	$-$	$-$	$+$
$2x + 3$	$-$	$+$	$+$
$(x - 4)(2x + 3)$	$+$	$-$	$+$

We see that when $x < -\frac{3}{2}$, both the factors $x - 4$ and $2x + 3$ are negative, so their product is positive. And when $x > 4$, both factors are positive, so their product is again positive. Thus $(x - 4)(2x + 3) > 0$ either when $x < -\frac{3}{2}$ or when $x > 4$. In this example, we are concerned with the weak inequality $(x - 4)(2x + 3) \geq 0$, so the solution set also contains those points for which $(x - 4)(2x + 3) = 0$. That is, the endpoints $x = -\frac{3}{2}$ and 4 are included. Thus the complete solution consists of the two intervals $x \leq -\frac{3}{2}$ and $x \geq 4$, as shown in Figure 9.

FIGURE 9

Factoring the quadratic expression $ax^2 + bx + c$ may sometimes be difficult. We can often use the following theorem to accomplish this factoring.

THEOREM 1 If α and β are the roots of the quadratic equation $ax^2 + bx + c = 0$, $(a \neq 0)$, then

$$ax^2 + bx + c = a(x - \alpha)(x - \beta).$$

Note that α and β can always be found from the quadratic formula.

Let us apply Theorem 1 to factor the expression $2x^2 - 5x - 12$ in Example 2. To do this, we first have to solve the equation $2x^2 - 5x - 12 = 0$. Here, $a = 2$, $b = -5$, and $c = -12$, so we have the following roots from the quadratic formula.

$$x = \frac{-b \pm \sqrt{b^2 - 4ac}}{2a}$$

$$= \frac{+5 \pm \sqrt{25 - 4(2)(-12)}}{2(2)}$$

$$= \frac{5 \pm \sqrt{121}}{4} = \frac{5 \pm 11}{4}$$

$$= 4 \quad \text{or} \quad -\tfrac{3}{2}$$

Thus, in this case, the two roots of the equation $2x^2 - 5x - 12 = 0$ are $\alpha = -\tfrac{3}{2}$ and $\beta = 4$. Applying the above theorem, we have the following.

$$ax^2 + bx + c = a(x - \alpha)(x - \beta)$$
$$2x^2 - 5x - 12 = 2[x - (-\tfrac{3}{2})](x - 4)$$
$$= [2(x + \tfrac{3}{2})](x - 4)$$
$$= (2x + 3)(x - 4)$$

These are, of course, the same factors found in Example 2.

EXAMPLE 3   The monthly sales x of a certain commodity when its price p dollars per unit is given by $p = 200 - 3x$. The cost of producing x units of the same commodity is $C = (650 + 5x)$ dollars. How many units of this commodity should be produced and sold so as to realize a monthly profit of at least 2500 dollars?

Solution   The revenue R (in dollars) obtained by selling x units at a price of p dollars per unit is

$$R = x \times \text{price per unit}$$
$$= xp$$
$$= x(200 - 3x)$$
$$= 200x - 3x^2.$$

The cost C (in dollars) of manufacturing x units is

$$C = 650 + 5x.$$

The profit P (in dollars) obtained by producing and selling x units is given as follows.

$$P = \text{Revenue} - \text{Cost}$$
$$= 200x - 3x^2 - (650 + 5x)$$
$$= 195x - 3x^2 - 650$$

Since the profit P has to be at least \$2500, we have

$$P \geq 2500.$$

Thus

$$195x - 3x^2 - 650 \geq 2500$$

or

$$-3x^2 + 195x - 3150 \geq 0.$$

We divide both sides by -3, reverse the direction of inequality, and factor.

$$x^2 - 65x + 1050 \leq 0$$
$$(x - 30)(x - 35) \leq 0$$

Solving this inequality as in Example 1, we get

$$30 \leq x \leq 35.$$

Thus, to obtain a profit of at least $2500 per month, the manufacturer must produce and sell any number of units between and including 30 and 35.

EXAMPLE 4   A hairdresser gets an average of 100 customers per week at a present charge of $3 per haircut. For each increase of 50¢ in the price, the hairdresser will lose 10 customers. What price should be charged so that the weekly earnings will not be less than they are at the $3 price?

Solution   Let there be x increases of 50¢ in price beyond $3. Then the price per haircut is $(3 + 0.5x)$ dollars and the number of customers at this rate will be $(100 - 10x)$ per week.

Total Weekly Earnings = Number of Customers × Price per Haircut

$$= (100 - 10x)(3 + 0.5x) \text{ dollars}$$

Earnings from the present 100 customers are $100 \times \$3 = \$300$. Therefore the new weekly earnings should be at least 300 dollars. Thus

$$(100 - 10x)(3 + 0.5x) \geq 300.$$

We simplify and factor.

$$300 + 20x - 5x^2 \geq 300$$
$$20x - 5x^2 \geq 0$$
$$5x(4 - x) \geq 0$$

Since x is positive, we can divide both sides by the factor $5x$, obtaining $4 - x \geq 0$, or $x \leq 4$. Thus there should be at most 4 increases of 50¢, that is, the rate should be increased by 4×50¢, or $2, at the most. The hairdresser therefore should charge a maximum rate of $3 + \$2 = \$5$ per haircut to obtain at least the same revenue as for 100 customers at $3 per haircut.

EXERCISES 3

(1–14)   Solve the following inequalities.

1. $(x - 2)(x - 5) < 0$ 2. $(x + 1)(x - 3) \leq 0$

3. $(2x - 5)(x + 3) \geq 0$ 4. $(3x - 1)(x + 2) > 0$

5. $x^2 - 7x + 12 \leq 0$ 6. $9x > x^2 + 14$ 7. $y(2y + 1) > 6$

8. $3y^2 \geq 4 - 11y$ 9. $x^2 + 3 > 0$ 10. $x^2 + 1 \leq 0$

11. $x^2 \geq 4$ 12. $x^2 < 9$ 13. $x^2 - 6x + 9 \leq 0$

14. $x^2 - 6x + 9 > 0$

15. At a price of p dollars per unit, x units of a certain commodity can be sold each month in the market, with $p = 600 - 5x$. How many units should be sold each month to obtain a revenue of at least $18,000?

16. A manufacturer can sell x units of a product each week at a price of p dollars per unit, where $p = 200 - x$. What number of units must be sold each week to obtain a minimum weekly revenue of $9900?

17. A manufacturer can sell all units of a product at $25 each. The cost C (in dollars) of producing x units each week is given by $C = 3000 + 20x - 0.1x^2$. How many units should be produced and sold each week to obtain a profit?

18. A publisher can sell 12,000 copies of a book at $25 each. For every dollar increase in price, sales will fall by 400 copies. What maximum price should be charged for each copy to obtain a revenue of at least $300,000?

19. A farmer wishes to enclose a rectangular field and has 200 yards of fencing available. Find the possible dimensions of the field if its area must be at least 2100 square yards.

20. A certain area of water is to be stocked with fish. If n fish are put in, it is known that the average gain in weight of each fish will be $(600 - 3n)$ grams. Find the restrictions on n if the total gain in weight of all the fish stock is to be greater than 28,800 grams.

21. An investor invests $100 at R percent interest per annum and $100 at $2R$ percent per annum. If the value of the two investments is to be at least $224.80 after 2 years, what restrictions must there be on R?

22. A supermarket finds itself with a large stock of apples on hand that must be sold quickly. The manager knows that if the apples are offered at p cents per pound, he will sell x pounds, where $x = 1000 - 20p$. What price should be charged in order to produce a revenue of at least $120?

3-4 ABSOLUTE VALUES

If x is a real number, then the **absolute value** of x, denoted by $|x|$, is defined by

$$|x| = \begin{cases} x & \text{if } x \geq 0 \\ -x & \text{if } x < 0. \end{cases}$$

For example, $|5| = 5$, $|-3| = -(-3) = 3$, and $|0| = 0$.

From this definition, it is clear that the *absolute value of a number is always a nonnegative real number*; that is,

$$|x| \geq 0.$$

The absolute value of x is a measure of the "size" of x without regard as to whether x is positive or negative.

EXAMPLE 1   Solve for x.

$$|2x - 3| = 5$$

Solution   According to the definition of absolute value, the given equation is satisfied if either

$$2x - 3 = 5 \quad \text{or} \quad 2x - 3 = -5$$

because in either case, the absolute value of $2x - 3$ is 5. If $2x - 3 = 5$, then $2x = 3 + 5 = 8$ and so $x = 4$. Similarly, if $2x - 3 = -5$, then $x = -1$. Thus there are two values of x, $x = 4$ and $x = -1$, that satisfy the given equation.

EXAMPLE 2   Solve for x.

$$|3x - 2| = |2x + 7|$$

Solution   This equation will be satisfied if either

$$3x - 2 = 2x + 7 \quad \text{or} \quad 3x - 2 = -(2x + 7).$$

Solving these two equations separately, we obtain $x = 9$ and $x = -1$.

From Examples 1 and 2, it is clear that we have the following general rules for solving equations involving absolute values.

> If $|a| = b$, where $b \geq 0$, then either $a = b$ or $a = -b$.
>
> If $|a| = |b|$, then either $a = b$ or $a = -b$.

The symbol $\sqrt{a}$ denotes the nonnegative square root of the real number a ($a \geq 0$). For example, $\sqrt{9} = 3$. The negative square root of 9 is denoted by $-\sqrt{9}$. Using the radical symbol, we can give the following alternative definition of absolute value.

> $$|x| = \sqrt{x^2}.$$

For example, $\sqrt{3^2} = \sqrt{9} = 3$, $\sqrt{(-5)^2} = \sqrt{25} = 5 = |-5|$, and $\sqrt{(x - 3)^2} = |x - 3|$.

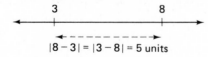

FIGURE 10

We can interpret $|x|$ geometrically. (See Figure 10.) The numbers 3 and 8 on the number line are 5 units apart. Also $|8 - 3| = |5| = 5$ and $|3 - 8| = |-5| = 5$. Thus $|8 - 3| = |3 - 8|$ gives the distance between two points 3 and 8 on a number line. In general, we may interpret $|x - c| = |c - x|$ as the distance between two points x and c on a number line, without regard to direction. For example, the equation $|x - 2| = 5$ states that the distance between x and 2 on a number line is 5 units, without regard to direction. Thus x can be either $2 + 5 = 7$ or $2 - 5 = -3$, as shown in Figure 11.

Since $|x| = |x - 0|$, $|x|$ represents the distance of the point x on the real

FIGURE 11

number line from the origin O, without regard to direction. (See Figure 12.) Also, since the distance between O and x is the same as the distance between O and $-x$, it follows that

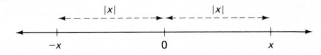

FIGURE 12

$$|x| = |-x|.$$

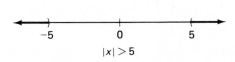

FIGURE 13

For example, $|7| = |-7| = 7$.

Let us now consider some inequalities involving absolute values. The inequality $|x| < 5$ implies that the distance of x from the origin is less than 5 units. Since x can be on either side of 0, x lies between -5 and 5, or $-5 < x < 5$. (See Figure 13.) Similarly, $|x| > 5$ implies that x is more than 5 units from the origin on either side, that is, $x < -5$ or $x > 5$. (See Figure 14.) This result is generalized in the following theorem:

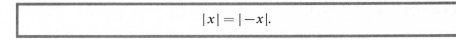

FIGURE 14

THEOREM 1 If $a > 0$, then

$$|x| < a \text{ if and only if } -a < x < a; \tag{1}$$
$$|x| > a \text{ if and only if either } x > a \text{ or } x < -a. \tag{2}$$

Figures 15 and 16 illustrate Theorem 1.

FIGURE 15

FIGURE 16

represents the number x on the x-axis and the point N represents the number y on the y-axis, then x and y are called the **Cartesian coordinates** of the point P. We write these two coordinates enclosed in a parentheses, in the order (x, y).

In this way, corresponding to each point P in the plane, there is a unique ordered pair of real numbers (x, y), which are the coordinates of the point. And conversely, we can see that corresponding to each ordered pair (x, y) of real numbers, there is a unique point in the plane. This representation of points in the plane by ordered pairs of real numbers is called the **Cartesian coordinate system**.

If the ordered pair (x, y) represents a point P in the plane, then x (the first member) is called the **abscissa** or **x-coordinate** of the point P and y (the second member) is called the **ordinate** or **y-coordinate** of P. The abscissa and ordinate of P together are called the **rectangular Cartesian coordinates** of the point P. The notation $P(x, y)$ is used to denote a point P with coordinates (x, y).

The coordinates of the origin are $(0, 0)$. For each point on the x-axis, the y-coordinate is zero; each point on the y-axis has an x-coordinate of zero. Figure 2 shows several ordered pairs of real numbers and the corresponding points.

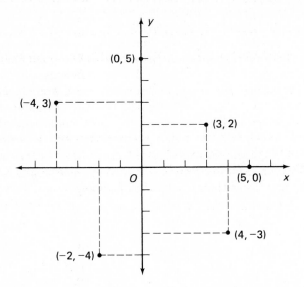

FIGURE 2

The coordinate axes divide the xy-plane into four parts, called **quadrants**. The quadrants are called the *first, second, third* and *fourth quadrants*, as shown in Figure 3.

(x, y) is in the first quadrant if $x > 0$ and $y > 0$,

(x, y) is in the second quadrant if $x < 0$ and $y > 0$,

(x, y) is in the third quadrant if $x < 0$ and $y < 0$,

(x, y) is in the fourth quadrant if $x > 0$ and $y < 0$.

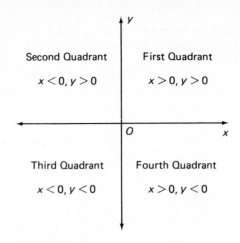

FIGURE 3

THEOREM 1 (DISTANCE FORMULA) If $P(x_1, y_1)$ and $Q(x_2, y_2)$ are any two points in the plane, then the distance d between P and Q is given by

$$d = \sqrt{(x_2 - x_1)^2 + (y_2 - y_1)^2}.$$

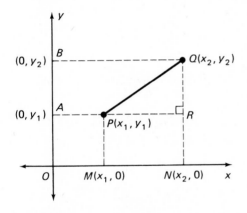

FIGURE 4

PROOF If PM and QN are perpendiculars from the two points $P(x_1, y_1)$ and $Q(x_2, y_2)$ onto the x-axis, and PA and QB are perpendiculars onto the y-axis, as shown in Figure 4, then the coordinates of the points M, N, A, and B are as given in Figure 4. Let the point where line PA meets line QN be R, so that PQR is a right triangle with right angle at R.

From Figure 4* we have

$$PR = MN = ON - OM = x_2 - x_1$$

and

$$RQ = AB = OB - OA = y_2 - y_1.$$

We next use the Pythagorean theorem with right triangle PQR.

$$PQ^2 = PR^2 + RQ^2$$

or

$$d^2 = (x_2 - x_1)^2 + (y_2 - y_1)^2.$$

*Figure 4 has been drawn with P and Q both in the first quadrant. The equations for PR and RQ apply in whatever quadrants the two points lie. However, in Figure 4, Q has been drawn above and to the right of P, so that $x_2 > x_1$ and $y_2 > y_1$. In the more general case—when these conditions are not satisfied—the horizontal and vertical distances between P and Q are given by $PR = |x_2 - x_1|$ and $RQ = |y_2 - y_1|$. It can be seen that Equation (1) for d continues to apply in this general case.

Taking the square root (the nonnegative square root because the distance is always nonnegative), we have

$$d = \sqrt{(x_2 - x_1)^2 + (y_2 - y_1)^2} \tag{1}$$

which proves the result. Equation (1) is known as the **distance formula in the plane.**

EXAMPLE 1　Find the distance between the two points $A(-1, 3)$ and $B(4, 15)$.

Solution　We identify the two given points as

$$(-1, 3) = (x_1, y_1) \quad \text{and} \quad (4, 15) = (x_2, y_2).$$

We now use the distance formula.

$$AB = \sqrt{(x_2 - x_1)^2 + (y_2 - y_1)^2}$$
$$= \sqrt{(4 - (-1))^2 + (15 - 3)^2}$$
$$= \sqrt{5^2 + 12^2} = \sqrt{169} = 13$$

EXAMPLE 2　The abscissa of a point is 7 and its distance from the point $(1, -2)$ is 10. Find the ordinate of the point.

Solution　Let P be the point whose ordinate is required, and A be the point $(1, -2)$. Let y be the ordinate of the point P. Then coordinates of P are $(7, y)$, because its abscissa is given to be 7. From the statement of the problem, we are given that

$$PA = 10. \tag{2}$$

Now identifying the two points P and A as

$$(7, y) = (x_1, y_1) \quad \text{and} \quad (1, -2) = (x_2, y_2)$$

and using the distance formula, we have

$$PA = \sqrt{(x_2 - x_1)^2 + (y_2 - y_1)^2}$$
$$= \sqrt{(1 - 7)^2 + (-2 - y)^2}$$

or

$$10 = \sqrt{36 + (2 + y)^2}$$

from Equation (2) above. We next square both sides.

$$100 = 36 + (2 + y)^2$$
$$= 36 + 4 + 4y + y^2$$

Therefore,

$$y^2 + 4y - 60 = 0$$

or

$$(y + 10)(y - 6) = 0.$$

Therefore one of the following conditions holds.

$$y + 10 = 0 \quad \text{or} \quad y - 6 = 0$$
$$y = -10 \qquad\qquad y = 6$$

The ordinate of the required point P is either 6 or -10.

DEFINITION The **graph** of an equation in two unknowns, such as x and y, is the set of all those points whose coordinates (x, y) satisfy the equation.

Consider, for example, the equation $2x - y - 3 = 0$. One of the points whose coordinates satisfy this equation is $(1, -1)$, since the equation is satisfied when we substitute $x = 1$ and $y = -1$. Other such points are $(0, -3)$ and $(2, 1)$. The graph of this equation is obtained by plotting these points and the many others which satisfy this equation. (There are, in fact, infinitely many points which satisfy this equation.)

Drawing the *exact* graph of an equation in two unknowns is usually an impossible task because it would involve plotting infinitely many points. In general practice, enough points satisfying the given equation are selected to exhibit the general nature of the graph. These points are plotted and joined by a smooth curve.

When finding the points satisfying a given equation, it is often useful to solve the equation for one unknown in terms of the other. For example, if we solve the equation $2x - y - 3 = 0$ for y in terms of x, we have

$$y = 2x - 3.$$

Now if we give values to x, we can calculate the corresponding values for y. For example, if $x = 1$, $y = 2(1) - 3 = -1$; if $x = 5$, $y = 10 - 3 = 7$; and so on.

EXAMPLE 3 Sketch the graph of the equation $2x - y - 3 = 0$.

Solution Solving the given equation for y, we have

$$y = 2x - 3.$$

The values of y corresponding to different values of x are given in Table 1.

TABLE 1

x	-2	-1	0	1	2	3	4
y	-7	-5	-3	-1	1	3	5

Plotting these points, we observe that they lie on a straight line. (See Figure 5 on next page.) This line is the graph of the given equation.

EXAMPLE 4 Sketch the graph of the equation $y = 5 - x^2$.

Solution Since x appears in the equation only in the second degree and $(x)^2 = (-x)^2$, the table of values of x and y can be abbreviated by combining positive and negative values of x. (See Table 2.)

TABLE 2.

x	0	± 1	± 2	± 3
y	5	4	1	-4

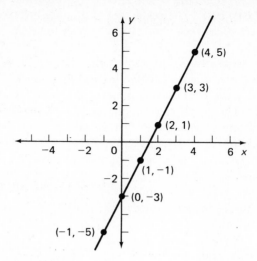

FIGURE 5

We plot these points and join them by a smooth curve, obtaining the graph of the equation $y = 5 - x^2$ shown in Figure 6.

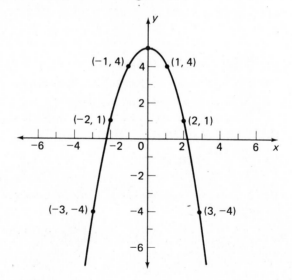

FIGURE 6

EXAMPLE 5   If a certain item is offered for sale at a price p per unit, the quantity q demanded in the market is given by the relation $3q + p = 10$. Sketch the graph of this relation.

Solution   We shall plot price p along the vertical axis, as is usual with demand relations. In this case, since neither the price p nor the quantity q demanded is negative, only that portion of the graph in the first quadrant is of any practical significance.

Solving the equation for p, we have

$$p = 10 - 3q.$$

Values of p corresponding to a number of different values of q are given in Table 3.

TABLE 3

q	0	1	2	3
p	10	7	4	1

For example, when the price is 7, the quantity demanded is only 1 unit. When the price is reduced to 4, 2 units are demanded by the market, and so on.

Plotting these points, we obtain the graph shown in Figure 7.

Observe that the graph is again a straight line, or rather the portion of a straight line that lies in the first quadrant.

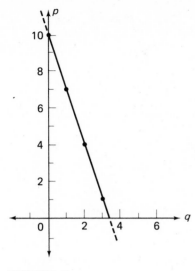

FIGURE 7

EXERCISES 1

1. Plot the following points:

$$(2, -5); (-1, 4); (0, 2); (-3, -2); (5, 0).$$

Label each point with its coordinates.

2. Determine the quadrants in which the points in Exercise 1 lie.

(3–6) Find the distance between each pair of points.

3. $(4, -1)$ and $(2, 0)$ 4. $(-3, 1)$ and $(-2, -3)$

5. $(\frac{1}{2}, 2)$ and $(-2, 1)$ 6. $(a, 2)$ and $(b, 2)$

7. The ordinate of a point is 6 and its distance from the point $(-3, 2)$ is 5. Find the abscissa of the point.

8. The abscissa of a point is 2 and its distance from the point $(3, -7)$ is $\sqrt{5}$. Find the ordinate of the point.

9. If P is the point $(1, a)$ and its distance from the point $(6, 7)$ is 13, find the value of a.

10. We are given the point $P(x, 2)$. The distance of P from the point $A(9, -6)$ is twice its distance from the point $B(-1, 5)$. Find the value of x.

11. If P is the point $(-1, y)$ and its distance from the origin is half of its distance from the point $(1, 3)$, determine the value of y.

(12–15) Find the equation that the coordinates of the point $P(x, y)$ must satisfy in order that the following conditions are met.

12. P is at a distance of 5 units from the point $(2, -3)$.

13. P is at a distance of 3 units from the point $(-1, 3)$.

14. The distance of P from the point $A(2, 1)$ is twice its distance from the point $B(-1, 3)$.

15. The sum of the squares of the distances of the points $A(0, 1)$ and $B(-1, 0)$ from P is 3.

(16–19) Sketch the graph of each equation.

16. $2x + 3y = 6$ **17.** $3x - 4y = 12$

18. $x^2 - y + 6 = 0$ **19.** $x = y^2 - 2$

(20–23) Sketch the graph of the following demand relations, where p denotes the price per unit and q is the quantity demanded.

20. $p = -2q + 5$ **21.** $2p + 3q = 8$

22. $p + q^2 = 14$ **23.** $p = 25 - q^2$

4-2 STRAIGHT LINES AND LINEAR EQUATIONS

In this section, we shall examine a number of properties of straight lines. Our first aim will be to investigate the algebraic equation that has a given line as its graph.

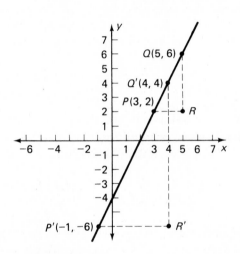

FIGURE 8

One of the most important properties of a straight line is how steeply it rises or falls, and we wish to introduce a quantity which will measure this steepness of a given line. Let us begin by considering an example. The equation $y = 2x - 4$ has as its graph the straight line shown in Figure 8. Let us choose two points on this line, such as the points $(3, 2)$ and $(5, 6)$, which are denoted, respectively, by P and Q in Figure 8. The difference between the x-coordinates of these two points, denoted by PR, is called the *run* from P to Q:

$$\text{run} = PR = 5 - 3 = 2.$$

The difference between the y-coordinates of P and Q, equal to the distance QR, is called the *rise* from P to Q:

$$\text{rise} = QR = 6 - 2 = 4.$$

We note that the rise is equal to twice the run. This will be the case no matter which pair of points we choose on the given graph. For example, let us take the two points $P'(-1, -6)$ and $Q'(4, 4)$. (See Figure 8.) Then

$$\text{run} = P'R' = 4 - (-1) = 5 \quad \text{and} \quad \text{rise} = Q'R' = 4 - (-6) = 10.$$

Again we see that the ratio of rise to run is equal to 2.

The same ratio of rise to run is obtained in the two cases because the two triangles PQR and $P'Q'R'$ are similar. Therefore the ratios of corresponding

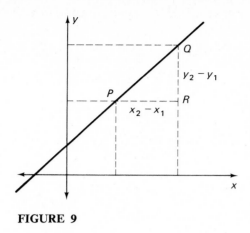

FIGURE 9

sides are equal: $QR/PR = Q'R'/P'R'$. This ratio is called the **slope** of the given straight line. The line in Figure 8 has a slope equal to 2.

The slope of a general straight line is defined similarly. Let P and Q be any two points on the given line. (See Figure 9.) Let them have coordinates (x_1, y_1) and (x_2, y_2), respectively. Let R be the intersection of the horizontal line through P and the vertical line through Q. Then the distance PR is called the **run** between P and Q and the distance QR is called the **rise** between P and Q.

In terms of the coordinates,

$$\text{rise} = QR = y_2 - y_1$$

and

$$\text{run} = PR = x_2 - x_1.$$

(Note that if Q turns out to lie below R, which happens when the line slopes downwards to the right, then the rise is negative. We could also choose Q to lie to the left of P, in which case $x_2 < x_1$ and the run would be negative.)

The **slope** of the line is defined to be the ratio of rise to run. It is usually denoted by the letter m. Hence

$$m = \frac{\text{rise}}{\text{run}} = \frac{y_2 - y_1}{x_2 - x_1}. \tag{1}$$

Note that Equation (1) for slope is meaningful as long as $x_2 - x_1 \neq 0$; that is, provided that the line is nonvertical. Slope is *not* defined for vertical lines.

It should be noted that the slope of a line remains the same, no matter how we choose the positions of the two points P and Q on the line.

If the slope m of a line is positive, the line ascends to the right. The larger the value of m, the more steeply the line is inclined to the horizontal. If m is negative, then the line descends to the right. If $m = 0$, then the line is horizontal. These properties are illustrated in Figure 10 on next page.

EXAMPLE 1 Find the slope of the line joining the two points $(1, -3)$ and $(3, 7)$.

Solution Using Equation (1), the slope is

$$m = \frac{7 - (-3)}{3 - 1} = \frac{10}{2} = 5.$$

EXAMPLE 2 The slope of the line joining the two points $(3, 2)$ and $(5, 2)$ is

$$m = \frac{2 - 2}{5 - 3} = 0.$$

Thus the line joining these two points is horizontal.

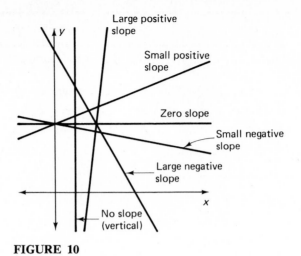

Large positive
slope

Small positive
slope

Zero slope

Small negative
slope

Large negative
slope

No slope
(vertical)

FIGURE 10

EXAMPLE 3   The slope of the line joining $P(2, 3)$ and $Q(2, 6)$ is given by

$$m = \frac{6 - 3}{2 - 2} = \frac{3}{0}$$

which is undefined. Thus the line joining P and Q has *no* slope. In this case, line PQ is vertical.

What information do we need to be given in order to be able to draw a particular straight line? One way in which a line can be specified is by giving two points that lie on it. Once two points are given, the whole line is determined, since there is only one straight line through any two points.

Through any *one* point, there are of course many different straight lines with slopes ranging from large to small, positive or negative. However if the slope is given, then there is only one line through the point in question. Thus a second way in which a straight line can be specified is by giving one point on it and its slope.

Our immediate task will be to determine the equation of a nonvertical straight line with slope m that passes through a given point, (x_1, y_1).

Let (x, y) be a point on the line different from the given point, (x_1, y_1). (See Figure 11.) Then the slope m of the line joining the two points (x_1, y_1) and (x, y) is given by

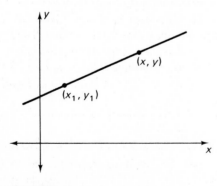

(x, y)

(x_1, y_1)

FIGURE 11

$$m = \frac{y - y_1}{x - x_1}.$$

It follows therefore that

$$y - y_1 = m(x - x_1). \tag{2}$$

This is called the **point-slope** formula for the line.

EXAMPLE 4 Find the equation of the line through the point $(5, -3)$ with slope -2.

Solution Using Equation (2) with $m = -2$ and $(x_1, y_1) = (5, -3)$, we find that the required equation of the straight line is as follows.

$$y - (-3) = -2(x - 5)$$
$$y + 3 = -2x + 10$$
$$y = -2x + 7$$

EXAMPLE 5 Find the equation of the straight line passing through the two points $(1, -2)$ and $(5, 6)$.

Solution The slope of the line joining $(1, -2)$ and $(5, 6)$ is

$$m = \frac{6 - (-2)}{5 - 1} = \frac{8}{4} = 2.$$

Using the point-slope formula, the equation of the straight line through $(1, -2)$ with slope $m = 2$ is

$$y - (-2) = 2(x - 1)$$
$$y = 2x - 4.$$

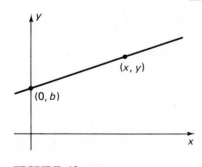

FIGURE 12

In the point-slope formula, let (x_1, y_1) be $(0, b)$. (See Figure 12.) Then Equation (2) becomes

$$y - b = m(x - 0)$$

or

$$y = mx + b. \tag{3}$$

The quantity b, which gives the distance along the y-axis that is cut off by the straight line, is called the y-**intercept** of the line. Equation (3) is called the **slope-intercept** formula of a line.

If the given line is horizontal, then its slope is $m = 0$ and Equation (3) reduces to

$$y = b. \tag{4}$$

This is the equation of a horizontal line at a distance b from the x-axis. (See Figure 13.) In particular, if we take $b = 0$ in Equation (4), we get $y = 0$, which is the equation of the x-axis itself.

Next, suppose that the line in question is *vertical* and let it intersect the x-axis at the point $A(a, 0)$ as shown in Figure 14. If $P(x, y)$ is a general point on

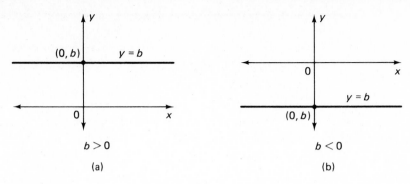

FIGURE 13

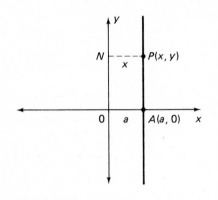

FIGURE 14

the line, then the two points P and A have the same abscissa; that is, $x = a$. Every point on the line satisfies this condition, so we can say that

$$x = a \qquad (5)$$

is the equation of a vertical line.

For example, if $a = 0$, we have the equation $x = 0$, which is the equation of the y-axis. Similarly, $x = 2$ is the equation of the vertical line lying 2 units to the right of the y-axis, and $x = -4$ is the equation of the vertical line lying 4 units to the left of the y-axis.

A **general linear equation** (or a first-degree equation) in two variables x and y is an equation of the form

$$Ax + By + C = 0 \qquad (6)$$

where A, B, and C are constants and A and B are *not both* zero.

In the light of the above discussion, we are in a position to describe the graph of the general linear equation, Equation (6), for different values of A and B.

1. $B \neq 0$, $A \neq 0$. In this case, Equation (6) takes the form

$$y = -\frac{A}{B} x - \frac{C}{B}$$

when solved for y. Using Equation (3), we see that this is the equation of a straight line whose slope is $-A/B$ and y-intercept is $-C/B$.

2. $B \neq 0$, $A = 0$. When solved for y, Equation (6) becomes

$$y = -\frac{C}{B}$$

From Equation (4), we see that this is the equation of a horizontal line whose y-intercept is $-C/B$.

3. $A \neq 0$, $B = 0$. When $B = 0$, Equation (6) can be written in the form

$$x = -\frac{C}{A}.$$

This is the equation of a vertical line that intersects the x-axis at the point $(-C/A, 0)$, using Equation (5).

Thus the graph of the general linear equation (6) is, in each case, a straight line. A linear equation of the form of Equation (6) is often referred to as the **general equation** of a straight line. Table 4 summarizes the various forms taken by the equation of a straight line.

TABLE 4

Formula Name	Equation
1. Point-slope Formula	$y - y_1 = m(x - x_1)$
2. Slope-intercept Formula	$y = mx + b$
3. General Formula	$Ax + By + C = 0$, A, B not both zero
4. Horizontal Line	$y = b$
5. Vertical Line	$x = a$

EXAMPLE 6 Given the linear equation $2x + 3y = 6$, find the slope and y-intercept of its graph.

Solution To find the slope and y-intercept of the line, we must express the given equation in the form

$$y = mx + b.$$

That is, we must solve the equation for y in terms of x.

$$2x + 3y = 6$$
$$3y = -2x + 6$$
$$y = -\tfrac{2}{3}x + 2$$

Comparing with the general form $y = mx + b$, we have $m = -\tfrac{2}{3}$ and $b = 2$. Thus the slope is equal to $-\tfrac{2}{3}$ and the y-intercept is equal to 2.

EXAMPLE 7 Find the equation of the straight line passing through the two points $(2, 5)$ and $(2, 9)$.

Solution The slope of the line joining $(2, 5)$ and $(2, 9)$ is given by

$$m = \frac{y_2 - y_1}{x_2 - x_1} = \frac{9 - 5}{2 - 2} = \frac{4}{0}$$

which is undefined. Thus the line joining the two given points is vertical. We know that the equation of any vertical line is of the form

$$x = a.$$

The given line passes through the point $(2, 5)$, which has an x-coordinate of 2. Therefore $a = 2$ and the equation of the straight line is

$$x = 2.$$

EXAMPLE 8   Sketch the graph of the linear equation $3x - 4y = 12$.

Solution   We know that the graph of a linear equation in two variables is always a straight line, and a straight line is completely determined by two points. Thus to sketch the graph of the given linear equation, we find two *different* points (x, y) satisfying the given equation, plot them, and then join these points by a straight line. Putting $x = 0$ in the given equation, we get

$$-4y = 12 \quad \text{or} \quad y = -3.$$

Thus one point on the line is $(0, -3)$. Putting $y = 0$ in the given equation, we get

$$3x = 12 \quad \text{or} \quad x = 4.$$

Hence $(4, 0)$ is a second point on the line. Plotting the two points $(0, -3)$ and $(4, 0)$, which lie on the two coordinate axes, and joining them by a straight line, we obtain the graph of the given equation as shown in Figure 15.

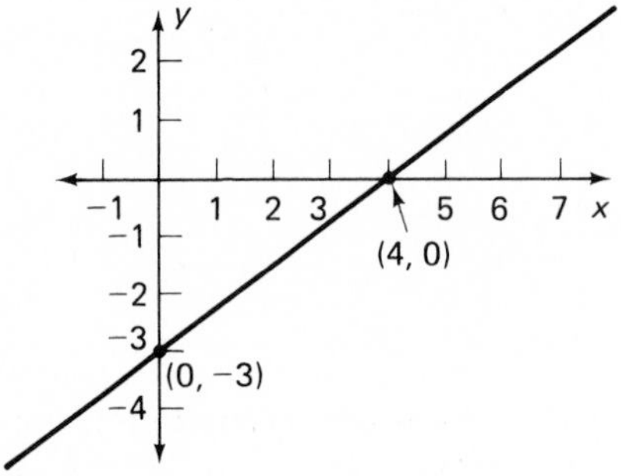

FIGURE 15

When plotting the graph of a linear relation, the simplest procedure in most cases is to find the two points where the graph crosses the coordinate axes, as we did in Example 8. There are occasions, however, when this is inconvenient; for example, one of these points of intersection may be off the graph paper we are using. It is also impossible to use this technique if the graph happens to pass through the origin. In such cases, we can use any pair of points on the graph in order to draw it, choosing the most convenient values of x at which to calculate y.

Alternatively, it is sometimes helpful to use the slope in order to sketch the graph. For example, the equation in Example 8 can be written in the form $y = \frac{3}{4}x - 3$, which shows that the slope is $\frac{3}{4}$ and the y-intercept is -3. Thus we can plot the point $(0, -3)$. In addition, for every 4 units we move along the positive x direction, the graph is going to rise by 3 units, since slope = rise/run $= \frac{3}{4}$. So if we move horizontally 4 units and vertically 3 units from the point $(0, -3)$ we obtain a second point on the graph. Or we can move horizontally 8 units and then vertically 6 units to get a second point, and so on. This is illustrated in Figure 16. From the y-intercept of -3, we have moved 8 units horizontally and then 6 units vertically to arrive at point B. A straight line can then be drawn connecting the point $(0, -3)$ and B.

EXAMPLE 9   A city government has a budget of \$200 million for capital expenditure on transportation, and it intends to use it to construct additional subways or highways. It costs \$2.5 million per mile to build highways and \$4 million per mile for subways. Find the relationship between the numbers of miles of highway and of subway that can be built to completely use the available budget. Interpret the slope of the linear relation that is obtained.

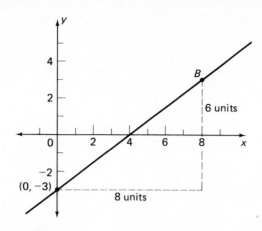

FIGURE 16

Solution   Suppose x miles of highway and y miles of subway are built. The cost of constructing x miles of highway at \$2.5 million per mile is $2.5x$ million dollars and the cost of building y miles of subway at \$4 million per mile is $4y$ million dollars. Since the total cost has to equal the budget allotted for the purpose,

$$2.5x + 4y = 200.$$

This equation provides the required relation between the numbers of miles that can be constructed within the budget.

Solving the given equation for y, we have

$$y = -\tfrac{5}{8}x + 50.$$

The slope of this line is $-\tfrac{5}{8}$, which expresses the fact that every additional mile of highway construction will be at the cost of $\tfrac{5}{8}$ miles of subway construction. Solving the original equation for x in terms of y, we get

$$x = -\tfrac{8}{5}y + 80.$$

Thus each additional mile of subway construction is traded off against $\tfrac{8}{5}$ miles of highway construction.

EXERCISES 2

(1–6)   Find the slopes of the lines joining each pair of points.

1. (2, 1) and (5, 7)   **2.** (5, −2) and (1, −6)

3. (2, −1) and (4, −1)   **4.** (3, 5) and (−1, 5)

5. (−3, 2) and (−3, 4)   **6.** (1, 2) and (1, 5)

(7–16)   Find the equation of the straight lines satisfying the conditions in each of the following exercises. Sketch the graph in each case.

7. Passing through (2, 1) with slope 5.

8. Passing through (1, −2) with slope −3.

9. Passing through (3, 4) with zero slope.

10. Passing through (2, −3) with no slope.

11. Passing through (3, −1) and (4, 5).

12. Passing through (2, 1) and (3, 4).

13. Passing through (3, −2) and (3, 7).

14. With slope −2 and y-intercept 5.

15. With slope $\frac{1}{3}$ and y-intercept −4.

16. With slope 3 and y-intercept 0.

(17–22) Find the slope and the y-intercept for each of the following linear relations.

17. $3x - 2y = 6$	18. $4x + 5y = 20$	19. $y - 2x + 3 = 0$
20. $\dfrac{x}{3} + \dfrac{y}{4} = 1$	21. $2y - 3 = 0$	22. $3x + 4 = 0$

23. A company manufactures two types of a certain product. Each unit of the first type requires 2 machine-hours and each unit of the second type requires 5 machine-hours. There are 280 machine-hours available each week.

   a. If x units of first type and y units of second type are made each week, find the relation between x and y if all the machine-hours are used.

   b. What is the slope of the equation in part (a)? What does it represent?

   c. How many units of the first type can be manufactured if 40 units of the second type are manufactured in a particular week?

24. The Boss-Toss Company manufactures two products, X and Y. Each unit of X requires 3 work-hours and each unit of Y requires 4 work-hours. There are 120 work-hours available each day.

   a. If x units of X and y units of Y are manufactured each day and all the available work-hours are used, find the relationship between x and y.

   b. Give the physical interpretation of the slope of the linear relation obtained.

   c. How many units of X can be made in one day if 15 units of Y are made the same day?

   d. How many units of Y can be made in one day if 16 units of X are made the same day?

25. Jackson Stores has 650 units of item X in stock and their average sales per day of this item is 25 units.

   a. If y represents the inventory (of items X in stock) at a time t (measured in days), determine the linear relation between y and t. (Use $t = 1$ to represent the end of the first day, and so on.)

   b. How long would it take to run out of stock?

   c. On what sales day is the new order placed if it is placed when the stock level reaches 125 units?

4-3 SYSTEMS OF EQUATIONS

Many problems in business and economics lead to what are called *systems of linear equations*. Consider for example, the following situation.

The owner of a television store wants to expand his business by buying and displaying two new types of television sets that have recently appeared on the market. Each television set of the first type costs $300 and each set of the second type costs $400. Each of the first type of set occupies 4 square feet of floor space, whereas each set of the second type occupies 5 square feet. If the owner has only $2000 available for this expansion and 26 square feet of floor space, how many sets of each type should be bought and displayed to make full use of the available capital and space?

Suppose the owner buys x television sets of the first type and y sets of the second type. Then it costs $300x$ to buy the first type of sets and $400y$ to buy the second type of sets. Since the total amount to be spent is $2000, it is necessary that

$$300x + 400y = 2000. \tag{1}$$

Also, the amounts of space occupied by the two types of sets are $4x$ square feet and $5y$ square feet, respectively. The total space available for these two types of sets is 26 square feet. Therefore

$$4x + 5y = 26. \tag{2}$$

To find the number of sets of each type that can be bought and displayed, we must solve the Equations (1) and (2) for x and y. That is, we must find the values of x and y that satisfy both Equations (1) and (2) simultaneously. Observe that each of these equations is a linear equation in x and y.

DEFINITION A **system of linear equations** in two variables x and y consists of two equations of the type

$$a_1x + b_1y = c_1 \tag{3}$$
$$a_2x + b_2y = c_2 \tag{4}$$

where a_1, b_1, c_1, a_2, b_2, and c_2 are six given constants. The **solution** of the system defined by Equations (3) and (4) is the set of values of x and y that satisfy both equations.

Equations (1) and (2) form such a system of linear equations. If we identify Equation (1) with Equation (3) and Equation (2) with Equation (4), the six coefficients have the values $a_1 = 300$, $b_1 = 400$, $c_1 = 2000$ $a_2 = 4$, $b_2 = 5$, and $c_2 = 26$.

Our main concern in this section is to solve systems of linear equations algebraically. Solution by the use of algebraic methods involves the elimination of one of the variables, either x or y, from the two equations; this allows determination of the value of the other variable. Elimination of one of the variables can be achieved either by substitution or by adding a suitable multiple of one equation to the other. The two processes are illustrated in Example 1.

EXAMPLE 1 Solve the two equations that resulted from the problem posed in the beginning of this section.

$$300x + 400y = 2000 \tag{1}$$
$$4x + 5y = 26 \tag{2}$$

Solution   (**Method of Substitution**)   In this case, we solve one of the given equations for x or y (whichever is simplest) and substitute the value of this variable in the other equation. From Equation (2) (solving for x), we have

$$4x = 26 - 5y$$
$$x = \frac{26 - 5y}{4}. \tag{5}$$

We substitute this value of x in Equation (1) and solve for y.

$$300\left(\frac{26 - 5y}{4}\right) + 400y = 2000$$
$$75(26 - 5y) + 400y = 2000$$
$$1950 - 375y + 400y = 2000$$
$$25y = 2000 - 1950 = 50$$
$$y = 2$$

Substituting $y = 2$ in (5) we have

$$x = \tfrac{1}{4}(26 - 10) = 4.$$

Thus the solution of the system of Equations (1) and (2) above is $x = 4$ and $y = 2$. In other words, the dealer should buy and display 4 sets of the first type and 2 sets of the second type to make use of all the available space and capital.

Alternative
Solution

(**Method of Addition**)

$$300x + 400y = 2000 \tag{1}$$
$$4x + 5y = 26 \tag{2}$$

According to this method, we make the coefficients of either x or y in the two equations exactly the same magnitude and opposite in sign; we then add the two equations to eliminate one of the variables. Observe that if we multiply both sides of Equation (2) by -80, we make the coefficient of y the same magnitude as the coefficient in Equation (1), but of opposite sign. Equation (2) becomes

$$-320x - 400y = -2080. \tag{6}$$

Recall that Equation (1) is

$$300x + 400y = 2000.$$

We add these two equations; the y-terms cancel and we obtain

$$(-320x - 400y) + (300x + 400y) = -2080 + 2000 \tag{7}$$

or

$$-20x = -80$$
$$x = 4.$$

Substituting $x = 4$ in one of the given equations (we use Equation (2)), we have

$$16 + 5y = 26$$
$$5y = 26 - 16 = 10$$
$$y = 2.$$

Thus the solution is $x = 4$ and $y = 2$, the same as obtained by the first method.

Note: The operations involved in these methods of solution do not change the set of solutions. For example, any x and y that satisfy Equation (2) also satisfy Equation (6); any x and y that satisfy both Equations (6) and (1) also satisfy Equation (7), and so on. Thus the methods yield values of x and y that are solutions of the original pair of equations.

EXAMPLE 2   Solve the following system.

$$\frac{x - y}{3} = \frac{y - 1}{4}$$

$$\frac{4x - 5y}{7} = x - 7$$

Solution   The first step is to get rid of fractions in the given equations. We multiply both sides of the first equation by 12, the common denominator, and simplify.

$$4(x - y) = 3(y - 1)$$
$$4x - 4y = 3y - 3$$
$$4x - 7y = -3$$

Multiplying both sides of the second equation by 7 and simplifying, we obtain

$$4x - 5y = 7(x - 7) = 7x - 49$$
$$-3x - 5y = -49.$$

Multiplying throughout by -1, we get

$$3x + 5y = 49.$$

Thus the given system of equations is equivalent to the following system of linear equations.

$$4x - 7y = -3 \tag{8}$$
$$3x + 5y = 49 \tag{9}$$

We use the substitution method. We solve Equation (8) for x.

$$4x = 7y - 3 \quad \text{or} \quad x = \tfrac{1}{4}(7y - 3) \tag{10}$$

Substituting this value of x into Equation (9) we obtain

$$\tfrac{3}{4}(7y - 3) + 5y = 49.$$

We multiply both sides by 4 and solve for y.

$$3(7y - 3) + 20y = 196$$
$$21y - 9 + 20y = 196$$
$$41y = 196 + 9 = 205$$
$$y = \frac{205}{41} = 5$$

Putting $y = 5$ in Equation (10) we get

$$x = \tfrac{1}{4}(35 - 3) = 8.$$

Thus the required solution is $x = 8$ and $y = 5$.

A system of linear equations and its solution has an important geometrical interpretation. For example, let us consider the following system.

$$x + y = 3 \tag{11}$$

$$3x - y = 1 \tag{12}$$

Using either of the above methods of solution, we can easily see that the solution in this case is $x = 1$ and $y = 2$.

Each of Equations (11) and (12) is a linear equation in x and y and so has as its graph a straight line in the xy-plane. In the case of Equation (11), we find the point where the line meets the x-axis by setting $y = 0$. This gives $x = 3$, so the line passes through the point $(3, 0)$. Similarly, setting $x = 0$, we find $y = 3$, so that the line meets the y-axis at the point $(0, 3)$. These two points are shown in Figure 17, and the graph of Equation (11) is drawn as the straight line joining them.

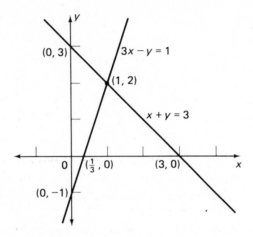

FIGURE 17

Proceeding in a similar way for Equation (12), we find the points $(0, -1)$ and $(\frac{1}{3}, 0)$ on the coordinate axes.

Any pair of values of x and y that satisfies Equation (11) corresponds to a point (x, y) on the first straight line. Any pair of values that satisfies Equation (12) corresponds to a point (x, y) on the second straight line. Thus if x and y satisfy *both* equations, then the point (x, y) must lie on *both* of the lines. In other words, (x, y) must be the point at which the lines intersect. From Figure 17, we see that this point is $(1, 2)$, so the solution in this case is $x = 1$ and $y = 2$, as stated earlier.

Now let us return to the general system of linear equations.

$$a_1 x + b_1 y = c_1 \tag{3}$$

$$a_2 x + b_2 y = c_2 \tag{4}$$

The graphs of these two equations consist of two straight lines in the xy-plane, since any linear equation always represents a straight line, as we saw in Section

2. Any pair of values of x and y that satisfy both Equations (3) and (4) must correspond to a point (x, y) that lies on both of the lines.

Let us denote the two straight lines by L and M, respectively. Then there are three possible kinds of behavior that can be found.

1. Lines L and M intersect each other. Since the point of intersection, (x_0, y_0), lies on both lines, the coordinates (x_0, y_0) satisfy the equations of both lines and hence they provide a solution of the given system. This solution is unique, because if the two straight lines intersect, they intersect each other at only one point. (See part (a) of Figure 18.)

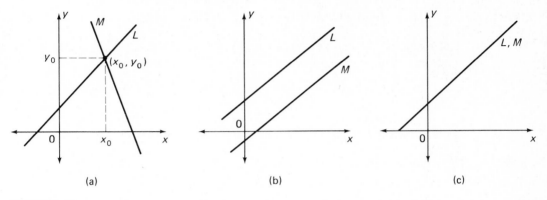

(a)　　　　　　　　　(b)　　　　　　　　　(c)

FIGURE 18

2. Lines L and M are parallel. In this case, the lines do not meet each other and there is no point that lies on both the lines. Thus there are no values of x and y that will satisfy both the equations. In other words, the equations have *no solution* in this case. (See part (b) of Figure 18.)

3. Lines L and M coincide. In such a case, every point on line L is also on line M. In this case, the system has an *infinite number of solutions*, namely, every ordered pair (x, y) that lies on $L (= M)$. (See part (c) of Figure 18.)

EXAMPLE 3　Solve the following system of equations.

$$x + 2y = 4$$
$$3x + 6y - 8 = 0$$

Solution　We solve the first equation for x.

$$x = 4 - 2y$$

We then substitute this value of x in the second equation and simplify.

$$3(4 - 2y) + 6y - 8 = 0$$
$$12 - 6y + 6y - 8 = 0$$
$$4 = 0$$

This is impossible. Thus the given equations have *no solution*. This is illustrated graphically in Figure 19. The two straight lines are parallel in this case and do

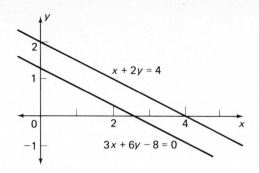

FIGURE 19

not intersect. We can see this easily by writing the given equations in slope-intercept form.

$$y = -\tfrac{1}{2}x + 2$$
$$y = -\tfrac{1}{2}x + \tfrac{4}{3}$$

The two lines have the *same slope* $(-\tfrac{1}{2})$ but different y-intercepts. Thus the two lines are parallel, with no common point of intersection.

EXAMPLE 4   Solve the system of equations.

$$2x - 3y = 6 \tag{13}$$

$$\frac{x}{3} - \frac{y}{2} = 1 \tag{14}$$

Solution   Multiplying both sides of the second equation by -6, we obtain

$$-2x + 3y = -6.$$

Adding this equation to the first equation, we get

$$0 = 0$$

an equation that is always true.

Writing the two equations in the slope-intercept form, we find that they both reduce to the equation

$$y = \tfrac{2}{3}x - 2.$$

Since the two equations are identical, the two lines coincide in this case and the two given equations are equivalent to one another. In fact, Equation (14) can be obtained from Equation (13) by multiplying the latter by $\tfrac{1}{6}$. We have an infinite number of solutions in this case: any pair of values (x, y) that satisfies Equation (13) provides a solution. One such pair is $(6, 2)$, for example, and another is $(0, -2)$.

The method of substitution is often useful when we have a system of equations in which one equation is linear and the other is not.

EXAMPLE 5   Solve the following system of equations.

$$2x - y = 3$$
$$x^2 + y^2 = 5$$

Solution In this system, one of the two equations is not linear. The method of solution still consists of elimination of one of the variables, x or y, from the two equations. From the first equation, we have

$$y = 2x - 3.$$

We substitute this value of y into the second equation and simplify.

$$x^2 + (2x - 3)^2 = 5$$
$$x^2 + 4x^2 - 12x + 9 = 5$$
$$5x^2 - 12x + 4 = 0$$

This factors to give

$$(x - 2)(5x - 2) = 0.$$

Therefore, either

$$x - 2 = 0 \quad \text{or} \quad 5x - 2 = 0$$
$$x = 2 \qquad\qquad x = \tfrac{2}{5}.$$

Next, we substitute these values into $y = 2x - 3$.

$$
\begin{aligned}
y &= 2x - 3 & y &= 2x - 3 \\
&= 2(2) - 3 & &= 2(\tfrac{2}{5}) - 3 \\
&= 1 & &= -\tfrac{11}{5}
\end{aligned}
$$

Hence there are two solutions,

$$x = 2, y = 1 \quad \text{and} \quad x = \tfrac{2}{5}, y = -\tfrac{11}{5}.$$

We shall conclude this section by solving an applied problem involving simultaneous equations.

EXAMPLE 6 The Britannia Store, which specializes in selling all kinds of nuts, sells peanuts at $0.70 per pound and cashews at $1.60 per pound. At the end of the month, the owner of the store finds that peanuts are not selling well and decides to mix peanuts and cashews to make a mixture of 45 pounds, which could sell for $1.00 per pound. How many pounds of peanuts and cashews should be mixed to keep the same revenue?

Solution Let the mixture contain x pounds of peanuts and y pounds of cashews. Since the total mixture is 45 pounds,

$$x + y = 45.$$

The revenue from x pounds of peanuts at $0.70 per pound is $0.7x$ dollars and the revenue from y pounds of cashews at $1.60 per pound is $1.6y$ dollars. The revenue obtained from the mixture of 45 pounds at $1.00 per pound will be $45. Since the revenue from the mixture must be the same as from the separate nuts, we have the following equation.

Revenue from Peanuts + Revenue from Cashews = Revenue from Mixture

$$0.7x + 1.6y = 45$$
$$7x + 16y = 450$$

Thus we arrive at the following system of linear equations.

$$x + y = 45$$
$$7x + 16y = 450$$

From the top equation, we have $x = 45 - y$. We then substitute this value of x into the bottom equation and solve for y.

$$7(45 - y) + 16y = 450$$
$$315 - 7y + 16y = 450$$
$$9y = 450 - 315 = 135$$
$$y = 15$$

Therefore $x = 45 - y = 45 - 15 = 30$.

Thus 30 pounds of peanuts should be mixed with 15 pounds of cashews to form the mixture.

_____

The method of substitution can also often be used to solve systems of equations with three or more variables.

EXERCISES 3

(1–18) Solve the following systems of linear equations.

1. $x - y = 1$ and $2x + 3y + 8 = 0$

2. $2x - 3y = 1$ and $5x + 4y = 14$

3. $4x - y = -2$ and $3x + 4y = 27$

4. $3u + 2v = 9$ and $u + 3v = 10$

5. $3x + 5t = 12$ and $4x - 3t = -13$

6. $2p - q = 3$ and $p = 5 - 3q$

7. $7x - 8y = 4$ and $\dfrac{x}{2} + \dfrac{y}{3} = 3$

8. $\dfrac{x+y}{2} - \dfrac{x-y}{3} = 8$ and $\dfrac{x+y}{3} + \dfrac{x-y}{4} = 11$

9. $\dfrac{x}{4} + \dfrac{y}{5} + 1 = \dfrac{x}{5} + \dfrac{y}{4} = 23$

10. $\dfrac{x - 2y}{3} = 2 + \dfrac{2x + 3y}{4}$ and $\dfrac{3x - 2y}{2} = \dfrac{-y + 5x + 11}{4}$

11. $5x - 7y + 2 = 0$ and $15x - 21y = 7$

12. $2u - 3v = 12$ and $-\dfrac{u}{3} + \dfrac{v}{2} = 4$

13. $x + 2y = 4$ and $3x + 6y = 12$

14. $2p + q = 3$ and $\frac{2}{3}p + \frac{1}{3}q = 1$

*15. $x + 3y + 4z = 1$, $2x + 7y + 3z = -5$, and $3x + 10y + 8z = -3$

*16. $3x - 2y + 4z = 3$, $4x + 3y = 9$, and $2x + 4y + z = 0$

17. $x + y = 3$ and $x^2 + y^2 = 29$

18. $2x + y = 5$ and $xy = 2$

19. Two metals, X and Y, can be extracted from two types of ore, I and II. One hundred pounds of ore I yields 3 ounces of X and 5 ounces of Y, and 100 pounds of ore II yields 4 ounces of X and 2.5 ounces of Y. How many pounds of ores I and II will be required to produce 72 ounces of X and 95 ounces of Y?

20. A firm manufactures two products, A and B. Each product has to be processed by two machines, I and II. Each unit of type A requires 1 hour of processing by machine I and 1.5 hours by machine II, and each unit of type B requires 3 hours on machine I and 2 hours on machine II. If machine I is available for 300 hours each month and machine II for 250 hours, how many units of each type can be manufactured in one month if the total available time on the two machines is to be utilized?

21. A company is trying to purchase and store two types of items, X and Y. Each item X costs $3 and each item Y costs $2.50. Each item X occupies 2 square feet of floor space and each item Y occupies 1 square foot of floor space. How many units of each type can be purchased and stored if $400 is available for purchasing and 240 square feet of floor space is available for storing these items?

22. A store sells two types of coffee, one at $2.00 per pound and the other at $1.50 per pound. The owner of the store makes 50 pounds of a new blend of coffee by mixing these two types of coffee and sells it at $1.60 per pound. How many pounds of coffee of each type should be mixed to keep the revenue unchanged?

23. A chemical store has two types of acid solutions. One contains 25% acid and the other contains 15% acid. How many gallons of each type should be mixed to obtain 200 gallons of a mixture containing 18% acid?

24. The income tax department has a certain tax rate on the first $5000 of taxable income and a different rate on taxable income over $5000 but less than $10,000. The government wishes to fix the tax rates in such a way that a person with taxable income of $7000 should pay $950 in tax, while one with taxable income of $9000 should pay $1400 in tax. Find the two rates.

25. A certain company employs 53 persons in its two branch offices. Of these people, 21 are university graduates. If one-third of those in the first office and three-sevenths of those in the second office are university graduates, how many persons are employed in each office?

4-4 APPLICATIONS TO BUSINESS ANALYSIS

In this section, we shall discuss some applications of linear equations and straight lines to problems in business and economics.

Linear Cost Model

In the production of any commodity by a firm, there are two types of costs involved; these are known as *fixed costs* and *variable costs*. **Fixed costs** are costs that have to be met no matter how much or how little of the commodity is produced: that is, they do not depend on the level of production. Examples of fixed costs are rents, interest on loans and bonds, and management salaries.

Variable costs are costs that depend on the level of production, that is, on the amount of commodity produced. Material costs and labor costs are examples of variable costs. The total cost is given by

$$\text{Total Cost} = \text{Variable Costs} + \text{Fixed Costs.}$$

Consider the case when the *variable cost per unit of commodity is constant*. In this case, the total variable costs are proportional to the amount of commodity produced. If m dollars denotes the variable cost per unit, then the total variable costs of producing x units of commodity is mx dollars. If the fixed costs are b dollars, then the total cost y_c (in dollars) of producing x units is given by

$$\text{Total cost} = \text{Total Variable Costs} + \text{Fixed Costs}$$
$$y_c = mx + b. \tag{1}$$

Equation (1) is an example of a **linear cost model**. The graph of Equation (1) is a straight line whose slope represents the variable cost per unit and whose y-intercept gives the fixed costs.

EXAMPLE 1   The variable cost of processing 1 pound of coffee beans is 50¢ and the fixed costs per day are $300.

(a) Give the linear cost equation and draw its graph.

(b) Find the cost of processing 1000 pounds of coffee beans in one day.

Solution   (a) If y_c represents the cost (in dollars) of processing x pounds of coffee beans per day, then according to the linear cost model, we have

$$y_c = mx + b$$

where m is the variable cost per unit and b the fixed cost. In our case, $m = 50¢ = \$0.50$ and $b = \$300$. Therefore

$$y_c = 0.5x + 300. \tag{2}$$

To sketch the graph of Equation (2), let us first find two points on it.

Letting $x = 0$ in Equation (2), we have $y = 300$; letting $x = 200$ in Equation (2), we have $y_c = 0.5(200) + 300 = 400$. Thus two points satisfying Cost Equation (2) are (0, 300) and (200, 400). Plotting these two points and joining them by a straight line, we obtain the graph shown in Figure 20. Note that the relevant portion of the graph lies totally in the first quadrant because x and y_c are both nonnegative quantities.

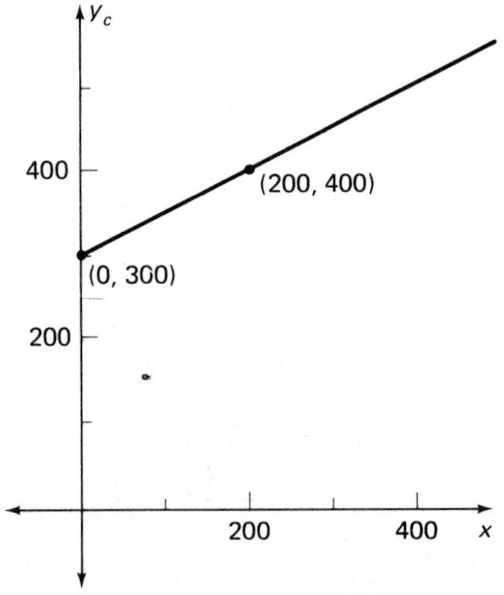

FIGURE 20

(b) Substituting $x = 1000$ in Equation (2), we get
$$y_c = 0.5(1000) + 300 = 800.$$
Thus the cost of processing 1000 pounds of coffee beans per day will be $800.

EXAMPLE 2   The cost of manufacturing 10 typewriters per day is $350, while it costs $600 to produce 20 typewriters per day. Assuming a linear cost model, determine the relationship representing the total cost y_c of producing x typewriters per day and draw its graph.

Solution   We are given two points (10, 350) and (20, 600) that lie on the graph of a linear cost model. The slope of the line joining these two points is
$$m = \frac{600 - 350}{20 - 10} = \frac{250}{10} = 25.$$

Using the point-slope formula, the required equation of the (linear cost model) straight line with slope $m = 25$ and passing through the point (10, 350) is
$$y - y_1 = m(x - x_1)$$
$$y_c - 350 = 25(x - 10) = 25x - 250;$$
that is,
$$y_c = 25x + 100. \tag{3}$$
The graph of Equation (3) in this case is not a continuous straight line, because x cannot take fractional values as it represents the number of typewriters produced. The variable x can take the integer values 0, 1, 2, 3, 4, 5, ... only. The corresponding values of y_c are given in Table 5.

TABLE 5

x	0	1	2	3	4	5	6....
y_c	100	125	150	175	200	225	250....

Plotting these points, we obtain the graph shown in Figure 21. Note that the

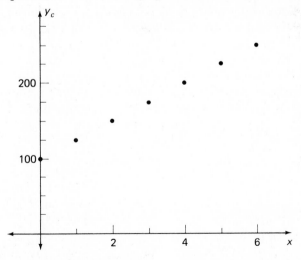

FIGURE 21

graph consists of separate (discrete) points rather than a continuous straight line.

Break-Even Analysis

If the total cost y_c of production exceeds the revenue y_R obtained from the sales, then a business is running at a loss. On the other hand, if the revenue exceeds the costs, there is a profit. If the cost of production equals the revenue obtained from the sales, there is no profit or loss, so the business breaks even. The number of units produced and sold in this case is called the **break-even point**.

EXAMPLE 3   For a watchmaker, the cost of labor and material per watch is $15 and the fixed costs are $2000 per day. If each watch sells for $20, how many watches should be produced and sold each day to guarantee that the business breaks even?

Solution   Let x watches be produced and sold each day. The total cost of producing x watches is

$$y_c = \text{Total Variable Costs} + \text{Fixed Costs}$$
$$= 15x + 2000.$$

Since each watch sells for $20, the revenue y_R obtained by selling x watches is

$$y_R = 20x.$$

The break-even point is obtained when the revenue equals costs, that is,

$$20x = 15x + 2000.$$

We have $5x = 2000$ or $x = 400$.

Thus 400 watches must be produced and sold each day to guarantee no profit or loss. Figure 22 illustrates the graphical interpretation of the break-even point. When $x < 400$, the cost y_c exceeds the revenue y_R and there is a loss. When $x > 400$, the revenue y_R exceeds the cost y_c so that a profit results.

Note that graphically, the break-even point corresponds to the intersection of two straight lines. One of the lines has the equation $y = 15x + 2000$, corresponding to the cost of production, and the other line has the equation $y = 20x$, corresponding to the revenue.

EXAMPLE 4   Suppose the total daily cost (in dollars) of producing x chairs is given by

$$y_c = 2.5x + 300.$$

(a) If each chair sells for $4, what is the break-even point?

(b) If the selling price is increased to $5 per chair, what is the new break-even point?

(c) If it is known that at least 150 chairs can be sold each day, what price should be charged to guarantee no loss?

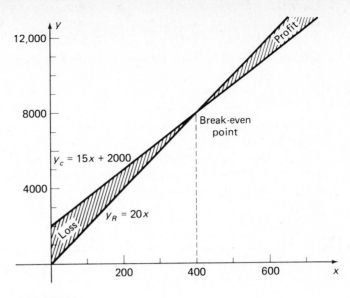

$y_c = 15x + 2000$

$y_R = 20x$

Break-even point

Profit

Loss

FIGURE 22

Solution   The cost is given by
$$y_c = 2.5x + 300.$$

(a) If each chair sells for \$4, the revenue (in dollars) obtained by the sale of x chairs is
$$y_R = 4x.$$
At the break-even point, we have $y_c = y_R$; that is,
$$4x = 2.5x + 300.$$
Thus $1.5x = 300$ or $x = 200$. The break-even point is 200 chairs.

(b) If the selling price is increased to \$5 per chair, the revenue in this case is
$$y_R = 5x.$$
The break-even point obeys $y_R = y_c$, so
$$5x = 2.5x + 300.$$
Thus $2.5x = 300$, or $x = 120$. With the new selling price, the break-even point is 120 chairs.

(c) Let p dollars be the price charged for each chair. Then the revenue obtained from the sale of 150 chairs is $y_R = 150p$ and the cost of producing 150 chairs is $y_c = 2.5(150) + 300 = 675$. To guarantee a break-even situation, we must have $y_R = y_c$; that is,
$$150p = 675 \quad \text{or} \quad p = 4.50.$$
Thus, \$4.50 per chair should be charged to guarantee break-even (at worst) if at least 150 chairs will be sold each day.

It should be pointed out that when an economist uses a linear relationship to describe a relation between two variables, it is not claimed that the true relationship is linear, but rather that a linear relationship is a good approximation to the observed data over the range of interest. If the observed data are found to lie on or close to a straight line when plotted on a graph, we can use a linear relationship as an approximate representation of the data. The way in which this can be carried out will be described in Section 6 of Chapter 18.

Although observed data often lie close to a straight line, there are also many cases in which they do not, and in such cases it is not reasonable to use a linear equation to approximate the relationship between two given variables. For example, the cost of manufacturing x items of a certain type may not be given by a linear cost model, $y_c = mx + b$, but may depend on x in some more complex way. In principle, a break-even analysis remains unchanged in such cases, but the algebra involved in finding the break-even point becomes more complicated.

EXAMPLE 5 A candy company sells its boxes of chocolates for $2 each. If x is the number of boxes produced per week (in thousands), then the management knows that the production costs are given in dollars by

$$y_c = 1000 + 1300x + 100x^2.$$

Determine the level of production at which the company will break even.

Solution The revenue from selling x thousands of boxes at $2 each is given by

$$y_R = 2000x.$$

In order to break even, revenue must equal costs; so

$$1000 + 1300x + 100x^2 = 2000x.$$

Dividing both sides of this equation by 100 and moving all the terms to the left, we have

$$x^2 - 7x + 10 = 0.$$

If we factor this expression, we get

$$(x - 2)(x - 5) = 0$$

and so $x = 2$ or $x = 5$.

We find, therefore, that there are two break-even points in this problem. The company can decide to make 2000 boxes per week ($x = 2$), with revenues and costs both $4000. Or they can make 5000 boxes per week ($x = 5$), when revenues and costs will again balance at $10,000.

It is instructive in this example to look at the profitability of the company. The weekly profit P is given by revenue minus costs.

$$P = y_R - y_c$$
$$= 2000x - (1000 + 1300x + 100x^2)$$
$$= -1000 + 700x - 100x^2$$
$$= -100(x - 2)(x - 5)$$

When $x = 2$ or 5, the profit is zero, and these are the break-even points. When $2 < x < 5$, we have $x - 2 > 0$ and $x - 5 < 0$. Because the product contains two negative signs, P is positive in this case. Thus the company makes a positive profit when $2 < x < 5$; that is, when it manufactures and sells between 2000 and 5000 boxes per week.

EXERCISES 4

1. The variable cost of manufacturing a table is $7 and the fixed cost is $150 per day. Determine the total cost y_c of manufacturing x tables per day. What is the cost of manufacturing 100 tables per day?

2. The total cost of manufacturing 100 cameras per week is $700 and of 120 cameras per week is $800.

   a. Determine the cost equation, assuming it to be linear.

   b. What are the fixed cost and the variable cost per unit?

3. It costs a company $75 to produce 10 units of a certain item per day and $120 to produce 25 units of the same item per day.

   a. Determine the cost equation, assuming it to be linear.

   b. What is the cost of producing 20 items per day?

   c. What are the variable cost per item and the fixed cost?

4. Johnson's Moving Company charges $70 to move a certain machine 15 miles and $100 to move the same machine 25 miles.

   a. Determine the relation between total charges and the distance moved, assuming it to be linear.

   b. What is the minimum charge for moving this machine?

   c. What is the rate for each mile the machine is moved?

5. Fixed costs of manufacturing a certain product are $300 per week and the total cost of manufacturing 20 units per week is $410. Determine the relationship between the total cost and the number of units manufactured, assuming it to be linear. What will it cost to manufacture 30 units per week?

6. A hotel rents a room to one person at the rate of $25 for the first night and $20 for each succeeding night. Express the cost y_c of the bill in terms of x, the number of nights the person stays at the hotel.

7. A catering company will provide banquets for groups of people at a cost of $10 per person plus an overhead charge of $150. Find the cost y_c they would charge for catering for x people.

8. The cost of a bus ticket in Jonesville depends linearly on the distance traveled. A journey of 2 miles costs 40 cents, while a journey of 6 miles costs 60 cents. Determine the cost of a ticket for a journey of x miles.

9. The variable cost of producing a certain item is 90¢ per item and the fixed costs are $240 per day. The item sells for $1.20 each. How many items should be produced and sold to guarantee no profit and no loss?

10. The fixed costs of producing a certain product are $5000 per month and the variable cost is $3.50 per unit. If the product sells for $6.00 each, find each of the following.

    a.   The break-even point.

    b.   The number of units that must be produced and sold each month to obtain a profit of $1000 per month.

    c.   The loss when only 1500 units are produced and sold each month.

11. The cost of producing x items is given by $y_c = 2.8x + 600$ and each item sells for $4.00.

    a.   Find the break-even point.

    b.   If it is known that at least 450 units will be sold, what should be the price charged for each item to guarantee no loss?

12. A manufacturer produces items at a variable cost of 85¢ per item and the fixed costs are $280 each day. If the item can be sold for $1.10, determine the break-even point.

13. In Exercise 12, if the manufacturer can reduce the variable cost to 70¢ per item by increasing the daily fixed costs to $350, is it advantageous to do so? (Such a reduction might be possible, for example, by purchasing a new machine that would cut production costs but would increase interest charges.)

14. The cost of producing x items per week is given by $y_c = 1000 + 5x$. If each item can be sold for $7, determine the break-even point. If the manufacturer can reduce variable costs to $4 per item by increasing fixed costs to $1200 per week, would it be wise to do so?

15. The cost of producing x items per day is given in dollars by $y_c = 80 + 4x + 0.1x^2$. If each item can be sold for $10, determine the break-even point.

*16. The cost of producing x items per day is given in dollars by $y_c = 2000 + 100\sqrt{x}$. If each item can be sold for $10, determine the break-even point.

*17. The cost of producing x items per day is given in dollars by $y_c = 1000 + 20\sqrt{x} + 8x$. If each item can be sold for $20, determine the break-even point.

4-5 SUPPLY AND DEMAND

The laws of demand and supply are two of the fundamental relationships in any economic analysis. The quantity x of any commodity that will be purchased by consumers depends on the price at which that commodity is made available. A relationship that specifies the amounts of a particular commodity that consumers are willing to buy at various price levels is called the **law of demand**. The simplest law is a linear relation of the type

$$p = mx + b \qquad (1)$$

where p is the price per unit of the commodity and m and b are constants. The graph of a demand law is called the **demand curve**. Observe that, as given, p is expressed in terms of x. This allows us to calculate the price level at which a certain amount x can be sold.

It is a well-recognized fact that if the price per unit of a commodity is increased, the demand for that commodity will decrease because fewer purchasers can afford it, whereas if the price per unit is decreased—that is, the

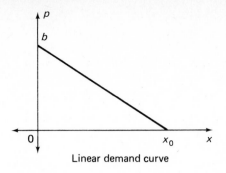

Linear demand curve

FIGURE 23

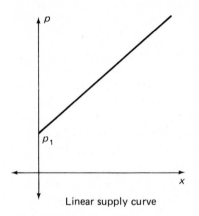

Linear supply curve

FIGURE 24

commodity is made cheaper—the demand will increase. In other words, slope m of the demand relation of Equation (1) is negative. Thus the graph of Equation (1) slopes downwards to the right, as shown in Figure 23. Since the price p per unit and the quantity x demanded are both nonnegative numbers, the graph of Equation (1) has been drawn only in the first quadrant.

The amount of a particular commodity that its suppliers are willing to make available depends on the price at which they can sell it. A relation specifying the amount of any commodity that manufacturers (or sellers) can make available in the market at various prices is called the **law of supply**.

The graph of a supply equation (or law of supply) is known as the **supply curve**. In general, suppliers will make a greater quantity available in the market if they can get a high price and a smaller quantity if they get a low price. In other words, the supply increases with increase in price. A typical linear supply curve is shown in Figure 24. The price p_1 corresponds to the price below which suppliers will not supply the commodity.

EXAMPLE 1 A dealer can sell 20 electric shavers per day at $25 per shaver, but he can sell 30 shavers if he charges $20 per shaver. Determine the demand equation, assuming it is linear.

Solution Taking the quantity x demanded as the abscissa (or x-coordinate) and the price p per unit as the ordinate (or y-coordinate) the two points on the demand curve have coordinates

$$x = 20, p = 25 \quad \text{and} \quad x = 30, p = 20.$$

Thus the points are $(20, 25)$ and $(30, 20)$. Since the demand equation is linear, it is given by the equation of the straight line passing through the two given points $(20, 25)$ and $(30, 20)$. The slope of the line joining these two points is

$$m = \frac{20 - 25}{30 - 20} = -\frac{5}{10} = -0.5.$$

From the point-slope formula, the equation of the line through $(20, 25)$ with slope $m = -0.5$ is

$$y - y_1 = m(x - x_1).$$

Since $y = p$, we have

$$p - 25 = -0.5(x - 20)$$
$$p = -0.5x + 35$$

which is the required demand equation. (See Figure 25.)

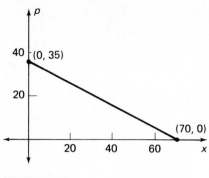

FIGURE 25

Market Equilibrium

If the price of a certain commodity is too high, consumers will not purchase it, whereas if the price is too low, suppliers will not sell it. In a competitive market, when the price per unit depends only on the quantity demanded and the supply available, there is always a tendency for the price to adjust itself so that the quantity demanded by purchasers matches the quantity which suppliers are willing to supply at the given price. **Market equilibrium** is said to occur at a price when the quantity demanded is equal to quantity supplied. This corresponds to the point of intersection of the demand and supply curves. (See Figure 26.)

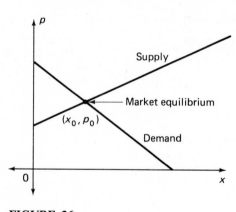

FIGURE 26

Algebraically, the market equilibrium price p_0 and quantity x_0 are determined by solving the demand and supply equations simultaneously for p and x. Note that equilibrium price and quantity are only meaningful if they are not negative.

EXAMPLE 2 Determine the equilibrium price and quantity for the following demand and supply laws.

$$D: \quad p = 25 - 2x \tag{2}$$
$$S: \quad p = 3x + 5 \tag{3}$$

Solution Equating the two values of p in Equations (2) and (3), we have

$$3x + 5 = 25 - 2x.$$

The solution is readily seen to be $x = 4$. Substituting $x = 4$ in Equation (2), we get

$$p = 25 - 8 = 17.$$

Thus the equilibrium price is 17 and quantity is 4 units. The graphs of the supply and demand curves are shown in Figure 27.

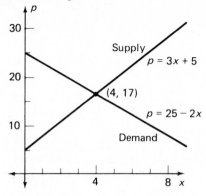

FIGURE 27

EXAMPLE 3   If the demand and supply equations are, respectively,

$$D: \quad 3p + 5x = 22 \tag{4}$$
$$S: \quad 2p - 3x = 2 \tag{5}$$

determine the values of x and p at market equilibrium.

Solution   Equations (4) and (5) form a system of linear equations for the two variables x and p. Let us solve them by the addition method. Multiplying both sides of Equation (4) by 3 and both sides of Equation (5) by 5, we obtain

$$9p + 15x = 66$$
$$10p - 15x = 10.$$

We next add these equations and simplify.

$$9p + 15x + 10p - 15x = 66 + 10$$
$$19p = 76$$

Thus $p = 4$. Substituting this value of p into Equation (4), we have

$$3(4) + 5x = 22.$$

Therefore $x = 2$. Market equilibrium thus occurs when $p = 4$ and $x = 2$.

Like most linear relations in economics, linear demand and supply equations provide an approximate representation of the true relations between price and quantity, and cases do arise in which such linear approximations are not good enough. The determination of market equilibrium when the demand equation or the supply equation (or both) is nonlinear can involve quite complicated calculations.

EXAMPLE 4   The demand for goods produced by an industry is given by the equation $p^2 + x^2 = 169$, where p is the price and x is the quantity demanded. The supply is given by $p = x + 7$. What are the equilibrium price and quantity?

Solution   The equilibrium price and quantity are the positive values of p and x that satisfy both the demand and supply equations.

$$p^2 + x^2 = 169 \tag{6}$$

$$p = x + 7 \tag{7}$$

Substituting the value of p from Equation (7) into Equation (6) and simplifying gives the following.

$$(x + 7)^2 + x^2 = 169$$

$$2x^2 + 14x + 49 = 169$$

$$x^2 + 7x - 60 = 0$$

Factoring, we find that

$$(x + 12)(x - 5) = 0$$

which gives $x = -12$ or 5. The negative value of x is inadmissible, so $x = 5$. Substituting $x = 5$ in Equation (7), we get

$$p = 5 + 7 = 12.$$

Thus the equilibrium price is 12 and the quantity is 5.

Additive Tax and Market Equilibrium

Often the government imposes additional taxes on certain commodities in order to raise more revenue or gives subsidies to producers of specified commodities to make these essential commodities available to consumers at reasonable prices. We shall consider the effect of an additional tax or subsidy on market equilibrium under the following two assumptions.

1. The quantity demanded by consumers depends on the price alone, that is, the demand equation does not change.

2. The quantity made available by suppliers is determined by the price received by them. The price received by the supplier is equal to the price paid by the consumer less the amount of taxation. If p denotes the price received per unit by the supplier and if t denotes the tax per unit, then the amount paid per unit by the consumer is $p_1 = p + t$.

EXAMPLE 5   The demand law for a certain commodity is $5p + 2x = 200$ and the supply law is $p = \frac{4}{3}x + 10$.
(a) Find the equilibrium price and quantity.
(b) Find the equilibrium price and quantity after a tax of 6 per unit is imposed. Find the increase in price and the decrease in quantity demanded.
(c) What subsidy will cause the quantity demanded to increase by 2 units?

Solution   The demand and supply equations are

$$D: \quad 5p + 2x = 200 \tag{8}$$

$$S: \quad p = \tfrac{4}{3}x + 10. \tag{9}$$

(a) Substituting the value of p from Equation (9) into Equation (8) and simplifying gives the following.

$$5(\tfrac{4}{5}x + 10) + 2x = 200$$
$$4x + 50 + 2x = 200$$
$$6x = 150$$
$$x = 25$$

Therefore, from Equation (9),

$$p = \tfrac{4}{5}(25) + 10 = 20 + 10 = 30.$$

Thus the equilibrium price and quantity before taxation are

$$p = 30 \quad \text{and} \quad x = 25.$$

(b) When a tax of 6 per unit is imposed, let the market price be p_1. Of this price p_1 paid by the consumer, 6 goes to the government, so the supplier gets $p_1 - 6$. The price received by the supplier is given still by the supply equation, Equation (9), so that

$$p_1 - 6 = \tfrac{4}{5}x_1 + 10$$

where x_1 is the quantity supplied at the new equilibrium. Therefore

$$p_1 = \tfrac{4}{5}x_1 + 16. \tag{10}$$

Since the demand equation remains unchanged, we use Equation (8), changing (x, p) to (x_1, p_1).

$$5p_1 + 2x_1 = 200 \tag{11}$$

Substituting the value of p_1 from Equation (10) into Equation (11), we get

$$5(\tfrac{4}{5}x_1 + 16) + 2x_1 = 200.$$

The solution is given by $x_1 = 20$. Therefore, from Equation (10), $p_1 = \tfrac{4}{5}(20) + 16 = 32$. Hence the equilibrium price and quantity after a tax of 6 per unit is imposed, are

$$p_1 = 32 \quad \text{and} \quad x_1 = 20.$$

The increase in price is $p_1 - p = 32 - 30 = 2$ and the decrease in quantity demanded is $x - x_1 = 25 - 20 = 5$.

(c) Let t be the subsidy per unit necessary to raise the equilibrium demand from 25 to $x_2 = 25 + 2 = 27$. Then the supply equation after subsidy of t per unit is given by

$$p_2 = \tfrac{4}{5}x_2 + 10 - t. \tag{12}$$

(In this case, $p_2 = p - t$, where p_2 is the market price and p is the price received by suppliers.) The demand equation, Equation (8), remains the same and, changing p and x to p_2 and x_2, respectively, gives

$$5p_2 + 2x_2 = 200. \tag{13}$$

Since $x_2 = 27$, we substitute this value in Equation (13).

$$5p_2 + 54 = 200$$

Therefore, $p_2 = \frac{146}{5} = 29.2$. Now substituting $p_2 = 29.2$ and $x_2 = 27$ in Equation (12), we obtain

$$29.2 = \tfrac{4}{5}(27) + 10 - t.$$

Therefore $t = 21.6 + 10 - 29.2 = 2.4$. A subsidy of 2.4 per unit will increase the demand by 2 units.

EXERCISES 5

1. A detergent manufacturer finds that weekly sales are 10,000 packets when the price is $1.20 per packet, but that the sales increase to 12,000 when the price is reduced to $1.10 per packet. Determine the demand relation, assuming that it is linear.

2. A television manufacturer finds that at $500 per television set, sales are 2000 sets per month. However, at $450 per set, sales are 2400 units. Determine the demand equation, assuming it to be linear.

3. At a price of $2.50 per unit, a firm will supply 8000 shirts per month; at $4 per unit, the firm will supply 14,000 shirts per month. Determine the supply equation, assuming it to be linear.

4. A tool manufacturer can sell 3000 hammers per month at $2 each, whereas only 2000 hammers can be sold at $2.75 each. Determine the demand law, assuming it to be linear.

(5–10) Find the equilibrium price and quantity for the following demand and supply curves:

5. D: $2p + 3x = 100$
   S: $p = \frac{1}{10}x + 2$

6. D: $3p + 5x = 200$
   S: $7p - 3x = 56$

7. D: $4p + x = 50$
   S: $6p - 5x = 10$

8. D: $5p + 8x = 80$
   S: $3x = 2p - 1$

9. D: $p^2 + x^2 = 25$
   S: $p = x + 1$

10. D: $p^2 + 2x^2 = 114$
    S: $p = x + 3$

11. A dealer can sell 200 units of a certain commodity per day at $30 per unit and 250 units at $27 per unit. The supply equation for that commodity is $6p = x + 48$.

    a. Find the demand equation for the commodity, assuming it to be linear.

    b. Find the equilibrium price and quantity.

    c. Find the equilibrium price and quantity if a tax of $3.40 per unit is imposed on the commodity. What is the increase in price and the decrease in quantity demanded?

    d. What subsidy per unit will increase the demand by 24 units?

    e. What additive tax per unit should be imposed on the commodity so that the equilibrium price per unit increases by $1.08?

12. At a price of $2400, the supply of a certain commodity is 120 units while its demand is 560 units. If the price is raised to $2700 per unit, the supply and demand will be 160 units and 380 units, respectively.

    a. Determine the demand and supply equations, assuming them to be linear.

b. Determine the market equilibrium price and quantity.

c. If a tax of $110 per unit is imposed on the commodity, what are the new equilibrium price and quantity? What is the increase in price and decrease in quantity?

d. What subsidy per unit will decrease the market price by $15?

(13–14) Solve the following supply and demand equations. Explain where market equilibrium would be.

13. S: $p = x + 5$
 D: $3p + 4x = 12$

14. S: $2p - 3x = 8$
 D: $3p + 6x = 9$

REVIEW EXERCISES FOR CHAPTER 4

1. State whether the following statements are true or false. If false, replace by the corresponding correct statement.

a. If a point lies on the x-axis, then its abscissa is zero.

b. Each point on the y-axis has its y-coordinate zero.

c. If a point (x, y) is in the first quadrant, then $x \geq 0$, $y \geq 0$.

d. The origin $(0, 0)$ lies in all the four quadrants.

e. A horizontal line has no slope.

f. If a line slopes down to the right, then its slope is negative.

g. A vertical line has zero slope.

h. The distance of the point (a, b) from the origin $(0, 0)$ is $a + b$.

i. The slope of the line joining two points (x_1, y_1), (x_2, y_2) is given by $m = \dfrac{y_2 - y_1}{x_2 - x_1}$ for all values of x_1, y_1, x_2, y_2.

j. The linear equation $Ax + By + C = 0$ represents a straight line for all values of the constants A, B, and C.

k. The slope of the line given by $x = my + b$ is m.

l. If the variable cost per unit of producing a certain commodity is constant, then the commodity obeys a linear cost model.

m. The equation of the x-axis is $y = 0$.

n. The equation $x = c$, c a constant, always represents a vertical line.

o. If the numbers x and y are of the same sign (that is, both positive or both negative), then the point $P(x, y)$ lies in either the first or the third quadrant.

p. If the point $P(x, y)$ lies in the second or fourth quadrant, then x and y are of opposite signs.

(2–6) Find the equation of each line.

2. Passing through (2, 3) and (3, 1).

3. Passing through $(-1, 2)$ and (5, 2).

4. Passing through (3, 0) and $(0, -4)$.

5. Passing through $(2, -1)$ with no slope.

6. Passing through $(-3, 2)$ with zero slope.

(7–12) Solve the following systems of equations.

7. $3x - 4y = 13; 2x + 3y = 3$

8. $\dfrac{2}{x} + \dfrac{3}{y} = 2; \dfrac{5}{x} + \dfrac{8}{y} = 5\dfrac{1}{6}$ $\left(\textit{Hint: Let } \dfrac{1}{x} = u \text{ and } \dfrac{1}{y} = v.\right)$

*9. $x + y - 2z = -1; 2x - 3y + z = 13; -3x + 2y + 5z = -8$

*10. $u + 2v + 3w = 17; 2u - v + 4w = 11; 3u + 7v - 8w = -14$

11. $x + y = 9; \dfrac{1}{x} + \dfrac{1}{y} = \dfrac{1}{2}$

*12. $\dfrac{1}{x} + \dfrac{1}{y} = \dfrac{7}{12}; xy = 12$

13. A company manufactures two types of products, A and B. Each product A requires 2.5 work-hours and each product B requires 4 work-hours. If 320 work-hours are available each week, find the relationship between the number of items of each type that can be made to make full use of the available work-hours.

14. A chemical plant is used to manufacture two chemicals, A and B. It can operate by 2 processes. Process 1 produces 2 tons per hour of A and 5 tons per hour of B; process 2 produces 3 tons per hour of A and 4 tons per hour of B. The company can sell 260 tons per week of A and 440 tons per week of B. How many hours per week should the plant be operated on each of the two processes?

15. A manufacturer has fixed costs of $3000 and the variable costs of $25 per unit. Find the equation relating costs to production. What is the cost of producing 100 units?

16. A mining firm finds that it can produce 7 tons of ore at a cost of $1500 and 15 tons at a cost of $1800. Assuming a linear cost-output model, find the fixed cost and the variable costs. What will be the cost of producing 20 tons of ore?

17. A tobacco dealer mixed 8 pounds of one grade of tobacco with 5 pounds of another grade to obtain a blend worth $35. A second blend worth $49 was then made mixing 10 pounds of the first grade with 8 pounds of the second grade. Find the price per pound of each grade.

18. An individual receives $1860 in interest on two investments, with the first earning 6% and the second earning 8%. The next year the rates were interchanged and the earnings were $1920. Find the amount of each investment.

19. A person made two investments, the first being $3750 less than the second. If, during the first year, the rate of the first investment was 2% more than that of the second and the income from each was $900, find the amount of the second investment and the rate that it earned.

20. A pharmacist wishes to obtain 30 fluid ounces of a solution containing 70%

alcohol. There are two solutions, containing 50% and 80% alcohol, respectively. How much of each solution should be used?

21. At a price of $50 per ton, the demand for a certain commodity is 4500 tons whereas the supply is 3300 tons. If the price is increased by $10 per ton, the demand and supply will be 4400 tons and 4200 tons, respectively.

    a. Assuming linearity, determine the laws of supply and demand.

    b. Find the equilibrium price and quantity.

    c. If an additional tax of $2 per ton is imposed on the supplier, find the increase in equilibrium price and decrease in equilibrium quantity.

    d. What subsidy per ton should be given to the supplier so that the equilibrium quantity increases by 55 tons?

22. At a price of $30 per pair of shoes, a manufacturer can supply 2000 pairs of shoes per month whereas the demand is 2800 pairs. At a price of $35 per pair, 400 more pairs per month can be supplied. However at this increased price, the demand reduces by 100 pairs.

    a. Assuming linear relationships, determine the supply and demand relations.

    b. Determine the equilibrium price and quantity.

    c. If the government imposes a tax of $1.50 per pair of shoes, find the new equilibrium price and quantity.

    d. What additive tax per pair should be imposed to raise the equilibrium price to $40?

23. A company has fixed costs of $2500 and the total costs of producing 200 units is $3300.

    a. Assuming linearity, write down the cost-output equation.

    b. If each item produced sells for $5.25, find the break-even point.

    c. How many units should be produced and sold so that a profit of $200 results?

24. A shoe manufacturing company breaks even if its sales are $180,000 per year. If the yearly fixed costs are $45,000 and each pair of shoes sells for $30, find the average variable cost per pair.

25. Atlas Motors buys fan belts for its "Atlas" cars for $2.50 each. The management is considering manufacturing its own belts at fixed costs of $6000 per year and a variable cost of $1.30 per belt. How many belts should be required each year to justify manufacturing by the firm itself?

FUNCTIONS AND GRAPHS

CHAPTER

5-1 FUNCTIONS

The concept of function is one of the basic ideas in all mathematics. Almost every study that concerns the application of mathematics to practical problems or that involves the analysis of empirical data makes use of this mathematical concept.

A function expresses the idea of one quantity depending on or being determined by another. The following are examples of this idea.

1. The area of a circle depends on the length of its radius; if the length of the radius is known then its area can be determined.

2. The cost of producing any commodity depends on the number of items produced.

3. The benefits paid out by the welfare system of a country depend on its unemployment rate.

4. The purchasing power of the dollar depends on the cost of living index.

5. The quantity of a certain commodity that will be supplied by the manufacturer depends on the price the manufacturer can get.

We shall begin by giving a formal definition of a function.

DEFINITION   Let X and Y be two nonempty sets. Then a **function** from X to Y is a *rule* that assigns to each element $x \in X$ a unique $y \in Y$.

If a function assigns y to a particular $x \in X$, then we say y is the **value** of the function at x. A function is generally denoted by a single letter such as f, g, F, or G.

Let f denote a given function. The set X for which f assigns a unique $y \in Y$ is called the **domain** of the function f. It is often denoted by D_f. The corresponding set of values $y \in Y$ is called the **range** of the function and is often denoted by R_f.

EXAMPLE 1   (a)   Let X be the set of students in a class. Let f be the rule which assigns to each student his or her final grade. Since each student is associated with exactly one final grade, this rule does define a function. In this case, the domain is the set of all students in the class and the range is the set of all the different grades awarded. (For example, R_f might be the set $\{A, B, C, D, F\}$.)

(b)   The growth of financial assets of a firm is a function of time. Here the domain is a set of values of time and the range of the function is the set of values of the assets (say in dollars).

If a function f assigns a value y in the range to a certain x in the domain, we write

$$y = f(x).$$

We read $f(x)$ as f of x; it is called the *value of f at x*. Note that $f(x)$ is *not* the product of f and x.

If a function f is expressed by a relation of the type $y = f(x)$, then x is called the **independent variable** or **argument of f** and y is called the **dependent variable**.

Generally, we shall encounter functions that are expressed by stating the value of the function by means of an algebraic formula in terms of the independent variable involved. For example, $f(x) = 5x^2 - 7x + 2$ and $g(p) = 2p^3 + 7/(p + 1)$.

EXAMPLE 2   Given $f(x) = 2x^2 - 5x + 1$, find the value of f when $x = a$, $x = 3$, $x = -2$, and $x = -\frac{1}{4}$; that is, find $f(a)$, $f(3)$, $f(-2)$ and $f(-\frac{1}{4})$.

Solution   We have

$$f(x) = 2x^2 - 5x + 1. \tag{1}$$

To find $f(a)$, we replace x by a in Equation (1).

$$f(a) = 2a^2 - 5a + 1$$

To evaluate $f(3)$, we substitute 3 for x on both sides of Equation (1).

$$f(3) = 2(3)^2 - 5(3) + 1$$
$$= 18 - 15 + 1 = 4$$

Similarly,

$$f(-2) = 2(-2)^2 - 5(-2) + 1 = 19$$

and

$$f(-\tfrac{1}{4}) = 2(-\tfrac{1}{4})^2 - 5(-\tfrac{1}{4}) + 1 = \tfrac{19}{8}.$$

EXAMPLE 3   Given $g(x) = 3x^2 - 2x + 5$, evaluate: (a) $g(1 + h)$; (b) $g(1) + g(h)$; (c) $[g(x + h) - g(x)]/h$.

Solution   We have

$$g(x) = 3x^2 - 2x + 5. \tag{2}$$

(a)   To evaluate $g(1 + h)$, we must replace x in Equation (2) by $1 + h$.

$$g(1 + h) = 3(1 + h)^2 - 2(1 + h) + 5$$
$$= 3(1 + 2h + h^2) - 2 - 2h + 5$$
$$= 3h^2 + 4h + 6$$

(b)   Replacing x by 1 and h, respectively, in Equation (2) we get

$$g(1) = 3(1^2) - 2(1) + 5 = 3 - 2 + 5 = 6$$

and

$$g(h) = 3h^2 - 2h + 5.$$

Therefore

$$g(1) + g(h) = 6 + 3h^2 - 2h + 5 = 3h^2 - 2h + 11.$$

(c)   Replacing the argument x in Equation (2) by $x + h$, we have the following.

$$g(x + h) = 3(x + h)^2 - 2(x + h) + 5$$
$$= 3(x^2 + 2xh + h^2) - 2x - 2h + 5$$
$$= 3x^2 - 2x + 5 + h(3h + 6x - 2)$$

Therefore

$$\frac{1}{h}[g(x + h) - g(x)]$$

$$= \frac{1}{h}[3x^2 - 2x + 5 + h(3h + 6x - 2) - (3x^2 - 2x + 5)]$$
$$= 3h + 6x - 2.$$

In most cases of interest, the domains and ranges of the functions with which we are concerned are subsets of the real numbers. In such cases, the function is commonly represented by its *graph*. The graph of a function f is obtained by plotting all of the points (x, y), where x belongs to the domain of f and $y = f(x)$, treating x and y as Cartesian coordinates.

EXAMPLE 4   Consider $f(x) = 2 + 0.5x^2$. The domain of f is the set of all real numbers, since we can evaluate $f(x)$ for any real value of x. Some of the values of this function are shown in Table 1, in which selected values of x are listed in the top row and the values of $y = f(x)$ are given beneath the corresponding values of x.

TABLE 1

x	0	1	2	3	4	-1	-2	-3	-4
$y = f(x)$	2	2.5	4	6.5	10	2.5	4	6.5	10

The points corresponding to the values of x and y are plotted as dots in Figure 1. The graph of the function $f(x) = 2 + 0.5x^2$ is shown as the U-shaped curve passing through the heavy dots.

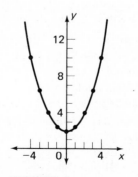

FIGURE 1

Let us now suppose that in Example 4, x denotes the number of items produced in a factory and $f(x)$ denotes the total cost of producing x units. The cost of producing no items at all is given by setting $x = 0$, that is,

$$f(0) = 2.$$

Thus 2 will be the minimum cost whether we produce any item or not. This is known as the **overhead cost**. For example, investment in machinery, rent of factory space, and management expenses are some examples of overhead costs. In this case, the domain of f is *not* the set of real numbers but the set of non-negative integers, since x now represents the number of items produced and must be a whole number. Thus

$$D_f = \{0, 1, 2, 3, 4, \ldots\}.$$

Now as the independent variable x takes the values $0, 1, 2, 3, \ldots,$ the dependent variable $y = f(x)$ assumes the values

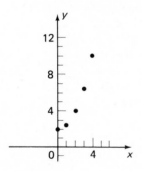

$$f(0) = 2 + 0.5(0) = 2$$
$$f(1) = 2 + 0.5(1^2) = 2.5$$
$$f(2) = 2 + 0.5(2^2) = 4$$
$$f(3) = 2 + 10.5(3^2) = 6.5$$

and so on.

FIGURE 2

The graph of f in this case is shown in Figure 2. Note that the graph in this case consists of a set of discrete points and not a continuous curve, as was the case earlier. From this example, we see that the domain and range of a function can or may depend on what the independent and dependent variables represent in a practical problem.

Any given curve (or set of points) in the xy-plane is the graph of a function provided that any vertical line meets the graph in at most one point.

Any vertical line corresponds to some particular value, say $x = x_0$, of the independent variable, and the point where this vertical line meets the graph determines the value of y that corresponds to x_0. That is, the graph itself provides the rule that relates each value of x to some value of y. If the vertical line $x = x_0$ does not meet the graph at all, then x_0 simply does not belong to the domain.

The graphs in Figure 3 represent functions. (Note that in part (c), the domain of the function is the set of integers $\{1, 2, 3, 4, 5\}$, so the graph simply consists of five points rather than a curve.)

On the other hand, the graphs in Figure 4 do not represent functions. These are not functions because there are vertical lines that meet the graphs in more than one point. Thus, corresponding to the value $x = x_0$ on the first graph, there are two values y_1 and y_2 for y. In such a case, the value of x does not determine a unique value of y.

On the graph of a function, the values along the x-axis at which the graph is defined constitute the domain of the function. Correspondingly, the values along the y-axis at which the graph has points constitute the range of the func-

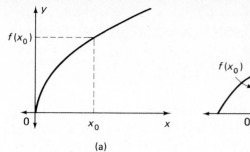

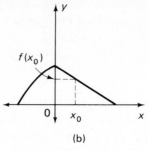

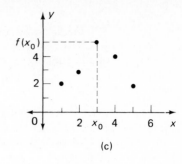

(a)   (b)   (c)

FIGURE 3

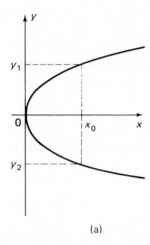

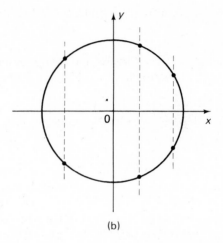

(a)   (b)

FIGURE 4

tion. This is illustrated in Figure 5. Here we have

$$D_f = \{x \,|\, -2 \le x \le 3\} \quad \text{and} \quad R_f = \{y \,|\, 0 \le y \le 2\}.$$

Often the domain of a function is not stated explicitly. In such cases, it is understood to be the set of all values of the argument for which the given rule makes sense. For a function f defined by an algebraic expression, the domain

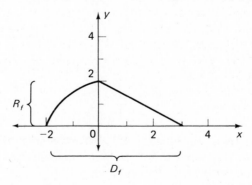

FIGURE 5

of f is the set of all real numbers x for which $f(x)$ is a well-defined real number. For example, the domain of the function $f(x) = \sqrt{x}$ is the set of nonnegative real numbers, since square root makes sense only if $x \geq 0$. Similarly, in the case of the function $g(x) = x^2/(x - 3)$, the domain is the set of all real numbers except $x = 3$, since when $x = 3$ the denominator becomes zero and $g(3)$ is not defined.

In general, when finding the domain of a function we must bear these two conditions in mind: *Any expression underneath a square root cannot be negative and the denominator of any fraction cannot be zero.* (More generally, any expression underneath a radical of even index such as $\sqrt[4]{}$ or $\sqrt[6]{}$ cannot be negative.)

EXAMPLE 5 Find the domain of g, where
$$g(x) = \frac{x + 3}{x - 2}.$$

Solution Clearly $g(x)$ is not a well-defined real number for $x = 2$. For any other value of x, $g(x)$ is a well-defined real number. Thus the domain of g is the set of all real numbers except 2.

EXAMPLE 6 Find the domain of f if $f(x) = \sqrt{x - 4}$.

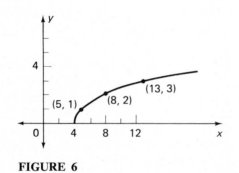

FIGURE 6

Solution The domain of f is the set of all values of x for which the expression under the radical sign is nonnegative. That is,

$$x - 4 \geq 0 \quad \text{or} \quad x \geq 4.$$

For $x < 4$, $f(x)$ is not a real number, since the quantity beneath the square root, $x - 4$, is negative. The graph of f is shown in Figure 6, in which a few explicit points are plotted.

In applied problems, it is often necessary to construct an algebraic function from certain verbal information.

EXAMPLE 7 A telephone link is to be constructed between two towns that are situated on opposite banks of a river at points A and B. The width of the river is 1 kilometer and B lies 2 kilometers downstream from A. It costs c dollars per kilometer to construct a line over land and $2c$ dollars per kilometer under water. The telephone line will follow the river bank from A for a distance x (kilometers) and then will cross the river diagonally in a straight line directly to B. Determine the total cost of the line as a function of x.

Solution Figure 7 illustrates this problem. The telephone line proceeds from A to C, a distance x along the bank, then diagonally across from C to B. The cost of the segment AC is cx while the cost of CB is $2c(CB)$. The total cost (call it y) is therefore given by
$$y = cx + 2c(CB).$$

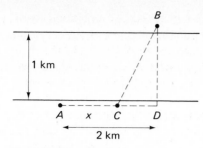

FIGURE 7

In order to complete the problem, we must express CB in terms of x. We apply the Pythagorean theorem to the triangle BCD.

$$BC^2 = BD^2 + CD^2$$

But $BD = 1$ (the width of the river) and

$$CD = AD - AC = 2 - x.$$

Therefore

$$BC^2 = 1^2 + (2 - x)^2 = 1 + (4 - 4x + x^2)$$
$$= x^2 - 4x + 5.$$

Thus the cost is given by

$$y = cx + 2c\sqrt{x^2 - 4x + 5}.$$

This is the required expression, giving y as a function of x.

In the preceding examples, we have been concerned with functions that are defined by a single algebraic expression for all values of the independent variable throughout the domain of the function. It sometimes happens that we need to use functions that are defined by more than one expression.

EXAMPLE 8   Electricity is charged to consumers at the rate of 10¢ per unit for the first 50 units and 3¢ per unit for amounts in excess of this. Find the function $c(x)$ that gives the cost of using x units of electricity.

Solution   For $x \leq 50$, each unit costs 10¢, so the total cost of x units is $10x$ cents. So $c(x) = 10x$ for $x \leq 50$. When $x = 50$, we get $c(50) = 500$: the cost of the first 50 units is equal to 500¢. When $x > 50$, the total cost is equal to the cost of the first 50 units (that is, 500¢) plus the cost of the rest of the units used. The number of these excess units is $x - 50$, and they cost 3¢ each, so their total cost is $3(x - 50)$ cents. Thus the total bill when $x > 50$ comes to

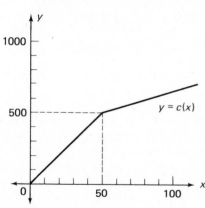

FIGURE 8

$$c(x) = 500 + 3(x - 50) = 500 + 3x - 150$$
$$= 350 + 3x.$$

We can write $c(x)$ in the form

$$c(x) = \begin{cases} 10x & (x \leq 50) \\ 350 + 3x & (x > 50). \end{cases}$$

The graph of $y = c(x)$ is shown in Figure 8. Observe how the nature of the graph changes at $x = 50$, where one formula takes over from the other.

EXAMPLE 9   Consider the following function.

$$f(x) = \begin{cases} 4 - x & (0 \leq x \leq 4) \\ \sqrt{x - 4} & (x > 4) \end{cases}$$

The domain of this function is the set of all nonnegative real numbers. For $0 \leq x \leq 4$, the function is defined by the algebraic expression $f(x) = 4 - x$, while for $x > 4$, it is defined by the expression $f(x) = \sqrt{x - 4}$. Some values of $f(x)$ are given in Table 2 and the graph of this function is shown in Figure 9.

TABLE 2

x	0	2	4	5	8	13
$y = f(x)$	4	2	0	1	2	3

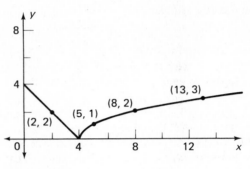

FIGURE 9

It consists of two segments: For x between 0 and 4, the graph consists of a straight line segment with equation $y = 4 - x$. For $x \geq 4$, the function is identical with that in Example 6.

In these examples, the function under consideration has been defined by two algebraic expressions. It is sometimes necessary to consider functions defined by three or more different expressions.

We close this section by discussing some simple functions. A function of the form

$$f(x) = b$$

where b is some constant is called a **constant function**. We have already encountered such functions in Section 2 of Chapter 4. The graph of f is a straight line parallel to the x-axis and at a distance $|b|$ above or below the x-axis depending on whether b is positive or negative. In this case

$$D_f = \text{set of all real numbers} \quad \text{and} \quad R_f = \{b\}.$$

A function f defined by the relation

$$f(x) = a_n x^n + a_{n-1}x^{n-1} + \cdots + a_1 x + a_0 \qquad (a_n \neq 0)$$

where $a_0, a_1, \ldots, a_n$ are constants and n is a nonnegative integer, is said to be a **polynomial function of degree n**. For example, the functions f and g defined by

$$f(x) = 3x^7 - 5x^4 + 2x - 1 \quad \text{and} \quad g(x) = x^3 + 7x^2 - 5x + 3$$

are polynomial functions of degree 7 and 3, respectively.

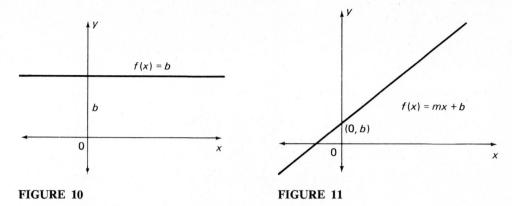

FIGURE 10   **FIGURE 11**

If the degree of the polynomial function is 1, then the function is a **linear function**. The general form of the linear function is given by

$$f(x) = mx + b \qquad (m \neq 0)$$

where m and b are constants. As we know from Section 2 of Chapter 4, the graph of a linear function is a straight line with slope m and y-intercept of b. Here D_f equals R_f equals the set of all real numbers.

If the degree of the polynomial function is 2, then the function is called a **quadratic function**. The general quadratic function may be defined by

$$g(x) = ax^2 + bx + c \qquad (a \neq 0)$$

where a, b, and c are constants. We shall discuss this function in detail in the next section.

Similarly, a polynomial function of degree 3 is called a **cubic function**. For example, the function f defined by

$$f(x) = 2x^3 - 5x^2 + 7x + 1$$

is a cubic function.

If the degree of the polynomial function is zero, then it reduces to a constant function.

If a function can be expressed as the quotient of two polynomial functions, then it is called a **rational function**. Examples of rational functions are

$$f(x) = \frac{x^2 - 9}{x - 4} \quad \text{and} \quad g(x) = \frac{2x^3 - 7x + 1}{5x^2 - 2}.$$

In general, any rational function has the form $f(x) = p(x)/q(x)$, where $p(x)$ and $q(x)$ are polynomials in x.

If the value $f(x)$ of a function f is found by a finite number of algebraic operations, f is called an **algebraic function**. The algebraic operations are addition, subtraction, multiplication, division, raising to powers, and extracting roots. For example, the functions f and g defined by

$$f(x) = \frac{(2x + 1)^2 - \sqrt{x^3 + 1}}{(x^2 + 1)^4} \quad \text{and} \quad g(x) = (2x^2 - 1)^{-1/7} + 5x^{3/4}$$

are algebraic functions.

Apart from algebraic functions, there are other functions called **transcendental functions**. Examples of transcendental functions are logarithmic functions, and exponential functions, which we shall discuss in Chapter 6.

EXERCISES 1

1. Given $f(x) = 3x^2 - 5x + 7$, find each of the following.

   a. $f(0)$ **b.** $f(2)$ **c.** $f(-3)$

   d. $f(\frac{1}{2})$ **e.** $f(-\frac{4}{3})$ **f.** $f(c)$

   g. $f(c + h)$ **h.** $\dfrac{f(c + h) - f(c)}{h}$

2. Given $g(x) = 2x^2 + 3x - 5$, evaluate each of the following.

   a. $g(1)$ **b.** $g(-2)$ **c.** $g(\frac{2}{3})$

   d. $g(a)$ **e.** $g(a + h)$ **f.** $\dfrac{g(a + h) - g(a)}{h}$

3. Given

   $$f(x) = \begin{cases} 2x - 3 & \text{if } x \geq 5 \\ 6 - 3x & \text{if } x < 5, \end{cases}$$

   find each of the following.

   a. $f(0)$ **b.** $f(7)$ **c.** $f(-2)$

   d. $f(5 + h)$ and $f(5 - h)$, where $h > 0$.

4. Given

   $$g(x) = \begin{cases} 4x + 3 & \text{if } -2 \leq x < 0 \\ 1 + x^2 & \text{if } 0 \leq x \leq 2 \\ 7 & \text{if } x > 2 \end{cases}$$

   evaluate each of the following.

   a. $g(1)$ **b.** $g(3)$ **c.** $g(-1)$

   d. $g(0)$ **e.** $g(-3)$

   f. $g(2 + h)$ and $g(2 - h)$ if $h > 0$.

5. If $F(t) = t/(1 + t)$ and $G(t) = t/(1 - t)$, show that $F(t) - G(t) = -2F(t^2)$.

6. If $y = f(x) = (x + 1)/(x - 1)$, show that $x = f(y)$.

7. If $f(x) = x^2 + 1$ and $g(x) = 2x - 1$, find $f[g(2)]$.

8. If $f(x) = g(x) + h(x)$, $g(x) = x^2 + 3$, and $f(x) = x^3$, find $h(2)$.

(9–16) Find the domain of each function.

9. $f(x) = 2x + 3$ 10. $g(x) = 2x^2 - 3x + 7$

11. $h(x) = \dfrac{x - 1}{x - 2}$ 12. $D(p) = \dfrac{2p + 3}{p - 1}$

13. $f(x) = \sqrt{x - 2}$ 14. $F(y) = -\sqrt{3y - 2}$

15. $g(t) = \dfrac{1}{\sqrt{2t - 3}}$ 16. $G(u) = \dfrac{2}{\sqrt{3 - 2u}}$

17. A radio manufacturing firm has fixed costs of \$3000 and the cost of labor and material is \$15 per radio. Determine the cost function, that is, the total cost as

a function of number of radios manufactured. If each radio is sold for $25, determine the revenue function and the profit function.

18. A manufacturer can sell 300 units of its product in a month at a charge of $20 per unit and 500 units at a charge of $15 per unit. Express the market demand x (the number of units that can be sold each month) as a function of the price per unit, assuming it to be a linear function. Express the revenue as a function: (a) of the price; (b) of x.

19. A farmer has 200 yards of fencing to enclose a rectangular field. Express the area A of the field as a function of the length of one side of it.

20. A rectangle is inscribed in a circle of radius 3 centimeters. Express the area A of the rectangle as a function of the length of one of its sides.

21. A cistern is constructed to hold 300 cubic feet of water. The cistern has a square base and four vertical sides, all made of concrete, and a square top made of steel. If concrete costs $1.50 per square foot and steel costs $4 per square foot, determine the total cost C as a function of the length of the side of the square base.

22. Repeat Exercise 21 if the cistern is a cylinder with circular base and top. Express the cost C as a function of radius r of the base of the cylinder.

23. Sugar costs 25¢ per pound for amounts up to 50 pounds and 20¢ per pound for amounts over 50 pounds. If $C(x)$ denotes the cost of x pounds of sugar, express $C(x)$ by means of suitable algebraic expressions and sketch its graph.

24. A retailer can buy oranges from the wholesaler at the following prices: 20¢ per pound if 20 pounds or less are purchased; 15¢ per pound for amounts over 20 pounds and up to 50 pounds, and 12¢ per pound for amounts over 50 pounds. Determine the cost $C(x)$ of purchasing x pounds of oranges.

(25–30) State whether or not the following graphs represent functions.

25.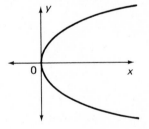

26.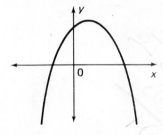

27.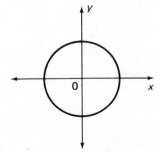

28.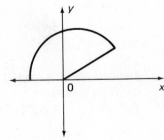

29.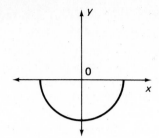

30.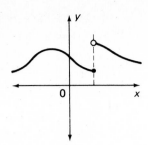

5-2 QUADRATIC FUNCTIONS AND PARABOLAS

A function of the form

$$f(x) = ax^2 + bx + c \qquad (a \neq 0)$$

where a, b, and c are constants, is called a *quadratic function*. The domain of $f(x)$ is the set of all real numbers. The graph of a quadratic function is a curve called a **parabola**.

The simplest quadratic function is obtained by setting b and c equal to zero, in which case we obtain $f(x) = ax^2$. Typical graphs of this function in the two cases when a is positive or negative are shown in Figure 12. The lowest point on the graph when $a > 0$ occurs at the origin, while the origin is the highest point when $a < 0$. In either case, this point is called the **vertex** of the parabola.

The general quadratic function $f(x) = ax^2 + bx + c$ has a graph identical in shape and size to the graph of $y = ax^2$; the only difference is that the vertex of $f(x) = ax^2 + bx + c$ is shifted away from the origin.

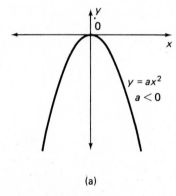

(a)   (b)

FIGURE 12

THEOREM 1 The graph of the function $f(x) = ax^2 + bx + c \,(a \neq 0)$ is a parabola that opens upwards if $a > 0$ and downwards if $a < 0$. Its vertex (which is the lowest point when $a > 0$ and the highest point when $a < 0$) is at the point

$$x = -\frac{b}{2a} \quad \text{and} \quad y = \frac{4ac - b^2}{4a}.$$

Typical graphs of the quadratic function $y = ax^2 + bx + c$ are shown in Figure 13.

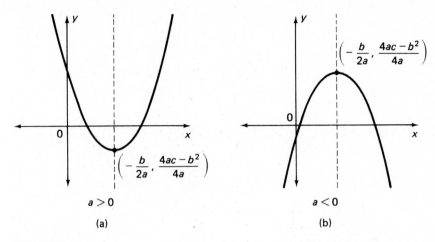

$a > 0$

(a)

$a < 0$

(b)

FIGURE 13

Notes: 1. If $b = c = 0$, the quadratic function reduces to $f(x) = ax^2$. The coordinates of the vertex given in Theorem 1 then reduce to $x = y = 0$, which is consistent with our earlier statements.

2. The y-coordinate of the vertex can also be found by substituting the value $x = -b/2a$ into the equation $y = ax^2 + bx + c$ of the parabola. This is often easier than using the formula for y given in Theorem 1.

3. Theorem 1 is most easily proved using the method of *completing the square*. We shall not prove it here.

EXAMPLE 1 Sketch the parabola $y = 2x^2 - 4x + 7$ and find its vertex.

Solution Comparing the given equation

$$y = 2x^2 - 4x + 7$$

with the standard quadratic function

$$y = ax^2 + bx + c$$

we have $a = 2$, $b = -4$, and $c = 7$. The x-coordinate of the vertex is

$$x = -\frac{b}{2a} = -\frac{(-4)}{2(2)} = 1.$$

To find the y-coordinate of the vertex, the simplest way is to substitute $x = 1$ in the given equation for the parabola.

$$y = 2(1)^2 - 4(1) + 7 = 5$$

Thus the vertex is at the point $(1, 5)$.

Alternatively, we could use the formula given in Theorem 1.

$$y = \frac{4ac - b^2}{4a} = \frac{4(2)(7) - (-4)^2}{4(2)} = \frac{56 - 16}{8} = 5$$

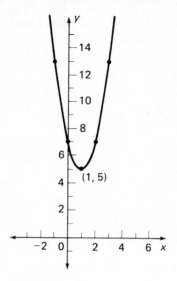

FIGURE 14

Since $a = 2 > 0$, the parabola opens upwards; that is, the vertex $(1, 5)$ is the lowest point on the parabola. The graph of this parabola can be sketched by plotting a few points (x, y) lying on it. Values of y corresponding to selected values of x are shown in Table 3.

TABLE 3

x	-1	0	1	2	3
y	13	7	5	7	13

Plotting these points and joining them by a smooth curve, we obtain the graph as shown in Figure 14. (Note that the graph in this example meets the y-axis at the point $(0,7)$ but does not meet the x-axis at all. It is often helpful when drawing the graph of some given function to find the points where this graph meets the coordinate axes.)

As stated before, the vertex of a parabola represents the lowest point when $a > 0$ or the highest point when $a < 0$. It follows, therefore, that for $a > 0$, the function $f(x) = ax^2 + bx + c$ takes its minimum value at the vertex of the corresponding parabola. That is, $f(x)$ is smallest when $x = -b/2a$ and this smallest value of $f(x)$ is equal to $(4ac - b^2)/4a$. Correspondingly, when $a < 0$, the function $f(x) = ax^2 + bx + c$ takes its largest value when $x = -b/2a$, and the maximum value of $f(x)$ is $(4ac - b^2)/4a$. This largest or the smallest value of $f(x) = ax^2 + bx + c$ can also be obtained by substituting $x = -b/2a$ in $f(x)$ if we do not remember the formula $(4ac - b^2)/4a$.

Problems in which we are required to calculate the maximum and minimum values of certain functions arise very frequently in applications. We shall study them at some length in Chapter 14. However, some of these problems can be solved by making use of the properties of parabolas. The following examples belong to this category.

EXAMPLE 2   A farmer has 200 yards of fencing with which to enclose a rectangular field. One side of the field can make use of a fence that already exists. What is the maximum area that can be enclosed?

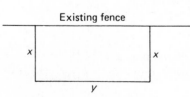

Existing fence

FIGURE 15

Solution   Let the sides of the field be denoted by x and y, as shown in Figure 15, with the side labeled y parallel to the fence that already exists. Then the length of new fence is $2x + y$, which must equal the 200 yards available.

$$2x + y = 200$$

The area enclosed is $A = xy$.

But $y = 200 - 2x$, so
$$A = x(200 - 2x) = 200x - 2x^2. \qquad (1)$$

Comparing this with $f(x) = ax^2 + bx + c$, we see that A is a quadratic function of x, with $a = -2$, $b = 200$, and $c = 0$. Therefore, since $a < 0$, the quadratic function has a maximum value at the vertex, that is, when

$$x = -\frac{b}{2a} = -\frac{200}{2(-2)} = 50.$$

The maximum value of A is obtained by substituting $x = 50$ in Equation (1).

$$A = 200(50) - 2(50^2) = 10{,}000 - 5{,}000 = 5{,}000$$

The maximum area that can be enclosed is 5000 square yards. The dimensions of this largest area are $x = 50$ yards and $y = 100$ yards. (*Note*: $y = 200 - 2x$.)

EXAMPLE 3   The demand per month, x, for a certain commodity at a price p dollars per unit is given by the relation

$$x = 1350 - 45p.$$

The cost of labor and material to manufacture this commodity is \$5 per unit and the fixed costs are \$2000 per month. What price p per unit should be charged to the consumers to obtain a maximum monthly profit?

Solution   The total cost C (in dollars) of producing x units per month is

$$C = \text{Variable Costs} + \text{Fixed Costs}$$
$$= 5x + 2000.$$

The demand x is given to be
$$x = 1350 - 45p.$$

Using this value of x in C, we have
$$C = 5(1350 - 45p) + 2000$$
$$= 8750 - 225p.$$

The revenue R (in dollars) obtained by selling x units at p dollars per unit is

$$R = \text{Price per Unit} \times \text{Number of Units Sold}$$
$$= px = p(1350 - 45p)$$
$$= 1350p - 45p^2.$$

The profit P (in dollars) is then given by the difference between revenue and cost.

$$P = R - C$$
$$= -45p^2 + 1350p - (8750 - 225p)$$
$$= -45p^2 + 1575p - 8750$$

The profit P is a quadratic function of p. Since $a = -45 < 0$, the graph is a parabola opening downwards and the maximum profit is realized at the vertex. In this case, we have

$$a = -45, \quad b = 1575, \quad \text{and} \quad c = -8750.$$

The vertex of the parabola is given by

$$p = -\frac{b}{2a} = -\frac{1575}{2(-45)} = \frac{1575}{90} = 17.5.$$

Thus a price of $p = \$17.50$ per unit must be charged to consumers to obtain a maximum profit. The maximum profit then will be

$$P = \frac{4ac - b^2}{4a} = \frac{4(-45)(-8750) - (1575)^2}{4(-45)}$$

or $5031.25 per month.

EXAMPLE 4   Mr. Woolhouse owns an apartment building with 60 suites. He can rent all the suites if he charges a monthly rent of $200 per suite. At a higher rent, some suites will remain vacant. On the average, for each increase in rent of $5, one suite remains vacant with no possibility of renting it. Determine the functional relationship between the total monthly revenue and the number of vacant units. What monthly rent will maximize the total revenue? What is this maximum revenue?

Solution   Let x denote the number of vacant units. The number of rented apartments is then $60 - x$ and the monthly rent per suite is $(200 + 5x)$ dollars. If R denotes the total monthly revenue (in dollars), then

$$R = (\text{Rent per Unit})(\text{Number of Units Rented})$$
$$= (200 + 5x)(60 - x)$$
$$= -5x^2 + 100x + 12,000.$$

The total monthly revenue R is a quadratic function of x with

$$a = -5, \quad b = 100, \quad \text{and} \quad c = 12,000.$$

The graph of R is a parabola which opens downwards (since $a < 0$) and has a vertex at the maximum point. The vertex is given by

$$\left(-\frac{b}{2a}, \ \frac{4ac - b^2}{4a} \right) \quad \text{or} \quad (10, \$12,500).$$

Thus when 10 units are unoccupied, the revenue is greatest. The rent per suite is then $(200 + 5x)$ dollars, or $250, and the total revenue is $12,500 per month.

EXERCISES 2

(1–4)   Sketch the following parabolas and determine their vertices.

1. $y = 2x^2 + 3x - 1$ 2. $y = 4x - x^2$
3. $y = 3 - x - 3x^2$ 4. $y = 4x^2 + 16x + 4$

5. The monthly revenue from selling x units of a certain commodity is given by $R(x) = 12x - 0.01x^2$ dollars. Determine the number of units that must be sold each month to maximize the revenue. What is the corresponding maximum revenue?

6. The profit $P(x)$ obtained by manufacturing and selling x units of a certain product is given by

$$P(x) = 60x - x^2.$$

Determine the number of units that must be produced and sold to maximize the profit. What is the maximum profit?

7. A firm has a monthly fixed costs of $2000, and the variable cost per unit of its product is $25.

   a. Determine the cost function.

   b. The revenue R obtained by selling x units is given by $R(x) = 60x - 0.01x^2$. Determine the number of units that must be sold each month so as to maximize the revenue. What is this maximum revenue?

   c. How many units must be produced and sold each month to obtain a maximum profit? What is this maximum profit?

8. The average cost per unit (in dollars) of producing x units of a certain commodity is $C(x) = 20 - 0.06x + 0.0002x^2$. What number of units produced will minimize the average cost? What is the corresponding minimum cost per unit?

9. A farmer has 500 yards of fencing with which to enclose a rectangular paddock. What is the largest area that can be enclosed?

10. The yield of apples from each tree in an orchard is $(500 - 5x)$ pounds, where x is the density with which the trees are planted (that is, the number of trees per acre). Find the value of x that makes the total yield per acre a maximum.

11. If rice plants are sown at a density of x plants per square foot, the yield of rice from a certain location is $x(10 - 0.5x)$ bushels per acre. What value of x maximizes the yield per acre?

12. If apple trees are planted at 30 per acre, the value of the crop produced by each tree is $180. For each additional tree planted per acre, the value of the crop falls by $3. What number of trees must be planted per acre to obtain the maximum value of the crop? What is this maximum value per acre of the crop?

13. If a publisher prices a book at $20 per book, 10,000 copies can be sold. For every dollar increase in the price, sales fall by 400 copies. What should be charged per book to obtain the maximum revenue? What is the value of this maximum revenue?

14. In Exercise 13, the cost of producing each copy is $13. What price should the publisher charge for each book to gain a maximum profit?

15. Chou-ching Realty has built a new rental unit of 40 apartments. It is known from market research that if a rent of $150 per month is charged, all the suites will be occupied. For each $5 increase in rent, one unit will remain vacant. What monthly rent should be charged for each unit to obtain the maximum monthly rental revenue? Find this maximum revenue.

16. The market demand for a certain product is x units when the price charged to consumers is p dollars, where

$$15p + 2x = 720.$$

The cost (in dollars) of producing x units is given by $C(x) = 200 + 6x$. What price p per unit should be charged to consumers to obtain a maximum profit?

5-3 MORE SIMPLE FUNCTIONS

In this section, we shall discuss a few more simple functions of common use and interest.

Power Functions

A function of the form

$$f(x) = ax^n$$

where a and n are nonzero constants, is called a **power function**. We shall consider some special cases of functions of this type.

1. **n = 2** In this case $f(x) = ax^2$, and we have a special case of the quadratic functions discussed in Section 2. The graph of $y = ax^2$ is a parabola with vertex at the origin, opening upwards if $a > 0$ and downwards if $a < 0$.

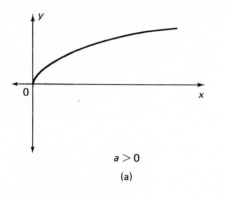

$a > 0$

(a)

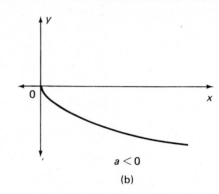

$a < 0$

(b)

FIGURE 16

2. **n = $\frac{1}{2}$** In this case, $f(x) = ax^{1/2} = a\sqrt{x}$. The graph of this function is *one-half of a parabola* that opens towards the right. If $a > 0$, the graph is the upper half of the parabola, while if $a < 0$, it is the lower half. Thus the graph rises or falls to the right depending on whether $a > 0$, or $a < 0$. The domain of f is the set of all nonnegative real numbers (See Fig. 16).

3. **n = -1** In this case, $f(x) = a/x$. The domain of $f(x)$ consists of all real numbers except zero. Figure 17 shows the graphs of $y = 1/x$ and $y = -1/x$ (that is, corresponding to $a = \pm 1$). The graph of $y = a/x$ for $a > 0$ is similar in form to that of $y = 1/x$ and that for $a < 0$ is similar in form to the graph of $y = -1/x$. The graph of $y = a/x$ is called a **rectangular hyperbola**. As x moves closer and closer to zero, the denominator in $f(x) = a/x$ becomes very small, so $f(x)$ becomes numerically very large. It may become large and positive or large and negative, depending on the signs of a and x. These possibilities are clear from Figure 17. It can be seen from the graph that as x becomes very large (positive or negative), $f(x)$ becomes closer and closer to zero; however, it is never quite equal to zero. The graph is said to be **asymptotic** to the coordinate axes.

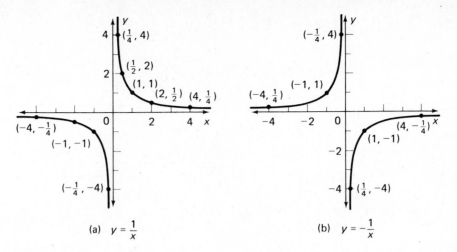

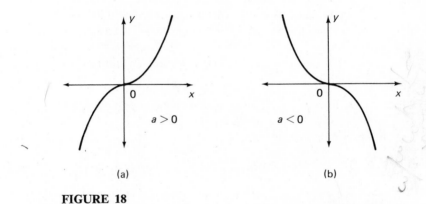

FIGURE 17

4. n = 3 In this case, $f(x) = ax^3$. The graph of $f(x)$ is the cubic curve shown in Figure 18. The domain is equal to the set of all real numbers.

FIGURE 18

Figure 19 provides a comparison of the graphs of the function $y = ax^n$ for various values of n. The case $a > 0$ is shown, and the graphs are drawn only for the quadrant in which x and y are nonnegative. (In business and economic applications, we are commonly concerned with variables that take only non-negative values.)

We see that all the graphs pass through the point $(1, a)$. When $n > 1$, the graph rises as we move to the right and, moreover, rises more and more steeply as x increases. The functions $y = ax^2$ and $y = ax^3$ encountered previously are examples that fall into this category. The case $n = 1$ corresponds to the straight line $y = ax$ passing through the origin and the point $(1, a)$.

When $0 < n < 1$, the graph of $y = ax^n$ still rises as we move to the right, but it rises less steeply as x increases. The function $y = ax^{1/2}$, which, as we saw before, has a graph that is half of a parabola, is an example of this type.

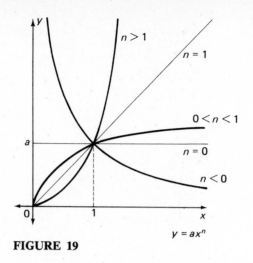

FIGURE 19

The case $n = 0$ corresponds to a horizontal straight line. Finally, when $n < 0$, the function $y = ax^n$ has a graph that falls as we move to the right and is asymptotic to the x- and y-axes. The rectangular hyperbola, with equation $y = ax^{-1}$, is an example of such a graph.

There exist situations in business where, in a given range of interest, the demand relation between quantity and price is based on inverse variation; that is, the quantity sold or demanded in the market is inversely proportional to the price. This means that every combination of quantity sold and price per unit will result in the same total revenue. Consider the following example.

EXAMPLE 1   A firm has a total revenue of \$500 per day regardless of the price of its product. If p denotes the price (in dollars) per unit of the product and x is the number of units that can be sold at the price p, then to obtain \$500, we must have

$$500 = \text{Price per Unit} \times \text{Number of Units Sold}$$
$$= px.$$

That is,

$$p = \frac{500}{x}.$$

Selected values of x and $p = 500/x$ are given in Table 4.

TABLE 4

x	25	50	100	125	250	500
p	20	10	5	4	2	1

Plotting these points and joining them by a smooth curve, we obtain the curve shown in Figure 20. We have restricted the graph to the first quadrant because neither the price nor the quantity sold can be negative. The graph is one-half of a rectangular hyperbola.

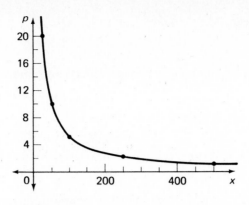

FIGURE 20

Circles

A **circle** is the set of all points that lie at a constant distance (called the **radius**) from a given point (called the **center**).

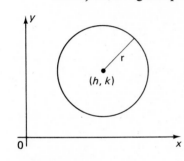

FIGURE 21

Let us find the equation of the circle with center at the point (h, k) and radius r. Let (x, y) be any point on the circle. Then the distance between this point (x, y) and the center (h, k) is given by the distance formula to be

$$\sqrt{(x - h)^2 + (y - k)^2}.$$

Setting this equal to the given radius r, we obtain the equation

$$\sqrt{(x - h)^2 + (y - k)^2} = r$$

which, on squaring, gives the following equation.

$$(x - h)^2 + (y - k)^2 = r^2 \qquad (1)$$

This is called the **center-radius** form of the equation of the circle. In particular, if the center is at the origin, $h = k = 0$ and Equation (1) reduces to

$$x^2 + y^2 = r^2. \qquad (2)$$

EXAMPLE 2   Find the equation of a circle with center at $(2, -3)$ and radius 5.

Solution   Here $h = 2$, $k = -3$, and $r = 5$. Using the standard equation of a circle, we have

$$(x - 2)^2 + (y - (-3))^2 = 5^2$$

or

$$(x - 2)^2 + (y + 3)^2 = 25.$$

We expand the squares and simplify.

$$x^2 + y^2 - 4x + 6y - 12 = 0$$

Equation (1), when expanded and simplified, can be written as

$$x^2 + y^2 - 2hx - 2ky + (h^2 + k^2 - r^2) = 0.$$

This is of the form

$$x^2 + y^2 + Bx + Cy + D = 0 \qquad (3)$$

where B, C, and D are constants given by

$$B = -2h, \qquad C = -2k, \quad \text{and} \quad D = h^2 + k^2 - r^2.$$

Equation (3) is called the **general form** of the equation of a circle.

Given any equation in general form, we can readily determine the center and radius of the circle that it represents. For

$$h = -\frac{B}{2} \quad \text{and} \quad k = -\frac{C}{2}$$

give the coordinates of the center immediately. The radius is then obtained as follows.

$$r^2 = h^2 + k^2 - D$$
$$= \tfrac{1}{4}(B^2 + C^2) - D$$

Thus

$$r = \tfrac{1}{2}\sqrt{B^2 + C^2 - 4D}.$$

Note that we must have $B^2 + C^2 - 4D > 0$; otherwise r would not be a real number. If this condition is not met, Equation (3) does not represent a circle.

EXAMPLE 3   Determine whether the graph of $2x^2 + 2y^2 - 5x + 4y - 1 = 0$ is a circle. If the graph is a circle, find its center and radius.

Solution   Dividing the equation throughout by 2 (to make the coefficients of x^2 and y^2 equal to 1), we get

$$x^2 + y^2 - \tfrac{5}{2}x + 2y - \tfrac{1}{2} = 0.$$

Comparing this with Equation (3), we see that

$$B = -\tfrac{5}{2}, \qquad C = 2, \quad \text{and} \quad D = -\tfrac{1}{2}.$$

Since

$$B^2 + C^2 - 4D = \tfrac{25}{4} + 4 + 2 = \tfrac{49}{4}$$

is positive, the graph of the given equation is a circle. The center of this circle is $(-B/2, -C/2)$ or $(\tfrac{5}{4}, -1)$ and the radius is $r = \tfrac{1}{2}\sqrt{B^2 + C^2 - 4D} = \tfrac{1}{2} \cdot \tfrac{7}{2} = \tfrac{7}{4}$ units.

It sometimes happens that a business firm has a choice between two (or more) ways of using certain of its resources to form different endproducts. Resources such as the available raw materials, plant and machinery, or labor may, in certain instances, be directed towards the production of several different items, and the company may choose how much of each to produce. For example, a shoe manufacturer can produce either men's or women's shoes from the same resources, an oil refinery can choose a variety of different grades of oil and gasoline to make from its crude oil, and so on.

In general, these different products compete for the use of the available resources—that is, an increase in the amount of one product must be accompanied by a decrease in the amounts of the others. These various amounts are related by an equation. When there are only two products involved, this equation can be graphed, and its graph is called the **product transformation curve**.

EXAMPLE 4   A shoe manufacturing firm can produce men's and women's shoes by varying the production process. The possible amounts x and y (in hundreds of pairs) are related by the equation

$$x^2 + y^2 + 40x + 30y = 975.$$

Plot the product transformation curve for this firm.

Solution   The given equation is of the general form of Equation (3) and hence has a circle as its graph. The coefficients are

$$B = 40, \qquad C = 30, \quad \text{and} \quad D = -975.$$

The coordinates of the center of the circle are

$$h = -\frac{B}{2} = -\frac{40}{2} = -20 \quad \text{and} \quad k = -\frac{C}{2} = -\frac{30}{2} = -15$$

so the center is the point $(-20, -15)$. The radius is

$$r = \tfrac{1}{2}\sqrt{B^2 + C^2 - 4D}$$
$$= \tfrac{1}{2}\sqrt{(40)^2 + (30)^2 - 4(-975)} = 40.$$

Figure 22 shows the product transformation curve. Note that since x and y must in practice both be positive, only the portion of the curve in the first

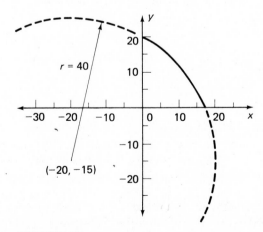

FIGURE 22

quadrant is of practical significance. The rest of the curve is shown as a dotted curve in the figure.

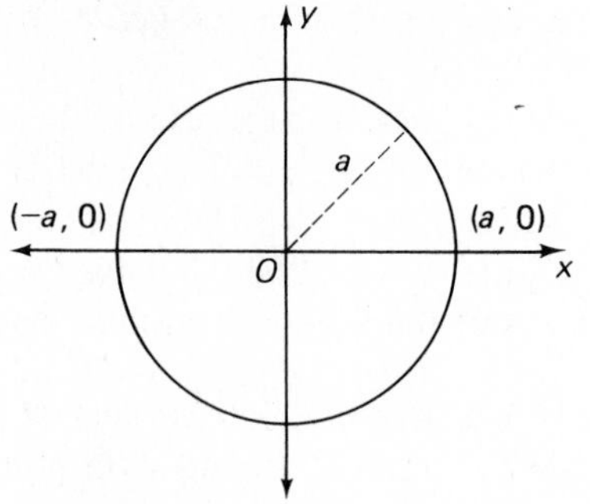

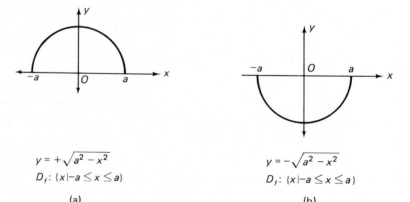

The set of points (x, y) that satisfy the relation $x^2 + y^2 = a^2$ consists of the points on the circle whose center is the origin and whose radius is a. We may speak of this circle as being the graph of the relation $x^2 + y^2 = a^2$. (See Figure 23.)

Clearly the circle cannot represent a function because for any value of x lying between $-a$ and $+a$ (excluding $x = \pm a$), there are two values of y. We can see this algebraically by solving the equation $x^2 + y^2 = a^2$ for y.

$$y = \pm\sqrt{a^2 - x^2}$$

FIGURE 23

This shows that there are two values of y for each x, depending on whether we choose the positive or the negative value.

In fact, the complete circle represents two functions. The upper semicircle is the graph of the function $y = +\sqrt{a^2 - x^2}$, in which the positive square root is taken for y; the lower semicircle is the graph of the function $y = -\sqrt{a^2 - x^2}$, in which the negative square root is taken. (See Figure 24.)

$$y = +\sqrt{a^2 - x^2}$$
$$D_f: \{x \mid -a \leq x \leq a\}$$

(a)

$$y = -\sqrt{a^2 - x^2}$$
$$D_f: \{x \mid -a \leq x \leq a\}$$

(b)

FIGURE 24

Absolute-Value Functions

If x is a real number, the absolute value of x, denoted by $|x|$, is defined as

$$|x| = \begin{cases} x & \text{if } x \geq 0 \\ -x & \text{if } x \leq 0. \end{cases}$$

Clearly, $|x| \geq 0$; that is, *the absolute value of a real number is always nonnegative.*

We call $f(x) = |x|$ the **absolute-value function**. The domain of f is the set of all real numbers and the range is the set of all nonnegative real numbers. The graph of $y = |x|$ is shown in Figure 25.

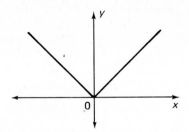

FIGURE 25

EXAMPLE 5   Consider the function

$$f(x) = |x - 2|.$$

The domain of f is the set of all real numbers and the range is the set of all nonnegative real numbers. Let us draw the graph of $f(x)$.

Setting $y = f(x)$, we have

$$y = |x - 2|$$

or, using the above definition of absolute value,

$$y = x - 2 \qquad \text{if } x - 2 \geq 0$$
$$\text{(that is, if } x \geq 2)$$

and

$$y = -(x - 2) \qquad \text{if } x - 2 \leq 0$$
$$\text{(that is, if } x \leq 2).$$

Therefore the graph of $f(x)$ consists of portions of the two straight lines

$$y = x - 2 \quad \text{and} \quad y = -(x - 2) = 2 - x$$

for $x \geq 2$ and $x \leq 2$, respectively. The graph is as shown in Figure 26. Note that $y \geq 0$ for all x.

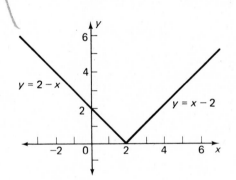

FIGURE 26

EXAMPLE 6   Consider the function

$$f(x) = \frac{|x|}{x}.$$

Clearly, the function is not defined for $x = 0$, since for this value of x the denominator becomes zero. Thus the domain of f is the set of all real numbers except zero.

$$\text{If } x > 0, f(x) = \frac{|x|}{x} = \frac{x}{x} = 1.$$

$$\text{If } x < 0, f(x) = \frac{|x|}{x} = \frac{-x}{x} = -1.$$

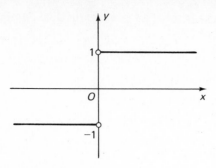

FIGURE 27

For example, $f(-3) = |-3|/(-3) = 3/(-3) = -1$. Thus the range consists of only two numbers, 1 and -1.

The graph of f consists of two straight lines (one above and one below the x-axis) that are parallel to the x-axis and at a distance 1 from it. This is shown in Figure 27. Note that the endpoints where the two lines meet the y-axis are *not* included in the graph. This is indicated by drawing small, open circles at the ends of the two lines.

EXERCISES 3

(1–14) Find the domains of the following functions and sketch their graphs.

1. $f(x) = \sqrt{4 - x^2}$ **2.** $f(x) = 2 - \sqrt{9 - x^2}$

3. $g(x) = -\sqrt{3 - x}$ **4.** $f(x) = \sqrt{x - 2}$ **5.** $f(x) = \dfrac{1}{x}$

6. $f(x) = \dfrac{-3}{x - 2}$ **7.** $f(x) = x^3$ **8.** $f(x) = 1 - x^3$

9. $f(x) = 2 - |x|$ **10.** $g(x) = |x| + 3$ **11.** $f(x) = |x + 3|$

12. $F(x) = -|x - 2|$ **13.** $f(x) = \dfrac{|x - 3|}{x - 3}$ **14.** $G(x) = \dfrac{2 - x}{|x - 2|}$

15. Which of the following half circles represent the graphs of functions? In each case where the answer is yes, determine the functional equation for the function from the graph.

a.

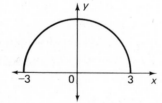

b.

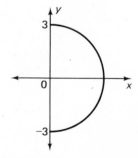

c.

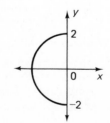

d.

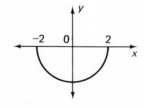

(16–21) Find the equation of each circle.

16. Center $(0, 2)$ and radius 5.   17. Center $(2, 5)$ and radius 3.

18. Center $(-3, 0)$ and radius 4.   19. Center $(0, 0)$ and radius 7.

20. Center $(1, -3)$ and passes through the point $(2, -1)$.

21. Center $(-2, 1)$ and passes through the point $(0, 4)$.

22. At a price of p dollars per unit, a manufacturer can sell x units of his product, where x and p are related by

$$x^2 + p^2 + 400x + 300p = 60,000.$$

Plot the demand curve. What is the highest price above which no sales are possible?

23. A car dealer can sell x cars of a particular model when he charges p dollars per car, where

$$x^2 + p^2 + 4000x + 2500p = 19,437,500.$$

Plot the demand curve for this model of car. What is the highest price up to which sales are still possible?

24. The owner of an apple orchard can produce either apples or apple cider. The possible amounts x of apples (in kilograms) and y of apple cider (in liters) are related by the equation

$$x^2 + y^2 + 8x + 250y = 6859.$$

Plot the graph of this relation (called the *product transformation curve*) and determine the maximum amounts of apples or apple cider that can be produced.

25. The Coronado cycle industries manufactures two types of bicycles called *Coronado* and *Eastern Star*. The possible quantities x and y (in thousands) that can be produced per year are related by

$$x^2 + y^2 + 6x + 10y = 47.$$

Sketch the product transformation curve for this industry. What are the maximum numbers of cycles of each type that can be produced?

5-4 COMBINATIONS OF FUNCTIONS

A variety of situations arise in which we have to combine two or more functions in one of several ways to get new functions. For example, let $f(t)$ and $g(t)$ denote the incomes of a person from two different sources at time t; then the combined income from the two sources is $f(t) + g(t)$. From the two functions f and g, we have in this way obtained a third function, the *sum* of f and g. If $C(x)$ denotes the cost of producing x units of a certain commodity and $R(x)$ is the revenue obtained from the sale of x units, then the profit $P(x)$ obtained by producing and selling x units is given by $P(x) = R(x) - C(x)$. The new function P so obtained is the *difference* of the two functions R and C.

If $P(t)$ denotes population of a country and $I(t)$ is the per capita income at time t, then the national income of that country is given by $P(t)I(t)$. This is an example in which a new function is formed as the *product* of two functions. Correspondingly, we can define the *quotient* of two functions: If $N(t)$ and $P(t)$ denote the national income and the population at any time t, then the per capita income of that country is given by $N(t)/P(t)$.

These kinds of examples lead us to the following abstract definitions.

DEFINITION Given two functions f and g, the **sum, difference, product**, and **quotient** functions are defined as follows.

Sum: $\quad (f + g)(x) = f(x) + g(x)$

Difference: $\quad (f - g)(x) = f(x) - g(x)$

Product: $\quad (f \cdot g)(x) = f(x) \cdot g(x)$

Quotient: $\quad \left(\dfrac{f}{g}\right)(x) = \dfrac{f(x)}{g(x)}, \qquad$ provided $g(x) \neq 0$

The domains of the sum, difference, and product functions are all equal to the common part of the domains of f and g, that is, the set of x at which both f and g are defined. In the case of the quotient function, the domain is the common part of the domains of f and g except for those values of x for which $g(x) = 0$.

EXAMPLE 1 Let $f(x) = 1/(x - 1)$ and $g(x) = \sqrt{x}$. Find $f + g$, $f - g$, $f \cdot g$, f/g, and g/f. Determine the domain in each case.

Solution We have:

$$(f + g)(x) = f(x) + g(x) = \frac{1}{x - 1} + \sqrt{x}$$

$$(f - g)(x) = f(x) - g(x) = \frac{1}{x - 1} - \sqrt{x}$$

$$(f \cdot g)(x) = f(x) \cdot g(x) = \frac{1}{x - 1} \cdot \sqrt{x} = \frac{\sqrt{x}}{x - 1}$$

$$\left(\frac{f}{g}\right)(x) = \frac{f(x)}{g(x)} = \frac{1/(x - 1)}{\sqrt{x}} = \frac{1}{\sqrt{x}\,(x - 1)}$$

$$\left(\frac{g}{f}\right)(x) = \frac{g(x)}{f(x)} = \frac{\sqrt{x}}{1/(x - 1)} = \sqrt{x}\,(x - 1)$$

Since its denominator becomes zero when $x = 1$, $f(x)$ is not defined for $x = 1$, so the domain of f is the set of all real numbers except 1.

Similarly, $g(x)$ is defined for values of x for which the expression under the radical sign is nonnegative, that is, for $x \geq 0$. Thus

$$D_f: \ \{x \mid x \neq 1\} \quad \text{and} \quad D_g: \ \{x \mid x \geq 0\}.$$

The common part of D_f and D_g is

$$\{x \mid x \geq 0 \quad \text{and} \quad x \neq 1\}. \tag{1}$$

This set provides the domain of $f + g$, $f - g$ and $f \cdot g$.

Since $g(x) = \sqrt{x}$ is zero when $x = 0$, this point must be excluded from the domain of f/g. Thus the domain of f/g is

$$\{x \mid x > 0 \quad \text{and} \quad x \neq 1\}.$$

Since $f(x)$ is never zero, the domain of g/f is again the common part of D_f and D_g, namely Set (1). It appears from the algebraic formula for $(g/f)(x)$ that this function is well-defined when $x = 1$. In spite of this, it is still necessary to exclude $x = 1$ from the domain of this function, as g/f can be defined only at points where both g and f are defined.

Another way in which two functions can be combined to yield a third function is called the *composition* of functions. Consider the following situation.

The monthly revenue R of a firm depends on the number x of the units that it produces and sells. In general, we can say $R = f(x)$. Clearly, the number x of units it can sell depends on the price p per unit it charges the customers, so that $x = g(p)$. If we eliminate x from the two relations $R = f(x)$ and $x = g(p)$, we have

$$R = f(x) = f(g(p)).$$

This gives R as a function of the price p. Observe how R is obtained as a function of p by using the function $g(p)$ as the argument of the function f. This leads to the following definition.

DEFINITION Let f and g be two functions. Let x belong to the domain of g and be such that $g(x)$ belongs to the domain of f. Then the **composite function** $f \circ g$ (read f *circle* g) is defined by

$$(f \circ g)(x) = f(g(x)).$$

EXAMPLE 2 Let $f(x) = 1/(x - 2)$ and $g(x) = \sqrt{x}$. Evaluate: (a) $(f \circ g)(9)$; (b) $(f \circ g)(4)$; (c) $(f \circ g)(x)$; (d) $(g \circ f)(6)$; (e) $(g \circ f)(1)$; (f) $(g \circ f)(x)$.

Solution (a) $g(9) = \sqrt{9} = 3$. Therefore,

$$(f \circ g)(9) = f(g(9)) = f(3) = 1/(3 - 2) = 1.$$

(b) $g(4) = \sqrt{4} = 2$. We have $(f \circ g)(4) = f(g(4)) = f(2) = 1/(2 - 2)$. This is not defined. The value $x = 4$ does not belong to the domain of $f \circ g$, so $(f \circ g)(4)$ cannot be found.

(c) $g(x) = \sqrt{x}$

$$(f \circ g)(x) = f(g(x)) = \frac{1}{g(x) - 2} = \frac{1}{\sqrt{x} - 2}$$

(d) $f(6) = 1/(6 - 2) = \frac{1}{4}$; $(g \circ f)(6) = g(f(6)) = g(\frac{1}{4}) = \sqrt{\frac{1}{4}} = \frac{1}{2}$.

(e) $f(1) = 1/(1 - 2) = -1$; $(g \circ f)(1) = g(f(1)) = g(-1) = \sqrt{-1}$ which is not a real number. We cannot evaluate $(g \circ f)(1)$ as 1 does not belong to the domain of $g \circ f$.

(f) $f(x) = 1/(x - 2)$

$$(g \circ f)(x) = g(f(x)) = \sqrt{f(x)} = \sqrt{\frac{1}{x - 2}} = \frac{1}{\sqrt{x - 2}}$$

The domain of $f \circ g$ is given by

$$D_{f \circ g} = \{x \mid x \in D_g \text{ and } g(x) \in D_f\}.$$

It can be shown that, for the functions in Example 2,

$$D_{f \circ g} = \{x \mid x \geq 0 \text{ and } x \neq 4\}$$

and

$$D_{g \circ f} = \{x \mid x > 2\}.$$

EXAMPLE 3   The monthly revenue R obtained by selling deluxe model shoes is a function of the demand x in the market. It is observed that, as a function of price p per pair, the monthly revenue and demand are

$$R = 300p - 2p^2 \quad \text{and} \quad x = 300 - 2p.$$

How does R depend on x?

Solution   If $R = f(p)$ and $p = g(x)$, then R is obtained as a function of x by means of the composition $R = (f \circ g)(x) = f(g(x))$. The function $f(p)$ is given by $R = f(p) = 300p - 2p^2$. However, in order to obtain $g(x)$, we must solve the demand relation $x = 300 - 2p$ to express p as a function of x. We get

$$p = \tfrac{1}{2}(300 - x).$$

We substitute this value of p in R and simplify.

$$R = 300p - 2p^2$$
$$= 300 \cdot \tfrac{1}{2}(300 - x) - 2 \cdot \tfrac{1}{4}(300 - x)^2$$
$$= (150)(300) - 150x - \tfrac{1}{2}(300^2 - 600x + x^2)$$
$$= 150x - 0.5x^2$$

This is the required result, expressing the monthly revenue R as a function of the demand x in the market.

EXERCISES 4

(1–5) Find the sum, difference, product, and quotient of the two functions f and g in each of the following exercises. Determine the domains of the resulting functions.

1. $f(x) = x^2; \quad g(x) = \dfrac{1}{x - 1}$ **2.** $f(x) = x^2 + 1; \quad g(x) = \sqrt{x}$

3. $f(x) = \sqrt{x - 1}; \quad g(x) = \dfrac{1}{x + 2}$

4. $f(x) = 1 + \sqrt{x}; \quad g(x) = \dfrac{2x + 1}{x + 2}$

5. $f(x) = (x + 1)^2; \quad g(x) = \dfrac{1}{x^2 - 1}$

(6–13) Given $f(x) = x^2$ and $g(x) = \sqrt{x - 1}$, evaluate each of the following.

6. $(f \circ g)(5)$ **7.** $(g \circ f)(3)$ **8.** $(f \circ g)(\tfrac{5}{4})$

9. $(g \circ f)(-2)$ **10.** $(f \circ g)(\tfrac{1}{2})$ **11.** $(g \circ f)(\tfrac{1}{3})$

12. $(f \circ g)(2)$ **13.** $(g \circ f)(1)$

(14–18) Determine $(f \circ g)(x)$ and $(g \circ f)(x)$ in the following exercises.

14. $f(x) = x^2; \quad g(x) = 1 + x$

15. $f(x) = \sqrt{x} + 1; \quad g(x) = x^2$

16. $f(x) = \dfrac{1}{x+1}; \quad g(x) = \sqrt{x} + 1$

17. $f(x) = 2 + \sqrt{x}; \quad g(x) = (x-2)^2$

18. $f(x) = x^2 + 2; \quad g(x) = x - 3$

(19–22) Find $f(x)$ and $g(x)$ such that each composite function $f \circ g$ is as described. (The answer is not unique. Choose f and g to be as simple as you can.)

19. $(f \circ g)(x) = (x^2 + 1)^3$

20. $(f \circ g)(x) = \sqrt{2x + 3}$

21. $(f \circ g)(x) = \dfrac{1}{x^2 + 7}$

22. $(f \circ g)(x) = \dfrac{1}{\sqrt{x^2 - 5}}$

23. The demand x for a certain commodity is given by $x = 2000 - 15p$, where p is the price per unit of the commodity. The monthly revenue R obtained from the sales of this commodity is given by $R = 2000p - 15p^2$. How does R depend on x?

24. A manufacturer can sell q units of a product at a price p per unit, where $20p + 3q = 600$. As a function of quantity q demanded in the market, the total weekly revenue R is given by $R = 30q - 0.15q^2$. How does R depend on the price p?

5-5 IMPLICIT RELATIONS AND INVERSE FUNCTIONS

When y is a given function of x, that is, $y = f(x)$, then we often say that y is an **explicit function** of the independent variable x. Examples of explicit functions are $y = 3x^2 - 7x + 5$, and $y = 5x + 1/(x - 1)$.

Sometimes the fact that y is a function of x is expressed indirectly by means of some equation of the type $F(x, y) = 0$, in which both x and y appear as arguments of the function F on the left side. An equation of this type is called an **implicit relation** between x and y.

EXAMPLE 1   Consider $xy + 3y - 7 = 0$. In this equation, we have a function on the left involving both x and y, and the equation provides an implicit relation between x and y. In this case we can solve for y.

$$y(x + 3) = 7$$
$$y = \frac{7}{x + 3}$$

Thus we can express y as an explicit function. In this example, the given implicit relation is equivalent to a certain explicit function. This is not always the case, as the following examples show.

EXAMPLE 2   Consider the implicit relation $x^2 + y^2 = 4$. In this case, we can again solve for y.

$$y^2 = 4 - x^2$$
$$y = +\sqrt{4 - x^2} \quad \text{or} \quad y = -\sqrt{4 - x^2}$$

These last two are explicit functions. Thus the implicit relation $x^2 + y^2 = 4$ leads to the two explicit functions,

$$y = +\sqrt{4 - x^2} \quad \text{and} \quad y = -\sqrt{4 - x^2}.$$

EXAMPLE 3   Consider the implicit relation $x^2 + y^2 + 4 = 0$. If we try to solve for y, we obtain

$$y^2 = -4 - x^2.$$

Whatever the value of x, the right side of the equation is always negative, so we cannot take the square root. In this case, the implicit relation has no solution. (We say that its domain is empty.)

EXAMPLE 4 $y^5 + x^3 - 3xy = 0$. This given relation does imply that y is a function of x, but we cannot solve for y in terms of x; that is, we cannot express y as an explicit function of x by means of any algebraic formula.

When the fact that y is a function of x is *implied* by some relation of the form $F(x, y) = 0$, we speak of y as an **implicit function** of x. As in Example 4, this does not necessarily mean that we can actually find a formula expressing y as a function of x.

Given an implicit relation $F(x, y) = 0$, we usually are free to choose which of the variables x or y to regard as the independent variable. Consider the demand relation

$$2p + 3x = 12 \tag{1}$$

where x is the quantity demanded at a price p per unit. This equation defines p as an implicit function of x. Solving for p, we get

$$p = 6 - \tfrac{3}{2}x \tag{2}$$

which expresses p as an explicit function of x. The graph of Equation (2) is shown in Figure 28.

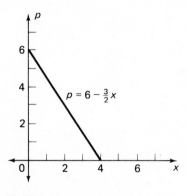

FIGURE 28

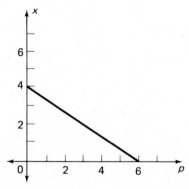

FIGURE 29

Equation (1) could also be viewed as defining x as an implicit function of p. Solving Equation (1) (or (2)) for x in terms of p, we obtain

$$x = 4 - \tfrac{2}{3}p. \tag{3}$$

Equation (3) expresses the demand x as a function of price p. Here p is treated as the independent variable and x as the dependent variable. The graph of Equation (3) is shown in Figure 29.

Thus the relation in Equation (1) defines not one but two implicit functions:

$$p = f(x) = 6 - \tfrac{3}{2}x \qquad \text{if } p \text{ is regarded as a function of } x$$

and

$$x = g(p) = 4 - \tfrac{2}{3}p \qquad \text{if } x \text{ is regarded as a function of } p.$$

The two functions f and g, where

$$f(x) = 6 - \tfrac{3}{2}x \quad \text{and} \quad g(p) = 4 - \tfrac{2}{3}p$$

are called **inverse functions** of each other.

In general, let $y = f(x)$ be some given function. The equation $y - f(x) = 0$ represents an implicit relation between x and y. If we regard x as the independent variable, we can solve this relation for y, obtaining our original function, $y = f(x)$. On the other hand, we may wish to regard y as the independent variable and to solve for x in terms of y. We will not always be able to do this, but if we can, the solution is written as $x = f^{-1}(y)$ and f^{-1} is called the *inverse function* of f.

Notes: 1. $f^{-1}(y)$ is not to be confused with the negative power

$$[f(y)]^{-1} = \frac{1}{f(y)}.$$

2. If we take the composition of f and its inverse function, we find that

$$(f^{-1} \circ f)(x) = x \quad \text{and} \quad (f \circ f^{-1})(y) = y.$$

In other words, the composition of f and f^{-1} gives the identity function, that is, the function which leaves the variable unchanged.

EXAMPLE 5   Find the inverse of the function $f(x) = 2x + 1$.

Solution   Setting $y = f(x) = 2x + 1$, we must solve for x as a function of y.

$$2x = y - 1$$

$$x = \frac{y - 1}{2}$$

Therefore the inverse function is given by $f^{-1}(y) = (y - 1)/2$. The graphs of $y = f(x)$ and $x = f^{-1}(y)$ are shown in Figures 30 and 31, respectively. Both graphs in this case are straight lines. Observe that when plotting the graph of $x = f^{-1}(y)$, the y-axis is taken as the horizontal axis and the x-axis as the vertical axis because y is the independent variable.

EXAMPLE 6   Find the inverse of the function $f(x) = x^3$ and sketch its graph.

Solution   Setting $y = f(x) = x^3$, we solve for x, obtaining $x = f^{-1}(y) = y^{1/3}$. The graphs of $y = f(x)$ and $x = f^{-1}(y)$ are shown in Figures 32 and 33, respectively.

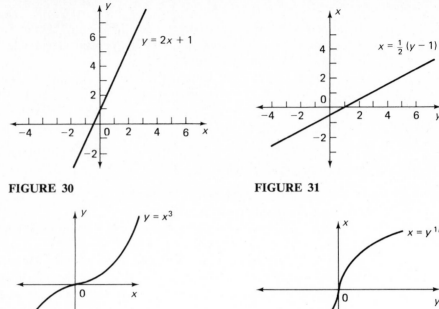

FIGURE 30

FIGURE 31

FIGURE 32

FIGURE 33

It can be seen from these two examples that the graphs of a function $y = f(x)$ and its inverse function $x = f^{-1}(y)$ are closely related. In fact, the graph of the inverse function is obtained by flipping over the graph of the original function so that the coordinate axes become interchanged. For example, hold the graph of $y = x^3$ in front of a mirror in such a way that the y-axis is horizontal and the x-axis points vertically upwards. The reflection you will see will be the graph $x = y^{1/3}$ that is shown in Figure 31.

The graphs of $y = f(x)$ and $x = f^{-1}(y)$ consist of precisely the same sets of points (x, y). The difference rests only in that the axes are drawn in different directions in the two cases.

Another way of seeing the relationship between the two graphs is to plot the functions $y = f(x)$ and $y = f^{-1}(x)$ on the same axes. Then the graph of either of these functions can be obtained by reflecting the other graph about the line $y = x$. Figure 34 shows the graphs of the function $f(x) = x^3$ and its inverse function, $f^{-1}(x) = x^{1/3}$, drawn on the same axes. Clearly the two graphs are reflections of one another about the line $y = x$.

In general, let (a, b) be any point on the graph of $y = f(x)$. Then $b = f(a)$. It follows, therefore, that $a = f^{-1}(b)$, so that (b, a) is a point on the graph of $y = f^{-1}(x)$. Now it can be shown that the two points (a, b) and (b, a) are reflections of one another about the line $y = x$. Consequently, to every point (a, b)

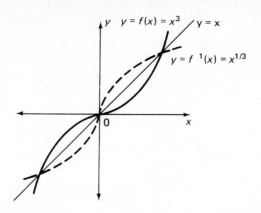

FIGURE 34

on the graph of $y = f(x)$, there exists a point (b, a) on the graph of $y = f^{-1}(x)$ that is the reflection of the first point about the line $y = x$.

Not every function has an inverse. Consider, for example, the function $y = x^2$. Solving for x in terms of y, we obtain

$$x^2 = y \quad \text{or} \quad x = \pm\sqrt{y}.$$

So, for any value of y in the region $y > 0$, there are two possible values of x. Thus we cannot say that x is a function of y.

This example is illustrated graphically in Figures 35 and 36. Figure 35 shows the graph of $y = x^2$, which is a parabola opening upwards. Figure 36 shows the same graph, but with the axes flipped over; that is, the y-axis is horizontal and the x-axis is vertical. For each $y > 0$, we have two values of x, $x = +\sqrt{y}$ and $x = -\sqrt{y}$; for example, when $y = 1$, x has the value $+1$ and -1, both of which satisfy the relation $y = x^2$.

The graph in Figure 36 corresponds to two functions rather than one. The upper branch of the parabola is the graph of $x = +\sqrt{y}$, while the lower branch is the graph of $x = -\sqrt{y}$. Thus we can say that the function $y = x^2$ has two inverse functions, one given by $x = +\sqrt{y}$ and the other by $x = -\sqrt{y}$.

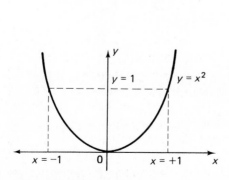

FIGURE 35

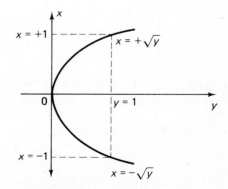

FIGURE 36

In a case such as this, it is possible to make the definition of f^{-1} unambiguous by restricting the values of x. For example, if x is restricted to the region $x \geq 0$, then $y = x^2$ has the unique inverse $x = +\sqrt{y}$. On the other hand, if x is restricted to the region $x \leq 0$, then the inverse is given by $x = -\sqrt{y}$. Placing a restriction on x in this way means restricting the domain of the original function f. We conclude, therefore, that in cases where a function $y = f(x)$ has more than one inverse function, the inverse can be made unique by placing a suitable restriction on the domain of f.

It is worth observing that *a function $f(x)$ has a unique inverse whenever horizontal lines intersect its graph in at most one point.*

EXERCISES 5

(1–12) Find the explicit function or functions corresponding to the following implicit relations.

1. $3x + 4y = 12$ | **2.** $5x - 2y = 20$

3. $xy + x - y = 0$ | **4.** $3xy + 2x - 4y = 1$

5. $x^2 - y^2 + x + y = 0$ | **6.** $x^2y + xy^2 - x - y = 0$

7. $x^2 + y^2 + 2xy = 4$ | **8.** $9x^2 + y^2 + 6xy = 25$

9. $4x^2 + 9y^2 = 36$ | **10.** $4x^2 - 9y^2 = 36$

11. $\sqrt{x} + \sqrt{y} = 1$ | **12.** $xy^2 + yx^2 = 6$

13. $xy^2 + (x^2 - 1)y - x = 0$ | **14.** $y^2 - 3xy + (2x^2 + x - 1) = 0$

(15–24) Find the inverse of each of the following functions. In each case, draw the graphs of the function and its inverse.

15. $y = -3x - 4$ | **16.** $y = x - 1$ | **17.** $p = 4 - \frac{2}{3}x$

18. $q = 3p + 6$ | **19.** $y = \sqrt{3x - 4}$ | **20.** $y = \sqrt{\frac{1}{4}x + 2}$

21. $y = x^5$ | **22.** $y = \sqrt{x}$ | **23.** $y = \sqrt{4 - x}$

24. $y = -\sqrt{2 - x}$

(25–28) By placing a suitable restriction on the domain of each of the following functions, find an inverse function.

25. $y = (x + 1)^2$ | **26.** $y = (3 - 2x)^2$

27. $y = x^{2/3}$ | **28.** $y = \sqrt{x^2 + 1}$

REVIEW EXERCISES FOR CHAPTER 5

1. State whether each of the following is true or false. Replace each false statement by a corresponding true statement.

a. The domain of $f(x) = |x - 3|$ is the set of all real numbers greater than or equal to 3.

b. The range of $f(x) = x/x$ is $\{1\}$.

c. The graph of $f(x) = (x^2 - 4)/(x - 2)$ is a straight line which is broken at the point $(2, 4)$.

d. If $x \neq 3$, then $|x^2 - 9|/(x - 3) = x + 3$.

e. A given curve is the graph of a function if any vertical line meets the curve in at least one point.

f. A function is a rule that assigns to each value in the domain at least one value in the range.

g. For all real numbers x, $\sqrt{x^2} = |x|$.

h. For all values of a, b, and c, $F(x) = ax^2 + bx + c$ represents a quadratic function.

i. The domain of a polynomial function is the set of all integers.

j. If f and g are two functions, then $f + g$, $f - g$, fg, and f/g have the same domain.

k. If f and g are two functions such that both the composite functions $f \circ g$ and $g \circ f$ are defined, then $f \circ g = g \circ f$.

l. The graph of a quadratic function is a parabola with the vertex at the origin.

m. In an implicit function of the form $F(x, y) = 0$, x and y are both independent variables.

n. The function $y = f(x)$ has a unique inverse if and only if any horizontal line meets the graph of $f(x)$ in at most one point.

o. The graph of f^{-1} is the reflection of the graph of f about the y-axis.

2. Give an example of a function f that satisfies each property for all values of x and y.

a. $f(x) = f(-x)$ (Such a function is called an *even function*.)

b. $f(-x) = -f(x)$ (Such a function is called an *odd function*.)

c. $f(x + y) = f(x) + f(y)$

3. Two functions f and g are said to be equal if $f(x) = g(x)$ for all x in the domain and $D_f = D_g$. Use this criterion to determine which of the following functions are equal to $f(x) = (2x^2 + x)/x$.

a. $g(x) = 2x + 1$

b. $h(x) = \sqrt{1 + 4x + 4x^2}$

c. $F(x) = \dfrac{2x^3 + x^2}{x^2}$

d. $G(x) = \dfrac{(x^3 + 2x)(1 + 2x)}{x(x^2 + 2)}$

4. Find an equation of the circle with center $(-1, 2)$ and that passes through the point $(3, 4)$.

5. A circle of radius 5 units has its center at $(p, -1)$ and passes through the point $(1, 2)$. Determine p.

6. Determine the radius of a circle that passes through the point $(-3, 1)$ and has its center at $(1, -2)$.

7. Find the domain of $f(x) = |x| - 2$. Sketch the graph of f.

8. Find the domain of $g(x) = (x^2 - 4)/(x - 2)$ and sketch its graph.

9. If $f(x) = |x|$ and $g(x) = x^2$, determine $f \circ g$ and $g \circ f$.

6-1 EXPONENTIAL FUNCTIONS

Consider a certain city with population at a given time of 1 million, with the population increasing at the rate of 10% per year. After 1 year, the population will have increased to 1.1 million. During the second year, the increase in population will be 10% of the size at the beginning of that year, that is, 10% of 1.1 million. Therefore the population size after 2 years will be

$$1.1 + (0.1)(1.1) = (1.1)^2 = 1.21 \text{ million.}$$

During the third year, the increase will be 10% of 1.21 million, giving a total population at the end of the third year equal to

$$1.21 + (0.1)(1.21) = (1.1)(1.21) = (1.1)^3 = 1.331 \text{ million.}$$

Continuing in this way, we see that the size of the population after n years is equal to $(1.1)^n$ million. A graph of this function is shown in Figure 1, in which the values $(1.1)^n$ are shown as dots for $n = 0, 1, 2, \ldots, 10$.

The formula $(1.1)^n$ may be used to calculate the size of the population in millions at fractional parts of a year as well as at integer values of n. For example, after 6 months (that is, half a year), the size of the population is $(1.1)^{1/2} = 1.049$ million (to 3 decimal places). After 2 years and 3 months ($2\frac{1}{4}$ years), the size of the population is $(1.1)^{9/4} = 1.239$ million, and so on.

If all these values of $(1.1)^n$ for fractional values of n are plotted on the graph in Figure 1, it is found that they lie on a smooth curve. This curve is shown in Figure 1, passing, of course, through the heavy dots, since these dots correspond to the values of $(1.1)^n$ for integer values of n.

We note that the value of $(1.1)^n$ can only be defined by elementary means when n is a rational number. For example, when $n = \frac{9}{4}$, $(1.1)^n = (1.1)^{9/4}$ can be defined as the 4th root of 1.1 raised to the 9th power. Similarly, $(1.1)^{7/5}$ can be defined as the 5th root of 1.1 raised to the 7th power. But such a definition in terms of powers and roots cannot be given for $(1.1)^n$ when n is an irrational

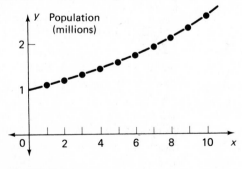

FIGURE 1

number: for example, $(1.1)^{\sqrt{2}}$ cannot be defined by powers and roots. However, once we have constructed the smooth curve in the preceding figure, we can use that curve to define $(1.1)^n$ for irrational values of n. For instance, to find $(1.1)^{\sqrt{2}}$, we simply use the ordinate of the point on the curve that corresponds to the abscissa $n = \sqrt{2}$. In this way, we see that the value of $(1.1)^n$ can be defined for all real values of n, both rational and irrational.

In a similar way, we may define the function $y = a^x$ for any positive real number a. When $x = 0$, $y = a^0 = 1$; when $x = 2$, $y = a^2$; when $x = 3$, $y = a^3$, and so on, for all positive integer values of x. When x is a positive rational number, a^x is defined in terms of an appropriate power and root: for example, $a^{11/3}$ is defined as the cube root of a raised to the 11th power. When x is a negative rational number, a^x can be defined in the usual way in terms of reciprocals. For example, when $x = -1$, $y = a^{-1} = 1/a$; when $x = -\frac{4}{3}$, $y = a^{-4/3} = 1/\sqrt[3]{a^4}$, and so on. In general, $a^{-x} = 1/a^x$.

We see then that the value of $y = a^x$ can be defined for all rational values of x. When plotted on a graph, it is found that all of the points (x, y) lie on a smooth curve. This curve may then be used in order to define the value of a^x when x is an irrational number simply by reading the ordinate of the point on the graph at which x has the given irrational value.

EXAMPLE 1   Construct the graphs of each function.

(a) $y = 2^x$ (b) $y = (\frac{1}{3})^x$

Solution   Table 1 gives values of these two functions for a selection of values of x.

TABLE 1

x	-2	-1.5	-1	-0.5	0	0.5	1	1.5	2	3
$y = 2^x$	0.25	0.354	0.5	0.707	1	1.414	2	2.828	4	8
$y = (\frac{1}{3})^x$	9	5.196	3	1.732	1	0.577	0.333	0.192	0.111	0.037

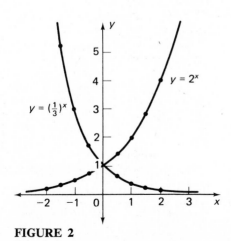

FIGURE 2

For example, when $x = -0.5$,

$$2^x = 2^{-1/2} = \frac{1}{\sqrt{2}} = \frac{1}{1.414} = 0.707$$

and

$$(\tfrac{1}{3})^x = (\tfrac{1}{3})^{-1/2} = 3^{1/2} = \sqrt{3} = 1.732.$$

When plotted, the points indicated by dots on Figure 2 are obtained, and these points can be joined by smooth curves as shown.

The graphs obtained in Example 1 are characteristic of *exponential functions*. Figure 3 illustrates the graphs of two functions, $y = a^x$ and $y = b^x$, when $a > b > 1$. It is seen

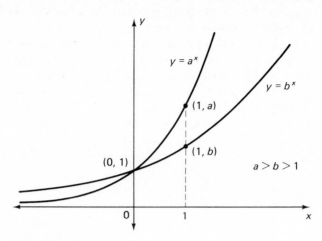

FIGURE 3

that for $x > 0$, these two functions grow at an ever-increasing rate as x increases. Since $a > b$, the graph of $y = a^x$ for positive values of x is above the graph of $y = b^x$ and, moreover, increases more steeply.

On the other hand, for $x < 0$, both functions decrease towards zero as x becomes larger and larger negatively. In this case, the function a^x falls more steeply than b^x and its graph is situated below the graph of $y = b^x$. The two graphs intersect when $x = 0$, since $a^0 = b^0 = 1$.

A function of the type $y = a^x$ is called an **exponential function**. When $a > 1$, the function is called a *growing exponential function*, whereas when $a < 1$, it is called a *decaying exponential function*. The graph of $y = a^x$ when $a < 1$ is illustrated in Figure 4. When $a < 1$, a^x decreases as x increases and approaches zero as x becomes larger. As a result, the graph approaches the x-axis more and more closely as x becomes very large.

The number a that appears in the exponential function a^x is called the **base**. The base can be any *positive* real number. It is often useful to use as base

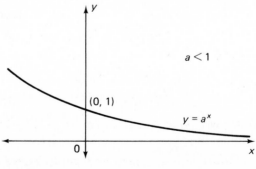

FIGURE 4

an irrational number denoted by e, which is given to five decimal places by $e = 2.71828$. The corresponding exponential function is written e^x and is called the **natural exponential function**.

The reason why this particular exponential function is so important cannot fully be explained without the use of calculus. However later in this chapter (Section 4), a partial explanation for its importance will be given.

The function e^x is in fact so important that a table giving some of its values is included in the Appendix. (See Table A-3-3.) Values of this function can also be obtained from many pocket calculators.

EXAMPLE 2 Using Table A-3-3 in the Appendix or a calculator, find the values of the following.

(a) e^2 (b) $e^{3.55}$ (c) $e^{-0.24}$

Solution We use Table A-3-3.

(a) $e^2 = 7.3891$

(b) $e^{3.55} = 34.813$

(c) $e^{-0.24} = 0.7866$

(In part (c), the value is read from the column headed e^{-x} adjacent to the value 0.24 in the x column.)

EXAMPLE 3 The population of a certain developing nation is found to be given in millions by the formula

$$P = 15e^{0.02t}$$

where t is the number of years measured from 1960. Determine the population in 1980 and the projected population in 1990, assuming this formula continues to hold until then.

Solution In 1980, $t = 20$ and so

$$P = 15e^{(0.02)(20)} = 15e^{0.4}$$

$$= 15(1.4918) = 22.4. \qquad \text{(to 1 decimal place)}$$

So in 1980, the population would be 22.4 million. After a further 10 years, $t = 30$ and so

$$P = 15e^{(0.02)(30)} = 15e^{0.6}$$

$$= 15(1.8221) = 27.3. \qquad \text{(to 1 decimal place)}$$

Thus in 1990 the projected population will be 27.3 million.

Further applications of exponential functions to the growth of populations are given in the following examples.

EXAMPLE 4   The population of the earth at the beginning of 1976 was 4 billion and it was growing at 2% per year. What will be the population in the year 2000, assuming that the rate of growth remains unchanged?

Solution   When a population grows by 2% a year, this means that its size at any time is 1.02 times what it was one year earlier. Thus at the beginning of 1977, the population was $(1.02) \times 4$ billion. Furthermore, at the beginning of 1978, it was (1.02) times the population at the beginning of 1977, that is, $(1.02)^2 \times 4$ billion. We continue to find the population in a similar fashion, multiplying by a factor of 1.02 for every year that passes. The population at the beginning of the year 2000, that is, after 24 years, will therefore be $(1.02)^{24} \times 4$ billion or

$$1.608 \times 4 \text{ billion} = 6.43 \text{ billion}.$$

Note   In this example, we needed to evaluate $(1.02)^{24}$. Quantities of this type can readily be evaluated using the y^x key on an electronic calculator. An alternative method of making such calculations is to use logarithm tables.

EXAMPLE 5   The population of a certain developing nation is increasing by 3% per year. By how much per year must the gross national product increase if the income per capita is to double in 20 years?

Solution   Let the present population be denoted by P_0. Then, since the population increases by a factor (1.03) each year, the size of the population after n years is given by

$$P = P_0(1.03)^n.$$

Let the present gross national product (GNP) be I_0. Then the present income per capita is obtained by dividing this quantity I_0 by the population size, so is equal to (I_0/P_0).

If the GNP increases by $R\%$ per year, then it changes by a factor of $1 + i$ for each year, where $i = R/100$. Therefore, after n years, the GNP is given by

$$I = I_0(1 + i)^n.$$

The income per capita after n years is therefore

$$\frac{I}{P} = \frac{I_0(1 + i)^n}{P_0(1.03)^n} = \frac{I_0}{P_0}\left(\frac{1 + i}{1.03}\right)^n.$$

We wish to find the value of R for which the income per capita when $n = 20$ is equal to twice its present value, I_0/P_0. Therefore we have the equation

$$\frac{I}{P} = \frac{I_0}{P_0}\left(\frac{1 + i}{1.03}\right)^{20} = 2\frac{I_0}{P_0}.$$

It follows that

$$\left(\frac{1 + i}{1.03}\right)^{20} = 2.$$

Therefore

$$\frac{1 + i}{1.03} = 2^{1/20}$$

and so $1 + i = (1.03)2^{1/20} = (1.03)(1.0353) = 1.066$. Thus $i = 0.066$ and $R = 100i = 6.6$. Thus the GNP would have to increase by 6.6% per annum if the stipulated goal is to be achieved.

The exponential growth equation must be applied to population problems with a certain amount of caution. A growing population will grow exponentially, provided there are no factors from its environment that limit or otherwise influence the growth. For instance, if the supply of food available to the population of a certain species is limited, then exponential growth must cease eventually as the food supply becomes insufficient to support the ever-growing population. Among other factors that inhibit indefinite growth are the supply of shelter for the species, which typically is limited, the interaction with predator species, sociological factors that might slow the expansion of the population in over-crowded circumstances, and, finally, simply the limited availability of physical space for the population. Such factors as these eventually operate to end the exponential growth of a population and cause it to level off at some value that is the maximum population which can be supported by the given habitat.

It is becoming apparent that such constraints are at this time being imposed on the human population, and it seems quite probable that the human population will not grow exponentially during the coming decades. Thus future projections of the human population over long periods of time based on the exponential growth equation are unlikely to turn out to be very accurate. They indicate what will happen if present trends continue, which may be different from what will happen in fact.

Another case in which exponential functions arise concerns investments made at compound interest. Consider a sum of money, say $100, that is invested at a fixed rate of interest, such as 6% per annum. After one year, the investment will have increased in value by 6%, to $106. If the interest is compounded, then during the second year, this whole sum of $106 earns interest at 6%. Thus the value of the investment at the end of the second year will consist of the $106 existing at the beginning of that year plus 6% of $106 in interest, giving a total value of $106 + (0.06)(\$106) = \$100(1.06)^2 = \$112.36$. During the third year, the value increases by an amount of interest equal to 6% of $112.36, giving a total value at the end of the year equal to

$$\$112.36 + \$112.36(0.06) = \$100(1.06)^3.$$

In general, the investment increases by a factor of 1.06 with each year that passes, so after n years its value is $\$100(1.06)^n$.

Let us consider the general case of an investment growing at compound interest. Let a sum P be invested at a rate of interest of R percent per annum. Then the interest in the first year is $(R/100)P$, so the value of the investment after one year is

$$P + \left(\frac{R}{100}\right)P = P\left(1 + \frac{R}{100}\right) = P(1 + i)$$

where we have let $i = (R/100)$.

The interest in the second year will be R percent of this new value, $P(1 + i)$:

$$\text{interest} = \left(\frac{R}{100}\right)P(1 + i).$$

Thus the value after 2 years is

$$P(1 + i) + \left(\frac{R}{100}\right)P(1 + i) = P(1 + i)\left(1 + \frac{R}{100}\right) = P(1 + i)^2.$$

We see that each year the value of the investment is multiplied by a factor of $1 + i$ from its value the previous year. After n years, the value is given by the formula

$$\text{Value after } n \text{ years} = P(1 + i)^n, \qquad i = \frac{R}{100}.$$

This is equivalent to the exponential function Pa^n, where the base is $a = 1 + i$.

EXAMPLE 6   A sum of \$200 is invested at 5% interest compounded annually. Find the value of the investment after 10 years.

Solution   In this case $R = 5$ and $i = R/100 = 0.05$. After n years, the value of the investment is

$$P(1 + i)^n = 200(1.05)^n.$$

When $n = 10$, this is

$$200(1.05)^{10} = 200(1.6289) = 325.78.$$

The value of the investment is therefore \$325.78.

In some cases, interest is compounded more than once per year, for example semiannually (2 times per year), quarterly (4 times per year) or monthly (12 times per year). In these cases, the annual rate of interest R percent which is usually quoted is called the **nominal rate**. If compounding occurs k times per year and if the nominal rate of interest is R percent, this means that the interest rate at each compounding is equal to $(R/k)\%$. In n years, the number of compoundings is kn.

For example, at 8% nominal interest compounded quarterly, an investment is increased by 2% every 3 months. In 5 years, there would be 20 such compoundings.

The formula which replaces the one given earlier for the value after n years is

$$\text{Value after } n \text{ years} = P\left(1 + \frac{i}{k}\right)^{nk}, \qquad i = \frac{R}{100}.$$

EXAMPLE 7   A sum of \$2000 is invested at a nominal rate of interest of 9% compounded monthly. Find the value of the investment after 3 years.

Solution   Here $k = 12$, the investment is compounded monthly and the interest rate at each compounding is $R/k = \frac{9}{12} = 0.75\%$. Thus at each compounding, the value is increased by a factor

$$\left(1 + \frac{R}{100k}\right) = \left(1 + \frac{0.75}{100}\right) = 1.0075.$$

During 3 years, there will be $nk = 3 \cdot 12 = 36$ such compoundings. Hence the value will be

$$2000(1.0075)^{36} = 2000(1.3086) = 2617.29 \text{ dollars.}$$

EXERCISES 1

(1–4) Construct the graphs of the following exponential functions by calculating a few points.

1. $y = (\frac{3}{2})^x$ **2.** $y = (\frac{1}{2})^x$

3. $y = (\frac{1}{2})^{-x}$ **4.** $y = 3^{-x}$

(5–10) Evaluate the following using Table A-3-3 in the Appendix.

5. $e^{0.41}$ **6.** $e^{2.75}$ **7.** e^8

8. $e^{-1.05}$ **9.** $e^{-0.68}$ **10.** $e^{-5.2}$

(11–12) If $2000 is invested at 6% compound interest per annum, find the following.

11. The value of the investment after 4 years.

12. The value of the investment after 12 years.

(13–14) If $100 is invested at 8% compound interest per annum find the following.

13. The value of the investment after 5 years.

14. The value of the investment after 10 years.

15. What rate of compound interest doubles the value of an investment in 10 years?

16. What rate of compound interest triples the value of an investment in 10 years?

17. A sum of money is invested for 5 years at 3% interest per annum and then for a further 4 years at $R\%$ interest. Find R if the money exactly doubles in value over the 9 years.

18. The population of the earth at the beginning of 1976 was 4 billion. If the growth rate continues at 2% per year, what will be the population in the year 2026?

19. With the data in Exercise 18, calculate the population in 2076.

20. The population of a certain city at time t (measured in years) is given by the formula

$$P = 50,000e^{0.05t}.$$

Calculate the population: (a) when $t = 10$; (b) when $t = 15$.

21. A certain depressed economic region has a population which is in decline. In 1970, its population was 500,000, and thereafter its population was given by the formula

$$P = 500,000e^{-0.02t}$$

where t is time in years. Find the population in 1980. Assuming this trend continues, find the projected population in the year 2000.

22. In Exercise 20, calculate the percentage growth of the population per year.

23. In Exercise 21, calculate the percentage decline in the population per year. Is it constant or does it depend on t?

24. The profits of a certain company have been increasing by an average of 12% per year between 1975 and 1980. In 1980, they were $5.2 million. Assuming that this growth rate continues, find the profits in 1985.

25. A machine is purchased for $10,000 and depreciates continuously from the date of purchase. Its value after t years is given by the fomula

$$V = 10,000e^{-0.2t}.$$

   a. Find the value of the machine after 8 years.

   b. Find the percentage decline in value each year.

6-2 LOGARITHMS

The inverse of a function $f(x)$ is obtained by solving the equation $y = f(x)$ for x, thus expressing x as a function of y: $x = f^{-1}(y)$. We can consider the possibility of constructing the inverse of the function a^x. In order to do so, we must solve the equation $y = a^x$ for x. Now such an equation cannot be solved in terms of the functions we know so far, so a new name must be invented for the solution. We write the solution in the form $x = \log_a y$, which we call the **logarithm of y with base a**. Thus

$$x = \log_a y \quad \text{if and only if} \quad y = a^x.$$

From the statement $y = a^x$, we see that a must be raised to the power x in order to obtain y. This leads us to an alternative verbal definition (since $x = \log_a y$).

$\log_a y$ is the power to which a must be raised in order to get y.

In these definitions, a can be any positive number except 1.

EXAMPLE 1 Construct the graph of the logarithm function with base 2.

Solution Let us use x as the independent variable and write

$$y = \log_2 x.$$

According to the definition this means the same thing as:

$$x = 2^y.$$

(Note that x and y have been interchanged and $a = 2$.) We can now construct Table 2, in which we give a series of values for y and calculate the corresponding values of x.

TABLE 2

y	-2	-1.5	-1	-0.5	0	0.5	1	1.5	2	3
x	0.25	0.354	0.5	0.707	1	1.414	2	2.828	4	8

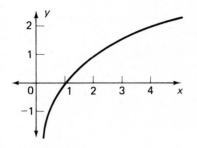

The tabulated values of (x, y) are plotted in Figure 5 and joined by the smooth curve that provides the required graph of $y = \log_2 x$. Note that when we write $y = \log_2 x$, we are regarding x as the independent variable, so the x-axis is drawn horizontally. In spite of this, the various plotted points can be obtained by giving y selected values and calculating the corresponding values of x.

FIGURE 5

As with any other inverse function, the graph of the logarithm function $x = \log_a y$ for a general base a can be obtained from the graph of the exponential function $y = a^x$ simply by flipping the axes. The two graphs are illustrated in Figure 6 for $a > 1$.

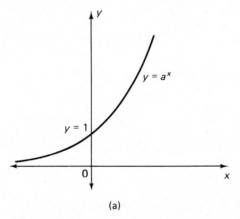

(a)

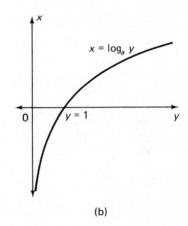

(b)

FIGURE 6

We note that $\log_a y$ is defined only for $y > 0$. In addition, $\log_a y$ is positive for $y > 1$ and negative for $y < 1$, and $\log_a 1 = 0$.

The statement that $x = \log_a y$ means exactly the same thing as the statement that $y = a^x$. For example, the statement $\log_3 9 = 2$ is true because it means the same as the statement $3^2 = 9$. (Here $a = 3$, $y = 9$, and $x = 2$.) Of these two equivalent statements, $x = \log_a y$ is called the **logarithmic form** and $y = a^x$ is called the **exponential form**.

EXAMPLE 2 Write each statement in logarithmic form.

(a) $2^4 = 16$ (b) $(\frac{1}{2})^{-3} = 8$

Write each statement in exponential form to verify that each is correct.

(c) $\log_4 8 = \frac{3}{2}$ (d) $\log_{27} \left(\frac{1}{9}\right) = -\frac{2}{3}$

Solution

(a) We have $2^4 = 16$. Comparing this with the equation $a^x = y$, we see that $a = 2$, $x = 4$, and $y = 16$. The logarithmic form, $x = \log_a y$, is $\log_2 16 = 4$.

(b) Comparing $\left(\frac{1}{2}\right)^{-3} = 8$ with $a^x = y$, we have $a = \frac{1}{2}$, $x = -3$, and $y = 8$. The logarithmic form is $\log_{1/2} 8 = -3$.

(c) Comparing $\log_4 8 = \frac{3}{2}$ with the equation $\log_a y = x$, we have $a = 4$, $y = 8$, and $x = \frac{3}{2}$. The exponential form, $y = a^x$, is $8 = 4^{3/2}$. Since this is clearly a true statement, it follows that the given logarithmic form must also be true.

(d) Here $a = 27$, $y = \frac{1}{9}$, and $x = -\frac{2}{3}$ and the exponential form is $27^{-2/3} = \frac{1}{9}$. Again, this is easily verified.

EXAMPLE 3   Find the values of: (a) $\log_2 16$; (b) $\log_{1/3} 243$.

Solution

(a) Let $x = \log_2 16$. Then from the definition of logarithm, it follows that $16 = 2^x$. But $16 = 2^4$, so $x = 4$. Therefore $\log_2 16 = 4$.

(b) Let $x = \log_{1/3} 243$. Then, from the definition, $243 = \left(\frac{1}{3}\right)^x$. But $243 = 3^5 = \left(\frac{1}{3}\right)^{-5}$. Therefore $x = -5$.

EXAMPLE 4   Evaluate $2^{\log_4 9}$.

Solution

Let $x = \log_4 9$, so that $9 = 4^x$. The quantity we wish to calculate is therefore

$$2^{\log_4 9} = 2^x = (4^{1/2})^x$$
$$= (4^x)^{1/2} = 9^{1/2} = 3.$$

If $y = a^x$, then $x = \log_a y$. Substituting for x in the first equation, we find

$$y = a^{\log_a y}.$$

This equation is often summarized in the following form: *A number y is equal to the base raised to the power of the logarithm of y with respect to that base.*

We can also substitute $y = a^x$ in the second equation. We get

$$x = \log_a (a^x).$$

In the definition of the logarithm, let us take $x = 0$. Then

$$y = a^x = a^0 = 1.$$

Therefore the statement $\log_a y = x$ takes the form

$$\log_a 1 = 0.$$

Thus we see that *the logarithm of 1 with any base is equal to 0.*

Next, let us take $x = 1$. Then
$$y = a^x = a^1 = a.$$
Therefore the statement $\log_a y = x$ becomes

$$\log_a a = 1.$$

So *the logarithm of any positive number with the same base is always equal to 1.* Logarithms have the following four properties.

$$\log_a (uv) = \log_a u + \log_a v \qquad\qquad a^x \cdot a^y = a^{x+y} \qquad (1)$$

$$\log_a \left(\frac{u}{v}\right) = \log_a u - \log_a v \qquad\qquad \frac{a^x}{a^y} = a^{x-y} \qquad (2)$$

$$\log_a \left(\frac{1}{v}\right) = -\log_a v \qquad\qquad a^{-x} = \frac{1}{a^x} \qquad (3)$$

$$\log_a (u^n) = n \log_a u \qquad\qquad (a^x)^n = a^{xn} \qquad (4)$$

(Beside each property, we have also given the related property of exponents.) These properties form the basis for the use of logarithms in performing arithmetic calculations. We shall prove them at the end of this section. Meanwhile, we shall illustrate them with a number of examples.

EXAMPLE 5   (a) Since $8 = 2^3$, it follows that $\log_2 8 = 3$. Since $16 = 2^4$, it follows that $\log_2 16 = 4$. From the Property (1), therefore,

$$\log_2 (8 \times 16) = \log_2 8 + \log_2 16$$

or

$$\log_2 (128) = 3 + 4 = 7.$$

This statement is obviously true since $128 = 2^7$.

(b) We can also calculate $\log_2 (128)$ by making use of Property (4) of logarithms.

$$\log_2 (128) = \log_2 (2^7) = 7 \log_2 2$$

But $\log_a a = 1$ for any $a > 0$, so $\log_2 2 = 1$. Therefore $\log_2 128 = 7$.

(c) Since $81 = \left(\frac{1}{3}\right)^{-4}$, it follows that $\log_{1/3} 81 = -4$. Therefore

$$\log_{1/3} \left(\frac{1}{81}\right) = -\log_{1/3} 81 = -(-4) = 4.$$

This result is clearly correct since $\frac{1}{81} = \left(\frac{1}{3}\right)^4$.

EXAMPLE 6   If $x = \log_2 3$, express the following quantities in terms of x.

(a) $\log_2 \left(\frac{1}{3}\right)$ (b) $\log_2 \left(\frac{2}{3}\right)$ (c) $\log_2 18$ (d) $\log_2 \sqrt{\frac{27}{2}}$

Solution   (a) $\log_2 \left(\frac{1}{3}\right) = -\log_2 3$ (Property 3)

$$= -x$$

(b) $\log_2 \left(\frac{2}{3}\right) = \log_2 2 - \log_2 3$ (Property 2)

$$= 1 - x$$

(Here we used the fact that $\log_a a = 1$ for any $a > 0$.)

(c) $\log_2 (18) = \log_2 (2 \cdot 3^2)$

$$= \log_2 2 + \log_2 3^2 \qquad \text{(Property 1)}$$

$$= 1 + 2 \log_2 3 \qquad \text{(Property 4)}$$

$$= 1 + 2x$$

(d) $\log_2 \sqrt{\frac{27}{2}} = \log_2 (\frac{27}{2})^{1/2}$

$$= \tfrac{1}{2} \log_2 (\tfrac{27}{2}) \qquad \text{(Property 4)}$$

$$= \tfrac{1}{2}[\log_2 27 - \log_2 2] \qquad \text{(Property 2)}$$

$$= \tfrac{1}{2}[\log_2 3^3 - 1]$$

$$= \tfrac{1}{2}[3 \log_2 3 - 1] \qquad \text{(Property 4)}$$

$$= \tfrac{1}{2}(3x - 1)$$

At one time, logarithms were used extensively in carrying out arithmetical calculations involving multiplication, division, and the calculation of powers and roots. With the widespread availability of electronic calculators, such usage has diminished considerably, although in some areas logarithms are still used. (For example, a ship's navigator must still learn how to use logarithm tables and other tables to guard against the possibility of electronics failure.)

The logarithms ordinarily used for this purpose are called **common logarithms** and are obtained by using the number 10 as base (that is, $a = 10$). Thus the common logarithm of a number y is $\log_{10} y$; however, to avoid cumbersome notation, the common logarithm is usually denoted by $\log y$, the base being omitted.* So when the base is not written, it should be understood to be 10.

These statements are thus equivalent:

$$x = \log y \quad \text{and} \quad y = 10^x.$$

The following examples demonstrate the application of Properties 1–4 to common logarithms.

EXAMPLE 7 Let us examine the general relations $y = 10^x$ and $x = \log y$ for certain values of x and y.

(a) $x = 1$: Then $y = 10^1 = 10$, so $\log 10 = 1$.

(b) $x = 2$: Then $y = 10^2 = 100$, so $\log 100 = 2$.

(c) $x = -1$: Then $y = 10^{-1} = 0.1$, so $\log 0.1 = -1$.

(d) To four places, we find from Table A-3-1 that $\log 3 = 0.4771$. This means that $3 = 10^{0.4771}$. Using Property 1 of logarithms stated above, it follows that

$$\log 30 = \log 3 + \log 10 = 1.4771$$

$$\log 300 = \log 3 + \log 100 = 2.4771$$

$$\log (0.3) = \log 3 + \log 0.1 = -1 + 0.4771 = -0.5229.$$

*In some books, the notation $\log y$ is used to mean the natural logarithm of y. (See page 194 in this section.)

(e) Also from Table A-3-1, we find that $\log 2 = 0.3010$. Thus $\log 6 = \log (3 \times 2) = \log 3 + \log 2 = 0.4771 + 0.3010 = 0.7781$ and $\log 4 = \log (2^2) = 2 \log 2 = 0.6020$.

EXAMPLE 8   Given that $\log 2 = 0.3010$ and $\log 3 = 0.4771$ (to four places), evaluate: (a) $\log 5$; (b) $\log 18$; (c) $\log \sqrt{54}$.

Solution

(a) $\log 5 = \log (10 \div 2) = \log 10 - \log 2$

$\qquad = 1 - 0.3010 = 0.6990$

(Note that $\log 2 + \log 3$ is not equal to $\log 5$, but is $\log 6$.)

(b) $\log 18 = \log (2 \times 3^2) = \log 2 + \log 3^2$

$\qquad = \log 2 + 2 \log 3$

$\qquad = 0.3010 + 2(0.4771) = 1.2552$

(c) $\log \sqrt{54} = \frac{1}{2} \log 54$

$\qquad = \frac{1}{2} \log (2 \times 3^3) = \frac{1}{2}[\log 2 + 3 \log 3]$

$\qquad = \frac{1}{2}[0.3010 + 3(0.4771)] = 0.8662$

EXAMPLE 9   Simplify the following expression without using tables or calculators.

$$E = \log 2 + 16 \log \left(\tfrac{16}{15}\right) + 12 \log \left(\tfrac{25}{24}\right) + 7 \log \left(\tfrac{81}{80}\right)$$

Solution

$$E = \log 2 + 16 \log \left(\frac{2^4}{3 \cdot 5}\right) + 12 \log \left(\frac{5^2}{2^3 \cdot 3}\right) + 7 \log \left(\frac{3^4}{2^4 \cdot 5}\right)$$

$$= \log 2 + 16(\log 2^4 - \log 3 - \log 5)$$

$$+ 12(\log 5^2 - \log 2^3 - \log 3) + 7(\log 3^4 - \log 2^4 - \log 5)$$

$$= \log 2 + 16(4 \log 2 - \log 3 - \log 5)$$

$$+ 12(2 \log 5 - 3 \log 2 - \log 3) + 7(4 \log 3 - 4 \log 2 - \log 5)$$

$$= (1 + 64 - 36 - 28) \log 2 + (-16 - 12 + 28) \log 3$$

$$+ (-16 + 24 - 7) \log 5$$

$$= \log 2 + \log 5$$

$$= \log (2 \times 5)$$

$$= \log 10 = 1$$

EXAMPLE 10   Solve the following equation for x.

$$2 \log (2x + 2) = \log \left(1 + \frac{12x}{25}\right) + 2$$

Solution   Using the properties of logarithms and the fact that $\log 100 = 2$, we can write the given equation in the form

$$\log (2x + 2)^2 = \log \left(1 + \frac{12x}{25}\right) + \log 100$$

$$= \log \left[100\left(1 + \frac{12x}{25}\right)\right] = \log (100 + 48x).$$

Therefore
$$(2x + 2)^2 = 100 + 48x.$$

This is a quadratic equation with solutions $x = 12$ and $x = -2$. However, when $x = -2$, the term $\log (2x + 2)$ in the original equation is not defined, so $x = -2$ cannot be a solution. Therefore $x = 12$ is the only solution.

We can also form logarithms with base e. These are called **natural logarithms** (or **Napierian logarithms**). They are denoted by the symbol ln.

$$y = e^x \qquad x = \log_e y = \ln y$$

The following identities are obtained by eliminating either x or y from these two equations.

$$e^{\ln y} = y \qquad \ln (e^x) = x$$

The natural logarithm is important because of certain mathematical properties it has in connection with calculus. This type of logarithm *can* be used to perform arithmetical calculations instead of the common logarithm, but much less conveniently. Its importance arises in other ways, as we shall see later.

The natural logarithm has all of the properties discussed earlier for logarithms with a general base a. In particular:

$$\ln (uv) = \ln u + \ln v$$
$$\ln \left(\frac{u}{v} \right) = \ln u - \ln v$$
$$\ln \left(\frac{1}{v} \right) = -\ln v$$
$$\ln u^n = n \ln u$$
$$\ln e = 1$$
$$\ln 1 = 0.$$

With a suitable pocket calculator, we can find the natural logarithm of any number by pressing the appropriate button. If no calculator is available, a table of natural logarithms is provided in the Appendix (see Table A-3-2); Example 11 illustrates its use.

EXAMPLE 11 Using Table A-3-2 in the Appendix, find the values of:

(a) $\ln 3.4$; (b) $\ln 100$; (c) $\ln 340$; (d) $\ln 0.34$.

Solution (a) From the table, we find directly that $\ln 3.4 = 1.2238$.

(b) At the bottom of the table, we find that $\ln 10 = 2.3026$. Therefore
$$\ln 100 = \ln 10^2 = 2 \ln 10 = 2(2.3026) = 4.6052.$$

(c) $\ln 340 = \ln (3.4 \times 100)$
$$= \ln 3.4 + \ln 100$$
$$= 1.2238 + 4.6052 = 5.8290$$

Observe that Table A-3-2 provides the natural logarithms only of numbers lying between 1 and 10. For numbers lying outside this range, an appropriate power of 10 has to be extracted (in this example, 100).

(d)
$$\ln (0.34) = \ln (3.4 \times 10^{-1})$$
$$= \ln 3.4 + \ln (10^{-1})$$
$$= \ln 3.4 - \ln 10$$
$$= 1.2238 - 2.3026 = -1.0788$$

PROOF OF BASIC PROPERTIES

1. Let $x = \log_a u$ and $y = \log_a v$. Then from the definition of logarithm,

$$u = a^x \quad \text{and} \quad v = a^y.$$

It follows, therefore, that

$$uv = (a^x)(a^y) = a^{x+y}$$

after using one of the fundamental properties of exponents. Consequently, from the definition of logarithm, it follows that $x + y$ must be the logarithm of uv with base a:

$$x + y = \log_a (uv).$$

In other words, substituting for x and y we have the required formula.

$$\log_a (uv) = \log_a u + \log_a v$$

2. The second result may be obtained by considering u/v.

$$\frac{u}{v} = \frac{a^x}{a^y} = a^x a^{-y} = a^{x-y}$$

Thus $x - y = \log_a (u/v)$, or equivalently, $\log_a (u/v) = \log_a u - \log_a v$.

3. We use Property (2) and let $u = 1$. When $u = 1$, $\log_a u = 0$, and we get

$$\log_a \left(\frac{1}{v}\right) = -\log_a v.$$

4. Fourth, let $y = \log_a v$, so that $v = a^y$. Then $v^n = (a^y)^n = a^{yn}$. Thus $yn = \log_a (v^n)$, or

$$\log_a v^n = n \log_a v.$$

EXERCISES 2

(1–6) Verify the following statements and rewrite them in logarithmic form with an appropriate base.

1. $(27)^{-4/3} = \frac{1}{81}$

2. $(16)^{3/4} = 8$

3. $(125)^{2/3} = 25$

4. $8^{-5/3} = \frac{1}{32}$

5. $\left(\frac{8}{27}\right)^{-1/3} = \frac{3}{2}$

6. $\left(\frac{625}{16}\right)^{-3/4} = \frac{8}{125}$

(7–10) Write the following equations in exponential form and hence verify them.

7. $\log_3 27 = 3$

8. $\log_{1/9} \left(\frac{1}{243}\right) = \frac{5}{2}$

9. $\log_4 \left(\frac{1}{2}\right) = -\frac{1}{2}$

10. $\log_2 \left(\frac{1}{4}\right) = -2$

(11–22) Find the values of the following expressions by using the definition of logarithm.

11. $\log_2 512$

12. $\log_{27} 243$

13. $\log_{\sqrt{2}} 16$

14. $\log_8 128$

15. $\log_2 0.125$

16. $\log_a 32 \div \log_a 4$

17. $10^{\log 100}$

18. $10^{\log 2}$

19. $\log_4 (2^p)$

20. $\log_2 (4^p)$

21. $2^{\log_{1/2} 3}$

22. $3^{\log_9 2}$

(23–28) Given that $\log 5 = 0.6990$ and $\log 9 = 0.9542$, evaluate the following expressions without using tables or calculators.

23. $\log 2$

24. $\log 3$

25. $\log 12$

26. $\log 75$

27. $\log 30$

28. $\log \sqrt{60}$

(29–32) Solve the following equations for x without using tables or calculators.

29. $\log (10x + 5) - \log (x - 4) = \log 2$

30. $\log_3 3 + \log_3 (x + 1) - \log_3 (2x - 7) = 4$

31. $\log x = \log 3 + 2 \log 2 - \frac{3}{4} \log 16$

32. $\log (4x - 3) = \log (x + 1) + \log 3$

(33–34) Prove the following without using tables or calculators.

33. $7 \log \left(\frac{16}{15}\right) + 5 \log \left(\frac{25}{24}\right) + 3 \log \left(\frac{81}{80}\right) = \log 2$

34. $3 \log \left(\frac{36}{25}\right) + \log \left(\frac{6}{27}\right)^3 - 2 \log \left(\frac{16}{125}\right) = \log 2$

(35–40) Evaluate the following using Table A-3-2 in the Appendix.

35. $\ln 3.41$

36. $\ln 2.68$

37. $\ln 84.2$

38. $\ln 593$

39. $\ln 0.341$

40. $\ln 0.00917$

6-3 APPLICATIONS OF LOGARITHMS

One of the most important applications of logarithms is to solve certain types of equations in which the unknown variable appears as an exponent. Consider the following examples.

EXAMPLE 1   In 1970, the population of a certain city was 2 million and was increasing at the rate of 5% each year. When will the population pass the 5 million mark, assuming this growth rate continues.

Solution   At a rate of increase of 5%, the population is multiplied by a factor 1.05 each year. After n years, starting from 1970, the population level is therefore

$$2(1.05)^n \text{ million.}$$

We require the value of n for which this level is 5 million, so we have

$$2(1.05)^n = 5 \quad \text{or} \quad (1.05)^n = 2.5.$$

Observe that in this equation, the unknown quantity n appears as an exponent. We can solve it by taking logarithms of both sides. It does not matter which base we use for the logarithms, but common logarithms are usually the most convenient. We obtain

$$\log (1.05)^n = \log 2.5$$

or, using Property 4 of logarithms,

$$n \log 1.05 = \log 2.5$$

Therefore

$$n = \frac{\log 2.5}{\log 1.05} = \frac{0.3979}{0.0212} \qquad \text{(from Table A-3-1 in the Appendix)}$$

$$= 18.8$$

It therefore takes 18.8 years for the population to climb to 5 million. This level will be reached during 1988.

EXAMPLE 2   The sum of \$100 is invested at 6% compound interest per annum. How long does it take the investment to increase in value to \$150?

Solution   At 6% interest per annum, the investment grows by a factor of 1.06 each year. Therefore, after n years, the value is $100(1.06)^n$. Setting this equal to 150, we obtain the following equation for n:

$$100(1.06)^n = 150 \quad \text{or} \quad (1.06)^n = 1.5.$$

We take logarithms of both sides and simplify.

$$\log (1.06)^n = n \log (1.06) = \log (1.5)$$

$$n = \frac{\log (1.5)}{\log (1.06)}$$

$$= \frac{0.1761}{0.0253} = 6.96$$

Thus it takes almost 7 years for the investment to increase in value to \$150.

It will be seen that these two examples lead to an equation of the type

$$a^x = b$$

where a and b are two given positive constants and x is the unknown variable. Such an equation can always be solved by taking logarithms of both sides.

$$\log (a^x) = x \log a = \log b$$

and so

$$x = \frac{\log b}{\log a}.$$

There is no difference in principle here between problems involving growing exponential functions ($a > 1$) and those involving decaying exponentials ($a < 1$). The following example involves a decaying exponential function.

EXAMPLE 3   Shortly after consuming a substantial dose of whiskey, the alcohol level in an individual's blood rises to a level of 0.3 milligrams per milliliter (mg/ml). Thereafter, this level decreases according to the formula $(0.3)(0.5)^t$, where t is the time measured in hours from the time at which the peak level is reached.

How long is it before the person can legally drive his automobile? (In his locality, the legal limit is 0.08 mg/ml of blood alcohol.)

Solution   We wish to find the value of t at which

$$(0.3)(0.5)^t = 0.08.$$

That is,

$$(0.5)^t = \frac{0.08}{0.3} = 0.267.$$

Taking logarithms, we obtain

$$\log (0.5)^t = t \log (0.5) = \log (0.267)$$

and so,

$$t = \frac{\log (0.267)}{\log (0.5)}$$

$$= \frac{(-0.5735)}{(-0.3010)} \qquad \text{(from Table A-3-1 in the Appendix)}$$

$$= 1.91$$

It therefore takes 1.91 hours before the individual is legally fit to drive.

Another application is to the **present value** of a future revenue or a future liability. Let us suppose that by pursuing a certain business activity, an individual expects to receive a certain sum of money, P, at a time n years in the future. This future revenue P is less valuable than would be a revenue of the same amount received at the present time since, if the person received P now, it could be invested at interest, and it would be worth more than P in n years time. We are interested in finding the sum Q which, if received at the present time and invested for n years, would be worth the same as the future revenue P that the person will receive.

Let us suppose that the interest rate that could be obtained on such an investment is equal to $R\%$. Then, after n years, the sum Q would have increased to $Q(1 + i)^n$, where $i = R/100$. Setting this equal to P, we obtain the equation

$$Q(1 + i)^n = P$$

or

$$Q = \frac{P}{(1 + i)^n} = P(1 + i)^{-n}.$$

We call Q the **present value** of the future revenue P.

In calculating present value, it is necessary to make some assumption about the rate of interest R that would be obtained over the n years. In such circumstances, R is called the **discount rate** and we say that the future revenue P is **discounted back** to the present time.

EXAMPLE 4   A real estate developer owns a piece of property that could be sold right away for \$100,000. Alternatively, the property could be held for five years. During this time, the developer would spend \$100,000 on developing it; it would then sell for $300,000. Assume that the development cost would be spent in a lump sum at the end of three years and must be borrowed from a bank at 12% interest per annum. If the discount rate is assumed to be 10%, calculate the present value of this second alternative and hence decide which of these two alternatives represents the developer's best strategy.

Solution   Consider first the money which must be borrowed in order to develop the property. Interest must be paid at 12% on this over a period of 2 years, so when the property is sold, this loan has increased to

$$\$100,000(1.12)^2 = \$125,440.$$

The net proceeds from the sale, after paying off this loan, will be

$$\$300,000 - \$125,440 = \$174,560.$$

This revenue is received 5 years in the future. Discounting back at a rate of 10%, we obtain a present value of

$$\$174,560(1.1)^{-5} = \$108,400.$$

Since the present value of an immediate sale is only $100,000, it is somewhat better if the developer holds the property and sells in 5 years.

Observe the way in which decisions can be made between alternative business strategies by comparing their present values.

Change of Base

Any exponential function can be written in terms of a natural exponential function. Let $y = a^x$. Then, since we can write $a = e^{\ln a}$, it follows that

$$y = (e^{\ln a})^x = e^{(\ln a)x}.$$

Thus any exponential function $y = a^x$ can be written in the equivalent form $y = e^{kx}$, where $k = \ln a$.

EXAMPLE 5   In Example 3, the alcohol level in a person's blood at a time t was given by the formula $(0.3)(0.5)^t$ mg/ml. We can write this in terms of e,

$$(0.5)^t = e^{kt}$$

where

$$k = \ln(0.5) = \ln 5 - \ln 10$$
$$= 1.6094 - 2.3026 = -0.69$$

to two decimal places. Therefore the alcohol level after t hours is $(0.3)e^{-(0.69)t}$.

It is the usual practice to write any growing exponential function a^x in the form e^{kx}, where $k = \ln a$. A decaying exponential function, defined by a^x with $a < 1$, would normally be written as e^{-kx}, where k is a positive constant given by $k = -\ln a$. The constant k is known as the **specific growth rate** for the function e^{kx} and as the **specific decay rate** for the decaying exponential e^{-kx}.

EXAMPLE 6   The population of a certain developing nation is given in millions by the formula

$$P = 15e^{0.02t}$$

where t is the time in years measured from 1960. When will the population reach 25 million, assuming this formula continues to hold?

Solution   Setting $P = 25$, we obtain the equation

$$15e^{0.02t} = 25$$

or

$$e^{0.02t} = \tfrac{25}{15} = 1.667.$$

Again, we have an equation in which the unknown variable appears in the exponent, and we can solve for t by taking the logarithm of both sides. However, because the exponential has base e, it is easiest to take natural logarithms, since $e^{0.02t} = 1.667$ means the same as $0.02t = \ln 1.667$. Therefore

$$t = (\ln 1.667)/0.02 = 0.5108/0.02 = 25.5.$$

It therefore takes 25.5 years for the population to reach 25 million, which it does therefore midway through 1985.

It is possible to express logarithms with respect to one base in terms of logarithms with respect to any other base. This is done by means of the **base-change formula**, which says that

$$\log_b y = (\log_a y)(\log_b a).$$

Before proving this formula, let us illustrate it by examining some special cases. First of all, let $b = 10$ so that $\log_b y = \log y$ and $\log_b a = \log a$. Then the base-change formula can be written

$$(\log_a y)(\log a) = \log y$$

or

$$\log_a y = \frac{\log y}{\log a}.$$

So *the logarithm of y with base a is equal to the common logarithm of y divided by the common logarithm of a.*

EXAMPLE 7   If $a = 2$, we have the following.

$$\log_2 y = \frac{\log y}{\log 2} = \frac{\log y}{0.3010}$$

For example,

$$\log_2 3 = \frac{(\log 3)}{(\log 2)} = \frac{(0.4771)}{(0.3010)} = 1.5850.$$

Secondly, let $y = b$ in the base-change formula. Then the left side becomes $\log_b b$, which equals 1. Therefore we obtain the following results.

$$(\log_a b)(\log_b a) = 1$$

$$\log_b a = \frac{1}{\log_a b}.$$

EXAMPLE 8   If $b = 10$, we have

$$\log_a 10 = \frac{1}{\log a}.$$

For example,

$$\log_2 10 = \frac{1}{\log 2} = \frac{1}{0.3010} = 3.3219$$

and

$$\log_3 10 = \frac{1}{\log 3} = \frac{1}{0.4771} = 2.0959.$$

$$\ln 10 = \log_e 10 = \frac{1}{\log e}$$

To 4 decimal places, the values of these two logarithms are

$$\log e = \log (2.7183) = 0.4343 \quad \text{and} \quad \ln 10 = 2.3026.$$

The two numbers are reciprocals of one another.

The base-change formula allows us to relate a logarithm with a general base a to a common logarithm. In particular, taking $a = e$, we can express the natural logarithm in terms of the common logarithm:

$$\log_e y = \frac{\log y}{\log e} = \frac{\log y}{0.4343}.$$

Thus

$$\ln y = 2.3026 \log y.$$

Thus, in order to find the natural logarithm of y, we can determine the common logarithm of y and multiply it by 2.3026. However, this method of finding the natural logarithm of a number is not very convenient when compared to the use of a separate table. The relationship between the two logarithms is of some theoretical importance, however.

EXAMPLE 9   From the Table A-3-1, we find that $\log 2 = 0.3010$, so $\log 0.2 = 0.3010 - 1 = -0.6990$. The natural logarithms of 2 and 0.2 are therefore

$$\ln 2 = 2.3026 \log 2 = (2.3026)(0.3010) = 0.6931$$

and

$$\ln 0.2 = 2.3026 \log 0.2 = (2.3026)(-0.6990) = -1.6095.$$

Let us now turn to the matter of proving the base-change formula. We have the pair of equivalent statements

$$y = a^x \quad \text{and} \quad x = \log_a y.$$

Similarly, if $a = b^c$, then $c = \log_b a$. But then

$$y = a^x = (b^c)^x = b^{cx}$$

and from this it follows that $cx = \log_b y$. Therefore, substituting for c and x, we obtain the required formula.

$$\log_b y = cx = (\log_b a)(\log_a y)$$

EXERCISES 3

(1–10) Solve the following equations for x.

1. $10^x = 25$
2. $2^x = 25$
3. $3^x 2^{3x} = 4$
4. $3^x 2^{1-x} = 10$
5. $3^x = 2^{2-x}$
6. $(3^x)^2 = 2\sqrt{2^x}$
7. $(2^x)^x = 25$
8. $(2^x)^x = 3^x$
9. $a^x = cb^x$
10. $(a^x)^2 = b^{x+1}$

11. The population of the earth in 1976 was 4 billion and was growing at 2% per year. If this rate of growth continues, when will the population reach 10 billion?

12. The population of China in 1970 was 750 million and was growing at 4% per year. When would this population reach 2 billion, assuming that the same growth rate continued?

13. Using the data of Exercises 11 and 12, calculate when the population of China will be equal to half the population of the earth.

14. The profits of a company have been increasing at an average of 12% per year between 1975 and 1980 and in 1980 they reached the level of $5.2 million. Assuming this rate of growth continues, how long will it be before they reach $8 million per year?

15. Two competing newspapers have circulations of 1 million and 2 million, respectively. If the first is increasing its circulation by 2% each month, while the circulation of the second is declining by 1% each month, calculate how long it will be before the two have equal circulations.

(16–17) Suppose $1000 is invested at 8% interest compounded annually.

16. How long does it take to increase to $1500?

17. How long does it take to increase to $3000?

18. The following rule of thumb is often employed by people in finance: If the rate of interest is R percent per annum, then the number of years, n, for an investment to double is given by dividing R into 70 (that is, $n = 70/R$). Calculate n *exactly* for the following values of R: 4, 8, 12, 16, and 20. Compare your answers to those obtained from the formula $n = 70/R$ and so assess the accuracy of the rule of thumb.

19. Calculate the rate of semiannual interest that is equivalent to an annual interest rate of 8%.

20. Calculate the rate of monthly interest that is equivalent to an annual interest rate of 8%.

21. An individual expects to receive $1,000 every year for the next 3 years, the first payment to arrive in 1 year's time. Calculate the present value of this income, assuming a discount rate of 8% per annum.

22. An individual owes a debt that is to be paid off in 3 equal annual installments of $5,000, the first payment to be made in 1 year's time. If, instead, the person decides to pay the debt off in a lump sum right away, calculate how much must be paid, assuming a discount rate of 8% per annum.

(23–26) Express the following functions in the form $y = ae^{kt}$.

23. $y = 2^t$

24. $y = (1000)2^{t/3}$

25. $y = 5(1.04)^t$

26. $y = 6 \times 10^8(1.05)^t$

27. The earth's population is 4 billion at present and is increasing by 2% each year. Express the population y at a time t years from now in the form $y = ae^{kt}$.

28. A company purchases a machine for $10,000. Each year the value of the machine decreases by 20%. Express the value in the form be^{kt}, where b and k are constants and the time $t = 0$ corresponds to the date of purchase.

29. Between January 1975 and January 1980, the consumer price index I rose from 121 to 196.

   a. Calculate the average percentage increase per annum during this period.

   b. Express I in the form be^{kt}, with $t = 0$ corresponding to January, 1975.

   c. Assuming this growth rate continues, determine when I will reach 250.

30. A population is growing according to the formula
$$P = 5 \times 10^6 e^{0.06t}$$
where t is in years. Calculate the percentage growth per annum. How long does it take the population to increase by 50%?

31. A population has a size given by formula
$$P = P_0 e^{kt}.$$
Find an expression for the percentage of growth per unit of time and for the length of time necessary for the population to double in size and to triple in size.

6-4 NATURAL EXPONENTIALS AND LOGARITHMS

Suppose a sum of money, say $100, is invested at a rate of interest of 8% compounded annually. Each year the value of the investment increases by a factor of 1.08, so that after x years, the value of the investment is equal to $100(1.08)^x$. For example, after 4 years, the investment is worth $100(1.08)^4 = \$136.05$.

Now let us suppose instead that the investment of $100 is compounded semiannually and that the nominal rate of interest is still 8% per annum. This means that the rate of interest per half-year is 4%. Then each half-year, the value of the investment increases by a factor of 1.04. In a period of x years, there are $2x$ such semiannual compoundings; thus after x years the investment is worth $100(1.04)^{2x}$. For example, after 4 years the value is $100(1.04)^8 = \$136.86$.

Next consider the possibility that the investment is compounded every 3 months, again with the nominal annual interest rate of 8%. Then the rate of interest per quarter is equal to $\frac{8}{4}$ or 2%. Each quarter the value increases by a factor of 1.02 and so each year it increases by a factor $(1.02)^4$. In a period of x years, the value increases to $100(1.02)^{4x}$. For example, after 4 years the value is $100(1.02)^{16} = 137.28$.

We can continue in this same manner: Let us divide the year into n equal periods and compound the interest at the end of each of these periods at a nominal annual interest rate of 8%. This means that the interest rate for each period is $(8/n)$ percent and the investment increases in value by a factor of $1 + 0.08/n$ for each of these small periods. During x years there are nx such compounding periods, so the value after x years is given by the formula $100(1 + 0.08/n)^{nx}$ dollars. For example, after 4 years the value is

$$100(1 + 0.08/n)^{4n} \text{ dollars.} \tag{1}$$

Table 3 shows these values for several different values of n. We first give $n = 1, 2,$ and 4 and then give $n = 12, 52,$ and 365, which correspond, respectively, to monthly compounding, weekly compounding and daily compounding.

TABLE 3

n	Value After 4 Years
1	$136.05
2	$136.86
4	$137.28
12	$137.57
52	$137.68
365	$137.71
1000	$137.71

Finally, we give $n = 1000$ for comparison. It can be seen that as the frequency of compounding is increased, the value of the investment also increases; however it does not increase indefinitely, but rather approaches closer and closer to a certain value. To the nearest cent, there is no difference between compounding 365 times a year and 1000 times a year: the value of the investment after 4 years would still be $137.71.

Because of this, we can envisage the possibility of what is called **continuous compounding**. By this we mean that the number n is allowed to become arbitrarily large; we say that n is allowed *to approach infinity* and we write this as $n \rightarrow \infty$. This corresponds to compounding the interest infinitely often during the year. With our $100 invested at the nominal rate of 8% per annum, continuous compounding gives a value of $137.71 after 4 years, the same value as daily compounding.

Let us write $n = (0.08)p$ in Expression (1), which is the value of the investment after 4 years. Then $4n = (0.32)p$ and the value after 4 years takes the form

$$100\left(1 + \frac{0.08}{n}\right)^{4n} = 100\left(1 + \frac{1}{p}\right)^{0.32p} = 100\left[\left(1 + \frac{1}{p}\right)^{p}\right]^{0.32}.$$

The reason for writing it in this form is that as $n \longrightarrow \infty$, then $p = n/(0.08)$ also becomes arbitrarily large. The quantity inside the square bracket, $(1 + 1/p)^p$, gets closer and closer to a certain value as $p \longrightarrow \infty$. This can be seen from Table 4, in which the values of $(1 + 1/p)^p$ are given for a series of increas-

TABLE 4

p	$\left(1 + \dfrac{1}{p}\right)^{p}$
1	2
2	2.25
10	2.594
100	2.705
1000	2.717
10,000	2.718

ingly large values of p. The eventual value to which $(1 + 1/p)^p$ approaches as p increases indefinitely is the number that we previously denoted by the letter e. (Recall that e is an irrational number and is equal to 2.71828 to 5 decimal places.)

Returning to the above example of continuous compounding, we see that as $p \longrightarrow \infty$, the value of the investment after 4 years gets closer and closer to $100e^{0.32}$ dollars.

Let us examine continuous compounding in the general case when a sum P is invested at an annual rate of interest of $R\%$. Each year the value increases by a factor $1 + i$, where i denotes $R/100$. After x years, the value is equal to $P(1 + i)^x$.

Now let the interest be compounded n times a year at the nominal annual interest rate of R percent. The rate of interest at each compounding is then (R/n) percent. At each compounding, the value increases by a factor $1 + i/n$. After x years, during which there will have been nx such compoundings, the value will be $P(1 + i/n)^{nx}$.

We introduce $p = n/i$, or $n = ip$. Then $nx = pix$ and the value after x years is

$$P\left(1 + \frac{1}{p}\right)^{pix} = P\left[\left(1 + \frac{1}{p}\right)^{p}\right]^{ix}.$$

For continuous compounding, we must let $n \longrightarrow \infty$; this means that $p = n/i$ also becomes infinitely large. The quantity inside the square bracket here becomes closer and closer to e as $p \longrightarrow \infty$, so the value of the investment becomes Pe^{ix}.

We have thus shown that if a sum P is compounded continuously at a nominal annual rate of interest of R percent, its value after x years is Pe^{ix}, where $i = R/100$. We see, therefore, that the natural exponential function arises in a very basic way in problems concerning continuous compounding.

EXAMPLE 1   An investment of $250 is compounded continuously at a nominal annual rate of interest of $7\frac{1}{2}\%$. What will be the value of the investment after 6 years?

Solution   We must use the formula Pe^{ix} for the value after x years. In this example, $P = 250$, $x = 6$, and $i = 7.5/100 = 0.075$. Therefore $ix = (0.075)(6) = 0.45$ and the value is

$$Pe^{ix} = 250e^{0.45} \text{ dollars.}$$

The value of $e^{0.45}$ can be found in Table A-3-3 in the Appendix, and we get

$$250e^{0.45} = 250(1.5683) = 392.08.$$

Thus the value of the investment after 6 years is $392.08.

EXAMPLE 2   What nominal rate of interest, when compounded continuously, gives the same growth over a whole year as a 10% annual rate of interest?

Solution   A sum P invested at a nominal rate of interest R percent compounded continuously has a value Pe^i after 1 year, with $i = R/100$. (Take $x = 1$ in the formula for continuous compounding.) If invested at 10% per annum, it would increase by a factor of 1.1 during each year. Therefore we must let

$$Pe^i = (1.1)P \quad \text{or} \quad e^i = 1.1.$$

If we take natural logarithms of both sides, we get

$$\ln (e^i) = \ln (1.1).$$

But $\ln (e^x) = x$ for any real number x, so

$$i = \ln (1.1) = 0.0953.$$

Therefore $R = 100i = 9.53$.

So 10% interest compounded annually is equivalent to the annual growth provided by a 9.53% nominal rate of interest compounded continuously.

EXAMPLE 3   On its savings accounts, the Piggy Bank of New York gives a nominal annual interest rate of 6%, compounded daily. The bank wishes to calculate an effective annual rate of interest to use in its advertisements.

Solution   We saw earlier that daily compounding amounts to the same thing as continuous compounding, to the nearest cent on a hundred dollars. Thus we use the continuous compounding formula. Here $R = 6$ and $i = \frac{6}{100} = 0.06$. In one year, any investment increases by a factor $e^i = e^{0.06} = 1.0618$. This is equivalent to an annual interest of 6.18%, so the bank should advertise its effective annual rate as 6.18%.

Earlier, when discussing the growth of populations, we mentioned that an exponential growth function can be used for populations growing without restraint from their environments. However when the habitat imposes limitations on growth, exponential growth does not continue indefinitely, and eventually the population size levels off. The function that is most commonly used to model a restricted growth of this kind is called a **logistic model**. It is based on the following equation for the population size.

$$y = \frac{y_m}{1 + Ce^{-kt}} \tag{2}$$

Here y is the population size at time t and y_m, C, and k are three positive constants.

A typical graph of y against t for this logistic function is shown in Figure 7. We note that when t becomes very large, e^{-kt} becomes very small, so the denominator in Equation (2) becomes closer and closer to 1. Therefore y itself gets closer and closer to y_m as t gets very large. This is apparent from the graph in Figure 7, which levels off and approaches the horizontal line $y = y_m$ as t becomes large.

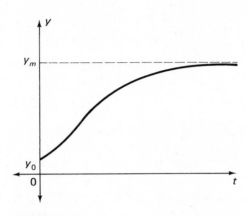

FIGURE 7

When $t = 0$, the value of y is denoted by y_0. Substituting $t = 0$ in Equation (2), we find that

$$y_0 = \frac{y_m}{1 + Ce^{-k(0)}} = \frac{y_m}{1 + C}$$

since $e^0 = 1$. It follows, therefore, that

$$1 + C = \frac{y_m}{y_0}$$

and so

$$C = \frac{y_m}{y_0} - 1 = \frac{y_m - y_0}{y_0}.$$

If the initial value y_0 of y is much smaller than the eventual value y_m, then the population size shows a period of growth for small values of t that is approximately exponential. Eventually, however, the growth slows down and finally levels off, approaching y_m as t becomes very large. This final level y_m represents the maximum population size that can be supported by the given environment.

EXAMPLE 4   A certain population grows according to the logistic equation, with constants $y_m = 275$ million, $C = 54$, and $k = (\ln 12)/100$. The variable t is measured in years. What are the population sizes when $t = 0$, 100, and 200?

Solution
When $t = 0$, the size is

$$y_0 = \frac{y_m}{1 + C} = \frac{275}{1 + 54} = 5 \quad \text{(million)}.$$

We substitute $t = 100$ into Equation (2).

$$y = \frac{y_m}{1 + Ce^{-k(100)}}$$

Now $100k = \ln 12$, so

$$e^{-100k} = e^{-\ln 12} = e^{\ln (1/12)} = \tfrac{1}{12}.$$

Therefore,

$$y = \frac{275}{1 + 54(\tfrac{1}{12})} = \frac{275}{1 + (\tfrac{9}{2})} = 50 \quad \text{(million)}.$$

When $t = 200$,

$$y = \frac{y_m}{1 + Ce^{-k(200)}} = \frac{y_m}{1 + C(e^{-100k})^2}$$

$$= \frac{275}{1 + 54(\tfrac{1}{12})^2} = \frac{275}{1 + (\tfrac{3}{8})} = 200 \quad \text{(million)}.$$

(This example provides an approximate application of the logistic equation to the population of the United States in the years 1777 ($t = 0$) to 1977 ($t = 200$). For this example, the eventual population size is 275 million.

The logistic equation is used in many situations other than the growth of populations. The essential qualitative features of the logistic function are that for small values of t, it resembles an exponential function, while for large values of t, it levels off and approaches closer and closer to a certain limiting value. These features occur in a number of phenomena and account for the widespread use of this function.

An example is the spread of information through a population. For example, the information may be a piece of news, a rumor, or knowledge about some new product that has recently come on the market. If p represents the proportion of the population that is aware of the information, then for small values of t, p is small and grows typically in an exponential manner. However p cannot exceed 1, and as t becomes large, p approaches closer and closer to this value as the information spreads through the whole population. Using the logistic equation, we would model p by means of the expression

$$p = \frac{1}{1 + Ce^{-kt}}.$$

EXAMPLE 5
At $t = 0$, 10% of all stockbrokers have heard about the impending financial collapse of a large airline. Two hours later, 25% have heard about it. How long will it be before 75% have heard about it?

Solution
If $t = 0$, we find that

$$p = \frac{1}{1 + Ce^{-k(0)}} = \frac{1}{1 + C} = 0.1.$$

Therefore $1 + C = 10$, or $C = 9$. Next, when $t = 2$, we have

$$p = \frac{1}{1 + Ce^{-k(2)}} = \frac{1}{1 + 9e^{-2k}} = 0.25.$$

Therefore

$$1 + 9e^{-2k} = 4$$
$$9e^{-2k} = 3$$
$$e^{-2k} = \tfrac{1}{3}.$$

Taking natural logarithms of both sides, we find that

$$-2k = \ln\left(\tfrac{1}{3}\right) = -\ln 3$$

and so

$$k = \tfrac{1}{2}\ln 3.$$

Having found the values of k and C, we know the precise form of p as a function of t. We wish to calculate the value of t at which $p = 0.75$.

$$p = \frac{1}{1 + 9e^{-kt}} = 0.75 = \frac{3}{4}$$
$$1 + 9e^{-kt} = \tfrac{4}{3}$$
$$9e^{-kt} = \tfrac{1}{3}$$
$$e^{-kt} = \tfrac{1}{27}$$

Again, taking natural logarithms of both sides, we get

$$-kt = \ln\left(\tfrac{1}{27}\right) = -\ln 27$$

and so

$$t = \frac{\ln 27}{k} = \frac{\ln 27}{\tfrac{1}{2}\ln 3}$$
$$= \frac{2\ln(3)^3}{\ln 3} = \frac{6\ln 3}{\ln 3} = 6.$$

Thus it takes 6 hours before 75% of stockbrokers have heard about the collapse of the airline.

EXERCISES 4

1. An investment is compounded continuously at a nominal rate of 8% per annum ($i = 0.08$). How long does it take the investment to double in value?

2. An investment of $100 is compounded continuously for 4 years, increasing in value to $150. Calculate the nominal rate of interest.

3. An investment is compounded continuously for 2 years at a nominal rate R percent and for a further 4 years at the nominal rate $2R$ percent. Find R if the value exactly doubles.

4. An investment of $100 is compounded continuously for 2 years at a nominal rate of interest of 9% and then for a further 5 years at a nominal rate of interest of 11%. Calculate the value of the investment after the 7 year period.

5. If a bank compounds interest daily with a nominal annual rate of $4\tfrac{1}{2}$%, what is the "effective annual rate of interest" that it can use in its advertisements?

6. Which is better for the investor, continuous compounding with a nominal annual rate of 8% or quarterly compounding with a nominal annual rate of 8.2%?

7. Calculate the nominal rate of interest that doubles an investment in 10 years when compounded continuously.

8. A new product was introduced onto the market at $t = 0$, and thereafter its monthly sales grew according to the formula

$$S = 4000(1 - e^{-kt})^3.$$

If $S = 2000$ when $t = 10$ (that is, after 10 months), find the value of k.

9. In a competitive market, the volume of sales depends on the amount spent on advertising the product in question. If x dollars are spent per month advertising a particular product, it is found that for a particular product the volume of sales S per month (in dollars) is given by the formula

$$S = 10{,}000(1 - e^{-0.001x}).$$

Find the volume of sales when $x = 500$ and $x = 1000$. If x is decreased from 500 to 100 dollars per month, what is the resulting percentage decrease in sales?

10. An individual's efficiency in performing a routine task improves with practice. Let t be the time spent learning the task and y a measure of the individual's output. (For example, y might be the number of times the task can be performed per hour.) Then one function often used to relate y to t is

$$y = A(1 - e^{-kt})$$

where A and k are constants. (The graph of such a relation between y and t is called a **learning curve**). After one hour of practice, a person on an assembly line can tighten 10 nuts in 5 minutes. After 2 hours, the person can tighten 15 nuts in 5 minutes. Find the constants A and k. How many nuts can the person tighten after 4 hours of practice?

11. A population grows according to the logistic model, with constants $y_m = (\frac{124}{3})$ $\times 10^7$, $C = \frac{245}{3}$, and $k = \ln (\frac{35}{4})$. Find the population sizes when $t = 0, 1$, and 2.

12. The weight of a culture of bacteria is given by

$$y = \frac{2}{1 + 3(2^{-t})}$$

where t is measured in hours. What are the weights when $t = 0, 1, 2$, and 4?

13. A new improved strain of rice is developed. After t years, the proportion of rice farmers who have switched to the new strain is found to be given by a logistic model

$$p = [1 + Ce^{-kt}]^{-1}.$$

At $t = 0$, 2% of farmers are using the new strain. Four years later, 50% are doing so. Evaluate C and k and calculate how many years it is before 90% have switched to the new strain.

*14. Another function sometimes used to describe restricted growth of a population is the *Gompertz function*

$$y = pe^{-ce^{-kt}}$$

where p, c, and k are constants. Show that at $t = 0$, $y = pe^{-c}$, and that as $t \to \infty$, y gets closer and closer to the value p.

REVIEW EXERCISES FOR CHAPTER 6

1. State whether each of the following is true or false. Replace each false statement by a corresponding true statement.

   a. The common logarithm of any base is always equal to 1.

   b. Since $(-2)^2 = 4$, we can say that $\log_{-2} 4 = 2$.

   c. $(\log_2 3)(\log_3 4) = 2$

   d. $\ln (78) = \ln (7.8) + 1$

   e. The function a^x represents exponential growth if $a > 1$ and exponential decay if $0 < a < 1$.

   f. The function e^{kx} represents exponential growth if $k > 0$ and exponential decay if $k < 0$.

   g. $\log_a (x + y) = \log_a x + \log_a y$.

   h. If $\ln x > 1$, then x must be greater than 10.

   i. $\ln 10 = (\log e)^{-1}$

   j. $\ln (1 + 2 + 3) = \ln 1 + \ln 2 + \ln 3$

   k. Any population with restricted growth must be given by a logistic equation.

(2–3) Evaluate each expression.

2. $\log_{\sqrt{27}} 81$ 3. $\log_{36} (1/\sqrt{6})$

(4–6) If $\log_{12} 2 = x$, express the following in terms of x.

4. $\log_{12} 3$ 5. $\log_{12} \sqrt{108}$ 6. $\log_{27} 12$

7. Solve for x: $\log_3 (x + 2) + \log_3 (2x + 7) = 3$.

8. Find the value of n for which $(0.081)^n = 0.24$.

(9–10) Solve the following equations for x.

9. $2^{x+1} = 3^{2-2x}$ 10. $(2^x)^x = 4^{1-x}$

11. If \$500 is invested at 7% interest per annum compounded annually, what is its value after 7 years?

12. If \$100 is added to the investment in Exercise 11 after each year, calculate the new value after 3 years.

13. The sum of \$1000 is borrowed at the rate of interest of 10%, compounded annually. The loan is to be repaid in two equal installments, at the end of 1 year and at the end of 2 years. How much must the installments be?

14. Repeat Exercise 13 in the case where the loan is repaid in 3 equal annual installments.

15. A man at the age of 45 purchases a deferred endowment from a life insurance company that will pay him a lump sum of $20,000 at the age of 65. The company charges him $5000 for the policy. What discount rate are they using?

16. The population of Britain in 1600 is believed to have been about 5 million. Three hundred fifty years later, it had increased to 50 million. What was the average percentage growth per year during that period? (Assume a uniform exponential growth.)

17. If a population increases from 5 million to 200 million over a period of 200 years, what is the average percentage growth per year?

18. A sum of $100 is invested at the nominal rate of interest of 12% per annum. How much is the investment worth after 5 years if compounded: (a) annually; (b) quarterly; (c) continuously?

19. At what nominal rate of interest does money triple in value in 10 years if compounded continuously?

20. The GNP of Nation A increased from $0.5 to $1.1 billion between 1970 and 1980.

    a. Calculate the average percentage growth per annum.

    b. Express the GNP at time t in the form be^{kt}.

    c. Assuming this growth rate continues, calculate when the GNP will reach $1.5 billion.

21. The GNP of Nation B during the same period (see Exercise 20) increased from $1.0 to $1.5 billion.

    a. Calculate the average percentage growth per annum for B.

    b. Express the GNP in the form $b'e^{k't}$.

    c. Calculate when the GNP of Nation A overtakes that of B.

FINITE MATHEMATICS

PART

PROGRESSIONS AND THE MATHEMATICS OF FINANCE

CHAPTER

7

A **sequence** is an ordered list of numbers. For example,

$$2, 5, 8, 11, 14, \ldots \tag{1}$$

$$3, 6, 12, 24, 48, \ldots \tag{2}$$

are examples of sequences. In Sequence (1), the **first term** is 2, the **second term** is 5, and so on. It can be seen that each term is obtained by adding 3 to the preceding term. In Sequence (2), the first term is 3 and the fourth term is 24, and any term can be obtained by doubling the preceding term. Sequences of these types arise in many problems, particularly in the mathematics of finance.

A sequence is said to be **finite** if it contains a limited number of terms, that is, if the sequence has a last term. If there is no last term in the sequence, it is called an **infinite** sequence. The terms of a sequence will be denoted by T_1, T_2, T_3, and so on. Thus, for example, T_7 denotes the seventh term, T_{10} the tenth term, and T_n the nth term. The nth term of a sequence is commonly called its **general term**.

7-1 ARITHMETIC PROGRESSIONS

Suppose Mr. Cernac borrows a sum of $5000 from the bank at 1 % interest per month. He agrees to pay $200 toward the principal each month, plus the interest on the balance. At the end of the first month, he pays $200 plus the interest on $5000 at 1 % per month, which is $50. Thus his first payment is $250 and he owes only $4800 to the bank. At the end of the second month, he pays $200 toward the principal plus the interest on $4800, which is $48 at 1 % for one month. Thus his second payment is $248. Continuing in this way, his successive payments (in dollars) are

$$250, 248, 246, 244, \ldots, 202.$$

This sequence is an example of an *arithmetic progression*.

DEFINITION A sequence is said to be an **arithmetic progression** (A.P.) if the difference between any term and the preceding term is the same throughout the sequence. The algebraic difference between each term and the preceding term is called the **common difference** and is denoted by d.

Mr. Cernac's sequence of payments is an A.P. because the difference between any term and its preceding term is -2. This A.P. has 250 as its first term and -2 ($= 248 - 250$) as its common difference. Similarly,

$$2, 5, 8, 11, 14, \ldots$$

is an A.P. with first term 2 and common difference 3.

If a is the first term and d the common difference of an A.P., then the successive terms of the A.P. are

$$a, a + d, a + 2d, a + 3d, \ldots$$

The nth term is given by the formula

$$T_n = a + (n - 1)d. \tag{3}$$

For example, letting $n = 1$, 2, and 3, we find

$$T_1 = a + (1 - 1)d = a$$
$$T_2 = a + (2 - 1)d = a + d$$
$$T_3 = a + (3 - 1)d = a + 2d.$$

Further values can be obtained in a similar manner.

Equation (3) contains four numbers, a, d, n, and T_n. If any three of them are given, we can find the fourth.

EXAMPLE 1   Given the sequence

$$1, 5, 9, 13, \ldots,$$

find: (a) the fifteenth term;   (b) the nth term.

Solution   The given sequence is an A.P. because

$$5 - 1 = 9 - 5 = 13 - 9 = 4.$$

Thus the common difference, d, is 4. Also, $a = 1$.

(a) Using Equation (3) with $n = 15$,

$$T_{15} = a + (15 - 1)d = a + 14d$$
$$= 1 + (14)(4) = 57.$$

(b) $T_n = a + (n - 1)d$
$$= 1 + (n - 1)4 = 4n - 3$$

Thus the fifteenth term is 57 and the nth term is $4n - 3$.

EXAMPLE 2   A firm installs a machine at a cost of \$1700. The value of the machine depreciates annually by \$150 and its scrap value is \$200. What is the life of the machine?

Solution   We are interested in finding the number of years after which the value of the machine has reduced to its scrap value of \$200. Since the value of the machine depreciates each year by \$150, its value at the end of the first year, second year, third year, and so on, will be

$$1700{-}150, 1700{-}2(150), 1700{-}3(150), \ldots$$

or

$$1550, 1400, 1250, \ldots.$$

This sequence of values forms an A.P. with first term $a = 1550$ and common difference $d = 1400 - 1550 = -150$. Thus the nth term is

$$T_n = a + (n - 1)d$$
$$= 1550 + (n - 1)(-150) = 1700 - 150n.$$

This quantity T_n gives the value of the machine in dollars at the end of the nth year.

We are interested in the value of n at which this value has reduced to the scrap value, since this gives the lifetime of the machine. Thus we let $T_n = 200$ and solve for n.

$$1700 - 150n = 200$$
$$150n = 1700 - 200 = 1500$$
$$n = 10$$

The lifetime of the machine is 10 years.

EXAMPLE 3   Michelle's monthly payments to the bank towards her loan form an A.P. If her sixth and tenth payments are \$345 and \$333, respectively, what will be her fifteenth payment to the bank?

Solution   Let a be the first term and d the common difference of the monthly payments of the A.P. Then successive payments (in dollars) are

$$a, a + d, a + 2d, \ldots.$$

Since the sixth and tenth payments (in dollars) are 345 and 333, $T_6 = 345$ and $T_{10} = 333$. Using Equation (3) for the nth term and the given values for T_6 and T_{10}, we have

$$T_6 = a + 5d = 345$$
$$T_{10} = a + 9d = 333.$$

We subtract the top equation from the second equation and simplify.

$$4d = 333 - 345 = -12$$
$$d = -3$$

Substituting this value of d in the top equation, we obtain

$$a - 15 = 345 \quad \text{or} \quad a = 360.$$

Now

$$T_{15} = a + 14d$$
$$= 360 + 14(-3) = 308.$$

Thus her fifteenth payment to the bank will be \$308.

Sum of n Terms of an A.P.

If a is the first term and d the common difference of an A.P., then the sequence is

$$a, a + d, a + 2d, \ldots.$$

If the sequence contains n terms and if l denotes the last term (that is, the nth term), then

$$l = a + (n - 1)d. \tag{4}$$

The next to last term will be $l - d$, the second from the last term will be $l - 2d$ and so on.

If S_n denotes the sum of these n terms, then

$$S_n = a + (a + d) + (a + 2d) + \cdots + (l - 2d) + (l - d) + l.$$

If we write this progression in the reverse order, the sum remains unaltered, so

$$S_n = l + (l - d) + (l - 2d) + \cdots + (a + 2d) + (a + d) + a.$$

Adding the two values for S_n, we get

$$2S_n = [a + l] + [a + d + l - d] + [a + 2d + l - 2d] + \cdots$$
$$+ [l - d + a + d] + [l + a].$$

There are n terms on the right side and each is equal to $a + l$. Thus,

$$2S_n = n(a + l)$$

or

$$S_n = \frac{n}{2}(a + l). \tag{5}$$

Substituting the value of l from Equation (4) into Equation (5), we get

$$S_n = \frac{n}{2}[a + a + (n - 1)d]$$

or

$$S_n = \frac{n}{2}[2a + (n - 1)d].$$

These results are summarized below.

THEOREM 1   The sum of n terms of an A.P. with first term a and common difference d is given by

$$S_n = \frac{n}{2}[2a + (n - 1)d].$$

We can also write this formula as

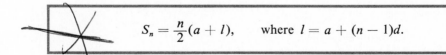

$$S_n = \frac{n}{2}(a + l), \qquad \text{where } l = a + (n - 1)d.$$

EXAMPLE 4   Find the sum of the first 20 terms of the progression

$$2 + 5 + 8 + 11 + 14 + \ldots.$$

Solution   The given sequence is an A.P. because

$$5 - 2 = 8 - 5 = 11 - 8 = 14 - 11 = 3.$$

Thus the common difference is 3, that is, $d = 3$. Also $a = 2$ and $n = 20$. Therefore

$$S_n = \frac{n}{2}[2a + (n-1)d]$$

$$S_{20} = \frac{20}{2}[2(2) + (20-1)3]$$

$$= 10(4 + 57) = 610.$$

EXAMPLE 5   Consider Mr. Cernac's loan of $5000 from the bank at 1% interest per month. Each month he pays back $200 towards the principal plus the monthly interest on the outstanding balance. How much will he have paid in all by the time he has repaid the loan?

Solution   As discussed at the beginning of this section, the sequence of repayments is

$$250, 248, 246, \ldots, 202.$$

These form an A.P. with $a = 250$ and $d = -2$. Since $200 of principal is repaid each month, the total number of payments is $n = 5000/200 = 25$. The last term is, therefore,

$$l = T_{25} = a + 24d = 250 + 24(-2) = 202$$

as indicated above.

The total payment is given by the sum of all 25 terms.

$$S_n = \frac{n}{2}(a + l) = \frac{25}{2}(250 + 202) = 5650$$

The total amount paid to the bank is $5650, which means that the interest paid will amount to $650.

EXAMPLE 6   A woman owning a small business borrowed money from a bank that used a simple discount rate of 9%. She could afford to repay $200 each month and she wished to repay the loan over the next 30 months. How much was she able to borrow?

Solution   To say that the bank charges a simple discount rate of R percent means the following: Let a sum P be borrowed from the bank and repaid in a single payment by an amount A at a time n months later. Then P and A are related by the formula

$$P = A\left(1 - \frac{R}{100} \cdot \frac{n}{12}\right).$$

For example, if the discount rate is 9%, then a payment of $200 after n months would provide a loan given by

$$P = 200\left(1 - \frac{9}{100} \cdot \frac{n}{12}\right).$$

A payment of $200 repaid after one month will secure a loan given by

$$P = 200\left(1 - \frac{9}{100} \cdot \frac{1}{12}\right) = 200\left(1 - \frac{3}{400}\right) = 198.50.$$

On the other hand, a sum of $200 repaid after two months will secure a loan given by

$$P = 200\left(1 - \frac{9}{100} \cdot \frac{2}{12}\right) = 200\left(1 - \frac{6}{400}\right) = 197.00.$$

Continuing, $200 repaid after three months will secure a loan of $195.50, $200 repaid after four months will secure a loan of $194, and so on.

We may regard the loan described in the problem as consisting of 30 separate loans, each repaid by $200, with varying durations of $n = 1, 2, 3, \ldots, 30$. Then the total sum borrowed is the sum of all the values of P for each of these 30 loans.

$$S = 200\left(1 - \frac{9}{100} \cdot \frac{1}{12}\right) + 200\left(1 - \frac{9}{100} \cdot \frac{2}{12}\right) + 200\left(1 - \frac{9}{100} \cdot \frac{3}{12}\right)$$

$$+ \cdots + 200\left(1 - \frac{9}{100} \cdot \frac{30}{12}\right)$$

$$= \left(200 - \frac{3}{2}\right) + \left(200 - \frac{6}{2}\right) + \left(200 - \frac{9}{2}\right) + \cdots + \left(200 - \frac{90}{2}\right)$$

The terms here clearly form an A.P. with first term $a = 200 - \frac{3}{2}$, common difference $d = -\frac{3}{2}$, and 30th term $l = 200 - \frac{90}{2}$. Therefore the sum is

$$S = \frac{n}{2}(a + l)$$

$$= \frac{30}{2}\left[\left(200 - \frac{3}{2}\right) + \left(200 - \frac{90}{2}\right)\right]$$

$$= 15\left(400 - \frac{93}{2}\right) = 5302.50.$$

So the businesswoman was able to borrow $5302.50.

EXAMPLE 7   A man agrees to pay an interest-free debt of $5800 in a number of installments, each installment (beginning with the second) exceeding the previous one by $20. If the first installment is $100, find how many installments will be necessary to repay the loan completely.

Solution   Since the first installment is $100 and each succeeding installment increases by $20, the installments (in dollars) are

$$100, 120, 140, 160, \ldots .$$

These numbers form an A.P. with $a = 100$ and $d = 20$. Let n installments be necessary to repay the loan of $5800. Then the sum of the first n terms of this sequence must equal 5800, that is, $S_n = 5800$. Using the formula for the sum of an A.P., we get

$$S_n = \frac{n}{2}[2a + (n - 1)d]$$

$$5800 = \frac{n}{2}[200 + (n - 1)20]$$

$$= \frac{n}{2}(20n + 180)$$

$$= 10n^2 + 90n.$$

Therefore
$$10n^2 + 90n - 5800 = 0.$$
Dividing through by 10, we get
$$n^2 + 9n - 580 = 0$$
or
$$(n - 20)(n + 29) = 0$$
which gives $n = 20$ or $n = -29$.

Since a negative value of n is not permissible, we have $n = 20$. Thus 20 installments will be necessary to repay the loan.

Arithmetic Mean

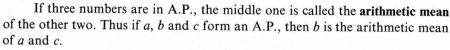

If three numbers are in A.P., the middle one is called the **arithmetic mean** of the other two. Thus if a, b and c form an A.P., then b is the arithmetic mean of a and c.

If $\bar{x}$ represents the arithmetic mean of two numbers x_1 and x_2, then, by definition, x_1, $\bar{x}$, x_2 form an A.P. Therefore,

$$\bar{x} - x_1 = x_2 - \bar{x}. \qquad \text{(Each is equal to the common difference.)}$$

That is,
$$2\bar{x} = x_1 + x_2$$
or
$$\bar{x} = \frac{x_1 + x_2}{2}.$$

Thus the arithmetic mean of two numbers is equal to half their sum—or, in other words, $\bar{x}$ is the **average** of x_1 and x_2.

If $x_1, x_2, \ldots, x_n$ are n given numbers (not necessarily an A.P.), their arithmetic mean or average $\bar{x}$ is defined by

$$\bar{x} = \frac{x_1 + x_2 + \cdots + x_n}{n}.$$

EXERCISES 1

(1–4) Find the indicated terms of the given sequences.

1. Tenth and fifteenth terms of $3, 7, 11, 15, 19, \ldots$

2. Seventh and nth terms of $5, 3, 1, -1, \ldots$

3. rth term of $72, 70, 68, 66, \ldots$

4. nth term of $4, 4\frac{1}{3}, 4\frac{2}{3}, 5, \ldots$

5. If the third and seventh terms of an A.P. are 18 and 30, respectively, find the fifteenth term.

6. If the fifth and tenth terms of an A.P. are 38 and 23, respectively, find the nth term.

7. Which term of the sequence $5, 14, 23, 32, \ldots$ is 239?

8. The last term of the sequence 20, 18, 16, . . . is −4. Find the number of terms in the sequence.

(9–14) Find the indicated sum of the following progressions.

9. $1 + 4 + 7 + 10 + \ldots$; 30 terms

10. $70 + 68 + 66 + 64 + \ldots$; 15 terms

11. $2 + 7 + 12 + 17 + \ldots$; n terms

12. $3 + 5 + 7 + 9 + \ldots$; p terms

13. $51 + 48 + 45 + 42 + \ldots + 18$

14. $15 + 17 + 19 + 21 + \ldots + 55$

15. How many terms of the sequence 9, 12, 15, . . . are needed to make the sum 306?

16. How many terms of the sequence −12, −7, −2, 3, 8, . . . must be added to obtain a sum of 105?

17. A manufacturing company installs a machine at a cost of $1500. At the end of 9 years, the machine has a value of $420. Assuming that yearly depreciation is a constant amount, find the annual depreciation.

18. It cost $2000 to install a machine which depreciated annually by $160. What was the life of the machine if its scrap value was $400?

19. Steve's monthly payments to the bank towards his loan form an A.P. If his eighth and fifteenth payments are $153 and $181, respectively, what will be his twentieth payment?

20. Carla's monthly salary is increased annually in an A.P. She earned $440 a month during her seventh year and $1160 a month during her 25th year.

    a. Find her starting salary and the annual increment.

    b. What should her salary be at the time of retirement, on completion of 38 years of service?

21. In Exercise 19, suppose Steve paid a total of $5490 to the bank.

    a. Find the number of payments he made to the bank.

    b. How much was his last payment to the bank?

22. A debt of $1800 is to be repaid in one year by making a payment of $150 at the end of each month, plus interest at the rate of 1 % per month on the outstanding balance. Find the total interest paid.

23. A person deposits $50 at the beginning of every month into a savings account in which interest is allowed at $\frac{1}{2}$% per month on the minimum monthly balance. Find the balance of the account at the end of the second year, calculating at simple interest.

24. The cost of boring a tube-well 600 feet deep is as follows: $15 is charged for the first foot and the cost per foot increases by $2 for every subsequent foot. Find the cost of boring the 500th foot and the total cost.

25. A man borrows money from a bank that uses a simple discount rate of 12%. He will repay the loan with payments of $100 at the end of each month for the next 12 months. How much can he borrow?

26. Miss Brookfield borrowed money from her credit union, which used a simple discount rate of 10%. She promised to repay $50 a month at the end of each month for the next 24 months. How much was the total interest charged by the credit union?

27. A man agrees to repay a debt of $1800 in a number of installments, each installment (beginning with the second) less than the previous one by $10. If his fifth installment is $200, find how many installments will be necessary to repay the debt.

28. On November 1 every year, a person buys savings bonds of a value exceeding the previous year's purchase by $50. After 10 years, the total cost of the bonds purchased was $4250. Find the value of the bonds purchased: (a) in the first year; (b) in the seventh year.

7-2 GEOMETRIC PROGRESSIONS

Suppose $1000 is deposited with a bank that calculates interest at the rate of 10% compounded annually. The value of this investment (in dollars) at the end of 1 year is equal to

$$1000 + 10\% \text{ of } 1000 = 1000(1 + 0.1) = 1000(1.1) = 1100.$$

The value of investment (in dollars) at the end of 2 years is

$$1100 + 10\% \text{ of } 1100 = 1100 + 0.1(1100)$$

$$= 1100 (1 + 0.1) = 1100(1.1) = 1000(1.1)^2.$$

Similarly, the value of the investment at the end of 3 years will be $1000(1.1)^3$ dollars, and so on. Thus the values of the investment (in dollars) at the end of 0 years, 1 year, 2 years, 3 years, and so on, are

$$1000, \quad 1000(1.1), \quad 1000(1.1)^2, \quad 1000(1.1)^3, \ldots.$$

This sequence is an example of a *geometric progression*.

DEFINITION A sequence of terms is said to be a **geometric progression (G.P.)** if the ratio of each term to its preceding term is the same throughout. This constant ratio is called the **common ratio** of the G.P.

Thus the sequence 2, 6, 18, 54, 162, . . . is a G.P. because

$$\tfrac{6}{2} = \tfrac{18}{6} = \tfrac{54}{18} = \tfrac{162}{54} = 3.$$

The common ratio is 3.

Similarly the sequence $\frac{1}{3}, -\frac{1}{6}, \frac{1}{12}, -\frac{1}{24}, \ldots$ is a G.P. with common ratio $-\frac{1}{2}$.

Each term in a G.P. is obtained by multiplying the preceding term by the common ratio. If a is the first term and r the common ratio, then successive terms of the G.P. are

$$a, ar, ar^2, ar^3, \ldots.$$

In this G.P., we observe that the power of r in any term is one less than the number of the term. Thus the *n*th term is given by

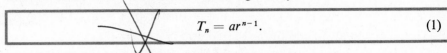

$$T_n = ar^{n-1}. \tag{1}$$

EXAMPLE 1   Find the fifth and *n*th terms of the sequence 2, 6, 18, 54, ...

Solution   The given sequence is a G.P. because

$$\tfrac{6}{2} = \tfrac{18}{6} = \tfrac{54}{18} = 3.$$

Thus successive terms have a constant ratio of 3; that is, $r = 3$. Also, $a = 2$. Therefore,

$$T_5 = ar^4 = 2(3^4) = 162$$

and

$$T_n = ar^{n-1} = 2(3^{n-1}) = 2 \times 3^{n-1}.$$

EXAMPLE 2   The fourth and ninth terms of a G.P. are $\tfrac{1}{2}$ and $\tfrac{16}{243}$. Find the sixth term.

Solution   Let *a* be the first term and *r* be the common ratio of the given G.P. Then, using our given values, we have

$$T_4 = ar^3 = \tfrac{1}{2}$$

and

$$T_9 = ar^8 = \tfrac{16}{243}.$$

We divide the second equation by the first and solve for *r*.

$$\frac{ar^8}{ar^3} = \frac{\tfrac{16}{243}}{\tfrac{1}{2}}$$

$$r^5 = \tfrac{16}{243} \times \tfrac{2}{1} = \tfrac{32}{243} = (\tfrac{2}{3})^5.$$

$$r = \tfrac{2}{3}$$

Substituting this value of *r* in the first equation, we have

$$a(\tfrac{2}{3})^3 = \tfrac{1}{2}.$$

Thus,

$$a = \tfrac{1}{2} \times \tfrac{27}{8} = \tfrac{27}{16}$$

and

$$T_6 = ar^5$$
$$= \tfrac{27}{16}(\tfrac{2}{3})^5 = \tfrac{27}{16} \times \tfrac{32}{243} = \tfrac{2}{9}.$$

Hence the sixth term is $\tfrac{2}{9}$.

EXAMPLE 3   A machine is depreciated annually at the rate of 20% on its declining value. The original cost was $10,000 and the ultimate scrap value is $3000. Find the effective life of the machine, that is, the number of years until the depreciated value is less than the scrap value.

Solution   Since the value of the machine depreciates each year by 20% of its value at the beginning of the year, the value of the machine at the end of any year is 80% or four-fifths of its value at the beginning of that year. Thus the value (in dollars) of the machine at the end of the first year is

$$\tfrac{4}{5} \text{ of } 10,000 = 10,000(\tfrac{4}{5})$$

and at the end of the second year is

$$\tfrac{4}{5} \text{ of } 10,000(\tfrac{4}{5}) = 10,000(\tfrac{4}{5})^2.$$

Similarly, its value (in dollars) at the end of the third year will be $10,000(\tfrac{4}{5})^3$, and so on. Therefore the value (in dollars) of the machine at the end of the first year, second year, third year, and so on, is

$$10,000(\tfrac{4}{5}), \qquad 10,000(\tfrac{4}{5})^2, \qquad 10,000(\tfrac{4}{5})^3, \ldots.$$

This sequence is clearly a G.P. with first term of $10,000(\tfrac{4}{5})$ and common ratio of $\tfrac{4}{5}$. The nth term, which gives the value of the machine at the end of the nth year, is, therefore

$$T_n = ar^{n-1} = 10,000(\tfrac{4}{5}) \cdot (\tfrac{4}{5})^{n-1} = 10,000(\tfrac{4}{5})^n.$$

Setting n successively equal to $1, 2, 3, \ldots$, we obtain the values in Table 1.

TABLE 1

n	1	2	3	4	5	6
T_n	8000	6400	5120	4096	3276.8	2621.44

We see, therefore, that after 5 years the value of the machine is still a little greater than its scrap value of $3000, but after 6 years, its value is below the scrap value. The lifetime of the machine is therefore 6 years.

The general case of an investment growing at compound interest was discussed at the end of Section 1 of Chapter 6. If a sum P is invested at a rate of interest of R percent per annum compounded annually, then the value of the investment at the end of the nth year is given by the formula

$$T_n = P(1 + i)^n, \qquad i = \frac{R}{100}.$$

These values for $n = 1, 2, 3, \ldots$ form a sequence that is a G.P. The common ratio is $r = 1 + i$ and the first term is $a = T_1 = P(1 + i)$.

More generally, an investment can be compounded more than once per year. If the nominal annual rate of interest* is R percent and if there are k compoundings per year, then the value after n years is given by the formula

$$T_n = P\left(1 + \frac{i}{k}\right)^{nk}, \qquad i = \frac{R}{100}.$$

Again this sequence forms a G.P. for $n = 1, 2, 3, \ldots$. The common ratio is now given by $r = (1 + i/k)^k$.

THEOREM 1   (SUM OF n TERMS OF A G.P.)

If a is the first term and r the common ratio of a G.P., then the sum S_n

---

*See Section 1 of Chapter 6.

of n terms of the G.P. is given by

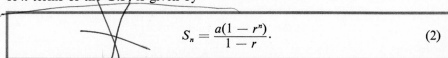

$$S_n = \frac{a(1 - r^n)}{1 - r}. \qquad (2)$$

PROOF The n terms of the given G.P. are

$$a, ar, ar^2, \ldots, ar^{n-2}, ar^{n-1}.$$

Therefore the sum of these terms is

$$S_n = a + ar + ar^2 + \cdots + ar^{n-2} + ar^{n-1}.$$

We multiply both sides by $-r$.

$$-rS_n = -ar - ar^2 - \cdots - ar^{n-1} - ar^n$$

Adding these two equations, we find that all the terms cancel except the first term in the first equation and the last term in the second equation, giving

$$S_n - rS_n = a - ar^n$$

We factor and solve for S_n.

$$S_n(1 - r) = a(1 - r^n)$$

$$S_n = \frac{a(1 - r^n)}{1 - r}$$

This proves the result.

Note The above formula for S_n is valid only when $r \neq 1$. When $r = 1$, the given G.P. becomes

$$a + a + a + \cdots + a \qquad (n \text{ terms})$$

which has the sum na.

Multiplying numerator and denominator of Equation (2) by -1, we obtain the alternative formula

$$S_n = \frac{a(r^n - 1)}{r - 1}$$

This formula is generally used when $r > 1$, whereas Equation (2) is more useful when $r < 1$.

EXAMPLE 4 Find the sum of the first 10 terms of the sequence $2 - 4 + 8 - 16 + \ldots.$

Solution The given sequence is a G.P. with $a = 2$ and $r = -\frac{4}{2} = -2$. Here $n = 10$. Therefore

$$S_n = \frac{a(1 - r^n)}{1 - r}$$

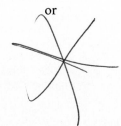

or

$$S_{10} = \frac{2(1 - (-2)^{10})}{1 - (-2)}$$

$$= \tfrac{2}{3}(1 - 2^{10}) = \tfrac{2}{3}(1 - 1024) = \tfrac{2}{3}(-1023)$$

$$= 2(-341) = -682.$$

EXAMPLE 5   Each year a person invests $1000 in a savings plan that pays interest at the fixed rate of 8% per annum. What is the value of this savings plan on the tenth anniversary of the first investment?

Solution   The first $1000 has been invested for ten years, so it has increased in value to

$$\$1000(1 + i)^{10}, \quad i = \frac{R}{100} = \frac{8}{100} = .08.$$

Thus the value is $\$1000(1.08)^{10}$.

The second $1000 was invested one year later; hence it has been in the plan for 9 years. Its value has therefore increased to $\$1000(1.08)^9$. The third $1000 has been in the plan for 8 years and has the value $\$1000(1.08)^8$. We continue in the same fashion until we reach the tenth payment of $1000, which was made 9 years after the first. Its value one year later is $\$1000(1.08)$.

Thus the total value of the plan on its tenth anniversary is obtained by adding all these amounts together.

$$S = 1000(1.08)^{10} + 1000(1.08)^9 + \cdots + 1000(1.08)$$

But this is a G.P. with $a = 100(1.08)$, $r = 1.08$, and $n = 10$. Therefore

$$S = 1000(1.08)\frac{(1.08)^{10} - 1}{1.08 - 1}$$

using the formula for the sum of a G.P. Simplifying,

$$S = 1000\frac{1.08}{0.08}[(1.08)^{10} - 1]$$

$$= 13,500[2.1589 - 1] = 15,645.$$

The value is thus $15,645.

The sum of the first n terms of the geometric sequence

$$a + ar + ar^2 + \ldots$$

is given by

$$S_n = \frac{a(1 - r^n)}{1 - r}. \tag{2}$$

Let us consider the behavior of r^n for large n when $-1 < r < 1$. To pick a specific example, let $r = \frac{1}{2}$. Then Table 2 gives the values of r^n for several different values of n.

TABLE 2

n	1	2	3	4	5	6	7
r^n	0.5	0.25	0.125	0.0625	0.03125	0.015625	0.0078125

From this table, we observe that as n gets larger and larger, r^n gets smaller and smaller. Ultimately, when n approaches infinity, r^n approaches zero. This behavior of r^n—namely, that r^n gets closer and closer to zero as n becomes larger and larger—is true whenever $-1 < r < 1$. Thus from Equation (2), we can say that the sum of an infinite number of terms in a G. P. is given by

$$S_\infty = \frac{a(1 - 0)}{1 - r} = \frac{a}{1 - r}.$$

This leads us to the following theorem.

THEOREM 2 (SUM OF AN INFINITE G.P.)
The sum S of an infinite geometric sequence

$$a + ar + ar^2 + \ldots$$

is given by

$$S = \frac{a}{1 - r}, \qquad \text{provided } -1 < r < 1. \tag{3}$$

EXAMPLE 6 Find the sum of the infinite sequence $1 - \frac{1}{3} + \frac{1}{9} - \frac{1}{27} + \ldots$.

Solution The given sequence is a G.P. with $a = 1$ and $r = -\frac{1}{3}$. The sum is given by

$$S = \frac{a}{1 - r}$$

$$= \frac{1}{1 - (-\frac{1}{3})} = \frac{1}{\frac{4}{3}} = \frac{3}{4}.$$

EXERCISES 2

(1–4) Find the specified term.

1. Ninth term of the sequence $3, 6, 12, 24, \ldots$

2. Sixth term of the sequence $\sqrt{3}, 3, 3\sqrt{3}, 9, \ldots$

3. nth term of the sequence $\frac{2}{9}, -\frac{1}{3}, \frac{1}{2}, \ldots$

4. pth term of the sequence $\frac{2}{5}, -\frac{1}{2}, \frac{5}{8}, \ldots$

(5–6) Which term of the sequence is the last given term?

5. $96, 48, 24, 12, \ldots; \frac{3}{16}$

6. $18, 12, 8, \ldots; \frac{512}{729}$

7. The second term of a G.P. is 24 and the fifth term is 81. Find the sequence and the tenth term.

8. The fifth, eighth, and eleventh terms of a G.P. are x, y, and z, respectively. Show that $y^2 = xz$.

(9–15) Find the indicated sum of the following sequences.

9. $2 + 6 + 18 + 54 + \ldots; 12$ terms

10. $\sqrt{3} - 3 + 3\sqrt{3} - 9 + \ldots; 10$ terms

11. $1 + 2 + 4 + 8 + \ldots; n$ terms

12. $3 + 1.5 + 0.75 + 0.375 + \ldots; p$ terms

13. $1 + \frac{1}{2} + \frac{1}{4} + \frac{1}{8} + \ldots$

14. $1 - \frac{1}{3} + \frac{1}{9} - \frac{1}{27} + \cdots$

15. $\sqrt{2} - \dfrac{1}{\sqrt{2}} + \dfrac{1}{2\sqrt{2}} - \cdots$

16. If $y = 1 + x + x^2 + x^3 + \cdots$ $(-1 < x < 1)$, show that

$$x = \frac{y-1}{y}.$$

17. If $v = 1/(1 + i)$, show that

$$v + v^2 + v^3 + \cdots = \frac{1}{i}.$$

18. Prove that $9^{1/3} \cdot 9^{1/9} \cdot 9^{1/27} \ldots = 3$.

19. Evaluate $4^{1/3} \cdot 4^{-1/9} \cdot 4^{1/27} \cdot 4^{-1/81} \ldots$.

20. Express $0.85555 \ldots$ as a fraction (*Hint:* Write $0.85555 = 0.8 + 0.05(1 + 0.1 + 0.01 + \ldots)$).

21. A machine is depreciated annually at the rate of 10% on its reducing value. The original cost was $10,000 and the ultimate scrap value was $5314.41. Find the effective life of the machine.

22. If $2000 is invested in a savings account at 8% interest compounded annually, find its value after 5 years.

23. In Exercise 22, the rate of interest decreases after 6 years to 6% per annum. Find the value of the investment after a further 6 years.

24. If $5000 is invested in a savings account on which interest is compounded quarterly at a nominal interest rate of 8% per annum, find its value after 3 years.

25. Suppose $4000 is invested in a fixed deposit at nominal annual interest rate of 6% compounded monthly. Find its value: (a) after 1 year; (b) after 4 years.

26. An individual wishes to invest a certain sum of money in a fixed deposit earning 10% interest per annum for a period of four years. At the end of this time the proceeds from the investment will be used to pay off a debt of $10,000 that will become due then. How much must be invested to have enough to pay off the debt?

27. Every year Mary invests $2000 in a savings account that earns interest at 10% per annum. Find the value of her investment on the twelfth anniversary of her first deposit.

28. At the beginning of every month, Joe deposits $200 in a savings account that earns interest at the rate of $\frac{1}{2}\%$ per month on the minimum monthly balance. How much is his investment worth after 2 years (that is, 25 deposits)?

7-3 MATHEMATICS OF FINANCE

In this section we shall describe briefly some very important applications of sequences that arise in the mathematics of finance.

Savings Plans

The simplest type of savings plan is one in which regular payments of a fixed amount are made into the plan (for example, at the end of every month or once per year), and the balance invested in the plan earns interest at some fixed rate.

EXAMPLE 1   Every month Jane pays $100 into a savings plan that earns interest at $\frac{1}{2}\%$ per month. Calculate the value of her savings: (a) at the time when she makes her 25th payment; (b) at the time when she makes her nth payment.

Solution   (a) The 25th payment is made 24 months after the first payment. Each investment increases by a factor of 1.005 per month (0.5% per month). Thus the first $100 that Jane invested is worth $100(1.005)^{24}$ after 24 months. The second $100 she saved will have been in the plan for 23 months, so it will be worth $100 (1.005)^{23}$. The third $100 will be worth $100 (1.005)^{22}$, and so on. The 24th payment of $100 will have been in the plan for only one month, so will be worth $100 (1.005)$. The last payment will not yet have earned any interest. Thus the total value of the plan will be the sum of all these amounts; that is,

$$S = 100(1.005)^{24} + 100(1.005)^{23} + 100(1.005)^{22} + \cdots$$
$$+ 100(1.005)^2 + 100(1.005) + 100.$$

But this expression is the sum of 25 terms in a G.P. The first term is $a = 100$ and the common ratio is $r = 1.005$. Therefore

$$S = \frac{a(r^n - 1)}{r - 1} = \frac{100[(1.005)^{25} - 1]}{1.005 - 1}$$

$$= \frac{100}{0.005}[(1.005)^{25} - 1]$$

$$= 20{,}000[1.13280 - 1] = 2655.91.$$

After 24 months, Jane's savings plan is therefore worth $2,655.91.

(b) The nth payment is made $(n - 1)$ months after the first payment. After $(n - 1)$ months, the first $100 invested will be worth $100 (1.005)^{n-1}$. The second $100 will be worth $100 (1.005)^{n-2}$ since it will have been in the plan for $(n - 2)$ months. The next-to-last payment will again be worth $100 (1.005)$ dollars, and the last (nth) payment will be just $100. Thus the total value of the plan will be the following sum.

$$S = 100(1.005)^{n-1} + 100(1.005)^{n-2} + \cdots + 100(1.005)^2$$
$$+ 100(1.005) + 100$$

Again the terms in this sum form a G.P. with $a = 100$ and $r = 1.005$. There are n terms, so

$$S = \frac{a(r^n - 1)}{r - 1} = \frac{100[(1.005)^n - 1]}{1.005 - 1}$$

$$= 20{,}000[(1.005)^n - 1].$$

From this formula, we can calculate the value of the plan after any number of months. For example, after 59 months (that is, when the 60th payment is made), the savings plan is worth

$$20,000[(1.005)^{60} - 1] = 20,000[1.34885 - 1] = 6977.00$$

or $6977.00.

The argument used in this example can be easily extended to the general case. Let us suppose that an amount P is saved each period, where the period may be a month, a quarter, a year, or any other fixed length of time. Let the interest rate be R percent per period. Then each period the investment increases by a factor of $1 + i$, where $i = R/100$. Now let us ask what will be the value of the savings plan after $n - 1$ periods from the first payment, that is, at the time when the nth payment is made.

The first payment of P will have been invested for the full $n - 1$ periods, so will have increased in value to $P(1 + i)^{n-1}$. The second payment will, however, only have been invested for $n - 2$ periods, so will have increased in value to $P(1 + i)^{n-2}$. (See figure 1.) The nth or last payment will just have been invested, so it will be worth P (Figure 1).

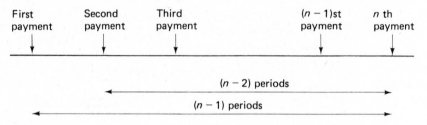

FIGURE 1

The total value of the savings plan will therefore be given by the sum

$$S = P(1 + i)^{n-1} + P(1 + i)^{n-2} + \cdots + P(1 + i) + P.$$

This is the sum of a G.P. with first term $a = P$ and common ratio $1 + i$. There are n terms, so

$$S = \frac{a(r^n - 1)}{r - 1} = \frac{P[(1 + i)^n - 1]}{(1 + i) - 1} = \frac{P}{i}[(1 + i)^n - 1].$$

If we substitute $P = 100$ and $i = 0.005$, we have the results of Example 1. In financial mathematics, it is common to use the notation

$$S = P\,s_{\overline{n}|i} \qquad \text{where } s_{\overline{n}|i} = i^{-1}[(1 + i)^n - 1].$$

The quantity $s_{\overline{n}|i}$ represents the value of a savings plan after n regular payments of $1 each. It depends only on the interest rate and the number n. In books concerned with financial mathematics, tables exist that give the value of $s_{\overline{n}|i}$ for different values of R and n.

Annuities

An annuity is like a negative savings plan. It is a typical method used after retirement by people in order to provide themselves with a pension. Typically an individual will, during his or her working life, make regular contributions to a retirement savings plan. Upon retirement, the sum thus accumulated can be used to purchase an annuity. Annuities are also used for other purposes, such as in income averaging by individuals whose incomes fluctuate greatly from year to year, but retirement pensions form their most common use.

A person purchasing an annuity deposits a fixed sum of money and then each year withdraws a certain fixed amount of it as pension. The balance remaining after each withdrawal gains interest until the following year, when the next withdrawal is made. This process continues until the whole sum deposited has been used up.

EXAMPLE 2 On his 65th birthday, Mr. Hoskins wishes to purchase an annuity that will pay him $5000 per year for the next 10 years, the first payment to be made to him on his 66th birthday. His insurance company will give him an interest rate of 8% per annum on the investment. How much must he pay in order to purchase such an annuity?

Solution Consider the first payment, which Mr. Hoskins will receive on his 66th birthday. This payment will be $5000, and it must be paid for by a deposit made 1 year earlier. Let this deposit be A_1. In the intervening year, A_1 will have gained 8% interest, so it will have increased to $(1.08)A_1$. This must be equal to 5000.

$$(1.08)A_1 = 5000$$
$$A_1 = 5000(1.08)^{-1}.$$

That is, if an amount equal to $5000(1.08)^{-1}$ is deposited on Mr. Hoskins' 65th birthday, it will have increased to $5000 by his 66th birthday.

Now consider the second payment, which he will receive on his 67th birthday. This must be paid by a deposit, A_2, made 2 years earlier. Since A_2 is accumulating interest for 2 years at 8%, we must have

$$A_2(1.08)^2 = 5000$$

if it is to be just enough to grow to $5000 on his 67th birthday. Thus

$$A_2 = 5000(1.08)^{-2}.$$

That is, if an amount equal to A_2 is deposited on Mr. Hoskins' 65th birthday, it will have increased to $5000 by his 67th birthday. Clearly, if Mr. Hoskins deposits the sum $A_1 + A_2$ on his 65th birthday, the investment will be just enough to enable him to collect $5000 on each of his 66th and 67th birthdays.

We can continue in this same way. A deposit of $A_3 = \$5000(1.08)^{-3}$ will increase to $5000 after 3 years (on his 68th birthday), and so on. The last $5000 will be paid on his 75th birthday, so it will have been invested for 10 years. Hence it will require a deposit of $5000(1.08)^{-10}$.

Thus in order to receive all ten payments, the total sum S that Mr. Hoskins must deposit on his 65th birthday is given by

$$S = A_1 + A_2 + A_3 + \cdots + A_{10}$$
$$= 5000(1.08)^{-1} + 5000(1.08)^{-2} + 5000(1.08)^{-3} + \cdots + 5000(1.08)^{-10}.$$

This expression represents the sum of 10 terms of a G.P. with first term $a = 5000(1.08)^{-1}$ and common ratio $r = (1.08)^{-1}$. Therefore

$$S = \frac{a(1 - r^n)}{1 - r} = \frac{5000(1.08)^{-1}[1 - (1.08)^{-10}]}{1 - (1.08)^{-1}}.$$

Multiplying numerator and denominator by 1.08, we obtain

$$S = \frac{5000[1 - (1.08)^{-10}]}{1.08[1 - (1.08)^{-1}]} = \frac{5000[1 - (1.08)^{-10}]}{1.08 - 1}$$

$$= \frac{5000}{0.08}[1 - (1.08)^{-10}]$$

$$= \frac{5000}{0.08}(1 - 0.4632)$$

$$= 33{,}550.$$

Thus Mr. Hoskins must deposit \$33,550 in order to buy his required annuity of \$5000 for 10 years.

Now let us generalize this example. Suppose an annuity is purchased with a down payment S and the annual payments made to the annuitant are equal to P. These payments are to be made once a year for n years, starting one year after the annuity is purchased. The interest rate is R percent per annum.

As in Example 2, the first payment of P—made 1 year after the annuity is purchased—requires a deposit A_1, where

$$A_1(1 + i) = P \qquad \left(i = \frac{R}{100} \right).$$

This is because an investment of A_1 would increase to a value $A_1(1 + i)$ during the intervening year. Therefore

$$A_1 = P(1 + i)^{-1}.$$

In a similar way, an investment of A_2 would increase to a value P after 2 years if

$$A_2(1 + i)^2 = P$$

or

$$A_2 = P(1 + i)^{-2}.$$

The nth and last payment requires a deposit A_n to be made n years beforehand, where

$$A_n(1 + i)^n = P$$

or

$$A_n = P(1 + i)^{-n}.$$

Thus if the sum S is to be sufficient to enable all n annuity payments to be made, we must have

$$S = A_1 + A_2 + \cdots + A_n$$
$$= P(1 + i)^{-1} + P(1 + i)^{-2} + \cdots + P(1 + i)^{-n}.$$

Again we have the sum of n terms of a G.P. The first term is $a = P(1 + i)^{-1}$ and common ratio is $r = (1 + i)^{-1}$. Therefore

$$S = \frac{a(1 - r^n)}{1 - r} = \frac{P(1 + i)^{-1}[1 - (1 + i)^{-n}]}{1 - (1 + i)^{-1}}.$$

Multiplying numerator and denominator by $1 + i$, the denominator becomes

$$(1 + i)[1 - (1 + i)^{-1}] = (1 + i) - (1 + i)(1 + i)^{-1} = (1 + i) - 1 = i.$$

Therefore we are left with

$$S = \frac{P}{i}[1 - (1 + i)^{-n}]. \tag{1}$$

When a life insurance company issues a pension policy to an individual, they usually do not issue it for a certain specified number of years, but rather for as long as the individual concerned remains alive. In such a case, the value of n used is the life expectancy of the individual, that is, the number of years (on the average) that individuals in his or her category survive.

EXAMPLE 3   Mrs. Josephs retires at the age of 63 and uses her life savings of \$120,000 to purchase an annuity. The life insurance company gives an interest rate of 6% and they estimate that her life expectancy is 15 years. How much annuity (that is, how big an annual pension) will she receive?

Solution   In Equation (1), we know that $S = 120{,}000$ and $i = R/100 = \frac{6}{100} = 0.06$. We wish to calculate P. We have

$$S = \frac{P}{i}[1 - (1 + i)^{-n}].$$

That is,

$$120{,}000 = \frac{P}{0.06}[1 - (1.06)^{-15}]$$

$$= \frac{P}{0.06}(1 - 0.4173)$$

$$= \frac{P}{0.06}(0.5827).$$

Therefore, $P = (120{,}000)(0.06)/0.5827 = 12{,}355.53$ and Mrs. Josephs will receive an annual pension of \$12,355.53.

It is common to write Equation (1) in the following form.

$$S = Pa_{\overline{n}|i} \qquad \text{where } a_{\overline{n}|i} = i^{-1}[1 - (1 + i)^{-n}]$$

Again, tables of $a_{\overline{n}|t}$ for different values of n and R can be found in books on mathematics of finance.

We often call S the **present value** of an annuity of P per annum for a period of n years: It is the amount that must be paid to purchase such an annuity. The quantity $a_{\overline{n}|t}$ represents the present value of an annuity of \$1 per year for n years.

Amortization

When a debt is repaid by regular payments over a period of time, we say that the debt is **amortized**. For example, an individual might borrow \$5000 from the bank to buy a new car with the arrangement that a specified amount will be paid back each month for the next 24 months. We would like to determine how much the monthly payments should be, given that the bank will charge interest at a certain rate on each outstanding balance. Another example of widespread importance are mortgages, which are again repaid by regular payments typically spread over 20 or 25 years.

Mathematically speaking, the amortization of a debt presents exactly the same problem as paying an annuity. With an annuity, we can view the annuitant as lending a certain sum S to the life insurance company; the company then repays this loan by n regular payments of amount P each. On each outstanding balance, the company adds interest to the credit of the annuitant at the rate of R percent per period. This is identical with the situation arising in the case of a loan. Here the bank lends a specified sum S to the borrower, who then repays this loan by n regular payments of P each. On each outstanding balance, the borrower must add interest at the rate of R percent per period.

Consequently, Equation (1) also applies to the amortization of a loan.

$$S = \frac{P}{i}[1 - (1 + i)^{-n}] \qquad \left(i = \frac{R}{100}\right) \qquad (2)$$

EXAMPLE 4 A small construction company wishes to borrow money from the bank for expansion of their operations. The bank charges interest at 1% per month, and insists that the loan be repaid within 24 months. The company estimates that they can afford to repay the loan at a rate of \$1500 per month. What is the maximum they can borrow?

Solution In the above formula, we can let $P = 1500$, $i = \frac{1}{100} = 0.01$ (since the interest rate is 1% per period, that is, per month in this case), and $n = 24$. Then

$$S = \frac{1500}{0.01}[1 - (1.01)^{-24}]$$

$$= 150{,}000(1 - 0.7876)$$

$$= 31{,}865.$$

Thus the company can borrow up to \$31,865.

Usually we want to use Equation (2) in order to calculate the magnitude of the payments P. Solving for P, we obtain

$$P = \frac{iS}{1 - (1 + i)^{-n}} = \frac{S}{a_{\overline{n}|i}}. \qquad (3)$$

EXAMPLE 5   During his years as an undergraduate, a student accumulates student loans so that, upon graduation, the debt is $8000. The loan accumulates interest at 10% per annum and is repaid in single installments at the end of each year. How much must the student pay each year to repay the debt in 5 years?

Solution   The initial debt is $S = 8000$. The repayment period is $n = 5$. Since the interest rate is $R = 10$, then $i = R/100 = 0.1$. The annual payment is obtained from Equation (3).

$$P = \frac{(0.1)(8000)}{1 - (1.1)^{-5}} = \frac{800}{1 - 0.6209} = 2110.$$

The student must therefore repay $2110 at the end of each year in order to amortize the debt within 5 years.

EXERCISES 3

1. If $50 is saved every month and the interest rate is $\frac{3}{4}$% per month, calculate the value of the investment: (a) 12 months after the first payment; (b) n months after the first payment.

2. At the beginning of every year, $2000 is invested in a savings plan. The interest rate is 8% per annum. Calculate the value of the investment: (a) at the end of the fifth year; (b) at the end of the nth year.

3. Jack is investing money every month in a savings plan which pays interest at $\frac{1}{2}$% per month. Five years (60 months) after starting the plan, he plans to withdraw the money and use it to pay off a second mortgage on his house. If he will require $8000 to repay the mortage, how much per month must he save?

4. Ms. Jones is due to retire in 4 years, and she and her husband plan to take a trip around the world. They estimate that they will require $20,000 for this. How much a month must she put aside in order to save the required amount in 48 months? The bank pays interest of $\frac{3}{4}$% per month on the savings account.

5. An individual wishes to purchase an annuity that will pay $8000 per year for the next 15 years. If the interest rate is 6%, how much will such an annuity cost?

6. If the life expectancy of a man is 12 years at retirement, how much will it cost him to buy an annuity for life of $10,000 per annum if the interest rate is 8%?

7. Repeat Exercise 6 if the interest rate is: (a) 7%; (b) 9%.

8. If the man in Exercise 6 has $100,000 with which to buy his annuity, how much annual pension will he receive?

9. Mary receives a legacy of $10,000 which she invests at 6% per annum. At the end of every year, she wishes to withdraw a sum P in order to take a trip to Hawaii. How much should P be if the money is to last 10 years?

10. When Cy retired, he had \$120,000 invested in long-term bonds paying 5% interest. At the beginning of every year, he withdraws a sum P to meet his expenses for the coming year. If the money is to last for 15 years, how much should he withdraw each year?

*11. In Exercise 10, calculate how much Cy has remaining in the bonds just after he has made his tenth withdrawal.

12. A loan of \$5000 is to be repaid by regular monthly installments over 12 months. If the interest rate is 1% per month, how big should the monthly payments be?

13. If the loan in Exercise 12 were paid back over 18 months, how big would be the monthly payments then?

14. Sam borrows \$6000 from the bank at 12% interest per annum. He repays it by regular installments at the end of every year. If the loan is to be paid off in 4 years, how much should his annual payments be?

15. A mortgage of \$40,000 is to be repaid by monthly payments over a period of 25 years (300 payments). If the rate of interest is $\frac{3}{4}$% per month, calculate the monthly payment.

16. Recalculate Exercise 15 if the mortgage is to be repaid over 20 years.

*17. In Exercise 15, calculate how much is owed on the mortgage: (a) after 5 years; (b) after 15 years.

REVIEW EXERCISES FOR CHAPTER 7

1. State whether each of the following is true or false. Replace each false statement by a corresponding true statement.

   a. The nth term of a sequence is given by $T_n = a + (n-1)d$.

   b. The sum of n terms of an A.P. is given by
$$S_n = \frac{a(1 - r^n)}{1 - r}.$$

   c. The sum of an infinite G.P. with a as first term and r as common ratio is given by $S = a/(1 - r)$ for all r.

   d. The pth term of a G.P. is given by $T_p = ar^p$.

   e. If a, l, and r are the first term, last term, and the common ratio, respectively, of a G.P., then its sum is given by
$$\frac{a - rl}{1 - r}.$$

   f. A sequence $T_1, T_2, T_3, \ldots$ is an A.P. if $T_2 - T_1 = T_3 - T_2 = T_4 - T_3 = \ldots$.

   g. A sequence $T_1, T_2, T_3, \ldots$ is a G.P. if $T_2/T_1 = T_3/T_2 = T_4/T_3 = \ldots$.

   h. The sum of n terms of the G.P. $a, ar, ar^2, \ldots$ is given by
$$S_n = \frac{a(r^n - 1)}{r - 1}.$$

i. The terms of an arithmetic progression satisfy the equation $T_n - T_{n-1} = d$ for all n, where d is the common difference.

j. The terms of a geometric progression satisfy the equation $T_n = rT_{n-1}$ for all n, where r is the common ratio.

k. The sequence $1, 2x, 3x^2, 4x^3, \ldots$ is a geometric progression.

2. If $-18, x, y, z$, and 4 form an A.P., find the values of x, y, and z.

3. Find an arithmetric progression of six terms if the first term is $\frac{2}{3}$ and the last term is $\frac{22}{3}$.

4. If $2, p, q$, and 54 form a G.P., find the values of p and q.

5. Find a geometric progression of six terms if the third term is 2 and the last term is 0.25.

6. If you save 1¢ today, 2¢ tomorrow, 3¢ the next day, and so on, what will be your savings in 365 days?

(7–12) Find the sum of the following progressions.

7. $3 + 7 + 11 + 15 + \ldots$; 20 terms

8. $20 + 19\frac{1}{3} + 18\frac{2}{3} + 18 + \cdots + 14$

9. $3 + 6 + 12 + 24 + \ldots$; n terms

10. $18 + 6\sqrt{3} + 6 + 2\sqrt{3} + \ldots$; p terms

11. $18 - 12 + 8 - \frac{16}{3} + \ldots$

12. $a + br + ar^2 + br^3 + ar^4 + br^5 + \ldots$; $|r| < 1$

13. A man secures an interest-free loan of $1530 from a friend and agrees to repay it in 12 installments. He pays $100 as the first installment and then increases each installment by an equal amount over the preceding one. What will be his last installment? How much does each installment differ from the previous one?

14. Susan's monthly payments to the bank toward her loan form an A.P. If her fourth and seventh payments are $236 and $242, respectively, what will be her tenth payment?

15. Joe borrows $4000 at 1% interest per month. Each month he repays $200 plus the interest on the outstanding balance. Write a formula for his nth payment. Calculate the total amount of interest he pays by the time the loan is repaid.

16. If $1200 is invested at 9% interest per annum, calculate the value of the investment: (a) after 4 years; (b) after n years.

17. How much does it cost to buy an annuity of $12,000 per year for 20 years if the interest rate is: (a) 6%; (b) 8% per annum?

18. Jake borrowed $5000 from the bank to buy a new car. The bank charges interest on the loan of 1% each month on the outstanding balance at the beginning of the month, and Jake makes regular repayments at the end of each month. If the loan is to be repaid in 24 months, what must the monthly payment be?

19. In Exercise 18, how large would Jake's monthly payments need to be in order to repay the loan in 48 months?

20. Jane regularly saves $250 at the beginning of each month. The bank pays interest of $\frac{1}{2}$% per month on her savings. Calculate the value of her savings account: (a) after 24 months; (b) after n months.

PROBABILITY

CHAPTER

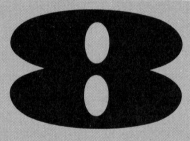

8-1 SAMPLE SPACES AND EVENTS

Historically, the theory of probability originated in investigations conducted by Blaise Pascal (1623–1662) and Pierre de Fermat (1601–1665) in the middle of the seventeenth century at the instigation of certain figures in the gambling world of the time. Today, besides its applications to games of chance, probability theory has become an important tool in such diverse fields as engineering, meteorology, insurance and actuarial work, business operations, and the experimental sciences. Probability theory underlies most of the methods of statistics, a field with widespread applications in almost every area of modern life.

Probability theory is used to handle situations that involve uncertainty. There exist many kinds of observations for which the precise outcome cannot be predicted, even though the set of all possible outcomes can be listed. For example, if a coin is tossed, we cannot predict whether it will fall heads or tails; however, we do know that it will come up one or the other, so that the set of possible outcomes is known. Similarly, when a political election takes place, we cannot predict with certainty how many seats each party will win, but we can make a list of all the possible outcomes. A sales manager may not be able to predict with certainty what sales will be next month, but it may be possible to say that they will be somewhere between 600 and 1000 units. In order to develop the theory of such observations we introduce the following definition.

DEFINITION The set of all possible outcomes of an experiment is called the **sample space** and is denoted by S. Each element of this set (that is, each outcome) is called a **sample point**. The sample space is said to be **finite** if the number of outcomes is finite. (In this chapter, we shall deal only with finite sample spaces.)

EXAMPLE 1 (a) The experiment consists of tossing a coin. In this case, there are two outcomes, namely heads (H) or tails (T), so that the sample space consists of just two elements. Using set notation, we can write

$$S = \{H, T\}.$$

(b) Two firms, A and B, are competing for two contracts. The set of outcomes can be denoted by

$$S = \{AA, AB, BA, BB\}$$

where, for example, AB means that A wins the first contract and B the second, AA means that A wins both contracts, and so on.

Tree diagrams are useful for listing the sample spaces of more complicated observations or experiments.

EXAMPLE 2   Suppose we flip two coins. In the tree diagram shown in Figure 1, we first draw branches from the starting point to H and T, the possible outcomes from flipping the first coin.

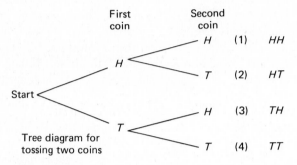

Tree diagram for tossing two coins

FIGURE 1

Then for each of these outcomes, we draw further branches corresponding to the possible outcomes from flipping the second coin: If the first was H, the second could be either H or T and if the first was T, the second could again be either H or T. The elements of the sample space are now obtained by reading from start to the ends of branches (1), (2), (3), and (4). Thus the sample space is

$$S = \{HH, HT, TH, TT\}.$$

We shall, when we come to the question of probability, be concerned with what are called *events*. Let us consider the example of tossing two coins. Then an example of the type of event with which we might be concerned is the event that "both coins fall alike." Looking at the list of elements or points in the sample space, we see that two of the four points satisfy the requirement that both coins fall alike, namely the outcomes HH and TT. We can say, therefore, that the event that both coins fall alike *consists of* the set of outcomes $\{HH, TT\}$.

As a second example, the event that "the first coin falls heads" occurs if and only if the outcome is either HH or HT. Thus this event can be identified with the set of outcomes $\{HH, HT\}$.

The event that "at least one coin falls heads" can be identified with the set of outcomes $\{HH, HT, TH\}$.

We see that in each of these examples, an event is associated with a certain set of outcomes of the experiment in question. This leads us to make the following formal definition.

DEFINITION   Any subset of a sample space S for a particular experiment is called an **event**. Usually the letter E is used to denote events.

EXAMPLE 3   Consider the experiment of rolling a die with six faces containing 1, 2, 3, 4, 5, and 6 spots, respectively. The sample space is

$$S = \{1, 2, 3, 4, 5, 6\}.$$

(a) $E_1 = \{2, 4, 6\}$ represents the event that the die will show an even number of spots.

(b) $E_2 = \{4, 5, 6\}$ represents the event that the die will show more than 3 spots.

(c) Suppose we are interested in the event that 7 spots will show up. Clearly this will never happen, because no face on the die has 7 spots. Thus this subset is empty, that is, $E_3 = \varnothing$. Such an event is called an **impossible event**.

(d) The event that either an odd or an even number of spots show up is given by the subset $E_4 = \{1, 2, 3, 4, 5, 6\}$. Clearly this is the whole sample space. An event consisting of all the sample points of the sample space is called a **certain event**.

It is often useful to represent sample spaces and events by means of what is called a **Venn diagram**. The sample space S itself is represented by a number of points enclosed within a rectangular boundary, each of the points representing one of the outcomes of the experiment. Any event would be represented by a closed region within the rectangle that contains all of the points corresponding to the outcomes in that event. For example, the sample space for rolling a die is shown in part (a) of Figure 2. The events E_1 and E_2 of Example 3 are shown in part (b).

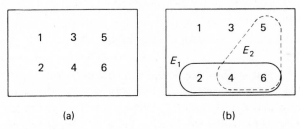

(a)   (b)

FIGURE 2

There exist many situations in which a given event can be related to two or more other events. For example, consider the tossing of two coins, for which the sample space consists of the four outcomes $S = \{HH, HT, TH, TT\}$. Then $E_1 = \{HT, TH\}$ represents the event that both coins fall differently and $E_2 = \{TT, TH\}$ is the event that the first coin falls tails. Suppose we are interested in the event that either the first coin falls tails or else both coins fall differently. This event will occur whenever E_1 happens or E_2 happens or both E_1 and E_2 happen together. That is, this event has the possibilities $\{HT, TH, TT\}$, which are the sample points contained in either of the two events E_1 or E_2. The Venn diagram for this experiment is shown in Figure 3. The event that E_1 or E_2 or both occur consists of all three of the circled points. More generally, we have the following definition.

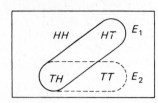

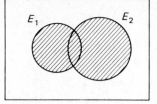

FIGURE 3 **FIGURE 4**

DEFINITION Let E_1 and E_2 be two events of a sample space S. Then the **union** of two events E_1 and E_2, denoted by $E_1 \cup E_2$, is the set of all the sample points which are in E_1 or E_2 or both. Thus

$$E_1 \cup E_2 = \{x \mid x \in E_1 \quad \text{or} \quad x \in E_2 \quad \text{or} \quad \text{both}\}.$$

$E_1 \cup E_2$ is read as E_1 *union* E_2. In terms of Venn diagrams, $E_1 \cup E_2$ represents the entire shaded region shown in Figure 4; $E_1 \cup E_2$ represents the event that E_1 *or* E_2 occurs. (Note that we use the inclusive *or*, which means that E_1, E_2, or both E_1 and E_2 occur.)

EXAMPLE 4 Given a sample space $S = \{1, 2, 3, 4, 5, 6\}$ for the rolling of a die, let E_1 be the event that an even number turns up, so $E_1 = \{2, 4, 6\}$; let E_2 be the event that an odd number turns up, so $E_2 = \{1, 3, 5\}$; and let E_3 be the event that the number turned up is less than 4, so $E_3 = \{1, 2, 3\}$.

(a) $E_1 \cup E_3 = \{1, 2, 3, 4, 6\}$ is the event that either the number turned up is even *or* the number turned up is less than 4.

(b) $E_1 \cup E_2 = \{1, 2, 3, 4, 5, 6\}$ is the event that either the number turned up is even *or* it is odd. Clearly in this case $E_1 \cup E_2 = S$, the whole sample space.

Let us once again consider the sample space $S = \{HH, HT, TH, TT\}$ for flipping two coins. Let $E_1 = \{HT, TH, TT\}$ be the event that at least 1 coin falls tails and $E_2 = \{HH, HT, TH\}$ be the event that at least 1 coin falls heads. Consider the event that at least 1 coin falls tails *and* at least 1 coin falls heads. This event has the possibilities $\{HT, TH\}$, which are the sample points common to events E_1 and E_2. This leads us to the following definition.

DEFINITION Let E_1 and E_2 be two events of a sample space S. Then the **intersection** of these events, denoted by $E_1 \cap E_2$, is the set of all the sample points that belong both to E_1 and E_2.

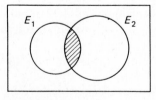

FIGURE 5

$$E_1 \cap E_2 = \{x \mid x \in E_1 \text{ and } x \in E_2\}$$

We read $E_1 \cap E_2$ as E_1 *intersection* E_2. The event $E_1 \cap E_2$ is shaded in Figure 5. The event $E_1 \cap E_2$ occurs when both E_1 *and* E_2 occur.

EXAMPLE 5 Consider the sample space $S = \{HH, HT, TH, TT\}$ for flipping two coins.

Let $E_1 = \{HH, TT\}$ be the event that both coins fall alike;

$E_2 = \{HT, TH\}$ be the event that both coins fall differently;

$E_3 = \{HH, HT, TH\}$ be the event that at least one coin falls heads;

$E_4 = \{TT, HT\}$ be the event that the second coin falls tails.

Then we have the following events.

$E_1 \cap E_4 = \{TT\}$ is the event that both coins fall alike *and* the second coin falls tails.

$E_2 \cap E_3 = \{HT, TH\}$ is the event that at least one coin falls heads *and* both coins fall differently.

$E_1 \cap E_2 = \varnothing$ is the event that both coins fall alike *and* both coins fall differently.

Note that $E_1 \cap E_2$ is an empty set because the sets E_1 and E_2 have no members in common. $E_1 \cap E_2$ is an **impossible event**.

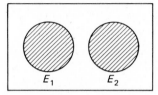

FIGURE 6

DEFINITION Two events E_1 and E_2 of a sample space are said to be **mutually exclusive** if there is no sample point which is in both E_1 and E_2, that is, if $E_1 \cap E_2 = \varnothing$. In other words, E_1 *and E_2 are mutually exclusive if they cannot occur at the same time.*

Figure 6 represents two mutually exclusive events. The regions representing E_1 and E_2 have no sample points in common.

EXAMPLE 6 Consider the sample space $\{1, 2, 3, 4, 5, 6\}$. Let $E_1 = \{2, 4, 6\}$, $E_2 = \{1, 5\}$, and $E_3 = \{2, 3\}$. Then E_1 and E_2 are mutually exclusive because $E_1 \cap E_2 = \varnothing$; however, E_1 and E_3 are *not* mutually exclusive because $E_1 \cap E_3 = \{2\}$ is not an empty set. We see that E_2 and E_3 are mutually exclusive.

EXAMPLE 7 Consider the sample space for drawing a single card from a deck of 52 cards. Then the events *drawing an 8* and *drawing a 10* are mutually exclusive because the card drawn cannot be both an 8 and a 10 at the same time. On the other hand, the events *drawing an ace* and *drawing a heart* are *not* mutually exclusive because it is possible to draw a card that is an ace as well as a heart.

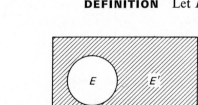

FIGURE 7

DEFINITION Let E be an event in a sample space S. Then the **complement** E' of the event E with respect to the sample space S is the set of all outcomes in S which are not in E.

$$E' = \{x \mid x \in S \quad \text{and} \quad x \notin E\}.$$

In terms of a Venn diagram, E' is the region inside the rectangle but outside the region representing event E. (See Figure 7.) The event E' occurs whenever E does not occur. It follows from the definition of E' that the events E and E' are mutually exclusive.

EXAMPLE 8   Consider the sample space $S = \{1, 2, 3, 4, 5, 6\}$ for the roll of a die. Let $E_1 = \{1, 2, 3\}$ and $E_2 = \{4, 6\}$. Then, E'_1 is the set of all outcomes in S which are not in E_1.

$$E'_1 = \{4, 5, 6\}.$$

Similarly, $E'_2 = \{1, 2, 3, 5\}$.

EXERCISES 1

(1–10)   Write the sample spaces for the following experiments.

1. Five persons named A, B, C, D, and E contest an election; the observation consists of naming the winner.

2. Three coins are tossed. Each may fall heads or tails with no other possibility.

3. A coin is tossed and at the same time a die is rolled. (The six faces of the die are marked with numbers $1, 2, \ldots, 6$.)

4. Two dice are rolled and the numbers turned up on the dice are observed.

5. The order in which three competing salesmen end the year in terms of their annual sales is observed.

6. The order in which four competing salesmen end the year is observed.

7. Three rats are chosen from a cage that contains three brown and two white rats. The colors of the selected rats are observed.

8. A card is selected from among the 4 aces in a deck of playing cards.

9. A spade is selected from a deck of cards.

10. A box contains 3 white balls and 2 black balls that are exactly alike except for color. Two balls are drawn from the box and their colors observed.

(11–14)   For the experiment in Exercise 4 above, write the events for which the sum of the numbers turned up on the two dice is equal to each of the following values.

11. 10   12. 5   13. 7   14. 13

(15–22)   A card is drawn from a pack of 52 cards. Let the events be defined as follows:

E_1:   The card drawn is a heart.

E_2:   The card drawn is a black card.

E_3:   The card drawn has a denomination less than 7 (ace counts low).

E_4:   The card drawn is an ace.

Express the following events in terms of sets, as well as in words.

15. $E_1 \cup E_2$ 16. $E_1 \cap E_2$ 17. $E_1 \cup E_3$

18. $E_1 \cap E_3$ 19. $E_3 \cap E_4$ 20. $E_1 \cup E_4$

21. E'_2 22. E'_3

23. Two coins are tossed. Which of the following events are mutually exclusive?

E_1:   Coins fall alike. E_2:   Coins fall with at least one head.

E_3:   Coins fall with two heads. E_4:   Coins fall differently.

E_5:   Coins fall with at least one tail. E_6:   Coins fall with three heads.

(24–27) A card is drawn from a deck of 52 cards. Which of the following pairs of events are mutually exclusive?

24. The card is a 7 and the card is an ace.

25. The card is a 4 and the card is a spade.

26. The card is a face card and the card is a heart.

27. The card is a 5 and the card is a face card.

28. On any given day, a stock on the stockmarket may go up, go down, or stay the same in price. An investor holds shares in two companies. List the outcomes for the investor's two stocks after trading on a particular day. How many outcomes would there be for an investor who holds three different stocks?

29. Among a group of applicants for a certain executive position with an insurance company, let U be the event that a given applicant has a university degree, let E be the event that the applicant has previous experience in insurance, and let F be the event that the applicant is over 40 years old. Express the following events in symbols.

    a. The event that an applicant is under 40 and has a university degree.

    b. The event that an applicant has neither a degree nor previous experience in insurance.

    c. The event that an applicant has a degree but no previous experience and is over 40.

    d. The event that an applicant has no degree, has previous experience and is under 40.

30. The Venn diagram shows the experiment in Exercise 29. Express the four events in parts a, b, c, and d of Exercise 29 in terms of the regions I, II, . . . , VIII into which the Venn diagram is divided. Which pairs of those events are mutually exclusive?

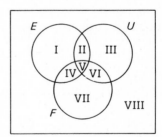

31. For the Venn diagram in Exercise 30, express in words the events represented by the following regions.

    a. Region IV   **b.** Region V   **c.** Regions I and VIII

    d. Regions III and VI   **e.** Regions VI and VIII

32. A corporation plans to promote one of its seven area managers to the position of vice-president of sales. Let S be the event that either Harry or Nick is promoted, T the event that either Harry or Laura is promoted, U the event that either Nick or Sarah is promoted, and V the event that either Fred or Nick is promoted.

List the outcomes belonging to each of the following events if the other two managers are Maureen and Joe.

a. $T \cup U$ b. $T \cup S$ c. S'

d. $V \cup U$ e. $V \cap U$ f. U'

g. $T \cap U$ h. $T \cap V$ i. $(T \cup U)'$

8-2 PROBABILITY

In an experiment or observation for which there are several possible outcomes, we associate with each possible outcome a non-negative number that we call its **probability**. The probability of any particular outcome indicates how likely that outcome is to occur: the bigger the probability, the more likely it is that the outcome will occur. The sum of the probabilities of all the possible outcomes for an experiment is always equal to 1.

To get an idea of the meaning of probability, suppose that the observation is repeated some large number N times, and let an outcome occur K times. Then the ratio K/N gives the proportion of the times that the given outcome occurs. As we make N larger and larger, this ratio can be expected to become closer and closer to the probability of the outcome in question.

EXAMPLE 1   Let a coin be tossed. The two outcomes H and T are clearly equally likely if the coin is tossed fairly, and they each have a probability of $\frac{1}{2}$. (Note that the sum of the probabilities of both possible outcomes is equal to 1.)

Let the coin be tossed N times and let H occur K times in these N tosses. The proportion of heads is then K/N. We know that in general K/N will not be equal to $\frac{1}{2}$; for example, if the coin is tossed twice, it does not have to land heads once and tails once. As a matter of fact, it can quite easily land heads both times or tails both times. However, if N is very large, the proportion K/N of heads will almost certainly be close to $\frac{1}{2}$. That is, K/N gets closer to the probability $\frac{1}{2}$ as N gets larger and larger.

EXAMPLE 2   A traffic survey shows that at a certain intersection, 15% of vehicles turn left, 31% turn right, and 54% make no turn. In this case, the experiment consists of randomly selecting a vehicle approaching the intersection and observing the direction that it turns. The sample space has three points, which can be denoted by

$$\{L, R, N\}$$

indicating left turn, right turn, and no turn, respectively.

The probabilities of these three outcomes are

$$P(L) = 0.15, \quad P(R) = 0.31, \quad \text{and} \quad P(N) = 0.54.$$

Observe that the sum of these probabilities is 1, as it should be:

$$P(L) + P(R) + P(N) = 0.15 + 0.31 + 0.54 = 1.$$

An event E was defined to be a subset of the outcomes in the sample space of a particular experiment. The event occurs whenever one of the outcomes in this subset occurs. We define the **probability of the event** E to be the sum of the probabilities of all the outcomes that belong to E. It is denoted by $P(E)$.

EXAMPLE 3   In Example 2, let the event E be that the selected vehicle makes a turn of some kind at the intersection. Then E consists of the outcomes $\{L, R\}$. The probability of E is then the sum of the probabilities of left and right turns:

$$P(E) = P(L) + P(R) = 0.15 + 0.31 = 0.46.$$

If the observation is repeated N times, let the event E occur on K of these repetitions. The ratio K/N gives the proportion of the observations in which E occured. If we make N very large, this proportion will almost certainly be close to the probability $P(E)$.

> ***Remarks***   1. If $E = \varnothing$, that is, if the event is impossible, then $P(E) = 0$.
> 2. If $E = S$, that is, the event is certain to happen since it consists of the whole set of possible outcomes, then $P(E) = P(S) = 1$.
> 3. The sum of probabilities of the outcomes of E cannot exceed the sum of all the possible outcomes, which is 1. Therefore, for any event E, $0 \leq P(E) \leq 1$.

Very often we find ourselves dealing with observations for which all of the outcomes in the sample space are equally likely to occur. For example, if a coin is tossed, the two outcomes of heads or tails can usually be presumed to be equally likely. Or if a well-balanced die is rolled, the outcomes 1, 2, 3, 4, 5, or 6 should be equally likely to occur. If the die is rolled a large number N of times, each of the six numbers should come up as readily as the rest; that is, each number should appear about one-sixth of the time as long as N is large enough.

DEFINITION   The outcomes of an experiment are said to be **equally likely** if their probabilities are all equal to one another. If the sample space contains n sample points, then the probability of each outcome must be $1/n$ if they are equally likely (since the sum of the probabilities of all the outcomes must equal 1).

It follows that if an event E contains k sample points in an experiment in which the outcomes are equally likely, then the probability $P(E) = k/n$:

$$P(E) = \frac{\text{number of sample points in } E}{\text{number of sample points in } S} = \frac{k}{n}.$$

EXAMPLE 4   What is the probability of throwing a number greater than 4 with a standard die?

Solution   When the die is rolled, the outcome can be any one of the six numbers 1, 2, 3, 4, 5, or 6, that is, $S = \{1, 2, 3, 4, 5, 6\}$. The event E of throwing a number greater than 4 will consist of the outcomes 5 or 6. Thus $E = \{5, 6\}$. In this case,

$$k = \text{number of sample points in } E = 2$$
$$n = \text{number of sample points in } S = 6.$$

Thus

$$P(E) = \frac{k}{n} = \frac{2}{6} = \frac{1}{3}.$$

EXAMPLE 5   What is the probability of throwing a 7 with a standard die?

Solution   As before, the sample space is $S = \{1, 2, 3, 4, 5, 6\}$. The event of throwing a 7 is clearly an impossible event because $7 \notin S$, so $E = \varnothing$. Thus we have $k = 0$, because the empty set has no element. Since $n = 6$,

$$P(E) = \frac{k}{n} = \frac{0}{6} = 0.$$

EXAMPLE 6   Find the probability of throwing at least two heads by tossing three fair coins.

Solution   The sample space for tossing three coins is easily obtained from the tree diagram in Figure 8. Thus $S = \{HHH, HHT, HTH, HTT, THH, THT, TTH, TTT\}$. The event of throwing at least two heads is

$$E = \{HHH, HHT, HTH, THH\}.$$

In this case, k is the number of elements in E, or $k = 4$, and n is the number of elements in S, or $n = 8$. Thus

$$P(E) = \frac{k}{n} = \frac{4}{8} = \frac{1}{2}.$$

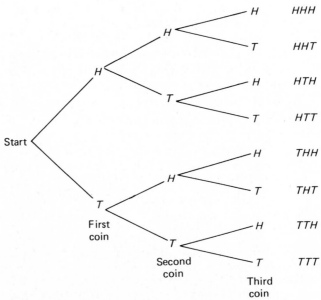

FIGURE 8

EXAMPLE 7   Find the probability of throwing a sum of 9 with the roll of two dice.

Solution   The sample space can easily be obtained by a tree diagram; it is given in ordered pair notation in Figure 9. In the ordered pair (x, y), x denotes the number on the first die and y denotes the number on the second die. There are 36 ordered pairs in this sample space, so $n = 36$. The sum of 9 on the two dice results if any one of the four pairs $(3, 6)$, $(4, 5)$, $(5, 4)$, or $(6, 3)$ is rolled. (These outcomes are circled in Figure 9.) Thus there are four sample points in the event *a sum of 9 is rolled*, that is, $k = 4$. Hence

$$P(\text{sum of 9 rolled}) = \frac{k}{n} = \frac{4}{36} = \frac{1}{9}.$$

(1, 1)	(1, 2)	(1, 3)	(1, 4)	(1, 5)	(1, 6)
(2, 1)	(2, 2)	(2, 3)	(2, 4)	(2, 5)	(2, 6)
(3, 1)	(3, 2)	(3, 3)	(3, 4)	(3, 5)	(3, 6)
(4, 1)	(4, 2)	(4, 3)	(4, 4)	(4, 5)	(4, 6)
(5, 1)	(5, 2)	(5, 3)	(5, 4)	(5, 5)	(5, 6)
(6, 1)	(6, 2)	(6, 3)	(6, 4)	(6, 5)	(6, 6)

FIGURE 9

Probability Formulas

$P(E')$ is the probability of the event E', which is complementary to E. Thus $P(E')$ is the probability that the event E does not occur. Similarly, $P(E_1 \cap E_2)$ is the probability of the intersection of E_1 and E_2, or the probability that E_1 *and* E_2 occur and $P(E_1 \cup E_2)$ is the probability that E_1 *or* E_2 occurs. There are certain formulas involving these three probabilities that are often useful in calculating probabilities of events.

Let us begin by considering the following example: Two dice are rolled and we want to find the probability that the sum of the two scores is different from 9.

In Example 7, we calculated the probability that the sum of the two numbers is *equal* to 9. This event corresponds to the four outcomes $(3, 6)$, $(4, 5)$, $(5, 4)$, and $(6, 3)$ and so has probability $\frac{4}{36}$, or $\frac{1}{9}$. The event that the sum of the two scores is different from 9 corresponds to the set of all the outcomes except these four. Since there are 32 other outcomes, the probability of getting a sum different from 9 is equal to $\frac{32}{36}$, or $\frac{8}{9}$.

Observe that in this example we are dealing with two events that are complementary to one another: the event that the sum is equal to 9 and the event that it is different from 9. These two events have probabilities of $\frac{1}{9}$ and $\frac{8}{9}$, respectively. The sum of the two probabilities equals 1. This property of complementary events is generalized in Rule 1.

RULE 1 If E' is the event complementary to E, then

$$P(E') = 1 - P(E).$$

PROOF $P(E)$ is equal to the sum of probabilities of all of the outcomes belonging to E. Since E' consists of all of the outcomes that do not belong to E, $P(E')$ is the sum of probabilities of these outcomes. Therefore the sum $P(E) + P(E')$ is equal to the sum of probabilities of all the possible outcomes in S and must equal $P(S)$, or 1:

$$P(E) + P(E') = 1.$$

The stated rule follows from this equation.

EXAMPLE 8   In a certain community, the probability of a 70-year-old individual living to be 80 is 0.64. What is the probability of an individual who is 70 and a member of this community dying sometime in the next 10 years?

Solution   If E denotes the event that a 70-year-old individual will live for the next 10 years, then the complementary event E' is that a 70-year-old person will die within the next 10 years. We are given that $P(E) = 0.64$ and we want $P(E')$.

$$P(E') = 1 - P(E)$$
$$= 1 - 0.64 = 0.36$$

Thus the probability of an individual who is 70 years old now dying within the next 10 years is 0.36.

In order to introduce the second probability formula, consider the example of rolling two dice. There are 36 outcomes, which are listed in Figure 9. Let E_1 be the event that the sum of the two scores is 8. Then $E_1 = \{(6, 2), (5, 3), (4, 4), (3, 5), (2, 6)\}$ and $P(E_1) = \frac{5}{36}$. Let E_2 be the event that both dice show an odd number of spots. Then

$$E_2 = \{(1, 1), (1, 3), (1, 5), (3, 1), (3, 3), (3, 5), (5, 1), (5, 3), (5, 5)\}.$$

There are 9 outcomes, so $P(E_2) = \frac{9}{36}$.

The event $E_1 \cap E_2$ is the event that both E_1 and E_2 occur and contains only the two outcomes (3, 5) and (5, 3). Therefore $P(E_1 \cap E_2) = \frac{2}{36}$.

Similarly, the event $E_1 \cup E_2$ is

$$E_1 \cup E_2 = \{(1, 1), (1, 3), (1, 5), (3, 1), (3, 3), (3, 5), (5, 1), (5, 3),$$
$$(5, 5), (6, 2), (4, 4), (2, 6)\},$$

which has 12 outcomes. Therefore $P(E_1 \cup E_2) = \frac{12}{36}$.

Note that $P(E_1) + P(E_2) = \frac{9}{36} + \frac{5}{36} = \frac{14}{36}$. This is not equal to $P(E_1 \cup E_2)$. The reason that these are not equal to one another is that in forming $P(E_1) + P(E_2)$, the two events (5, 3) and (3, 5) are counted twice—once in E_1 and once in E_2. We see, however, that the difference

$$P(E_1) + P(E_2) - P(E_1 \cup E_2) = \frac{14}{36} - \frac{12}{36}$$

is equal to $\frac{2}{36}$, the probability of the two outcomes (5, 3) and (3, 5). But this is precisely equal to $P(E_1 \cap E_2)$, so we have

$$P(E_1) + P(E_2) - P(E_1 \cup E_2) = P(E_1 \cap E_2).$$

This relation is true in general.

RULE 2 Let E_1 and E_2 be two events that are subsets of the same sample space S. Then,

$$\boxed{P(E_1 \cup E_2) = P(E_1) + P(E_2) - P(E_1 \cap E_2).}$$

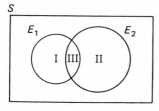

FIGURE 10

PROOF Figure 10 illustrates the Venn diagram for the experiment in question. The sets of sample points corresponding to E_1 and E_2 are shown. Region I consists of sample points that are in E_1 but outside E_2. Similarly, Region II consists of sample points in E_2 but not in E_1. Region III denotes the sample points that are in both E_1 and E_2, that is, the intersection $E_1 \cap E_2$.

$P(E_1) =$ sum of probabilities of the outcomes in Regions I and III

$P(E_2) =$ sum of probabilities of the outcomes in Regions II and III

Therefore if $P(E_1)$ and $P(E_2)$ are added, we obtain the sum of the probabilities of the outcomes in all three regions, I, II and III, except that those in III are counted twice. But the sum of probabilities in III is equal to $P(E_1 \cap E_2)$, and so

$$P(E_1) + P(E_2) - P(E_1 \cap E_2) = \text{sum of probabilities of the outcomes}$$
$$\text{in Regions I, II, and III}$$
$$= P(E_1 \cup E_2)$$

as required.

In particular, if the events E_1 and E_2 are mutually exclusive, $E_1 \cap E_2 = \varnothing$, so that $P(E_1 \cap E_2) = 0$. The formula in Rule 2 reduces to

$$\boxed{P(E_1 \cup E_2) = P(E_1) + P(E_2) \qquad \text{for mutually exclusive events.}}$$

EXAMPLE 9   Find the probability of drawing an ace *or* a spade from a deck of 52 cards in a single draw.

Solution   A single card can be drawn from a deck of 52 cards in 52 different ways, so that the sample space consists of 52 elements. The event E_1 of drawing an ace can be achieved in 4 ways because there are 4 aces. Thus $P(E_1) = \frac{4}{52}$. The event E_2 of drawing a spade can be achieved in 13 ways because there are 13 spades in the deck. Thus $P(E_2) = \frac{13}{52}$. There is only one card that is both an ace and a spade, so the event $E_1 \cap E_2$ can happen in only one way and $P(E_1 \cap E_2) = \frac{1}{52}$. We are interested in the probability of drawing an ace *or* a spade, that

27. A computer firm has 60 college graduates on its staff, 28 of whom had their college training in computer science. Of these employees, 39 are under 40 years old; among these 39, 21 had college training in computer science. If an individual is chosen at random from among the 60, what is the probability that he or she will be over 40 and have no training in computer science?

28. Of the customers at a supermarket, 20% buy 10 items or less, 70% spend more than $10, and 68% spend more than $10 and buy more than 10 items. What is the probability that a customer chosen at random: (a) spends more than $10 and buys 10 items or less; (b) spends less than $10 and buys 10 items or less?

29. Prove the following probability statements by appropriate Venn diagrams.

   a. $P(E_1 \cap E_2) + P(E_1 \cap E_2') = P(E_1)$

   b. $P(E_1' \cap E_2') = 1 - P(E_2) - P(E_1 \cap E_2')$

30. Two cards are drawn from a pack of 52 cards one by one without replacement; that is, the first card is not replaced before the second card is drawn. What is the probability in each case?

   a. The first card is an ace and the second is a heart.

   b. The first card is a 5 and the second is a 10.

8-3 CONDITIONAL PROBABILITY

Additional information about the outcome of an experiment can change the probabilities of associated events. For example, if a card is drawn at random from an ordinary deck of 52 cards, the probability that it is a spade is $\frac{1}{4}$. However, if we are told in addition that the drawn card is black, then the probability that it is a spade is $\frac{1}{2}$. The difference between these two situations is that in the first case, the sample space consists of all 52 cards, while in the second case, the additional information effectively reduces the sample space to the 26 black cards. In each case, 13 of the cards are spades, so that the probabilities of the drawn card being a spade are $\frac{13}{52} = \frac{1}{4}$ and $\frac{13}{26} = \frac{1}{2}$, respectively.

As a second example, let us suppose that an insurance company is choosing a person to fill a certain job from among 50 applicants. Among the applicants, some have a university degree, some have previous experience in the insurance field, and some have both. Suppose that the breakdown is given in Table 1. For example, 5 applicants have both a degree and previous experience in insurance, 20 applicants have neither, and so on. If an applicant is chosen at

TABLE 1

	Degree	No Degree
Previous Experience	5	10
No Experience	15	20

random from among the 50, the probability that this applicant will have had previous experience is $\frac{15}{50} = 0.3$, since 15 of the applicants altogether have had experience. However, let us suppose that the company considers only those applicants who have university degrees, and that an applicant is chosen at random from this subset. There are 20 such applicants, 5 of whom have had previous experience, so the probability of selecting one with experience is now $\frac{5}{20}$ or 0.25.

In the second case, the sample space is again effectively reduced by the company's restriction to applicants with degrees. This change of sample space changes the probability of the chosen applicant having previous experience. We can say that for the whole set of applicants, the probability of choosing one with previous experience is 0.3. However, the probability of choosing an applicant with experience given that he or she must also have a degree is 0.25.

This is an example of what is called a *conditional probability*.

DEFINITION   Let E_1 and E_2 be two events. Then the **conditional probability of E_2 given E_1**, written $P(E_2 | E_1)$, is the probability that E_2 occurs given that E_1 is known to have occurred.

In the last discussion, if E_1 is the event that the chosen applicant has a degree and E_2 the event that he or she has had previous experience, then $P(E_2) = 0.3$ and the conditional probability $P(E_2 | E_1) = 0.25$.

EXAMPLE 1   Three coins are tossed. Let E_1 be the event that the first coin falls heads and E_2 the event that two coins fall heads and one falls tails. Calculate $P(E_1)$, $P(E_2)$, $P(E_2 | E_1)$, and $P(E_1 | E_2)$.

Solution   The sample space consists of the eight points shown in Figure 11. Here E_1 contains the four outcomes whose first letter is H, and E_2 contains the three outcomes with 2 H's and 1 T. Therefore $P(E_1) = \frac{4}{8} = \frac{1}{2}$ and $P(E_2) = \frac{3}{8}$.

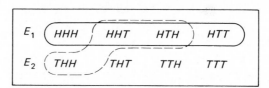

FIGURE 11

$P(E_2 | E_1)$ is the probability of two heads and one tail given that the first coin falls heads. To calculate this, we must restrict attention to the four outcomes in E_1. Of these, two outcomes also belong to E_2, namely HHT and HTH. Therefore E_2 occurs twice out of the four outcomes in E_1 and we have $P(E_2 | E_1) = \frac{2}{4} = \frac{1}{2}$.

$P(E_1 | E_2)$ is the probability that the first coin fell heads given that there were two heads and one tail. To calculate it, we must restrict our attention to the three outcomes in E_2. Of these, two also belong to E_1, so E_1 occurs twice out of the three outcomes in E_2. Therefore $P(E_1 | E_2) = \frac{2}{3}$.

Note that in calculating these two conditional probabilities, the two outcomes *HHT* and *HTH*, which belong to both E_1 and E_2, play a key role. These two outcomes form the intersection of E_1 and E_2. We can see that

$$P(E_2 \mid E_1) = \text{(Number of Outcomes in } E_1 \cap E_2)$$
$$\div \text{(Number of Outcomes in } E_1)$$
$$= 2 \div 4$$

and

$$P(E_1 \mid E_2) = \text{(Number of Outcomes in } E_1 \cap E_2)$$
$$\div \text{(Number of Outcomes in } E_2)$$
$$= 2 \div 3.$$

Alternatively, since the outcomes are all equally likely, we can write the following.

RULE 3

$$P(E_2 \mid E_1) = \frac{P(E_1 \cap E_2)}{P(E_1)} \quad \text{and} \quad P(E_1 \mid E_2) = \frac{P(E_1 \cap E_2)}{P(E_2)}$$

This result is, in fact, generally true for any pair of events E_1 and E_2. The first relation can be rewritten in the form

RULE 3′

$$P(E_1 \cap E_2) = P(E_1)P(E_2 \mid E_1).$$

In words, this says that *the probability that both E_1 and E_2 occur is equal to the probability that E_1 occurs multiplied by the conditional probability that E_2 occurs given that E_1 has already occurred.* In these verbal terms, the equation is intuitively plausible.

EXAMPLE 2   Among the male population in between the ages of 30 and 35 living in a certain city, 25% have a university degree, 15% earn more than $25,000 per year, and 65% have no degree and earn less than $25,000 per year. What is the probability that an individual chosen at random from this group earns more than $25,000 per year given that : (a) he has a degree;   (b) he has no degree?

Solution   Let D be the event that the individual has a degree and E be the event that he earns more than $25,000 per year. We are given that $P(D) = 0.25$ and $P(E) = 0.15$.

The complementary events are D', that he has no degree, and E', that he earns less than $25,000 per year. We are given that the probability of both these events is 0.65, that is, $P(E' \cap D') = 0.65$. The given information is summarized in Table 2. In this table, we have used Rule 1 to calculate $P(E') = 1 - P(E) = 1 - 0.15 = 0.85$ and $P(D') = 1 - P(D) = 1 - 0.25 = 0.75$. In

TABLE 2

	D (Degree)	D' (No Degree)	
E (Earns more than \$25,000)	$P(E \cap D)$	$P(E \cap D')$	$P(E) = 0.15$
E' (Earns less than \$25,000)	$P(E' \cap D)$	$P(E' \cap D')$ $= 0.65$	$P(E') = 0.85$
	$P(D) = 0.25$	$P(D') = 0.75$	

verbal terms, 25% of the given age group have a degree, so 75% do not have a degree; 15% earn more than \$25,000, so 85% must earn less.

In the main part of the table, the sample space is divided into the four segments $E \cap D$, $E \cap D'$, $E' \cap D$, and $E' \cap D'$. For example, the subset $E' \cap D$ corresponds to individuals who have a degree and earn less than \$25,000, while $E' \cap D'$ corresponds to those who have no degree and earn less than \$25,000. We are told that this latter group comprises 65% of the whole group, that is, $P(E' \cap D') = 0.65$.

Of the 85% who earn less than \$25,000, 65% have no degree. The remaining 20% must have a degree, so this 20% forms the membership of $E' \cap D$. In terms of probability, we can write

$$P(E' \cap D) + 0.65 = P(E') = 0.85$$

and so $P(E' \cap D) = 0.2$. Similarly, in the column headed by D', we have a total of 75% of the age group. Of these, 65% earn less than \$25,000, so the remaining 10% earn more. That is, $P(E \cap D') = 0.1$. Finally, in the top row, we have $P(E \cap D) + P(E \cap D') = P(E) = 0.15$. Since we now know that $P(E \cap D') = 0.1$, it follows that $P(E \cap D) = 0.05$. The completed table is shown as Table 3.

TABLE 3

	D	D'	
E	0.05	0.1	$P(E) = 0.15$
E'	0.2	0.65	$P(E') = 0.85$
	$P(D) = 0.25$	$P(D') = 0.75$	

We wish to calculate the two conditional probabilities

$$P(E \mid D) \quad \text{and} \quad P(E \mid D').$$

From Rule 3,

$$P(E \mid D) = \frac{P(E \cap D)}{P(D)} = \frac{0.05}{0.25} = 0.2$$

and

$$P(E|D') = \frac{P(E \cap D')}{P(D')} = \frac{0.1}{0.75} = \frac{2}{15} = 0.133$$

Thus the probability of an individual with a degree earning more than $25,000 is 0.2. The probability of one without a degree doing the same is 0.133.

DEFINITION Two events E_1 and E_2 are **independent** if the probability of either one occurring does not depend on whether or not the other occurs. That is, E_1 and E_2 are independent if

$$P(E_1 | E_2) = P(E_1) \tag{1}$$

or if

$$P(E_2 | E_1) = P(E_2). \tag{2}$$

These two conditions are, in fact, identical. Making use of Rule 3' for independent events, we have from Equation 1 that

$$P(E_1 \cap E_2) = P(E_1 | E_2)P(E_2) = P(E_1)P(E_2).$$

If this is substituted into the first part of Rule 3, then Equation (2) is obtained. Thus we have the following rule.

RULE 4

> $$P(E_1 \cap E_2) = P(E_1)P(E_2) \qquad \text{if } E_1 \text{ and } E_2 \text{ are independent.}$$

Thus *if E_1 and E_2 are independent, the probability of E_1 and E_2 both occurring is equal to the product of the separate probabilities of E_1 and E_2.* This result is often called the **multiplication rule** for independent events.

It is often intuitively obvious whether or not two events are independent. For example, let a coin be tossed and a die rolled at the same time and let E_1 be the event that the coin falls heads and E_2 the event that the die shows 5 or 6. Clearly E_1 and E_2 are independent, since there is no reason why the fall of the coin should influence the number of spots showing on the die.

EXAMPLE 3 Find the probability of tossing a head with a coin and then drawing an ace from a deck of 52 cards.

Solution The probability of getting a head (H) with the flip of a coin is $P(H) = \frac{1}{2}$. The probability of drawing an ace (A) from a pack of 52 cards is $P(A) = \frac{4}{52}$. The two events, tossing a head and drawing an ace, are independent events. Therefore

$$P(A \text{ and } H) = P(A) \cdot P(H)$$
$$= \frac{4}{52} \cdot \frac{1}{2} = \frac{1}{26}.$$

EXAMPLE 4 A card is drawn from a deck of 52 cards. It is replaced, the cards are shuffled, and a second card is drawn. Find the probability that the first card is a 7 and the second card is a spade.

Solution   These events are independent; the result of the second drawing is not affected by the first drawing since the first card is replaced in the deck before the second card is drawn. We can draw a card out of 52 cards in 52 ways. The card 7 can be drawn in 4 ways, so the probability of drawing a 7 is

$$P(7) = \tfrac{4}{52} = \tfrac{1}{13}.$$

Similarly, the probability of drawing a spade in the second drawing is

$$P(\text{spade}) = \tfrac{13}{52} = \tfrac{1}{4}.$$

Using Rule 4, the probability of drawing a 7 in the first drawing and a spade in the second drawing is

$$P(7 \text{ and spade}) = P(7) \cdot P(\text{spade})$$
$$= \tfrac{1}{13} \cdot \tfrac{1}{4} = \tfrac{1}{52}.$$

In cases where the independence of two events is not intuitively obvious, their independence can be verified by demonstrating that the multiplication rule holds or disproved by showing that the rule does not hold.

EXAMPLE 5   Over a certain period of time, an automobile plant turns out 5000 automobiles. Of these, 1000 were built on a Monday, 1000 on a Tuesday, and so on, with 1000 built on a Friday. It was necessary to return 400 of these automobiles for repair of a serious defect during the guarantee period. Of the cars built on a Friday, 150 were returned. Are the two events, a car was built on a Friday and it was defective, independent of one another?

Solution   Let F be the event that a car chosen at random was built on a Friday and D be the event that it turned out to be defective. Then the probabilities of these events are

$$P(F) = \tfrac{1000}{5000} = 0.2$$
$$P(D) = \tfrac{400}{5000} = 0.08.$$

Since 150 cars belong to both of these events,

$$P(F \cap D) = \tfrac{150}{5000} = 0.03.$$

But $P(D) \cdot P(F) = (0.08)(0.2) = 0.016 \neq P(F \cap D)$, so the events F and D are not independent.

The probability that a car built on a Friday being defective is the conditional probability $P(D|F)$. It is given by Rule 3:

$$P(D|F) = \frac{P(F \cap D)}{P(F)} = \frac{0.03}{0.2} = 0.15.$$

This probability is not equal to $P(D)$, again showing that the two events are not independent.

EXERCISES 3

(1–2) Two coins are tossed. Find each probability.

1. The second coin falls heads given that both coins fall alike.

2. The second coin falls heads given that the coins fall with at least one head.

(3–4) Two coins are tossed. Are the following events independent?

3. A: The coins fall at least one head.
    B: The coins fall both alike.

4. C: The first coin falls tails.
    D: The second coin falls either heads or different from the first coin.

(5–10) Two dice are rolled. Find each probability.

5. The sum of the scores is at least 9, given that the first die shows 5 spots.

6. The sum of the scores is at least 9, given that the sum of the scores is at least 8.

7. The difference between the scores is 1, given that the sum of the scores is 7.

8. The second die scores more than the first, given that the sum of the scores is 8.

9. At least one of the dice scores 5 or 6, given that the sum of the scores is 6 or more.

10. The two dice fall alike, given that the sum of the scores is: (a) even; (b) odd.

(11–14) Three coins are tossed. Find each probability.

11. The coins fall two heads and one tail, given that they do not all fall alike.

12. The first two coins fall tails, given that at least two of the coins fall tails.

13. There are more heads than tails, given that the first coin falls heads.

14. The coins do not all fall alike, given that the first two coins fall alike.

15. A manufacturer's product is examined by two inspectors, A and B. Of the defective products, 20% get by inspector A; and if a defective product gets by A, there is a probability of 0.5 that it will then be passed by inspector B. What is the probability that a defective part gets by both inspectors?

16. Of the cans of meat produced by a firm, 5% are underweight and 1% of the cans are both underweight and have a canning defect. If an underweight can is chosen at random, what is the probability that it will have a canning defect?

17. A can manufacturer stores its cans in batches of 500. In one particular batch, 150 of the cans are substandard. An inspector selects 2 cans at random from the batch. What is the probability: (a) that both are substandard; (b) that both are good?

18. 35% of married men and 50% of married women drink tea regularly. 50% of the men whose wives drink tea also drink tea themselves. Find each probability.

    a. That a given married couple both drink tea.

    b. That of a married couple, neither drinks tea.

    c. That a woman whose husband drinks tea also drinks tea herself.

19. A company estimates that 30% of the population has seen a television ad for its soap powder. Of those who see the ad, 10% later buy the product. What proportion of the population has both seen the ad and bought the product? If 5% of those who have not seen the ad have also bought the soap powder, find each probability.

    a. That a randomly selected individual has bought the soap powder.

    b. That an individual who has bought the soap powder has not seen the ad.

20. When spot-checked for safety, automobiles are found to have defective tires 15% of the time, defective lights 25% of the time, and both defective tires and lights 8% of the time. Find the probability that a randomly chosen car

    a. has defective lights, given that its tires have been found defective.

    b. has defective tires, given that its lights have been found defective.

    c. has good tires, given that its lights are good.

21. A credit-card company finds that 40% of its customers live in urban areas and 60% live in suburban or rural areas. Of the customers, 30% average more than $200 per month on their credit card and 10% both live in urban areas and spend over $200 per month. Find the probability that a given customer lives in an urban area given that the customer spends less than $200 per month on his or her credit card.

22. In a certain population, 35% are wealthy according to some standard and 30% have wealthy parents. One in six of those with wealthy parents are not wealthy themselves. Find the probability that an individual's parents are not wealthy given that the person is not wealthy.

23. A manufacturer buys a certain component from two suppliers, A and B. Over a certain period of time, the company used 20,000 of these components, 6,000 of which came from supplier A. Of these components, 3% of those supplied by A and $1\frac{1}{2}\%$ of those supplied by B turned out to be defective. Find the probability that a given defective component came from supplier A.

24. A company employs 8 unskilled laborers and 12 skilled tradesmen. Over a period of 100 working days, the company found that it lost 40 work-days of unskilled labor and 40 work-days of skilled labor through absenteeism. Find the probability that a randomly chosen absentee employee is one of the skilled tradesmen.

8-4 PERMUTATIONS AND COMBINATIONS

It is clear from the examples of the last two sections that we very often find ourselves dealing with observations for which the outcomes are all equally likely. In these situations, all we need to know to compute the probability of any event is the number of outcomes that lead to the event in question and the total number of outcomes of the observation. One way of evaluating these two numbers is to make a complete list of all of the outcomes and simply count those that belong to the event, as well as the total number of outcomes. This essentially was the method used in Section 2. But for some observations, the number of outcomes may be exceedingly large, and listing them all may be a difficult or even impossibly long task. The following example illustrates this point.

EXAMPLE 1   (a) What is the probability of rolling at least two 6's in six rolls of a die? The total number of outcomes when a die is rolled six times is 46,656, and it would clearly be foolish to attempt to list them all.

    (b) What is the probability of drawing a full house in a poker hand of five cards? What is the probability of drawing a royal flush? Such questions involve large numbers, since the total number of different poker hands, which is the number of points in the sample space, is about 2.5 million.

(c) A telephone cable containing 10 wires is cut. If the wires in the two broken ends are joined together in a random manner, what is the probability that they will be joined correctly? In this case, these are about 3.6 million ways of joining the two sets of wires together.

(d) In a reorganization of its senior personnel, a large corporation intends to promote 4 of its 20 area managers to positions in its central administration. The number of ways in which the 4 positions can be filled is 116,280. We could ask questions such as, "What is the probability that two of the area managers who are good friends will both be promoted to head office?"

What is needed in situations like this (which, in fact, arise very often) is a method of counting the numbers of outcomes in various events without actually listing them. In this section, we shall briefly outline several techniques that are useful in this situation.

The following fundamental principle underlies many counting methods. Consider an experiment that consists of several (p, for example) independent operations. Let the first operation have n_1 possible outcomes, the second operation have n_2 possible outcomes, and so on, the pth operation having n_p outcomes. Then the total number of outcomes of the whole experiment is given by the product

$$n_1 \times n_2 \times \cdots \times n_p.$$

EXAMPLE 2   (a) Let the experiment consist of flipping 3 coins. We can break this experiment up into three independent operations, each operation being the flip of one of the coins. Each of these has 2 outcomes, heads or tails. The total number of outcomes of the experiment is therefore given by the product $2 \times 2 \times 2 = 8$. (See Example 6 in Section 2.)

(b) Let the experiment consist of rolling 2 dice. Each of these rolls has 6 possible outcomes. Therefore the complete experiment, consisting of the 2 rolls, has $6 \times 6 = 36$ outcomes. (See Example 7 in Section 2.)

(c) A North American corporation is in the process of expanding its business into Europe and intends to send 3 representatives, one to Brussels, one to Frankfurt, and one to Zurich. If there are 10 representatives from which to choose, in how many ways can the 3 be selected?

There are 10 ways of selecting the representative to be sent to Brussels. Having made that choice however, there are only 9 left from which to make the next choice. Thus, if the Frankfurt representative is chosen next, this second choice can be made in 9 ways. Similarly, the Zurich representative can be chosen in only 8 ways once the other two have been selected. Consequently, the number of ways in which the 3 representatives can be chosen is given by the product $10 \times 9 \times 8 = 720$.

Part (c) of Example 2 provides an example of what are called **ordered selections** or **permutations**. We have a group of 10 individuals and we wish to select 3 of them for a certain purpose. Since each of the 3 individuals is needed for a different purpose, the *order* in which the selection is made is important. On the other hand, if the corporation intended to send all 3 representatives to the same place, then the order would not matter, and we would obtain a different answer.

Consider the general case in which we have n objects or individuals and we wish to make an ordered selection of r objects from among these n.

Since there are n objects from which to choose, the first object may be chosen in n ways. However, since the first object is not replaced, there are only $n - 1$ objects from which the second can be chosen. Hence the second object can be selected in $n - 1$ ways. Similarly, the third object can be selected in $n - 2$ ways once the first two have been chosen, and so on. The last (rth) object can be chosen in $n - r + 1$ ways. Thus the number of ways in which the whole permutation can be selected is given by the product

$$n(n - 1)(n - 2) \cdots (n - r + 1).$$

This product is denoted by the symbol $_nP_r$ and is called the **number of permutations of r objects from n objects**. The value of $_nP_r$ is given by the product of r consecutive integers, starting with n and decreasing to $n - r + 1$. For example,

$$_8P_3 = 8(8 - 1)(8 - 2) = 8 \cdot 7 \cdot 6 = 336$$

and

$$_{15}P_2 = 15 \cdot 14 = 210.$$

The quantity $n!$, called **n factorial**, is defined to be the product of all the positive integers from 1 up to n. Thus, for example, $1! = 1$, $2! = 1 \cdot 2 = 2$, $3! = 1 \cdot 2 \cdot 3 = 6$, $4! = 1 \cdot 2 \cdot 3 \cdot 4 = 24$, and $5! = 1 \cdot 2 \cdot 3 \cdot 4 \cdot 5 = 120$. In general, we can write

$$n! = 1 \cdot 2 \cdot 3 \cdots (n - 1)n.$$

We also define $0!$ to be 1 as a matter of convention.

We can express $_nP_r$ in terms of factorials.

EXAMPLE 3   (a) $_8P_3 = 8 \cdot 7 \cdot 6$

$$= \frac{8 \cdot 7 \cdot 6 \cdot 5 \cdot 4 \cdot 3 \cdot 2 \cdot 1}{5 \cdot 4 \cdot 3 \cdot 2 \cdot 1} = \frac{8!}{5!}$$

(b) $_{15}P_2 = 15 \cdot 14$

$$= \frac{15 \cdot 14 \cdot 13 \cdot 12 \cdots 2 \cdot 1}{13 \cdot 12 \cdots 2 \cdot 1} = \frac{15!}{13!}$$

In general,

$$_nP_r = n(n - 1) \cdots (n - r + 1)$$

$$= \frac{n(n - 1) \cdots (n - r + 1)(n - r)(n - r - 1) \cdots 2 \cdot 1}{(n - r)(n - r - 1) \cdots 2 \cdot 1}.$$

We introduced the factors $n - r, n - r - 1, \ldots, 2, 1$ into both numerator and denominator, so the value of the expression has not changed. But the numerator is now equal to $n!$ and the denominator is equal to $(n - r)!$, so we have

$$_nP_r = \frac{n!}{(n - r)!}.$$

Letting $r = n$, we obtain the result that

$$_nP_n = \frac{n!}{0!} = n!.$$

EXAMPLE 4   From a group of 4 people, we are required to select individuals to participate in 3 different tests. In how many ways can the selection be made?

Solution   Since the tests are *different*, the order in which the 3 are chosen is significant. The number of ways in which the choice can be made is therefore the number of permutations

$$_4P_3 = 4 \cdot 3 \cdot 2 = 24.$$

Now let us consider the case when r objects are selected from n objects, but when the order in which the objects are chosen is of no significance. For instance, in the last example, we could suppose that the 3 individuals are chosen from the 4 available people in order to participate in the *same* test. Then the order in which the 3 are chosen would be immaterial, and all we would need to know would be which 3 formed the chosen group.

Let us label the available individuals by the letters a, b, c, and d. If the order in which the choice is made is important, then the number of choices is equal to $_4P_3 = 4 \cdot 3 \cdot 2 = 24$. We can list these 24 choices as follows.

bcd,	*bdc,*	*cbd,*	*cdb,*	*dcb,*	*dbc*
acd,	*adc,*	*cad,*	*cda,*	*dac,*	*dca*
abd,	*adb,*	*bad,*	*bda,*	*dab,*	*dba*
abc,	*acb,*	*bac,*	*bca,*	*cab,*	*cba*

We observe from this list that each group of 3 individuals appears 6 times, corresponding to the 6 different ways in which the 3 individuals can be ordered. If the order in which the 3 individuals are selected is of no importance, all of these 6 permutations of each group are equivalent to one another; for example, *bcd* is equivalent to *bdc*, to *cbd*, and so on. When order is immaterial, there are only 4 different choices, corresponding to the 4 rows in the above table.

Now consider the general problem in which r objects are chosen from among n, where the order of selection is of no significance. Each such choice is called a **combination** of r objects from among n, and the number of combinations is denoted by the symbol $\binom{n}{r}$.

Any permutation of r objects from among n can be formed by first choosing the r objects and then arranging these r objects in an appropriate order. The number of permutations, $_nP_r$, is therefore equal to the number of ways of choosing particular combinations of r objects from among n multiplied by the number of ways in which each combination can be ordered. That is,

$$_nP_r = \binom{n}{r} \times N(r)$$

where $N(r)$ is the number of ordered arrangements of the chosen r objects. But $N(r)$ must be equal to $_rP_r = r!$, the number of permutations of r objects from among r. Therefore

$$_nP_r = \binom{n}{r}r!$$

and so

$$\binom{n}{r} = \frac{_nP_r}{r!} = \frac{n!}{(n-r)!r!}. \tag{1}$$

We can also write the number of combinations in the form

$$\binom{n}{r} = \frac{n(n-1)\cdots(n-r+1)}{r(r-1)\cdots 2 \cdot 1}.$$

Note that both the numerator and denominator in this fraction contain r consecutive integers as factors.

EXAMPLE 5   (a) $\binom{8}{3} = \frac{8(8-1)(8-2)}{3(3-1)(3-2)} = \frac{8\cdot7\cdot6}{3\cdot2\cdot1} = 56$

(b) $\binom{7}{5} = \frac{7\cdot6\cdot5\cdot4\cdot3}{5\cdot4\cdot3\cdot2\cdot1} = \frac{7\cdot6}{2\cdot1} = 21$

In the first case, three factors occur in numerator and denominator, while in the second, five factors occur.

Remarks

$$\binom{n}{n} = \binom{n}{0} = 1$$

$$\binom{n}{r} = \binom{n}{n-r} \quad \text{for all } r$$

The first two values follow by setting $r = n$ and $r = 0$, respectively, in Equation (1). The last result follows by replacing r by $n - r$ in Equation (1).

EXAMPLE 6   Compute the number of different poker hands.

Solution   A poker hand consists of a set of 5 cards chosen from the available 52 in the deck. The number of different hands is then simply the number of ways of choosing 5 cards from among 52. The order of selection is of no significance, so the number is

$$\binom{52}{5} = \frac{52\cdot51\cdot50\cdot49\cdot48}{1\cdot2\cdot3\cdot4\cdot5} = 2{,}598{,}960.$$

EXAMPLE 7   What is the probability of a poker hand of 5 cards containing 4 cards of a kind?

Solution   The number of points n in the sample space is the number of different poker hands that are possible. From Example 6, this is

$$n = \binom{52}{5} = \frac{52 \cdot 51 \cdot 50 \cdot 49 \cdot 48}{1 \cdot 2 \cdot 3 \cdot 4 \cdot 5}.$$

The event for which we wish to calculate the probability is that the poker hand contains 4 cards of the same denomination (that is, 4 aces, 4 sevens, and so on). If there are k different ways in which such a hand can be chosen, then the required probability is equal to k/n.

Consider first the possibility that the hand contains 4 aces. The number of hands that have this property is equal simply to the number of ways in which the fifth card can be selected, namely 48 (since there are 48 cards remaining after the four aces have gone).

Similarly, there are 48 poker hands containing four 2's, 48 hands containing four 3's, and so on. Since there are 13 possible denominations, the number of ways of choosing a hand with 4 of a kind, regardless of denomination, is given by

$$k = 13 \cdot 48.$$

The required probability is therefore

$$P = \frac{k}{n} = \frac{13 \cdot 48}{(52 \cdot 51 \cdot 50 \cdot 49 \cdot 48/1 \cdot 2 \cdot 3 \cdot 4 \cdot 5)} = \frac{1}{4165}.$$

EXAMPLE 8   A box contains 10 electric batteries, 4 of which are defective. If 4 of the batteries are chosen at random from the box, what is the probability that the chosen group contains: (a) 2 defective batteries; (b) at least 2 defective batteries?

Solution   The number of points in the sample space is the number of ways of choosing 4 batteries from among 10, that is,

$$n = \binom{10}{4} = \frac{10 \cdot 9 \cdot 8 \cdot 7}{1 \cdot 2 \cdot 3 \cdot 4} = 210.$$

(a) If the selection is to contain 2 defective batteries, it must contain 2 good ones. The number of ways of choosing 2 defective batteries from among the 4 available is $\binom{4}{2} = 6$ ways. The number of ways of choosing the 2 good batteries from among the 6 available is $\binom{6}{2} = 6 \cdot 5/1 \cdot 2 = 15$. Therefore the total number of ways of choosing 2 defective and 2 good batteries is $6 \times 15 = 90$.

Thus, for this event, the number of sample points is $k = 90$ and so the probability is $k/n = \frac{90}{210} = \frac{3}{7}$.

(b) If the selection is to contain at least 2 defective batteries, it can have 2 defective and 2 good batteries, 3 defective and 1 good batteries, or 4 defective and 0 good batteries. The first of these selections has a probability $\frac{90}{210}$. (See part a.) Three defective batteries can be chosen in $\binom{4}{3} = 4$ ways and 1 good battery can be chosen in $\binom{6}{1} = 6$ ways. So a group of 3 defective batteries and 1 good one can be chosen in $4 \times 6 = 24$ different ways. Hence the probability of such a selection is $\frac{24}{210}$.

For the third alternative, there is just 1 way of choosing 4 defective batteries. So the probability of such a choice is $\frac{1}{210}$.

The required event is the union of these three events, which are mutually exclusive. The probability of at least 2 defective batteries is therefore the sum of these three probabilities: $\frac{90}{210} + \frac{24}{210} + \frac{1}{210} = \frac{23}{42}$.

EXAMPLE 9   An office manager must locate 16 typists into three offices, which hold respectively 8, 5, and 3 typists. In how many ways can the three groups be chosen to occupy the three offices?

Solution   Let us suppose that the manager first selects the 8 typists for the largest office. This choice can be made in $\binom{16}{8}$ ways. Having made this choice, there remain 8 typists from whom to select 5 for the second largest office. This choice can be made in $\binom{8}{5}$ ways. After this, there is no choice left: the remaining 3 typists automatically occupy the remaining office. Thus the number of ways of making the complete choice is given by the product:

$$\binom{16}{8}\binom{8}{5} = \frac{16!}{8!8!} \cdot \frac{8!}{5!3!} = \frac{16!}{8!5!3!}$$

You should verify that this same result is obtained if the offices are filled in a different order.

EXERCISES 4

(1–9)   Evaluate the following.

1. $_{10}P_2$ **2.** $_6P_4$ **3.** $_5P_5$

4. $\binom{10}{2}$ **5.** $\binom{30}{28}$ **6.** $\binom{20}{17}$

7. $\frac{20!}{18!}$ **8.** $\frac{10!}{7!}$ **9.** $\frac{8!}{7! + 6!}$

10.   Given $(n + 1)! = 20n!$, find the value of n.

11.   Three cards are selected one at a time, with replacement, from a deck of 52 cards. What is the probability of selecting an ace, a king, and a queen in that order?

12.   Three individuals are selected from a group of 5 men and 4 women to fill 3 executive positions in a business firm. Find each probability.

    a.   All the selected individuals are men.

    b.   The selected group consists of 2 men and 1 woman.

    c.   The selected group contains more women than men.

13.   Two machine parts are randomly selected from a bag containing 10 good parts and 5 defective parts. Find each probability.

    a.   Both selected parts are defective.

    b.   One good and one defective part are selected.

14. Three balls are selected from a box that contains 5 white, 6 red, and 4 yellow balls. Find each probability.

   a. All 3 balls are red.

   b. The 3 balls are different colors.

   c. The 3 balls are the same color.

15. A sample of 6 individuals is selected for a test from a group containing 20 smokers and 10 nonsmokers. What is the probability that the sample contains 4 smokers?

16. Two teams play off a final series of 3 matches in a sports competition. The first team to win 2 matches wins the competition. How many different outcomes are there for the series? (*Hint:* Use a tree diagram.)

17. Repeat Exercise 16 for the case when the series consists of 5 matches and the first team to win 3 matches wins the competition.

18. A taxicab company has 5 cabs and 4 drivers available when requests for 3 cabs are received. How many different ways are there of selecting the cabs and the drivers to meet these requests? (Assume that any driver can be given any cab to drive.)

19. Repeat Exercise 18 for the case when a single request for 3 cabs is received, rather than 3 separate requests.

20. Four men and 4 women attend the theatre and sit in 8 adjacent seats. How many different seating arrangements are there if men and women alternate along the row?

*21. Four men and 4 women sit around a circular dining table. If men and women alternate around the table, how many different orderings are there? (Two orderings are the same if everyone has the same two neighbors in each.)

*22. Repeat Exercise 21 for the case when the dinner party consists of 4 married couples and no husband and wife sit next to one another.

23. Out of a team of 12 astronauts, 7 have been on a space flight and 5 have not. If 4 of the team are selected at random for a project, what is the probability that at least 2 of those selected have already had experience in space?

24. Six individuals are chosen from a group consisting of 4 men, 3 women, and 6 children. What is the probability that the selected group contains: (a) 2 men; (b) 3 women and 2 children?

25. A test consists of 10 true-false questions. In how many ways can a student fill in the answer sheet?

26. A driving examination contains 20 multiple-choice questions with 3 answers given for each. If an applicant fills out the answer sheet entirely by guesswork, what is the probability that he or she will pass the examination? (At least 19 correct answers are necessary to pass.)

27. If a monkey playing with a typewriter types out 11 letters at random, what is the probability that it will spell out the word *Shakespeare*?

28. A government agency must distribute 10 orders among 3 different firms A, B, and C such that A receives 3 orders, B receives 2 orders, and C receives 5 orders. In how many ways can the orders be distributed?

29. In Exercise 28, 3 of the orders are highly sought after. What is the probability that firm C receives at least two of these orders?

*30. Find the probability that a poker hand of 5 cards contains a full house (2 cards of one denomination and 3 of another).

8-5 BINOMIAL PROBABILITIES

In this section, we shall deal with a particular type of observation, in which there are exactly two mutually exclusive outcomes. Such observations are known as **Bernoulli trials**, named after the eighteenth-century Swiss mathematician Jacob Bernoulli. For example, winning or losing in a lottery is a Bernoulli trial since there are two outcomes (win or lose) and these two outcomes are mutually exclusive. Similarly, the flip of a single coin is a Bernoulli trial, since it has only two mutually exclusive outcomes, heads or tails. If such a Bernoulli trial is repeated a certain number of times with the trials independent of one another, we are interested in calculating the probabilities of different numbers of occurrences of one of the outcomes.

The study of Bernoulli trials has many applications in many areas. For example, the probability of an individual living or not living beyond a certain age is of interest to his insurance company and is a Bernoulli trial. An opinion poll on a question with a simple *yes* or *no* answer constitutes a sequence of Bernoulli trials.

It is customary to denote the two outcomes of a Bernoulli trial by the terms success (S) and failure (F). If p denotes the probability of success in a Bernoulli trial, then the probability of failure is $q = 1 - p$, because the two outcomes (success and failure) are mutually exclusive and the two probabilities p and q must add up to 1. We assume that the probability of success in each Bernoulli trial remains unchanged from one trial to the next.

For example, let us consider individuals insured by a certain life-insurance company. In such a case, we can define a success to be when the individual lives past the age of 65 and failure to occur if he or she does not. Then p is the probability of living and q the probability of not living beyond 65 years. (It would in principle be quite possible, though perhaps macabre, to define success and failure the other way round. In such a case, the values of p and q would be interchanged.)

Now let us consider a group of three such individuals, and let us calculate the probabilities that all three live past 65, that two do so, that only one does and that all three die before 65. The set of outcomes can be listed as follows:

$$SSS, \ SSF, \ SFS, \ FSS, \ SFF, \ FSF, \ FFS, \ FFF.$$

Here for example, *SSF* means that the first two individuals live past 65 (successes) and the third dies before 65 (failure).

The outcome *SSS*, in which all three survive past 65, has a probability $p \times p \times p = p^3$, since each Bernoulli trial has a probability p of resulting in a success.

Similarly, the outcome *SSF* has probability $p \times p \times q = p^2q$, since the two successes each have probability p and the failure has probability q. In the same way, the other two outcomes *SFS* and *FSS*, in which there are two successes and one failure, also have probabilities p^2q. Therefore the total probability of two individuals surviving and one dying before 65 is equal to the sum of the probabilities of the three outcomes *SSF*, *SFS*, and *FSS*, and hence is given by $3p^2q$.

Continuing in this way, we see that the probability of one individual surviving and two dying before 65 is equal to $3pq^2$ and the probability of all three dying before 65 is equal to q^3.

EXAMPLE 1   Let a success be rolling a 6 with a dice. Then $p = \frac{1}{6}$ and $q = \frac{5}{6}$. The probability of getting two 6's when rolling 3 dice is equal to

$$3p^2q = 3(\tfrac{1}{6})^2(\tfrac{5}{6}) = \tfrac{5}{72}.$$

These results are special cases of a general expression for the probability of obtaining r successes in a sequence of n Bernoulli trials ($0 \le r \le n$). The general result is given in the following theorem.

THEOREM 1   If p is the probability of success and q the probability of failure in a single Bernoulli trial, then the probability of exactly r successes in a sequence of n independent trials is

$$P(r) = \binom{n}{r} p^r q^{n-r}.$$

EXAMPLE 2   A fair coin is tossed 5 times. What is the probability of getting 3 heads?

Solution   Tossing a coin is a Bernoulli trial, because there are two mutually exclusive outcomes, heads (success) and tails (failure). The probability of getting a head in a single trial is $p = \frac{1}{2}$. Thus $q = 1 - p = \frac{1}{2}$. Since the coin is tossed 5 times, we have $n = 5$ trials.

In this case $r = 3$, because we want 3 heads (successes). Using Theorem 1, the required probability of 3 heads is

$$P(3) = \binom{n}{r} p^r q^{n-r}$$

$$= \binom{5}{3}\left(\frac{1}{2}\right)^3\left(\frac{1}{2}\right)^{5-3}$$

$$= \frac{5 \cdot 4 \cdot 3}{3 \cdot 2 \cdot 1} \cdot \left(\frac{1}{2}\right)^5$$

$$= 10 \cdot \frac{1}{32} = \frac{5}{16}.$$

EXAMPLE 3   An airplane with 2 or 4 engines can remain airborne as long as half its engines are functioning. If the probability of any engine breaking down is 10^{-3}, calculate the probability of engine failure causing a crash for each of these types of airplanes.

Solution   Let success occur if any engine does not break down. Then the probability of failure, q, is $q = 10^{-3} = 0.001$, and $p = 1 - q = 0.999$. For the two-engine airplane, we have 2 Bernoulli trials (each engine can fail or it can not fail) and the plane crashes if there are 2 failures. Therefore, $P(\text{crashing}) = P(2 \text{ failures}) = q^2 = 10^{-6}$.

For the four-engine airplane, there are 4 Bernoulli trials and the plane crashes if there are 3 or 4 failures. Therefore

$$P(\text{crashing}) = P(3 \text{ failures}) + P(3 \text{ failures})$$

$$= \binom{4}{3} pq^3 + \binom{4}{4} q^4$$

$$= 4pq^3 + q^4$$

$$= 4(0.999)(10^{-3})^3 + (10^{-3})^4$$

$$= 3.997 \times 10^{-9}.$$

(A comparison of these probabilities shows that the four-engine design is much safer from the danger of engine failure than is the two-engine design.)

EXAMPLE 4   Just before an election, 40% of the population support the Square Party, 40% support the Round Party, and 20% are undecided. If 6 people are chosen at random from the population and their opinions are sampled, what is the probability that at least half of them will express support for the Squares?

Solution   Let a success be the expression of support for the Squares. Then its probability, p, is $p = 0.4$. Correspondingly, $q = 1 - p = 0.6$. There are 6 Bernoulli trials and we want to find the probability of at least 3 successes.

$$P(r \geq 3) = P(3) + P(4) + P(5) + P(6)$$

$$= \binom{6}{3}(0.4)^3(0.6)^3 + \binom{6}{4}(0.4)^4(0.6)^2 + \binom{6}{5}(0.4)^5(0.6) + \binom{6}{6}(0.4)^6(0.6)^0$$

$$= 20(0.01382) + 15(0.00922) + 6(0.00614) + 1(0.00410)$$

$$= 0.4557$$

As an alternative solution, the event that $r \geq 3$ is complementary to the event that $r \leq 2$. Therefore

$$P(r \geq 3) = 1 - [P(0) + P(1) + P(2)]$$

$$= 1 - \left[\binom{6}{0}(0.4)^0(0.6)^6 + \binom{6}{1}(0.4)(0.6)^5 + \binom{6}{2}(0.4)^2(0.6)^4 \right]$$

$$= 1 - [0.04666 + 6(0.03110) + 15(0.02074)]$$

$$= 1 - 0.5443$$

$$= 0.4557.$$

This example illustrates the principle of opinion sampling, commonly carried out prior to elections by numerous newspapers, opinion survey organizations, and so on. Of course, the samples used in such surveys are much bigger than six, typically being 2000 in size. With such large samples, the use of binomial probabilities becomes quite cumbersome. Suppose, for example, that 2000 people are asked their opinions in Example 4 and we want to calculate the probability that at least half of them express support for the Square party. This is the probability of 1000, 1001, 1002, on up to 2000 successes and is given by the sum of all the probabilities

$$\binom{2000}{r}(0.4)^r(0.6)^{2000-r}$$

with r ranging from 1000 up to 2000. Clearly finding this sum involves a prodigious amount of work (although a modern computer could do it fairly rapidly). We should mention, however, that it is possible to calculate such probabilities as this one relatively easily using the *normal probability distribution*.

EXERCISES 5

(1–2) A fair coin is tossed four times. What is the probability of getting:

1. One head?

2. At least one head?

(3–4) A fair die is rolled 5 times. Find the probability of rolling 4 spots each of the following number of times.

3. Exactly 2 times.

4. At least 2 times.

(5–7) The probability that a couple will have a left-handed child is $\frac{1}{5}$.

5. If the couple has 5 children, what is the probability that exactly 2 are left-handed?

6. If the couple has 4 children, what is the probability that exactly 2 are right-handed?

7. If the couple has 6 children, what is the probability that at least 1 is left-handed?

(8–9) On the average, 25% of the adult population watch a certain television show. A group of 8 people are chosen at random and independently of one another.

8. What is the probability that exactly two of them watched the show the last time it was on television?

9. What is the probability that more than two of them watched the show?

10. Suppose that 40% of the patients diagnosed as having a certain disease die from it. What is the probability that exactly 1 will die from a group of 4 who have this disease?

11. Six rats are administered a dose of poison and the number of rats dying within 24 hours is observed. Suppose that each rat has a probability $\frac{1}{4}$ of dying and that the survival of each rat is independent of the survival of the other rats. What is the probability that: (a) four rats die; (b) all the rats die?

12. Of the trees planted by a landscaping firm, 85% survive. What is the probability that 8 or more out of a group of 10 trees planted will survive?

13. A multiple choice examination contains 10 true-false questions. If a student fills in the answers by random guessing, what is the probability that 5 answers will be correct?

14. In Exercise 13, find the probability that the student gets 4 answers correct by guessing.

15. A multiple-choice examination contains 10 questions. Five answers are given to each question, only one of which is correct. If a student fills in the answers by random guessing, what is the probability that half of them will be correct?

16. In Exercise 15, find the probability that the student gets 4 correct answers.

17. A typist makes at least one error on average in every fifth letter typed. If eight letters are typed in one afternoon, what is the probability that: a) none of them has an error; b) at least two of them have an error?

18. An encyclopedia salesperson makes a sale one time out of three once she is admitted into a home. Over one weekend, she is admitted to 6 homes. What is the probability that she makes: (a) 1 sale; (b) 2 sales; (c) 3 sales during this weekend?

19. A boat charter firm has 8 boats that it hires out by the day. It supplies skippers for those clients who want them; otherwise it charters only the boat. On the basis of long experience, it is known that 1 client in every 5 will want a skipper. If the firm has 3 skippers available, on what fraction of the days will they be unable to meet the demand for skippers? (Assume that all the boats are chartered on each day).

20. A bank manager knows from experience that, on the average, 10% of the loan customers fall behind in their payments. One day the manager authorizes 7 loans. What is the probability that:

    a. None of these 7 borrowers will fall behind in their payments.

    b. One of them will fall behind.

    c. At least two of them will fall behind.

21. A defective canning machine seals the lids on the cans incorrectly on 1 can out of 6. If an inspector chooses 2 cans for inspection at random from the output of the machine, what is the probability that the defect will remain unnoticed? If 4 cans are chosen, what is the probability that 2 or more will be found to have defective lids?

22. A cereal manufacturer states that every box of cereal contains at least 1 card with a photograph of a hockey player and two-thirds of the boxes contain 2 such cards. If Jimmy's mother buys 8 boxes of cereal one week, what is the probability that Jimmy will get: (a) exactly 12 cards; (b) at least 12 cards out of these boxes?

23. Just before an election for mayor, 60% of the voters prefer Smith and 40% prefer Jones. If 10 people are chosen at random and asked their preference, find the probability that: (a) 6; (b) 7; (c) 5 of them express a preference for Smith.

24. In Exercise 23, suppose that 100 voters are asked their opinion and let $P(r)$ denote the probability that exactly r of them express a preference for Smith. Calculate: (a) $P(60)/P(59)$; (b) $P(59)/P(58)$; (c) $P(60)/P(61)$; and (d) $P(61)/P(62)$. What conclusion can you draw regarding the outcome $r = 60$?

1. State whether each of the following statements is true or false. Replace each false statement by a true statement.

   a. If two events are mutually exclusive, then they are independent.

   b. The probability of any event is a nonnegative real number.

   c. If E_1 and E_2 are two independent events, then $P(E_1 \cap E_2) = P(E_1) + P(E_2)$.

   d. If E_1 and E_2 are two mutually exclusive events, then $P(E_1 \cap E_2) = 0$.

   e. The sample points in a sample space are equally likely outcomes.

   f. The probabilities of complementary events are always equal.

   g. If E_1 and E_2 are independent, they must be mutually exclusive.

   h. If A and B are mutually exclusive, then $P(A) + P(B) \leq 1$.

   i. $P(A \mid A) = 1$

   j. $P(A \mid B) = P(B \mid A)$

   k. $P(\varnothing \mid A) = 0$

   l. If $P(B) = 1$, then $P(A \mid B) = P(A)$.

   m. $P(A \mid A') = 1$

   n. If $E_2 \subseteq E_1$, then $P(E_2 \mid E_1) = 1$.

   o. The probability of E_1 given E_2 is equal to one minus the probability of E_2 given E_1.

   p. If E_1 and E_2 are independent, then $P(E_1 \mid E_2) = P(E_1 \cap E_2)$.

   q. For any two events, $P(E_1 \cap E_2) + P(E'_1 \cap E_2) = P(E_2)$.

   r. If E_1 and E_2 are independent events, then E'_1 and E_2 are independent events.

   s. If A and B are independent events and if A and C are independent events, then B and C are independent events.

   (2–6) Evaluate the following.

2. $_7P_4$ 3. $\binom{8}{5}$ 4. $_9P_{12}$

5. $\binom{n}{r} \div \binom{n-1}{r-1}$ 6. $\binom{6}{3}\binom{5}{3} + \binom{6}{2}\binom{5}{4} + \binom{6}{1}\binom{5}{5}$

7. Of 10 girls in a class, 4 have blue eyes. If two of the girls are chosen at random, what is the probability that: (a) both have blue eyes; (b) neither has blue eyes; (c) at least one has blue eyes?

8. Two people are selected at random from a group of 10 married couples. Find each probability.

   a. They are husband and wife. b. One is male and one is female.

9. The probability that a person over 50 years old is a smoker in a certain community is $\frac{3}{5}$ and the probability that a person over 50 years old has cancer is $\frac{1}{20}$. The probability that a person over 50 years old will be a smoker and have a cancer is $\frac{1}{25}$. Are smoking and cancer disorders independent?

10. Of the patients examined at the local clinic, 30% have high blood pressure, 35% have excessive weight, and 15% have both. What is the probability that a patient selected at random will have at least one of these characteristics? Are the events *excessive weight* and *high blood pressure* independent? Explain.

11. In a certain community, 40% of the people smoke, 32% of the people drink, and 60% either smoke or drink. What percentage of the people smoke as well as drink?

12. The probability that a man will live 10 more years is $\frac{1}{5}$ and the probability that his wife will live 10 more years is $\frac{1}{4}$. Find each probability.

   a. Both will live 10 more years.

   b. At least one of them will be alive for 10 more years.

   c. Only the wife will be alive for 10 more years.

13. Let E_1 be the event that a family has children of both sexes and E_2 be the event that a family has at most one boy. Show that the events E_1 and E_2 are:

   a. independent if the family has three children;

   b. not independent if the family has two children.

14. If the events E_1 and E_2 are independent, show that E_1 and E_2' are also independent. (*Hint:* Make a Venn diagram for $E_1 \cap E_2'$.)

15. A family has 8 children. Assuming that the probability that any child is a boy is $\frac{1}{2}$, find the probability that the family will have fewer girls than boys.

16. A batch of 12 new high-grade tires is shipped to a store which accepts the whole batch if a sample of 3 chosen at random from the batch has no defective tires. If the batch contains 3 defective tires, find the probability that it is accepted.

17. Of a firm's customers, 12% subsequently make some kind of complaint about the quality of the service they have received. One salesman named Dick is responsible for one-third of the firm's customers, and 15% of his customers subsequently make a complaint. What proportion of the customers who make complaints are Dick's responsibility? What percentage of the customers who are not Dick's responsibility make complaints?

18. A bank manager arrives late for work 45% of the time and leaves early at the end of the day 50% of the time. She does both 15% of the time. What is the probability that she does not leave early on a day on which she arrives late?

19. In a certain town, 60% of the adults are smokers and 40% nonsmokers. If each smoker has a probability of 25% of living to be 75 and each nonsmoker has a probability of 40%, what proportion of the town's residents aged 75 and over are nonsmokers?

20. An individual has a probability p of winning a prize in a lottery. What is the probability that the person will win a prize on the first, second, or third try in the lottery? What is the probability of winning a prize sometime in the first n tries at the lottery? (*Hint:* Consider the event of failure n times in a row.)

21. Three dice are rolled. Let E_1 be the event that the scores total 15 or more and E_2 be the event that two 6's are rolled. Find $P(E_1 | E_2)$ and $P(E_2 | E_1)$.

*22. An event A is independent of each of the events B, C, and $B \cup C$. Prove that A is independent of $B \cap C$.

23. The coordinator of a cooperative education program has 36 available jobs for the next semester and 30 students in the program. In how many ways can the students be assigned jobs? What would be the answer if only 26 jobs were available?

24. In a certain country, automobile registration numbers consist of 3 letters followed by 3 digits, where the first digit is nonzero. What is the total number of available registration numbers?

25. Because of a decline in business, 2 of 6 salespeople employed by a company are to be fired by putting the 6 names in a hat and randomly choosing 2 of them. If Ramon and Carole are two of the salespeople, what is the probability that neither of them will be fired? What is the probability that one and not the other will be fired?

26. Six airlines provide direct flights between two cities. An individual makes a round trip between these cities, choosing an airline at random for each leg of the journey (not necessarily flying both ways with the same airline). What is the probability that on at least one leg of the journey the individual flies with XYZ Airline, which is one of the six.

27. A real estate saleswoman fails to complete a sale one week out of every three, on the average. What is the probability that she will fail to make a sale in 3 weeks out of the 4 weeks in one month?

28. In Exercise 27, find the probability that the saleswoman fails to make sales in at most 2 weeks during a given five-week period.

*29. Two cards are dealt from a deck of 52 playing cards. One of the two is chosen at random and turns out to be an ace. What is the probability that the two cards were both aces?

30. In a certain country, 20% of the income tax returns are subjected to more than routine scrutiny. Of those scrutinized, it is found that 15% are fraudulent; it is estimated that 5% of the returns that are not scrutinized are also fraudulent. What is the probability that a random fraudulent return will be scrutinized?

MATRIX ALGEBRA

CHAPTER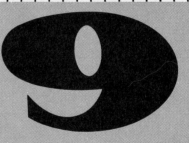

9-1 MATRICES

A firm produces four products, A, B, C, and D. The manufacture of each product involves specified quantities of two raw materials, X and Y, and also fixed amounts of labor. Suppose the firm wants to compare the numbers of units of X and Y and of labor that are involved in the weekly output of these four products. Sample information for such a case is shown in Table 1. For example, the weekly output of A involves 250 units of X, 160 units of Y, and 80 units of labor.

TABLE 1

Product	A	B	C	D
Units of Material X	250	300	170	200
Units of Material Y	160	230	75	120
Units of Labor	80	85	120	100

Observe that the data in this table naturally forms a rectangular array. If the headings are removed, we obtain the following rectangular array of numbers.

$$\begin{bmatrix} 250 & 300 & 170 & 200 \\ 160 & 230 & 75 & 120 \\ 80 & 85 & 120 & 100 \end{bmatrix}$$

This array is an example of a *matrix*.

In this example, it is clear that a rectangular array is a natural way in which to store the twelve given numbers. Each column of three numbers in the array relates to one of the products A, B, C, or D, while each row of four numbers applies to one of the inputs, X, Y, or labor. Thus the number 75 that is in the second row and the third column gives the number of units of the second input (Y) used in the weekly output of the third product (C). The number 80 in the third row and first column represents the number of units of the third input (labor) that is involved in the weekly output of the first product (A), and so on.

Many other sets of tabulated data naturally form rectangular arrays. We shall see later that a number of the calculations that we might wish to make with such data correspond to certain "matrix operations" that are defined in this and following sections.

DEFINITION A **matrix** (plural **matrices**), is a rectangular array of real numbers, which is enclosed in large brackets. Matrices are generally denoted by boldface capital letters such as **A**, **B**, or **C**.

Some examples of matrices are given below.

$$\mathbf{A} = \begin{bmatrix} 2 & -3 & 7 \\ 1 & 0 & 4 \end{bmatrix} \qquad \mathbf{B} = \begin{bmatrix} 3 & 4 & 5 & 6 \\ 7 & 8 & 9 & 1 \\ 5 & 4 & 3 & 2 \end{bmatrix} \qquad \mathbf{C} = \begin{bmatrix} 4 \\ 2 \\ 3 \\ 1 \end{bmatrix}$$

$$\mathbf{D} = \begin{bmatrix} 1 & 2 & 3 & 5 & 6 \end{bmatrix} \qquad \mathbf{E} = \begin{bmatrix} 3 \end{bmatrix}$$

The real numbers which form the array are called the **entries** or **elements** of the matrix. The elements in any horizontal line form a **row** and those in any vertical line form a **column** of the matrix. For example, matrix **B** (above) has three rows and four columns. The elements of first row are 3, 4, 5, and 6 and those of third column are 5, 9, and 3.

If a matrix has m rows and n columns, then it is said to be of **size** $m \times n$ (read m *by* n). Of the matrices given above, **A** is a 2×3 matrix, **B** is a 3×4 matrix, and **C** is a 4×1 matrix.

A matrix of size $1 \times n$ has only one row and a matrix of size $m \times 1$ has only one column. A matrix having only one row is often called a **row matrix** or a **row vector**. Similarly, a matrix having only one column is called a **column matrix** or a **column vector**. In the above examples, **D** is a row vector and **C** is a column vector.

It is often convenient to use a double subscript notation for the elements of a matrix. In this notation, for example, a_{ij} denotes the element of the matrix **A** that is in the ith row and the jth column. Thus a_{24} denotes the entry in the second row and fourth column of **A**. If **A** is the 2×3 matrix

$$\mathbf{A} = \begin{bmatrix} 2 & -3 & 7 \\ 1 & 0 & 4 \end{bmatrix}$$

then $a_{11} = 2$, $a_{12} = -3$, $a_{13} = 7$, $a_{21} = 1$, $a_{22} = 0$, and $a_{23} = 4$.

In general, if **A** is an $m \times n$ matrix, we can write the following.

$$\mathbf{A} = \begin{bmatrix} a_{11} & a_{12} & a_{13} & \cdots & a_{1n} \\ a_{21} & a_{22} & a_{23} & \cdots & a_{2n} \\ \cdot & \cdot & \cdot & & \cdot \\ \cdot & \cdot & \cdot & & \cdot \\ \cdot & \cdot & \cdot & & \cdot \\ a_{m1} & a_{m2} & a_{m3} & \cdots & a_{mn} \end{bmatrix}$$

The matrix **A** can be denoted by $[a_{ij}]$ when its size is understood. If the size is also to be specified, then we write $\mathbf{A} = [a_{ij}]_{m \times n}$.

If all the elements of a matrix are zero, we call the matrix a **zero matrix** and denote it by **O**. Thus the following is the zero matrix of size 2×3.

$$\mathbf{O} = \begin{bmatrix} 0 & 0 & 0 \\ 0 & 0 & 0 \end{bmatrix}$$

A matrix with the same number of rows as columns is called a **square matrix**. The following are examples of square matrices.

$$\mathbf{P} = \begin{bmatrix} 1 & 2 \\ 3 & 4 \end{bmatrix}, \qquad \mathbf{Q} = \begin{bmatrix} 2 & 1 & 3 \\ 4 & -2 & 1 \\ 3 & 0 & 2 \end{bmatrix}, \qquad \mathbf{R} = [2]$$

If $A = [a_{ij}]$ is a square matrix, then the elements a_{ij} for which $i = j$, (that is, the elements a_{11}, a_{22}, a_{33}, and so on) are called the **diagonal elements** of the matrix.

A square matrix is called an **identity matrix** if all the elements of its diagonal are equal to 1 and all the elements not on the diagonal are equal to zero. The following are identity matrices of sizes 2×2 and 3×3, respectively.

$$\begin{bmatrix} 1 & 0 \\ 0 & 1 \end{bmatrix} \qquad \begin{bmatrix} 1 & 0 & 0 \\ 0 & 1 & 0 \\ 0 & 0 & 1 \end{bmatrix}$$

The identity matrix is usually denoted by **I** when its size is understood without ambiguity.

DEFINITION   Two matrices **A** and **B** are said to be **equal** if
1. they are of the same size, and
2. their corresponding elements are equal.

For example, let

$$\mathbf{A} = \begin{bmatrix} 2 & x & 3 \\ y & -1 & 4 \end{bmatrix} \quad \text{and} \quad \mathbf{B} = \begin{bmatrix} a & 5 & 3 \\ 0 & b & 4 \end{bmatrix}.$$

Clearly **A** and **B** are of same size and $A = B$ if and only if $a = 2$, $x = 5$, $y = 0$, and $b = -1$.

Scalar Multiplication of a Matrix

Scalar multiplication of a matrix refers to the operation of multiplying the matrix by a real number. If $\mathbf{A} = [a_{ij}]$ is an $m \times n$ matrix and c is any real number, then the product $c\mathbf{A}$ is an $m \times n$ matrix obtained by multiplying each element of **A** by the constant c. In other words, $c\mathbf{A} = [ca_{ij}]$.
For example, if

$$\mathbf{A} = \begin{bmatrix} 1 & 0 & -1 \\ 0 & -2 & 4 \end{bmatrix}$$

then

$$2\mathbf{A} = 2\begin{bmatrix} 1 & 0 & -1 \\ 0 & -2 & 4 \end{bmatrix} = \begin{bmatrix} 2(1) & 2(0) & 2(-1) \\ 2(0) & 2(-2) & 2(4) \end{bmatrix} = \begin{bmatrix} 2 & 0 & -2 \\ 0 & -4 & 8 \end{bmatrix}$$

Addition and Subtraction of Matrices

Two matrices **A** and **B** of the *same size* can be added (or subtracted) by adding (or subtracting) their corresponding elements. In other words, if $\mathbf{A} = [a_{ij}]$ and $\mathbf{B} = [b_{ij}]$ are two matrices of the same size, then $\mathbf{A} + \mathbf{B} = [a_{ij} + b_{ij}]$

and $\mathbf{A} - \mathbf{B} = [a_{ij} - b_{ij}]$. Thus

$$\begin{bmatrix} 2 & 0 & -1 \\ 3 & 4 & 5 \\ 1 & -2 & 3 \end{bmatrix} + \begin{bmatrix} 3 & 1 & 2 \\ 2 & 0 & -3 \\ 3 & 2 & -4 \end{bmatrix} = \begin{bmatrix} 2+3 & 0+1 & -1+2 \\ 3+2 & 4+0 & 5+(-3) \\ 1+3 & -2+2 & 3+(-4) \end{bmatrix} = \begin{bmatrix} 5 & 1 & 1 \\ 5 & 4 & 2 \\ 4 & 0 & -1 \end{bmatrix}$$

and

$$\begin{bmatrix} 2 & 0 & -1 \\ 3 & 4 & 5 \end{bmatrix} - \begin{bmatrix} 4 & 1 & -2 \\ 2 & 6 & 1 \end{bmatrix} = \begin{bmatrix} -2 & -1 & 1 \\ 1 & -2 & 4 \end{bmatrix}$$

EXAMPLE 1   Given

$$\mathbf{A} = \begin{bmatrix} 3 & 1 & 4 \\ 2 & -3 & 5 \end{bmatrix} \quad \text{and} \quad \mathbf{B} = \begin{bmatrix} 1 & 2 & 3 \\ 4 & 5 & 6 \end{bmatrix}$$

determine the matrix $\mathbf{X}$ such that $\mathbf{X} + \mathbf{A} = 2\mathbf{B}$.

Solution   We have $\mathbf{X} + \mathbf{A} = 2\mathbf{B}$, or $\mathbf{X} = 2\mathbf{B} - \mathbf{A}$.

$$\mathbf{X} = 2\begin{bmatrix} 1 & 2 & 3 \\ 4 & 5 & 6 \end{bmatrix} - \begin{bmatrix} 3 & 1 & 4 \\ 2 & -3 & 5 \end{bmatrix}$$

$$= \begin{bmatrix} 2 & 4 & 6 \\ 8 & 10 & 12 \end{bmatrix} - \begin{bmatrix} 3 & 1 & 4 \\ 2 & -3 & 5 \end{bmatrix} = \begin{bmatrix} -1 & 3 & 2 \\ 6 & 13 & 7 \end{bmatrix} .$$

EXAMPLE 2   A firm manufacturing television sets makes three models of sets of different qualities in three different sizes. The production capacity (in thousands) at its New York plant is given by matrix $\mathbf{A}$.

		Model I	Model II	Model III	
Size 1	(20″)	5	3	2	
Size 2	(23″)	7	4	5	$= \mathbf{A}$
Size 3	(26″)	10	8	4	

(In other words, the capacity of the plant is 5000 Model I, 20-inch sets, 8000 Model II, 26-inch sets, and so on.) The production capacity at the California plant is given by matrix $\mathbf{B}$.

	Model I	Model II	Model III	
Size 1	4	5	3	
Size 2	9	6	4	$= \mathbf{B}$
Size 3	8	12	2	

(a) What is the total production capacity at the two plants?
(b) If the firm decides to increase production at its New York plant by 20%, what will be the new production at that plant?

Solution   (a) The combined production (in thousands) at the two plants is given by the sum of the two matrices **A** and **B**.

$$\mathbf{A} + \mathbf{B} = \begin{bmatrix} 5 & 3 & 2 \\ 7 & 4 & 5 \\ 10 & 8 & 4 \end{bmatrix} + \begin{bmatrix} 4 & 5 & 3 \\ 9 & 6 & 4 \\ 8 & 12 & 2 \end{bmatrix} = \begin{bmatrix} 9 & 8 & 5 \\ 16 & 10 & 9 \\ 18 & 20 & 6 \end{bmatrix}$$

(For example, the two plants make 9,000 Model I, 20-inch sets.)

(b) If the production at New York increases by 20%, the new production (in thousands) will be given by the matrix 1.2**A**.

$$1.2\mathbf{A} = 1.2\begin{bmatrix} 5 & 3 & 2 \\ 7 & 4 & 5 \\ 10 & 8 & 4 \end{bmatrix} = \begin{bmatrix} 6 & 3.6 & 2.4 \\ 8.4 & 4.8 & 6 \\ 12 & 9.6 & 4.8 \end{bmatrix}$$

(Thus, 4800 Model II, 23-inch sets will be made, and so on.)

EXERCISES 1

1. Give the size of each matrix.

$$\mathbf{A} = \begin{bmatrix} 1 & 0 \\ 2 & 3 \end{bmatrix} \qquad \mathbf{B} = \begin{bmatrix} 2 & 3 & 1 \\ -1 & 2 & 3 \end{bmatrix} \qquad \mathbf{C} = \begin{bmatrix} 3 \\ 1 \\ 2 \end{bmatrix}$$

$$\mathbf{D} = \begin{bmatrix} 1 & 2 & 3 \\ 4 & 5 & 6 \\ 9 & 8 & 7 \end{bmatrix} \qquad \mathbf{E} = \begin{bmatrix} 3 & 4 & 5 \\ 1 & 0 & 2 \end{bmatrix} \qquad \mathbf{F} = \begin{bmatrix} 2 & -1 \\ -1 & 1 \end{bmatrix}$$

$$\mathbf{G} = [4 \quad 1 \quad 3] \qquad \mathbf{H} = [1]$$

2. In Exercise 1, if $\mathbf{B} = [b_{ij}]$, find $b_{12}, b_{22}, b_{21}, b_{23}$, and b_{32}.

3. Give the 2×2 matrix $\mathbf{A} = [a_{ij}]$ for which $a_{ij} = i + j - 2$.

4. Give the 3×2 matrix $\mathbf{B} = [b_{ij}]$ for which $b_{ij} = 2i + 3j - 4$.

5. Give an example of a 3×3 matrix $[c_{ij}]$ for which $c_{ij} = -c_{ji}$.

6. Give the 3×4 matrix $\mathbf{A} = [a_{ij}]$ for which

$$a_{ij} = \begin{cases} i + j & \text{if } i \neq j \\ 0 & \text{if } i = j \end{cases}.$$

(7–14) Perform the indicated operations and simplify.

7. $3\begin{bmatrix} 2 & 4 \\ 1 & 3 \end{bmatrix}$

8. $-2\begin{bmatrix} 1 & -2 & 3 \\ -2 & 1 & -4 \\ 3 & 0 & 2 \end{bmatrix}$

9. $\begin{bmatrix} 2 & 1 & 3 \\ -1 & 4 & 7 \end{bmatrix} + \begin{bmatrix} 0 & -1 & 2 \\ 1 & 2 & -8 \end{bmatrix}$

10. $\begin{bmatrix} 3 & 1 & 4 \\ -2 & 5 & -3 \\ 0 & -1 & 2 \end{bmatrix} - \begin{bmatrix} 1 & -2 & 5 \\ 2 & -1 & -4 \\ -3 & 2 & 1 \end{bmatrix}$

11. $2\begin{bmatrix} 1 & 2 \\ -1 & 3 \end{bmatrix} + 3\begin{bmatrix} -2 & 3 \\ 1 & 0 \end{bmatrix}$

12. $3\begin{bmatrix} 2 & 1 \\ -1 & 3 \\ 4 & 7 \end{bmatrix} - 2\begin{bmatrix} 1 & -2 \\ 2 & 3 \\ -3 & 0 \end{bmatrix}$

13. $2\begin{bmatrix} 1 & 2 & 3 \\ 2 & -1 & 0 \\ 4 & 5 & 6 \end{bmatrix} + 3\begin{bmatrix} 0 & -1 & 2 \\ 3 & 2 & -4 \\ -1 & 0 & 3 \end{bmatrix}$

14. $4\begin{bmatrix} 1 & 0 & -3 & 4 \\ 2 & -1 & 5 & 1 \\ 3 & 2 & 0 & -2 \end{bmatrix} - 5\begin{bmatrix} 2 & -1 & 2 & 3 \\ 1 & 0 & -3 & 4 \\ 3 & 1 & 0 & -5 \end{bmatrix}$

(15–24) Determine the values of the variables for which the following matrix equations are true.

15. $\begin{bmatrix} x & 2 \\ 3 & y \end{bmatrix} = \begin{bmatrix} 1 & 2 \\ 3 & 4 \end{bmatrix}$

16. $\begin{bmatrix} 3 & -1 \\ x & 0 \end{bmatrix} = \begin{bmatrix} y+2 & z \\ 4 & t-1 \end{bmatrix}$

17. $\begin{bmatrix} 4 & x & 3 \\ y & -1 & 2 \end{bmatrix} = \begin{bmatrix} y-1 & 2-x & 3 \\ 5 & z+1 & 2 \end{bmatrix}$

18. $\begin{bmatrix} x+2 & 5 & y-3 \\ 4 & z-6 & 7 \end{bmatrix} = \begin{bmatrix} 3 & t+1 & 2y-5 \\ 4 & 2 & z-1 \end{bmatrix}$

19. $\begin{bmatrix} 1 & -2 & x \\ y & 3 & 4 \\ 2 & z & 3 \end{bmatrix} = \begin{bmatrix} 1 & t & 6 \\ 5 & 3 & 4 \\ u & 2 & v \end{bmatrix}$

20. $\begin{bmatrix} x+1 & 2 & 3 \\ 4 & y-1 & 5 \\ u & -1 & z+2 \end{bmatrix} = \begin{bmatrix} 2x-1 & t+1 & 3 \\ v+1 & -3 & 5 \\ -4 & w-1 & 2z-1 \end{bmatrix}$

21. $\begin{bmatrix} x & 3 & 4 \\ 2 & -1 & y \\ 1 & z & -3 \end{bmatrix} + \begin{bmatrix} 1 & t & -1 \\ 3 & 4 & x \\ u & y & 2 \end{bmatrix} = \begin{bmatrix} 2 & 7 & v+1 \\ 5 & w-2 & 3 \\ 0 & 5 & -1 \end{bmatrix}$

22. $\begin{bmatrix} x+1 & -2 & 3 \\ 4 & 1 & z+2 \\ -1 & y & 2 \end{bmatrix} + 2\begin{bmatrix} 3 & -1 & 2 \\ 1 & 2 & -3 \\ 4 & -1 & 0 \end{bmatrix} = \begin{bmatrix} 6 & u+2 & 7 \\ v+1 & 5 & -7 \\ 7 & 0 & w \end{bmatrix}$

23. $3\begin{bmatrix} x & 1 & -1 \\ 0 & -2 & 3 \\ 1 & y & 2 \end{bmatrix} + 2\begin{bmatrix} -2 & t & 0 \\ z & 1 & -1 \\ u & 2 & v \end{bmatrix} = \begin{bmatrix} w-4 & 1 & -v \\ 4 & 2u & 2v+y \\ -1 & x+7 & 12 \end{bmatrix}$

24. $2\begin{bmatrix} 1 & x+1 & 0 \\ 0 & -2 & y-1 \\ z & 1 & 2 \end{bmatrix} - 3\begin{bmatrix} u & -1 & 2 \\ 1 & v+2 & 3 \\ 0 & -3 & 1 \end{bmatrix} = \begin{bmatrix} 8 & 7 & 2v-2z \\ u+y & -7 & 1-7z \\ 4 & w+11 & t \end{bmatrix}$

25. A company has plants at three locations, X, Y, and Z, and four warehouses at the locations A, B, C, and D. The cost (in dollars) of transporting each unit of its product from a plant to a warehouse is given by the following matrix.

$$\begin{array}{c} \text{To} \quad \text{X} \quad \text{Y} \quad \text{Z} \; \leftarrow \text{From} \\ \downarrow \\ \begin{array}{c} \text{A} \\ \text{B} \\ \text{C} \\ \text{D} \end{array} \begin{bmatrix} 10 & 12 & 15 \\ 13 & 10 & 12 \\ 8 & 15 & 6 \\ 16 & 9 & 10 \end{bmatrix} \end{array}$$

a. If the transportation costs are increased uniformly by $1 per unit what is the new matrix?

b. If the transportation costs go up by 20%, write the new costs in matrix form.

26. A building contractor finds that the costs (in dollars) of purchasing and transporting specific units of concrete, wood, and steel from three different locations are given by the following matrices (one matrix for each location).

$$\begin{array}{cccc} & \text{Concrete} & \text{Wood} & \text{Steel} \\ \mathbf{A} = & \begin{bmatrix} 20 & 35 & 25 \\ 8 & 10 & 6 \end{bmatrix} & & \begin{array}{l} \text{MATERIAL COSTS} \\ \text{TRANSPORTATION COSTS} \end{array} \end{array}$$

$$\mathbf{B} = \begin{bmatrix} 22 & 36 & 24 \\ 9 & 9 & 8 \end{bmatrix} \begin{array}{l} \text{MATERIAL COSTS} \\ \text{TRANSPORTATION COSTS} \end{array}$$

$$\mathbf{C} = \begin{bmatrix} 18 & 32 & 26 \\ 11 & 8 & 5 \end{bmatrix} \begin{array}{l} \text{MATERIAL COSTS} \\ \text{TRANSPORTATION COSTS} \end{array}$$

Write the matrix representing the total costs of material and transportation for one unit of concrete, wood, and steel from each of the three locations.

27. The trade between three countries I, II, and III during 1976 (in millions of United States dollars) is given by the matrix $\mathbf{A} = [a_{ij}]$, where a_{ij} represents the exports from the ith country to the jth country.

$$\mathbf{A} = \begin{bmatrix} 0 & 16 & 20 \\ 17 & 0 & 18 \\ 21 & 14 & 0 \end{bmatrix}$$

The trade between these three countries during the year 1977 (in millions of United States dollars) is given by matrix $\mathbf{B}$.

$$\mathbf{B} = \begin{bmatrix} 0 & 17 & 19 \\ 18 & 0 & 20 \\ 24 & 16 & 0 \end{bmatrix}$$

a. Write a matrix representing the total trade between the three countries for the two-year period 1976 and 1977.

b. If in 1976 and 1977, 1 United States dollar was equal to 5 Hong-Kong dollars, write the matrix representing the total trade for the two years in Hong-Kong dollars.

28. A firm produces three sizes of recording tapes in two different qualities. The production (in thousands) at its California plant is given by the following matrix.

$$\begin{array}{c} \qquad\qquad\quad \text{Size 1} \quad \text{Size 2} \quad \text{Size 3} \\ \begin{array}{c} \text{Quality 1} \\ \text{Quality 2} \end{array} \begin{bmatrix} 27 & 36 & 30 \\ 18 & 26 & 21 \end{bmatrix} \end{array}$$

The production (in thousands) at its New York plant is given by this matrix:

	Size 1	Size 2	Size 3
Quality 1	32	40	35
Quality 2	25	38	30

a. Write a matrix that represents the total production of recording tapes at both plants.

b. The firm's management is planning to open a third plant at Chicago, which would have one and one-half times the capacity of its plant in California. Write the matrix representing the production at the Chicago plant.

c. What will be the total production of all the three plants?

29. A shoe manufacturer makes black, white, and brown shoes for children, women, and men. The production capacity (in thousands of pairs) at the Seattle plant is given by the following matrix.

	Men's	Women's	Children's
Black	30	34	20
Brown	45	20	16
White	14	26	25

The production at the Denver plant is given by:

	Men's	Women's	Children's
Black	35	30	26
Brown	52	25	18
White	23	24	32

a. Give the matrix representing the total production of each type of shoe at both plants.

b. If the production at Seattle is increased by 50% and that at Denver is increased by 25%, give the matrix representing the new total production of each type of shoe.

9-2 MULTIPLICATION OF MATRICES

Suppose a firm manufactures a product using different amounts of three inputs, P, Q, and R (raw materials or labor, for example). Let the number of units of these inputs used for each unit of the product be given by the following row matrix.

$$\begin{array}{ccc} P & Q & R \end{array}$$
$$A = [3 \quad 2 \quad 4]$$

Then let the cost per unit of each of the three inputs be given by the following column matrix.

$$B = \begin{bmatrix} 10 \\ 8 \\ 6 \end{bmatrix} \begin{array}{c} P \\ Q \\ R \end{array}$$

Then the total cost of the three inputs per unit of product is obtained by adding the costs of 3 units of P at a cost of 10 each, 2 units of Q at 8 each, and 4 units of R at 6 each:

$$3 \cdot 10 + 2 \cdot 8 + 4 \cdot 6 = 30 + 16 + 24 = 70$$

We refer to this number as the *product* of the row matrix **A** and the column matrix **B**, written **AB**. Observe that in forming **AB**, the first elements of **A** and **B** are multiplied together, the second elements are multiplied together, the third are multiplied together, and then these three products are added. This method of forming products applies to row and column matrices of any size.

DEFINITION Let **C** be a $1 \times n$ row matrix and **D** be an $n \times 1$ column matrix. Then the **product CD** is obtained by calculating the products of corresponding elements in **C** and **D** and then finding the sum of all n of these products.

EXAMPLE 1 Given the following matrices:

$$\mathbf{K} = [2 \quad 5] \qquad \mathbf{L} = [1 \quad -2 \quad -3 \quad 2]$$

$$\mathbf{M} = \begin{bmatrix} -3 \\ 2 \end{bmatrix} \qquad \mathbf{N} = \begin{bmatrix} 2 \\ 5 \\ -3 \\ 4 \end{bmatrix}$$

Then

$$\mathbf{KM} = 2(-3) + 5(2) = -6 + 10 = 4$$

and

$$\mathbf{LN} = 1(2) + (-2)5 + (-3)(-3) + 2(4) = 9.$$

Notes: 1. The row matrix is always written on the left and the column matrix on the right in such products (for example, **KM**, not **MK**).
2. The row and column matrices *must* have the same number of elements. In Example 1, the products **LM** and **KN** are not defined.

The method of forming products can be extended to matrices in general. Consider the following example. Suppose that a firm manufactures two products, I and II, by using different amounts of the three raw materials P, Q, and R. Let the units of raw materials used for the two products be given by the following matrix.

$$\mathbf{A} = \begin{array}{c} \begin{array}{ccc} \text{P} & \text{Q} & \text{R} \end{array} \\ \begin{bmatrix} 3 & 2 & 4 \\ 2 & 5 & 1 \end{bmatrix} \end{array} \begin{array}{l} \text{Product I} \\ \text{Product II} \end{array}$$

Suppose the firm produces these two products at two plants, X and Y. Let the costs of the raw materials (per unit) at the two locations X and Y be given by matrix **B**.

$$\begin{matrix} & \text{X} & \text{Y} \\ \mathbf{B} = & \begin{bmatrix} 10 & 12 \\ 8 & 7 \\ 6 & 5 \end{bmatrix} & \begin{matrix} \text{P} \\ \text{Q} \\ \text{R} \end{matrix} \end{matrix}$$

The total cost of raw materials for each unit of product I produced at location X is obtained by multiplying the elements of the first row in $\mathbf{A}$ by the corresponding elements of the first column in $\mathbf{B}$ and adding them.

$$3(10) + 2(8) + 4(6) = 30 + 16 + 24 = 70$$

Similarly, the total cost of raw materials for each unit of product I produced at plant Y is obtained by multiplying the elements of the first row in $\mathbf{A}$ by the elements of the *second* column in $\mathbf{B}$ and adding them.

$$3(12) + 2(7) + 4(5) = 36 + 14 + 20 = 70$$

The total cost of raw materials for each unit of product II produced at plant X is obtained by multiplying the elements of the second row in $\mathbf{A}$ by the elements in the first column in $\mathbf{B}$.

$$2(10) + 5(8) + 1(6) = 20 + 40 + 6 = 66$$

Finally, the total cost of materials for each unit of product II produced at location Y is

$$2(12) + 5(7) + 1(5) = 24 + 35 + 5 = 64.$$

The total costs of raw materials for the two products produced at the two plants X and Y can be arranged in matrix form.

$$\begin{matrix} & \text{X} & \text{Y} \\ \mathbf{C} = & \begin{bmatrix} 70 & 70 \\ 66 & 64 \end{bmatrix} & \begin{matrix} \text{Product I} \\ \text{Product II} \end{matrix} \end{matrix}$$

We say that the matrix $\mathbf{C}$ is equal to the product $\mathbf{AB}$ of the original matrices $\mathbf{A}$ and $\mathbf{B}$. This is written as $\mathbf{AB} = \mathbf{C}$ or, in full,

$$\begin{bmatrix} 3 & 2 & 4 \\ 2 & 5 & 1 \end{bmatrix} \begin{bmatrix} 10 & 12 \\ 8 & 7 \\ 6 & 5 \end{bmatrix} = \begin{bmatrix} 70 & 70 \\ 66 & 64 \end{bmatrix}.$$

Observe that in forming the product matrix $\mathbf{C}$, each row of $\mathbf{A}$ is multiplied by each column of $\mathbf{B}$, just as a row matrix is multiplied by a column matrix. For example, the element c_{21} is obtained by multiplying the second row of $\mathbf{A}$ by the first column of $\mathbf{B}$:

$$c_{21} = 2(10) + 5(8) + 1(6) = 66.$$

In general, *the element c_{ij} of the product matrix is obtained by multiplying the ith row of $\mathbf{A}$ by the jth column of $\mathbf{B}$.*

In forming the product of two matrices, each row of the first matrix is multiplied in turn by each column of the second matrix. Note that such products can be formed only if the rows of the first matrix have the same number of elements as the columns of the second matrix. In *other words, the product* **AB** *of two matrices can only be formed if the number of columns in* **A** *is equal to the number of rows in* **B**. That is, if **A** is an $m \times n$ matrix and **B** a $q \times p$ matrix, then the product **AB** is defined only if $n = q$.

DEFINITION If $\mathbf{A} = [a_{ij}]$ is an $m \times n$ matrix and $\mathbf{B} = [b_{ij}]$ is an $n \times p$ matrix, then the product **AB** is an $m \times p$ matrix $\mathbf{C} = [c_{ij}]$, where the ijth element c_{ij} is obtained by multiplying the ith row of **A** and the jth column of **B**.

EXAMPLE 2 Let

$$\mathbf{A} = \begin{bmatrix} 2 & 3 \\ 4 & 1 \end{bmatrix} \quad \text{and} \quad \mathbf{B} = \begin{bmatrix} 3 & 1 & 0 \\ 2 & -3 & 4 \end{bmatrix}$$

Find **AB** and **BA** if they exist.

Solution Here **A** is 2×2 and **B** is 2×3. Since the number of columns in **A** is equal to the number of rows in **B**, the product **AB** is defined. It is of size 2×3. If $\mathbf{C} = \mathbf{AB}$, then we can write **C** as follows.

$$\mathbf{C} = \begin{bmatrix} c_{11} & c_{12} & c_{13} \\ c_{21} & c_{22} & c_{23} \end{bmatrix}$$

The element c_{ij} is found by multiplying the ith row of **A** and the jth column of **B**. For example, to obtain the element in the first row and second column, that is, c_{12}, we add the products of the elements in the first row of **A** and the elements in the second column of **B**.

Row 1 of **A**	Column 2 of **B**	Product
2	1	2
3	-3	-9
	Sum	$-7 = c_{12}$

Thus, in full,

$$\mathbf{AB} = \begin{bmatrix} 2 & 3 \\ 4 & 1 \end{bmatrix}\begin{bmatrix} 3 & 1 & 0 \\ 2 & -3 & 4 \end{bmatrix}$$

$$= \begin{bmatrix} 2(3) + 3(2) & 2(1) + 3(-3) & 2(0) + 3(4) \\ 4(3) + 1(2) & 4(1) + 1(-3) & 4(0) + 1(4) \end{bmatrix}$$

$$= \begin{bmatrix} 12 & -7 & 12 \\ 14 & 1 & 4 \end{bmatrix}$$

In this case, the product **BA** is *not* defined because the number of columns in **B** is not equal to the number of rows in **A**.

EXAMPLE 3 Given

$$\mathbf{A} = \begin{bmatrix} 1 & 2 & 3 \\ 4 & 5 & 6 \\ 2 & 1 & 4 \end{bmatrix} \quad \text{and} \quad \mathbf{B} = \begin{bmatrix} -2 & 1 & 2 \\ 3 & 2 & 1 \\ 1 & 3 & 2 \end{bmatrix}$$

find **AB** and **BA**.

Solution   Here **A** and **B** are both of size 3×3. Thus **AB** and **BA** are both defined and both have size 3×3. We have the following.

$$\mathbf{AB} = \begin{bmatrix} 1 & 2 & 3 \\ 4 & 5 & 6 \\ 2 & 1 & 4 \end{bmatrix} \begin{bmatrix} -2 & 1 & 2 \\ 3 & 2 & 1 \\ 1 & 3 & 2 \end{bmatrix}$$

$$= \begin{bmatrix} 1(-2) + 2(3) + 3(1) & 1(1) + 2(2) + 3(3) & 1(2) + 2(1) + 3(2) \\ 4(-2) + 5(3) + 6(1) & 4(1) + 5(2) + 6(3) & 4(2) + 5(1) + 6(2) \\ 2(-2) + 1(3) + 4(1) & 2(1) + 1(2) + 4(3) & 2(2) + 1(1) + 4(2) \end{bmatrix}$$

$$= \begin{bmatrix} 7 & 14 & 10 \\ 13 & 32 & 25 \\ 3 & 16 & 13 \end{bmatrix}$$

$$\mathbf{BA} = \begin{bmatrix} -2 & 1 & 2 \\ 3 & 2 & 1 \\ 1 & 3 & 2 \end{bmatrix} \begin{bmatrix} 1 & 2 & 3 \\ 4 & 5 & 6 \\ 2 & 1 & 4 \end{bmatrix}$$

$$= \begin{bmatrix} -2(1) + 1(4) + 2(2) & -2(2) + 1(5) + 2(1) & -2(3) + 1(6) + 2(4) \\ 3(1) + 2(4) + 1(2) & 3(2) + 2(5) + 1(1) & 3(3) + 2(6) + 1(4) \\ 1(1) + 3(4) + 2(2) & 1(2) + 3(5) + 2(1) & 1(3) + 3(6) + 2(4) \end{bmatrix}$$

$$= \begin{bmatrix} 6 & 3 & 8 \\ 13 & 17 & 25 \\ 17 & 19 & 29 \end{bmatrix}$$

Clearly $\mathbf{AB} \neq \mathbf{BA}$, even though both products are defined.

If **A** *is an* $m \times n$ *matrix, then the products* **AB** *and* **BA** *are both defined only if* **B** *is of size* $n \times m$. *In particular, if* **A** *is a square matrix, then* **AB** *and* **BA** *are both defined, provided* **B** *is also a square matrix of the same size as* **A**. In general, $\mathbf{AB} \neq \mathbf{BA}$ (in contrast to addition of matrices, where the commutative property $\mathbf{A} + \mathbf{B} = \mathbf{B} + \mathbf{A}$ does hold.)

If **A**, **B**, and **C** are three matrices of sizes $m \times n$, $n \times p$, and $p \times q$, respectively, then the products **AB**, **BC**, **(AB)C** and **A(BC)** are all defined. The following property can be shown.

$$\mathbf{(AB)C} = \mathbf{A(BC)} \qquad \text{Associative Law}$$

In such products, we can therefore omit the brackets and write simply **ABC**. The product matrix **ABC** is of size $m \times q$.

EXAMPLE 4   Let

$$\mathbf{A} = \begin{bmatrix} a & b \\ c & d \end{bmatrix}.$$

Find **AI** and **IA**, where **I** denotes the identity matrix.

Solution   The products $\mathbf{AI}$ and $\mathbf{IA}$ are both defined if $\mathbf{A}$ and $\mathbf{I}$ are square matrices of the same size. Since $\mathbf{A}$ is a 2×2 matrix, the identity matrix $\mathbf{I}$ must also be of the size 2×2; that is,

$$\mathbf{I} = \begin{bmatrix} 1 & 0 \\ 0 & 1 \end{bmatrix}.$$

Thus

$$\mathbf{AI} = \begin{bmatrix} a & b \\ c & d \end{bmatrix}\begin{bmatrix} 1 & 0 \\ 0 & 1 \end{bmatrix} = \begin{bmatrix} a(1) + b(0) & a(0) + b(1) \\ c(1) + d(0) & c(0) + d(1) \end{bmatrix}$$

$$= \begin{bmatrix} a & b \\ c & d \end{bmatrix} = \mathbf{A}.$$

Similarly,

$$\mathbf{IA} = \begin{bmatrix} 1 & 0 \\ 0 & 1 \end{bmatrix}\begin{bmatrix} a & b \\ c & d \end{bmatrix} = \begin{bmatrix} a & b \\ c & d \end{bmatrix} = \mathbf{A}.$$

Therefore $\mathbf{AI} = \mathbf{IA} = \mathbf{A}$.

We see from this example that when any 2×2 matrix is multiplied by the identity matrix, it remains unchanged. It is easily seen that this result holds for square matrices of any size. In other words, $\mathbf{I}$ behaves the same way in matrix multiplication as the number 1 behaves in multiplication of real numbers. This justifies the name *identity matrix* for $\mathbf{I}$. If $\mathbf{A}$ is a *square matrix* of any size, then it is always true that

$$\mathbf{AI} = \mathbf{IA} = \mathbf{A}.$$

If $\mathbf{A}$ is a square matrix of size $n \times n$, we can form the product $\mathbf{AA}$ of $\mathbf{A}$ with itself. This product is of the same size as $\mathbf{A}$, $n \times n$, so we can multiply it again by $\mathbf{A}$, forming $\mathbf{AAA}$. For real numbers, a^2 stands for the product $a \cdot a$ and a^3 stands for $a \cdot a \cdot a$, so for matrices we use the notation $\mathbf{A}^2$ to denote the product $\mathbf{AA}$, $\mathbf{A}^3$ to denote the product $\mathbf{AAA}$, and so on. Note that $\mathbf{A}^2$, $\mathbf{A}^3$, $\ldots$, are defined only if $\mathbf{A}$ is a square matrix.

Note: The product of two matrices can be the zero matrix $\mathbf{O}$ even though neither matrix is the zero matrix. For example, if

$$\mathbf{A} = \begin{bmatrix} 1 & 0 \\ 0 & 0 \end{bmatrix} \quad \text{and} \quad \mathbf{B} = \begin{bmatrix} 0 & 0 \\ 1 & 0 \end{bmatrix}$$

it is easily seen that $\mathbf{AB} = \mathbf{O}$ even though $\mathbf{A} \neq \mathbf{O}$ and $\mathbf{B} \neq \mathbf{O}$.

By using the idea of matrix multiplication, systems of linear equations can be written in the form of matrix equations. Consider, for example, the system

$$2x - 3y = 7$$
$$4x + y = 21$$

consisting of two simultaneous linear equations for the variables x and y. We have the following matrix product.

$$\begin{bmatrix} 2 & -3 \\ 4 & 1 \end{bmatrix} \begin{bmatrix} x \\ y \end{bmatrix} = \begin{bmatrix} 2x - 3y \\ 4x + y \end{bmatrix}$$

But from the given simultaneous equations, we have the following equality.

$$\begin{bmatrix} 2x - 3y \\ 4x + y \end{bmatrix} = \begin{bmatrix} 7 \\ 21 \end{bmatrix}$$

Therefore

$$\begin{bmatrix} 2 & -3 \\ 4 & 1 \end{bmatrix} \begin{bmatrix} x \\ y \end{bmatrix} = \begin{bmatrix} 7 \\ 21 \end{bmatrix}.$$

If we define matrices $\mathbf{A}$, $\mathbf{B}$, and $\mathbf{X}$ as

$$\mathbf{A} = \begin{bmatrix} 2 & -3 \\ 4 & 1 \end{bmatrix}, \quad \mathbf{X} = \begin{bmatrix} x \\ y \end{bmatrix}, \quad \text{and} \quad \mathbf{B} = \begin{bmatrix} 7 \\ 21 \end{bmatrix}$$

then this matrix equation can be written simply as

$$\mathbf{AX} = \mathbf{B}.$$

Observe that the matrices $\mathbf{A}$ and $\mathbf{B}$ have elements whose values are given numbers. Matrix $\mathbf{X}$ contains the unknown quantities x and y. The column matrix $\mathbf{X}$ is commonly called the **variable vector**, $\mathbf{A}$ is called the **coefficient matrix**, and $\mathbf{B}$ is called the **value vector**.

By introducing appropriate matrices $\mathbf{A}$, $\mathbf{B}$, and $\mathbf{X}$, any system of linear equations can be expressed as a matrix equation.

EXAMPLE 5   Express the following system of equations in matrix form.

$$2x + 3y + 4z = 7$$
$$4y = 2 + 5z$$
$$3z - 2x + 6 = 0$$

Solution   We first rearrange the equations so that the constant terms are on the right and the variables x, y, and z are aligned in columns on the left.

$$2x + 3y + 4z = 7$$
$$0x + 4y - 5z = 2$$
$$-2x + 0y + 3z = -6$$

Observe that the missing terms are written as $0x$ and $0y$ in the second and third equations. If we define

$$\mathbf{A} = \begin{bmatrix} 2 & 3 & 4 \\ 0 & 4 & -5 \\ -2 & 0 & 3 \end{bmatrix}, \quad \mathbf{X} = \begin{bmatrix} x \\ y \\ z \end{bmatrix}, \quad \text{and} \quad \mathbf{B} = \begin{bmatrix} 7 \\ 2 \\ -6 \end{bmatrix}$$

the given system can be written in the form $\mathbf{AX} = \mathbf{B}$. Again, $\mathbf{A}$ and $\mathbf{B}$ are known matrices of numbers and $\mathbf{X}$ is the matrix whose elements are the unknown variables.

Let us suppose now that we are given a general system of m linear equations involving n variables. We denote the variables by $x_1, x_2, \ldots, x_n$, and suppose that the system takes the following form.

$$
\begin{aligned}
a_{11}x_1 + a_{12}x_2 + &\cdots + a_{1n}x_n = b_1 \\
a_{21}x_1 + a_{22}x_2 + &\cdots + a_{2n}x_n = b_2 \\
a_{31}x_1 + a_{32}x_2 + &\cdots + a_{3n}x_n = b_3 \\
&\ \ \vdots \\
a_{m1}x_1 + a_{m2}x_2 + &\cdots + a_{mn}x_n = b_m
\end{aligned}
\tag{1}
$$

Here the coefficients a_{ij} are certain given numbers, with a_{ij} the coefficient of x_j in the ith equation, and $b_1, b_2, \cdots, b_m$ are the given right sides of the equations.

Let us introduce the $m \times n$ matrix A whose elements consist of the coefficients of $x_1, x_2, \ldots, x_n$; $A = [a_{ij}]$.

Note that the first column of A contains all the coefficients of x_1, the second column contains all the coefficients of x_2, and so on. Let X be the column vector formed by the n variables $x_1, x_2, \cdots, x_n$, and B be the column vector formed by the m constants on the right sides of the equations. Thus

$$
X = \begin{bmatrix} x_1 \\ x_2 \\ x_3 \\ \vdots \\ x_n \end{bmatrix}
\quad \text{and} \quad
B = \begin{bmatrix} b_1 \\ b_2 \\ b_3 \\ \vdots \\ b_m \end{bmatrix}
$$

Now consider the product AX. This product is defined because the number of columns in A is equal to the number of rows in X. We have

$$
AX = \begin{bmatrix}
a_{11} & a_{12} & \cdots & a_{1n} \\
a_{21} & a_{22} & \cdots & a_{2n} \\
a_{31} & a_{32} & \cdots & a_{3n} \\
\vdots & \vdots & & \vdots \\
a_{m1} & a_{m2} & \cdots & a_{mn}
\end{bmatrix}
\begin{bmatrix} x_1 \\ x_2 \\ x_3 \\ \vdots \\ x_n \end{bmatrix}
$$

$$
= \begin{bmatrix}
a_{11}x_1 + a_{12}x_2 + \cdots + a_{1n}x_n \\
a_{21}x_1 + a_{22}x_2 + \cdots + a_{2n}x_n \\
a_{31}x_1 + a_{32}x_2 + \cdots + a_{3n}x_n \\
\vdots \\
a_{m1}x_1 + a_{m2}x_2 + \cdots + a_{mn}x_n
\end{bmatrix}
= \begin{bmatrix} b_1 \\ b_2 \\ b_3 \\ \vdots \\ b_m \end{bmatrix}
= B
$$

where we have used Equations (1). Thus the system of Equations (1) is again equivalent to the single matrix equation $\mathbf{AX} = \mathbf{B}$.

EXERCISES 2

(1–6) If $\mathbf{A}$ is a 3×4 matrix, $\mathbf{B}$ is 4×3, $\mathbf{C}$ is 2×3, and $\mathbf{D}$ is 4×5, find the sizes of the following product matrices.

1. **AB**
2. **BA**
3. **CA**
4. **AD**
5. **CAD**
6. **CBA**

(7–18) Perform the indicated operations and simplify.

7. $[2 \quad 3] \begin{bmatrix} 4 \\ 5 \end{bmatrix}$

8. $[2 \quad 0 \quad 1] \begin{bmatrix} 0 & 2 \\ 1 & -1 \\ 3 & 0 \end{bmatrix}$

9. $\begin{bmatrix} 3 & 0 & 1 \\ 2 & 4 & 0 \end{bmatrix} \begin{bmatrix} 4 \\ 5 \\ 6 \end{bmatrix}$

10. $\begin{bmatrix} 1 & -2 \\ -3 & 4 \\ 5 & 6 \end{bmatrix} \begin{bmatrix} 2 \\ 0 \end{bmatrix}$

11. $\begin{bmatrix} 1 & 0 & 2 \\ 0 & 2 & -1 \\ -2 & 1 & 0 \end{bmatrix} \begin{bmatrix} 3 & -2 \\ 2 & 1 \\ -1 & 3 \end{bmatrix}$

12. $\begin{bmatrix} 2 & -1 & 0 \\ 1 & 3 & 2 \\ 4 & 0 & -3 \end{bmatrix} \begin{bmatrix} 1 & 0 & 2 \\ 0 & 2 & 1 \\ 2 & 1 & 0 \end{bmatrix}$

13. $\begin{bmatrix} 2 & 3 & 1 \\ -1 & 2 & -3 \\ 4 & 5 & 6 \end{bmatrix} \begin{bmatrix} 1 \\ 2 \\ 3 \end{bmatrix}$

14. $\begin{bmatrix} 2 & 1 & 4 \\ 5 & 3 & 6 \end{bmatrix} \begin{bmatrix} 1 & 0 & 2 & 4 \\ 3 & -1 & 0 & 1 \\ 0 & 2 & 1 & 3 \end{bmatrix}$

15. $\begin{bmatrix} 1 & 2 & 3 \\ 4 & 5 & 6 \end{bmatrix} \begin{bmatrix} -1 & 0 \\ 2 & 4 \\ 0 & 3 \end{bmatrix} \begin{bmatrix} 3 & -1 \\ -2 & 1 \end{bmatrix}$

16. $\begin{bmatrix} 1 & 0 & 2 \\ 0 & 2 & -1 \\ 3 & 1 & 0 \end{bmatrix} \begin{bmatrix} 2 & -1 \\ 1 & 0 \\ 0 & 3 \end{bmatrix} \begin{bmatrix} 0 & 1 & -2 \\ 3 & 0 & 1 \end{bmatrix}$

17. $\begin{bmatrix} 4 & 1 & -2 \\ -3 & 2 & 1 \end{bmatrix} \left(\begin{bmatrix} 5 & 6 \\ 1 & 0 \\ 2 & -3 \end{bmatrix} + \begin{bmatrix} -4 & 2 \\ 3 & 1 \\ -2 & 3 \end{bmatrix} \right)$

18. $\begin{bmatrix} 2 & 1 \\ 0 & 2 \\ 3 & -1 \end{bmatrix} \left(\begin{bmatrix} 1 & -2 \\ 2 & -1 \end{bmatrix} + 3 \begin{bmatrix} 2 & 0 \\ 1 & 2 \end{bmatrix} \right)$

19. Evaluate $\mathbf{A}^2 + 2\mathbf{A} - 3\mathbf{I}$ for

$$\mathbf{A} = \begin{bmatrix} 1 & 2 \\ 2 & 3 \end{bmatrix}.$$

20. Evaluate $\mathbf{A}^2 - 5\mathbf{A} + 2\mathbf{I}$ for

$$\mathbf{A} = \begin{bmatrix} 1 & 0 & 0 \\ 0 & 2 & 1 \\ 0 & 0 & 3 \end{bmatrix}.$$

21. Given

$$A = \begin{bmatrix} 1 & 2 \\ 3 & 4 \end{bmatrix} \quad \text{and} \quad B = \begin{bmatrix} 2 & -1 \\ -3 & -2 \end{bmatrix}.$$

a. Find $(A + B)^2$.   **b.** Find $A^2 + 2AB + B^2$.

c. Is $(A + B)^2 = A^2 + 2AB + B^2$?

22. Given

$$A = \begin{bmatrix} 2 & 3 \\ 1 & 2 \end{bmatrix} \quad \text{and} \quad B = \begin{bmatrix} 1 & 0 \\ 2 & -1 \end{bmatrix}.$$

Compute $A^2 - B^2$ and $(A - B)(A + B)$ and show that $A^2 - B^2 \neq (A - B)(A + B)$.

(23–26) Determine the matrix A for which each matrix equation is true.

*23. $A \begin{bmatrix} 2 & 1 \\ 1 & 0 \end{bmatrix} = [5 \quad 3]$

*24. $\begin{bmatrix} 1 & 0 & 2 \\ 2 & -1 & 0 \\ 0 & 1 & 3 \end{bmatrix} A = \begin{bmatrix} 7 \\ 0 \\ 11 \end{bmatrix}$

*25. $\begin{bmatrix} 2 & 0 \\ 1 & -1 \\ 0 & 1 \end{bmatrix} A = \begin{bmatrix} 6 & 0 \\ 3 & -1 \\ 0 & 1 \end{bmatrix}$

*26. $A \begin{bmatrix} 1 & 2 \\ 3 & 4 \end{bmatrix} = \begin{bmatrix} 7 & 10 \\ 15 & 22 \end{bmatrix}$

(27–32) Express the following systems of linear equations in matrix form.

27. $2x + 3y = 7$
$x + 4y = 5$

28. $3x - 2y = 4$
$4x + 5y = 7$

29. $x + 2y + 3z = 8$
$2x - y + 4z = 13$
$3y - 2z = 5$

30. $2x - y = 3$
$3y + 4z = 7$
$5z + x = 9$

31. $2x + y \quad - u = 0$
$3y + 2z + 4u = 5$
$x - 2y + 4z + u = 12$

32. $2x_1 - 3x_2 + 4x_3 = 5$
$3x_3 + 5x_4 - x_1 = 7$
$x_1 + x_2 \quad = x_3 + 2x_4$

33. For the following value of A, find a 2×2 nonzero matrix B such that AB is a zero matrix. (There is more than one answer.)

$$A = \begin{bmatrix} 1 & 2 \\ 3 & 6 \end{bmatrix}$$

34. Give an example of two nonzero matrices A and B of different sizes such that the product AB is defined and is a zero matrix. (There are many possible answers.)

(35–38) Determine the matrix A^n for a general positive integer n, where A is as given.

35. $A = \begin{bmatrix} 1 & 0 \\ 0 & 1 \end{bmatrix}$

36. $A = \begin{bmatrix} 0 & 1 \\ 1 & 0 \end{bmatrix}$

*37. $A = \begin{bmatrix} 1 & 0 \\ \frac{1}{2} & \frac{1}{2} \end{bmatrix}$

38. $A = \begin{bmatrix} 0 & 1 & 0 \\ 1 & 0 & 0 \\ 0 & 0 & 1 \end{bmatrix}$

39. A dealer in color television sets has five 26-inch sets, eight 20-inch sets, four 18-inch sets, and ten 12-inch sets. The 26-inch sets sell for $650 each, the 20-inch sets sell for $550 each, the 18-inch sets sell for $500 each, and the 12-inch sets sell for $300 each. Express the total selling price of his television stock as the product of two matrices.

40. A firm uses four different raw materials M_1, M_2, M_3, and M_4 in the production of its product. The number of units of M_1, M_2, M_3, and M_4 used per unit of the product are 4, 3, 2, and 5, respectively. The cost per unit of the four raw materials is $5, $7, $6, and $3, respectively. Express the total cost of raw materials per unit of the product as the product of two matrices.

41. A firm uses three types of raw materials M_1, M_2, and M_3 in the production of two products P_1 and P_2. The numbers of units of M_1, M_2, and M_3 used for each unit of P_1 are 3, 2, and 4, respectively, and for each unit of P_2 are 4, 1, and 3, respectively. Suppose the firm produces 20 units of P_1 and 30 units of P_2 each week. Express the answers to the following questions as matrix products.

    a. What is the weekly consumption of the three raw materials?

    b. If the unit costs (in dollars) for M_1, M_2, and M_3 are 6, 10, and 12, respectively, what are the costs of raw materials per unit of P_1 and P_2?

    c. What is the total amount spent on raw materials per week on the production of P_1 and P_2?

42. A building contractor can purchase the required lumber, bricks, concrete, glass, and paint from any one of three suppliers. The prices that each supplier charges for each unit of these five materials are given in matrix $\mathbf{A}$.

$$\mathbf{A} = \begin{bmatrix} 8 & 5 & 7 & 2 & 4 \\ 9 & 4 & 5 & 2 & 5 \\ 9 & 5 & 6 & 1 & 5 \end{bmatrix}$$

In this matrix, each row refers to one supplier and the columns to the materials, in the order listed above. The contractor has the policy of purchasing all the required materials for any particular job from the same supplier in order to minimize transportation costs. There are three jobs underway at present: Job I requires 20 units of lumber, 4 of bricks, 5 of concrete, 3 of glass, and 3 of paint; job II requires 15, 0, 8, 8, and 2 units, respectively; and job III requires 30, 10, 20, 10, and 12 units, respectively. Arrange this information as a 5×3 matrix $\mathbf{B}$ and form the matrix product $\mathbf{AB}$. Interpret the entries in this product and use them to decide which supplier should be used for each job.

9-3 SOLUTION OF LINEAR SYSTEMS BY ROW REDUCTION

In Section 3 of Chapter 4, we discussed how systems of linear equations arise in certain areas of business and economics. In that section, we solved systems consisting of two linear equations in two unknowns. We shall now develop a method of solving systems of linear equations that can be used regardless of the number of equations involved in the system. Let us illustrate the principles of the method by solving the following simple system of two equations.

$$2x + 3y = 3$$
$$x - 2y = 5$$

(1)

If we interchange the two equations (the reason for this will become clear later), we get the following equivalent system.

$$x - 2y = 5$$
$$2x + 3y = 3$$

(2)

If we multiply the first of these equations by -2, we obtain $-2x + 4y = -10$; we add this equation to the second equation in System (2) and simplify.

$$2x + 3y + (-2x + 4y) = 3 + (-10)$$
$$0x + 7y = -7$$

System (2) then becomes

$$x - 2y = 5$$
$$0x + 7y = -7.$$

(3)

We multiply both sides of the second equation by $\frac{1}{7}$, which gives the equivalent system

$$x - 2y = 5$$
$$0x + y = -1.$$

(4)

From the second equation in System (4), we have $y = -1$. Thus $2y = -2$. Adding this to the first equation in System (4), we have the following system.

$$x + 0y = 3$$
$$0x + y = -1$$

(5)

Therefore $x = 3$ and $y = -1$ and we have solved the given system of equations.

In the above method, we performed specific operations on the original equations of System (1), transforming them into those of System (5), from which the values of the unknowns x and y can be read directly. With each operation, the system is transformed into a new system that is equivalent to the old one. The operations consisted of the following basic types.

1. Interchanging two equations.
2. Multiplying or dividing an equation by a nonzero constant.
3. Adding (or subtracting) a constant multiple of one equation to (or from) another equation.

If we keep track of the positions of various variables and the equality signs, then a system of linear equations can be written as a matrix with the variables omitted. For example, System (1) above,

$$2x + 3y = 3$$
$$x - 2y = 5$$

can be abbreviated as

$$\begin{bmatrix} 2 & 3 & | & 3 \\ 1 & -2 & | & 5 \end{bmatrix}.$$

This array of numbers is called the **augmented matrix** for the given system. Note that in writing this augmented matrix, we have written the coefficient matrix elements to the left of the vertical line and the elements of the value vector, (that is, the constants on the right sides of the equations) to the right of the vertical line. Thus, if the given system of equations in matrix form is $\mathbf{AX} = \mathbf{B}$, the augmented matrix may be denoted by $\mathbf{A}|\mathbf{B}$. The augmented matrix is simply a way of writing the system of equations without writing down the variables every time.

EXAMPLE 1   For the variables x, y, z, and t, in that order, the augmented matrix

$$\begin{bmatrix} 2 & -1 & 3 & 4 & | & 5 \\ 1 & 3 & -2 & 0 & | & 7 \\ -4 & 0 & 5 & 1 & | & -3 \end{bmatrix}$$

corresponds to the following linear system.

$$2x - y + 3z + 4t = 5$$
$$x + 3y - 2z = 7$$
$$-4x + 5z + t = -3$$

Since each row of the augmented matrix corresponds to an equation in the linear system, the three operations listed earlier correspond to the following three **row operations** of the augmented matrix.

1. Interchanging two rows.
2. Multiplying or dividing a row by a nonzero constant.
3. Adding (or subtracting) a constant multiple of one row to (or from) another row.

We shall illustrate the use of row operations on an augmented matrix to solve the following system.

$$3x - 2y = 4$$
$$x + 3y = 5$$

The augmented matrix in this case is

$$\begin{bmatrix} 3 & -2 & | & 4 \\ 1 & 3 & | & 5 \end{bmatrix}.$$

To clarify the use of these operations, we shall also solve the system by operating on the equations, side-by-side with the corresponding operations on the augmented matrix.

SYSTEM	AUGMENTED MATRIX

$$3x - 2y = 4$$
$$x + 3y = 5$$

$$\begin{bmatrix} 3 & -2 & | & 4 \\ 1 & 3 & | & 5 \end{bmatrix}$$

Interchange the first and second equations:

Interchange the first and second rows:

$$x + 3y = 5$$
$$3x - 2y = 4$$

$$\begin{bmatrix} 1 & 3 & | & 5 \\ 3 & -2 & | & 4 \end{bmatrix}$$

Add -3 times the first equation to the second equation:

Add -3 times the first row to the second row:

$$x + 3y = 5$$
$$0x - 11y = -11$$

$$\begin{bmatrix} 1 & 3 & | & 5 \\ 0 & -11 & | & -11 \end{bmatrix}$$

Divide both sides of the second equation by -11:

Divide the second row by -11:

$$x + 3y = 5$$
$$0x + y = 1$$

$$\begin{bmatrix} 1 & 3 & | & 5 \\ 0 & 1 & | & 1 \end{bmatrix}$$

Subtract 3 times the second equation from the first equation:

Subtract 3 times the second row from the first row:

$$x + 0y = 2$$
$$0x + y = 1$$

$$\begin{bmatrix} 1 & 0 & | & 2 \\ 0 & 1 & | & 1 \end{bmatrix}$$

The solution is therefore $x = 2$ and $y = 1$. Observe that the values of x and y are given by the entries in the last column of this final augmented matrix.

The final augmented matrix from which we read the solution is of the form $I \,|\, C$, where I is the identity matrix and C is a certain column vector. Thus, to obtain the solution of a given system $AX = B$, we first write the augmented matrix $A \,|\, B$ and then use row operations to change it to the form $I \,|\, C$. This is not always possible; however, if we succeed, the solution for the variables is given by the entries in the last column C. The final form of the matrix $I \,|\, C$ that gives the solutions to a system is called the **reduced matrix**. This method of solving linear systems is called the **method of row reduction**.

Before we explain how to select the order of row operations to obtain the reduced matrix from the original augmented matrix, we introduce some notation to avoid repeating lengthy expressions. We shall use the symbol R_p for the pth row of the augmented matrix. Thus R_1 denotes the first row, R_2 the second row, and so on. When we say "apply $R_2 - 2R_1$," this means "subtract twice the first row from the second row," while the operation $R_3 + 4R_2$ consists of adding four times the second row to the third row and $R_2 + R_3$ means adding the third row to the second row (*not* the second row to the third row). Similarly, the operation $2R_3$ means multiplying the third row of the augmented matrix by 2 and $-\frac{1}{2}R_1$ means multiplying the first row by $-\frac{1}{2}$. Finally, notation such as $R_1 \leftrightarrow R_3$ means the operation of interchanging the first and third rows. We shall also use notation such as

$$\text{matrix } \mathbf{A} \xrightarrow{R_1 - 2R_2} \text{matrix } \mathbf{B}$$

which means that matrix $\mathbf{B}$ is obtained by applying the operation $R_1 - 2R_2$ (that is, subtracting twice the second row from the first row) on matrix $\mathbf{A}$.

Now we are in a position to explain the method of row reduction in detail. We shall do this through an example.

EXAMPLE 2   Use the method of row reduction to solve the following system of linear equations.

$$2x - 3y + 4z = 13$$
$$x + y + 2z = 4$$
$$3x + 5y - z = -4$$

Solution   The augmented matrix for this system is

$$\begin{bmatrix} 2 & -3 & 4 & \bigm| & 13 \\ 1 & 1 & 2 & \bigm| & 4 \\ 3 & 5 & -1 & \bigm| & -4 \end{bmatrix}.$$

Our purpose is to apply row operations on this matrix until we obtain its reduced form, that is, until the first three columns form an identity matrix. The best method, generally, is to attack the columns one by one, changing the main diagonal elements to 1 and making the other entries in the columns zero. In the first column of our matrix, the first entry is 2. To change this entry to 1, we could divide R_1 by 2 or, alternatively, we could interchange R_1 and R_2. If we apply $\frac{1}{2}R_1$, we immediately introduce fractions, whereas if we interchange R_1 and R_2 (that is, apply $R_1 \leftrightarrow R_2$), we shall avoid fractions (at least for the time being). Thus it is preferable to apply $R_1 \leftrightarrow R_2$ and obtain

$$\begin{bmatrix} 1 & 1 & 2 & \bigm| & 4 \\ 2 & -3 & 4 & \bigm| & 13 \\ 3 & 5 & -1 & \bigm| & -4 \end{bmatrix}.$$

Now that we have obtained a diagonal entry of 1 in the first column, we use the first row to change the other elements in the first column to zero. This can be done by applying the operations $R_2 - 2R_1$ and $R_3 - 3R_1$. This gives us the matrix

$$\begin{bmatrix} 1 & 1 & 2 & \bigm| & 4 \\ 2 - 2(1) & -3 - 2(1) & 4 - 2(2) & \bigm| & 13 - 2(4) \\ 3 - 3(1) & 5 - 3(1) & -1 - 3(2) & \bigm| & -4 - 3(4) \end{bmatrix} = \begin{bmatrix} 1 & 1 & 2 & \bigm| & 4 \\ 0 & -5 & 0 & \bigm| & 5 \\ 0 & 2 & -7 & \bigm| & -16 \end{bmatrix}.$$

We have now reduced the first column to the required form (that is, to the first column of the identity matrix). We now attack the second column. In this column, we must have 1 in the second row and zero in the first and third row. While achieving this goal, *we must be careful not to change the first column.* (This means, for instance, that we cannot add 6 times the first row to the second row because this will change the first column entries). There are many ways that yield 1 in the second entry in the second column. For example, we can apply $-\frac{1}{3}R_2$ or $R_2 + 3R_3$. Application of $-\frac{1}{3}R_2$ is simpler in this case; it leads to the following matrix.

$$\begin{bmatrix} 1 & 1 & 2 & 4 \\ 0 & 1 & 0 & -1 \\ 0 & 2 & -7 & -16 \end{bmatrix}$$

We now use the second row to make the other two entries in the second column zero. We apply the operations $R_1 - R_2$ and $R_3 - 2R_2$, which gives

$$\begin{bmatrix} 1-0 & 1-1 & 2-0 & 4-(-1) \\ 0 & 1 & 0 & -1 \\ 0-2(0) & 2-2(1) & -7-2(0) & -16-2(-1) \end{bmatrix} = \begin{bmatrix} 1 & 0 & 2 & 5 \\ 0 & 1 & 0 & -1 \\ 0 & 0 & -7 & -14 \end{bmatrix}.$$

Notice that these operations have not changed the first column. Thus we have also reduced the second column to the required form, with 1 on the main diagonal and 0 elsewhere.

Finally we attack the third column. We must make the third entry in this column equal to 1; this can be done by applying $-\frac{1}{7}R_3$. This leads to

$$\begin{bmatrix} 1 & 0 & 2 & 5 \\ 0 & 1 & 0 & -1 \\ 0 & 0 & 1 & 2 \end{bmatrix}.$$

In the third column, the entries in the first and second row must also be zero. We already have zero in the second row. To obtain zero in the first row, we apply the operation $R_1 - 2R_2$. This gives

$$\begin{bmatrix} 1 & 0 & 2-2(1) & 5-2(2) \\ 0 & 1 & 0 & -1 \\ 0 & 0 & 1 & 2 \end{bmatrix} = \begin{bmatrix} 1 & 0 & 0 & 1 \\ 0 & 1 & 0 & -1 \\ 0 & 0 & 1 & 2 \end{bmatrix}.$$

Thus we have attained our goal, that is, we have changed the first three columns of the augmented matrix of the system to an identity matrix. The final matrix represents the system

$$\begin{aligned} x + 0y + 0z &= 1 & & x = 1 \\ 0x + 1y + 0z &= -1 & \text{or} \quad & y = -1 \\ 0x + 0y + 1z &= 2 & & z = 2 \end{aligned}$$

from which the required solution can be read directly.

In light of the above example, we may summarize the steps involved in changing the augmented matrix to its reduced form as follows.* Each step is carried out by means of one or more of the row operations given earlier.

*The procedure does not always work and must be modified in certain cases (see Section 4).

1. Use row operations to obtain a top entry in the first column equal to 1.

2. Add or subtract the appropriate multiples of the first row to the other rows so that the remaining entries in the first column become zero.

3. Without disturbing the first column, use row operations to make the second entry in the second column equal to 1. Then add or subtract suitable multiples of the second row to the other rows to obtain zeros in the rest of the second column.

4. Without disturbing the first two columns, make the third entry in the third column equal to 1. Then use the third row to obtain zeros in the rest of the third column.

5. Continue the process column by column until the reduced form of the matrix is obtained; that is, until the matrix takes the form $\mathbf{I}\,|\,\mathbf{C}$, with an identity matrix $\mathbf{I}$ on the left of the vertical line. The solutions for the variables are then given by the entries in the last column, $\mathbf{C}$.

EXAMPLE 3 Two products A and B are competitive. The demands x_A and x_B for these products are related to their prices P_A and P_B according to the demand equations

$$x_A = 17 - 2P_A + \tfrac{1}{2}P_B \quad \text{and} \quad x_B = 20 - 3P_B + \tfrac{1}{2}P_A.$$

The supply equations are

$$P_A = 2 + x_A + \tfrac{1}{3}x_B \quad \text{and} \quad P_B = 2 + \tfrac{1}{2}x_B + \tfrac{1}{4}x_A$$

giving the prices at which the quantities x_A and x_B of the two products will be available on the market. For market equilibrium, all four equations must be satisfied (since demand and supply must be equal). Find the equilibrium values of x_A, x_B, P_A, and P_B.

Solution Rearranging the four equations, we obtain the following system.

$$
\begin{aligned}
x_A \quad\quad\;\; + 2P_A - \tfrac{1}{2}P_B &= 17 \\
x_B - \tfrac{1}{2}P_A + 3P_B &= 20 \\
x_A + \tfrac{1}{3}x_B - P_A \quad\quad\;\; &= -2 \\
\tfrac{1}{4}x_A + \tfrac{1}{2}x_B \quad\quad\; - P_B &= -2
\end{aligned}
$$

Note that the variables in each equation have been put in the order x_A, x_B, P_A, and P_B. The augmented matrix is as follows.

$$
\left[
\begin{array}{cccc|c}
1 & 0 & 2 & -\tfrac{1}{2} & 17 \\
0 & 1 & -\tfrac{1}{2} & 3 & 20 \\
1 & \tfrac{1}{3} & -1 & 0 & -2 \\
\tfrac{1}{4} & \tfrac{1}{2} & 0 & -1 & -2
\end{array}
\right]
$$

We apply the sequence of row operations $R_3 - R_1$, $R_4 - \tfrac{1}{4}R_1$, $R_3 - \tfrac{1}{3}R_2$, and $R_4 - \tfrac{1}{2}R_2$. This gives the following.

$$
\left[
\begin{array}{cccc|c}
1 & 0 & 2 & -\tfrac{1}{2} & 17 \\
0 & 1 & -\tfrac{1}{2} & 3 & 20 \\
0 & 0 & -\tfrac{17}{6} & -\tfrac{1}{2} & -\tfrac{77}{3} \\
0 & 0 & -\tfrac{1}{4} & -\tfrac{19}{8} & -\tfrac{65}{4}
\end{array}
\right]
$$

Before reducing the matrix further, we observe that interchanging the third and fourth rows will help to avoid complicated fractions, since the entry in the third column is $-\frac{1}{4}$ rather than $-\frac{17}{6}$. So making this interchange and multiplying the new R_3 by -4 we have the following.

$$
\begin{bmatrix}
1 & 0 & 2 & -\frac{1}{2} & \bigg| & 17 \\
0 & 1 & -\frac{1}{2} & 3 & \bigg| & 20 \\
0 & 0 & 1 & \frac{19}{2} & \bigg| & 65 \\
0 & 0 & -\frac{17}{6} & -\frac{1}{2} & \bigg| & -\frac{77}{3}
\end{bmatrix}
\begin{array}{l} R_1 - 2R_3 \\ R_2 + \frac{1}{2}R_3 \\ R_4 + \frac{17}{6}R_3 \\ \longrightarrow \end{array}
\begin{bmatrix}
1 & 0 & 0 & -\frac{39}{2} & \bigg| & -113 \\
0 & 1 & 0 & \frac{31}{4} & \bigg| & \frac{105}{2} \\
0 & 0 & 1 & \frac{19}{2} & \bigg| & 65 \\
0 & 0 & 0 & \frac{317}{12} & \bigg| & \frac{317}{2}
\end{bmatrix}
$$

$$
\xrightarrow{\frac{12}{317}R_4}
\begin{bmatrix}
1 & 0 & 0 & -\frac{39}{2} & \bigg| & -113 \\
0 & 1 & 0 & \frac{31}{4} & \bigg| & \frac{105}{2} \\
0 & 0 & 1 & \frac{19}{2} & \bigg| & 65 \\
0 & 0 & 0 & 1 & \bigg| & 6
\end{bmatrix}
$$

$$
\begin{array}{l} R_1 + \frac{39}{2}R_4 \\ R_2 - \frac{31}{4}R_4 \\ R_3 - \frac{19}{2}R_4 \\ \longrightarrow \end{array}
\begin{bmatrix}
1 & 0 & 0 & 0 & \bigg| & 4 \\
0 & 1 & 0 & 0 & \bigg| & 6 \\
0 & 0 & 1 & 0 & \bigg| & 8 \\
0 & 0 & 0 & 1 & \bigg| & 6
\end{bmatrix}
$$

The solution for market equilibrium is therefore $x_A = 4$, $x_B = 6$, $P_A = 8$, and $P_B = 6$.

EXERCISES 3

(1–14) In the following problems, solve the given system (if the solution exists) by using the row reduction method.

1. $2x + 3y = 7$
$3x - y = 5$

2. $x + 2y = 1$
$3y + 2x = 3$

3. $u + 3v = 1$
$2u - v = 9$

4. $3p + 2q = 5$
$p - 3q + 2 = 0$

5. $x + y + z = 6$
$2x - y + 3z = 9$
$-x + 2y + z = 6$

6. $x + 2y - z = -3$
$3y + 4z = 5$
$2x - y + 3z = 9$

7. $3x_1 + 2x_2 + x_3 = 6$
$2x_1 - x_2 + 4x_3 = -4$
$x_1 + x_2 - 2x_3 = 5$

8. $2u - 3v + 4w = 13$
$u + v + w = 6$
$-3u + 2v + w + 1 = 0$

9. $p - q + r = -1$
$3p - 2r = -7$
$r + 4q = 10$

10. $b = 3 - a$
$c = 4 - a - b$
$3a + 2b + c = 8$

11.
$$x + 2y + z - t = 0$$
$$y - 2z + 2t = 13$$
$$2x + 4y - z + 2t = 19$$
$$y - z - 3t = 0$$

12.
$$p - q - r = 4$$
$$q - r - s = -5$$
$$r - s - p = -8$$
$$p + 2q + 2r + s = -5$$

13.
$$x + y + z \quad = 1$$
$$2x + 3y \quad - w = 3$$
$$-x \quad + 2z + 3w = 3$$
$$2y - z + w = 5$$

14.
$$x_1 + x_2 + x_3 + x_4 = 2$$
$$x_1 - x_2 + x_3 + 2x_4 = -4$$
$$2x_1 + x_2 - x_3 + x_4 = 1$$
$$-x_1 + x_2 + x_3 - x_4 = 4$$

15. Find x, y, and z such that
$$x[1 \quad 2 \quad -1] - y[2 \quad -1 \quad 3] + z[3 \quad -2 \quad 1] = [9 \quad -1 \quad -2].$$

16. Find a, b, and c such that
$$a[2 \quad 3 \quad -1] + b[1 \quad 2 \quad 3] + c[1 \quad 0 \quad 2] = [3 \quad 7 \quad 3].$$

(17–24) Use the method of row reduction to solve the following problems.

17. The demand equation for a certain product is $p + 2x = 25$ and the supply equation is $p - 3x = 5$, where p is the price and x is the quantity demanded or supplied, as the case may be. Find the values of x and p at market equilibrium.

18. The demand and supply equations for a certain commodity are $3p + 5x = 200$ and $7p - 3x = 56$, respectively. Find the values of x and p at market equilibrium.

19. If a sales tax of 11 is imposed on each item in Exercise 18, find the new values of quantity x and the price p_1 paid by consumers (see Section 5 of Chapter 4).

20. The cost in dollars of producing x items per week of a certain product is given by $C = 3x + 500$. If the items sell for \$5 each, how many should be produced to give a weekly profit equal to \$300 plus 10% of the production costs?

21. A firm produces three products, A, B, and C, which require processing by three machines. The time (in hours) required for processing one unit of each product by the three machines is given below.

	A	B	C
Machine I	3	1	2
Machine II	1	2	4
Machine III	2	1	1

Machine I is available for 850 hours, machine II for 1200 hours, and machine III for 550 hours. How many units of each product should be produced to make use of all the available time on the machines?

22. A shipping company loaded three types of cargo on its light transport plane. The space required by each unit of the three types of cargo was 5, 2, and 4 cubic feet, respectively. Each unit of the three types of cargo weighed 2, 3, and 1 kilograms, respectively, whereas the unit values of the three types of cargo were \$10, \$40, and \$60, respectively. Determine the number of units of each type of cargo loaded if the total value of the cargo was \$13,500, it occupied 1050 cubic feet of space, and it weighed 550 kilograms.

23. A person invested a total of \$20,000 in three different investments at 6%, 8%, and 10%. The total annual return was \$1624 and the return from the 10% investment was twice the return from the 6% investment. How much was invested in each?

24. A contractor has 5000 work-hours of labor available for three projects. The costs per work-hour of the three projects are $8, $10, and $12, respectively, and the total cost is $53,000. If the number of work-hours for the third project is equal to the sum of the work-hours for the first two projects, find the work-hours that can be used for each project.

9-4 SINGULAR SYSTEMS

All the systems of linear equations that we solved in the last section had unique solutions. There exist systems of equations that have more than one solution and other systems that have no solutions at all. Such systems are said to be **singular**. Consider the following example.

EXAMPLE 1 Solve the following system.

$$
\begin{aligned}
x + y - z &= 4 \\
3x - 2y + 4z &= 9 \\
9x - y + 5z &= 30
\end{aligned}
$$

Solution We reduce the augmented matrix for this system as follows.

$$
\begin{bmatrix} 1 & 1 & -1 & 4 \\ 3 & -2 & 4 & 9 \\ 9 & -1 & 5 & 30 \end{bmatrix}
\xrightarrow[R_3 - 9R_1]{R_2 - 3R_1}
\begin{bmatrix} 1 & 1 & -1 & 4 \\ 0 & -5 & 7 & -3 \\ 0 & -10 & 14 & -6 \end{bmatrix}
$$

$$
\xrightarrow{-\frac{1}{5}R_2}
\begin{bmatrix} 1 & 1 & -1 & 4 \\ 0 & 1 & -\frac{7}{5} & \frac{3}{5} \\ 0 & -10 & 14 & -6 \end{bmatrix}
\xrightarrow[R_3 + 10R_2]{R_1 - R_2}
\begin{bmatrix} 1 & 0 & \frac{2}{5} & \frac{17}{5} \\ 0 & 1 & -\frac{7}{5} & \frac{3}{5} \\ 0 & 0 & 0 & 0 \end{bmatrix}
$$

So far we have obtained the first two columns in the desired form. However, the third row now consists entirely of zeros, so we are unable to obtain 1 in the third entry of the third column without disturbing the first and second columns. Thus we cannot continue the process of row reduction any further.

The matrix we have obtained corresponds to the following equations.

$$
\begin{aligned}
x + \tfrac{2}{5}z &= \tfrac{17}{5} \\
y - \tfrac{7}{5}z &= \tfrac{3}{5}
\end{aligned}
\tag{1}
$$

The third equations is $0x + 0y + 0z = 0$, or $0 = 0$, which is true for all values of x, y, and z and can be ignored. We see therefore that the given system of three equations can be reduced to only two independent equations. The two equations in System (1) can be solved for x and y in terms of z.

$$
\begin{aligned}
x &= \tfrac{17}{5} - \tfrac{2}{5}z = \tfrac{1}{5}(17 - 2z) \\
y &= \tfrac{3}{5} + \tfrac{7}{5}z = \tfrac{1}{5}(3 + 7z)
\end{aligned}
\tag{2}
$$

The variable z is arbitrary and can take any value. For example, if $z = 1$, then $x = \tfrac{1}{5}(17 - 2) = 3$ and $y = \tfrac{1}{5}(3 + 7) = 2$. Thus $x = 3$, $y = 2$, and $z = 1$ is one solution. By changing the values of z, we get different values of x and y from System (2) and, therefore, different solutions of the given system. Thus the system has an infinite number of solutions. The general form of solution is $x = \frac{1}{5}(17 - 2z)$, $y = \frac{1}{5}(3 + 7z)$, z, where z is arbitrary.

The solution in Example 1 is only one form of the general solution. We can, in fact, solve for any two of the variables in terms of the third. For example, if we want to solve for x and z in terms of y, we reduce the matrix to a form containing a second-order identity matrix in the columns corresponding to x and z.

Example 2 illustrates a different situation in which an infinite number of solutions can occur.

EXAMPLE 2   Solve the following system of four equations.

$$x - y + z - t = 5$$
$$2x - 2y + z + 3t = 2$$
$$-x + y + 2z + t = 4$$
$$3x - 3y + z + 3t = 3$$

Solution   The augmented matrix for this system is

$$
\begin{bmatrix}
1 & -1 & 1 & -1 & 5 \\
2 & -2 & 1 & 3 & 2 \\
-1 & 1 & 2 & 1 & 4 \\
3 & -3 & 1 & 3 & 3
\end{bmatrix}
\begin{array}{l} R_2 - 2R_1 \\ R_3 + R_1 \\ R_4 - 3R_1 \\ \longrightarrow \end{array}
\begin{bmatrix}
1 & -1 & 1 & -1 & 5 \\
0 & 0 & -1 & 5 & -8 \\
0 & 0 & 3 & 0 & 9 \\
0 & 0 & -2 & 6 & -12
\end{bmatrix}.
$$

At this stage, we observe that the second column contains all zeros below the first row. Thus it is impossible to obtain a 1 in the second position in this column without changing the zeros in the first column. In this kind of predicament, what we do is to forget about the second column and move on to the third. The sequence of row operations $(-1)R_2$ followed by $R_1 - R_2$, $R_3 - 3R_2$, and $R_4 + 2R_2$ gives the matrix in the following form.

$$
\begin{bmatrix}
1 & -1 & 1-1 & -1-(-5) & 5-8 \\
0 & 0 & 1 & -5 & 8 \\
0 & 0 & 3-3(1) & 0-3(-5) & 9-3(8) \\
0 & 0 & -2+2(1) & 6+2(-5) & -12+2(8)
\end{bmatrix}
=
\begin{bmatrix}
1 & -1 & 0 & 4 & -3 \\
0 & 0 & 1 & -5 & 8 \\
0 & 0 & 0 & 15 & -15 \\
0 & 0 & 0 & -4 & 4
\end{bmatrix}
$$

Having disregarded the second column, we have reduced the third column to the form that the second column would normally have—that is, 1 in the second entry and zeros elsewhere. Applying $\frac{1}{15}R_3$, we how obtain

$$
\begin{bmatrix}
1 & -1 & 0 & 4 & -3 \\
0 & 0 & 1 & -5 & 8 \\
0 & 0 & 0 & 1 & -1 \\
0 & 0 & 0 & -4 & 4
\end{bmatrix}
\begin{array}{l} R_1 - 4R_3 \\ R_2 + 5R_3 \\ R_4 + 4R_3 \\ \longrightarrow \end{array}
\begin{bmatrix}
1 & -1 & 0 & 0 & 1 \\
0 & 0 & 1 & 0 & 3 \\
0 & 0 & 0 & 1 & -1 \\
0 & 0 & 0 & 0 & 0
\end{bmatrix}.
$$

As in Example 1, we have obtained an entire row of zeros in the matrix, corresponding to the trivial equation $0 = 0$. The other three rows correspond to the equations

$$x - y = 1, \qquad z = 3, \quad \text{and} \quad t = -1.$$

Thus we see that in this case certain of the variables (z and t) have definite values, while others (x and y) do not. Again the number of solutions is infinite, since we can allow y to have any value whatsoever; x is then given by $x = y + 1$.

There are also systems of equations that have no solution at all.

EXAMPLE 3   Solve the following system.

$$x + y + 2z = 9$$
$$3x - 2y + 7z = 20$$
$$2x + 7y + 3z = 27$$

Solution   We reduce the augmented matrix for the system as follows.

$$\begin{bmatrix} 1 & 1 & 2 & | & 9 \\ 3 & -2 & 7 & | & 20 \\ 2 & 7 & 3 & | & 27 \end{bmatrix} \xrightarrow[\substack{R_2 - 3R_1 \\ R_3 - 2R_1}]{} \begin{bmatrix} 1 & 1 & 2 & | & 9 \\ 0 & -5 & 1 & | & -7 \\ 0 & 5 & -1 & | & 9 \end{bmatrix}$$

$$\xrightarrow{-\frac{1}{5}R_2} \begin{bmatrix} 1 & 1 & 2 & | & 9 \\ 0 & 1 & -\frac{1}{5} & | & \frac{7}{5} \\ 0 & 5 & -1 & | & 9 \end{bmatrix} \xrightarrow[\substack{R_1 - R_2 \\ R_3 - 5R_2}]{} \begin{bmatrix} 1 & 0 & \frac{11}{5} & | & \frac{38}{5} \\ 0 & 1 & -\frac{1}{5} & | & \frac{7}{5} \\ 0 & 0 & 0 & | & 2 \end{bmatrix}$$

The first two columns are in the desired form of an identity matrix. However, we cannot put 1 in the third column and third row without affecting these two columns, so the reduction cannot proceed any further. Let us examine the equation represented by the third row.

$$0x + 0y + 0z = 2, \quad \text{or} \quad 0 = 2$$

Clearly this equation is absurd. Thus the system does not have a solution, that is, there are no values of x, y, and z that satisfy all the three equations of the system.

In general, *a system will have no solution if a row is obtained in which all the entries except the last are zero.*

We have seen three possibilities for the solution of a system. It may have a unique solution, infinitely many solutions, or no solution at all. A system is said to be **consistent** if it has at least one solution, whereas it is said to be **inconsistent** if it has no solution. The system in Example 3 is inconsistent, but Examples 1 and 2 (as well as all the examples in Section 3) involve consistent systems.

It is clear from the examples of this section that the procedure of row reduction outlined in Section 3 is not sufficiently general to cope with all cases. We cannot always reduce an augmented matrix to the form $\mathbf{I} \,|\, \mathbf{C}$. More generally, we can reduce it to a form that has the following properties.

1. The first nonzero entry in each row is 1.
2. In the column in which a 1 appears, all other entries are 0.
3. The first nonzero entry in any row is to the right of the first nonzero entry in every preceding row.
4. Any rows consisting entirely of zeros are below the rows with nonzero entries.

In this form, the method of row reduction can be used for any system, regardless of the numbers of equations and variables. If the final reduced form contains a row in which only the last entry is nonzero, then the system is inconsistent. Otherwise it is consistent.

All the systems we have considered so far had the same number of equations as variables. The method of row reduction is also useful in cases where the number of equations is different from the number of unknowns involved in the system.

If a system has fewer equations than the number of variables, the system will always have more than one solution, provided it is not inconsistent. We use the method of Examples 1 and 2 above and try to obtain an identity matrix in the columns corresponding to some of the variables. This then gives the solution for the corresponding variables in terms of the others. This is illustrated in Example 4.

EXAMPLE 4 Solve the following system.

$$3x - 2y + 4z + \quad w = -2$$
$$x + \quad y - 3z + 2w = 12$$

Solution The augmented matrix is

$$\begin{bmatrix} 3 & -2 & 4 & 1 & | & -2 \\ 1 & 1 & -3 & 2 & | & 12 \end{bmatrix}.$$

Since there are only two equations in this case, we can obtain an identity matrix of size 2×2 at most. Let us suppose we want to solve for y and w in terms of the remaining variables x and z. Then we must obtain an identity matrix in the two columns corresponding to y and w (that is, the second and fourth columns). Applying $R_1 \leftrightarrow R_2$, we have

$$\begin{bmatrix} 1 & 1 & -3 & 2 & | & 12 \\ 3 & -2 & 4 & 1 & | & -2 \end{bmatrix} \xrightarrow{R_2 + 2R_1} \begin{bmatrix} 1 & 1 & -3 & 2 & | & 12 \\ 5 & 0 & -2 & 5 & | & 22 \end{bmatrix}.$$

Thus we have obtained the y-column, as desired. Now we have to change the entries in the w-column to obtain zero in the top row and 1 in the bottom row. To obtain 1 in R_2, we apply $\frac{1}{5}R_2$.

$$\begin{bmatrix} 1 & 1 & -3 & 2 & | & 12 \\ 1 & 0 & -\frac{2}{5} & 1 & | & \frac{22}{5} \end{bmatrix} \xrightarrow{R_1 - 2R_2} \begin{bmatrix} -1 & 1 & -\frac{11}{5} & 0 & | & \frac{16}{5} \\ 1 & 0 & -\frac{2}{5} & 1 & | & \frac{22}{5} \end{bmatrix}$$

Thus we have obtained an identity matrix in the columns corresponding to y

and w, as we set out to do. The system represented by the final matrix is

$$-x + \;\; y - \tfrac{11}{5}z + 0w = \tfrac{16}{5}$$
$$x + 0y - \;\; \tfrac{2}{5}z + 1w = \tfrac{22}{5}.$$

After solving for y and w, we have the following equations.

$$y = \tfrac{16}{5} + x + \tfrac{11}{5}z$$
$$w = \tfrac{22}{5} - x + \tfrac{2}{5}z$$

Thus we have expressed y and w in terms of the other two variables, x and z.

EXAMPLE 5   The system

$$2x - 3y + \;\; 4z = 7$$
$$6x - 9y + 12z = 22$$

contains two equations involving three variables. It is left as an exercise to verify that this system is inconsistent. (If the process of row reduction is carried out, it will be found that the second row reduces to zeros, except for the last entry.)

EXERCISES 4

(1–18)   Find the solutions of the following systems where solutions exist.

1.
$$x + y + z = 5$$
$$-x + y + 3z = 1$$
$$x + 2y + 3z = 8$$

2.
$$x + y \qquad = 3$$
$$2x + y + z = 4$$
$$2x + 2y - 2z = 5$$

3.
$$x + y + z = 3$$
$$-x - y + z = -1$$
$$3x + 3y + 4z = 8$$

4.
$$6x - 5y + 6z = 7$$
$$2x + y + 6z = 5$$
$$2x - y + 3z = 3$$

5.
$$u - v + 2w = 5$$
$$4u + v + 3w = 15$$
$$5u - 2v + 7w = 31$$

6.
$$-x + y + z = 4$$
$$3x - y + 2z = -3$$
$$4x - 2y + z = 3$$

7.
$$2x + y - z = 2$$
$$3x + 2y + 4z = 8$$
$$5x + 4y + 14z = 20$$

8.
$$a + b - 2c = 3$$
$$2a + 3b + c = 13$$
$$7a + 9b - 4c = 35$$

9.
$$x + 2y - 3z - t = 2$$
$$2x + 4y + z - t = 1$$
$$3x + 6y + 2z + t = -7$$
$$x + 2y + z + t = 6$$

10.
$$p + 2q - r + 2s = 6$$
$$-2p + q + 2r + 3s = 6$$
$$3p + 5q - 3r + s = 0$$
$$p + 2q - r + s = 2$$

11.
$$u + v - w = 4$$
$$3u - v + 2w = -1$$
$$2u + 3v + w = 7$$
$$u + 2v + 3w = 2$$

12.
$$3x + 2y + z = 10$$
$$2x - y + 3z = 9$$
$$x + y - 2z = -3$$
$$2x + 3y + 4z = 20$$

13.
$$x + y - 2z = -3$$
$$2x + 3y + z = 10$$
$$-x + 2y + 3z = 9$$
$$3x + y - z = 4$$
$$x - 2y - z = 2$$

14.
$$x_1 + 2x_2 - x_3 = 2$$
$$3x_1 + x_2 + 4x_3 = 17$$
$$-2x_1 + 3x_2 + 5x_3 = 19$$
$$x_1 + x_2 + 2x_3 = 9$$
$$4x_1 - x_2 + x_3 = 4$$

15.
$$2x - y + 3z = 9$$
$$3y - 6x - 9z = 12$$

16.
$$u - 2v + w = 7$$
$$5u - 10v + 5w = 36$$

17.
$$x + y - z = 2$$
$$2x - 3y + 4z = -3$$

18.
$$2x + y - 3z = 10$$
$$3x + 2y + z = 11$$

REVIEW EXERCISES FOR CHAPTER 9

1. Are the following statements true or false? If false, explain why.

a. The following array of numbers

$$\begin{bmatrix} 2 & 3 & 4 \\ 0 & 1 & 3 \\ 3 & 2 & \end{bmatrix}$$

represents a matrix.

b. If

$$\mathbf{A} = [a_1 \quad b_1] \quad \text{and} \quad \mathbf{B} = \begin{bmatrix} a_2 \\ b_2 \end{bmatrix}$$

then $\mathbf{A} + \mathbf{B} = [a_1 + a_2 \quad b_1 + b_2]$.

c. If $\mathbf{A}$ and $\mathbf{B}$ are two matrices of the same size, then $\mathbf{A} + \mathbf{B} = \mathbf{B} + \mathbf{A}$.

d. If $\mathbf{A} + \mathbf{B}$ is defined for two matrices $\mathbf{A}$ and $\mathbf{B}$, then the size of $\mathbf{A} + \mathbf{B}$ is the same as that of $\mathbf{A}$ or $\mathbf{B}$.

e. The product $\mathbf{AB}$ is defined only if the number of rows in $\mathbf{A}$ is equal to the number of columns in $\mathbf{B}$.

f. If $\mathbf{A}$ and $\mathbf{B}$ are two matrices of the same size, then $\mathbf{AB}$ and $\mathbf{BA}$ are both defined.

g. If $\mathbf{A}$ and $\mathbf{B}$ are two matrices such that $\mathbf{AB}$ and $\mathbf{BA}$ are both defined, then $\mathbf{AB}$ is never equal to $\mathbf{BA}$.

h. If $\mathbf{AB}$ and $\mathbf{BA}$ are both defined, then the size of $\mathbf{AB}$ or $\mathbf{BA}$ is the same as the size of $\mathbf{A}$ or $\mathbf{B}$.

i. If $\mathbf{A}$ is a matrix of any size and $\mathbf{I}$ is the identity matrix, then $\mathbf{AI} = \mathbf{IA} = \mathbf{A}$.

j. If $\mathbf{A}$ and $\mathbf{B}$ are two square matrices of the same size, then the size of $\mathbf{AB}$ or $\mathbf{BA}$ is the same as that of $\mathbf{A}$ or $\mathbf{B}$.

k. If $\mathbf{A} = \mathbf{A} + \mathbf{B}$, then $\mathbf{B}$ is a zero matrix.

l. If $\mathbf{AB} = \mathbf{0}$, then either $\mathbf{A}$ or $\mathbf{B}$ is a zero matrix.

m. If a system has the same number of equations as the number of variables, then the system has a unique solution.

n. If there are more variables than the number of equations, then the system has infinitely many solutions.

o. A system of linear equations is said to be consistent if it has a unique solution.

2. Give an example of a 2×2 nonzero matrix $\mathbf{A}$ such that $\mathbf{A}^2 = \mathbf{0}$.

(3–8) Perform the indicated matrix operations and simplify.

3. $\begin{bmatrix} 2 & -1 \\ 3 & 4 \end{bmatrix} + 2\begin{bmatrix} 1 & -2 \\ 4 & 3 \end{bmatrix} - 3\begin{bmatrix} 1 & 2 \\ -3 & 0 \end{bmatrix}$

4. $\begin{bmatrix} 1 & 2 & 3 \\ 3 & -1 & 2 \\ -2 & 3 & 1 \end{bmatrix} - 3\begin{bmatrix} 0 & 1 & -1 \\ -2 & 3 & 0 \\ 1 & 0 & 2 \end{bmatrix} + 5\begin{bmatrix} 1 & 0 & 2 \\ -1 & 2 & 3 \\ 0 & -1 & 0 \end{bmatrix}$

5. $\begin{bmatrix} 1 & 0 & -1 \\ 2 & 1 & 0 \end{bmatrix}\begin{bmatrix} 2 & -1 \\ 1 & 3 \\ -3 & 2 \end{bmatrix} + 2\begin{bmatrix} 1 & 2 \\ 3 & 4 \end{bmatrix}$

6. $\begin{bmatrix} 2 & 3 \\ 1 & 0 \\ -3 & 1 \end{bmatrix} - 2\begin{bmatrix} -1 & 2 \\ 0 & -1 \\ 2 & 3 \end{bmatrix}\begin{bmatrix} 2 & 1 \\ 3 & -1 \end{bmatrix}$

7. $\begin{bmatrix} 1 & 2 & 3 \\ 0 & -1 & 2 \end{bmatrix}\begin{bmatrix} 2 & -1 \\ 3 & 4 \\ 1 & 0 \end{bmatrix} - \begin{bmatrix} 3 & 1 \\ -1 & 2 \end{bmatrix}\begin{bmatrix} 0 & 1 \\ 2 & 3 \end{bmatrix}$

8. $\begin{bmatrix} 1 & 0 & -1 \\ 0 & 1 & 2 \end{bmatrix}\left(\begin{bmatrix} 2 & 0 \\ 1 & -1 \\ 0 & 1 \end{bmatrix} + 3\begin{bmatrix} 0 & -1 \\ 1 & 2 \\ 0 & 0 \end{bmatrix}\right) + \begin{bmatrix} 2 & 1 \\ 3 & 0 \end{bmatrix}\begin{bmatrix} -1 & 2 \\ 0 & 1 \end{bmatrix}$

(9–16) Solve the following matrix equations.

9. $x[3 \quad -1] + y[2 \quad 1] = [7 \quad 1]$

10. $x\begin{bmatrix} 2 \\ -1 \\ 3 \end{bmatrix} + y\begin{bmatrix} 1 \\ 2 \\ -1 \end{bmatrix} - z\begin{bmatrix} 3 \\ -1 \\ 2 \end{bmatrix} = \begin{bmatrix} -5 \\ -1 \\ 0 \end{bmatrix}$

11. $x[3 \quad 1 \quad 2] + y[2 \quad -3 \quad 1] = [1 \quad 4 \quad 1]$

12. $x\begin{bmatrix} 1 \\ 2 \\ 3 \end{bmatrix} + 2y\begin{bmatrix} -1 \\ 3 \\ 1 \end{bmatrix} = \begin{bmatrix} 4 \\ 10 \\ 3 \end{bmatrix}$

13. $\begin{bmatrix} 2 & -1 \\ 1 & 3 \end{bmatrix}\begin{bmatrix} x \\ y \end{bmatrix} = \begin{bmatrix} -4 \\ 5 \end{bmatrix}$

14. $\begin{bmatrix} 3 & 2 \\ 4 & -1 \end{bmatrix}\begin{bmatrix} x \\ y \end{bmatrix} + \begin{bmatrix} 5 \\ -3 \end{bmatrix} = \begin{bmatrix} 9 \\ 6 \end{bmatrix}$

15.
$$\begin{bmatrix} 1 & -1 & 1 \\ 2 & 1 & 3 \\ 1 & 0 & 2 \\ 3 & -2 & 4 \end{bmatrix} \begin{bmatrix} x \\ y \\ z \end{bmatrix} = \begin{bmatrix} 2 \\ 8 \\ 4 \\ 5 \end{bmatrix}$$

16.
$$\begin{bmatrix} 1 & 2 & -1 \\ 3 & 4 & 2 \\ 2 & -1 & 1 \\ 1 & 1 & 3 \end{bmatrix} \begin{bmatrix} x \\ y \\ z \end{bmatrix} = \begin{bmatrix} 4 \\ 5 \\ 0 \\ -1 \end{bmatrix}$$

(17–20) Determine the matrix X such that each of the following equations is satisfied.

*17.
$$\begin{bmatrix} 2 & 1 \\ 3 & 4 \end{bmatrix} X = \begin{bmatrix} 2 & -1 \\ 3 & 1 \end{bmatrix}$$

*18.
$$\begin{bmatrix} 2 & 1 & 3 \\ 1 & 2 & -1 \\ -1 & 1 & 1 \end{bmatrix} X = \begin{bmatrix} 7 & 14 \\ -3 & 1 \\ 0 & 2 \end{bmatrix}$$

*19.
$$X \begin{bmatrix} 1 & 2 & 3 \\ 3 & -1 & 2 \end{bmatrix} = \begin{bmatrix} -1 & 5 & 4 \\ 7 & 0 & 7 \end{bmatrix}$$

*20.
$$X \begin{bmatrix} 1 & 2 & 3 \\ 2 & -1 & 0 \\ 3 & 1 & -1 \end{bmatrix} = \begin{bmatrix} -1 & -2 & 1 \\ 6 & 7 & 8 \end{bmatrix}$$

21. A number of people were interviewed about their political affiliation and their annual income. The following information was obtained:

517 were Liberals earning over \$15,000 per year.

345 were Conservatives earning over \$15,000 per year.

189 were Democrats earning over \$15,000 per year.

257 were Liberals earning under \$15,000 per year.

284 were Conservatives earning under \$15,000 per year.

408 were Democrats earning under \$15,000 per year.

Represent the above information in the form of a matrix. Is this representation unique?

22. The inventory (in gallons) of a small paint store at the beginning of a week is given by matrix A.

	Black	White	Red	
$A = $	80	72	45	Regular
	50	58	60	Deluxe

Its sales during the week are given by matrix S.

	Black	White	Red	
$S = $	65	70	39	Regular
	27	47	35	Deluxe

Write the inventory at the end of the week.

23. The Western Brewery Limited produces three brands of beer in two different sizes. The production (in thousands) per week at its Vancouver plant is

	Brand		
	I	II	III
Size 1	13	27	15
Size 2	12	14	24

and the weekly production at its Toronto plant is

$$
\begin{array}{c}
\textit{Brand} \\
\begin{array}{ccc}
\text{I} & \text{II} & \text{III}
\end{array} \\
\begin{array}{c}
\text{Size 1} \\
\text{Size 2}
\end{array}
\begin{bmatrix}
20 & 32 & 18 \\
35 & 24 & 30
\end{bmatrix}.
\end{array}
$$

a. What is the total weekly production at the two plants?

b. If the production at the Vancouver plant is increased by 20%, what will the total production be at the two plants now?

24. A firm produces two types of coffee in three different sizes. The production (in thousands of units) at its plant at location A is given by:

$$
\begin{array}{cccc}
 & \text{Size 1} & \text{Size 2} & \text{Size 3} \\
\begin{array}{c}
\text{Type 1} \\
\text{Type 2}
\end{array}
&
\begin{bmatrix}
20 & 28 & 30 \\
16 & 22 & 20
\end{bmatrix}
\end{array}
$$

whereas the production (in thousands) at its plant at location B is given by

$$
\begin{array}{cccc}
 & \text{Size 1} & \text{Size 2} & \text{Size 3} \\
\begin{array}{c}
\text{Type 1} \\
\text{Type 2}
\end{array}
&
\begin{bmatrix}
30 & 40 & 36 \\
24 & 20 & 28
\end{bmatrix}.
\end{array}
$$

a. Write the matrix that represents the total production at both plants.

b. The firm's management is planning to open a third plant at a location C, which would have a capacity 20% more than that at location B. Write the matrix representing the production at location C.

c. What will be the total production at all three locations?

25. Steve bought 3 pants, 5 shirts, 2 ties, and 3 jackets from a department store. If the pants are $12 each, the shirts $5 each, the ties $3 each, and the jackets $20 each, use matrix multiplication to represent the total amount Steve spent at the department store.

26. A consulting firm has offices in Miami and Atlanta. The office at Miami has 5 chairs, 7 tables, and 4 typewriters. The Atlanta office has 12 chairs, 16 tables, and 8 typewriters. If the chairs are $10 each, tables $15 each, and typewriters $200 each, express the total amounts spent on these items at the two offices in terms of matrix products.

27. Susan earns $5 an hour by tutoring, $6 an hour by typing, and $1.50 an hour by babysitting. The numbers of hours she worked at each type of work over a four-week period are given by matrix **A**.

$$
\begin{array}{c}
\textit{Week} \\
\begin{array}{cccc}
\text{I} & \text{II} & \text{III} & \text{IV}
\end{array} \\
\mathbf{A} =
\begin{bmatrix}
15 & 10 & 16 & 12 \\
6 & 4 & 2 & 3 \\
2 & 7 & 0 & 4
\end{bmatrix}
\begin{array}{l}
\text{Tutoring} \\
\text{Typing} \\
\text{Babysitting}
\end{array}
\end{array}
$$

If $\mathbf{P} = [5 \quad 6 \quad 1.5]$ denotes her earnings matrix, determine the matrix **PA** and interpret its elements.

28. A small contracting firm charges $6 per hour for a truck without a driver, $20 per hour for a tractor without a driver, and $10 per hour for each driver. The firm uses matrix **A** for various types of work.

$$
\begin{array}{c}
\textit{Type of Work} \\
\begin{array}{cccc}
\text{I} & \text{II} & \text{III} & \text{IV}
\end{array} \\
\mathbf{A} = \begin{bmatrix} 1 & 1 & 1 & 2 \\ 2 & 0 & 1 & 1 \\ 3 & 1 & 3 & 4 \end{bmatrix}
\begin{array}{l}
\text{Trucks} \\
\text{Tractors} \\
\text{Drivers}
\end{array}
\end{array}
$$

a. If **P** denotes the price matrix that the firm charges, with $\mathbf{P} = [6 \quad 20 \quad 10]$, determine the product **PA** and interpret its elements.

b. Suppose for a small project, the firm used 20 hours of type I work and 30 hours of type II work. If **S** denotes the supply matrix,

$$
\mathbf{S} = \begin{bmatrix} 20 \\ 30 \\ 0 \\ 0 \end{bmatrix}.
$$

determine and interpret the elements of **AS**.

c. Evaluate and interpret the matrix product **PAS**.

INVERSES AND DETERMINANTS

CHAPTER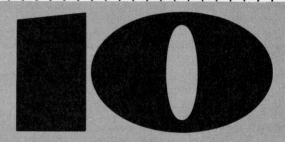

10-1 THE INVERSE OF A MATRIX

DEFINITION   Let **A** be an $n \times n$ square matrix. Then a matrix **B** is said to be an **inverse** of **A** if it satisfies the two matrix equations

$$\mathbf{AB} = \mathbf{I} \quad \text{and} \quad \mathbf{BA} = \mathbf{I}$$

where **I** is the identity matrix of size $n \times n$. In other words, the product of the matrices **A** and **B** in either order is the identity matrix.

It is clear from this definition that **B** must be a square matrix of the same size as **A**; otherwise one or both of the products **AB** and **BA** will not be defined.

EXAMPLE 1   Show that $\mathbf{B} = \begin{bmatrix} -2 & 1 \\ \frac{3}{2} & -\frac{1}{2} \end{bmatrix}$ is an inverse of $\mathbf{A} = \begin{bmatrix} 1 & 2 \\ 3 & 4 \end{bmatrix}$.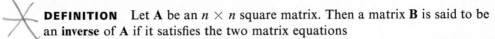

Solution   To show that **B** is an inverse of **A**, all we need prove is that $\mathbf{AB} = \mathbf{I}$ and $\mathbf{BA} = \mathbf{I}$.

$$\mathbf{AB} = \begin{bmatrix} 1 & 2 \\ 3 & 4 \end{bmatrix} \begin{bmatrix} -2 & 1 \\ \frac{3}{2} & -\frac{1}{2} \end{bmatrix}$$

$$= \begin{bmatrix} 1(-2) + 2(\frac{3}{2}) & 1(1) + 2(-\frac{1}{2}) \\ 3(-2) + 4(\frac{3}{2}) & 3(1) + 4(-\frac{1}{2}) \end{bmatrix} = \begin{bmatrix} 1 & 0 \\ 0 & 1 \end{bmatrix} = \mathbf{I}$$

$$\mathbf{BA} = \begin{bmatrix} -2 & 1 \\ \frac{3}{2} & -\frac{1}{2} \end{bmatrix} \begin{bmatrix} 1 & 2 \\ 3 & 4 \end{bmatrix}$$

$$= \begin{bmatrix} -2(1) + 1(3) & -2(2) + 1(4) \\ \frac{3}{2}(1) - \frac{1}{2}(3) & \frac{3}{2}(2) - \frac{1}{2}(4) \end{bmatrix} = \begin{bmatrix} 1 & 0 \\ 0 & 1 \end{bmatrix} = \mathbf{I}$$

Thus **B** is an inverse of **A**.

Not every square matrix has an inverse. This is illustrated by Example 2.

EXAMPLE 2   Find an inverse of the matrix **A**, if such an inverse exists, for

$$\mathbf{A} = \begin{bmatrix} 1 & 2 \\ 2 & 4 \end{bmatrix}.$$

Solution   Let **B** be an inverse of **A**. If **B** exists, it is a square matrix of the same size as **A** and so must be of the form

$$\mathbf{B} = \begin{bmatrix} a & b \\ c & d \end{bmatrix}$$

where a, b, c, and d are specific entries.

Now the equation $\mathbf{AB} = \mathbf{I}$ implies that

$$\begin{bmatrix} 1 & 2 \\ 2 & 4 \end{bmatrix}\begin{bmatrix} a & b \\ c & d \end{bmatrix} = \begin{bmatrix} 1 & 0 \\ 0 & 1 \end{bmatrix}$$

or

$$\begin{bmatrix} a + 2c & b + 2d \\ 2a + 4c & 2b + 4d \end{bmatrix} = \begin{bmatrix} 1 & 0 \\ 0 & 1 \end{bmatrix}.$$

Therefore, comparing entries in these matrices, we find that

$$\begin{matrix} a + 2c = 1 \\ 2a + 4c = 0 \end{matrix} \quad \text{and} \quad \begin{matrix} b + 2d = 0 \\ 2b + 4d = 1 \end{matrix}.$$

These systems of equations are inconsistent, as we see if we divide the lower two equations by 2. Thus these systems *have no solution*, so there is no matrix $\mathbf{B}$ that satisfies the condition that $\mathbf{AB} = \mathbf{I}$. Thus $\mathbf{A}$ does not have an inverse.

DEFINITION   A matrix $\mathbf{A}$ is said to be **invertible** or **nonsingular** if it has an inverse. If $\mathbf{A}$ does not have an inverse, then it is said to be a **singular matrix**.

It can be shown that the inverse of any nonsingular matrix is unique. That is, if $\mathbf{A}$ has an inverse at all, then it has only one inverse. Because of this, we denote the inverse of $\mathbf{A}$ by $\mathbf{A}^{-1}$ (read $\mathbf{A}$ *inverse*). Thus we have the two equations

$$\mathbf{AA}^{-1} = \mathbf{I} \quad \text{and} \quad \mathbf{A}^{-1}\mathbf{A} = \mathbf{I}.$$

Let us now turn to the problem of finding the inverse of a nonsingular matrix. As an example, suppose we want to find the inverse of

$$\mathbf{A} = \begin{bmatrix} 1 & 3 \\ 2 & 5 \end{bmatrix}.$$

Let

$$\mathbf{B} = \begin{bmatrix} a & b \\ c & d \end{bmatrix}$$

denote the inverse of $\mathbf{A}$. Then $\mathbf{B}$ must satisfy the two equations

$$\mathbf{AB} = \mathbf{I} \quad \text{and} \quad \mathbf{BA} = \mathbf{I}.$$

The matrix equation $\mathbf{AB} = \mathbf{I}$, when written out in full, is

$$\begin{bmatrix} 1 & 3 \\ 2 & 5 \end{bmatrix}\begin{bmatrix} a & b \\ c & d \end{bmatrix} = \begin{bmatrix} 1 & 0 \\ 0 & 1 \end{bmatrix}$$

or

$$\begin{bmatrix} a + 3c & b + 3d \\ 2a + 5c & 2b + 5d \end{bmatrix} = \begin{bmatrix} 1 & 0 \\ 0 & 1 \end{bmatrix}.$$

Therefore

$$a + 3c = 1 \quad \text{and} \quad b + 3d = 0$$
$$2a + 5c = 0 \qquad\qquad 2b + 5d = 1. \tag{1}$$

Note that the two equations on the left form a system of equations for the unknown entries a and c, while the two equations on the right form a system of equations for b and d. To solve these two systems of equations, we must transform the corresponding augmented matrices

$$\left[\begin{array}{cc|c} 1 & 3 & 1 \\ 2 & 5 & 0 \end{array}\right] \quad \text{and} \quad \left[\begin{array}{cc|c} 1 & 3 & 0 \\ 2 & 5 & 1 \end{array}\right] \tag{2}$$

to their reduced forms. You can verify that these reduced forms are, respectively,

$$\left[\begin{array}{cc|c} 1 & 0 & -5 \\ 0 & 1 & 2 \end{array}\right] \quad \text{and} \quad \left[\begin{array}{cc|c} 1 & 0 & 3 \\ 0 & 1 & -1 \end{array}\right].$$

Therefore $a = -5$, $c = 2$, $b = 3$, and $d = -1$. Consequently the matrix $\mathbf{B}$ that satisfies the equation $\mathbf{AB} = \mathbf{I}$ is

$$\mathbf{B} = \begin{bmatrix} a & b \\ c & d \end{bmatrix} = \begin{bmatrix} -5 & 3 \\ 2 & -1 \end{bmatrix}.$$

It is now easy to verify that this matrix $\mathbf{B}$ also satisfies the equation $\mathbf{BA} = \mathbf{I}$.* Therefore $\mathbf{B}$ is the inverse of $\mathbf{A}$, and we can write

$$\mathbf{A}^{-1} = \begin{bmatrix} -5 & 3 \\ 2 & -1 \end{bmatrix}.$$

In this example, to find the inverse, we solved the two linear systems in Equation (1) by reducing their augmented matrices (Equation (2)). Now it can be observed that the two systems in Equation (1) have the same coefficient matrix $\mathbf{A}$, so it is possible to reduce both augmented matrices in the same calculation since both of them require the same sequence of row operations. The procedure we can use for this simultaneous reduction is to write the coefficient matrix $\mathbf{A}$, draw a vertical line, and write the constants appearing in the right sides of the systems in Equation (1) in two columns, as shown below.

$$\left[\begin{array}{cc|cc} 1 & 3 & 1 & 0 \\ 2 & 5 & 0 & 1 \end{array}\right] \tag{3}$$

We now perform row operations in the usual way to reduce the left half of this augmented matrix to an identity matrix.

It may be observed that the elements to the right of the vertical line in the augmented matrix (3), form a 2×2 identity matrix. Thus this augmented matrix can be abbreviated as simply $\mathbf{A} \,|\, \mathbf{I}$. If we transform $\mathbf{A} \,|\, \mathbf{I}$ to reduced form, we shall be simultaneously reducing the two augmented matrices in Equation (2) and therefore solving the two linear systems in Equation (1) at the same time.

*It can be shown (though the proof is quite difficult) that if either one of the two conditions $\mathbf{AB} = \mathbf{I}$ or $\mathbf{BA} = \mathbf{I}$ is satisfied, then the other one is satisfied automatically. This is why we need to use only one of these conditions in order to determine $\mathbf{B}$.

In this example, $\mathbf{A}\,|\,\mathbf{I}$ is reduced by the following sequence of row operations.

$$\mathbf{A}\,|\,\mathbf{I} = \begin{bmatrix} 1 & 3 & | & 1 & 0 \\ 2 & 5 & | & 0 & 1 \end{bmatrix} \xrightarrow{R_2 - 2R_1} \begin{bmatrix} 1 & 3 & | & 1 & 0 \\ 0 & -1 & | & -2 & 1 \end{bmatrix}$$

$$\xrightarrow{-R_2} \begin{bmatrix} 1 & 3 & | & 1 & 0 \\ 0 & 1 & | & 2 & -1 \end{bmatrix}$$

$$\xrightarrow{R_1 - 3R_2} \begin{bmatrix} 1 & 0 & | & -5 & 3 \\ 0 & 1 & | & 2 & -1 \end{bmatrix}$$

This is now the required reduced matrix, since it has an identity matrix to the left of the vertical line. The elements to the right of this line are the solutions of the two systems in Equation (1)—in other words, they form the matrix

$$\begin{bmatrix} a & b \\ c & d \end{bmatrix} = \begin{bmatrix} -5 & 3 \\ 2 & -1 \end{bmatrix}.$$

But this matrix is the inverse of $\mathbf{A}$. We conclude, therefore, that in the reduced form of the augmented matrix $\mathbf{A}\,|\,\mathbf{I}$, the inverse of $\mathbf{A}$ appears to the right of the vertical line. To summarize: *Let $\mathbf{A}$ be an invertible square matrix of size $n \times n$, and let $\mathbf{I}$ be the identity matrix of the same size. Then the reduced form of $\mathbf{A}\,|\,\mathbf{I}$ is $\mathbf{I}\,|\,\mathbf{A}^{-1}$.*

EXAMPLE 3   Find $\mathbf{A}^{-1}$, given

$$\mathbf{A} = \begin{bmatrix} 1 & 2 & 3 \\ 2 & 5 & 7 \\ 3 & 7 & 8 \end{bmatrix}.$$

Solution

$$\mathbf{A}\,|\,\mathbf{I} = \begin{bmatrix} 1 & 2 & 3 & | & 1 & 0 & 0 \\ 2 & 5 & 7 & | & 0 & 1 & 0 \\ 3 & 7 & 8 & | & 0 & 0 & 1 \end{bmatrix} \xrightarrow[R_3 - 3R_1]{R_2 - 2R_1} \begin{bmatrix} 1 & 2 & 3 & | & 1 & 0 & 0 \\ 0 & 1 & 1 & | & -2 & 1 & 0 \\ 0 & 1 & -1 & | & -3 & 0 & 1 \end{bmatrix}$$

$$\xrightarrow[R_3 - R_2]{R_1 - 2R_2} \begin{bmatrix} 1 & 0 & 1 & | & 5 & -2 & 0 \\ 0 & 1 & 1 & | & -2 & 1 & 0 \\ 0 & 0 & -2 & | & -1 & -1 & 1 \end{bmatrix}$$

$$\xrightarrow{-\frac{1}{2}R_3} \begin{bmatrix} 1 & 0 & 1 & | & 5 & -2 & 0 \\ 0 & 1 & 1 & | & -2 & 1 & 0 \\ 0 & 0 & 1 & | & \frac{1}{2} & \frac{1}{2} & -\frac{1}{2} \end{bmatrix}$$

$$\xrightarrow[R_2 - R_3]{R_1 - R_3} \begin{bmatrix} 1 & 0 & 0 & | & \frac{9}{2} & -\frac{5}{2} & \frac{1}{2} \\ 0 & 1 & 0 & | & -\frac{5}{2} & \frac{1}{2} & \frac{1}{2} \\ 0 & 0 & 1 & | & \frac{1}{2} & \frac{1}{2} & -\frac{1}{2} \end{bmatrix}$$

This matrix is now in the reduced form $\mathbf{I}\,|\,\mathbf{A}^{-1}$.

Thus

$$\mathbf{A}^{-1} = \begin{bmatrix} \frac{9}{2} & -\frac{5}{2} & \frac{1}{2} \\ -\frac{5}{2} & \frac{1}{2} & \frac{1}{2} \\ \frac{1}{2} & \frac{1}{2} & -\frac{1}{2} \end{bmatrix} = \frac{1}{2}\begin{bmatrix} 9 & -5 & 1 \\ -5 & 1 & 1 \\ 1 & 1 & -1 \end{bmatrix}$$

You may verify that this is, in fact, the inverse matrix of $\mathbf{A}$ by checking the two equations

$$\mathbf{A}\mathbf{A}^{-1} = \mathbf{I} \quad \text{and} \quad \mathbf{A}^{-1}\mathbf{A} = \mathbf{I}.$$

How do we know whether a given matrix $\mathbf{A}$ is invertible or not? If we carry out the process of transforming $\mathbf{A}\,|\,\mathbf{I}$ to its reduced form and if at any step we find that one of the rows on the left of the vertical line consists entirely of zeros, then it can be shown that $\mathbf{A}^{-1}$ does not exist.

EXAMPLE 4   Find $\mathbf{A}^{-1}$ if it exists, given

$$\mathbf{A} = \begin{bmatrix} 1 & 2 & 3 \\ 2 & 5 & 7 \\ 3 & 7 & 10 \end{bmatrix}.$$

Solution

$$\mathbf{A}\,|\,\mathbf{I} = \begin{bmatrix} 1 & 2 & 3 & | & 1 & 0 & 0 \\ 2 & 5 & 7 & | & 0 & 1 & 0 \\ 3 & 7 & 10 & | & 0 & 0 & 1 \end{bmatrix} \xrightarrow[R_3 - 3R_1]{R_2 - 2R_1} \begin{bmatrix} 1 & 2 & 3 & | & 1 & 0 & 0 \\ 0 & 1 & 1 & | & -2 & 1 & 0 \\ 0 & 1 & 1 & | & -3 & 0 & 1 \end{bmatrix}$$

$$\xrightarrow{R_3 - R_2} \begin{bmatrix} 1 & 2 & 3 & | & 1 & 0 & 0 \\ 0 & 1 & 1 & | & -2 & 1 & 0 \\ 0 & 0 & 0 & | & -1 & -1 & 1 \end{bmatrix}$$

Since the third row to the left of the vertical line consists entirely of zeros, the reduction cannot be completed. We must conclude that $\mathbf{A}^{-1}$ does not exist and that $\mathbf{A}$ is a *singular* matrix. (See also Example 4 in Section 4.)

Inverses of matrices have many uses, one of which is in the solution of systems of equations. In Section 3 of Chapter 9, we solved systems of linear equations by transforming an augmented matrix to its reduced form. In the case when we have n equations in n variables, we can also solve the system by finding the inverse of the coefficient matrix.

A system of equations can be written in matrix form as $\mathbf{A}\mathbf{X} = \mathbf{B}$. If the coefficient matrix $\mathbf{A}$ is invertible, then $\mathbf{A}^{-1}$ exists. Multiplying both sides of the given matrix equation by $\mathbf{A}^{-1}$ on the left, we obtain

$$\mathbf{A}^{-1}(\mathbf{A}\mathbf{X}) = \mathbf{A}^{-1}\mathbf{B}.$$

Using the associative property and simplifying, we can write this as follows.

$$(\mathbf{A}^{-1}\mathbf{A})\mathbf{X} = \mathbf{A}^{-1}\mathbf{B}$$

$$\mathbf{I}\mathbf{X} = \mathbf{A}^{-1}\mathbf{B}$$

$$\mathbf{X} = \mathbf{A}^{-1}\mathbf{B}$$

Thus we have obtained an expression for the solution **X** of the given system of equations.

EXAMPLE 5   Solve the following system of linear equations.

$$x + 2y + 3z = 3$$
$$2x + 5y + 7z = 6$$
$$3x + 7y + 8z = 5$$

Solution   The given system of equations in matrix form is

$$\mathbf{AX = B} \tag{4}$$

where

$$\mathbf{A} = \begin{bmatrix} 1 & 2 & 3 \\ 2 & 5 & 7 \\ 3 & 7 & 8 \end{bmatrix}, \quad \mathbf{X} = \begin{bmatrix} x \\ y \\ z \end{bmatrix} \quad \text{and} \quad \mathbf{B} = \begin{bmatrix} 3 \\ 6 \\ 5 \end{bmatrix}.$$

Then $\mathbf{A}^{-1}$ (as found in Example 3) is given by

$$\mathbf{A}^{-1} = \tfrac{1}{2} \begin{bmatrix} 9 & -5 & 1 \\ -5 & 1 & 1 \\ 1 & 1 & -1 \end{bmatrix}.$$

It follows that the solution of Equation (4) is given by

$$\mathbf{X} = \mathbf{A}^{-1}\mathbf{B} = \tfrac{1}{2} \begin{bmatrix} 9 & -5 & 1 \\ -5 & 1 & 1 \\ 1 & 1 & -1 \end{bmatrix} \begin{bmatrix} 3 \\ 6 \\ 5 \end{bmatrix}$$

$$= \tfrac{1}{2} \begin{bmatrix} 27 - 30 + 5 \\ -15 + 6 + 5 \\ 3 + 6 - 5 \end{bmatrix} = \tfrac{1}{2} \begin{bmatrix} 2 \\ -4 \\ 4 \end{bmatrix} = \begin{bmatrix} 1 \\ -2 \\ 2 \end{bmatrix}.$$

That is,

$$\begin{bmatrix} x \\ y \\ z \end{bmatrix} = \begin{bmatrix} 1 \\ -2 \\ 2 \end{bmatrix}.$$

Therefore $x = 1$, $y = -2$, and $z = 2$.

At first glance, it may appear that this method of solving a system of equations is much less convenient than the simple method of row reduction described in Section 3 of Chapter 9. The advantage of using the inverse matrix occurs in cases where several systems of equations with the same coefficient matrix must be solved. For such problems as this, the solutions of *all* the systems can be determined immediately once the inverse of the coefficient matrix has been found; it is not necessary to use row reduction over and over again for each system. (See the final remark in the next section.)

EXERCISES 1

(1–16) In the following problems, find the inverse of the given matrix (if it exists).

1. $\begin{bmatrix} 2 & 5 \\ 3 & 4 \end{bmatrix}$

2. $\begin{bmatrix} 3 & 1 \\ 4 & 2 \end{bmatrix}$

3. $\begin{bmatrix} 1 & -2 \\ -3 & 4 \end{bmatrix}$

4. $\begin{bmatrix} 1 & -3 \\ -2 & 6 \end{bmatrix}$

5. $\begin{bmatrix} 3 & -2 \\ -6 & 4 \end{bmatrix}$

6. $\begin{bmatrix} 1 & 2 \\ 0 & 0 \end{bmatrix}$

7. $\begin{bmatrix} 1 & 0 & 2 \\ 0 & 3 & 1 \\ 2 & -1 & 0 \end{bmatrix}$

8. $\begin{bmatrix} 2 & 1 & 0 \\ 1 & 0 & 3 \\ 0 & 2 & 1 \end{bmatrix}$

9. $\begin{bmatrix} 2 & 3 & 4 \\ 1 & 2 & 0 \\ 4 & 5 & 6 \end{bmatrix}$

10. $\begin{bmatrix} 1 & 2 & 3 \\ -2 & 1 & 4 \\ -3 & -4 & 1 \end{bmatrix}$

11. $\begin{bmatrix} 2 & 1 & -1 \\ 3 & 2 & 0 \\ 4 & 3 & 1 \end{bmatrix}$

12. $\begin{bmatrix} 3 & -4 & 5 \\ 4 & -3 & 6 \\ 6 & -8 & 10 \end{bmatrix}$

13. $\begin{bmatrix} -1 & 2 & -3 \\ 2 & -1 & 1 \\ 3 & 1 & 2 \end{bmatrix}$

14. $\begin{bmatrix} -3 & 2 & 1 \\ 2 & -1 & 3 \\ 1 & -3 & 2 \end{bmatrix}$

15. $\begin{bmatrix} 1 & -1 & 1 & 2 \\ 2 & -3 & 0 & 3 \\ 1 & 1 & 1 & 1 \\ 3 & 0 & -1 & 2 \end{bmatrix}$

16. $\begin{bmatrix} 2 & 1 & 3 & 4 \\ 1 & 1 & 1 & -1 \\ -1 & 1 & -1 & 0 \\ 3 & 0 & 1 & 2 \end{bmatrix}$

(17–24) Solve the following systems of equations by finding the inverse of the coefficient matrix.

17. $2x - 3y = 1$
    $3x + 4y = 10$

18. $3x_1 + 2x_2 = 1$
    $2x_1 - x_2 = 3$

19. $4u + 5v = 14$
    $2v - 3u = 1$

20. $3y - 2z = -4$
    $5z + 4y = -13$

21. $2x - y + 3z = -3$
    $x + y + z = 2$
    $3x + 2y - z = 8$

22. $x + 2y - z = 1$
    $2z - 3x = 2$
    $3y + 2z = 5$

23. $2u + 3v - 4w = -10$
    $w - 2u - 1 = 0$
    $u + 2v = 1$

24. $p + 2q - 3r = 1$
    $q - 2p + r = 3$
    $2r + p - 2 = 0$

25. Two metals, X and Y, can be extracted from two types of ores, P and Q. One hundred pounds of ore P yield 3 ounces of X and 5 ounces of Y, and 100 pounds of ore Q yield 4 ounces of X and 2.5 ounces of Y. How many pounds of ores P and Q will be required to produce 72 ounces of X and 95 ounces of Y?

26. A person invested a total of $20,000 in three different investments that yield 5%, 6%, and 8%, respectively. The income from the 8% investment is twice the income from the 5% investment and the total income per year from all the three investments is $1296. Find the amount invested in each investment.

27. If A is a nonsingular matrix and $AB = AC$, show that $B = C$.

28. If $AB = A$ and A is nonsingular, show that $B = I$.

29. Given

$$\mathbf{A} = \begin{bmatrix} 1 & 3 \\ 2 & 4 \end{bmatrix} \quad \text{and} \quad \mathbf{B} = \begin{bmatrix} 2 & -1 \\ -3 & 1 \end{bmatrix}.$$

verify the result $(\mathbf{AB})^{-1} = \mathbf{B}^{-1}\mathbf{A}^{-1}$.

30. Use the matrices $\mathbf{A}$ and $\mathbf{B}$ in Exercise 29 to verify that $(\mathbf{A}^{-1}\mathbf{B})^{-1} = \mathbf{B}^{-1}\mathbf{A}$.

*31. Show that $(\mathbf{A}^{-1})^{-1} = \mathbf{A}$ for any invertible matrix $\mathbf{A}$.

*32. Show that for any two invertible $n \times n$ matrices $\mathbf{A}$ and $\mathbf{B}$,

$$(\mathbf{AB})^{-1} = \mathbf{B}^{-1}\mathbf{A}^{-1}.$$

*33. Show that if two matrices $\mathbf{B}$ and $\mathbf{C}$ are both inverses of a matrix $\mathbf{A}$, then $\mathbf{B} = \mathbf{C}$. (*Hint:* Consider $\mathbf{BAC}$.)

10-2 INPUT-OUTPUT ANALYSIS

The input-output model was first introduced in the late forties by Leontief, the recipient of a 1973 Nobel prize, in a study of the United States economy. The main feature of this model is that it incorporates the interactions between different industries or sectors which make up the economy. The aim of the model is to allow economists to forecast the future production levels of each industry in order to meet future demands for the various products. Such forecasting is complicated by the linkages between the different industries, through which a change in the demand for the product of one industry can induce a change in the production levels of other industries. For example, an increase in the demand for automobiles leads not only to an increase in the production levels of automobile manufacturers, but also in the levels of a variety of other industries in the economy, such as the steel industry, the rubber industry, and so on. In Leontief's original model, he divided the United States economy into 500 interacting sectors of this type.

In order to describe the model in the simplest possible terms, we consider an economy that consists of only two industries, P and Q. To clarify our ideas, suppose that the interactions between these two industries are those given in Table 1. The first two columns in this table give the *inputs* of the two industries,

TABLE 1

	Industry P	Industry Q	Final Demands	Gross Output
Industry P	60	64	76	200
Industry Q	100	48	12	160
Primary Inputs	40	48		

measured in suitable units. (For example, the units might be millions of dollars per year.) From the first column, we see that in its annual production, industry

P uses 60 units of its own product and 100 units of the product of industry Q. Similarly, Q uses 64 units of P's product and 48 units of its own product. In addition, from the last row we see that P uses 40 units of *primary inputs*, which include inputs such as labor, land, or raw materials, while Q uses 48 units of primary inputs.

Totaling the columns, we see that the total inputs are 200 units for P and 160 units for Q. It is an assumption of the model that whatever is produced is consumed, or, in other words, the output of each industry must equal the sum of all the inputs (measured in common units). Thus the gross output of the two industries must be 200 units for P and 160 units for Q.

Now consider the first two rows in Table 1, which show how the outputs of each industry are used. Of the 200 units produced by P, 60 are used by that industry itself and 64 are used by Q. This leaves 76 units available to meet the *final demand*, that is, the goods that are not used internally by the producing industries themselves. These would consist primarily of goods produced for household consumption, government consumption, or export. Similarly, of the 160 units produced by Q, 100 are used by P, 48 are used by Q itself, and 12 units are left to meet the final demand.

Suppose that market research predicts that in 5 years, the final demand for P will decrease from 76 to 70 units, whereas for Q, it will increase considerably from 12 to 60 units. The question arises concerning how much each industry should adjust its production level in order to meet these projected final demands.

It is clear that the two industries do not operate independently of one another—for example, the gross output of P depends on the final demand for Q's product, and vice versa. Thus the output of one industry is linked to the outputs of the other industry or industries. Let us suppose that in order to meet the projected final demands in 5 years, P must produce x_1 units and Q must produce x_2 units.

From Table 1, we see that to produce 200 units, industry P uses 60 units of its own product and 100 units of Q's product. Thus to produce x_1 units, industry P must use $\frac{60}{200}x_1$ units of its own product and $\frac{100}{200}x_1$ units of Q's product. Similarly, to produce x_2 units, industry Q should use $\frac{64}{160}x_2$ units of P's product and $\frac{48}{160}x_2$ units of its own product. But we have the following equation:

$$\begin{matrix} \text{Gross Output} \\ \text{of Industry P} \end{matrix} = \begin{matrix} \text{Units Consumed} \\ \text{by P} \end{matrix} + \begin{matrix} \text{Units Consumed} \\ \text{by Q} \end{matrix} + \text{Final Demands.}$$

That is,

$$x_1 = \tfrac{60}{200}x_1 + \tfrac{64}{160}x_2 + 70$$

since the new final demand is 70 units.

Similarly, out of x_2 units produced by industry Q, $\frac{100}{200}x_1$ units are used up by P and $\frac{48}{160}x_2$ units are used by Q itself. Thus we have,

$$\begin{matrix} \text{Gross Output} \\ \text{of Industry Q} \end{matrix} = \begin{matrix} \text{Units Consumed} \\ \text{by P} \end{matrix} + \begin{matrix} \text{Units Consumed} \\ \text{by Q} \end{matrix} + \text{Final Demands}$$

That is,

$$x_2 = \tfrac{100}{200}x_1 + \tfrac{48}{160}x_2 + 60.$$

These two equations can be written in matrix form as

$$\begin{bmatrix} x_1 \\ x_2 \end{bmatrix} = \begin{bmatrix} \frac{60}{200} & \frac{64}{160} \\ \frac{100}{200} & \frac{48}{160} \end{bmatrix} \begin{bmatrix} x_1 \\ x_2 \end{bmatrix} + \begin{bmatrix} 70 \\ 60 \end{bmatrix}.$$

Thus

$$\mathbf{X} = \mathbf{AX} + \mathbf{D} \qquad (1)$$

where

$$\mathbf{X} = \begin{bmatrix} x_1 \\ x_2 \end{bmatrix}, \quad \mathbf{A} = \begin{bmatrix} \frac{60}{200} & \frac{64}{160} \\ \frac{100}{200} & \frac{48}{160} \end{bmatrix} \quad \text{and} \quad \mathbf{D} = \begin{bmatrix} 70 \\ 60 \end{bmatrix}.$$

We call $\mathbf{X}$ the **output matrix**, $\mathbf{D}$ the **demand matrix**, and $\mathbf{A}$ **the input-output matrix**. The entries in matrix $\mathbf{A}$ are called the **input-output coefficients**.

Let us consider the interpretation of the elements of the input-output matrix. As usual, let a_{ij} denote the general element in $\mathbf{A}$. We note that of the 200 units of total input into industry P, 60 consist of units of its own product and 100 consist of units of Q's product. Thus the entries $\frac{60}{200}$ and $\frac{100}{200}$ in the first column of the input-output matrix represent the proportion of P's inputs which come from the industries P and Q, respectively. In general, a_{ij} represents the fractional part of the input of industry j that is the product of industry i.

Each entry in the input-output matrix is between 0 and 1, and the sum of the entries in any column is never greater than 1. Note that, the input-output matrix

$$\mathbf{A} = \begin{bmatrix} \frac{60}{200} & \frac{64}{160} \\ \frac{100}{200} & \frac{48}{160} \end{bmatrix} = \begin{bmatrix} 0.3 & 0.4 \\ 0.5 & 0.3 \end{bmatrix}$$

in the above example can be obtained directly from Table 1 by dividing each number in the interior rectangle of the table by the gross output of the industry that heads the column. For example, in the first column headed by P, we divide each entry by 200, which is the gross output of industry P. Thus we obtain $\frac{60}{200}$ and $\frac{100}{200}$ as the elements of the first column in the input-output matrix.

Equation (1), $\mathbf{X} = \mathbf{AX} + \mathbf{D}$, is called the **input-output equation**. To find the output matrix $\mathbf{X}$ that will meet the projected new final demands, we must solve Equation (1) for $\mathbf{X}$. We have

$$\mathbf{X} = \mathbf{AX} + \mathbf{D}$$

$$\mathbf{X} - \mathbf{AX} = \mathbf{D}.$$

We can write this as

$$\mathbf{IX} - \mathbf{AX} = \mathbf{D}$$

or

$$(\mathbf{I} - \mathbf{A})\mathbf{X} = \mathbf{D}.$$

Suppose that $(\mathbf{I} - \mathbf{A})^{-1}$ exists. Then

$$(\mathbf{I} - \mathbf{A})^{-1}(\mathbf{I} - \mathbf{A})\mathbf{X} = (\mathbf{I} - \mathbf{A})^{-1}\mathbf{D}$$

$$\mathbf{X} = (\mathbf{I} - \mathbf{A})^{-1}\mathbf{D}.$$

Thus we see that the output matrix **X** is determined once the inverse of the matrix $(I - A)$ has been found. This inverse can be calculated using the methods of the last section.

In our example, we have

$$I - A = \begin{bmatrix} 1 & 0 \\ 0 & 1 \end{bmatrix} - \begin{bmatrix} 0.3 & 0.4 \\ 0.5 & 0.3 \end{bmatrix} = \begin{bmatrix} 0.7 & -0.4 \\ -0.5 & 0.7 \end{bmatrix}.$$

Using the methods of Section 1, we find that

$$(I - A)^{-1} = \tfrac{1}{29} \begin{bmatrix} 70 & 40 \\ 50 & 70 \end{bmatrix}.$$

Therefore

$$X = (I - A)^{-1} D$$

$$= \tfrac{1}{29} \begin{bmatrix} 70 & 40 \\ 50 & 70 \end{bmatrix} \begin{bmatrix} 70 \\ 60 \end{bmatrix} = \begin{bmatrix} \frac{7300}{29} \\ \frac{7700}{29} \end{bmatrix} = \begin{bmatrix} 251.7 \\ 265.5 \end{bmatrix}.$$

Thus industry P must produce 251.7 units and Q should produce 265.5 units to meet the projected final demands in 5 years.

EXAMPLE 1 Suppose that in a hypothetical economy with only two industries, I and II, the interaction between the industries is as shown in Table 2.

TABLE 2

	Industry I	Industry II	Final Demands	Gross Output
Industry I	240	750	210	1200
Industry II	720	450	330	1500
Primary Inputs	240	300		

(a) Determine the input-output matrix **A**.

(b) Determine the output matrix if the final demands change to 312 units for industry I and 299 units for industry II.

(c) What will then be the new primary inputs for the two industries?

Solution (a) Dividing the first column (headed by industry I) by the gross output of industry I, 1200, and the second column (headed by industry II) by the gross output of industry II, 1500, we obtain input-output matrix **A**.

$$A = \begin{bmatrix} \frac{240}{1200} & \frac{750}{1500} \\ \frac{720}{1200} & \frac{450}{1500} \end{bmatrix} = \begin{bmatrix} 0.2 & 0.5 \\ 0.6 & 0.3 \end{bmatrix}$$

(b) If **I** denotes the 2×2 identity matrix, then

$$I - A = \begin{bmatrix} 1 & 0 \\ 0 & 1 \end{bmatrix} - \begin{bmatrix} 0.2 & 0.5 \\ 0.6 & 0.3 \end{bmatrix} = \begin{bmatrix} 0.8 & -0.5 \\ -0.6 & 0.7 \end{bmatrix}$$

Using the methods of Section 1, we obtain

$$(\mathbf{I} - \mathbf{A})^{-1} = \begin{bmatrix} \frac{35}{13} & \frac{25}{13} \\ \frac{30}{13} & \frac{40}{13} \end{bmatrix} = \frac{5}{13}\begin{bmatrix} 7 & 5 \\ 6 & 8 \end{bmatrix}.$$

If $\mathbf{D}$ denotes the new demand vector, that is,

$$\mathbf{D} = \begin{bmatrix} 312 \\ 299 \end{bmatrix}$$

and $\mathbf{X}$ the new output matrix, then we have

$$\mathbf{X} = (\mathbf{I} - \mathbf{A})^{-1}\mathbf{D}$$
$$= \frac{5}{13}\begin{bmatrix} 7 & 5 \\ 6 & 8 \end{bmatrix}\begin{bmatrix} 312 \\ 299 \end{bmatrix} = \frac{5}{13}\begin{bmatrix} 3679 \\ 4264 \end{bmatrix} = \begin{bmatrix} 1415 \\ 1640 \end{bmatrix}.$$

Thus industry I must produce 1415 units and industry II must produce 1640 units to meet the new final demands.

(c) For industry I, 240 units of primary inputs are needed to produce a gross output of 1200 units. That is, primary inputs are $\frac{240}{1200} = 0.2$ of the gross output. Thus 0.2 of the new output, 1415, gives the new primary inputs for industry I. The primary inputs for industry I are $(0.2)(1415) = 283$ units. Similarly, the primary inputs for industry II are $\frac{300}{1500} = 0.2$ of the gross output, and so equal $(0.2)(1640) = 328$ units. The new primary inputs for the two industries will thus be 283 units and 328 units, respectively.

The basic assumptions of the input-output model can be seen in these simple examples involving only two interacting sectors. In a realistic model of a national economy, it is necessary to consider a much larger number of sectors. Such an enlargement of the model introduces great complications in the calculations, and it becomes necessary to use a computer to solve the system of equations. However, the principles involved in the model remain essentially the same as those in our two-sector examples.

We can summarize these basic assumptions as follows.

1. Each industry or sector of the economy produces a single commodity and no two industries produce the same commodity.

2. For each industry, the total value of the output is equal to the total value of all the inputs, and all the outputs are consumed either by other producing sectors or as final demands.

3. The input-output matrix remains constant over the period of time under consideration. Over long periods, technological advances do cause changes in the input-output matrix and this means that predictions based on this model must be relatively short-term to be reliable.

It may happen that an economist is uncertain about his or her prediction of future final demands. Thus he or she may wish to calculate the output matrix $\mathbf{X}$ for a number of different demand matrices $\mathbf{D}$. In such a case, it is much more convenient to use the formula $\mathbf{X} = (\mathbf{I} - \mathbf{A})^{-1}\mathbf{D}$, involving the inverse matrix, than to use row reduction to solve for $\mathbf{X}$ for each different $\mathbf{D}$.

EXERCISES 2

1. Table 3 gives the interaction between two sectors in a hypothetical economy.

   ### TABLE 3

	Industry I	Industry II	Final Demands	Gross Output
Industry I	20	56	24	100
Industry II	50	8	22	80
Primary Inputs	30	16		

   a. Find the input-output matrix **A**.
   b. If in five years, the final demands change to 74 for industry I and 37 for industry II, how much should each industry produce to meet this projected demand?
   c. What will be the new primary input requirements in five years for the two industries?

2. The interaction between the two sectors of a hypothetical economy is given in Table 4.

   ### TABLE 4

	Agriculture	Manufacturing	Final Demands	Total Output
Agriculture	240	270	90	600
Manufacturing	300	90	60	450
Labor	60	90		

   a. Find the input-output matrix **A**.
   b. Suppose that in 3 years the demand for agricultural products decreases to 63 units and increases to 105 units for manufactured goods. Determine the new output vector to meet these new demands.
   c. What will the new labor requirements be for each sector?

3. Table 5 gives the interaction between two sectors of a hypothetical economy:

   ### TABLE 5

	Industry P	Industry Q	Final Demands	Total Output
Industry P	60	75	65	200
Industry Q	80	30	40	150
Labor	60	45		

a. Determine the input-output matrix **A**.

b. Determine the output matrix if the final demands change to 104 for P and 172 for Q.

c. What are the new labor requirements?

4. The interaction between two industries P and Q that form a hypothetical economy is given in Table 6.

TABLE 6

	Industry P	Industry Q	Consumer Demand	Total Output
Industry P	46	342	72	460
Industry Q	322	114	234	570
Labor Inputs	92	114		

a. Determine the input-output matrix **A**.

b. Determine the output matrix if the consumer demands change to 129 for P and 213 for Q.

c. What will the new labor requirements be for the two industries?

*5. For the economy of Exercise 3, it is anticipated that the final demand for the output of industry Q will increase by twice as much over the next few years as the final demand for the output of industry P. During the next five years, the total labor pool available to the two industries will increase from 105 units to 150 units. How much must the two final demands increase to cover this period if this whole labor pool is to be employed?

10-3 DETERMINANTS

Corresponding to any square matrix there is a real number called its *determinant*. The determinant is denoted by enclosing the matrix in vertical bars. For example if **A** is the 2×2 matrix given by

$$\mathbf{A} = \begin{bmatrix} 2 & 3 \\ 4 & 5 \end{bmatrix}$$

then its determinant is denoted by $|\mathbf{A}|$, or, in full, by

$$\begin{vmatrix} 2 & 3 \\ 4 & 5 \end{vmatrix}.$$

The determinant of an $n \times n$ matrix is said to be a *determinant of order n*. For example, $|\mathbf{A}|$ just given is a determinant of order 2.

The symbol Δ (delta) is also often used to denote a given determinant.

We shall begin by defining determinants of order 2, discussing higher orders later.

DEFINITION A **determinant of order 2** is defined by the following expression.

$$\begin{vmatrix} a_1 & b_1 \\ a_2 & b_2 \end{vmatrix} = a_1 b_2 - a_2 b_1$$

In other words, the determinant is given by the product of the elements a_1 and b_2 on the main diagonal minus the product of the elements a_2 and b_1 on the cross-diagonal. We can indicate these two diagonals by means of arrows.

$$(+) \quad (-)$$

$$\begin{vmatrix} a_1 & b_1 \\ a_2 & b_2 \end{vmatrix} = a_1 b_2 - a_2 b_1$$

The $(+)$ and $(-)$ signs indicate the signs associated with the two products.

EXAMPLE 1 Evaluate the following determinants.

(a) $\begin{vmatrix} 2 & -3 \\ 4 & 5 \end{vmatrix}$ (b) $\begin{vmatrix} 3 & 2 \\ 0 & 4 \end{vmatrix}$

Solution (a) $(+) \quad (-)$

$$\Delta = \begin{vmatrix} 2 & -3 \\ 4 & 5 \end{vmatrix} = 2(5) - 4(-3) = 10 + 12 = 22$$

(b) $(+) \quad (-)$

$$\Delta = \begin{vmatrix} 3 & 2 \\ 0 & 4 \end{vmatrix} = 3(4) - 0(2) = 12 - 0 = 12$$

DEFINITION A **determinant of order 3** is defined by the following expression.

$$\Delta = \begin{vmatrix} a_1 & b_1 & c_1 \\ a_2 & b_2 & c_2 \\ a_3 & b_3 & c_3 \end{vmatrix} = a_1 b_2 c_3 + a_2 b_3 c_1 + a_3 b_1 c_2 - a_1 b_3 c_2 - a_3 b_2 c_1 - a_2 b_1 c_3$$

The expression on the right is called the **complete expansion** of the third order determinant Δ. Observe that it contains six terms, three positive and three negative. Each term consists of a product of three elements in the determinant.

When evaluating a third-order determinant, we usually do not use the complete expansion; instead, we use what are called *cofactors*. Each element in the determinant has a cofactor, which is denoted by the corresponding capital letter. For example, A_2 denotes the cofactor of a_2, B_3 denotes the cofactor of b_3, and so on. They are defined as follows.

DEFINITION The **minor** of an element in a determinant Δ is equal to the determinant obtained by deleting the row and column in Δ that contain the given element. If the given element occurs in the ith row and the jth column of Δ, then its **cofactor** is equal to $(-1)^{i+j}$ times its minor.

EXAMPLE 2   (a) In the above determinant Δ, a_2 occurs in the second row and first column ($i = 2$ and $j = 1$), so its cofactor is

$$A_2 = (-1)^{2+1} \begin{vmatrix} a_1 & b_1 & c_1 \\ a_2 & b_2 & c_2 \\ a_3 & b_3 & c_3 \end{vmatrix} = (-1)^3 \begin{vmatrix} b_1 & c_1 \\ b_3 & c_3 \end{vmatrix} = - \begin{vmatrix} b_1 & c_1 \\ b_3 & c_3 \end{vmatrix}.$$

(b) Since c_3 occurs in the third row and third column ($i = j = 3$), its cofactor is

$$C_3 = (-1)^{3+3} \begin{vmatrix} a_1 & b_1 & c_1 \\ a_2 & b_2 & c_2 \\ a_3 & b_3 & c_3 \end{vmatrix} = (-1)^6 \begin{vmatrix} a_1 & b_1 \\ a_2 & b_2 \end{vmatrix} = \begin{vmatrix} a_1 & b_1 \\ a_2 & b_2 \end{vmatrix}.$$

The connection between a determinant and its various cofactors is given by Theorem 1.

THEOREM 1   The value of a determinant can be found by multiplying the elements in any row (or column) by their cofactors and adding the products for all elements in the given row (or column).

Let us verify that this theorem holds for expansion by the first row. The theorem states that

$$\Delta = a_1 A_1 + b_1 B_1 + c_1 C_1. \tag{1}$$

The three cofactors here are as follows.

$$A_1 = (-1)^{1+1} \begin{vmatrix} b_2 & c_2 \\ b_3 & c_3 \end{vmatrix} = (b_2 c_3 - b_3 c_2)$$

$$B_1 = (-1)^{1+2} \begin{vmatrix} a_2 & c_2 \\ a_3 & c_3 \end{vmatrix} = -(a_2 c_3 - a_3 c_2)$$

$$C_1 = (-1)^{1+3} \begin{vmatrix} a_2 & b_2 \\ a_3 & b_3 \end{vmatrix} = (a_2 b_3 - a_3 b_2)$$

Substituting these into Equation (1), we obtain

$$\Delta = a_1(b_2 c_3 - b_3 c_2) - b_1(a_2 c_3 - a_3 c_2) + c_1(a_2 b_3 - a_3 b_2).$$

It is easily seen that this expression agrees with the complete expansion given in the definition of the third-order determinant.

EXAMPLE 3   Evaluate the determinant

$$\Delta = \begin{vmatrix} 2 & 3 & -1 \\ 1 & 4 & 2 \\ -3 & 1 & 4 \end{vmatrix}.$$

Solution   Expanding by the first row, we have

$$\Delta = a_1 A_1 + b_1 B_1 + c_1 C_1$$

$$= 2 \begin{vmatrix} 4 & 2 \\ 1 & 4 \end{vmatrix} - 3 \begin{vmatrix} 1 & 2 \\ -3 & 4 \end{vmatrix} + (-1) \begin{vmatrix} 1 & 4 \\ -3 & 1 \end{vmatrix}$$

$$= 2(4 \cdot 4 - 1 \cdot 2) - 3[1 \cdot 4 - (-3)2] + (-1)[1 \cdot 1 - (-3)4]$$

$$= 2(16 - 2) - 3(4 + 6) - 1(1 + 12) = -15.$$

Let us now return to Theorem 1 and verify that it gives the determinant when we expand by the second column. In this case, the theorem states that

$$\Delta = b_1 B_1 + b_2 B_2 + b_3 B_3. \tag{2}$$

Here, the cofactors are

$$B_1 = (-1)^{1+2} \begin{vmatrix} a_2 & c_2 \\ a_3 & c_3 \end{vmatrix} = -(a_2 c_3 - a_3 c_2)$$

$$B_2 = (-1)^{2+2} \begin{vmatrix} a_1 & c_1 \\ a_3 & c_3 \end{vmatrix} = (a_1 c_3 - a_3 c_1)$$

$$B_3 = (-1)^{3+2} \begin{vmatrix} a_1 & c_1 \\ a_2 & c_2 \end{vmatrix} = -(a_1 c_2 - a_2 c_1).$$

Therefore, from Equation (2),

$$\Delta = -b_1(a_2 c_3 - a_3 c_2) + b_2(a_1 c_3 - a_3 c_1) - b_3(a_1 c_2 - a_2 c_1).$$

Again, we can verify that the terms here are the same as the six terms given in the complete expansion.

In a similar way, we can verify that a determinant can be evaluated by expanding by any row or column.

EXAMPLE 4   Evaluate the determinant:

$$\Delta = \begin{vmatrix} 2 & -3 & 0 \\ 1 & 4 & 3 \\ -5 & 6 & 0 \end{vmatrix}$$

(a) by expanding by the second column;   (b) by expanding by the third column.

Solution   (a) Expanding by the second column, we get

$$\Delta = b_1 B_1 + b_2 B_2 + b_3 B_3$$

$$= -(-3) \begin{vmatrix} 1 & 3 \\ -5 & 0 \end{vmatrix} + 4 \begin{vmatrix} 2 & 0 \\ -5 & 0 \end{vmatrix} - 6 \begin{vmatrix} 2 & 0 \\ 1 & 3 \end{vmatrix}$$

$$= 3[(1(0) - 3(-5)] + 4[2(0) - (-5)(0)] - 6[2(3) - 1(0)]$$

$$= 3(15) + 4(0) - 6(6) = 9.$$

(b) Expanding by the third column, we get

$$\Delta = c_1 C_1 + c_2 C_2 + c_3 C_3$$

$$= (0) \begin{vmatrix} 1 & 4 \\ -5 & 6 \end{vmatrix} - 3 \begin{vmatrix} 2 & -3 \\ -5 & 6 \end{vmatrix} + (0) \begin{vmatrix} 2 & -3 \\ 1 & 4 \end{vmatrix}$$

In this expansion, two of the terms are zero, so $\Delta = -3[2(6) - (-3)(-5)] = 9$.

In Example 4, the same answer was obtained using both methods, but the calculations involved in the second method were a little easier because the third column had two zeros, and two of the three terms in the expansion could immediately be set equal to zero. *It is generally easier to choose a row or column with the maximum number of zeros when expanding a determinant.*

From the above discussion, it will be clear that we can expand a determinant of order 3 by any row or column. In such an expansion, the terms alternate in sign and each element in the given row or column multiplies the 2×2 determinant (the minor) obtained by deleting from Δ the row and column that contain that element.

We observe that sometimes the sign of the first term in such an expansion is positive (as in Example 3 and part (b) of Example 4) and sometimes it is negative (as in part (a) of Example 4.) In fact, *the first term in an expansion is positive when expanding by the first or third row (or column) and is negative when expanding by the second row (or column).*

These rules extend in a natural way to determinants of orders higher than 3. Any such determinant can be evaluated by expansion along any row or column. The determinant is obtained by multiplying each element in the row (or column) by its cofactor and adding all the products so obtained. The rule for evaluating the cofactors is exactly the same as for 3×3 determinants: the cofactor of the element in the ith row and jth column is equal to $(-1)^{i+j}$ multiplied by the determinant obtained by deleting the ith row and the jth column. For example, consider the following determinant of order 4.

$$\Delta = \begin{vmatrix} a_1 & b_1 & c_1 & d_1 \\ a_2 & b_2 & c_2 & d_2 \\ a_3 & b_3 & c_3 & d_3 \\ a_4 & b_4 & c_4 & d_4 \end{vmatrix}$$

Its expansion by the first row is given by

$$\Delta = a_1 \begin{vmatrix} b_2 & c_2 & d_2 \\ b_3 & c_3 & d_3 \\ b_4 & c_4 & d_4 \end{vmatrix} - b_1 \begin{vmatrix} a_2 & c_2 & d_2 \\ a_3 & c_3 & d_3 \\ a_4 & c_4 & d_4 \end{vmatrix} + c_1 \begin{vmatrix} a_2 & b_2 & d_2 \\ a_3 & b_3 & d_3 \\ a_4 & b_4 & d_4 \end{vmatrix} - d_1 \begin{vmatrix} a_2 & b_2 & c_2 \\ a_3 & b_3 & c_3 \\ a_4 & b_4 & c_4 \end{vmatrix}$$

$$= a_1 A_1 + b_1 B_1 + c_1 C_1 + d_1 D_1$$

where $A_1, B_1, C_1,$ and D_1 denote the cofactors of $a_1, b_1, c_1,$ and d_1, respectively, in Δ.

One important application of determinants is to the solution of systems of linear equations when the number of equations is equal to the number of unknowns. In fact, the concept of determinants originated from the study of such systems of equations. The main result, known as *Cramer's rule*, is stated in Theorem 2 for systems of three equations. The theorem generalizes in a straightforward way to systems of n equations in n unknowns.

THEOREM 2 (CRAMER'S RULE)

Consider the following system of three equations in three unknowns, x, y, and z.

$$a_1 x + b_1 y + c_1 z = k_1$$
$$a_2 x + b_2 y + c_2 z = k_2$$
$$a_3 x + b_3 y + c_3 z = k_3$$

Let

$$\Delta = \begin{vmatrix} a_1 & b_1 & c_1 \\ a_2 & b_2 & c_2 \\ a_3 & b_3 & c_3 \end{vmatrix}$$

be the determinant of coefficients and let Δ_1, Δ_2, and Δ_3 be obtained by replacing the first, second, and third columns in Δ, respectively, by the constant terms. In other words,

$$\Delta_1 = \begin{vmatrix} k_1 & b_1 & c_1 \\ k_2 & b_2 & c_2 \\ k_3 & b_3 & c_3 \end{vmatrix}, \qquad \Delta_2 = \begin{vmatrix} a_1 & k_1 & c_1 \\ a_2 & k_2 & c_2 \\ a_3 & k_3 & c_3 \end{vmatrix} \quad \text{and} \quad \Delta_3 = \begin{vmatrix} a_1 & b_1 & k_1 \\ a_2 & b_2 & k_2 \\ a_3 & b_3 & k_3 \end{vmatrix}.$$

Then *if $\Delta \neq 0$, the given system has a unique solution given by*

$$x = \frac{\Delta_1}{\Delta}, \qquad y = \frac{\Delta_2}{\Delta}, \qquad z = \frac{\Delta_3}{\Delta}.$$

If $\Delta = 0$ and $\Delta_1 = \Delta_2 = \Delta_3 = 0$, then the system has an infinite number of solutions. If $\Delta = 0$ and either $\Delta_1 \neq 0$ or $\Delta_2 \neq 0$ or $\Delta_3 \neq 0$, then the system has no solution.

EXAMPLE 6   Use determinants to solve the following system of equations.

$$2x - 3y + z = 5$$
$$x + 2y - z = 7$$
$$6x - 9y + 3z = 4$$

Solution   The determinant of coefficients is

$$\Delta = \begin{vmatrix} 2 & -3 & 1 \\ 1 & 2 & -1 \\ 6 & -9 & 3 \end{vmatrix} = 0$$

as can be seen by expanding by the first row. Replacing the first column elements in Δ by the constant terms, we have

$$\Delta_1 = \begin{vmatrix} 5 & -3 & 1 \\ 7 & 2 & -1 \\ 4 & -9 & 3 \end{vmatrix} = -11.$$

Since $\Delta = 0$ and $\Delta_1 \neq 0$, the given system has *no* solution.

EXAMPLE 7   Use determinants to solve the following system of equations.

$$3x - y + 2z = -1$$
$$2x + y - z = 5$$
$$x + 2y + z = 4$$

Solution   The determinant of coefficients is

$$\Delta = \begin{vmatrix} 3 & -1 & 2 \\ 2 & 1 & -1 \\ 1 & 2 & 1 \end{vmatrix}.$$

Expanding by the first row, we obtain

$$\Delta = 3\begin{vmatrix} 1 & -1 \\ 2 & 1 \end{vmatrix} - (-1)\begin{vmatrix} 2 & -1 \\ 1 & 1 \end{vmatrix} + 2\begin{vmatrix} 2 & 1 \\ 1 & 2 \end{vmatrix}$$
$$= 3(1 + 2) + 1(2 + 1) + 2(4 - 1) = 18.$$

Since $\Delta \neq 0$, the system has a unique solution given by

$$x = \frac{\Delta_1}{\Delta}, \qquad y = \frac{\Delta_2}{\Delta}, \qquad z = \frac{\Delta_3}{\Delta}.$$

Replacing the first, second, and third columns in Δ, respectively, by the constant terms, we have the following values.

$$\Delta_1 = \begin{vmatrix} -1 & -1 & 2 \\ 5 & 1 & -1 \\ 4 & 2 & 1 \end{vmatrix} = 18$$

$$\Delta_2 = \begin{vmatrix} 3 & -1 & 2 \\ 2 & 5 & -1 \\ 1 & 4 & 1 \end{vmatrix} = 36$$

$$\Delta_3 = \begin{vmatrix} 3 & -1 & -1 \\ 2 & 1 & 5 \\ 1 & 2 & 4 \end{vmatrix} = -18$$

Therefore we have the following values for x, y, and z.

$$x = \frac{\Delta_1}{\Delta} = \frac{18}{18} = 1$$

$$y = \frac{\Delta_2}{\Delta} = \frac{36}{18} = 2$$

$$z = \frac{\Delta_3}{\Delta} = -\frac{18}{18} = -1$$

Hence the required solution is $x = 1$, $y = 2$, and $z = -1$.

It should be pointed out that Cramer's rule is not usually the most efficient method of solving a system of equations. As a rule, the method of row reduction described in Chapter 9 involves shorter calculations. Cramer's rule is important mainly from a theoretical standpoint. One of the most significant results arising from it is that *a system of n linear equations in n unknowns has a unique solution if and only if the determinant of coefficients is nonzero.*

EXERCISES 3

(1–4) Write each of the following, given

$$\Delta = \begin{vmatrix} a & b & c \\ p & q & r \\ l & m & n \end{vmatrix}.$$

1. The minor of q.   **2.** The minor of n.

3. The cofactor of r.   **4.** The cofactor of m.

(5–28) Evaluate the following determinants.

5. $\begin{vmatrix} 3 & -1 \\ 4 & 7 \end{vmatrix}$ **6.** $\begin{vmatrix} 5 & 8 \\ 3 & -2 \end{vmatrix}$ **7.** $\begin{vmatrix} -6 & -7 \\ -8 & -3 \end{vmatrix}$

8. $\begin{vmatrix} 2 & x \\ 0 & 1 \end{vmatrix}$ **9.** $\begin{vmatrix} a & -2 \\ b & 3 \end{vmatrix}$ **10.** $\begin{vmatrix} 5 & a \\ -a & 4 \end{vmatrix}$

11. $\begin{vmatrix} 32 & 2 \\ 64 & 5 \end{vmatrix}$ **12.** $\begin{vmatrix} 274 & 3 \\ 558 & 7 \end{vmatrix}$ **13.** $\begin{vmatrix} 59 & 3 \\ 64 & 0 \end{vmatrix}$

14. $\begin{vmatrix} a+1 & 2-a \\ 2a+3 & 5-2a \end{vmatrix}$ **15.** $\begin{vmatrix} a & b \\ a+b & b+c \end{vmatrix}$ **16.** $\begin{vmatrix} x+2 & x-1 \\ 3 & x \end{vmatrix}$

17. $\begin{vmatrix} 2 & 1 & 4 \\ 3 & 5 & -1 \\ 1 & 0 & 0 \end{vmatrix}$ **18.** $\begin{vmatrix} 1 & -2 & 3 \\ 4 & 0 & 5 \\ 6 & 0 & 7 \end{vmatrix}$ **19.** $\begin{vmatrix} 1 & 3 & -2 \\ 0 & 2 & 1 \\ 4 & -1 & 3 \end{vmatrix}$

20. $\begin{vmatrix} 3 & 1 & 0 \\ 0 & -2 & 1 \\ 2 & 0 & 5 \end{vmatrix}$ **21.** $\begin{vmatrix} 2 & 3 & 4 \\ 5 & 6 & 7 \\ 8 & 9 & 10 \end{vmatrix}$ **22.** $\begin{vmatrix} 5 & 10 & 1 \\ 8 & 5 & 4 \\ 1 & 4 & 2 \end{vmatrix}$

23. $\begin{vmatrix} 1 & 2 & 4 \\ 2 & 5 & 1 \\ 3 & 8 & 4 \end{vmatrix}$ **24.** $\begin{vmatrix} 7 & 9 & 3 \\ 8 & 2 & 0 \\ 0 & 5 & 4 \end{vmatrix}$ **25.** $\begin{vmatrix} a & b & c \\ 0 & d & e \\ 0 & 0 & f \end{vmatrix}$

26. $\begin{vmatrix} x & 0 & 0 & 0 \\ a & y & 0 & 0 \\ b & c & z & 0 \\ d & e & f & w \end{vmatrix}$ **27.** $\begin{vmatrix} 1 & 0 & -1 & 0 \\ 2 & 1 & 0 & -3 \\ 0 & -2 & 1 & 1 \\ 1 & 2 & 0 & -1 \end{vmatrix}$ **28.** $\begin{vmatrix} 2 & 3 & 4 & 5 \\ 1 & 0 & -1 & 2 \\ 0 & -2 & 1 & 0 \\ 3 & 0 & 2 & 1 \end{vmatrix}$

(29–32) Determine x such in each case.

29. $\begin{vmatrix} x & 3 \\ 2 & 5 \end{vmatrix} = 9$ **30.** $\begin{vmatrix} x+3 & 2 \\ x & x+1 \end{vmatrix} = 3$

31. $\begin{vmatrix} 1 & 0 & 0 \\ x^2 & x-2 & 3 \\ x & x+1 & x \end{vmatrix} = 3$

32. $\begin{vmatrix} x+1 & 2 & x \\ x & x^2 & 2 \\ 0 & 1 & 0 \end{vmatrix} = 1$

(33–50) Use Cramer's rule to solve the following systems of equations.

33. $3x + 2y = 1$
$\quad\ 2x - y = 3$

34. $2x - 5y = 8$
$\quad\ 3y + 7x = -13$

35. $4x + 5y - 14 = 0$
$\quad\ 3y = 7 - x$

36. $2(x - y) = 5$
$\quad\ 4(1 - y) = 3x$

37. $\frac{1}{3}x + \frac{1}{2}y = 7$
$\quad\ \frac{1}{2}x - \frac{1}{5}y = 1$

38. $\frac{2}{3}u + \frac{3}{4}v = 13$
$\quad\ \frac{5}{2}u + \frac{1}{3}v = 19$

39. $2x + 3y = 13$
$\quad\ 6x + 9y = 40$

40. $3x = 2(2 + y)$
$\quad\ 4y = 7 + 6x$

41. $x + y + z = -1$
$\quad\ 2x + 3y - z = 0$
$\quad\ 3x - 2y + z = 4$

42. $2x - y + z = 2$
$\quad\ 3x + y - 2z = 9$
$\quad\ -x + 2y + 5z = -5$

43. $2x + y + z = 0$
$\quad\ x + 2y - z = -6$
$\quad\ x + 5y + 2z = 0$

44. $x + 3y - z = 0$
$\quad\ 3x - y + 2z = 0$
$\quad\ 2x - 5y + z = 5$

45. $x + 2y = 5$
$\quad\ 3y - z = 1$
$\quad\ 2x - y + 3z = 11$

46. $2v + 5w = 3$
$\quad\ 4u - 3w = 5$
$\quad\ 3u - 4v + 2w = 12$

47. $2x - y + 3z = 4$
$\quad\ x + 3y - z = 5$
$\quad\ 6x - 3y + 9z = 10$

48. $4x + 2y - 6z = 7$
$\quad\ 3x - y + 2z = 12$
$\quad\ 6x + 3y - 9z = 10$

49. $x + 2y - z = 2$
$\quad\ 2x - 3y + 4z = -4$
$\quad\ 3x + y + z = 0$

50. $2p - r = 5$
$\quad\ p + 3q = 9$
$\quad\ 3p - q + 5r = 12$

10-4 INVERSES BY DETERMINANT

In Section 1, we used row operations to find the inverse of a nonsingular matrix. It is also possible to calculate inverses by the the use of determinants and, in fact, for small matrices (2×2 or 3×3), this method is usually more convenient than using row operations.

DEFINITION Let $\mathbf{A} = [a_{ij}]$ be a matrix of any size. The matrix obtained by interchanging the rows and columns of $\mathbf{A}$ is called the **transpose** of $\mathbf{A}$ and is denoted by $\mathbf{A}^T$. The first, second, third, $\ldots$, rows of $\mathbf{A}$ become the first, second, third, $\ldots$, columns of $\mathbf{A}^T$.

EXAMPLE 1   (a) If $\mathbf{A} = \begin{bmatrix} 2 & 3 \\ 5 & 7 \end{bmatrix}$, then $\mathbf{A}^T = \begin{bmatrix} 2 & 5 \\ 3 & 7 \end{bmatrix}$.

(b) If $\mathbf{A} = \begin{bmatrix} a & b \\ p & q \\ u & v \end{bmatrix}$, then $\mathbf{A}^T = \begin{bmatrix} a & p & u \\ b & q & v \end{bmatrix}$.

DEFINITION   Let $\mathbf{A} = [a_{ij}]$ be a square matrix and let A_{ij} denote the cofactor of the element a_{ij} in the determinant of $\mathbf{A}$. (That is, A_{11} denotes the cofactor of a_{11}, the first element in the first row of $\mathbf{A}$; A_{32} denotes the cofactor of a_{32}, the second element in the third row of $\mathbf{A}$; and so on.) The matrix $[A_{ij}]$ whose ij-element is the cofactor A_{ij} is called the **cofactor matrix** of $\mathbf{A}$. The transpose of the cofactor matrix is called the **adjoint** of $\mathbf{A}$ and is denoted by adj $\mathbf{A}$.

EXAMPLE 2   Find the adjoint of the matrix $\mathbf{A}$.

$$\mathbf{A} = \begin{bmatrix} 1 & 2 & 3 \\ 4 & 5 & 6 \\ 3 & 1 & 2 \end{bmatrix}$$

Solution   Let us first find the cofactors A_{ij} of the various elements a_{ij} of $\mathbf{A} = [a_{ij}]$.

$$A_{11} = (-1)^{1+1} \begin{vmatrix} 1 & 2 & 3 \\ 4 & 5 & 6 \\ 3 & 1 & 2 \end{vmatrix} = \begin{vmatrix} 5 & 6 \\ 1 & 2 \end{vmatrix} = 10 - 6 = 4$$

$$A_{12} = (-1)^{1+2} \begin{vmatrix} 1 & 2 & 3 \\ 4 & 5 & 6 \\ 3 & 1 & 2 \end{vmatrix} = -\begin{vmatrix} 4 & 6 \\ 3 & 2 \end{vmatrix} = -(8 - 18) = 10$$

Similarly,

$$A_{13} = (-1)^{1+3} \begin{vmatrix} 4 & 5 \\ 3 & 1 \end{vmatrix} = 4 - 15 = -11$$

$$A_{21} = (-1)^{2+1} \begin{vmatrix} 2 & 3 \\ 1 & 2 \end{vmatrix} = -(4 - 3) = -1$$

and so on, the other cofactors being $A_{22} = -7$, $A_{23} = 5$, $A_{31} = -3$, $A_{32} = 6$, and $A_{33} = -3$.

Thus the cofactor matrix is

$$[A_{ij}] = \begin{bmatrix} A_{11} & A_{12} & A_{13} \\ A_{21} & A_{22} & A_{23} \\ A_{31} & A_{32} & A_{33} \end{bmatrix} = \begin{bmatrix} 4 & 10 & -11 \\ -1 & -7 & 5 \\ -3 & 6 & -3 \end{bmatrix}.$$

Then adj $\mathbf{A}$ is the transpose of $[A_{ij}]$ and so is given by

$$\text{adj } \mathbf{A} = \begin{bmatrix} 4 & -1 & -3 \\ 10 & -7 & 6 \\ -11 & 5 & -3 \end{bmatrix}.$$

The importance of the adjoint matrix is shown in Theorem 1, which we state without proof.

THEOREM 1 The inverse of a square matrix $\mathbf{A}$ exists if and only if $|\mathbf{A}|$ is nonzero; in such a case, it is given by the formula

$$\mathbf{A}^{-1} = \frac{1}{|\mathbf{A}|} \cdot \text{adj } \mathbf{A}.$$

In the case of a 2×2 matrix, this result takes the following explicit form. If

$$\mathbf{A} = \begin{bmatrix} a_{11} & a_{12} \\ a_{21} & a_{22} \end{bmatrix},$$

then

$$\mathbf{A}^{-1} = \frac{1}{|\mathbf{A}|} \begin{bmatrix} a_{22} & -a_{12} \\ -a_{21} & a_{11} \end{bmatrix}.$$

EXAMPLE 3 Find $\mathbf{A}^{-1}$ for the matrix of Example 2,

$$\mathbf{A} = \begin{bmatrix} 1 & 2 & 3 \\ 4 & 5 & 6 \\ 3 & 1 & 2 \end{bmatrix}.$$

Solution We find by expanding by the first row that $|\mathbf{A}| = -9$. Since $|\mathbf{A}| \neq 0$, $\mathbf{A}^{-1}$ exists and is given by

$$\mathbf{A}^{-1} = \frac{1}{|\mathbf{A}|} \cdot \text{adj } \mathbf{A}.$$

Taking the matrix adj $\mathbf{A}$ from Example 2, we obtain

$$\mathbf{A}^{-1} = \frac{1}{-9} \begin{bmatrix} 4 & -1 & -3 \\ 10 & -7 & 6 \\ -11 & 5 & -3 \end{bmatrix}$$

$$= \begin{bmatrix} -\frac{4}{9} & \frac{1}{9} & \frac{1}{3} \\ -\frac{10}{9} & \frac{7}{9} & -\frac{2}{3} \\ \frac{11}{9} & -\frac{5}{9} & \frac{1}{3} \end{bmatrix}.$$

Again, it is readily verified using matrix multiplication that $\mathbf{A}\mathbf{A}^{-1} = \mathbf{I}$ and $\mathbf{A}^{-1}\mathbf{A} = \mathbf{I}$.

EXAMPLE 4 Show that the matrix

$$\mathbf{A} = \begin{bmatrix} 1 & 2 & 3 \\ 2 & 5 & 7 \\ 3 & 7 & 10 \end{bmatrix}$$

is not invertible. (See Example 4 in Section 1.)

Solution   The simplest way of showing this is to demonstrate that the determinant of **A** is zero. By expansion, we readily verify that

$$|\mathbf{A}| = \begin{vmatrix} 1 & 2 & 3 \\ 2 & 5 & 7 \\ 3 & 7 & 10 \end{vmatrix} = 0$$

as required.

EXAMPLE 5   Table 7 below gives the interaction between various sectors of a hypothetical economy.

TABLE 7

	Industry I	Industry II	Industry III	Final Demands	Gross Output
Industry I	20	48	18	14	100
Industry II	30	12	54	24	120
Industry III	30	36	36	72	180
Labor Inputs	20	24	72		

(a) Determine the input-output matrix **A**.

(b) Suppose that in three years, the final demands are anticipated to change to 24, 33, and 75 for the three industries I, II, and III, respectively. How much should each industry produce to meet this projected demand?

Solution   (a) Dividing each column in the inner rectangle by the gross output of the corresponding industry, we obtain the input-output matrix.

$$\mathbf{A} = \begin{bmatrix} \frac{20}{100} & \frac{48}{120} & \frac{18}{180} \\ \frac{30}{100} & \frac{12}{120} & \frac{54}{180} \\ \frac{30}{100} & \frac{36}{120} & \frac{36}{180} \end{bmatrix} = \begin{bmatrix} 0.2 & 0.4 & 0.1 \\ 0.3 & 0.1 & 0.3 \\ 0.3 & 0.3 & 0.2 \end{bmatrix}$$

(b) If **I** denotes the 3×3 identity matrix, then

$$\mathbf{I} - \mathbf{A} = \begin{bmatrix} 1 & 0 & 0 \\ 0 & 1 & 0 \\ 0 & 0 & 1 \end{bmatrix} - \begin{bmatrix} 0.2 & 0.4 & 0.1 \\ 0.3 & 0.1 & 0.3 \\ 0.3 & 0.3 & 0.2 \end{bmatrix}$$

$$= \begin{bmatrix} 0.8 & -0.4 & -0.1 \\ -0.3 & 0.9 & -0.3 \\ -0.3 & -0.3 & 0.8 \end{bmatrix}$$

Let $\mathbf{B} = \mathbf{I} - \mathbf{A}$. Then, in order to calculate the future outputs, we need to find the inverse of **B** (see Section 2). We can use the method of determinants. We have

$$|\mathbf{B}| = \begin{vmatrix} 0.8 & -0.4 & -0.1 \\ -0.3 & 0.9 & -0.3 \\ -0.3 & -0.3 & 0.8 \end{vmatrix} = 0.336.$$

Since $|\mathbf{B}| = 0.336 \neq 0$, $\mathbf{B}^{-1}$ exists. The cofactors B_{ij} in the determinant $|\mathbf{B}|$ are as follows.

$$B_{11} = (-1)^{1+1} \begin{vmatrix} 0.9 & -0.3 \\ -0.3 & 0.8 \end{vmatrix} = 0.72 - 0.09 = 0.63$$

$$B_{12} = (-1)^{1+2} \begin{vmatrix} -0.3 & -0.3 \\ -0.3 & 0.8 \end{vmatrix} = -(-0.24 - 0.09) = 0.33$$

Continuing in the same manner, we have $B_{13} = 0.36$, $B_{21} = 0.35$, $B_{22} = 0.61$, $B_{23} = 0.36$, $B_{31} = 0.21$, $B_{32} = 0.27$, and $B_{33} = 0.60$.

Taking the transpose of the cofactor matrix, we obtain

$$\text{adj } \mathbf{B} = \begin{bmatrix} 0.63 & 0.35 & 0.21 \\ 0.33 & 0.61 & 0.27 \\ 0.36 & 0.36 & 0.60 \end{bmatrix}.$$

Consequently the inverse of $\mathbf{B}$ (or $\mathbf{I} - \mathbf{A}$) is given by

$$(\mathbf{I} - \mathbf{A})^{-1} = \mathbf{B}^{-1} = \frac{1}{|\mathbf{B}|} \text{adj } \mathbf{B}$$

$$= \left(\frac{1}{0.336}\right) \begin{bmatrix} 0.63 & 0.35 & 0.21 \\ 0.33 & 0.61 & 0.27 \\ 0.36 & 0.36 & 0.60 \end{bmatrix}.$$

If $\mathbf{D}$ denotes the new demand vector, that is,

$$\mathbf{D} = \begin{bmatrix} 24 \\ 33 \\ 75 \end{bmatrix}$$

and $\mathbf{X}$ is the new output matrix, then we showed in Section 2 that $\mathbf{X} = (\mathbf{I} - \mathbf{A})^{-1}\mathbf{D}$.

Therefore

$$\mathbf{X} = \left(\frac{1}{0.336}\right) \begin{bmatrix} 0.63 & 0.35 & 0.21 \\ 0.33 & 0.61 & 0.27 \\ 0.36 & 0.36 & 0.60 \end{bmatrix} \begin{bmatrix} 24 \\ 33 \\ 75 \end{bmatrix}$$

$$= \begin{bmatrix} 126.25 \\ 143.75 \\ 195 \end{bmatrix}.$$

Thus industry I should produce 126.25 units, industry II should produce 143.75 units, and industry III should produce 195 units to meet the projected final demands in three years.

EXERCISES 4

(1–6) Write the transposes of the following matrices.

1. $\begin{bmatrix} 2 & 5 \\ 3 & -7 \end{bmatrix}$

2. $\begin{bmatrix} 3 & 2 & 1 \\ -5 & 7 & 6 \\ 0 & 3 & 2 \end{bmatrix}$

3. $\begin{bmatrix} a_1 & a_2 & a_3 \\ b_1 & b_2 & b_3 \end{bmatrix}$

4.
$$\begin{bmatrix} 1 & 2 & 3 \\ 3 & 1 & 2 \\ 5 & 4 & 6 \\ 6 & 5 & 4 \end{bmatrix}$$

5.
$$\begin{bmatrix} 1 & 0 \\ 0 & 1 \end{bmatrix}$$

6. $[2]$

(7–16) Use the method of determinants to find the inverses of the following matrices (when they exist).

7.
$$\begin{bmatrix} 3 & 2 \\ -1 & 1 \end{bmatrix}$$

8.
$$\begin{bmatrix} -2 & 5 \\ 1 & -3 \end{bmatrix}$$

9.
$$\begin{bmatrix} -\frac{5}{2} & \frac{3}{2} \\ 2 & -1 \end{bmatrix}$$

10.
$$\begin{bmatrix} 0.3 & -0.1 \\ -0.2 & 0.4 \end{bmatrix}$$

11.
$$\begin{bmatrix} 2 & 1 & -1 \\ 1 & 2 & 3 \\ -1 & 1 & 2 \end{bmatrix}$$

12.
$$\begin{bmatrix} 1 & -1 & 1 \\ -1 & 1 & 1 \\ 1 & 1 & -1 \end{bmatrix}$$

13.
$$\begin{bmatrix} 1 & 0 & 2 \\ 0 & 2 & 1 \\ 2 & 1 & 0 \end{bmatrix}$$

14.
$$\begin{bmatrix} 1 & -1 & 2 \\ 2 & 1 & 0 \\ -1 & 2 & 1 \end{bmatrix}$$

15.
$$\begin{bmatrix} 1 & 2 & 3 \\ 4 & 5 & 6 \\ 7 & 8 & 9 \end{bmatrix}$$

16.
$$\begin{bmatrix} 2 & 1 & 3 \\ 5 & 3 & 7 \\ 7 & 4 & 10 \end{bmatrix}$$

17. Table 8 gives the interaction between various sectors of a hypothetical economy:

TABLE 8

	Industry I	Industry II	Industry III	Final Demands	Gross Output
Industry I	20	40	30	10	100
Industry II	30	20	90	60	200
Industry III	40	100	60	100	300
Primary Inputs	10	40	120		

a. Determine the input-output matrix **A**.

b. Suppose that in 5 years, the final demands change to 150, 280, and 420 for the industries I, II, and III, respectively. How much must each industry produce to meet these projected demands?

c. What will be the new primary inputs requirements for the three industries in 5 years?

18. The interaction between various sectors of a hypothetical economy is given by Table 9.

TABLE 9

	Industry I	Industry II	Industry III	Consumer Demands	Total Outputs
Industry I	16	30	20	14	80
Industry II	32	15	80	23	150
Industry III	24	75	40	61	200
Labor Inputs	8	30	60		

a. What is the input-output matrix **A**?

b. Suppose that in 3 years, the consumer demands change to 20 for industry I, 50 for industry II, and 70 for industry III. How much must each industry produce in 3 years to meet this projected demand?

c. What will be the new labor inputs requirements for the three industries in 3 years' time?

19. An economy consists of three sectors, A, B, and C, whose interactions are given in Table 10.

TABLE 10

	A	B	C	Final Demands	Gross Output
A	60	16	80	44	200
B	60	48	20	32	160
C	40	32	60	68	200
Primary Inputs	40	64	40		

a. Determine the input-output matrix.

b. If the final demands change to 50, 60, and 80 units for the products of A, B, and C, respectively, what will be the required production levels to meet these new demands?

20. The interaction between three sectors in an economy is given in the Table 11.

TABLE 11

	Primary Industry	Secondary Industry	Agriculture	Final Demands	Gross Output
Primary Industry	4	12	3	1	20
Secondary Industry	8	9	6	7	30
Agriculture	2	3	3	7	15
Primary Inputs	6	6	3		

a. Determine the input-output matrix.

b. If the final demand for secondary industrial products increases to 10 units, determine the new output levels for the three sectors.

c. If the final demand for primary industrial products falls to zero, determine the new output levels for the three sectors.

1. State whether each of the following is true or false? Replace each false statement by a true statement.

   a. If **A** is invertible, then the size of $\mathbf{A}^{-1}$ is the same as that of **A**.

   b. The identity matrix is its own inverse.

   c. The zero matrix has as its inverse a zero matrix.

   d. If **A**, **B**, and **C** are three matrices such that $\mathbf{AB} = \mathbf{AC}$, then $\mathbf{B} = \mathbf{C}$.

   e. If a matrix **A** contains a zero element, then it is not invertible.

   f. A matrix is invertible as long as at least one of its elements is nonzero.

   g. The square matrix **A** is invertible if and only if the determinant $|\mathbf{A}| \neq 0$.

   h. The adjoint of **A** is the cofactor matrix of $\mathbf{A}^T$.

   i. If **A** is an $n \times n$ square matrix, then the determinant of the matrix $k\mathbf{A}$ $(k \neq 0)$ is equal to $k|\mathbf{A}|$.

   j. If **A** is a square matrix and $\mathbf{A}^T$ its transpose, then $|\mathbf{A}| = |\mathbf{A}^T|$.

   k. The cofactor of an element in a determinant Δ is the determinant obtained by deleting the row and column in Δ in which the element occurs.

   l. The cofactor and minor of an element are equal in absolute value but differ in sign.

   m. If **A** and **B** are two square matrices of the same size and if their inverses exist, then $(\mathbf{AB})^{-1} = \mathbf{A}^{-1}\mathbf{B}^{-1}$.

   n. If **A** and **B** are two invertible square matrices of the same size, then $(\mathbf{A}^{-1}\mathbf{B})^{-1} = \mathbf{B}^{-1}\mathbf{A}$.

2. Show that if **A** and **B** are 2×2 matrices such that $\mathbf{A} = k\mathbf{B}$, where k is a constant, then $|\mathbf{A}| = k^2|\mathbf{B}|$. Does this still hold if **A** and **B** are 3×3? $n \times n$?

(3–14) Find the inverses of the matrices given below, when they exist.

3. $\begin{bmatrix} 1 & -3 \\ 2 & 5 \end{bmatrix}$
   4. $\begin{bmatrix} 2 & 4 \\ 5 & -3 \end{bmatrix}$

5. $\begin{bmatrix} a & b \\ -b & a \end{bmatrix}$ $(a, b \neq 0)$
   6. $\begin{bmatrix} 1 & 1 \\ a & b \end{bmatrix}$ $(a \neq b)$

7. $\begin{bmatrix} 1 & 0 & 0 \\ 0 & 2 & 0 \\ 0 & 0 & 3 \end{bmatrix}$
   8. $\begin{bmatrix} 1 & 0 & 2 \\ 0 & 2 & 1 \\ 2 & 1 & 0 \end{bmatrix}$
   9. $\begin{bmatrix} 1 & 2 & 3 \\ 2 & 3 & 4 \\ 3 & 1 & 2 \end{bmatrix}$

10. $\begin{bmatrix} 2 & -1 & 1 \\ 1 & 2 & -1 \\ -1 & 1 & 2 \end{bmatrix}$
    11. $\begin{bmatrix} 1 & -2 & 3 \\ 4 & 1 & 6 \\ 7 & 4 & 9 \end{bmatrix}$
    12. $\begin{bmatrix} 2 & -1 & -3 \\ 4 & 1 & -1 \\ 7 & -2 & -8 \end{bmatrix}$

13. $\begin{bmatrix} 2 & 1 & 3 \\ 1 & 4 & 2 \end{bmatrix}$
    14. $\begin{bmatrix} 1 & 2 & 3 & 4 \\ 5 & 6 & 7 & 8 \\ 2 & 1 & 4 & 3 \end{bmatrix}$

(15–18) Solve the following systems of equations by using the inverse of the coefficient matrix.

15. $4x - 3y = 1$
$3x + 2y = 5$

16. $2u - 5v = 11$
$3u + 4v = 5$

17. $x + y + z = 1$
$2x - y + 3z = -2$
$3x + 2y - z = 6$

18. $3p - 2q + 4r = 13$
$p + q - 2r = 1$
$2p - 3q + 5r = 11$

(19–24) Use determinants to solve the following systems of equations.

19. $3x + 5y = 1$
$2x - 4y = -3$

20. $3u - 2v = 4$
$3v = -5 + 4u$

21. $x - y + z = 2$
$-x + y + z = 4$
$x + y - z = 0$

22. $2x - y - z = 3$
$x - 2y + z = 6$
$x + y - 2z = -3$

23. $2x - 6y + 4z = 9$
$3x + y - 2z = 5$
$3x - 9y + 6z = 13$

24. $6x - 3y + 12z = 15$
$2x + 3y + 5z = 10$
$4x - 2y + 8z = 21$

(25–30) Factor the following determinants.

25. $\begin{vmatrix} a & 2 \\ 8 & a \end{vmatrix}$

26. $\begin{vmatrix} a & -b \\ b & a + 2b \end{vmatrix}$

27. $\begin{vmatrix} x + 1 & 7 \\ 6 & x + 2 \end{vmatrix}$

28. $\begin{vmatrix} x + 4 & x + 14 \\ x & 2x + 1 \end{vmatrix}$

29. $\begin{vmatrix} 1 & 1 & 1 \\ x & 0 & 1 \\ 1 & 1 & x \end{vmatrix}$

30. $\begin{vmatrix} 1 & -1 & 9 \\ x + 1 & x & 2 \\ x + 2 & x + 1 & x - 1 \end{vmatrix}$

31. Table 12 gives the interaction between various sectors of a hypothetical economy.

TABLE 12

	Industry I	Industry II.	Final Demands	Gross Outputs
Industry I	8	52	20	80
Industry II	56	26	48	130
Primary Inputs	16	52		

a. Find the input-output matrix **A**.

b. Suppose in two years the final demands change to 58 for industry I and 79 for industry II. How much should each industry produce to meet these projected demands?

c. What will be the new primary inputs requirements for the two industries in two years?

32. The interaction between various sectors of a hypothetical economy is given in Table 13 below:

TABLE 13

	Industry I	Industry II	Final Demands	Gross Outputs
Industry I	120	384	96	600
Industry II	420	288	252	960
Primary Inputs	60	288		

a. Give the input-output matrix **A**.

b. Suppose that in 5 years the final demands change to 140 for industry I and 287 for industry II. How much must each industry produce to meet these projected demands?

c. What will be the new primary inputs requirements for the two industries in 5 years?

LINEAR PROGRAMMING

CHAPTER

11-1 LINEAR INEQUALITIES

The inequality $y > 2x - 4$, relating the two variables x and y, is an example of what are called *linear inequalities*. Let us begin by examining this particular example in terms of a graph.

The equation $y = 2x - 4$ has as its graph a straight line whose slope is 2 and whose y-intercept is -4. It is shown as a dotted line in Figure 1. As an example, when $x = 4$, $y = 2(4) - 4 = 4$, so the point $(4, 4)$ lies on the line, as shown in Figure 1.

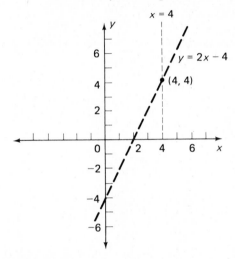

FIGURE 1

Now consider the inequality $y > 2x - 4$. When $x = 4$, this takes the form $y > 2(4) - 4$, or $y > 4$. Thus the inequality is satisfied at all the points $(4, y)$ where $y > 4$. Graphically, this means that on the vertical line $x = 4$, the inequality $y > 2x - 4$ is satisfied at all points that lie *above* the point $(4, 4)$.

Similarly we can take *any* vertical line, $x = x_1$. On this line, the inequality $y > 2x - 4$ becomes $y > y_1$, where $y_1 = 2x_1 - 4$. It is satisfied by the points (x_1, y) that lie on this vertical line above the point (x_1, y_1) where the vertical line meets the line $y = 2x - 4$.

We conclude from this, therefore, that the inequality $y > 2x - 4$ is satisfied at all of the points (x, y) that lie *above* the straight line $y = 2x - 4$. This region in the xy-plane is said to be the **graph** of the given inequality.

A linear inequality between two variables x and y is any relationship of the form $ax + by + c > 0$ (or < 0) or $ax + by + c \geq 0$ (or ≤ 0). The graph of a linear inequality consists of all those points (x, y) that satisfy the inequality. It consists of a region in the xy-plane, not simply a line or a curve.

The graph of the inequality $ax + by + c > 0$ is a half-plane bounded by the straight line whose equation is $ax + by + c = 0$. Parts (a)–(d) of Figure 2 illustrate some linear inequalities.

In each case, the half-plane of points that satisfy the inequality is shaded. The graph of $y > mx + c$ is the half-plane above the line $y = mx + c$, and the graph of $y < mx + c$ is the half-plane below the line $y = mx + c$. If the graph includes the line, we show it by a solid line; otherwise we use a dotted line. A dotted line always corresponds to a strict inequality ($>$ or $<$) and a solid line corresponds to a weak inequality ($\geq$ or $\leq$).

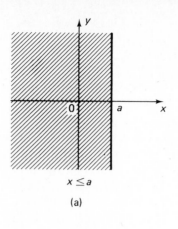

$x \leq a$

(a)

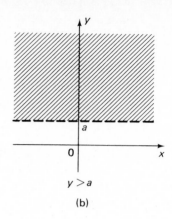

$y > a$

(b)

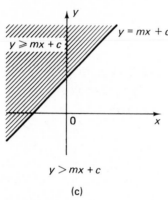

$y \geq mx + c$

(c)

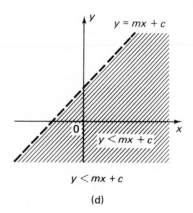

$y < mx + c$

(d)

FIGURE 2

EXAMPLE 1   Sketch the graph of the linear inequality $2x - 3y < 6$.

Solution   First we solve the given inequality for y in terms of x (that is, we express it in one of the forms $y > mx + c$ or $y < mx + c$).

$$2x - 3y < 6$$

$$-3y < -2x + 6$$

We now divide both sides by -3. (Recall that when we divide the terms of an inequality by a negative number, the sign of the inequality changes. See Section 2 of Chapter 3.)

$$y > \tfrac{2}{3}x - 2$$

Next we graph the line $y = \tfrac{2}{3}x - 2$. For $x = 0$, we have $y = -2$. Thus $(0, -2)$ is a point on this line. Again, when $y = 0$, we have $\tfrac{2}{3}x - 2 = 0$ or $x = 3$. Thus $(3, 0)$ is another point on the line. We plot these two points and join them by a dotted line (because we have a strict inequality). Since the given inequality, when solved for y, involves the *greater than* sign, the graph is the half-plane *above* the dotted line (see Figure 3).

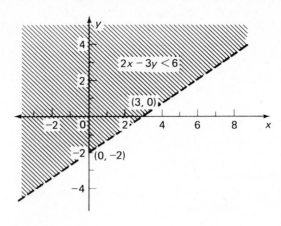

FIGURE 3

Linear inequalities arise in many problems of practical interest. This will become clear in the subsequent sections of this chapter, where we shall study an area of mathematics called *linear programming*. The following examples will provide some typical illustrations of situations that give rise to linear inequalities.

EXAMPLE 2   An investor plans to invest up to $30,000 in two stocks, A and B. Stock A is currently priced at $165 and stock B at $90 per share. If the investor buys x shares of A and y shares of B, graph the region in the xy-plane that corresponds to possible investment strategies.

Solution   The x shares of stock A at $165 per share cost $165x$ dollars. Similarly, y shares of stock B at $90 cost $90y$ dollars. The total sum invested is therefore

$$(165x + 90y) \text{ dollars}$$

and this cannot exceed $30,000. Thus

$$165x + 90y \le 30{,}000.$$

We solve for y.

$$90y \le 30{,}000 - 165x$$

$$y \le -\frac{165}{90}x + \frac{30{,}000}{90}$$

$$y \le -\frac{11}{6}x + \frac{1000}{3}$$

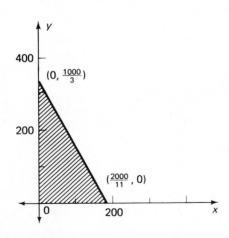

FIGURE 4

The graph of this inequality is shown in Figure 4. In this example, only the region for which $x \ge 0$ and $y \ge 0$ has any significance, so the shaded region is a triangular region rather than a half-plane).

In many practical situations, problems arise involving more than one linear inequality. Example 3 illustrates a case in which two such inequalities occur.

EXAMPLE 3   In the preceding example, stock A is currently paying a dividend of $6 per share and stock B is paying $5 per share. If the investor requires that the investment should pay more than $1400 in dividends, draw the graph of the allowed region.

Solution   Again let x and y be the numbers of shares of stocks A and B, respectively. The previous inequality, $165x + 90y \leq 30,000$, still applies. In addition, the dividend payments are $6x$ dollars from stock A and $5y$ dollars from stock B, giving a total of $(6x + 5y)$ dollars. Since this must exceed $1400, we have the second condition that

$$6x + 5y > 1400.$$

This can be rewritten as

$$y > -\tfrac{6}{5}x + 280.$$

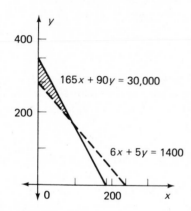

FIGURE 5

This inequality is satisfied by the points above the line $6x + 5y = 1400$. Since it is a strict inequality, the line is not included and is drawn as a dotted line in Figure 5.

The allowed values of x and y must satisfy both the inequalities $165x + 90y \leq 30,000$ and $6x + 5y > 1400$. Hence the region of allowed points (x, y) consists of the region below the line $165x + 90y = 30,000$ and above the line $6x + 5y = 1400$ (see Figure 5). Again, negative values of x or y are not allowed.

When more than two variables are involved in a system of inequalities, graphical techniques are much less helpful. With three variables, the graphs can still be drawn, but often at some inconvenience; with four or more variables, it becomes impossible to use graphs. Example 4 illustrates a simple problem involving three variables.

EXAMPLE 4   An electronics company makes television sets at two factories, F_1 and F_2. Factory F_1 can produce up to 100 sets per week and F_2 can produce up to 200 sets per week. The company has three distribution centers, X, Y, and Z. Center X requires 50 television sets per week, Y requires 75 sets per week, and Z requires 125 sets per week in order to meet the demands in their respective areas. If factory F_1 supplies x sets per week to distribution center X, y sets to Y, and z sets to Z, write the inequalities satisfied by x, y, and z.

Solution   The situation is illustrated in Figure 6. If factory F_1 supplies x sets to center X, then F_2 must supply $(50 - x)$ sets since a total of 50 sets are required at this distribution center. Similarly, F_2 must supply $(75 - y)$ sets to center Y and $(125 - z)$ sets to center Z.

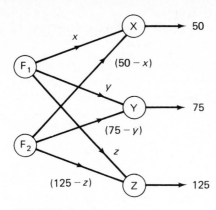

FIGURE 6

The total number of sets supplied by factory F_1 to all three distribution centers is $x + y + z$; this cannot exceed the productive capacity of this factory, which is 100 sets per week. Thus we arrive at the condition

$$x + y + z \leq 100.$$

Similarly, the total number of sets supplied by factory F_2 is equal to

$$(50 - x) + (75 - y) + (125 - z)$$
$$= 250 - x - y - z.$$

This number cannot exceed 200, which is the most this factory can produce.

$$250 - x - y - z \leq 200$$

that is,

$$x + y + z \geq 50.$$

Since the number of sets supplied by any factory to any distribution center cannot be negative, each of the six quantities x, y, z, $(50 - x)$, $(75 - y)$, and $(125 - z)$ must be greater than or equal to zero. Hence x, y, and z must satisfy the following system of inequalities.

$$x \geq 0 \qquad y \geq 0 \qquad z \geq 0 \qquad x \leq 50 \qquad y \leq 75 \qquad z \leq 125$$
$$x + y + z \geq 50 \qquad x + y + z \leq 100$$

In order to represent these inequalities geometrically, we must use three-dimensional coordinates (x, y, z). It is quite possible to draw a suitable figure, but a certain degree of drawing skill is needed to obtain an accurate representation.

EXERCISES 1

(1–6) Sketch the graphs of the following inequalities in the xy-plane.

1. $x + y > 1$ 2. $2x + 3y < 6$ 3. $2x - y \leq 4$

4. $3x \geq y - 6$ 5. $2x + 3 > 0$ 6. $4 - 3y < 0$

(7–12) Sketch the graphs of the following sets of inequalities.

7. $x + y > 2$, $3x + y < 3$

8. $2x + y > 4$, $x + 2y < 4$, $2x - 3y < 3$

9. $0 \leq x \leq 10$, $0 \leq y \leq 15$, $5 \leq x + y \leq 12$

10. $2 \leq x \leq 5$, $1 \leq y \leq 5$, $x + y > 4$, $2x + y < 10$

11. $x \geq 0$, $y \geq 0$, $x + 3y \leq 4$, $2x + y \leq 6$

12. $1 \leq x + y \leq 4$, $y - x \geq 0$, $y - 2x \leq 1$

13. A company has 100 tons of sheet aluminum stored at one location and 120 tons stored at a second location. Some of this material must be delivered to two construction projects. The first project requires 70 tons and the second project

requires 90 tons. Let x and y denote the amounts delivered from the first storage location to the two projects, respectively. Write the inequalities that must be satisfied by x and y and represent them graphically.

14. In Exercise 13, suppose that it costs $10 and $15 per ton to deliver the aluminum from the first storage location to the first and second construction projects, respectively, and $15 and $25 per ton, respectively, to deliver it from the second storage location. If the company requires that the total delivery cost should not exceed $2700, write the further condition on x and y and represent the allowed region graphically.

15. Repeat Exercise 14 if the four delivery costs are $15 and $10, respectively, from the first storage location and $10 and $20, respectively, from the second storage location.

16. A storage company wishes to store up to 120 television sets in its warehouse. It keeps two models in stock, a table model and a floor model. The number of table models must not be less than 40 and the number of floor models must not be less than 30. Represent graphically the possible numbers of sets that can be stored.

17. In Exercise 16, suppose that the floor model requires 12 cubic feet of storage space and the table model requires 8 cubic feet. If the company has 1200 cubic feet of space available for storing the sets, represent the new allowed numbers of sets by a graph.

18. A company makes two products, A and B. These products each require a certain amount of time on two machines in their manufacture. Each unit of product A requires 1 hour on machine I and 2 hours on machine II; each unit of product B requires 3 hours on machine I and 2 hours on machine II. The company has 100 hours per week available on each machine. If x units of product A and y units of product B are produced per week, give the inequalities satisfied by x and y and represent them graphically.

19. In Exercise 18, suppose that the company makes profits of $20 on each item A and $30 on each item B. If it is required that the total weekly profit should be at least $1100, represent the allowed values of x and y graphically.

20. In Exercise 19, represent the allowed region graphically if at least 15 of each type of product must be produced per week in order to fulfill contracts.

21. Sirloin steak costs 15¢ per ounce, and each ounce contains 110 calories and 7 grams of protein. Roast chicken costs 8¢ per ounce, and each ounce contains 83 calories and 7 grams of protein. Represent algebraically the combinations of x ounces of steak and y ounces of chicken that do not exceed $1.00 in cost and that contain less than 900 calories and at least 60 grams of protein.

22. A fish pool is stocked each spring with two species of fish, S and T. The average weight of the fish stocked is 3 pounds for S and 2 pounds for T. Two foods F_1 and F_2 are available in the pool. The average daily requirement of a fish of species S is 2 units of F_1 and 3 units of F_2, whereas for species T, it is 3 units of F_1 and 1 unit of F_2. If at most 600 units of F_1 and 300 units of F_2 are available each day, how should the pool be stocked so that the total weight of the fish in the pool is at least 400 pounds?

11-2 LINEAR OPTIMIZATION (GEOMETRIC APPROACH)

A linear programming problem is one that involves finding the maximum or minimum value of some linear algebraic expression when the variables in this expression are subject to a number of linear inequalities. The following simple example is typical of such problems.

EXAMPLE 1 A company manufactures two products, X and Y. Each of these products requires a certain amount of time on the assembly line and a further amount of time in the finishing shop. Each item of type X needs 5 hours for assembly and 2 hours for finishing, and each item of type Y needs 3 hours for assembly and 4 hours for finishing. In any week, the firm has available 105 hours on the assembly line and 70 hours in the finishing shop. The firm can sell all it can produce of each item and makes a profit of $200 on each item of X and $160 on each item of Y. Find the number of items of each type that should be manufactured per week to maximize the total profit?

It is usually convenient when handling problems of this type to summarize the information in the form of a table. Table 1 shows the information in Example 1.

TABLE 1

	Assembly	Finishing	Profit
X	5	2	200
Y	3	4	160
Available	105	70	

Suppose that the firm produces x items of type X per week and y items of type Y per week. Then the time needed on the assembly line will be $5x$ hours for product X and $3y$ hours for product Y, or $(5x + 3y)$ hours in all. Since only 105 hours are available, we must have $5x + 3y \leq 105$.

Similarly, it requires $2x$ hours in the finishing shop to finish x items of product X, and $4y$ hours to finish y items of product Y. The total number of hours, $2x + 4y$, cannot exceed the 70 which are available, so we have the second condition, $2x + 4y \leq 70$.

Each item of type X produces a profit of $200, so x items produce $200x$ dollars in profit. Similarly, y items of type Y produce $160y$ dollars in profit. Hence the total weekly profit P (in dollars) is given by

$$P = 200x + 160y.$$

We can therefore restate the problem in the following terms: Find the values of x and y that maximize the quantity $P = 200x + 160y$ when x and y are subject to the conditions

$$5x + 3y \leq 105, \quad 2x + 4y \leq 70, \quad x \geq 0, \quad \text{and} \quad y \geq 0. \quad (1)$$

(Observe the conditions that x and y must be nonnegative. These are added for completeness.)

This example is a typical linear programming problem. We have an expression $P = 200x + 160y$, which is linear in the variables x and y, and we wish to find the maximum value of P when x and y satisfy Inequalities (1). A more general problem might involve more than two variables and a larger number of inequalities than the four in this example, but otherwise the example is quite representative of problems in the linear programming area.

When investigating any problem in linear programming, especially when only two variables are involved, a graphical approach is often helpful. Consider Inequalities (1). The set of points (x, y) that satisfy all of these inequalities is shown shaded in Figure 7. This shaded region represents the set of *feasible solutions*, that is, the set of values of x and y that the firm is able to adopt. Any point (x, y) that lies outside this shaded region cannot be adopted.

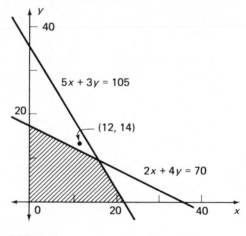

FIGURE 7

For example, consider the point $x = 12$, $y = 14$, which lies outside the feasible region. To produce 12 items of type X and 14 items of type Y would require $12(5) + 14(3) = 102$ hours on the assembly line and $12(2) + 14(4) = 80$ hours in the finishing shop. Although this would not exceed the available hours on the assembly line, it does exceed those available for finishing; so it does not represent a possible production schedule.

Now consider the set of values of x and y that lead to some fixed profit. For example, giving P the value 4000, we see that x and y must satisfy the equation

$$200x + 160y = 4000. \tag{2}$$

All values of x and y satisfying this equation produce a profit of \$4000 per week. This is the equation of a straight line that meets the x-axis at the point $(20, 0)$ and the y-axis at the point $(0, 25)$, as shown in Figure 8. This line passes through part of the region of feasible solutions. Because of this, we conclude that it is possible for the firm to achieve a profit of 4000 dollars per week. It can do this by choosing any value of (x, y) that lies on the segment AB shown in Figure 8. These values of (x, y) are in the feasible region and they also lie on the straight line of Equation (2), which corresponds to $P = 4000$.

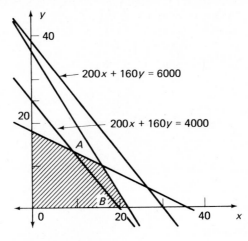

FIGURE 8

On the other hand, consider $P = 6000$. The corresponding values of x and y must satisfy $200x + 160y = 6000$, which again is the equation of a straight line, this time meeting the coordinate axes at the points $(30, 0)$ and $(0, 37.5)$. This straight line does not cross through the shaded region of feasible solutions (see Figure 8) and hence it is not possible for the firm to make a profit as large as \$6000 per week. The maximum possible profit must lie somewhere between \$4000 and \$6000 per week.

The set of points (x, y) that lead to a given profit P satisfy the equation $200x + 160y = P$. This equation, for a fixed P, has as its graph a straight line in the xy-plane called a **constant profit line** or an **indifference curve**. The two lines shown in Figure 8 are constant profit lines corresponding to the values $P = 4000$ and $P = 6000$.

The equation of a constant profit line can be written in the form:

$$160y = P - 200x$$

or

$$y = -\frac{5}{4}x + \frac{P}{160}.$$

The line therefore has a slope of $-\frac{5}{4}$ and a y-intercept of $P/160$. It is an important feature that the slope of any constant profit line is the same regardless of the value of P. This means that all the constant profit lines are parallel to one another. As the value of P is increased, the corresponding line of constant profit moves farther from the origin (the y-intercept increases), always with the same slope.

In order to obtain the maximum profit, we must move the constant profit line away from the origin until it just touches the edge of the region of feasible solutions. It is clear from Figure 9 that the line of maximum profit is the one that passes through the corner C on the boundary of the feasible region. The values of x and y at C provide the production volumes of the two products X and Y that lead to the maximum profit.

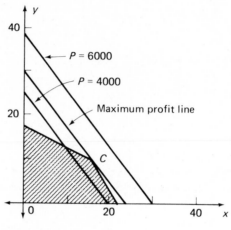

FIGURE 9

C is the point of intersection of the two straight lines which bound the feasible region. Its coordinates are obtained by solving the equations of these two lines, $5x + 3y = 105$ and $2x + 4y = 70$. Solving these equations, we find that $x = 15$ and $y = 10$. Thus the profit is maximum when the firm manufactures 15 items of type X and 10 items of type Y per week. The maximum weekly profit is given by

$$P_{max} = 200x + 160y$$
$$= 200(15) + 160(10)$$
$$= 4600.$$

The maximum profit is thus $4600.

The procedure used to solve this problem can also be used when a greater number of inequalities occur.

EXAMPLE 2   A chemical firm makes two brands of fertilizer. Their regular brand contains nitrates, phosphates, and potash in the ratio 3:6:1 (by weight) and their super brand contains these three ingredients in the ratio 4:3:3. Each month the firm can rely on a supply of 9 tons of nitrates, 13.5 tons of phosphates, and 6 tons of potash. Their manufacturing plant can produce at most 25 tons of fertilizer per month. If the firm makes a profit of $300 on each ton of regular fertilizer and $480 on each ton of the super grade, what amounts of each grade should be produced in order to yield the maximum profit?

Solution   The information given is summarized in Table 2.

TABLE 2

	Nitrates	Phosphates	Potash	Profit
Regular Grade	0.3	0.6	0.1	300
Super Grade	0.4	0.3	0.3	480
Available Supply	9	13.5	6	

Let the firm manufacture x tons of regular grade and y tons of super grade fertilizer per month. Then, since each ton of regular contains 0.3 tons of nitrates and each ton of super contains 0.4 tons of nitrates, the total amount of nitrates used is $0.3x + 0.4y$. This cannot exceed the available supply of 9 tons, so we have the condition $0.3x + 0.4y \leq 9$.

Proceeding similarly with the phosphates and potash, we obtain the two further conditions, $0.6x + 0.3y \leq 13.5$ and $0.1x + 0.3y \leq 6$.

In addition to these inequalities, there is also the condition that the total production of fertilizer, $x + y$, cannot exceed the plant capacity of 25 tons, so $x + y < 25$. After removing the decimals, we obtain the following system of inequalities that must be satisfied by x and y.

$$3x + 4y \leq 90 \qquad 6x + 3y \leq 135$$
$$x + 3y \leq 60 \qquad x + y \leq 25$$
$$x \geq 0 \qquad\qquad y \geq 0$$

The feasible region satisfying all these inequalities is shown in Figure 10. It is the interior of polygon $ABCDEO$, which is shaded.

Each ton of fertilizer yields a profit of $300 for the regular grade and $480 for the super grade. When the production volumes are x and y tons per month,

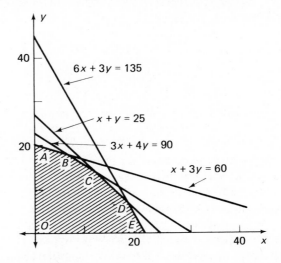

FIGURE 10

respectively, the total monthly profit P is

$$P = 300x + 480y.$$

By setting P at some fixed value, this equation again determines a straight line in the xy-plane, a constant profit line. A number of these lines are shown in Figure 11. The lines corresponding to different values of P are all parallel to one another and lie farther from the origin as the values of P increase. For example, we see that the line corresponding to $P = 7200$ passes across the feasible region, whereas the line for $P = 12,000$ does not. It is geometrically obvious that the constant profit line with the largest value of P that still intersects the feasible region is the one which passes through corner point B. Point B is the point of intersection of the two straight lines

$$x + 3y = 60 \quad \text{and} \quad 3x + 4y = 90.$$

Its coordinates are $x = 6$ and $y = 18$.

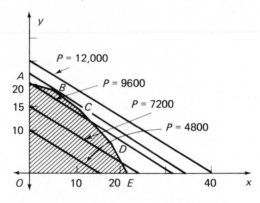

FIGURE 11

We conclude therefore that the maximum profit is obtained by manufacturing 6 tons of regular and 18 tons of super grade of fertilizer per month. The maximum profit is given by

$$\begin{aligned}
P_{\max} &= 300x + 480y \\
&= 300(6) + 480(18) \\
&= 10{,}440 \text{ dollars.}
\end{aligned}$$

It is worth noting that the production schedule that maximizes the profit uses all the available nitrates and potash, but does not use all of the available phosphates and does not make full use of the plant's capacity. You may find it instructive to consider what the firm should do (a) if more potash becomes available, or (b) if more nitrates become available. In considering questions like this, it is helpful to examine what happens to the boundaries of the feasible region in the two cases.

DEFINITION The inequalities that must be satisfied by the variables in a linear programming problem are called the **constraints**. The linear function that is to be maximized or minimized is called the **objective function**.

In the applications in business analysis, the objective function is very often either a profit function (which must be maximized) or a cost function (which must be minimized). It is usual to denote the objective function by the letter Z, and we shall do this from now on.

The following example illustrates a linear programming problem involving the minimization of a cost.

EXAMPLE 3   A chemical company is designing a plant for producing two types of polymer, P_1 and P_2. The plant must be capable of producing at least 100 units of P_1 and 420 units of P_2 per day. There are two possible designs for the basic reaction chambers which are to be included in the plant: each chamber of type A costs \$600,000 and is capable of producing 10 units of P_1 and 20 units of P_2 per day; type B is a cheaper design costing \$300,000 and capable of producing 4 units of P_1 and 30 units of P_2 per day. Because of operating costs it is necessary to have at least 4 chambers of each type in the plant. How many chambers of each type should be included to minimize the cost of construction and still meet the required production schedule?

Solution   The given information is summarized in Table 3.

TABLE 3

	P_1	P_2	Cost
Chamber A	10	20	6
Chamber B	4	30	3
Required	100	420	

(Costs are given in hundreds of thousands of dollars.) Let the design include x chambers of type A and y chambers of type B. Then the following inequalities must be satisfied.

$$x \geq 4, \quad y \geq 4;$$
$$10x + 4y \geq 100 \qquad \text{(production of } P_1)$$
$$20x + 30y \geq 420 \qquad \text{(production of } P_2)$$

The total cost of the chambers is given by

$$Z = 6x + 3y$$

and Z must be minimized subject to the above constraints. The feasible region (that is, the region satisfying the constraints) is shaded in Figure 12. Observe that this region is unbounded in this example.

The lines of constant cost are obtained by setting Z equal to different constants. Two of these lines are shown in the figure. As Z is decreased, the corresponding line moves closer to the origin, always keeping the same slope; the line of minimum cost is the one that passes through the vertex C of the feasible region.

At C we have the two simultaneous equations

$$10x + 4y = 100 \quad \text{and} \quad 20x + 30y = 420.$$

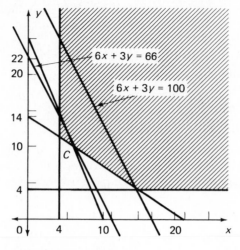

FIGURE 12

Their solution is $x = 6$ and $y = 10$. Therefore the optimal design for the plant is to include 6 reaction chambers of type A and 10 of type B. The minimum cost is

$$Z = 6x + 3y = 6(6) + 3(10) = 66$$

that is $6.6 million.

Consider a general linear programming problem with two variables, x and y. The feasible region, that is, the points (x, y) that satisfy the given set of linear inequalities, will consist of a polygon in the xy-plane. The equation obtained by setting the objective function equal to a constant will always represent a straight line in the xy-plane (for example, the constant profit line). It is intuitively obvious that the extreme (maximum or minimum) values of the objective function within the feasible region will be obtained when this straight line passes through a vertex of the polygon, since as we move the straight line parallel to itself in the direction of increasing (or of decreasing) the value of the objective function, the last point of contact with the feasible region must occur at one of the vertices.

This is illustrated in parts (a) and (b) of Figure 13, which show a series of lines of constant Z (where Z denotes the objective function). As Z increases, the line is moved across the feasible region. The largest and smallest values of Z occur when the line makes its first and last contacts with the feasible region.

In part (b), the lines of constant Z are parallel to one of the sides of the feasible region. In this case the largest value of Z occurs when the line of constant Z coincides with that side. Note, however, that it is still true that the maximum value of Z occurs when the line passes through a vertex of the polygon. In fact it passes through two vertices.

This suggests that instead of using the graphical technique of solving a linear programming problem, all we need do is to work out the value of the

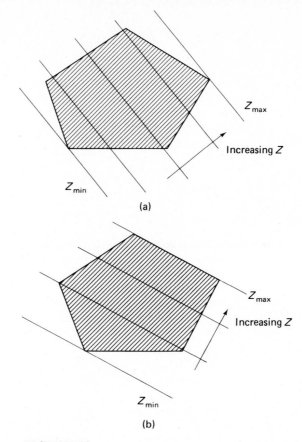

(a)

(b)

FIGURE 13

objective function at each of the vertices of the feasible region. The largest of these vertex values will give the maximum value of the objective function and the smallest of them will give its minimum value.* This method of solving such problems can be used quite easily when there are only two variables, although it has no real computational advantage over the graphical method. For more than two variables, neither of these methods offers a practical tool for optimisation. Fortunately an alternative method does exist, called the simplex method, and we shall devote the rest of this chapter to introducing it.

EXERCISES 2

(**1–6**) Find the maximum value of the objective function Z subject to the given constraints.

1. $Z = 3x + 2y;$ $x \geq 0,$ $y \geq 0,$ $x + y \leq 5$
2. $Z = 3x + 4y;$ $x \geq 0,$ $y \geq 0,$ $2x + y \leq 3$
3. $Z = 3x + 2y;$ $x \geq 0,$ $y \geq 0,$ $2x + y \leq 4,$ $x + 2y \leq 5$

*When the feasible region is unbounded, Z may not have a finite maximum or minimum value.

4. $Z = 2(x + y);$ $x \geq 0,$ $y \geq 0,$ $6x + 5y \leq 17,$ $4x + 9y \leq 17$

5. $Z = 5x + y;$ $x \geq 0,$ $y \geq 0,$ $3x + y \leq 7,$ $x + y \leq 3,$ $x + 2y \leq 5$

6. $Z = x + 3y;$ $x \geq 0,$ $y \geq 0,$ $2x + 3y \leq 6,$ $2x + y \leq 5,$ $x + 4y \leq 6.$

(7–12) Find the minimum values of the objective function Z subject to the given constraints.

7. $Z = x + y;$ $x \geq 0,$ $y \geq 0,$ $x + 3y \geq 6,$ $2x + y \geq 7$

8. $Z = x + 2y;$ $x \geq 0,$ $y \geq 0,$ $x + y \geq 5,$ $x + 4y \geq 8$

9. $Z = x + 4y;$ $0 \leq x \leq 4,$ $0 \leq y \leq 4,$ $5 \leq x + y \leq 7$

10. $Z = x - y;$ $x \geq 0,$ $y \geq 0,$ $x + y \geq 4,$ $x + 2y \leq 10$

11. $Z = x + 2y;$ $x \geq 0,$ $y \geq 0,$ $2x + y \geq 7,$ $2y - x \geq -1,$ $2x - y \geq -3$

12. $Z = x + y;$ $-\frac{1}{2} \leq y - x \leq 2,$ $y + 2x \leq 8,$ $y + 4x \geq 7$

13. A distilling company has two grades of raw (unblended) whisky, I and II, from which it makes two different blends. Regular blend contains 50% each of grades I and II, while super blend consists of two-thirds of grade I and one-third of grade II. The company has 3000 gallons of grade I and 2000 gallons of grade II available for blending. Each gallon of regular blend produces a profit of $5, whereas each gallon of super blend produces profit of $6. How many gallons of each blend should the company produce in order to maximize their profits?

14. A nut company sells two different mixtures of nuts. The cheaper mixture contains 80% peanuts and 20% walnuts, while the more expensive one contains 50% of each type of nut. Each week the company can obtain up to 1800 pounds of peanuts and up to 1200 pounds of walnuts from its sources of supply. How many pounds of each mixture should be produced in order to maximize profits if the profit is 10¢ from each pound of the cheaper mix and 15¢ from each pound of the more expensive mix?

15. A company produces two products, A and B. Each unit of A requires 2 hours on one machine and 5 hours on a second machine. Each unit of B requires 4 hours on the first machine and 3 hours on the second. There are 100 hours available per week on the first machine and 110 hours on the second machine. If the company makes a profit of $70 on each unit of A and $50 on each unit of B, how many of each unit should be produced to maximize the total profit?

16. In Exercise 15, suppose that a single order is received for 16 units of A per week. If it is decided that this order must be filled, determine the new value of the maximum profit.

17. A manufacturer makes two products, A and B, each of which requires time on three machines. Each unit of A requires 2 hours on the first machine, 4 hours on the second machine, and three hours on the third machine. The corresponding numbers for each unit of B are 5, 1, and 2, respectively. The company makes profits of $250 and $300 on each unit of A and B, respectively. If the numbers of machine hours available per month are 200, 240, and 190 for the first, second, and third machines, respectively, determine how many units of each product must be produced to maximize the total profit.

18. In Exercise 17, suppose that there is a sudden shortage of the product A on the market so that the company is able to increase its price of that product. If the

profit on each unit of A is increased to $600, determine the new production schedule that maximizes the total profit.

19. In Exercise 17, suppose that the manufacturer is forced by competition to reduce the profit margin on product B. How low can the profit per unit of B become before the manufacturer is obliged to change his production schedule? (The production schedule should always be chosen to maximize the total profit.)

20. An investment manager has $1 million of a pension fund, part or all of which is to be invested. The manager has two investments in mind, a conservative corporate bond that yields 6% per annum and a more risky mortgage that yields 10% per annum. According to government regulations, no more than 25% of the amount invested can be in mortgages. Furthermore, the minimum that can be put into a mortgage is $100,000. Determine the amounts of the two investments that will maximize the total yield.

21. A farmer has 100 acres on which to plant two crops. The cost of planting the first crop is $20 per acre and the second crop is $40 per acre, and up to $3000 is available to cover the cost of planting. Each acre of the first crop will require 5 work-hours for harvesting and each acre of the second crop will require 20 work-hours. The farmer can rely on having only a total of 1350 work-hours for harvesting the two crops. If the profit is $100 per acre for the first crop and $300 per acre for the second crop, determine the acreage that should be planted with each crop in order to maximize the total profit.

22. In Exercise 21, determine the acreage that should be planted with each crop if the profit from the second crop rises to $450 per acre.

23. A hospital dietician wishes to find the cheapest combination of two foods, A and B, that contains at least 0.5 milligrams of thiamin and at least 600 calories. Each ounce of A contains 0.12 milligram of thiamin and 100 calories, while each ounce of B contains 0.08 milligram of thiamin and 150 calories. If each food costs 10¢ per ounce, how many ounces of each should be combined?

24. A mining company has two mines, P and Q. Each ton of ore from the mine P yields 50 pounds of copper, 4 pounds of zinc, and 1 pound of molybdenum. Each ton of ore from Q yields 25 pounds of copper, 8 pounds of zinc, and 3 pounds of molybdenum. The company must produce at least 87,500, 16,000, and 5,000 pounds per week of these three metals, respectively. If it costs $50 per ton to obtain ore from P and $60 per ton from Q, how much ore should be obtained from each mine in order to meet the production requirements at minimum cost?

25. An automobile manufacturer has two plants located at D and C with capacities of 5,000 and 4,000 cars per day. These two plants supply three distribution centers, W, E, and N, which require 3,000, 4,000 and 2,000 cars per day, respectively. The shipping costs per car from each plant to each distribution center are given in Table 4.

TABLE 4

	W	E	N
D	45	15	25
C	60	10	50

Let x and y denote the numbers of cars per day shipped from plant D to W and E, respectively; determine the values of x and y that minimize the total shipping cost.

11-3 THE SIMPLEX TABLEAU

The geometric method and the method of inspection of vertices become impractical as methods of solution of linear programming problems when the number of variables is more than two, and particularly when the number of inequalities is large. For these more complex problems, an alternative, called the *simplex method*, does exist and provides a straightforward and economical way of finding the extrema. We shall describe the simplex method in Section 4; in this section, we shall outline certain constructions and operations that are basic to the method.

Suppose we are given the inequality $x + 3y \le 2$ satisfied by two variables x and y. We can write the inequality in the form

$$2 - x - 3y \ge 0.$$

If we define a new variable t by the equation

$$t = 2 - x - 3y$$

then the inequality takes the form $t \ge 0$. In this way, the original inequality $x + 3y \le 2$ is replaced by the following equation and inequality.

$$x + 3y + t = 2, \qquad t \ge 0$$

The variable t introduced in this way is called a **slack variable**. The reason for this name is that t is equal to the amount by which $x + 3y$ is less than 2, that is, t measures the *amount of slack* in the given inequality $x + 3y \le 2$.

The first step in using the simplex method is to introduce slack variables so that each inequality in the problem is changed to an equality and in such a way that all slack variables are nonnegative.

EXAMPLE 1   Suppose that a linear programming problem leads to the system of inequalities

$$x \ge 0, \qquad 0 \le y \le 1.5, \qquad 2x + 3y \le 6, \qquad x + y \le 2.5.$$

We introduce the slack variables

$$t = 1.5 - y, \qquad u = 6 - 2x - 3y, \qquad v = 2.5 - x - y.$$

Then the five variables (x, y, t, u, and v) satisfy the inequalities

$$x \ge 0, \qquad y \ge 0, \qquad t \ge 0, \qquad u \ge 0, \qquad v \ge 0$$

and the linear equations

$$y + t = 1.5, \qquad 2x + 3y + u = 6, \qquad x + y + v = 2.5.$$

Observe that in this example, the original set of inequalities has been replaced by three linear equations together with the condition that all of the five variables which occur in these equations are nonnegative. We say that the linear programming problem has been reduced to **standard form**. In general a linear programming problem is said to be in *standard form if it consists of finding the maximum values of an objective function Z which is a linear function of a number of variables such as* $x_1, x_2, \ldots, x_k$, *where* $x_1, x_2, \ldots, x_k$ *are all nonnegative and satisfy a certain number of linear equations.*

EXAMPLE 2   Reduce the problem given in Example 2 of Section 2 to standard form.

Solution   The given problem concerned a manufacturer of fertilizer who makes x tons of regular grade fertilizer and y tons of super grade. The profit function $Z = 300x + 480y$ is to be maximized subject to the following conditions.

$$x \geq 0, \quad y \geq 0, \quad 0.3x + 0.4y \leq 9$$

$$0.6x + 0.3y \leq 13.5, \quad 0.1x + 0.3y \leq 6, \quad x + y \leq 25$$

We define slack variables t, u, v, and w in such a way that the last four of these inequalities become equalities:

$$
\begin{aligned}
0.3x + 0.4y + t &= 9 & 0.6x + 0.3y + u &= 13.5 \\
0.1x + 0.3y + v &= 6 & x + y + w &= 25.
\end{aligned}
\tag{1}
$$

Then the linear programming problem can be stated in standard form in the following way: Maximize the linear function

$$Z = 300x + 480y$$

where x, y, t, u, v, and w are nonnegative variables satisfying the Equations (1).

Let us consider the significance of the slack variables in the context of this example. The manufacture of x tons of regular and y tons of super grade fertilizer uses $0.3x + 0.4y$ tons of nitrates. The condition $0.3x + 0.4y \leq 9$ states that this amount cannot exceed the available supply of 9 tons. The slack variable $t = 9 - (0.3x + 0.4y)$ equals the amount of nitrates that are left over, or unused. The condition $t \geq 0$ has the simple interpretation that the amount of nitrates left over can be zero or positive but cannot be negative.

Similarly the slack variables u and v represent the amounts of phosphates and potash, respectively, left over when x tons of regular and y tons of super grade fertilizer are produced. The variable w represents the unused plant capacity, that is, the number of additional tons of fertilizer that could be produced if the plant were working at full capacity. As mentioned before, the slack variables measure the amount of slack in the corresponding inequalities.

When a linear programming problem is changed to standard form, the solution remains unchanged. That is, the values of the variables that optimize the objective function for the new problem are the same as the values which optimize the objective function in the original problem. (Of course, the new problem has extra variables too.)

In the examples so far, the inequalities have all involved the symbol $\leq$ (except for those that state that the variables x and y themselves are nonnegative). The introduction of slack variables also can be done when inequalities of the $\geq$ variety occur.

EXAMPLE 3   Introduce slack variables for the system of inequalities

$$x \geq 0, \qquad y \geq 0, \qquad 3 \leq x + y \leq 9, \qquad 2y - x \geq -6, \qquad y - x \leq 6.$$

Solution   Define $t = x + y - 3$ and $u = 9 - x - y$. Then the condition $3 \leq x + y \leq 9$ implies that $t \geq 0$ and $u \geq 0$.

Similarly, if we define $v = 2y - x + 6$, then the condition $2y - x \geq -6$ implies that $v \geq 0$. Finally, setting $w = 6 + x - y$, we also have $w \geq 0$.

Then the six variables $x, y, t, u, v,$ and w are nonnegative and satisfy the following four linear equations.

$$x + y - t = 3 \qquad\qquad x + y + u = 9$$
$$x - 2y + v = 6 \qquad\qquad -x + y + w = 6$$

Observe that the slack variables are always introduced into the inequalities in such a way that they are nonnegative. This is done by defining each slack variable to be the high side of the associated inequality minus the low side.

Let us suppose that the original linear programming problem involved n nonnegative variables, which we denote by $x_1, x_2, \ldots, x_n$. In addition these variables satisfy a certain number (say m) of linear inequalities (not counting the conditions $x_j \geq 0$). In reducing the problem to standard form, we introduce m nonnegative slack variables (one for each inequality), which, in general, we denote by $x_{n+1}, x_{n+2}, \ldots, x_{n+m}$. These variables are introduced in such a way that the m inequalities change to m linear equations. Although the number of variables is enlarged from n to $n + m$ by this change, the problem is simplified to the extent that the inequalities are reduced to the simple requirement that the $n + m$ variables $x_1, x_2, \ldots, x_{n+m}$ are all nonnegative.

Consider, for example, the system of inequalities in Example 1 of this section. There are two original variables x and y (so $n = 2$) and three inequalities apart from the conditions $x \geq 0$ and $y \geq 0$ (so $m = 3$). It is therefore necessary to introduce three slack variables $t, u,$ and v, bringing the total number of variables in the problem to $n + m = 2 + 3 = 5$. These five variables are all nonnegative and satisfy the $m = 3$ linear equations

$$y + t = 1.5, \qquad 2x + 3y + u = 6, \qquad x + y + v = 2.5.$$

The feasible region for this problem is shown in Figure 14 in terms of the original variables x and y. We know that the optimum value of any linear objective function must be attained at one (or more than one) of the vertices of this region. But at each vertex, two of the five variables in the standard problem are always zero: at O, $x = y = 0$; at A, $x = 0$ and $y = 1.5$ so $t = 0$; at C, $x + y = 2.5$ and $2x + 3y = 6$ so that u and v are both zero; at D, $v = y = 0$; and at B, $t = u = 0$.

We conclude that the optimum value of any objective function for this example occurs when two of the five variables $x, y, t, u,$ and v are equal to zero.

This result generalizes. Consider the general case in which the original problem involves n variables $x_1, x_2, \ldots, x_n$ and m linear inequalities, so that m slack variables are introduced. The optimum value of the objective function (if such an optimum exists) always occurs at a vertex of the original feasible

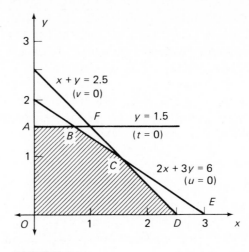

FIGURE 14

region. But at any vertex of the feasible region, we must have a certain number, say p, of the original variables equal to zero and $n - p$ of the linear inequalities satisfied as equalities. (p may be any number from 0 up to n.) But when a linear inequality is satisfied as an equality, the corresponding slack variable is zero. So at any vertex, a certain number p of the original variables are zero and $n - p$ of the slack variables are zero. Thus, out of all the $n + m$ variables together, $p + (n - p) = n$ of them are zero. So *in the optimal solution of the linear programming problem, n of the enlarged set of variables will always be zero.*

A feasible solution of the linear programming problem written in standard form in which n of the variables are equal to zero is called a **basic feasible solution** (BFS). The optimum value of the objective function always occurs at one of these basic feasible solutions, since they correspond to the vertices of the feasible region. The problem is, of course, to find out at which one—that is, to discover which n of the variables in the standard problem must be set equal to zero in order to optimize Z.

It should be pointed out that we cannot arbitrarily select the n variables to set equal to zero since some of these selections will not correspond to vertices of the feasible region. For example, in Figure 13, the point E corresponds to $y = 0$, $u = 0$, but this is not a BFS since E lies outside the feasible region. (It is easily seen that v is negative at E: E has coordinates $(3, 0)$ and so $v = 2.5 - x - y = -0.5$). Similarly point F, which corresponds to $t = v = 0$, is not a BFS since $u < 0$ there.

The essence of the simplex method consists first of choosing a particular BFS as a starting point and then of transforming from this to another BFS in such a way that the objective function becomes closer to being optimal. This transformation process is called **pivoting** and is continued until the optimal basic solution is determined. The criterion used to choose the particular pivot that will be made will be the subject of the next section. In this section, we shall simply discuss the transformations themselves.

Let us take an elementary example. Suppose there are two variables, x and y, which satisfy the constraints $x \geq 0$, $y \geq 0$, $2x + 3y \leq 12$, and $4x + y \leq 14$. We introduce slack variables t and u such that $t \geq 0$ and $u \geq 0$ and the inequalities become

$$2x + 3y + t = 12$$
$$4x + y + u = 14.$$

These equations can be summarized by means of the following augmented matrix of coefficients.

$$
\begin{array}{c}
\\ t \\ u
\end{array}
\begin{array}{cccc}
x & y & t & u \\
\end{array}
\left[
\begin{array}{cccc|c}
2 & 3 & 1 & 0 & 12 \\
4 & 1 & 0 & 1 & 14
\end{array}
\right]
$$

This matrix is called the **simplex tableau**.

Observe that the variables are listed in the tableau at the head of the column of coefficients corresponding to that variable. Certain of the variables are listed on the left side of the tableau, in this case t and u. We do this for the following reason: Suppose that all of the other variables except t and u are set equal to zero (that is, $x = 0$ and $y = 0$). Then the two equations reduce to:

$$2(0) + 3(0) + t = 12 \quad \text{and} \quad 4(0) + 0 + u = 14$$

or $t = 12$ and $u = 14$. So the values of t and u are given by the elements in the augmented matrix that lie in the last column. This is why t and u are set next to the corresponding rows of the tableau.

Looking at the columns headed by t and u in the above tableau, we see that they form a 2×2 unit matrix. It is for this reason that the values of t and u can be read off directly from the last column when $x = y = 0$.

Setting $x = y = 0$ gives one BFS. The corresponding values of t and u are given by the elements of the last column. Since these elements are positive, this solution is a feasible one. The variables t and u are said to form the **basis** for this feasible solution.

In using the simplex method, we move from one BFS to another (that is, from one vertex to another) by replacing the variables in the basis one at a time by variables outside the basis. The variable that is removed from the basis is called the **departing variable** and the variable that replaces it is called the **entering variable**. For example, we might change from the basis (t, u) in the above tableau to the basis (y, u). Then the departing variable would be t and the entering variable would be y.

Figure 15 illustrates this example. The BFS with basis (t, u) corresponds to vertex O and the BFS with basis (y, u) corresponds to vertex A. A pivot from the one BFS to the other corresponds to moving from O to A.

When the basis is (y, u), we require that the values of y and u can be read off from the last column of the tableau if $x = t = 0$. This means that the tableau must be transformed to the form

$$
\begin{array}{c}
\\ y \\ u
\end{array}
\begin{array}{cccc}
x & y & t & u \\
\end{array}
\left[
\begin{array}{cccc|c}
- & 1 & - & 0 & - \\
- & 0 & - & 1 & -
\end{array}
\right].
$$

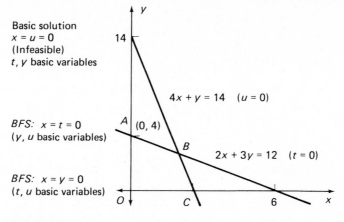

Basic solution
$x = u = 0$
(Infeasible)
t, y basic variables

$4x + y = 14$ $(u = 0)$

BFS: $x = t = 0$
(y, u basic variables)

A $(0, 4)$

B

$2x + 3y = 12$ $(t = 0)$

BFS: $x = y = 0$
(t, u basic variables)

O

C

6

FIGURE 15

where the dashes denote unknown entries. This transformation is accomplished by means of elementary row operations. For instance, the operation $R_2 - \frac{1}{3}R_1$ (subtracting one-third of the first row from the second row) changes the tableau to

$$\begin{bmatrix} 2 & 3 & 1 & 0 & 12 \\ \frac{10}{3} & 0 & -\frac{1}{3} & 1 & 10 \end{bmatrix}.$$

This places a zero in the y-column, as required. Dividing the first row by 3 reduces the tableau to the desired form.

$$\begin{array}{c} \quad x \quad\; y \quad\; t \quad\; u \\ \begin{array}{c} y \\ u \end{array} \begin{bmatrix} \frac{2}{3} & 1 & \frac{1}{3} & 0 & 4 \\ \frac{10}{3} & 0 & -\frac{1}{3} & 1 & 10 \end{bmatrix} \end{array}$$

From this tableau, we conclude that for the BFS in which $x = t = 0$, the values of y and u are 4 and 10, respectively. This second tableau corresponds to the equations

$$\frac{2}{3}x + y + \frac{1}{3}t = 4$$
$$\frac{10}{3}x - \frac{1}{3}t + u = 10$$

and it is readily seen that setting $x = t = 0$ gives $y = 4$ and $u = 10$.

EXAMPLE 4   A linear programming problem involves finding the maximum value of $Z = x + 4y + 2z$ when $x, y,$ and z are nonnegative variables satisfying the constraints

$$3x + y + 2z \leq 6 \quad \text{and} \quad 2x + 3y + z \leq 6.$$

We introduce the nonnegative slack variables t and u so that

$$3x + y + 2z + t = 6$$
$$2x + 3y + z + u = 6.$$

The simplex tableau then has the following form.

$$\begin{array}{c} \\ t \\ u \end{array} \begin{array}{ccccc} x & y & z & t & u \\ \left[\begin{array}{ccccc|c} 3 & 1 & 2 & 1 & 0 & 6 \\ 2 & 3 & 1 & 0 & 1 & 6 \end{array}\right] \end{array}$$

Let us transform this tableau to one in which t and y form the basis. This means that u will be the departing variable and y the entering variable, so we must perform row operations in such a way as to change the second column to

$$\begin{bmatrix} 0 \\ 1 \end{bmatrix}.$$

The operation $R_1 - \frac{1}{3}R_2$ (subtracting one-third of the second row from the first row) gives

$$\left[\begin{array}{ccccc|c} \frac{7}{3} & 0 & \frac{5}{3} & 1 & -\frac{1}{3} & 4 \\ 2 & 3 & 1 & 0 & 1 & 6 \end{array}\right]$$

and then the operation $\frac{1}{3}R_2$ (dividing the second row by 3) gives the required form.

$$\begin{array}{c} \\ t \\ y \end{array} \begin{array}{ccccc} x & y & z & t & u \\ \left[\begin{array}{ccccc|c} \frac{7}{3} & 0 & \frac{5}{3} & 1 & -\frac{1}{3} & 4 \\ \frac{2}{3} & 1 & \frac{1}{3} & 0 & \frac{1}{3} & 2 \end{array}\right] \end{array}$$

From this, we conclude that the basic feasible solution for which $x = z = u = 0$ has the values $t = 4$ and $y = 2$ for these variables.

Observe that the values of t and y for this basic solution have turned out to be nonnegative. If they had not, the solution would not have been a feasible one. But the values of t and y are given directly by the elements in the last column of the tableau. We see then that *any change of basis must result in a tableau in which the last column has nonnegative elements*; otherwise the corresponding basic solution will not be feasible. (Geometrically, this means it will not be a vertex of the feasible region, such as E and F in Figure 14.)

For example, suppose in Example 4 we transform from the basis (t, u) to the basis (t, z). This is accomplished simply by the row operation $R_1 - 2R_2$, which results in the following tableau.

$$\begin{array}{c} \\ t \\ z \end{array} \begin{array}{ccccc} x & y & z & t & u \\ \left[\begin{array}{ccccc|c} -1 & -5 & 0 & 1 & -2 & -6 \\ 2 & 3 & 1 & 0 & 1 & 6 \end{array}\right] \end{array}$$

Setting $x = y = u = 0$, we then find that $t = -6$ and $z = 6$. This is not a feasible solution since t is negative.

As we use the simplex method to transform from one basis to another, we must bear in mind this criterion that the elements in the last column of the tableau must remain nonnegative.

The preceding examples have involved tableaux with two rows. The number of rows in a tableau is equal to the number of slack variables, which in turn is equal to the number of inequalities in the original problem (not counting those of the type $x \geq 0$).

EXAMPLE 5   In Example 2 of this section, we considered the problem of maximizing the function $Z = 300x + 480y$, where the nonnegative variables x, y, t, u, v, and w satisfy the following equations.

$$\begin{aligned}
0.3x + 0.4y + t &&&&= 9 \\
0.6x + 0.3y &+ u &&&= 13.5 \\
0.1x + 0.3y &&+ v &&= 6 \\
x + y &&&+ w &= 25
\end{aligned}$$

Write the simplex tableau for this problem. Transform it first to the basis (t, u, y, w) and then to the basis (x, u, y, w).

Solution   The tableau is as follows.

$$
\begin{array}{c}
\\ t \\ u \\ \rightarrow v \\ w
\end{array}
\begin{array}{cccccc}
x & y & t & u & v & w \\
\left[\begin{array}{cccccc|c}
0.3 & 0.4 & 1 & 0 & 0 & 0 & 9 \\
0.6 & 0.3 & 0 & 1 & 0 & 0 & 13.5 \\
0.1 & 0.3 & 0 & 0 & 1 & 0 & 6 \\
1 & 1 & 0 & 0 & 0 & 1 & 25
\end{array}\right]
\end{array}
$$

In the first transformation, v is the departing variable and y the entering variable, as indicated by the two arrows. This means that the second column of the tableau must be transformed to the form

$$\begin{bmatrix} 0 \\ 0 \\ 1 \\ 0 \end{bmatrix}$$

by means of elementary row operations. This is accomplished by the sequence of operations $R_1 - \frac{4}{3}R_3$, $R_2 - R_3$, $R_4 - \frac{10}{3}R_3$, and $\frac{10}{3}R_3$. The result is the following tableau.

$$
\begin{array}{c}
\\ \rightarrow t \\ u \\ y \\ w
\end{array}
\begin{array}{cccccc}
x & y & t & u & v & w \\
\left[\begin{array}{cccccc|c}
\frac{1}{6} & 0 & 1 & 0 & -\frac{4}{3} & 0 & 1 \\
\frac{1}{2} & 0 & 0 & 1 & -1 & 0 & \frac{15}{2} \\
\frac{1}{3} & 1 & 0 & 0 & \frac{10}{3} & 0 & 20 \\
\frac{2}{3} & 0 & 0 & 0 & -\frac{10}{3} & 1 & 5
\end{array}\right]
\end{array}
$$

From the last column, we see that in the BFS for which $x = v = 0$, the other variables are $t = 1$, $u = \frac{15}{2}$, $y = 20$, and $w = 5$.

Figure 10 shows the feasible region for this example. The first tableau corresponds to the vertex O $(x = y = 0)$, while the second tableau corresponds to A $(x = v = 0)$. In the next step, we move to the basis (x, u, y, w), which corresponds to B $(t = v = 0)$. In this step, x is the entering variable and t the departing variable. The sequence of operations $R_2 - 3R_1$, $R_3 - 2R_1$, $R_4 - 4R_1$, and $6R_1$ result in the following tableau.

$$
\begin{array}{c}
x \\
u \\
y \\
w
\end{array}
\begin{array}{c}
\begin{array}{cccccccc}
x & y & t & u & v & w & \\
\end{array} \\
\left[
\begin{array}{cccccc|c}
1 & 0 & 6 & 0 & -8 & 0 & 6 \\
0 & 0 & -3 & 1 & 3 & 0 & \frac{9}{2} \\
0 & 1 & -2 & 0 & 6 & 0 & 18 \\
0 & 0 & -4 & 0 & 2 & 1 & 1 \\
\end{array}
\right]
\end{array}
$$

Again we see that for the basic feasible solution $t = v = 0$, $x = 6$, $u = \frac{9}{2}$, $y = 18$, and $w = 1$. (This basic feasible solution is, in fact, the optimal one for this problem.)

EXERCISES 3

(1–12) Introduce slack variables and write the simplex tableaux for Exercises 1–6, 13–17, and 21 of Section 2.

(13–14) Introduce slack variables and write the simplex tableaux for each of the following problems.

13. Maximize $Z = x + 3y + 2z$ subject to $x \geq 0$, $y \geq 0$, $z \geq 0$, $2x + y + z \leq 5$, $x + 2y + z \leq 4$.

14. Maximize $Z = x + y + z$ subject to $x \geq 0$, $y \geq 0$, $z \geq 0$, $4x + 2y + z \leq 11$, $2x + 2y + 3z \leq 15$, $x + 2y + 2z \leq 11$.

(15–22) For the simplex tableaux given below, perform the appropriate row operations to make the indicated change of basis. In each case decide whether the new basis gives a feasible solution. In Exercises 15, 16, and 19–22, illustrate the change of basis with a diagram showing the corresponding change of vertex of the feasible region.

15.
$$
\begin{array}{c}
t \\
u
\end{array}
\begin{array}{c}
\begin{array}{cccc}
x & y & t & u \\
\end{array} \\
\left[
\begin{array}{cccc|c}
2 & 3 & 1 & 0 & 8 \\
7 & 6 & 0 & 1 & 19 \\
\end{array}
\right]
\end{array}
\quad (t, u) \longrightarrow (y, u) \longrightarrow (y, x)
$$

16.
$$
\begin{array}{c}
s \\
t
\end{array}
\begin{array}{c}
\begin{array}{cccc}
x & y & s & t \\
\end{array} \\
\left[
\begin{array}{cccc|c}
2 & 1 & 1 & 0 & 10 \\
2 & 5 & 0 & 1 & 18 \\
\end{array}
\right]
\end{array}
\quad (s, t) \longrightarrow (s, x) \longrightarrow (y, x)
$$

17.
$$
\begin{array}{c}
t \\
u
\end{array}
\begin{array}{c}
\begin{array}{ccccc}
x & y & z & t & u \\
\end{array} \\
\left[
\begin{array}{ccccc|c}
1 & 2 & 1 & 1 & 0 & 5 \\
3 & 2 & 4 & 0 & 1 & 16 \\
\end{array}
\right]
\end{array}
\quad (t, u) \longrightarrow (y, u) \longrightarrow (y, x)
$$

18.
$$
\begin{array}{c}
t \\
u
\end{array}
\begin{array}{c}
\begin{array}{ccccc}
x & y & z & t & u \\
\end{array} \\
\left[
\begin{array}{ccccc|c}
3 & 1 & 1 & 1 & 0 & 4 \\
2 & 2 & 4 & 0 & 1 & 10 \\
\end{array}
\right]
\end{array}
\quad (t, u) \longrightarrow (y, u) \longrightarrow (y, z)
$$

19.
$$
\begin{array}{c}
s \\
t \\
u
\end{array}
\begin{array}{c}
\begin{array}{ccccc}
x & y & s & t & u \\
\end{array} \\
\left[
\begin{array}{ccccc|c}
6 & 5 & 1 & 0 & 0 & 17 \\
4 & 9 & 0 & 1 & 0 & 17 \\
2 & 3 & 0 & 0 & 1 & 6 \\
\end{array}
\right]
\end{array}
\quad
\begin{array}{l}
(s, t, u) \longrightarrow (s, x, u) \\
\qquad \longrightarrow (s, x, y) \\
\qquad \longrightarrow (u, x, y)
\end{array}
$$

20.

$$\begin{array}{c} \\ s \\ t \\ u \end{array} \begin{array}{ccccc} x & y & s & t & u \\ \left[\begin{array}{ccccc|c} 4 & 1 & 1 & 0 & 0 & 17 \\ 1 & 1 & 0 & 1 & 0 & 5 \\ 2 & 3 & 0 & 0 & 1 & 12 \end{array}\right] \end{array} \quad (s, t, u) \longrightarrow (y, t, u) \longrightarrow (y, x, u)$$

21.

$$\begin{array}{c} \\ p \\ q \\ r \end{array} \begin{array}{ccccc} x & y & p & q & r \\ \left[\begin{array}{ccccc|c} 3 & 2 & 1 & 0 & 0 & 5 \\ 1 & 2 & 0 & 1 & 0 & 3 \\ 1 & 5 & 0 & 0 & 1 & 6 \end{array}\right] \end{array} \quad \begin{array}{l} (p, q, r) \longrightarrow (x, q, r) \\ \qquad\qquad \longrightarrow (x, y, r) \\ \qquad\qquad \longrightarrow (x, y, q) \end{array}$$

22.

$$\begin{array}{c} \\ p \\ q \\ r \end{array} \begin{array}{ccccc} x & y & p & q & r \\ \left[\begin{array}{ccccc|c} 4 & 1 & 1 & 0 & 0 & 6 \\ 3 & 3 & 0 & 1 & 0 & 9 \\ 2 & 5 & 0 & 0 & 1 & 15 \end{array}\right] \end{array} \quad \begin{array}{l} (p, q, r) \longrightarrow (p, y, r) \\ \qquad\qquad \longrightarrow (p, y, x) \\ \qquad\qquad \longrightarrow (q, y, x) \end{array}$$

11-4 THE SIMPLEX METHOD

The procedure used in the simplex method is to continue making changes in the basis variables of the type discussed in the last section until the set of variables that optimizes the objective function is obtained. Each change of variables is made in such a way as to improve the value of the objective function.

Let us consider the method with reference to a particular example. Suppose that we wish to maximize $Z = 2x + 3y$ subject to the constraints $x \geq 0$, $y \geq 0$, $x + 4y \leq 9$, and $2x + y \leq 4$. As usual, we introduce slack variables t and u such that

$$x + 4y + t = 9, \qquad 2x + y + u = 4 \tag{1}$$

where the four variables x, y, t, and u are nonnegative. The simplex tableau is

$$\begin{array}{c} \\ t \\ u \\ {} \end{array} \begin{array}{cccc} x & y & t & u \\ \left[\begin{array}{cccc|c} 1 & 4 & 1 & 0 & 9 \\ 2 & 1 & 0 & 1 & 4 \\ 2 & 3 & 0 & 0 & Z \end{array}\right] \end{array}.$$

Observe that we have now added an additional row to the tableau that contains the coefficients in the objective function

$$2x + 3y + 0 \cdot t + 0 \cdot u = Z.$$

We start with the BFS in which $x = y = 0$. For this solution, $t = 9$ and $u = 4$. The objective function has the value zero for this BFS. Our aim is to replace one of the variables t or u with either x or y in such a way that Z is increased. Looking at the last row of the tableau, we see that if x is increased by 1, Z increases by 2, whereas if y is increased by 1, Z increases by 3. That is, any increase in y has a bigger effect on Z than the same increase in x. It therefore appears reasonable to take y as the entering variable in forming the new basis.

The elements in the bottom row of the tableau are called the **indicators**.

At each stage of the simplex procedure, *the entering variable is the one with the largest positive indicator.* (If the largest indicator occurs twice, we can choose arbitrarily between the two variables).

We must next decide whether to take t or u as the departing variable. Let us consider these two possibilities in turn.

t **departing:** In this case the basis will consist of (y, u), since y enters and t departs. The BFS for this basis will be obtained by setting $x = t = 0$. From Equations (1), we have $0 + 4y + 0 = 9$ and $2(0) + y + u = 4$. Thus $y = \frac{9}{4}$ and $u = 4 - y = 4 - \frac{9}{4} = \frac{7}{4}$. This solution is acceptable since y and u are both positive.

u **departing:** In this case, the basis will consist of (t, y) and the BFS corresponds to setting $x = u = 0$. From Equations (1), we have $0 + 4y + t = 9$ and $2(0) + y + 0 = 4$. Therefore $y = 4$ and $t = 9 - 4y = 9 - (4)4 = -7$.

The second solution is not acceptable because t is negative. It follows therefore that we must take t as departing variable.

This method of deciding on the departing variable can be shortened quite appreciably. Suppose that the tableau has the general form

$$
\begin{array}{c}
 \\
t \\
u
\end{array}
\begin{array}{cccc}
x & y & t & u \\
\left[\begin{array}{cccc|c}
p_1 & q_1 & 1 & 0 & b_1 \\
p_2 & q_2 & 0 & 1 & b_2
\end{array}\right]
\end{array}
$$

where p_i, q_i, and b_i denote the indicated entries in the tableau. The corresponding equations would be

$$
\begin{aligned}
p_1 x + q_1 y + t \phantom{{}+u} &= b_1 \\
p_2 x + q_2 y \phantom{{}+t} + u &= b_2.
\end{aligned}
\tag{2}
$$

Let us suppose that it has already been decided that y is the entering variable, and let us consider the two possibilities that t or u could be the departing variable.

t **departing:** In this case, the basis will consist of (y, u). The BFS will be obtained by setting $x = t = 0$, in which case Equations (2) give

$$
q_1 y = b_1 \text{ and } q_2 y + u = b_2.
$$

Therefore

$$
y = b_1/q_1 \text{ and } u = b_2 - q_2 y = b_2 - q_2(b_1/q_1).
$$

Since y and u must both be nonnegative if this is to be a feasible solution, we require that

$$
b_1/q_1 \geq 0 \text{ and } b_2 - q_2(b_1/q_1) \geq 0.
$$

Since b_1 is nonnegative (the elements in the last column must always be nonnegative), the first condition is met as long as $q_1 > 0$. Now q_1 is the element in the tableau that lies in the row of the departing variable t and the column of the entering variable y. It is called the *pivot element* for this change of basis. We conclude that in any change of basic variables *the pivot element must be positive.*

The second of the conditions will automatically be satisfied if $q_2 \leq 0$, since then the term $q_2(b_1/q_1)$ will be negative or zero. (Note that $b_2 \geq 0$). If $q_2 > 0$, this second condition can be written as $b_2 \geq q_2(b_1/q_1)$ or

$$(b_2/q_2) \geq (b_1/q_1).$$

u **departing:**   By a similar analysis, we conclude that a valid BFS will be obtained with (t, y) as basis provided that the pivot element $q_2 > 0$ and provided that either $q_1 \leq 0$ or, if $q_1 > 0$, then $(b_1/q_1) \geq (b_2/q_2)$.

Observe that the two ratios b_1/q_1 and b_2/q_2 are obtained by dividing the element in the last column of the tableau by the corresponding element in the column of the entering variable. (See Figure 16.) Thus if $q_1 > 0$ and $q_2 \leq 0$, t is the departing variable. If $q_2 > 0$ and $q_1 \leq 0$, u is the departing variable. If both $q_1 > 0$ and $q_2 > 0$, t is the departing variable if $b_1/q_1 \leq b_2/q_2$ and u is the departing variable if $b_2/q_2 \leq b_1/q_1$.* Thus *the departing variable is the one whose row in the tableau corresponds to the smallest nonnegative ratio b_i/q_i.*

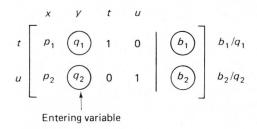

FIGURE 16

Let us return to the earlier example. The first two rows of the tableau are shown in Figure 17. Since y is to be the entering variable, we divide each element in the last column by the corresponding element in the column headed by y. The ratios are given at the right of the tableau. Both ratios are positive,

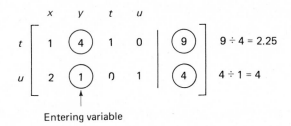

FIGURE 17

*If both $q_1 \leq 0$ and $q_2 \leq 0$, then the problem is unbounded—that is, Z does not have a finite maximum value.

and the smaller is $9 \div 4 = 2.25$, which belongs to the t-row in the tableau. So we must take t as the departing variable and the pivot element is 4.

The two row operations $R_2 - \frac{1}{4}R_1$ and $\frac{1}{4}R_1$ then reduce the tableau to the following form.

$$
\begin{array}{c}
y \\
u \\
\\
\end{array}
\begin{bmatrix}
\begin{array}{cccc|c}
x & y & t & u & \\
\frac{1}{4} & 1 & \frac{1}{4} & 0 & \frac{9}{4} \\
\frac{7}{4} & 0 & -\frac{1}{4} & 1 & \frac{7}{4} \\
2 & 3 & 0 & 0 & Z
\end{array}
\end{bmatrix}
$$

In this form, the values of the basis variables y and u can be read directly from the last column for the BFS in which $x = t = 0$.

We see that Z is still expressed in terms of x and y. We would like to express it in terms of x and t so that when x and t are set equal to zero, the value of Z can be read immediately from the tableau. We can do this by the operation $R_3 - 3R_1$.

$$
\begin{array}{c}
y \\
u \\
\\
\end{array}
\begin{bmatrix}
\begin{array}{cccc|c}
x & y & t & u & \\
\frac{1}{4} & 1 & \frac{1}{4} & 0 & \frac{9}{4} \\
\frac{7}{4} & 0 & -\frac{1}{4} & 1 & \frac{7}{4} \\
\frac{5}{4} & 0 & -\frac{3}{4} & 0 & Z - \frac{27}{4}
\end{array}
\end{bmatrix}
$$

The last row in this new tableau stands for the equation

$$Z - \tfrac{27}{4} = \tfrac{5}{4}x - \tfrac{3}{4}t. \tag{3}$$

When $x = t = 0$, this becomes $Z - \frac{27}{4} = 0$, or $Z = \frac{27}{4}$. Thus for the basic feasible solution at which $x = t = 0$, the objective function has the value $\frac{27}{4}$. This certainly represents an improvement over the previous value of zero.

In Equation (3), we observe that if t is made positive, Z would actually decrease. The corresponding indicator (namely $-\frac{3}{4}$) is negative. Therefore we do not want to allow t to enter the basis. The largest positive indicator (in fact, the only positive indicator) is $\frac{5}{4}$, which belongs to x, so x will be the entering variable for the next step in the simplex procedure.

To determine the departing variable, we again divide the last column by the corresponding elements of the column headed by the entering variable. The results are given in Figure 18. The smallest of these quotients is 1, which comes from the u-row, so u will be the departing variable.

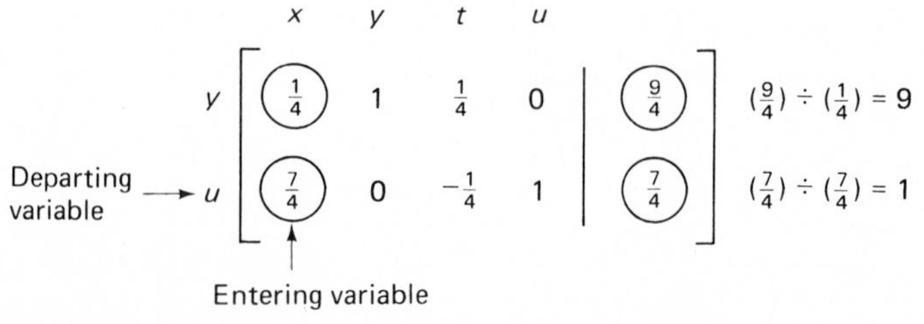

FIGURE 18

The sequence of row operations $R_1 - \frac{1}{7}R_2$, $R_3 - \frac{5}{7}R_2$, and $\frac{4}{7}R_2$ then reduces the tableau to

$$
\begin{array}{c}
\\ y \\ x \\ \;
\end{array}
\begin{array}{cccc}
x & y & t & u \\
\end{array}
\left[
\begin{array}{cccc|c}
0 & 1 & \frac{2}{7} & -\frac{1}{7} & 2 \\
1 & 0 & -\frac{1}{7} & \frac{4}{7} & 1 \\
0 & 0 & -\frac{4}{7} & -\frac{5}{7} & Z-8
\end{array}
\right].
$$

The BFS for this tableau corresponds to $t = u = 0$. Observe that the last row in the tableau corresponds to the equation

$$ Z - 8 = -\tfrac{4}{7}t - \tfrac{5}{7}u, $$

so that when t and u are zero, the value of Z can immediately be determined: $Z - 8 = 0$, or $Z = 8$. The corresponding values of x and y can be read from the last column: $y = 2$ and $x = 1$.

The indicators are now all negative. This means that if either of the variables t or u were given a positive value, Z would decrease. Hence the maximum value of Z is obtained by setting $t = u = 0$, that is by taking the BFS in which $x = 1$ and $y = 2$. In general, *the simplex procedure should be stopped when there remain no positive indicators*.

EXAMPLE 1   A company makes two types of electronic calculators, a standard model, on which its profit is $5, and a deluxe model, on which its profit is $8. The company estimates that at most 1000 calculators per week can be handled by its distribution network. Because of the rapid growth of the calculator industry, there is a shortage of both the parts and the skilled labor necessary to assemble the calculators. The company can obtain a regular weekly supply of only 5000 electronic circuitry units (chips) necessary for the calculators; each regular calculator needs 3 of these chips and each deluxe calculator needs 6. Furthermore, the company has only 2500 work-hours of skilled labor available per week; each regular calculator requires 3 work-hours to assemble and each deluxe calculator needs 2. How many calculators of each type should be made each week in order to maximize the total profit?

Solution   Let x regular calculators and y deluxe calculators be made each week. This requires $3x + 6y$ chips and $3x + 2y$ work-hours of labor. Thus x and y must satisfy the constraints $x \geq 0$, $y \geq 0$, $x + y \leq 1000$, $3x + 6y \leq 5000$, and $3x + 2y \leq 2500$. The weekly profit is then

$$ Z = 5x + 8y. $$

Introducing the slack variables t, u, and v, the constraints can be written in the following form.

$$
\begin{aligned}
x + y + t &\qquad\qquad = 1000 \\
3x + 6y &\quad + u \qquad = 5000 \\
3x + 2y &\qquad\quad + v = 2500
\end{aligned}
$$

where x, y, t, u, and v are all greater than or equal zero. We then have the simplex tableau below.

$$\begin{array}{c c} & \begin{array}{c c c c c} x & y & t & u & v \end{array} \\ \begin{array}{c} t \\ \rightarrow u \\ v \\ \\ \end{array} & \left[\begin{array}{c c c c c|c} 1 & 1 & 1 & 0 & 0 & 1000 \\ 3 & 6 & 0 & 1 & 0 & 5000 \\ 3 & 2 & 0 & 0 & 1 & 2500 \\ 5 & 8 & 0 & 0 & 0 & Z \end{array}\right] \end{array} \quad \begin{array}{l} 1000 \div 1 = 1000 \\ 5000 \div 6 = 833.3 \\ 2500 \div 2 = 1250 \end{array}$$

The largest of the indicators is 8, in the y-column, so that y becomes the entering variable. To decide on the departing variable, we take the ratios of the entries in the last column to those in the y-column: the smallest of these ratios, $5000 \div 6$, occurs in the u-row, so that u is the departing variable.

We must therefore transform the y-column to the form

$$\begin{bmatrix} 0 \\ 1 \\ 0 \\ 0 \end{bmatrix}$$

leaving the t- and v-columns unchanged. The sequence of row operations $R_1 - \frac{1}{6}R_2$, $R_3 - \frac{1}{3}R_2$, $R_4 - \frac{4}{3}R_2$, and $\frac{1}{6}R_2$ achieve this.

$$\begin{array}{c c} & \begin{array}{c c c c c} x & y & t & u & v \end{array} \\ \begin{array}{c} \rightarrow t \\ y \\ v \\ \\ \end{array} & \left[\begin{array}{c c c c c|c} \frac{1}{2} & 0 & 1 & -\frac{1}{6} & 0 & \frac{500}{3} \\ \frac{1}{2} & 1 & 0 & \frac{1}{6} & 0 & \frac{2500}{3} \\ 2 & 0 & 0 & -\frac{1}{3} & 1 & \frac{2500}{3} \\ 1 & 0 & 0 & -\frac{4}{3} & 0 & Z - \frac{20{,}000}{3} \end{array}\right] \end{array} \quad \begin{array}{l} \frac{500}{3} \div \frac{1}{2} \approx 333 \\ \frac{2500}{3} \div \frac{1}{2} \approx 1667 \\ \frac{2500}{3} \div 2 \approx 417 \end{array}$$

The largest positive indicator is now 1, in the x-column, so x is the entering variable for the next step. Finding the ratios involving the last column and the x-column, we find the smallest ratio occurs in the t-row, so t is the departing variable. Consequently we perform the row operations $R_2 - R_1$, $R_3 - 4R_1$, $R_4 - 2R_1$, and $2R_1$.

$$\begin{array}{c c} & \begin{array}{c c c c c} x & y & t & u & v \end{array} \\ \begin{array}{c} x \\ y \\ v \\ \\ \end{array} & \left[\begin{array}{c c c c c|c} 1 & 0 & 2 & -\frac{1}{3} & 0 & \frac{1000}{3} \\ 0 & 1 & -1 & \frac{1}{3} & 0 & \frac{2000}{3} \\ 0 & 0 & -4 & \frac{1}{3} & 1 & \frac{500}{3} \\ 0 & 0 & -2 & -1 & 0 & Z - 7000 \end{array}\right] \end{array}$$

At this stage, all the indicators are negative or zero, so we cannot improve the value of Z by further change of basis. The optimum value of Z is 7000, and is achieved by taking $x = \frac{1000}{3}$ and $y = \frac{2000}{3}$. Thus the company should make 333 regular calculators and 667 deluxe calculators per week.

_____

The simplex method can be summarized by the following sequence of steps.

Step 1 Introduce nonnegative slack variables to turn the inequalities into equations.

Step 2 Construct the simplex tableau.

Step 3 Select the entering variable on the basis of the largest positive indicator.

Step 4 Compute the ratios of the entries in the last column of the tableau to the entries in the column of the entering variable. The smallest nonnegative quotient determines the departing variable.

Step 5 Perform row operations on the tableau to transform the column headed by the entering variable into the form that the column of the departing variable had previously. This should be done without changing the columns headed by the other basic variables.

Step 6 Repeat Steps 3, 4, and 5 until none of the indicators are positive. The maximum value of the objective function will then be given in the lower right entry of the tableau.

The simplex method can be used for problems involving more than two variables and any number of inequalities. When these numbers are large, it is necessary to use a computer to perform the calculations, but problems with three variables can generally be computed by hand without too much difficulty.

EXAMPLE 2 Use the simplex method to find the maximum value of the objective function $Z = 4x + y + 3z$, where x, y, and z are nonnegative variables satisfying the constraints $x + y + z \leq 4$, $3x + y + 2z \leq 7$, and $x + 2y + 4z \leq 9$.

Solution We introduce t, u, and v as nonnegative slack variables such that

$$
\begin{aligned}
x + y + z + t &= 4 \\
3x + y + 2z + u &= 7 \\
x + 2y + 4z + v &= 9.
\end{aligned}
$$

The simplex tableau is given below. The largest indicator is 4, belonging to the x-column, so x becomes the entering variable. The quotients of entries in the last column to those in the x-column are calculated on the right. The smallest quo-

$$
\begin{array}{c}
\begin{array}{cccccc}
x & y & z & t & u & v
\end{array} \\
\begin{array}{c}
t \\
\text{Departing} \rightarrow u \\
\text{Variable} \quad v \\
{}
\end{array}
\left[
\begin{array}{cccccc|c}
1 & 1 & 1 & 1 & 0 & 0 & 4 \\
3 & 1 & 2 & 0 & 1 & 0 & 7 \\
1 & 2 & 4 & 0 & 0 & 1 & 9 \\
4 & 1 & 3 & 0 & 0 & 0 & Z
\end{array}
\right]
\begin{array}{l}
4 \div 1 = 4 \\
7 \div 3 = 2.33 \\
9 \div 1 = 9 \\
{}
\end{array}
\end{array}
$$

↑
Entering
Variable

tient belongs to the u-row, so u becomes the departing variable.

The row operations $R_1 - \frac{1}{3}R_2$, $R_3 - \frac{1}{3}R_2$, $R_4 - \frac{4}{3}R_2$, and $\frac{1}{3}R_2$ then reduce the tableau to the following form.

$$\begin{array}{c} \\ t \\ x \\ \text{Departing} \rightarrow v \\ \text{Variable} \\ \\ \end{array} \begin{array}{cccccc} x & y & z & t & u & v \\ \end{array}$$

	x	y	z	t	u	v		
t	0	$\frac{2}{3}$	$\frac{1}{3}$	1	$-\frac{1}{3}$	0	$\frac{5}{3}$	$\frac{5}{3} \div \frac{1}{3} = 5$
x	1	$\frac{1}{3}$	$\frac{2}{3}$	0	$\frac{1}{3}$	0	$\frac{7}{3}$	$\frac{7}{3} \div \frac{2}{3} = 3.5$
v	0	$\frac{5}{3}$	$\frac{10}{3}$	0	$-\frac{1}{3}$	1	$\frac{20}{3}$	$\frac{20}{3} \div \frac{10}{3} = 2$
	0	$-\frac{1}{3}$	$\frac{1}{3}$	0	$-\frac{4}{3}$	0	$Z - \frac{28}{3}$	

Entering
Variable

The only positive indicator now belongs to z, so this variable enters the basis. According to the quotients calculated on the right, v is the departing variable. We perform the sequence of operations $R_1 - \frac{1}{10}R_3$, $R_2 - \frac{1}{3}R_3$, $R_4 - \frac{1}{10}R_3$, and $\frac{3}{10}R_3$. The result is as follows.

	x	y	z	t	u	v	
t	0	$\frac{1}{2}$	0	1	$-\frac{3}{10}$	$-\frac{1}{10}$	1
x	1	0	0	0	$\frac{1}{10}$	$-\frac{1}{5}$	1
z	0	$\frac{1}{2}$	1	0	$-\frac{1}{10}$	$\frac{3}{10}$	2
	0	$-\frac{1}{2}$	0	0	$-\frac{13}{10}$	$-\frac{1}{10}$	$Z - 10$

The indicators are now all negative, showing that the maximum value of Z is attained for the corresponding BFS. This is given by $y = u = v = 0$ and the values of t, x, and z can be read from the last column. They are $t = 1$, $x = 1$, and $z = 2$. Thus the maximum value of Z is 10 and is achieved when $x = 1$, $y = 0$, and $z = 2$.

We have described the simplex method for a maximization problem. The easiest way of using it to solve a *minimization* problem is to convert the given problem into one involving maximization. For example, suppose we want to find the values of x and y subject to certain constraints that minimize a cost C given by $C = 2x + 6y + 3$. Then we define $Z = -2x - 6y$, so that $C = 3 - Z$. Then when C has its minimum value, Z must be maximum. We can thus replace the objective in the given problem by the new objective: Maximize $Z = -2x - 6y$. The constraints remain unchanged, and we can proceed by the simplex method as described above because we now have a maximization problem.

In our examples of the simplex method, we have started with a BFS in which the slack variables form the basis and the original variables are all zero. Sometimes, however, such a solution is not a feasible one, and the procedure must be modified.

Consider Exercise 10 in Section 2. Here we were required to minimize $Z = x - y$ subject to the constraints $x, y \geq 0$, $x + y \geq 4$, and $x + 2y \leq 10$. Introducing slack variables as usual, we can write the constraints in the form

$$x + y - t = 4, \quad x + 2y + u = 10$$

where $x, y, t, u \geq 0$. Now let us try to find a BFS by setting $x = y = 0$ in order to start the simplex method. We get $t = -4$ and $u = 10$, and this is not a feasible solution because $t < 0$.

It is possible to get around this kind of difficulty by introducing what are called *artificial variables*. If you wish to learn the details of how this is done, consult one of the many specialized books on linear programming.

EXERCISES 4

(1–16) Use the simplex method to solve the linear programming problems given in Exercises 1–6, 13–18, 21, and 22 of Section 2 and Exercises 13 and 14 of Section 3.

17. A nut company sells three different assortments of nuts. The regular assortment contains 80% peanuts, 20% walnuts, and no pecans; the super assortment contains 50% peanuts, 30% walnuts, and 20% pecans; and the deluxe assortment contains 30% peanuts, 30% walnuts, and 40% pecans. The firm has available supplies of up to 4300 pounds of peanuts, 2500 pounds of walnuts, and 2200 pounds of pecans per week. If the profit per pound is 10¢ for each assortment, how many pounds of each should be produced in order to maximize the total profit?

(18–22) Use the simplex method to find the maximum value of the given objective function subject to the constraints stated.

18. $Z = x + y + z;$ $x, y, z \geq 0,$ $x \leq 6,$ $x + 2y + 3z \leq 12,$
$2x + 4y + z \leq 16$

19. $Z = x + 2y - z;$ $x, y, z \geq 0,$ $2x + y + z \leq 4,$ $x + 4y + 2z \leq 5$

20. $Z = 2x - y + 3z;$ $x, y, z \geq 0,$ $x + 3y + z \leq 5,$ $2x + 2y + z \leq 7$

21. $Z = x + y + z;$ $x, y, z \geq 0,$ $x + 2y + z \leq 5,$ $2x + y + 2z \leq 7,$
$2x + 3y + 4z \leq 13$

22. $Z = 3x + y + 4z;$ $x, y, z \geq 0,$ $x + 2y + 2z \leq 9,$ $2x + y + 3z \leq 13,$
$3x + 2y + z \leq 13$

REVIEW EXERCISES FOR CHAPTER 11

1. State whether each of the following is true or false. Replace each false statement by a corresponding true statement.

a. The graph of a linear inequality is a dotted line if the inequality is weak and a solid line if the inequality is a strict one.

b. If $y - 2x \geq 1,$ then $2x - y \leq 1.$

c. If $y - 3x \leq 2,$ then $3x - y > -2.$

d. If $y > a$ and $x > b,$ then $y - x > a - b.$

e. If $y > a$ and $x < b,$ then $y - x > a - b.$

f. If $y - x > a - b,$ then $y > a$ and $x < b.$

g. If $x < a$ and $y < b,$ then $x + y < a + b.$

h. $4x - 2y > 6$ is equivalent to $-2x + y > -3.$

(2–4) Draw the graphs of the following sets of inequalities.

2. $x \geq 0$, $y \geq 0$, $x + y \leq 4$, $x + 2y \leq 6$

3. $1 \leq x \leq 5$, $2 \leq y \leq 5$, $2x + y \geq 5$, $3x + 2y \leq 20$

4. $0 \leq y - x \leq 6$, $x + 2y \geq 4$, $x + y \leq 10$, $x \geq 0$

(5–12) Solve each of the following linear programming problems: (a) by the geometric approach; (b) using the simplex method.

5. Maximize $Z = 5x + 7y$ subject to the conditions $x \geq 0$, $y \geq 0$, $3x + 2y \leq 7$, and $2x + 5y \leq 12$.

6. Maximize $Z = 2y - x$ subject to the conditions $x \geq 0$, $y \geq 0$, $x + y \leq 5$, and $x + 2y \leq 6$.

7. Find the maximum and minimum values of $Z = x - y$ subject to the conditions in Exercise 5.

8. Minimize $Z = 4y - 3x$ subject to the conditions $x \geq 0$, $y \geq 0$, $3x + 4y \leq 4$, and $x + 6y \leq 8$.

9. Maximize $Z = 3x - y$ subject to the conditions $2 \leq x \leq 5$, $y \geq 0$, and $x + y \leq 6$. (*Hint:* Set $x - 2 = z$).

10. Maximize $Z = x + 2y$ subject to the conditions $x \geq 0$, $y \geq 0$, $2y - x \geq -2$, and $4y + x \leq 9$.

11. Minimize $Z = 2y + x$ subject to the conditions $x \geq 0$, $y \geq 0$, $-y + x \geq -1$, and $3y - x \geq -2$.

12. Maximize $Z = 3y + x$ subject to the conditions $x \geq 0$, $y \geq 0$, $5y - x \geq -5$, $y - x \leq 2$, and $y + 2x \leq 4$.

(13–15) Solve each of the following linear programming problems by the simplex method.

13. Maximize $Z = x + 3y + 4z$ subject to the conditions $x, y, z \geq 0$, $x + y + z \leq 4$, $2x + y + 2z \leq 6$, and $3x + 2y + z \leq 8$.

14. Maximize $Z = x - 2y + 2z$ subject to the conditions $x, z \geq 0$, $2 \leq y \leq 5$, $x + 2y + z \leq 14$, and $2x + y + 3z \leq 14$.

15. Find the maximum and minimum values of $Z = x + 2y - z$ subject to the conditions $x + y + z \leq 8$, $x - y + 2z \leq 6$, $2x + y - 3z \leq 4$, and $x, y, z \geq 0$.

16. In Exercises 13 and 14 of Section 1, find the values of x and y that minimize the total delivery cost for the aluminum.

17. For Exercise 15 of Section 1, find the values of x and y that minimize the total delivery cost.

18. In Exercises 18 and 19 of Section 1, find the values of x and y that maximize the total weekly profit.

19. In Exercise 22 of Section 1, find the numbers of the two species of fish that produce the maximum weight of fish.

20. In Exercise 19, suppose that a third species of fish, U, is introduced into the pool. This species consumes 3 units of the food F_1 and 3 units of F_2 per day; the average weight of each fish of species U is 4 lbs. Find the numbers of the three species that produce the maximum weight of fish in the pool.

CALCULUS

PART

THE DERIVATIVE

12-1 INCREMENTS AND RATES

Differential calculus is the study of the changes that occur in a quantity when changes occur in other quantities on which the original quantity depends. The following are examples of such situations.

1. The change in the total cost of operation of a manufacturing plant that results from each additional unit produced.

2. The change in the demand for a certain product that results from an increase of one unit (for example, $1) in the price.

3. The change in the gross national product of a country with each additional year that passes.

DEFINITION Let a variable x have a first value x_1 and a second value x_2. Then the change in the value of x, which is $x_2 - x_1$, is called the **increment** in x and is denoted by Δx.

We use the Greek letter Δ (delta) to denote a change or increment in any variable.

Δx denotes the change in the variable x.

Δp denotes the change in the variable p.

Δq denotes the change in the variable q.

Let $y = f(x)$ be a variable dependent on x. When x has the value x_1, y has the value $y_1 = f(x_1)$. Similarly, when $x = x_2$, y has the value $y_2 = f(x_2)$. The increment in y is then

$$\Delta y = y_2 - y_1$$
$$= f(x_2) - f(x_1)$$

EXAMPLE 1 The volume of gasoline sales from a certain service station depends on the price per gallon. If p is the price per gallon in cents, it is found that the sales volume q (in gallons per day) is given by

$$q = 500(150 - p).$$

Find the increment in sales volume that corresponds to an increase in price from 120 to 130 cents per gallon.

Solution Here p is the independent variable and q is a function of p. The first value of p is $p_1 = 120$ and the second value is $p_2 = 130$. The increment in p is

$$\Delta p = p_2 - p_1 = 130 - 120 = 10.$$

The corresponding values of q are as follows.

$$q_1 = 500(150 - p_1) = 500(150 - 120) = 15,000$$
$$q_2 = 500(150 - p_2) = 500(150 - 130) = 10,000$$

Hence the increment in q is given by

$$\Delta q = q_2 - q_1 = 10,000 - 15,000 = -5000.$$

The increment in q measures the *increase* in q, and the fact that it is negative means that q actually decreases. The sales volume decreases by 5000 gallons per day if the price is increased from 120 to 130 cents.

Solving the equation $\Delta x = x_2 - x_1$ for x_2, we have $x_2 = x_1 + \Delta x$. Using this value of x_2 in the definition of Δy, we get

$$\Delta y = f(x_1 + \Delta x) - f(x_1).$$

Since x_1 can be any arbitrary value of x, we can drop the subscript and write

$$\boxed{\Delta y = f(x + \Delta x) - f(x).}$$

Alternatively, since $f(x) = y$, we can write

$$\boxed{y + \Delta y = f(x + \Delta x).}$$

Let P be the point (x_1, y_1) and Q be the point (x_2, y_2), both of which lie on the graph of the function $y = f(x)$. (See Figure 1.) Then the increment Δx is equal to the horizontal distance from P to Q, whereas Δy is equal to the vertical distance from P to Q. In other words, Δx is the *run* and Δy is the *rise* from P to Q.

In the case illustrated in part (a) of Figure 1, both Δx and Δy are positive. It is possible for either or both Δx and Δy to be negative, and Δy can also be zero. A typical example of a case when $\Delta x > 0$ and $\Delta y < 0$ is illustrated in part (b) of Figure 1.

In some of the applications we shall make later on, we shall want to think of the increment Δx as being small—that is, we shall want to consider only small changes in the independent variable. It is, in fact, often understood that Δx means a small increment in x rather than just any increment. In this section, however, no restriction will be placed on the size of increments considered; they may be as small or as large as we like.

EXAMPLE 2 Given $f(x) = x^2$, find Δy if $x = 1$ and $\Delta x = 0.2$.

Solution Substituting the values of x and Δx in the formula for Δy, we have the following.

$$\Delta y = f(x + \Delta x) - f(x)$$
$$= f(1 + 0.2) - f(1)$$
$$= f(1.2) - f(1)$$
$$= (1.2)^2 - (1)^2$$
$$= 1.44 - 1 = 0.44$$

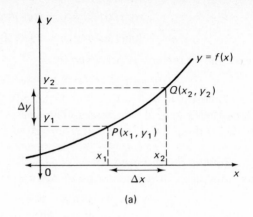

(a)

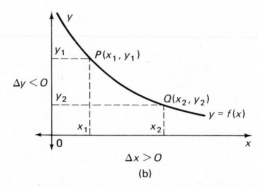

$\Delta y < O$

$\Delta x > O$

(b)

FIGURE 1

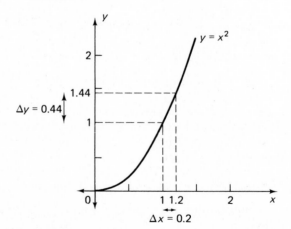

$\Delta x = 0.2$

FIGURE 2

Thus a change of 0.2 in the value of x results in a change in y of 0.44. This is illustrated graphically in Figure 2.

EXAMPLE 3   For the function $y = x^2$, find Δy when $x = 1$ for any increment Δx.

Solution

$$\Delta y = f(x + \Delta x) - f(x)$$
$$= f(1 + \Delta x) - f(1)$$
$$= (1 + \Delta x)^2 - (1)^2$$
$$= (1 + 2\Delta x + (\Delta x)^2) - 1 = 2\Delta x + (\Delta x)^2$$

Since the expression for Δy in Example 3 holds for all increments Δx, we may solve Example 2 by substituting $\Delta x = 0.2$ in this result. We get

$$\Delta y = 2(0.2) + (0.2)^2 = 0.4 + 0.04 = 0.44$$

as before.

EXAMPLE 4   For the function $y = x^2$, find Δy for general values of x and Δx.

Solution
$$\Delta y = f(x + \Delta x) - f(x)$$
$$= (x + \Delta x)^2 - x^2 = 2x\Delta x + (\Delta x)^2$$

It is again clear that we recover the result of Example 3 by substituting $x = 1$ in the expression of Example 4. However, this expression provides the increment in y for any values of x and Δx.

When stated in absolute terms (as in the above examples), changes in the dependent variable are less informative than they would be if stated in relative terms. For example, absolute statements such as, "The temperature dropped by 10°C" or "The revenue will increase by $3000" are less informative than relative statements such as, "The temperature dropped by 10°C in the last five hours" or "The revenue will increase by $3000 dollars if 60 extra units are sold." From these last statements, we not only know by how much the variable (temperature or revenue) changes, but also we can calculate the average *rate* at which it is changing with respect to a second variable. Thus the average drop in temperature during the last five hours is $\frac{10}{5} = 2$°C per hour; and the average increase in revenue if 60 more units are sold is $\frac{3000}{60} = 50$ dollars per unit.

DEFINITION   The **average rate of change** of a function f over an interval x to $x + \Delta x$ is defined by the ratio $\Delta y / \Delta x$. Thus the average rate of change of y with respect to x is

$$\frac{\Delta y}{\Delta x} = \frac{f(x + \Delta x) - f(x)}{\Delta x}.$$

Note: It is necessary that the whole interval from x to $x + \Delta x$ belong to the domain of f.

Graphically, if P is the point $(x, f(x))$ and Q the point $(x + \Delta x, f(x + \Delta x))$ on the graph of $y = f(x)$, then $\Delta y = f(x + \Delta x) - f(x)$ is the rise and Δx is the run from P to Q. From the definition of slope, we can say that $\Delta y / \Delta x$ is the slope of the straight line segment PQ. Thus the average rate of change of y with respect to x is equal to the slope of the chord PQ joining the two points P and Q on the graph of $y = f(x)$. (See Figure 3.) These points correspond to the values x and $x + \Delta x$ of the independent variable.

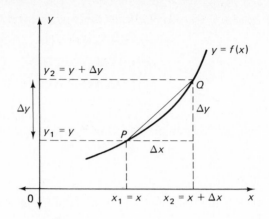

FIGURE 3

EXAMPLE 5   A chemical manufacturer finds that the cost per week of making x tons of a certain fertilizer is given by $C(x) = 20,000 + 40x$ dollars and the revenue obtained from selling x tons per week is given by $R(x) = 100x - 0.01x^2$. The company is currently manufacturing 3100 tons per week, but is considering an increase in production to 3200 tons per week. Calculate the resulting increments in cost, revenue, and profit. Find the average rate of change of profit per extra ton produced.

Solution   The first value of x is 3100 and $x + \Delta x = 3200$.

$$\Delta C = C(x + \Delta x) - C(x)$$
$$= C(3200) - C(3100)$$
$$= [20,000 + 40(3200)] - [20,000 + 40(3100)]$$
$$= 148,000 - 144,000 = 4000$$

$$\Delta R = R(x + \Delta x) - R(x)$$
$$= R(3200) - R(3100)$$
$$= [100(3200) - 0.01(3200)^2] - [100(3100) - 0.01(3100)^2]$$
$$= 217,600 - 213,900 = 3700$$

So the costs increase by \$4000 under the given increment in production, whereas the revenue increases by \$3700.

It is clear from these results that the profit must decrease by \$300. We can see this more fully if we consider that the profits made by the firm are equal to its revenues minus its costs, so the profit $P(x)$ from the sale of x tons of fertilizer is

$$P(x) = R(x) - C(x)$$
$$= 100x - 0.01x^2 - (20,000 + 40x)$$
$$= 60x - 0.01x^2 - 20,000.$$

Consequently the increment in profit when x changes from 3100 to 3200 is

$$\Delta P = P(3200) - P(3100)$$
$$= [60(3200) - 0.01(3200)^2 - 20{,}000]$$
$$- [60(3100) - 0.01(3100)^2 - 20{,}000]$$
$$= 69{,}600 - 69{,}900 = -300.$$

The profit therefore decreases by $300. The average rate of change of profit per extra ton is

$$\frac{\Delta P}{\Delta x} = \frac{-300}{100} = -3$$

where $\Delta x = 3200 - 3100 = 100$. So the profit decreases by an average of $3 per ton under the given increase in production.

EXAMPLE 6   When any object is released from rest and allowed to fall freely under the force of gravity, the distance s (in feet) traveled in time t (in seconds) is given by

$$s(t) = 16t^2.$$

Determine the average speed of the object during the following intervals of time.
(a) The time interval from 3 to 5 seconds.
(b) The fourth second (from $t = 3$ to $t = 4$ seconds).
(c) The interval between the times 3 and $3\frac{1}{2}$ seconds.
(d) The time interval from t to $t + \Delta t$.

Solution   The average speed of any moving object is equal to the distance traveled divided by the interval of time involved. During the interval of time from t to $t + \Delta t$, the distance traveled is the increment Δs, and so the average speed is the ratio $\Delta s / \Delta t$.
(a) Here $t = 3$ and $t + \Delta t = 5$.

$$\frac{\Delta s}{\Delta t} = \frac{s(t + \Delta t) - s(t)}{\Delta t} = \frac{s(5) - s(3)}{5 - 3}$$
$$= \frac{16(5^2) - 16(3^2)}{2} = \frac{400 - 144}{2}$$
$$= \frac{256}{2} = 128$$

Thus during the interval of time $t = 3$ to $t = 5$, the body falls a distance of 256 feet and has an average speed of 128 feet/second.
(b) Here $t = 3$ and $t + \Delta t = 4$.

$$\frac{\Delta s}{\Delta t} = \frac{s(t + \Delta t) - s(t)}{\Delta t} = \frac{s(4) - s(3)}{4 - 3}$$
$$= \frac{16(4^2) - 16(3^2)}{1} = 256 - 144$$
$$= 112$$

The body has an average speed of 112 feet/second during the 4th second of fall.

(c) Here $t = 3$ and $\Delta t = 3\frac{1}{2} - 3 = \frac{1}{2}$.

$$\frac{\Delta s}{\Delta t} = \frac{s(t + \Delta t) - s(t)}{\Delta t} = \frac{16(3\frac{1}{2})^2 - 16(3)^2}{\frac{1}{2}}$$

$$= \frac{196 - 144}{\frac{1}{2}} = \frac{52}{\frac{1}{2}}$$

$$= 104$$

Thus the body has an average speed of 104 feet/second during the time interval 3 to $3\frac{1}{2}$ seconds.

(d) In the general case,

$$\frac{\Delta s}{\Delta t} = \frac{s(t + \Delta t) - s(t)}{\Delta t}$$

$$= \frac{16(t + \Delta t)^2 - 16t^2}{\Delta t}$$

$$= \frac{16[t^2 + 2t \cdot \Delta t + (\Delta t)^2] - 16t^2}{\Delta t}$$

$$= \frac{32t \cdot \Delta t + 16(\Delta t)^2}{\Delta t}$$

$$= 32t + 16\Delta t$$

which is the required average speed during the interval from t to $t + \Delta t$.

All the specific results in Example 6 can be obtained as special cases of part (d) by putting in the appropriate values for t and Δt. For example, the result of part (a) is obtained by setting $t = 3$ and $\Delta t = 2$:

$$\frac{\Delta s}{\Delta t} = 32t + 16\Delta t = 32(3) + 16(2) = 96 + 32 = 128.$$

EXERCISES 1

(1–8) Find the increments of the following functions for the given intervals.

1. $f(x) = 2x + 7;\quad x = 3, \Delta x = 0.2$

2. $f(x) = 2x^2 + 3x - 5;\quad x = 2, \Delta x = 0.5$

3. $g(x) = \dfrac{x^2 - 4}{x - 2};\quad x = 1, \Delta x = 2$

4. $f(t) = \dfrac{900}{t};\quad t = 25, \Delta t = 5$

5. $p(t) = 2000 + \dfrac{500}{1 + t^2};\quad t = 2, \Delta t = 1$

6. $h(x) = ax^2 + bx + c;\quad x$ to $x + \Delta x$

7. $F(x) = x + \dfrac{2}{x};\quad x$ to $x + \Delta x$

8. $G(t) = 300 + \dfrac{5}{t + 1};\quad t$ to $t + \Delta t$

(9–16) Determine the average rate of change of each function for the given interval.

9. $f(x) = 3 - 7x; \quad x = 2, \Delta x = 0.5$

10. $f(x) = 3x^2 - 5x + 1; \quad x = 3, \Delta x = 0.2$

11. $g(x) = \dfrac{x^2 - 9}{x - 3}; \quad x = 2, \Delta x = 0.5$

12. $h(x) = \dfrac{3x^2 + 1}{x}; \quad x = 5, \Delta x = 0.3$

13. $f(t) = \sqrt{4 + t}; \quad t = 5, \Delta t = 1.24$

14. $F(x) = \dfrac{3}{x}; \quad x$ to $x + \Delta x$

15. $G(t) = t^3 + t; \quad t = a$ to $a + h$

16. $f(x) = \dfrac{3}{2x + 1}; \quad x$ to $x + \Delta x$

17. The size of the population of a certain mining town at time t (measured in years) is given by
$$p(t) = 10,000 + 1,000t - 120t^2.$$
Determine the average rate of growth between each pair of times.

   a. $t = 3$ and $t = 5$ years   **b.** $t = 3$ and $t = 4$ years

   c. $t = 3$ and $t = 3\frac{1}{2}$ years   **d.** $t = 3$ and $t = 3\frac{1}{4}$ years

   e. t and $t + \Delta t$ years

18. A manufacturer finds that the cost of producing x items is given by
$$C = 0.001x^3 - 0.3x^2 + 40x + 1000.$$
Find the increment in cost when the number of units is increased from 50 to 60. Find the average cost per additional unit in increasing the production from 50 to 60 units.

19. For the cost function in Exercise 18, find the average cost per additional unit in increasing the production from 90 to 100 units.

20. When the price of a certain item is equal to p, the number of items which can be sold per week (that is, the demand) is given by the formula
$$x = \frac{1000}{\sqrt{p} + 1}.$$
Determine the increment in demand when the price is increased from \$1 to \$2.25.

21. For the demand function in Exercise 20, determine the increment in gross revenue when the price per item is increased from \$4 to \$6.25. (*Note:* Revenue $= xp$) Determine the average increase in total revenue per dollar of increase in price which occurs with this increment in p.

22. During the period from 1950 to 1970, the gross national product of a certain nation was found to be given by the formula $I = 5 + 0.1x + 0.01x^2$ in billions of dollars. (Here the variable x is used to measure years, with $x = 0$ being 1950 and $x = 20$ being 1970.) Determine the average growth in GNP per year between 1955 and 1960.

23. After television was introduced in a certain developing country, the proportion of households owning a television set t years later was found to be given by the formula $p = 1 - e^{-0.1t}$. Find the increment in p between $t = 3$ and $t = 6$ and the average rate of change of p per year.

24. The population of a certain island as a function of time t is found to be given by the formula

$$y = \frac{20,000}{1 + 6(2)^{-0.1t}}.$$

Find the increment in y between $t = 10$ and $t = 30$ and the average population growth per year during that period.

25. A body thrown upwards with a velocity of 100 feet/second reaches a height s after t seconds, where $s = 100t - 16t^2$. Find the average upward velocity in each case.

    a. between $t = 2$ and $t = 3$ seconds   **b.** between $t = 3$ and $t = 5$ seconds

    c. between t and $t + \Delta t$

26. The total weekly revenue R (in dollars) obtained by producing and marketing x units of a certain commodity is given by

$$R = f(x) = 500x - 2x^2.$$

Determine the average change of revenue per extra unit as the number of units produced and marketed per week is increased from 100 to 120.

12-2   LIMITS

        In Example 6 of Section 1, we discussed the average speeds of a falling body during a number of different time intervals. However, in many instances in both science and everyday life, the average speed of a moving object does not provide the information of most importance. For example, if a person traveling in an automobile hits a concrete wall, it is not the average speed from the start to the point where he or she hits the wall, but the speed at the *instant of collision* that determines whether the person will survive the accident.

        What do we mean by the speed of a moving object at a certain instant of time (or *instantaneous speed*, as it is usually called)? Most people would accept that there is such a thing as instantaneous speed—it is precisely the quantity which is measured by the speedometer of an automobile—but the definition of instantaneous speed presents some difficulty. Speed is defined as the distance traveled in a certain interval of time divided by the length of time. But if we are concerned with the speed at a particular instant of time, we ought to consider an interval of time of zero duration. However the distance traveled during such an interval would be zero, and we would obtain $\frac{0}{0}$, a meaningless quantity, for the speed—distance divided by time.

        In order to define the instantaneous speed of a moving object at a certain time t, we proceed as follows. During any interval of time from t to $t + \Delta t$, an increment of distance Δs is traveled. The average speed is $\Delta s/\Delta t$. Now let us imagine that the increment Δt becomes smaller and smaller, so that the corresponding interval of time is very short. Then it is reasonable to suppose that the average speed $\Delta s/\Delta t$ over such a very short interval will be very close to the instantaneous speed at time t. Furthermore, the shorter the interval Δt, the better the average speed will approximate the instantaneous speed. In fact, we can imagine that Δt is allowed to get arbitrarily close to zero, so that the average speed $\Delta s/\Delta t$ can be made as close as we like to the instantaneous speed.

In Example 6 of Section 1, we saw that the average speed during the time interval from t to $t + \Delta t$, for a body falling under gravity is given by

$$\frac{\Delta s}{\Delta t} = 32t + 16\Delta t.$$

Setting $t = 3$, we obtain the average speed during a time interval of length Δt following 3 seconds of fall.

$$\frac{\Delta s}{\Delta t} = 96 + 16\Delta t$$

Some values of this velocity are given in Table 1 for different values of the increment Δt. For example, the average velocity between 3 and 3.1 seconds is obtained by setting $\Delta t = 0.1$: $\Delta s/\Delta t = 96 + 16(0.1) = 96 + 1.6 = 97.6$ feet/second.

TABLE 1

Δt	0.5	0.25	0.1	0.01	0.001
$\Delta s/\Delta t$	104	100	97.6	96.16	96.016

It is clear from the values in Table 1 that as Δt gets smaller and smaller, the average velocity gets closer and closer to 96 feet/second. We can reasonably conclude therefore that 96 feet/second is the instantaneous speed at $t = 3$.

This example is typical of a whole class of problems in which we need to examine the behavior of a certain function as its argument, gets closer and closer to a particular value.* In this case, we are concerned with the behavior of the average speed $\Delta s/\Delta t$ as Δt gets closer and closer to zero. In general, we can be interested in the behavior of a function $f(x)$ of a variable x as x approaches a particular value, say c. When we say that x approaches c, we mean that x takes a succession of values that get arbitrarily close to the value c, although x may never be exactly equal to c. (Note that the average speed $\Delta s/\Delta t$ is not defined for $\Delta t = 0$. We can only take a very, very small value of Δt, never a zero value.) We write $x \longrightarrow c$ to mean x *approaches* c; for example, we would write $\Delta t \longrightarrow 0$ in the above example.

Let us examine the behavior of the function $f(x) = 2x + 3$ as $x \longrightarrow 1$. We shall allow x to assume the succession of values 0.8, 0.9, 0.99, 0.999, and 0.9999, which clearly are getting closer and closer to 1. The corresponding values of $f(x)$ are given in Table 2.

It is clear from the table that as x gets closer to 1, $f(x)$ gets closer to 5. We write $f(x) \longrightarrow 5$ as $x \longrightarrow 1$.

*The term *argument* was defined on page 142 of Chapter 5.

TABLE 2

x	0.8	0.9	0.99	0.999	0.9999
$f(x)$	4.6	4.8	4.98	4.998	4.9998

The values of x considered in Table 2 were all less than 1. In such a case, we say that x approaches 1 from below. We can also consider the alternative case in which x approaches 1 from above, that is, x takes a succession of values getting closer and closer to 1 but always greater than 1. For example, we might allow x to take the sequence of values 1.5, 1.1, 1.01, 1.001, and 1.0001. The corresponding values of $f(x)$ are given in Table 3.

TABLE 3

x	1.5	1.1	1.01	1.001	1.0001
$f(x)$	6	5.2	5.02	5.002	5.0002

Again it is clear that $f(x)$ gets closer and closer to 5 as x approaches 1 from above.

Thus as x approaches 1 either from below or from above, $f(x) = 2x + 3$ approaches 5. We say that the *limit* (or *limiting value*) of $f(x)$ as x approaches 1 is equal to 5. This is written

$$\lim_{x \to 1} (2x + 3) = 5.$$

We now give a formal definition of a limit.

DEFINITION   Let $f(x)$ be a function that is defined for all values of x close to c, except possibly at the point c itself. Then *L is said to be the* **limit** *of $f(x)$ as x approaches c, if the difference between $f(x)$ and L can be made as small as we wish simply by restricting x to be sufficiently close to c.* In symbols, we write

$$\lim_{x \to c} f(x) = L$$

or

$$f(x) \to L \quad \text{as} \quad x \to c.$$

In our earlier example, $f(x) = 2x + 3$, $c = 1$, and $L = 5$. We can make the value of the function $2x + 3$ as close as we like to 5 by choosing x sufficiently close to 1.

In this example, the limiting value of the function $f(x) = 2x + 3$ as $x \to 1$ can be obtained simply by substituting $x = 1$ into the formula $2x + 3$ that defines the function. The question arises as to whether limits can always be found by substituting the value of x into the given expression. The answer to this question is: Sometimes, but not always. The discussion of instantaneous speed on page 397 made this point already. Example 1 illustrates another case when direct substitution does not work.

EXAMPLE 1   If $f(x) = (x^2 - 9)/(x - 3)$, evaluate $\lim\limits_{x \to 3} f(x)$.

Solution   If we substitute $x = 3$ into $f(x)$, we obtain $\frac{0}{0}$, and so we conclude that $f(x)$ is not defined for $x = 3$. However, $\lim\limits_{x \to 3} f(x)$ does exist, since we can write

$$f(x) = \frac{x^2 - 9}{x - 3} = \frac{(x - 3)(x + 3)}{x - 3} = x + 3.$$

Dividing out the factor $x - 3$ is valid for all $x \neq 3$, but, of course, is not valid for $x = 3$. It is readily seen that as x approaches 3, the function $x + 3$ gets closer and closer to 6 in value. Consequently,

$$\lim_{x \to 3} f(x) = \lim_{x \to 3} (x + 3) = 3 + 3 = 6.$$

When evaluating $\lim\limits_{x \to c} f(x)$, it is quite legitimate to divide numerator and denominator by a common factor of $x - c$, as we did in Example 1, in spite of the fact that when $x = c$, these factors are zero. This is because *the limit is concerned with the behavior of $f(x)$ close to $x = c$, but is not concerned at all with the value of f at $x = c$ itself.* As long as $x \neq c$, factors of $x - c$ can be divided out. In fact, Example 1 illustrates a case where $f(x)$ is not even defined for $x = c$ and yet $\lim\limits_{x \to c} f(x)$ exists.

Let us examine the idea of limits from the point of view of the graph of the function involved. We shall first consider our initial example in which $f(x) = 2x + 3$. The graph of this function is a straight line of slope 2 and intercept 3. When $x = 1$, $y = 5$.

Consider any sequence of points $P_1, P_2, P_3, \ldots$, on the graph (see Figure 4) such that the x-coordinates of the points are getting closer to 1. Then clearly the points themselves must get closer to the point (1, 5) on the graph, and their y-

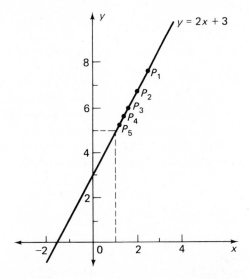

FIGURE 4

coordinates approach the limiting value 5. This corresponds to our earlier statement that $\lim_{x \to 1} (2x + 3) = 5$.

The example $f(x) = (x^2 - 9)/(x - 3)$ is a little different. We saw before that as long as $x \neq 3$, we can write $f(x) = x + 3$. So this function also has a straight line as its graph, with slope of 1 and intercept of 3. However $f(x)$ is not defined for $x = 3$, so that the point $(3, 6)$ is missing from the graph. This fact is indicated in Figure 5 by the use of a small circle at this point on the straight line. Again, if we consider a sequence of points $P_1, P_2, P_3, \ldots$, on the graph with x-coordinates approaching 3, then the points themselves must approach the point $(3, 6)$, even though this point is missing from the graph. Thus, in spite of the fact that $f(3)$ does not exist, the limit of $f(x)$ as $x \longrightarrow 3$ does exist and is equal to 6.

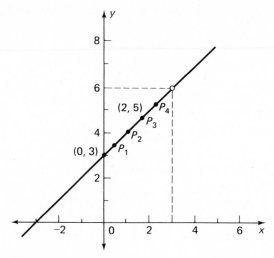

FIGURE 5

In the first of these two examples, we have a function $f(x) = 2x + 3$ for which the limit as $x \longrightarrow 1$ exists and is equal to the value of the function at $x = 1$. In the second example, we have a function $f(x) = (x^2 - 9)/(x - 3)$ for which the limit as $x \longrightarrow 3$ exists, but this limit is not equal to $f(3)$—in fact, $f(3)$ does not even exist in this case. The first function is said to be *continuous* at $x = 1$; the second function is *discontinuous* at $x = 3$. Roughly speaking, a function is continuous at $x = c$ if its graph passes through this value of x without a jump or a break. For example, the graph in Figure 5 does not pass through $x = 3$ without a break because the point $(3, 6)$ is missing from the graph. More precisely, we have the following definition.

DEFINITION A function $f(x)$ is **continuous** at $x = c$ if $f(c)$ and $\lim_{x \to c} f(x)$ both exist and are equal to one another.

We shall discuss continuous and discontinuous functions at greater length in Section 6.

The calculation of the limiting values of functions in more complicated cases rests on a number of theorems concerning limits. We shall now state these theorems and illustrate their significance with a number of examples, but shall not give proofs of them.

THEOREM 1   If m, b, and c are any three constants, then

$$\lim_{x \to c} (mx + b) = mc + b.$$

We note that the function $y = mx + b$ has as its graph a straight line with slope m and y-intercept b. When $x = c$, y is always defined and $y = mc + b$. As x approaches c, the point (x, y) on the graph of this function gets closer and closer to the point $(c, mc + b)$. That is, the value of y gets closer and closer to $mc + b$, as stated in the theorem.

EXAMPLE 2   (a) Taking $m = 2$, $b = 3$, and $c = 1$, we get the result

$$\lim_{x \to 1} (2x + 3) = 2(1) + 3 = 5$$

that we discussed earlier.

(b) Taking $m = 1$, $b = 3$, and $c = 3$, we get

$$\lim_{x \to 3} (x + 3) = 3 + 3 = 6$$

again reproducing a result stated earlier.

THEOREM 2

(a) $\lim\limits_{x \to c} bf(x) = b \lim\limits_{x \to c} f(x)$

(b) $\lim\limits_{x \to c} [f(x)]^n = [\lim\limits_{x \to c} f(x)]^n$ provided that $[f(x)]^n$ is defined for x close to

$$x = c.$$

EXAMPLE 3   (a) $\lim\limits_{x \to 3} x^2 = [\lim\limits_{x \to 3} x]^2$ (by Theorem 2(b))

$\qquad\qquad = 3^2$ (by Theorem 1)

$\qquad\qquad = 9$

(b) $\lim\limits_{x \to 1} 5(2x + 3)^{-1} = 5 \lim\limits_{x \to 1} (2x + 3)^{-1}$ (by Theorem 2(a))

$\qquad\qquad\qquad = 5[\lim\limits_{x \to 1} (2x + 3)]^{-1}$ (by Theorem 2(b))

$\qquad\qquad\qquad = 5[2(1) + 3]^{-1}$ (by Theorem 1)

$\qquad\qquad\qquad = 5(5)^{-1} = 1$

(c) $\lim\limits_{x \to 3} \dfrac{(x^2 - 9)^3}{12(x - 3)^3} = \dfrac{1}{12} \lim\limits_{x \to 3} \left(\dfrac{x^2 - 9}{x - 3}\right)^3$ (by Theorem 2(a))

$\qquad\qquad\qquad = \dfrac{1}{12}\left[\lim\limits_{x \to 3} \left(\dfrac{x^2 - 9}{x - 3}\right)\right]^3$ (by Theorem 2(b))

$\qquad\qquad\qquad = \dfrac{1}{12}(6)^3$ (by the result of Example 1)

$\qquad\qquad\qquad = 18$

THEOREM 3

(a) $\lim\limits_{x \to c} [f(x) + g(x)] = \lim\limits_{x \to c} f(x) + \lim\limits_{x \to c} g(x)$

(b) $\lim\limits_{x \to c} [f(x) - g(x)] = \lim\limits_{x \to c} f(x) - \lim\limits_{x \to c} g(x)$

(c) $\lim\limits_{x \to c} [f(x)g(x)] = \left[\lim\limits_{x \to c} f(x)\right]\left[\lim\limits_{x \to c} g(x)\right]$

(d) $\lim\limits_{x \to c} \left[\dfrac{f(x)}{g(x)}\right] = \dfrac{\left[\lim\limits_{x \to c} f(x)\right]}{\left[\lim\limits_{xr \to c} g(x)\right]}$

provided that the denominator on the right side is different from zero.

EXAMPLE 4
(a) $\lim\limits_{x \to 3} (x^2 + 2x) = \lim\limits_{x \to 3} x^2 + \lim\limits_{x \to 3} 2x$ (by Theorem 3(a))

$= 3^2 + 2(3)$ (by Example 3(a) and Theorem 1)

$= 9 + 6 = 15$

(b) $\lim\limits_{x \to -1} \left(2x^3 - \dfrac{3}{x - 1}\right) = \lim\limits_{x \to -1} (2x^3) - \lim\limits_{x \to -1} \left(\dfrac{3}{x - 1}\right)$

(by Theorem 3(b))

$= 2 \lim\limits_{x \to -1} x^3 - 3 \lim\limits_{x \to -1} (x - 1)^{-1}$

(by Theorem 2(a))

$= 2\left[\lim\limits_{x \to -1} x\right]^3 - 3\left[\lim\limits_{x \to -1} (x - 1)\right]^{-1}$

(by Theorem 2(b))

$= 2(-1)^3 - 3(-1 - 1)^{-1}$

(by Theorem 1)

$= -2 + \tfrac{3}{2} = -\tfrac{1}{2}$

(c) $\lim\limits_{x \to 3} \dfrac{(x - 1)(x^2 - 9)}{x - 3} = \lim\limits_{x \to 3} (x - 1) \lim\limits_{x \to 3} \left(\dfrac{x^2 - 9}{x - 3}\right)$

(by Theorem 3(c))

$= \lim\limits_{x \to 3} (x - 1) \lim\limits_{x \to 3} (x + 3)$

$= (3 - 1)(3 + 3) = 12$ (by Theorem 1)

(d) $\lim\limits_{x \to -2} \left(\dfrac{x^2}{x - 1}\right) = \dfrac{\lim\limits_{x \to -2} x^2}{\lim\limits_{x \to -2} (x - 1)}$ (by Theorem 3(d))

$= \dfrac{\left(\lim\limits_{x \to -2} x\right)^2}{(-2 - 1)}$ (by Theorems 2(b) and 1)

$= \dfrac{(-2)^2}{-3}$ (by Theorem 1)

$= -\tfrac{4}{3}$

It probably will not have escaped your notice that in most of these examples the limiting value of the function involved could have been obtained simply by substituting the limiting value of x into the given function. This method of simple substitution will in fact always produce the right answer when the function whose limit is being evaluated is continuous. This follows directly from the definition of a continuous function. All polynomials are continuous functions, and any rational function is continuous except at points where the denominator vanishes. So in the case of a rational function, we can always evaluate a limiting value by substitution, provided that the result after substitution is a well-defined number and is not of the form $\frac{0}{0}$ or constant/0. This same remark also applies to algebraic functions of x provided that they are defined on some interval which includes the limiting value of x.

In the examples that follow, we shall evaluate limits by simple substitution. However, it is recommended that you do a number of exercises using the above limit theorems in the manner illustrated by the preceding examples. The reason for this is that we shall encounter cases in later chapters in which use of the theorems plays an essential role, and the limits will not be capable of evaluation by substitution. Only after having mastered the use of the theorems should you adopt the method of substitution as a means of evaluating limits.

It may happen that upon substituting $x = c$ into $f(x)$, we obtain a result of the type constant/0. For example, suppose we tried to evaluate $\lim_{x \to 0} \left(\frac{1}{x} \right)$. Substituting $x = 0$, we obtain the result $1/0$, which is not defined. In such a case we would say that *the limit does not exist*. The function $1/x$ becomes indefinitely large as x approaches zero, and does not approach any limiting value. This can be seen from Table 4, which shows a series of values of $1/x$ as

TABLE 4

x	1	0.5	0.1	0.02	0.002	0.0002
$\dfrac{1}{x}$	1	2	10	50	500	5000

x takes a succession of smaller and smaller values. It is clear that the corresponding values of $1/x$ get larger and larger and cannot approach any finite limiting value.

A further, very important case, that can arise is that we obtain the result $0/0$, which is undefined, upon substituting $x = c$ into $f(x)$. Limits of this type can often be evaluated by dividing out common factors of $(x - c)$ from numerator and denominator of fractions that occur in $f(x)$. This technique was illustrated earlier in the section, and other examples will now be given.

EXAMPLE 5   Evaluate

$$\lim_{x \to -1} \frac{x^2 + 3x + 2}{1 - x^2}.$$

Solution   Letting $x = -1$, we have

$$\frac{(-1)^2 + 3(-1) + 2}{1 - (-1)^2} = \frac{1 - 3 + 2}{1 - 1} = \frac{0}{0}.$$

Consequently, we factor the numerator and denominator and cancel the factor $x + 1$ before substituting $x = -1$.

$$\lim_{x \to -1} \frac{x^2 + 3x + 2}{1 - x^2} = \lim_{x \to -1} \frac{(x + 1)(x + 2)}{(1 - x)(1 + x)}$$

$$= \lim_{x \to -1} \frac{x + 2}{1 - x} = \frac{-1 + 2}{1 - (-1)} = \frac{1}{2}$$

EXAMPLE 6   Evaluate

$$\lim_{x \to 0} \frac{\sqrt{1 + x} - 1}{x}.$$

Solution   When we substitute 0 for x, we get

$$\frac{\sqrt{1 + 0} - 1}{0} = \frac{0}{0}.$$

In this case, we cannot factor the numerator directly to get the factor x that is needed to cancel the x in the denominator. We overcome this difficulty by rationalizing the numerator, which is accomplished by multiplying the numerator and denominator by $(\sqrt{1 + x} + 1)$.*

$$\lim_{x \to 0} \frac{\sqrt{1 + x} - 1}{x} = \lim_{x \to 0} \frac{\sqrt{1 + x} - 1}{x} \cdot \frac{\sqrt{1 + x} + 1}{\sqrt{1 + x} + 1}$$

$$= \lim_{x \to 0} \frac{(\sqrt{1 + x})^2 - 1^2}{x(\sqrt{1 + x} + 1)} = \lim_{x \to 0} \frac{(1 + x) - 1}{x(\sqrt{1 + x} + 1)}$$

$$= \lim_{x \to 0} \frac{x}{x(\sqrt{1 + x} + 1)}$$

$$= \lim_{x \to 0} \frac{1}{\sqrt{1 + x} + 1}$$

$$= \frac{1}{\sqrt{1 + 0} + 1} = \frac{1}{2}$$

Note that in these examples, the final limit has been evaluated by substitution. In reality, the theorems on limits underlie this substitution procedure.

EXERCISES 2

(1–18)   Evaluate the following limits.

1. $\lim_{x \to 2} (3x^2 + 7x - 1)$ 2. $\lim_{x \to -1} (2x^2 + 3x + 1)$

3. $\lim_{x \to 3} \dfrac{x + 1}{x - 2}$ 4. $\lim_{x \to 3} \dfrac{x^2 + 1}{x + 3}$

*See Section 5 of Chapter 1.

5. $\displaystyle \lim_{x \to 5} \frac{x^2 - 25}{\sqrt{x^2 + 11}}$

6. $\displaystyle \lim_{x \to 4} \frac{x^2 - 16}{x - 4}$

7. $\displaystyle \lim_{x \to -2} \frac{x^2 - 4}{x^2 + 3x + 2}$

8. $\displaystyle \lim_{x \to 1} \frac{x^2 - 1}{x^2 + x - 2}$

9. $\displaystyle \lim_{x \to 3} \frac{x^2 - 5x + 6}{x - 3}$

10. $\displaystyle \lim_{x \to 1} \frac{x^3 - 1}{x^2 - 1}$

11. $\displaystyle \lim_{x \to 2} \frac{x + 1}{x - 2}$

12. $\displaystyle \lim_{x \to 0} \frac{2x^2 + 5x + 7}{x}$

13. $\displaystyle \lim_{x \to 0} \frac{\sqrt{4 + x} - 2}{x}$

14. $\displaystyle \lim_{x \to 2} \frac{\sqrt{x + 7} - 3}{x - 2}$

15. $\displaystyle \lim_{x \to 1} \frac{\sqrt{x + 3} - 2}{x^2 - 1}$

16. $\displaystyle \lim_{x \to 0} \frac{\sqrt{9 + x} - 3}{x^2 + 2x}$

17. $\displaystyle \lim_{x \to 0} \frac{\sqrt{1 + x} - 1}{\sqrt{4 + x} - 2}$

18. $\displaystyle \lim_{x \to 1} \frac{\sqrt{2 - x} - 1}{2 - \sqrt{x + 3}}$

(19–20) Evaluate $\displaystyle \lim_{x \to c} f(x)$ where $f(x)$ and c are given below.

19. $f(x) = \begin{cases} \dfrac{x^2 - 1}{x - 1} & \text{for } x \neq 1 \\ 3 & \text{for } x = 1 \end{cases}, \quad c = 1$

20. $f(x) = \begin{cases} \dfrac{x - 9}{\sqrt{x} - 3} & \text{for } x \neq 9 \\ 7 & \text{for } x = 9 \end{cases}, \quad c = 9$

(21–25) The functions $f(x)$ and the values of a are given below. Evaluate

$$\lim_{h \to 0} \frac{f(a + h) - f(a)}{h}$$

in each case.

21. $f(x) = 2x^2 + 3x + 1, \quad a = 1$

22. $f(x) = 3x^2 - 5x + 7, \quad a = 2$

23. $f(x) = x^2 - 1, \quad a = 0$

24. $f(x) = x^2 + x + 1, \quad a = x$

25. $f(x) = 2x^2 + 5x + 1, \quad a = x$

26. A body falls from rest under gravity. What is the instantaneous velocity after $1\frac{1}{2}$ seconds?

27. A ball is thrown vertically upwards with velocity 40 feet/second. The distance traveled in feet after t seconds is given by the formula $s = 40t - 16t^2$. Find the instantaneous velocity: (a) after 1 second; (b) after 2 seconds.

28. In Exercise 27, find the instantaneous velocity after t seconds. What occurs when $t = \frac{5}{4}$? What is the instantaneous velocity when $t = \frac{5}{2}$?

12-3 THE DERIVATIVE

In Section 2, we saw how the definition of the instantaneous velocity of a moving object leads naturally to a limiting process. The average velocity $\Delta s / \Delta t$ is first found for an interval of time from t to $t + \Delta t$, and then its limiting value is calculated as $\Delta t \to 0$. We might describe $\Delta s / \Delta t$ as the *average rate* of change of position, s, with respect to time, and its limit is the instantaneous rate of change of s with respect to t.

Now there are many examples of processes that develop in time and that can be described by one or more functions of t. In each case, a corresponding definition may be given of the rate of change of the appropriate quantity with respect to time. Example 1 illustrates a typical case in point.

EXAMPLE 1   During the 10-year period from 1960 to 1970, the population of a certain city was found to be given by the formula

$$P(t) = 1 + 0.03t + 0.001t^2$$

where P is in millions and t is time measured in years from the beginning of 1960. Find the instantaneous rate of growth at the beginning of 1965.

Solution   We want the rate of growth at $t = 5$. The increment in P between $t = 5$ and $t = 5 + \Delta t$ is

$$\begin{aligned}
\Delta P &= P(5 + \Delta t) - P(5) \\
&= [1 + 0.03(5 + \Delta t) + 0.001(5 + \Delta t)^2] \\
&\quad - [1 + 0.03(5) + 0.001(5)^2] \\
&= 1 + 0.15 + 0.03\,\Delta t + 0.001(25 + 10\,\Delta t + (\Delta t)^2) \\
&\quad - [1 + 0.15 + 0.001(25)] \\
&= 0.04\,\Delta t + 0.001\,(\Delta t)^2.
\end{aligned}$$

The average rate of growth during this time interval is therefore given by

$$\frac{\Delta P}{\Delta t} = 0.04 + 0.001\,\Delta t.$$

In order to obtain the instantaneous rate of growth, we must take the limit as $\Delta t \to 0$.

$$\lim_{\Delta t \to 0} \frac{\Delta P}{\Delta t} = \lim_{\Delta t \to 0} [0.04 + 0.001\,\Delta t] = 0.04$$

Thus at the beginning of 1965, the population of the city was growing at the rate of 0.04 million per year (that is, 40,000 per year).

The instantaneous rate of change of a function such as the one in Example 1 is one case of what we call the *derivative* of a function. We shall now give a formal definition of the derivative.

DEFINITION   Let $y = f(x)$ be a given function. Then the **derivative of y with respect to x**, denoted by dy/dx, is defined to be

$$\frac{dy}{dx} = \lim_{\Delta x \to 0} \frac{\Delta y}{\Delta x}$$

or

$$\frac{dy}{dx} = \lim_{\Delta x \to 0} \frac{f(x + \Delta x) - f(x)}{\Delta x}$$

provided this limit exists.

The derivative is also given the name **differential coefficient**, and the operation of calculating the derivative of a function is called **differentiation**.

If the derivative of a function f exists at a particular point, then we say that f is **differentiable** at that point.

The derivative of $y = f(x)$ with respect to x is also denoted by any one of the following symbols.

$$\frac{d}{dx}(y), \quad \frac{df}{dx}, \quad \frac{d}{dx}(f), \quad y', \quad f'(x), \quad D_x y, \quad D_x f$$

Every one of these notations means exactly the same thing as dy/dx.

Note: dy/dx represents a single symbol and should not be interpreted as the ratio of two quantities dy and dx. To amplify the notation further, note that dy/dx denotes the derivative of y with respect to (w.r.t.) x if y is a function of the independent variable x; dC/dq denotes the derivative of C w.r.t. q if C is a function of the independent variable q; dx/du denotes the derivative of x w.r.t. u if x is a function of the independent variable u.

From the definition,

$$\frac{dy}{dx} = \lim_{\Delta x \to 0} \frac{\Delta y}{\Delta x}, \quad \frac{dC}{dq} = \lim_{\Delta q \to 0} \frac{\Delta C}{\Delta q} \quad \text{and} \quad \frac{dx}{du} = \lim_{\Delta u \to 0} \frac{\Delta x}{\Delta u}.$$

In order to calculate the derivative dy/dx, we can proceed as follows:

1. Calculate $y = f(x)$ and $y + \Delta y = f(x + \Delta x)$;
2. Subtract the first from the second to get Δy and simplify the result;
3. Divide Δy by Δx and then take the limit of the resulting expression as $\Delta x \to 0$.

EXAMPLE 2 Find the derivative of $2x^2 + 3x + 1$ with respect to x.

Solution Let $y = f(x) = 2x^2 + 3x + 1$. Then

$$\begin{aligned}
y + \Delta y = f(x + \Delta x) &= 2(x + \Delta x)^2 + 3(x + \Delta x) + 1 \\
&= 2[x^2 + 2x \cdot \Delta x + (\Delta x)^2] + 3x + 3\Delta x + 1 \\
&= 2x^2 + 4x \cdot \Delta x + 2(\Delta x)^2 + 3x + 3\Delta x + 1 \\
&= 2x^2 + 3x + 1 + \Delta x(4x + 3 + 2\Delta x).
\end{aligned}$$

Subtracting y from $y + \Delta y$, we have

$$\Delta y = \Delta x(4x + 3 + 2\Delta x)$$

and so $\Delta y/\Delta x = 4x + 3 + 2\Delta x$. Thus

$$\frac{dy}{dx} = \lim_{\Delta x \to 0} \frac{\Delta y}{\Delta x} = \lim_{\Delta x \to 0} (4x + 3 + 2\Delta x)$$
$$= 4x + 3.$$

If $f(x) = 2x^2 + 3x + 1$, then $f'(x) = 4x + 3$. In particular, for example, $f'(-2) = 4(-2) + 3 = -5$.

Geometric Interpretation

We have already seen that in the case where the independent variable in a function $y = f(t)$ represents time, the derivative dy/dt gives the instantaneous rate of change of y. For example, if $s = f(t)$ represents the distance traveled by a moving object, then ds/dt provides the instantaneous velocity. Apart from this kind of application of derivatives, however, they also have a very great significance from a geometric point of view.

If P and Q are the two points $(x, f(x))$ and $(x + \Delta x, f(x + \Delta x))$ on the graph of $y = f(x)$, then, as stated in Section 1, the ratio

$$\frac{\Delta y}{\Delta x} = \frac{f(x + \Delta x) - f(x)}{\Delta x}$$

represents the slope of the line segment PQ. As Δx becomes smaller and smaller, the point Q moves closer and closer to P and the chord segment PQ becomes more and more nearly a tangent. As $\Delta x \longrightarrow 0$, the slope of the chord PQ approaches the slope of the tangent line at P. Thus,

$$\lim_{\Delta x \to 0} \frac{\Delta y}{\Delta x} = \frac{dy}{dx}$$

represents the slope of the tangent line to $y = f(x)$ at the point $P(x, f(x))$. (See Figure 6.) As long as the curve $y = f(x)$ is "smooth" at P; that is, as long as we can draw a nonvertical tangent at P, the limit will exist.

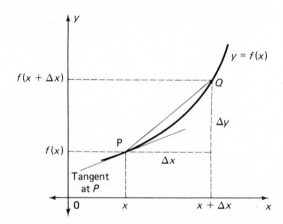

FIGURE 6

EXAMPLE 3   Find the slope of the tangent and the equation of the tangent line to the curve $y = \sqrt{x}$ at the point $(4, 2)$.

Solution   First let us calculate the derivative dy/dx. We have $y = \sqrt{x}$, so that $y + \Delta y = \sqrt{x + \Delta x}$ and therefore

$$\Delta y = \sqrt{x + \Delta x} - \sqrt{x}.$$

Thus

$$\frac{\Delta y}{\Delta x} = \frac{\sqrt{x + \Delta x} - \sqrt{x}}{\Delta x}.$$

We wish to take the limit as $\Delta x \to 0$; before doing so, we must rationalize the numerator. We do this by multiplying numerator and denominator by $(\sqrt{x + \Delta x} + \sqrt{x})$.

$$\frac{\Delta y}{\Delta x} = \frac{(\sqrt{x + \Delta x} - \sqrt{x})(\sqrt{x + \Delta x} + \sqrt{x})}{\Delta x(\sqrt{x + \Delta x} + \sqrt{x})}$$

$$= \frac{(\sqrt{x + \Delta x})^2 - (\sqrt{x})^2}{\Delta x(\sqrt{x + \Delta x} + \sqrt{x})}$$

$$= \frac{(x + \Delta x) - x}{\Delta x(\sqrt{x + \Delta x} + \sqrt{x})} = \frac{1}{\sqrt{x + \Delta x} + \sqrt{x}}$$

Therefore

$$\frac{dy}{dx} = \lim_{\Delta x \to 0} \frac{\Delta y}{\Delta x} = \lim_{\Delta x \to 0} \frac{1}{\sqrt{x + \Delta x} + \sqrt{x}}$$

$$= \frac{1}{\sqrt{x} + \sqrt{x}} = \frac{1}{2\sqrt{x}}.$$

Hence $f'(x) = 1/2\sqrt{x}$. When $x = 4$, $f'(4) = 1/2\sqrt{4} = \frac{1}{4}$. Thus the slope of the tangent to $y = \sqrt{x}$ when $x = 4$ is $\frac{1}{4}$.

To obtain the equation of the tangent line, we can use the point-slope formula

$$y - y_1 = m(x - x_1)$$

with slope $m = \frac{1}{4}$ and $(x_1, y_1) = (4, 2)$. (See Figure 7.) We obtain

$$y - 2 = \tfrac{1}{4}(x - 4)$$

$$y = \tfrac{1}{4}x + 1$$

which is the required equation.

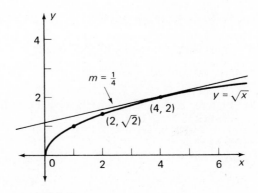

FIGURE 7

EXAMPLE 4   Evaluate dy/dx for the cubic function

$$y = Ax^3 + Bx^2 + Cx + D$$

where A, B, C, and D are four constants.

Solution   Replacing x by $x + \Delta x$, we find that

$$y + \Delta y = A(x + \Delta x)^3 + B(x + \Delta x)^2 + C(x + \Delta x) + D$$
$$= A[x^3 + 3x^2\,\Delta x + 3x\,(\Delta x)^2 + (\Delta x)^3]$$
$$+ B[x^2 + 2x\,\Delta x + (\Delta x)^2] + C(x + \Delta x) + D.$$

If we now subtract the given expression for y, we find that

$$\Delta y = (y + \Delta y) - y$$
$$= A[x^3 + 3x^2\,\Delta x + 3x(\Delta x)^2 + (\Delta x)^3]$$
$$+ B[x^2 + 2x\,\Delta x + (\Delta x)^2]$$
$$+ C(x + \Delta x) + D - (Ax^3 + Bx^2 + Cx + D)$$
$$= A[3x^2\,\Delta x + 3x\,(\Delta x)^2 + (\Delta x)^3] + B[2x\,\Delta x + (\Delta x)^2] + C\Delta x.$$

Therefore

$$\frac{\Delta y}{\Delta x} = A[3x^2 + 3x\,\Delta x + (\Delta x)^2] + B(2x + \Delta x) + C.$$

Allowing Δx to approach zero, we see that the three terms on the right that involve Δx as a factor all approach zero in the limit. The remaining terms give the following result.

$$\frac{dy}{dx} = \lim_{\Delta x \to 0} \frac{\Delta y}{\Delta x} = 3Ax^2 + 2Bx + C \tag{1}$$

From the result of this example, it is possible to retrieve some of the results in preceding examples. For instance, if we set $A = 0$, $B = 2$, $C = 3$, and $D = 1$, the cubic function in Example 4 becomes $y = 0x^3 + 2x^2 + 3x + 1 = 2x^2 + 3x + 1$, which was discussed in Example 2. From Equation (1), we obtain

$$\frac{dy}{dx} = 3Ax^2 + 2Bx + C = 3(0)x^2 + 2(2)x + 3 = 4x + 3$$

which agrees with the results of Example 2.

EXERCISES 3

(1–8)   Find the derivatives of the following functions w.r.t. the independent variables involved.

1. $f(x) = 2x - 5$ 2. $f(x) = 2 - 5x$

3. $g(u) = 3u^2 + 1$ 4. $h(t) = t^2 + t + 1$

5. $f(t) = \dfrac{1}{t + 1}$ 6. $g(x) = \dfrac{2}{1 - x}$

7. $g(y) = \dfrac{1}{y^2}$ 8. $H(u) = \dfrac{u}{u + 1}$

9. Find dy/dx if: (a) $y = 3 - 2x^2$; (b) $y = 3x + 7$.

10. Find du/dt if: (a) $u = 2t + 3$; (b) $u = 1/(2t + 1)$.

11. Find dx/dy if: (a) $x = \sqrt{y}$; (b) $x = (y + 1)/y^2$.

12. Find dp/dq if: (a) $p = 1/(3 + 2q)$; (b) $p = 1/\sqrt{q}$.

13. Find $f'(2)$ if $f(x) = 5 - 2x$. **14.** Find $g'(4)$ if $g(x) = (x + 1)^2$.

15. Find $F'(3)$ if $F(t) = t^2 - 3t$. **16.** Find $G'(1)$ if $G(u) = u^2 - u + 3$.

17. Find $h'(0)$ if $h(y) = y^2 + 7y$. **18.** Find $H'(2)$ if $H(t) = 1/(t - 1)$.

(19–22) Find the slope of the tangent line to the graphs of the following functions at the indicated points. Determine the equation of the tangent line in each case.

19. $y = \dfrac{x + 1}{x}$ at $x = 1$ **20.** $f(x) = \sqrt{x - 1}$ at $x = 5$

21. $f(x) = \dfrac{x + 1}{x - 1}$ at $x = 2$ **22.** $g(t) = 5t^2 + 1$ at $t = -3$

23. The sales volume of a particular phonograph record is given as a function of time t by the formula

$$S(t) = 10,000 + 2,000t - 200t^2$$

where t is measured in weeks and S is the number of records sold per week. Determine the rate at which S is changing when: (a) $t = 0$; (b) $t = 4$; (c) $t = 8$.

24. A certain population grows according to the formula

$$p(t) = 30,000 + 60t^2$$

where t is measured in years. Find the growth rate when: (a) $t = 2$; (b) $t = 0$; (c) $t = 5$.

12-4 DERIVATIVES OF POWER FUNCTIONS

It is clear from the previous section that finding derivatives of functions by direct use of the definition of the derivative is not always very easy and is generally time consuming. This task can be appreciably lightened by the use of certain standard formulas. In this section, we shall develop formulas for finding the derivatives of power functions and combinations of power functions.

Let us begin by going back to Example 4 in Section 3. By taking special cases for the coefficients A, B, C, and D in that example, we obtain the following results.

THEOREM 1
 (a) The derivative of a constant function is zero.
 (b) If $y = x$, then $dy/dx = 1$.
 (c) If $y = x^2$, then $dy/dx = 2x$.
 (d) If $y = x^3$, then $dy/dx = 3x^2$.

PROOF
 (a) In the function $y = Ax^3 + Bx^2 + Cx + D$, let A, B, and C equal zero. Then $y = D$, a constant function. The general expression for dy/dx is $3Ax^2 + 2Bx + C$ (from Example 4 of Section 3) and this is zero when $A = B = C = 0$.

(b) If we let $A = B = D = 0$ and $C = 1$, we get $y = x$ and $dy/dx = 1$, as required.

(c) and **(d)** are proved in a similar manner.

Geometrically, part (a) of Theorem 1 asserts that the slope of the line $y = c$ is zero at every point on it. This is obviously true because the graph of $y = c$ is a horizontal line, and any horizontal line has zero slope.

EXAMPLE 1 $\dfrac{d}{dx}(6) = 0$ and $\dfrac{d}{dt}(\tfrac{3}{2}) = 0$

From the results in parts (a)–(d) of Theorem 1, we can observe a certain pattern developing for the derivatives of powers of x, $y = x^n$. We have the following result that holds for any real value of n.

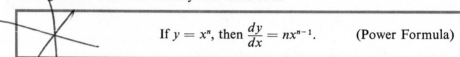

$$\text{If } y = x^n, \text{ then } \frac{dy}{dx} = nx^{n-1}. \qquad \text{(Power Formula)}$$

In words, *to find the derivative of any constant power of x, we decrease the power of x by 1 and multiply by the original exponent of x.*

At the end of this section, we shall prove this formula for the derivative of x^n for the case when n is a positive integer. It is, however, true for all real values of n.

EXAMPLE 2   **(a)** $\dfrac{d}{dx}(x^7) = 7x^{7-1} = 7x^6$

(b) $\dfrac{d}{dy}(y^{3/2}) = \tfrac{3}{2}y^{3/2-1} = \tfrac{3}{2}y^{1/2}$

(c) $\dfrac{d}{dt}\left(\dfrac{1}{\sqrt{t}}\right) = \dfrac{d}{dt}(t^{-1/2}) = -\tfrac{1}{2}t^{-1/2-1} = -\tfrac{1}{2}t^{-3/2}$

(d) $\dfrac{d}{du}\left(\dfrac{1}{u^2}\right) = \dfrac{d}{du}(u^{-2}) = -2u^{-2-1} = -2u^{-3} = -\dfrac{2}{u^3}$

(e) $\dfrac{d}{dx}(x) = \dfrac{d}{dx}(x^1) = 1 \cdot x^{1-1} = x^0 = 1$ (because $x^0 = 1$)

THEOREM 2   If $u(x)$ is a differentiable function of x and c is a constant, then

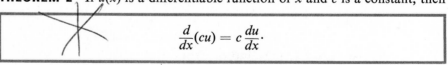

$$\frac{d}{dx}(cu) = c\frac{du}{dx}.$$

That is, *the derivative of the product of a constant and a function of x is equal to the product of the constant and the derivative of the function.*

EXAMPLE 3   **(a)** $\dfrac{d}{dx}(cx^n) = c\dfrac{d}{dx}(x^n) = c(nx^{n-1}) = ncx^{n-1}$

(b) $\dfrac{d}{dt}\left(\dfrac{4}{t}\right) = \dfrac{d}{dt}(4t^{-1}) = 4\dfrac{d}{dt}(t^{-1}) = 4(-1 \cdot t^{-2}) = -\dfrac{4}{t^2}$

(c) $\frac{d}{du}(2\sqrt{u}) = \frac{d}{du}(2u^{1/2}) = 2\frac{d}{du}(u^{1/2}) = 2 \cdot \frac{1}{2}u^{-1/2} = u^{-1/2}$

THEOREM 3 If $u(x)$ and $u(x)$ are two differentiable functions of x, then

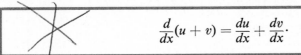

$$\frac{d}{dx}(u + v) = \frac{du}{dx} + \frac{dv}{dx}.$$

In other words, *the derivative of the sum of two functions is equal to the sum of the derivatives of the two functions.*

EXAMPLE 4   Find dy/dx if $y = x^2 + \sqrt{x}$.

Solution   The given function is the sum of x^2 and $x^{1/2}$. Therefore, by Theorem 3, we can differentiate these two powers separately.

$$\frac{dy}{dx} = \frac{d}{dx}(x^2) + \frac{d}{dx}(x^{1/2})$$

$$= 2x + \tfrac{1}{2}x^{-1/2}$$

This theorem can be readily extended to the sum of any number of functions and also to the differences between functions. For example,

$$\frac{d}{dx}(u - v) = \frac{du}{dx} - \frac{dv}{dx}$$

$$\frac{d}{dx}(u + v - w) = \frac{du}{dx} + \frac{dv}{dx} - \frac{dw}{dx}$$

and so on.

EXAMPLE 5   Find the derivative of $3x^4 - 5x^3 + 7x + 2$ w.r.t. x.

Solution   Let $y = 3x^4 - 5x^3 + 7x + 2$.

Then

$$\frac{dy}{dx} = \frac{d}{dx}(3x^4 - 5x^3 + 7x + 2)$$

$$= \frac{d}{dx}(3x^4) - \frac{d}{dx}(5x^3) + \frac{d}{dx}(7x) + \frac{d}{dx}(2).$$

We have used Theorem 3 to express the derivative of the sum $3x^4 - 5x^3 + 7x + 2$ as the sum of the derivatives of $3x^4$, $-5x^3$, $7x$, and 2. Evaluating these four derivatives, we obtain

$$\frac{dy}{dx} = 3(4x^3) - 5(3x^2) + 7(1x^0) + 0$$

$$= 12x^3 - 15x^2 + 7$$

because $x^0 = 1$.

Expressions involving parentheses can be differentiated after removing the parentheses. For example, if we wish to calculate dy/dx when $y = x^2(2x - 3)$, we first write $y = 2x^3 - 3x^2$. In this form, we can differentiate y as in Example 5, and we obtain $dy/dx = 6x^2 - 6x$. Or if $y = (x + 2)(x^2 - 3)$, then we begin by expanding the parentheses, obtaining $y = x^3 + 2x^2 - 3x - 6$. From this stage, we again proceed as in Example 5, and we obtain $dy/dx = 3x^2 + 4x - 3$.

Similarly, we can simplify fractions with monomial denominators before we differentiate. For example, if

$$y = \frac{5t^4 + 7t^2 - 3}{2t^2}$$

we first write $y = \frac{5}{2}t^2 + \frac{7}{2} - \frac{3}{2}t^{-2}$. After differentiating the three terms separately, we obtain

$$\frac{dy}{dt} = 5t + 3t^{-3}.$$

PROOF OF THEOREM 2 Let $y = cu(x)$. Then if x is replaced by $x + \Delta x$, u becomes $u + \Delta u$ and y becomes $y + \Delta y$, so that

$$y + \Delta y = cu(x + \Delta x)$$
$$= c(u + \Delta u).$$

Subtracting, we have $\Delta y = c(u + \Delta u) - cu = c \, \Delta u$. Dividing both sides by Δx gives

$$\frac{\Delta y}{\Delta x} = c \frac{\Delta u}{\Delta x}.$$

Taking the limit as $\Delta x \rightarrow 0$, we have

$$\lim_{\Delta x \to 0} \frac{\Delta y}{\Delta x} = \lim_{\Delta x \to 0} \left(c \frac{\Delta u}{\Delta x} \right) = c \lim_{\Delta x \to 0} \frac{\Delta u}{\Delta x}.$$

That is,

$$\frac{dy}{dx} = c \frac{du}{dx},$$

as required. Alternatively, we can write

$$\frac{d}{dx}[cf(x)] = c \frac{d}{dx}[f(x)].$$

PROOF OF THEOREM 3 Let $y = u(x) + v(x)$. Let x be given an increment Δx. Since y, u, and v are all functions of x, they become $y + \Delta y$, $u + \Delta u$, and $v + \Delta v$, where

$$y + \Delta y = u(x + \Delta x) + v(x + \Delta x)$$
$$= (u + \Delta u) + (v + \Delta v).$$

Subtracting y from $y + \Delta y$, gives

$$\Delta y = (u + \Delta u + v + \Delta v) - (u + v) = \Delta u + \Delta v.$$

Dividing by Δx, we have

$$\frac{\Delta y}{\Delta x} = \frac{\Delta u}{\Delta x} + \frac{\Delta v}{\Delta x}.$$

If we now allow Δx to approach zero, we obtain

$$\lim_{\Delta x \to 0} \frac{\Delta y}{\Delta x} = \lim_{\Delta x \to 0} \frac{\Delta u}{\Delta x} + \lim_{\Delta x \to 0} \frac{\Delta v}{\Delta x} \qquad \text{(by Theorem 3(a), Section 2)}$$

That is,

$$\frac{dy}{dx} = \frac{du}{dx} + \frac{dv}{dx}$$

which is the required result.

Finally, let us prove the power formula when n is a positive integer. The proof to be given makes use of the following result from algebra.

If n is a positive integer,

$$a^n - b^n = (a - b)(a^{n-1} + a^{n-2}b + a^{n-3}b^2 + \cdots + ab^{n-2} + b^{n-1}).$$

This result is easy to verify by multiplying the two expressions on the right side term by term. It should be noted that the number of terms in the second parentheses on the right is equal to n, the power of a and b on the left side. Consider the following examples.

$$\mathbf{n = 2:} \quad a^2 - b^2 = (a - b)\underbrace{(a + b)}_{\text{2 terms}}$$

$$\mathbf{n = 3:} \quad a^3 - b^3 = (a - b)\underbrace{(a^2 + ab + b^2)}_{\text{3 terms}}$$

$$\mathbf{n = 4:} \quad a^4 - b^4 = (a - b)\underbrace{(a^3 + a^2b + ab^2 + b^3)}_{\text{4 terms}}, \text{ etc.}$$

THEOREM 4 The derivative of x^n with respect to x is nx^{n-1}, when n is a positive integer.

PROOF Let $y = x^n$. When x changes to $x + \Delta x$, y changes to $y + \Delta y$, where

$$y + \Delta y = (x + \Delta x)^n.$$

Subtracting the value for y from that for $y + \Delta y$, we have

$$\Delta y = (x + \Delta x)^n - x^n.$$

In order to simplify this expression for Δy, we make use of the algebraic identity given above, letting $a = x + \Delta x$ and $b = x$. Then $a - b = (x + \Delta x) - x = \Delta x$, and so

$$\Delta y = \Delta x[(x + \Delta x)^{n-1} + (x + \Delta x)^{n-2} \cdot x + (x + \Delta x)^{n-3} \cdot x^2 + \cdots$$
$$+ (x + \Delta x) \cdot x^{n-2} + x^{n-1}].$$

Dividing both sides by Δx and taking the limit as $\Delta x \to 0$, we have

$$\frac{dy}{dx} = \lim_{\Delta x \to 0} \frac{\Delta y}{\Delta x} = \lim_{\Delta x \to 0} [(x + \Delta x)^{n-1} + (x + \Delta x)^{n-2} \cdot x + (x + \Delta x)^{n-3} \cdot x^2 + \cdots$$
$$+ (x + \Delta x) \cdot x^{n-2} + x^{n-1}].$$

Now as $\Delta x \longrightarrow 0$, each term in the brackets approaches the limit x^{n-1}. For example, the second term $(x + \Delta x)^{n-2} \cdot x$ approaches $x^{n-2} \cdot x = x^{n-1}$ as $\Delta x \longrightarrow 0$. Furthermore, there are n such terms added together, so

$$\frac{dy}{dx} = \underbrace{x^{n-1} + x^{n-1} + x^{n-1} + \cdots + x^{n-1} + x^{n-1}}_{n \text{ terms}}$$

$$= nx^{n-1}$$

as required.

EXERCISES 4

(1–36)   Find the derivatives of the following functions w.r.t. the independent variable involved.

1. $4x^3 - 3x^2 + 7$ 2. $2x - x^3$

3. $3x^4 - 7x^3 + 5x^2 + 8$ 4. $5 - 2x^2 + x^4$

5. $3u^2 + \dfrac{3}{u^2}$ 6. $\dfrac{1}{t} + 2 + t$ 7. $5 - \dfrac{1}{t}$

8. $\sqrt{x} - \dfrac{1}{x}$ 9. $\sqrt{y} + \dfrac{1}{\sqrt{y}}$ 10. $2x^{3/2} + 4x^{3/4}$

11. $3x^4 + (2x - 1)^2$ 12. $(y - 2)(2y - 3)$

13. $(x - 7)(2x - 9)$ 14. $\left(x + \dfrac{1}{x}\right)^2$ 15. $(u + 1)(2u + 1)$

16. $\left(\sqrt{x} + \dfrac{1}{\sqrt{x}}\right)^2 - \left(\sqrt{x} - \dfrac{1}{\sqrt{x}}\right)^2$

17. $(t + 1)(3t - 1)^2$ 18. $(u - 2)^3$ 19. $5 - 3t + 4t^2 - \dfrac{7}{t}$

20. $\dfrac{(x + 1)^2}{x}$ 21. $\dfrac{2y^2 + 3y - 7}{y}$ 22. $\dfrac{t + 3/t}{\sqrt{t}}$

23. $\dfrac{x^2 - 3x + 1}{\sqrt{x}}$ 24. $\dfrac{(x + 1)^2 + (x - 1)^2}{x^2}$

25. $\dfrac{u^3 + 2u + 2}{u^3}$ 26. $\left(\sqrt{x} + \dfrac{1}{\sqrt{x}}\right)^3$ 27. $\sqrt{2y} + (3y)^{-1}$

28. $(8y)^{2/3} + (8y)^{-2/3}$ 29. $(\ln 2)/x$ 30. x^e

31. $x^{1.2} + 1/x^{0.6}$ 32. $x^{-0.4} - x^{0.4}$ 33. $\dfrac{3.7x^{0.6} + 1}{x}$

34. $\dfrac{x^3 - x^{1.6}}{x^{2.3}}$ 35. $x^{\log 2}$ 36. $x^{2 \ln e}$

37. Find dy/dx if $y = x^3 + 1/x^3$.

38. Find du/dx if $u = x^2 - 7x + 5/x$.

39. Find dy/du if $y = u^3 - 5u^2 + \dfrac{7}{3u^2} + 6$.

40. Find dx/dt if $x = (t^3 - 5t^2 + 7t - 1)/t^2$.

41. If $y = \sqrt{x}$, prove that $2y(dy/dx) = 1$.

42. If $u = 1/\sqrt{x}$, prove that $2u^{-3}(du/dx) + 1 = 0$.

43. The distance traveled by a moving object at a time t is equal to $2t^3 - t^{1/2}$. Find the instantaneous velocity: (a) at time t; (b) at time 4.

44. A ball is thrown vertically upward with an initial velocity of 60 feet/second. After t seconds, its height above the ground is given by $s = 60t - 16t^2$. Find its instantaneous velocity after t seconds. What is special about $t = 15/8$?

45. In Exercise 22 of Section 1, find the instantaneous rates of growth of the GNP in: (a) 1950; (b) 1960; (c) 1970. (The answer will be in billions of dollars per year.)

12-5 MARGINAL ANALYSIS

Derivatives have a number of applications in business and economics in constructing what are called *marginal rates*. We shall begin by considering the example of *marginal cost*.

Marginal Cost

Suppose that the manufacturer of a certain item finds that in order to make x of these items per week, the total cost in dollars is given by $C = 200 + 0.03x^2$. For example, if 100 items are produced per week, the cost is given by $C = 200 + 0.03(100)^2 = 500$. The average cost per item of producing 100 items is therefore $\frac{500}{100} = \$5$.

Now let us suppose that the manufacturer is considering changing the rate of production from 100 to $(100 + \Delta x)$ units per week, where Δx represents the increment in weekly production. The cost becomes

$$C + \Delta C = 200 + (0.03)(100 + \Delta x)^2$$
$$= 200 + 0.03[10,000 + 200\Delta x + (\Delta x)^2]$$
$$= 500 + 6\Delta x + 0.03(\Delta x)^2.$$

Therefore the extra cost involved in producing the additional items is

$$\Delta C = (C + \Delta C) - C = 500 + 6\Delta x + 0.03(\Delta x)^2 - 500$$
$$= 6\Delta x + 0.03(\Delta x)^2.$$

The average cost per item of the extra items is therefore

$$\frac{\Delta C}{\Delta x} = 6 + 0.03\,\Delta x.$$

For example, if the production is increased from 100 to 150 per week (so $\Delta x = 50$), then the average cost of the additional 50 items is equal to $6 + 0.03(50) = \$7.50$ each. If the increase is from 100 to 110 (so $\Delta x = 10$), then the average cost of the extra 10 items is equal to $\$6.30$ each.

We define the **marginal cost** to be the limiting value of the average cost per extra item as the number of extra items approaches zero. Thus we can think of the marginal cost as the average cost per extra item when a very small change is made in the amount produced. In the above example,

$$\text{Marginal Cost} = \lim_{\Delta x \to 0} \frac{\Delta C}{\Delta x} = \lim_{\Delta x \to 0} (6 + 0.03\,\Delta x) = 6.$$

In the case of a general cost function $C(x)$ representing the cost of producing an amount x of a certain item, the marginal cost is similarly given by

$$\text{Marginal Cost} = \lim_{\Delta x \to 0} \frac{\Delta C}{\Delta x} = \lim_{\Delta x \to 0} \frac{C(x + \Delta x) - C(x)}{\Delta x}.$$

Clearly the marginal cost is nothing but the derivative of the cost function with respect to the amount produced.

$$\text{Marginal Cost} = \frac{dC}{dx}$$

The marginal cost measures the rate at which the cost is increasing with respect to increases in the amount produced.

EXAMPLE 1 For the cost function

$$C(x) = 0.001x^3 - 0.3x^2 + 40x + 1000$$

determine the marginal cost as a function of x. Evaluate the marginal cost when the production is given by $x = 50$, $x = 100$, and $x = 150$.

Solution We wish to calculate $C'(x)$. The given function $C(x)$ is a combination of powers of x and so can be differentiated by means of the power formula discussed in the last section. We obtain

$$C'(x) = \frac{d}{dx}(0.001x^3 - 0.3x^2 + 40x + 1000)$$

$$= 0.001(3x^2) - 0.3(2x) + 40(1) + 0$$

$$= 0.003x^2 - 0.6x + 40.$$

This function, the marginal cost, gives the average cost per item of increasing the production by a small amount given that x items are already being produced. When 50 units are being produced, the marginal cost of extra items is given by

$$C'(50) = (0.003)(50)^2 - (0.6)(50) + 40$$

$$= 7.5 - 30 + 40 = 17.5.$$

When $x = 100$, the marginal cost is

$$C'(100) = (0.003)(100)^2 - (0.6)(100) + 40$$

$$= 30 - 60 + 40 = 10.$$

When $x = 150$, the marginal cost is

$$C'(150) = (0.003)(150)^2 - (0.6)(150) + 40$$

$$= 67.5 - 90 + 40 = 17.5.$$

Roughly speaking, we can say that the 51st item costs $17.50 to produce, the 101st item costs $10, and the 151st item costs $17.50. (Such statements as these are not *quite* accurate, since the derivative gives the rate for an infinitesimally small increment in production, not for a unit increment.)

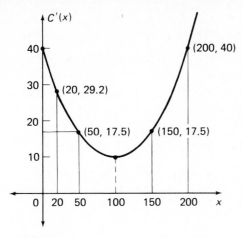

FIGURE 8

In Example 1, we observe that the marginal cost decreases as the production is increased from 50 to 100 units and then increases again as the production is further increased from 100 to 150. The graph of $C'(x)$ as a function of x is shown in Figure 8.

This type of behavior is quite typical of marginal cost. When the production x increases from small values, the marginal cost decreases—that is, the average cost of the next small increase in production becomes lower. The reason for this lies in the economies of scale, which make the manufacture of small quantities of goods relatively more expensive than the manufacture of larger quantities. However, when x becomes very large, costs start to increase again as the capacity of the existing production units becomes exhausted and it becomes necessary to invest in new plant or machinery or to pay overtime rates for labor, and so on. This causes an eventual rise in the marginal cost. Thus it is the usual case that the marginal cost first decreases as the production increases, then rises again.

It is important not to confuse the marginal cost with the average cost. If $C(x)$ is the cost function, then the **average cost** of producing x items is the total cost, $C(x)$, divided by the number of items produced.

$$\text{Average Cost per Item} = \frac{C(x)}{x}$$

This is quite different from the marginal cost, which is given by the derivative $C'(x)$. The marginal cost represents the average cost per *additional* unit of a small increase in production. The average cost is commonly denoted by $\bar{C}(x)$.

EXAMPLE 2   For the cost function $C(x) = 1000 + 10x + 0.1x^2$, the marginal cost is $C'(x) = 10 + 0.2x$. The average cost of producing x items is

$$\bar{C}(x) = \frac{C(x)}{x} = \frac{1000}{x} + 10 + 0.1x.$$

These two functions are quite distinct from one another.

Marginal Revenue and Profit

Now consider the revenues derived from the sale of a firm's products or services. If $R(x)$ denotes the revenue in dollars from the sale of x items, we define the **marginal revenue** to be the derivative $R'(x)$.

$$\text{Marginal Revenue} = R'(x) = \lim_{\Delta x \to 0} \frac{\Delta R}{\Delta x}$$

If the number of items sold increases from x to $x + \Delta x$, there is a corresponding increment in revenue given by

$$\Delta R = \text{New Revenue} - \text{Old Revenue} = R(x + \Delta x) - R(x).$$

The average increase in revenue per additional item sold is obtained by dividing ΔR by the number of additional items, giving $\Delta R / \Delta x$. The limiting value of this average as $\Delta x \to 0$ gives the marginal revenue. Thus the marginal revenue represents the additional income to a firm per additional item sold when a very small increase is made in the number of items sold. That is, it is the rate at which revenue is increasing with respect to increase in the volume of sales.

EXAMPLE 3 If the revenue function is given by

$$R(x) = 10x - 0.01x^2$$

where x is the number of items sold, determine the marginal revenue. Evaluate the marginal revenue when $x = 200$.

Solution We need to evaluate $R'(x)$. Since $R(x)$ is a combination of powers of x, we can use the power formula, obtaining the result

$$R'(x) = \frac{d}{dx}(10x - 0.01x^2)$$

$$= 10(1) - 0.01(2x) = 10 - 0.02x.$$

This provides the marginal revenue when a general number x items are sold. When $x = 200$, we get a marginal revenue of

$$R'(200) = 10 - (0.02)(200) = 10 - 4 = 6.$$

Thus when 200 items are sold, any small increase in sales provides an increase of revenue of \$6 per item.

The revenue function can be written in the form

$$R(x) = xp$$

where p is the price per item and x is the number of items sold. We saw in Section 5 of Chapter 4 that in many cases there exists a relationship between x and p characterized by the demand equation. The more items the firm wishes to sell, the lower it must set its price; the higher the price is set, in general, the smaller the volume of sales will be.

EXAMPLE 4 Determine the marginal revenue when $x = 300$ if the demand equation is

$$x = 1000 - 100p.$$

Solution We must first write the demand equation in a form in which p is expressed as a function of x.

$$100p = 1000 - x$$

$$p = 10 - 0.01x$$

Then the revenue function is given by

$$R(x) = xp = x(10 - 0.01x)$$
$$= 10x - 0.01x^2.$$

We observe that this revenue function is the same as the one in the previous example, so we can make use of the result for the marginal revenue:

$$R'(x) = 10 - 0.02x.$$

When the volume of sales is 300, the marginal revenue is therefore given by

$$R'(300) = 10 - (0.02)(300) = 10 - 6 = 4.$$

The profit that a business firm makes is given by the difference between its revenue and its costs. If the revenue function is $R(x)$ when x items are sold and if the cost function is $C(x)$ when x items are produced, then the profit $P(x)$ obtained by producing and selling x items is given by

$$P(x) = R(x) - C(x).$$

The derivative $P'(x)$ is called the **marginal profit**. It represents the additional profit per item if the production changes by a small increment.

EXAMPLE 5   The demand equation for a certain item is

$$p + 0.1x = 80$$

and the cost function is

$$C(x) = 5,000 + 20x.$$

Compute the marginal profit when 150 units are produced and sold and when 400 units are produced and sold.

Solution   The revenue function is given by

$$R(x) = xp = x(80 - 0.1x)$$
$$= 80x - 0.1x^2.$$

Therefore the profit from producing and selling x items is

$$P(x) = R(x) - C(x)$$
$$= (80x - 0.1x^2) - (5000 + 20x)$$
$$= 60x - 0.1x^2 - 5000.$$

The marginal profit is given by the derivative $P'(x)$. Since $P(x)$ is a combination of powers, we use the power formula to calculate its derivative.

$$P'(x) = \frac{d}{dx}(60x - 0.1x^2 - 5000)$$

$$= 60 - 0.2x$$

When $x = 150$, we get $P'(x) = 60 - (0.2)(150) = 30$. Thus when 150 items are being produced, the marginal profit, that is, the extra profit per additional item when the production is increased by a small amount, is $30.

When $x = 400$, the marginal profit is $P'(400) = 60 - (0.2)(400) = -20$. Thus when 400 units are being produced, a small increase in production results in a loss (that is, a negative profit) of $20 per additional unit.

The use of marginal rates is widespread in the fields of business and economics. Aside from the above examples of marginal cost, marginal revenue and marginal profit, a number of other uses occur. A few of these are summarized briefly below.

Marginal Productivity

Consider a manufacturer with a fixed amount of manufacturing capacity available but with a variable number of employees. Let u denote the amount of labor employed (for example, u might be the number of work-hours per week by the firm's employees) and let x be the amount of output (for example, the total number of items produced per week). Then x is a function of u and we can write $x = f(u)$.

If the amount of labor is given an increment Δu, then the production x changes to $x + \Delta x$ where, as usual, the increment in production is given by

$$\Delta x = f(u + \Delta u) - f(u).$$

The ratio

$$\frac{\Delta x}{\Delta u} = \frac{f(u + \Delta u) - f(u)}{\Delta u}$$

then gives the average additional production per extra unit of labor corresponding to the given increment Δu. If we now allow Δu to approach zero, this ratio approaches the derivative dx/du, which is called the **marginal productivity of labor**. Thus

$$\text{Marginal Productivity} = \frac{dx}{du} = \lim_{\Delta u \to 0} \frac{\Delta x}{\Delta u} = \lim_{\Delta u \to 0} \frac{f(u + \Delta u) - f(u)}{\Delta u}.$$

So the marginal productivity of labor measures the increase in production per additional unit of labor, for instance, per additional work-hour, when a small change is made in the amount of labor employed. It is given by the derivative $f'(u)$.

Marginal Yield

Suppose that an investor is faced with the question of how much capital to invest in a business or financial enterprise. If an amount S is invested, the investor will receive a certain return in the form of an income of, let us say, Y dollars per year. In general, the yield Y will be a function of the capital S which is invested: $Y = f(S)$. In a typical case, if S is small, the yield will be small or even zero since the enterprise would not have enough capital to operate efficiently. As S increases, the efficiency of operation improves and the yield increases rapidly. However, when S becomes very large, the efficiency may again deteriorate if the other resources necessary to the operation, such as labor or supplies, cannot increase sufficiently to keep pace with the extra capital. Thus for large S, the yield Y may again level off as S continues to increase.

The **marginal yield** is defined as the derivative dY/dS. It is obtained as the limiting value of $\Delta Y/\Delta S$ and it represents the yield per additional dollar invested when a small increase in capital is made.

Marginal Tax Rate

Let T be the amount of taxes paid by an individual or by a corporation when the income is I. Then we can write $T = f(I)$. If everything else is fixed, then a small increase ΔI in I leads to an increment in T given by $\Delta T = f(I + \Delta I) - f(I)$. The ratio $\Delta T/\Delta I$ represents the fraction of the increment of income that disappears in the form of taxation. If we allow ΔI to approach zero, this ratio approaches the derivative dT/dI, which is called the **marginal rate of taxation**. It represents the proportion of an infinitesimally small increment in income that must be paid in tax.

The marginal rate of taxation is determined by the graduated tax scales. Individuals with very low incomes pay no income tax, and below a certain income level the marginal rate is zero. As income rises, the marginal rate of taxation rises until it reaches a maximum level equal to the maximum proportion payable according to the scale. (See Example 8 in next section.)

Marginal Propensities to Save and to Consume

Let I be the total income (gross national product) of a nation. Each individual among the population who receives part of this income makes a decision to spend part of his or her income on consumable goods and services and to save the rest. Let C be the total amount spent by the population on consumables and S be the total amount of savings. Then $S + C = I$.

In general, the amount of savings is determined by the national income, and we can write $S = f(I)$. The amount of consumption is then given by $C = I - f(I)$.

If the national income receives an increment ΔI, then the savings and consumption also obtain increments ΔS and ΔC, respectively, where

$$\Delta S + \Delta C = \Delta I \quad \text{and} \quad \Delta S = f(I + \Delta I) - f(I).$$

The ratio $\Delta S/\Delta I$ represents the fraction of the increment of income that is saved and $\Delta C/\Delta I$ represents the fraction that is consumed. Since

$$\frac{\Delta S}{\Delta I} + \frac{\Delta C}{\Delta I} = \frac{\Delta S + \Delta C}{\Delta I} = \frac{\Delta I}{\Delta I} = 1$$

the sum of these two fractions is equal to 1.

In the limit as $\Delta I \to 0$, these fractions become the corresponding derivatives. We call dS/dI the **marginal propensity to save** and dC/dI the **marginal propensity to consume**. They represent the proportions of a small increment in national income that are saved and consumed, respectively. They are related by the equation

$$\frac{dS}{dI} + \frac{dC}{dI} = 1.$$

EXERCISES 5

(1–4) Calculate the marginal cost for the following cost functions.

1. $C(x) = 100 + 2x$ **2.** $C(x) = 40 + (\ln 2)x^2$

3. $C(x) = 0.0001x^3 - 0.09x^2 + 20x + 1200$

4. $C(x) = 10^{-6}x^3 - (3 \times 10^{-3})x^2 + 36x + 2000$

(5–8) Calculate the marginal revenue for the following revenue functions.

5. $R(x) = x - 0.01x^2$ **6.** $R(x) = 5x - 0.01x^{5/2}$

7. $R(x) = 0.1x - 10^{-3}x^2 - 10^{-5}x^{5/2}$ **8.** $R(x) = 100x - (\log 5)x^3(1 + \sqrt{x})$

9. If the demand equation is $x + 4p = 100$, calculate the marginal revenue, $R'(x)$.

10. If the demand equation is $\sqrt{x} + p = 10$, calculate the marginal revenue.

11. If the demand equation is $x^{3/2} + 50p = 1000$, calculate the marginal revenue when $p = 16$.

12. If the demand equation is $10p + x + 0.01x^2 = 700$, calculate the marginal revenue when $p = 10$.

13. If, in Exercise 9, the cost function is $C(x) = 100 + 5x$, calculate the marginal profit.

14. If, in Exercise 10, the cost function is $C(x) = 60 + x$, calculate the marginal profit.

15. If, in Exercise 11, the cost function is $C(x) = 50 + x^{3/2}$, evaluate the marginal profit when: (a) $p = 16$; (b) $x = 25$.

16. If, in Exercise 12, the cost function is $C(x) = 1000 + 0.1x^2$, evaluate the marginal profit when: (a) $x = 100$; (b) $p = 10$.

17–18. In Exercises 13 and 14, find the value of x that makes $P'(x) = 0$ and calculate the corresponding profit. This represents the maximum profit that can be obtained from sale of the item in question. Find the price p that gives this maximum profit.

19. When a barber charged $4 for a haircut, she found that she gave 100 haircuts a week, on the average. When she raised her price to $5, the number of customers per week fell to 80. Assuming a linear demand equation relating price and number of customers, find the marginal revenue function. Then find the price that makes the marginal revenue zero.

20. A magazine publisher finds that if he charges $1 for his magazine, he will sell 20,000 copies per month; however, if he charges $1.50, his sales will be only 15,000 copies. It costs him $0.80 to produce each issue and he has fixed overhead costs of $10,000 per month. Assuming a linear demand equation, calculate his marginal profit function and find the price of the magazine that makes the marginal profit equal to zero. Evaluate the profit itself when the price is: (a) $1.80; (b) $1.90; (c) $2.

21. Show that if the cost function is of the form $C(x) = ax^2 + bx + c$, then at the value of x for which the marginal cost is equal to the average cost $\bar{C}(x)$, the derivative $(d/dx)\bar{C}(x)$ is zero.

*22. Show that the result in Exercise 21 is true for any cost function $C(x)$ that is a polynomial function of x. (That is, $C(x)$ consists of a sum of powers of x, with each power multiplied by a constant.)

12-6 CONTINUITY AND DIFFERENTIABILITY (OPTIONAL SECTION)

In considering the limiting value of a function $f(x)$ as x approaches c, we must consider values of x both less than and greater than c. However, in some cases the behavior of a given function is different for $x < c$ than for $x > c$. In such a case, we may wish to consider separately the possiblities that x might approach c from above or from below.

We say that x **approaches** c **from above** and write $x \rightarrow c^+$ if x takes a sequence of values that get closer and closer to c but always remain greater than c (see page 398). We say that x **approaches** c **from below** and write $x \rightarrow c^-$ if x takes a sequence of values that get closer and closer to c, but remain less than c. If $f(x)$ approaches the limiting value L as $x \rightarrow c^+$, we write

$$\lim_{x \to c^+} f(x) = L.$$

If $f(x)$ approaches the limiting value M as $x \rightarrow c^-$, we write

$$\lim_{x \to c^-} f(x) = M.$$

Limits of this kind are called **one-sided limits**.

EXAMPLE 1 Investigate the limiting values of $f(x) = \sqrt{x - 1}$ as x approaches 1 from above and from below.

Solution As $x \rightarrow 1^+$, $x - 1$ approaches zero through positive values. Therefore

$$\lim_{x \to 1^+} \sqrt{x - 1} = 0.$$

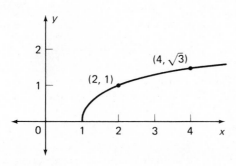

FIGURE 9

On the other hand, as $x \rightarrow 1^-$, $x - 1$ still approaches zero, but it is always negative. Hence $\sqrt{x - 1}$ is not defined for $x < 1$, so $\lim_{x \to 1^-} \sqrt{x - 1}$ does not exist.

The graph of $y = \sqrt{x - 1}$ is shown in Figure 9. The domain of this function does not extend to values of x less than 1, so the limit from below cannot exist.

EXAMPLE 2 Investigate the limiting values of $f(x) = |x|/x$ as x approaches 0 from above and from below.

Solution   For $x > 0$, $|x| = x$, and so

$$f(x) = \frac{|x|}{x} = \frac{x}{x} = 1.$$

The given function has the value 1 for all $x > 0$ and so must have the limiting value 1 as x approaches 0 from above:

$$\lim_{x \to 0^+} \frac{|x|}{x} = 1.$$

For $x < 0$, $|x| = -x$, and so

$$f(x) = \frac{|x|}{x} = \frac{-x}{x} = -1.$$

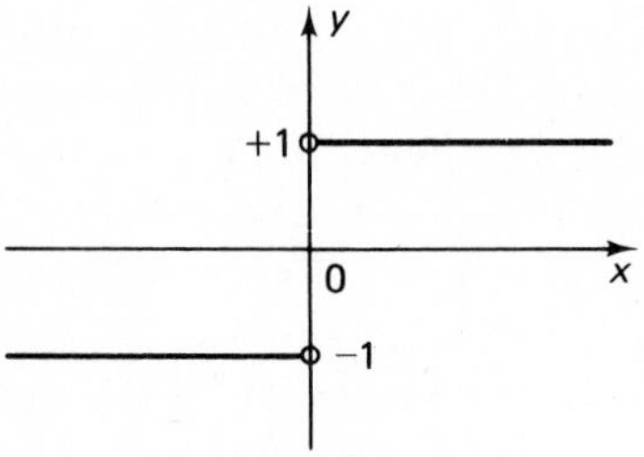

(For example, when $x = -6$, $f(-6) = |-6|/(-6) = 6/(-6) = -1$.)

Hence $f(x)$ is identically equal to -1 for all $x < 0$ and therefore

$$\lim_{x \to 0^-} \frac{|x|}{x} = -1.$$

The graph of $y = f(x)$ is shown in Figure 10. Note that $f(x)$ is not defined for $x = 0$ and that the graph makes a jump from -1 to $+1$ as x passes from below zero to above zero.

FIGURE 10

The preceding examples illustrate two basic types of behavior. In the first case, only one of the two limits from above and from below existed. In the second case, both limits existed, but their values were different from one another. In both cases, the relevant two-sided limit, $\lim_{x \to c} f(x)$, does not exist. For a general $f(x)$, as illustrated in Figure 11, if the graph of $f(x)$ makes a jump at $x = c$, then the two limits from above and from below are not equal to one another. Note that $\lim_{x \to c} f(x)$ exists if both $\lim_{x \to c^-} f(x)$ and $\lim_{x \to c^+} f(x)$ exist and are equal to one another.

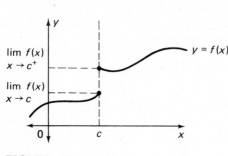

FIGURE 11

EXAMPLE 3   Given

$$f(x) = \begin{cases} 2x + 5 & \text{for } x > 3 \\ x^2 + 2 & \text{for } x \le 3 \end{cases}$$

find $\lim_{x \to 3} f(x)$.

Solution   In this case, $f(x)$ is defined by two different formulas, one for $x \le 3$ and one for $x > 3$. So we must find the limits separately from above and below. Since $f(x) = 2x + 5$ for $x > 3$, for the limit from above we find

$$\lim_{x \to 3^+} f(x) = \lim_{x \to 3} (2x + 5) = 2(3) + 5 = 11.$$

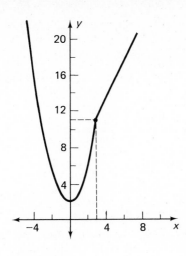

FIGURE 12

Similarly, for $x < 3$, we have $f(x) = x^2 + 2$ and therefore, for the limit from below,

$$\lim_{x \to 3^-} f(x) = \lim_{x \to 3} (x^2 + 2) = 3^2 + 2 = 11.$$

Since $\lim_{x \to 3^+} f(x) = \lim_{x \to 3^-} f(x) = 11$, it follows that $\lim_{x \to 3} f(x)$ exists and is equal to 11.

The graph of $f(x)$ in this case is shown in Figure 12. Note that the graph changes type at $x = 3$, but it does not make a jump at this point.

If the two limits of $f(x)$ as x approaches c from above and below are different from one another, we say that $f(x)$ has a **jump discontinuity** at $x = c$. Let us recall the definition of the continuity of a function from Section 2.

DEFINITION   A function $f(x)$ is said to be **continuous** at a point $x = c$ if the following three conditions are met.

1. $f(x)$ is defined at $x = c$. That is, $f(c)$ is well-defined.
2. $\lim_{x \to c} f(x)$ exists.
3. $\lim_{x \to c} f(x) = f(c)$

If any one of these three conditions is not satisfied, then the function is said to be **discontinuous** at $x = c$.

EXAMPLE 4   The function $f(x) = |x|$ is continuous at $x = 0$.

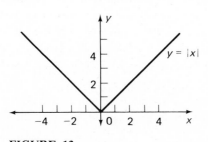

FIGURE 13

We note that $f(0) = |0| = 0$, so that condition (1) is satisfied. Also $\lim_{x \to 0} f(x)$ exists since, as x approaches zero, $|x|$ approaches the limit zero. Finally, condition (3) is met, since $\lim_{x \to 0} f(x)$ and $f(0)$ are equal to one another, both being zero. The graph of $y = |x|$ is shown in Figure 13. The graph clearly passes through $x = 0$ without a break. It does have a corner (or change of slope) at $x = 0$, but this does not make it discontinuous.

In Example 2, we discussed the function $f(x) = |x|/x$. This function is discontinuous at $x = 0$ because $\lim_{x \to 0} f(x)$ does not exist: the limits from above and from below are not equal to one another. The graph makes a jump from -1 to $+1$ as x passes through 0. Another example of a discontinuous function is given in Example 5.

EXAMPLE 5   Given

$$f(x) = \begin{cases} \dfrac{x^2 - 9}{x - 3} & \text{if } x \neq 3 \\ 5 & \text{if } x = 3. \end{cases}$$

Is $f(x)$ continuous at $x = 3$?

Solution   **Condition (1)**   Clearly $f(x)$ is defined at $x = 3$ and $f(3) = 5$.

Condition (2) $\displaystyle\lim_{x \to 3} f(x) = \lim_{x \to 3} \frac{x^2 - 9}{x - 3} = \lim_{x \to 3} \frac{(x - 3)(x + 3)}{x - 3}$

$$= \lim_{x \to 3} (x + 3) = 3 + 3 = 6$$

Condition (3) $\displaystyle\lim_{x \to 3} f(x) = 6$ and $f(3) = 5$ are not equal.

In this case, the first two conditions are satisfied, but the third condition is *not* met, so the given function is discontinuous at $x = 3$. This is shown graphically in Figure 14. The graph of $f(x)$ has a break at $x = 3$ and the isolated point $(3, 5)$ on the graph is not joined continuously to the rest of the graph.

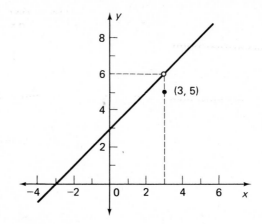

FIGURE 14

It may seem at first sight that discontinuous functions would be of little relevance to practical problems. This is not the case however, as the following example illustrates.

EXAMPLE 6   A wholesaler sells sugar at 50 cents a pound for amounts up to 100 pounds. For orders greater than 100 and up to 200 pounds, the charge is 45 cents a pound, and for orders over 200 pounds the charge is 40 cents a pound. Let $y = f(x)$ denote the cost in dollars of x pounds of sugar. Then for $x \leq 100$, $y = (0.5)x$. For $100 < x \leq 200$, the cost is $0.45 per pound, so $y = 0.45x$. Finally, for $x > 200$, $y = 0.4x$. The graph of this function is shown in Figure 15. Clearly, the function is discontinuous at $x = 100$ and 200.

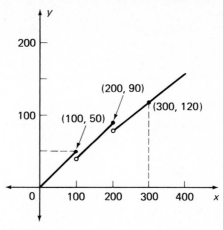

FIGURE 15

In Section 3, we defined the term differentiability: a function $f(x)$ is said to be differentiable at the point x if the derivative

$$f'(x) = \lim_{\Delta x \to 0} \frac{f(x + \Delta x) - f(x)}{\Delta x}$$

exists at that point.

EXAMPLE 7   Show that the function $f(x) = |x|$ is not differentiable at $x = 0$.

Solution   We must take $x = 0$, so that $f(x) = f(0) = 0$ and $f(x + \Delta x) = f(0 + \Delta x)$ $= f(\Delta x) = |\Delta x|$. So

$$\Delta y = f(x + \Delta x) - f(x) = |\Delta x| - 0 = |\Delta x|.$$

Then

$$\frac{dy}{dx} = \lim_{\Delta x \to 0} \frac{\Delta y}{\Delta x} = \lim_{\Delta x \to 0} \frac{|\Delta x|}{\Delta x}.$$

But in Example 2, we discussed this limit and we showed that the limit does not exist. In fact, the two limits from above and below exist but are unequal.

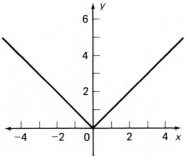

$$\lim_{\Delta x \to 0^+} \frac{|\Delta x|}{\Delta x} = 1$$

$$\lim_{\Delta x \to 0^-} \frac{|\Delta x|}{\Delta x} = -1$$

The graph of $y = |x|$ is shown in Figure 16. For $x > 0$, the graph has a constant slope of 1, while for $x < 0$ it has a constant slope of -1. For $x = 0$, there is no slope since the graph has a corner at this value of x. This is why $|x|$ is not differentiable at $x = 0$.

FIGURE 16

A function $y = f(x)$ is differentiable at a certain value of x if its graph is "smooth" at the corresponding point (x, y), by which we mean that the graph has a well-defined tangent line with a well-defined slope. If the graph has a corner at the point (x, y), then $f(x)$ is not differentiable at that value of x. The preceding example illustrates such a function.

EXAMPLE 8   In the mythical country of Erehwon, the fortunate inhabitants pay no income tax on their first $10,000 of taxable earnings. The graduated tax rates for higher income levels are given in Table 5. Let I denote taxable earnings and T

TABLE 5

Taxable Earnings	Tax Rate
$10,001–$20,000	20%
$20,001–$30,000	30%
Over $30,000	40%

denote the amount of taxes. Express T as a function of I, draw the graph of this function and discuss its differentiability.

Solution   For $0 \leq I \leq 10,000$, $T = 0$. When $10,000 < I \leq 20,000$, the amount by which I exceeds 10,000 is taxed at 20%. Therefore, in this range,

$$T = 0 \cdot 2(I - 10,000) = 0 \cdot 2I - 2000.$$

When $I = 20,000$, $T = 0 \cdot 2(20,000 - 10,000) = 2000$, so the tax on $20,000 is $2000.

When $20,000 < I \leq 30,000$, the amount by which I exceeds 20,000 is taxed at 30%. Thus, in this range,

$$T = 2000 + 0.3(I - 20,000)$$

$$= 0.3I - 4000.$$

When $I = 30,000$, $T = 0.3(30,000) - 4000 = 5000$, so the tax is $5000.

Continuing in this way, we construct a table of values of T as a function of I (see Table 6) and the graph as shown in Figure 17.

TABLE 6

I	T
$I \leq 10,000$	0
$10,000 < I \leq 20,000$	$0.2I - 2000$
20,000	2,000
$20,000 < I \leq 30,000$	$0.3I - 4000$
30,000	5000
$I > 30,000$	$0.4I - 7000$

The graph consists of a number of line segments. Clearly the amount of tax is a continuous function of taxable earnings, but it is not differentiable at the

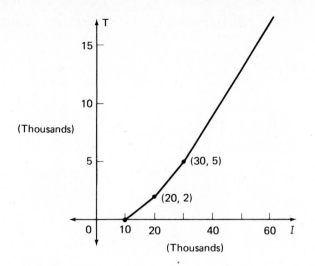

FIGURE 17

points where the graph has corners. These occur at the values of I that mark the divisions on the graduated tax scale. In between these dividing points, T is differentiable, and its derivative gives the marginal tax rate.

Another case in which a function is not differentiable arises when the tangent line at a certain point becomes vertical. In such a case, the slope of the tangent line is not defined at the point in question, so the function is not differentiable at that value of x. For example, we leave it as an exercise for the more ambitious student to show that the function $f(x) = x^{1/3}$ is not differentiable at $x = 0$.

We observe that in Example 7 we have a function that is defined and is continuous for all values of x, but that is not differentiable for all x. At $x = 0$, $f(x) = |x|$ is continuous but not differentiable. Clearly, therefore, *the fact that a function is continuous does not imply that it is differentiable*. However, the converse of this implication is true: *If $f(x)$ is differentiable at a point $x = c$, then it is continuous at $x = c$*. Thus differentiability implies continuity, but not conversely. We shall not give a proof of this result, although it is an important one.

EXERCISES 6

(1–12) Evaluate the following one-sided limits.

1. $\displaystyle\lim_{x \to 1^+} \sqrt{x - 1}$

2. $\displaystyle\lim_{x \to 1/2^-} \sqrt{1 - 2x}$

3. $\displaystyle\lim_{x \to 4/3^+} \sqrt{4 - 3x}$

4. $\displaystyle\lim_{x \to -1^-} \sqrt{x + 1}$

5. $\displaystyle\lim_{x \to 1^+} \frac{|x - 1|}{x - 1}$

6. $\displaystyle\lim_{x \to -1^-} \frac{x + 1}{|x + 1|}$

7. $\displaystyle\lim_{x \to 3^-} \frac{|x - 3|}{9 - x^2}$

8. $\displaystyle\lim_{x \to 2^-} \frac{x^2 - x - 2}{|x - 2|}$

9. $\displaystyle\lim_{x \to 0^-} \frac{1}{x^2}$

10. $\displaystyle\lim_{x \to -1^+} \frac{x - 1}{x + 1}$

11. $\displaystyle\lim_{x \to 1^-} \frac{2 - x^2}{|x - 1|}$

12. $\displaystyle\lim_{x \to 2^-} \frac{x^2 - 6}{(x - 2)^3}$

(13–18) Discuss the continuity of the following functions at $x = 0$ and sketch their graphs.

13. $f(x) = \dfrac{x^2}{x}$

14. $g(x) = \sqrt{x^2}$

15. $h(x) = \begin{cases} |x| & \text{for } x \neq 0 \\ 1 & \text{for } x = 0 \end{cases}$

16. $F(x) = \begin{cases} \dfrac{|x|}{x} & \text{if } x \neq 0 \\ 0 & \text{if } x = 0 \end{cases}$

17. $G(x) = \begin{cases} 0 & \text{if } x < 0 \\ 1 & \text{if } x > 0 \end{cases}$

18. $H(x) = \begin{cases} 0 & \text{if } x < 0 \\ x & \text{if } x > 0 \end{cases}$

(19–24) Discuss the continuity of the following functions at the indicated points and sketch their graphs.

19. $f(x) = x^2 + 4x + 7, \quad x = 1$

20. $g(x) = \dfrac{2x - 1}{x - 1}; \quad x = 1$

21. $f(x) = \begin{cases} \dfrac{|x - 3|}{x - 3} & \text{if } x \neq 3 \\ 0 & \text{if } x = 3 \end{cases}; \quad x = 3$

22. $G(x) = \begin{cases} \dfrac{x^2 - 4}{x - 2} & \text{for } x \neq 2 \\ 4 & \text{for } x = 2 \end{cases}; \quad x = 2$

23. $f(x) = \begin{cases} 5x + 7 & \text{for } x > 2 \\ 2x + 3 & \text{for } x \leq 2 \end{cases}; \quad x = 2$

24. $f(x) = \begin{cases} 3x + 5 & \text{for } x < 1 \\ 10 - 2x & \text{for } x > 1 \end{cases}; \quad x = 1$

(25–26) Find the value of h in the following exercises so that $f(x)$ is continuous at $x = 1$.

25. $f(x) = \begin{cases} x^2 - 3x + 4 & \text{if } x \neq 1 \\ h & \text{if } x = 1 \end{cases}$

26. $f(x) = \begin{cases} hx + 3 & \text{if } x \geq 1 \\ 3 - hx & \text{if } x < 1 \end{cases}$

*(27–30) Find the values of x for which the following functions are not differentiable.

*27. $f(x) = x^{2/3}$

*28. $f(x) = \begin{cases} 0 & \text{for } x \leq 0 \\ x & \text{for } x > 0 \end{cases}$

*29. $f(x) = \begin{cases} 0 & \text{for } x \leq 0 \\ x^2 & \text{for } x > 0 \end{cases}$

*30. $f(x) = (x - 1)^{1/2}$

31. A power company charges 10 cents per unit of electricity for the first 50 units used by a household each month and 3 cents per unit for amounts over this. If $c(x)$ denotes the cost of x units per month, discuss the continuity and differentiability of $c(x)$ and draw its graph.

32. Let $f(x)$ denote the cost per week to a firm of hiring an employee who works x hours per week. This cost consists of (a) an overhead cost of $20, (b) a wage of $6 per hour for the first 35 hours, (c) an overtime wage of $9 per hour for hours worked over 35 hours but not more than 45 hours, and (d) a double overtime wage of $12 per hour for hours worked in excess of 45. Discuss the continuity and differentiability of $f(x)$ and draw its graph.

33. A first-class letter costs 12 cents per ounce or fraction thereof. Let $f(x)$ denote the cost of mailing a letter weighing x ounces. Discuss the continuity and differentiability of $f(x)$ and draw its graph for $0 < x < 8$.

REVIEW EXERCISES FOR CHAPTER 12

1. State whether each of the following is true or false. Replace each false statement by a corresponding true statement.

   a. An increment in the independent variable must be positive.

   b. An increment in the dependent variable can be positive, negative, or zero.

   c. A function must be defined at a point if the limit of the function exists at this point.

   d. $x/x = 1$ for all x.

   e. If $g(x) \longrightarrow 0$ as $x \longrightarrow c$ and if $\lim_{x \to c} f(x)/g(x)$ exists, then $f(x)$ must approach zero as $x \longrightarrow c$.

   f. A function must be defined at a point if the derivative of the function exists at this point.

   g. The derivative of y w.r.t. x represents the average rate of change of y w.r.t. x.

   h. A function $f(x)$ is continuous at $x = c$ if and only if $\lim_{x \to c} f(x)$ exists.

   i. If a function is continuous at a point then it is differentiable at this point.

   j. The derivative of the sum of any number of functions is equal to the sum of their derivatives.

   k. If $f(x) = |x|$, then $f'(0) = 0$.

2. Find Δy when $x = 2$ and $\Delta x = 0.5$ for the function $y = x^3 - 2x^{-1}$.

3. For the cost function $C(x) = 3000 + 10x + 0.1x^2$, find the increment in cost when production is increased from 100 to 120 units. Find the average cost per additional unit.

4. For an object falling under gravity, find the average velocity between $t = 4$ and $t = 5$ seconds ($t = 0$ is the instant at which the object is released).

(5–8) Evaluate the following limits.

5. $\lim_{x \to 5} \dfrac{x^2 - 25}{x + 15}$

6. $\lim_{x \to a} \dfrac{\sqrt{x} - \sqrt{a}}{x - a}$

7. $\lim_{h \to 0} \dfrac{\sqrt{x + h} - \sqrt{x}}{h}$

8. $\lim_{x \to 1} \dfrac{\sqrt{x + 3} - 2}{\sqrt{2 - x} - x}$

(9–10) Find the derivatives of the following functions by using the definition of the derivative as a limit.

9. $f(x) = (x + 1)^{-2}$

10. $g(x) = (x + 1)^{-1/2}$

(11–14) Differentiate the following functions w.r.t. the argument given.

11. $x^{3/2} - 2x^{-3/2}$

12. $(x + 1)(2x - 1)/\sqrt{x}$

13. $x^e \sqrt{x}$

14. $(x^2 + 1)/x^{\sqrt{2}}$

(15–16) Find the marginal cost for the following cost functions.

15. $C(x) = 500 + 10x^2$

16. $C(x) = (2 \times 10^{-4})x^3 - 0.1x^2 + 25x + 2000$

17. If the demand equation is $x + 20p = 1000$, calculate the marginal revenue.

18. If the demand equation is $x^2 + 400p = 10,000$, calculate the marginal revenue.

19–20. Calculate the marginal profit in Exercises 17 and 18 if the cost function is $C(x) = 1000 + 10x$.

(21–22) Determine whether the following functions are continuous at the indicated points.

21. $f(x) = \dfrac{x^3 + 3x}{x}; \quad x = 0$

22. $f(x) = \begin{cases} \dfrac{|x^2 - 9|}{x - 3} & \text{if } x \neq 3 \\ 6 & \text{if } x = 3 \end{cases}; \quad x = 3$

23. Determine the value of h if

$$f(x) = \begin{cases} x^2 + h & \text{for } x \neq 1 \\ 3 & \text{for } x = 1 \end{cases}$$

is continuous at $x = 1$.

CALCULATION OF DERIVATIVES

CHAPTER

13-1 DERIVATIVES OF PRODUCTS AND QUOTIENTS

In this section, we shall prove and explain the use of two important theorems that provide useful techniques for differentiating complicated functions.

THEOREM 1 (PRODUCT RULE)
If $u(x)$ and $v(x)$ are any two differentiable functions of x, then

$$\frac{d}{dx}(u \cdot v) = u\frac{dv}{dx} + v\frac{du}{dx}.$$

That is, $(uv)' = uv' + vu'$.

In words, *the derivative of the product of two functions is equal to the first function times the derivative of the second plus the second function times the derivative of the first.*

EXAMPLE 1 Find y' if $y = (5x^2 - 3x)(2x^3 + 8x + 7)$.

Solution The given function y can be written as a product $y = uv$ if we let

$$u = 5x^2 - 3x \quad \text{and} \quad v = 2x^3 + 8x + 7.$$

Then, by the methods of Section 4 in Chapter 12, we see that

$$u' = 10x - 3 \quad \text{and} \quad v' = 6x^2 + 8.$$

Therefore, by the product rule,

$$
\begin{aligned}
y' &= uv' + vu' \\
&= (5x^2 - 3x)(6x^2 + 8) + (2x^3 + 8x + 7)(10x - 3) \\
&= 50x^4 - 24x^3 + 120x^2 + 22x - 21.
\end{aligned}
$$

In Example 1, we do not actually need the product rule in order to differentiate the given function. We could have calculated y' by multiplying out the right side and expressing y as a sum of powers of x.

$$
\begin{aligned}
y &= (5x^2 - 3x)(2x^3 + 8x + 7) \\
&= 10x^5 - 6x^4 + 40x^3 + 11x^2 - 21x \\
y' &= 10(5x^4) - 6(4x^3) + 40(3x^2) + 11(2x) - 21(1) \\
&= 50x^4 - 24x^3 + 120x^2 + 22x - 21
\end{aligned}
$$

The examples that we shall now give on the use of the product rule can likewise be solved using the methods of the last chapter. However, later we shall come across functions for which such an alternative method does not exist. For these functions, it will be essential to use the product rule in order to find their derivatives.

EXAMPLE 2 Given $f(t) = (2\sqrt{t} + 1)(t^2 + 3)$, find $f'(t)$.

Solution We use the product rule with $u = 2\sqrt{t} + 1 = 2t^{1/2} + 1$ and $v = t^2 + 3$.

$$f'(t) = (2t^{1/2} + 1)\frac{d}{dt}(t^2 + 3) + (t^2 + 3)\frac{d}{dt}(2t^{1/2} + 1)$$

$$= (2t^{1/2} + 1)(2t) + (t^2 + 3)(2 \cdot \tfrac{1}{2}t^{-1/2})$$

$$= 4t^{3/2} + 2t + t^{3/2} + 3t^{-1/2}$$

$$= 5t^{3/2} + 2t + \frac{3}{\sqrt{t}}$$

The demand equation gives the price p at which a quantity x of a certain item can be sold during a given span of time. In general, we can write $p = f(x)$. The revenue from the sale of this number of items is then

$$R = xp.$$

Since R is given as a product of two quantities, the marginal revenue, which is the derivative of R with respect to x, can be obtained from the product rule.

$$\frac{dR}{dx} = p\frac{d}{dx}(x) + x\frac{d}{dx}(p)$$

$$= 1 \cdot p + x\frac{dp}{dx}$$

$$= p + x\frac{dp}{dx}$$

EXAMPLE 3 If the demand equation is linear, we have

$$p = a - bx$$

where a and b are two positive constants. Then $dp/dx = -b$ and the marginal revenue is

$$\frac{dR}{dx} = p + x\frac{dp}{dx}$$

$$= a - bx + x(-b) = a - 2bx.$$

We note that the marginal revenue in this example can in fact be calculated directly.

$$R = xp = x(a - bx) = ax - bx^2$$

Therefore $R'(x) = a - 2bx$, as before.

It is also sometimes useful to talk about the marginal revenue with respect to price. In this situation, we regard the revenue R as a function of the price p; the marginal revenue with respect to price is defined as the derivative dR/dp. It represents the increase in revenue for each unit increase in the price per item when the price is given a small increase.

Since $R = xp$, it follows from the product rule that

$$\frac{dR}{dp} = x \frac{d}{dp}(p) + p \frac{d}{dp}(x)$$

$$= x + p \frac{dx}{dp}.$$

The derivative dx/dp that occurs in this equation is often called the **marginal demand with respect to price**. It represents the increase in demand per unit increase in the price per item when the price is given a small increase.

EXAMPLE 4   Let us again consider the linear demand equation $p = a - bx$. Then $x = (a/b) - (p/b)$ and so

$$\frac{dx}{dp} = -\frac{1}{b}.$$

Therefore the marginal revenue with respect to price is

$$\frac{dR}{dp} = x + p \frac{dx}{dp}$$

$$= \frac{a}{b} - \frac{p}{b} + p\left(-\frac{1}{b}\right)$$

$$= \frac{a - 2p}{b}.$$

Once again, we could have calculated dR/dp directly by differentiating the function $R = xp = (ap - p^2)/b$.

PROOF OF THEOREM 1   Let $y = u \cdot v$. Then

$$y + \Delta y = (u + \Delta u) \cdot (v + \Delta v)$$

$$= uv + u \cdot \Delta v + v \cdot \Delta u + \Delta u \cdot \Delta v$$

$$= y + u \, \Delta v + v \, \Delta u + \Delta u \, \Delta v.$$

We subtract y from both sides.

$$\Delta y = u\Delta v + v\Delta u + \Delta u \Delta v$$

$$\frac{\Delta y}{\Delta x} = u \frac{\Delta v}{\Delta x} + v \frac{\Delta u}{\Delta x} + \Delta u \cdot \frac{\Delta v}{\Delta x}$$

Taking limits as $\Delta x \to 0$, we have

$$\lim_{\Delta x \to 0} \frac{\Delta y}{\Delta x} = u \lim_{\Delta x \to 0} \frac{\Delta v}{\Delta x} + v \lim_{\Delta x \to 0} \frac{\Delta u}{\Delta x} + \lim_{\Delta x \to 0} \Delta u \cdot \lim_{\Delta x \to 0} \frac{\Delta v}{\Delta x}.$$

(Note that parts (a) and (c) of Theorem 3, in Section 2 of Chapter 12 have been used.) In the last term on the right, $\Delta u \to 0$ as $\Delta x \to 0$, so we get

$$\frac{dy}{dx} = u \cdot \frac{dv}{dx} + v \cdot \frac{du}{dx}$$

as required.

THEOREM 2 (QUOTIENT RULE)

If $u(x)$ and $v(x)$ are differentiable functions of x, then

$$\frac{d}{dx}\left(\frac{u}{v}\right) = \frac{v\dfrac{du}{dx} - u\dfrac{dv}{dx}}{v^2}$$

or

$$\left(\frac{u}{v}\right)' = \frac{vu' - uv'}{v^2}.$$

That is, *the derivative of a quotient of two functions is equal to the denominator times the derivative of the numerator minus the numerator times the derivative of the denominator all divided by the square of the denominator.*

EXAMPLE 5   Find y' if

$$y = \frac{x^2 + 1}{x^3 + 4}.$$

Solution   We use the quotient rule (with $u = x^2 + 1$ and $v = x^3 + 4$).

$$y' = \frac{(x^3 + 4)\dfrac{d}{dx}(x^2 + 1) - (x^2 + 1)\dfrac{d}{dx}(x^3 + 4)}{(x^3 + 4)^2}$$

$$= \frac{(x^3 + 4)(2x) - (x^2 + 1)(3x^2)}{(x^3 + 4)^2}$$

$$= \frac{2x^4 + 8x - (3x^4 + 3x^2)}{(x^3 + 4)^2}$$

$$= \frac{-x^4 - 3x^2 + 8x}{(x^3 + 4)^2}$$

EXAMPLE 6   The gross national product of a certain country increases with time t according to the formula $I = I_0 + at$, where I_0 and a are constants. The population at time t is $P = P_0 + bt$, P_0 and b being constants. Find the rate of change of per capita income at time t.

Solution   The per capita income, which we denote by y, is equal to GNP divided by population size.

$$y = \frac{I}{P} = \frac{I_0 + at}{P_0 + bt}$$

From the quotient rule, the rate of change of y (that is, the derivative of y w.r.t. time) is

$$\frac{dy}{dt} = \frac{P\dfrac{dI}{dt} - I\dfrac{dP}{dt}}{P^2}.$$

But $dI/dt = a$ and $dP/dt = b$, so

$$\frac{dy}{dt} = \frac{(P_0 + bt)a - (I_0 + at)b}{(P_0 + bt)^2}$$

$$= \frac{P_0 a - I_0 b}{(P_0 + bt)^2}.$$

Let $C(x)$ be the cost function for a certain item—that is, $C(x)$ is the cost of manufacturing and marketing a quantity x of the items in question. The derivative $C'(x)$ gives the marginal cost. The ratio $C(x)/x$ equals the total cost divided by the quantity produced and so represents the average cost per unit of producing these items. The derivative of this ratio w.r.t. x is called the **marginal average cost**. It gives the increase in the average cost per item for each increase of one unit in the amount produced.

In order to compute the marginal average cost from the cost function, we must differentiate the ratio $C(x)/x$. For this, we can use the quotient rule.

$$\text{Marginal Average Cost} = \frac{d}{dx}\left(\frac{C(x)}{x}\right)$$

$$= \frac{x\,\frac{d}{dx}C(x) - C(x)\,\frac{d}{dx}x}{x^2}$$

$$= \frac{xC'(x) - C(x)}{x^2}$$

$$= \frac{1}{x}\left[C'(x) - \frac{C(x)}{x}\right]$$

Observe that in this final expression square brackets represent the difference between the marginal cost, $C'(x)$, and the average cost, $C(x)/x$. Thus we conclude that *the marginal average cost is equal to marginal cost minus average cost all divided by the quantity produced.* In particular, the marginal average cost is zero when marginal cost and average cost are equal to one another.

EXAMPLE 7   Compute the marginal average cost for the cost function

$$C(x) = 0.001x^3 - 0.3x^2 + 40x + 1000$$

when $x = 100$.

Solution $C'(x) = 0.003x^2 - 0.6x + 40$ and so

$$C'(100) = 0.003(100)^2 - 0.6(100) + 40 = 10$$

$$C(100) = 0.001(100)^3 - 0.3(100)^2 + 40(100) + 1000 = 3000.$$

Therefore the marginal average cost when $x = 100$ is

$$\frac{1}{x}\left[C'(x) - \frac{C(x)}{x}\right] = \frac{1}{100}\left[10 - \frac{3000}{100}\right] = -0.2.$$

So when $x = 100$, the average cost per unit decreases by 0.2 for each additional unit produced.

PROOF OF THEOREM 2   Let $y = u/v$. When x changes to $x + \Delta x$, then y changes to $y + \Delta y$, u to $u + \Delta u$, and v to $v + \Delta v$, so that

$$y + \Delta y = \frac{u + \Delta u}{v + \Delta v}.$$

We subtract $y = u/v$ from both sides.

$$\Delta y = \frac{u + \Delta u}{v + \Delta v} - \frac{u}{v}$$

$$= \frac{v(u + \Delta u) - u(v + \Delta v)}{v(v + \Delta v)}$$

$$= \frac{v \, \Delta u - u \, \Delta v}{v(v + \Delta v)}$$

Dividing by Δx, we obtain

$$\frac{\Delta y}{\Delta x} = \frac{v \dfrac{\Delta u}{\Delta x} - u \dfrac{\Delta v}{\Delta x}}{v(v + \Delta v)}.$$

If we now take the limits as $\Delta x \longrightarrow 0$, so that $\Delta y/\Delta x \longrightarrow dy/dx$, $\Delta u/\Delta x \longrightarrow du/dx$, and $\Delta v/\Delta x \longrightarrow dv/dx$, we have

$$\frac{dy}{dx} = \frac{v \dfrac{du}{dx} - u \dfrac{dv}{dx}}{v(v + 0)} = \frac{vu' - uv'}{v^2}$$

since the extra Δv in the denominator tends to zero. Thus we have proved the result stated in the theorem.

EXERCISES 1

(1–8) Using the product rule, find the derivatives of the following functions with respect to the variable involved.

1. $y = (x + 1)(x^3 + 3)$ 2. $y = (x^3 + 6x^2)(x^2 - 1)$

3. $u = (7x + 1)(2 - 3x)$ 4. $u = (x^2 + 7x)(x^2 + 3x + 1)$

5. $f(x) = (x^2 - 5x + 1)(2x + 3)$ 6. $g(t) = \left(t + \dfrac{1}{t}\right)\left(5t^2 - \dfrac{1}{t^2}\right)$

7. $g(x) = (x^2 + 1)(3x - 1)(2x - 3)$ 8. $f(x) = (2x + 1)(3x^2 + 1)(x^3 + 7)$

(9–12) Using the product rule, calculate the marginal revenue for the following demand relations.

9. $x = 1000 - 2p$ 10. $p = 40 - \frac{1}{2}\sqrt{x}$

11. $x = 4000 - 10\sqrt{p}$ 12. $p = 15 - 0.1x^{0.6} - 0.3x^{0.3}$

13. The average income per capita in a certain country at time t is equal to $W = 6{,}000 + 500t + 10t^2$. ($W$ is in dollars and t is in years.) The population size at time t (in millions) is $P = 10 + 0.2t + 0.01t^2$. Calculate the rate of change of GNP at time t. (*Hint:* GNP = population size $\times$ per capita income.)

14. Repeat Exercise 13 for the case when $W = 1000 + 60t + t^2$ and $P = 4 + 0.1t + 0.01t^2$.

(15–22) Use the quotient rule to find the derivatives of the following functions with respect to the independent variable involved.

15. $f(x) = \dfrac{x + 2}{x - 1}$ 16. $g(x) = \dfrac{3 - x}{x^2 - 3}$ 17. $y = \dfrac{t^2 - 7t}{t - 5}$

18. $y = \dfrac{u^2 - u + 1}{u^2 + u + 1}$ 19. $x = \dfrac{\sqrt{u} + 1}{\sqrt{u} - 1}$ 20. $t = \dfrac{x^2 - 1}{x^2 + 1}$

21. $y = \dfrac{1}{x^2 + 1}$ **22.** $y = \dfrac{1}{(t + 1)^2}$

(23–24) Compute the marginal average cost for the following cost functions (a, b, and n are constants).

23. $C(x) = a + bx$ **24.** $C(x) = a + bx^n$

25. If the GNP of a nation at time t is $I = 10 + 0.4t + 0.01t^2$ (in billions of dollars) and the population size (in millions) is $P = 4 + 0.1t + 0.01t^2$, find the rate of change of per capita income.

26. Use the quotient rule to *prove* that $(d/dx)(x^{-7}) = -7x^{-8}$. (*Hint:* Write $x^{-7} = 1/x^7$.)

*27. Generalize Exercise 26 to prove that $(d/dx)(x^n) = nx^{n-1}$ when n is any negative integer. (*Hint:* Write $x^n = 1/x^m$, where $m = -n$.)

13-2 THE CHAIN RULE

Let $y = f(u)$ be a function of u and $u = g(x)$ be a function of x. Then we can write

$$y = f[g(x)]$$

representing y as a function of x, called the *composite function of f and g*. It is denoted by $(f \circ g)(x)$. (See Section 4 of Chapter 5.)

The derivatives of composite functions can be found by the use of the following theorem. A proof will be given at the end of this section.

THEOREM 1 (CHAIN RULE)

If y is a function of u and u is a function of x, then

$$\frac{dy}{dx} = \frac{dy}{du} \cdot \frac{du}{dx}.$$

The chain rule provides what is probably the most useful of all the aids to differentiation, as will soon become apparent. It is a tool that is constantly in use when you work with the differential calculus, and you should master its use as soon as possible. When using it to differentiate a complicated function, it is necessary at the start to spot how to write the given function as the composition of two simpler functions. The following examples provide some illustrations.

EXAMPLE 1   Find dy/dx when $y = (x^2 + 1)^5$.

Solution   We could solve this problem by expanding $(x^2 + 1)^5$ as a polynomial in x. However, it is much simpler to use the chain rule.

Observe that y can be written as a composite function in the following way.

$$y = u^5 \quad \text{where} \quad u = x^2 + 1$$

Then

$$\frac{dy}{du} = 5u^4 \quad \text{and} \quad \frac{du}{dx} = 2x.$$

From the chain rule, we have the following.

$$\frac{dy}{dx} = \frac{dy}{du} \cdot \frac{du}{dx}$$

$$= 5u^4 \cdot 2x$$

$$= 5(x^2 + 1)^4 \cdot 2x = 10x(x^2 + 1)^4$$

Another way of writing the chain rule is that if $y = f(u)$, then

$$\frac{dy}{dx} = f'(u) \frac{du}{dx}$$

(since $f'(u) = dy/du$). In particular, if $f(u) = u^n$, then $f'(u) = nu^{n-1}$. Thus we have the following special case of the chain rule.

> If $y = [u(x)]^n$, then $\dfrac{dy}{dx} = nu^{n-1} \dfrac{du}{dx}$.

Think of a composite function as having different layers that you peel off one by one. The outside layer of the function corresponds to the part you would compute last if you were evaluating it. For example, if $y = (x^2 + 1)^5$, the *outside* part of the function is the fifth power and the *inside* part is $(x^2 + 1)$. If you were evaluating y for a particular value of x, you would first evaluate the inside part, $x^2 + 1$, and then you would raise it to the fifth power. For example, if $x = 2$, then *inside* $= x^2 + 1 = 2^2 + 1 = 5$ and $y = (\textit{inside})^5 = 5^5 = 3125$.

When differentiating a composite function, you first differentiate the outside layer of the function, then multiply by the derivative of the inside. In these verbal terms we can rephrase the chain rule as follows.

If $y = f(\textit{inside})$, then $\dfrac{dy}{dx} = f'(\textit{inside}) \cdot (\text{derivative of } \textit{inside} \text{ w.r.t. } x)$.

If $y = (\textit{inside})^n$, then $\dfrac{dy}{dx} = n(\textit{inside})^{n-1} \cdot (\text{derivative of } \textit{inside} \text{ w.r.t. } x)$.

Here *inside* stands for any differentiable function of x.

For example, in the example in which $y = (x^2 + 1)^5$, we would take *inside* to be $x^2 + 1$ and $y = f(\textit{inside}) = (\textit{inside})^5$. Then immediately,

$$\frac{dy}{dx} = 5(\textit{inside})^4 \cdot \frac{d}{dx}(\textit{inside})$$

$$= 5(x^2 + 1)^4 \cdot \frac{d}{dx}(x^2 + 1)$$

$$= 5(x^2 + 1)^4 \cdot 2x = 10x(x^2 + 1)^4$$

giving the same answer as before.

EXAMPLE 2   Given $f(t) = 1/\sqrt{t^2 + 3}$, find $f'(t)$.

Solution   Let $u = t^2 + 3$, so that $y = f(t) = 1/\sqrt{u} = u^{-1/2}$. Then

$$\frac{du}{dt} = 2t \quad \text{and} \quad \frac{dy}{du} = -\tfrac{1}{2}u^{-3/2} = -\tfrac{1}{2}(t^2 + 3)^{-3/2}.$$

Thus, by the chain rule,

$$\frac{dy}{dt} = \frac{dy}{du} \cdot \frac{du}{dt}$$

$$= -\tfrac{1}{2}(t^2 + 3)^{-3/2} \cdot 2t = -t(t^2 + 3)^{-3/2}.$$

Alternately we can solve directly.

$$f(t) = \frac{1}{\sqrt{t^2 + 3}} = (t^2 + 3)^{-1/2}$$

Here *inside* is $(t^2 + 3)$ and *outside* is the power $-\tfrac{1}{2}$. Using the power formula to differentiate this outside part, we have

$$f'(t) = -\tfrac{1}{2}(t^2 + 3)^{-1/2-1} \cdot \frac{d}{dt}(t^2 + 3)$$

$$= -\tfrac{1}{2}(t^2 + 3)^{-3/2} \cdot 2t = -t(t^2 + 3)^{-3/2}.$$

EXAMPLE 3   Given $y = (x^2 + 5x + 1)(2 - x^2)^4$, find dy/dx.

Solution   Using the product rule for derivatives, we get

$$\frac{dy}{dx} = (x^2 + 5x + 1)\frac{d}{dx}(2 - x^2)^4 + (2 - x^2)^4 \cdot \frac{d}{dx}(x^2 + 5x + 1).$$

In order to evaluate $(d/dx)(2 - x^2)^4$, we can use the chain rule with *inside* $= (2 - x^2)$.

$$\frac{dy}{dx} = (x^2 + 5x + 1)\left[4(2 - x^2)^3 \frac{d}{dx}(2 - x^2)\right] + (2 - x^2)^4(2x + 5)$$

$$= (x^2 + 5x + 1)[4(2 - x^2)^3 \cdot (-2x)] + (2 - x^2)^4(2x + 5)$$

$$= -8x(2 - x^2)^3(x^2 + 5x + 1) + (2x + 5)(2 - x^2)^4$$

Factoring then yields

$$\frac{dy}{dx} = (2 - x^2)^3[-8x(x^2 + 5x + 1) + (2x + 5)(2 - x^2)]$$

$$= (2 - x^2)^3[10 - 4x - 45x^2 - 10x^3].$$

EXAMPLE 4   A shoe manufacturer can use his plant to make either men's or women's shoes. If he makes x (in thousands of pairs) men's shoes and y (in thousands of pairs) women's shoes per week, then x and y are related by the equation

$$2x^2 + y^2 = 25.$$

(This equation is the product transformation equation; see Section 3 of Chapter 5.) If the profit is $10 on each pair of shoes, calculate the marginal profit with respect to x when $x = 2$.

Solution   The weekly profit P in thousands of dollars is given by

$$P = 10x + 10y$$

since each thousand pairs of shoes brings in ten thousand dollars in profit, and so $(x + y)$ thousand pairs give $10(x + y)$ thousand dollars profit. But

$$y^2 = 25 - 2x^2$$

or

$$y = \sqrt{25 - 2x^2}.$$

Therefore we can express P in terms of x alone as

$$P = 10x + 10\sqrt{25 - 2x^2}.$$

The marginal profit w.r.t. x is just the derivative dP/dx. It measures the increase in profit per unit increase in x when x, the production of men's shoes, is given a small increment. It is

$$\frac{dP}{dx} = \frac{d}{dx}[10x + 10(25 - 2x^2)^{1/2}].$$

In order to differentiate the second term, we must use the chain rule with $inside = (25 - 2x^2)$.

$$\frac{d}{dx}(25 - 2x^2)^{1/2} = \tfrac{1}{2}(25 - 2x^2)^{-1/2} \cdot \frac{d}{dx}(25 - 2x^2)$$

$$= \tfrac{1}{2}(25 - 2x^2)^{-1/2}(-4x)$$

$$= -2x(25 - 2x^2)^{-1/2}$$

Therefore

$$\frac{dP}{dx} = 10 + 10\frac{d}{dx}(25 - 2x^2)^{1/2}$$

$$= 10 + 10[-2x(25 - 2x^2)^{-1/2}]$$

$$= 10 - 20x(25 - 2x^2)^{-1/2}.$$

When $x = 2$, the value of y is

$$y = \sqrt{25 - 2x^2} = \sqrt{25 - 2(4)} = \sqrt{17} = 4.1.$$

Thus the firm is producing 2000 pairs of men's shoes and 4100 pairs of women's shoes per week. Its weekly profit is

$$P = 10(x + y) = 10(2 + 4.1) = 61$$

(or \$61,000). The marginal profit

$$\frac{dP}{dx} = 10 - 20(2)[25 - 2(4)]^{-1/2}$$

$$\doteq 10 - \frac{40}{\sqrt{17}} = 0.30.$$

Thus an increase of Δx thousands of pairs of men's shoes gives an approximate increase of $(0.30)\,\Delta x$ thousand dollars in the profit.

Related Rates

Let $y = f(x)$ and suppose that x varies as a function of time t. Then since y is a function of x, y also will vary with time. By using the chain rule, it is possible to find an expression for the rate at which y varies in terms of the rate at which x varies. For we have

$$\frac{dy}{dt} = \frac{dy}{dx} \cdot \frac{dx}{dt} = f'(x)\frac{dx}{dt}$$

and we have a direct relation between the two rates dy/dt and dx/dt. This is called the equation of **related rates**.

EXAMPLE 5   A firm has the cost function $C(x) = 25 + 2x - \frac{1}{20}x^2$, where x is the production level. If the production level is equal to 5 at present and is increasing at the rate of 0.7 per year, find the rate at which the production costs are rising.

Solution   We are given that $dx/dt = 0.7$ (when time is measured in years). The marginal cost is given by

$$\frac{dC}{dx} = 2 - \frac{x}{10}.$$

Therefore

$$\frac{dC}{dt} = \frac{dC}{dx}\frac{dx}{dt} = \left(2 - \frac{x}{10}\right)\frac{dx}{dt}.$$

Substituting $x = 5$, the current production level, we obtain

$$\frac{dC}{dt} = (2 - \tfrac{5}{10})(0.7) = 1.05.$$

Thus the production costs are increasing at the rate of 1.05 per year.

PROOF OF CHAIN RULE   The proof of the chain rule, if given in complete detail, would be a little more complicated than we wish to include. We shall therefore provide a proof which, although covering most cases that arise, does have certain restrictions on its range of applicability.

Let Δx be an increment in x. Since u and y are functions of x, they will change whenever x changes, so we denote their increments by Δu and Δy. Then, as long as $\Delta u \neq 0$, we have

$$\frac{\Delta y}{\Delta x} = \frac{\Delta y}{\Delta u}\frac{\Delta u}{\Delta x}.$$

We now let $\Delta x \longrightarrow 0$. In this limit, we also have that $\Delta u \longrightarrow 0$ and $\Delta y \longrightarrow 0$, and so

$$\lim_{\Delta x \to 0} \frac{\Delta y}{\Delta x} = \lim_{\Delta x \to 0}\left(\frac{\Delta y}{\Delta u}\frac{\Delta u}{\Delta x}\right)$$

$$= \left(\lim_{\Delta x \to 0}\frac{\Delta y}{\Delta u}\right)\left(\lim_{\Delta x \to 0}\frac{\Delta u}{\Delta x}\right)$$

$$= \left(\lim_{\Delta u \to 0}\frac{\Delta y}{\Delta u}\right)\left(\frac{du}{dx}\right)$$

$$= \frac{dy}{du} \cdot \frac{du}{dx}$$

as required.

The reason that this proof is incomplete lies in the assumption that $\Delta u \neq 0$. For most functions $u(x)$, it will be the case that Δu never vanishes when Δx is sufficiently small (but $\Delta x \neq 0$). However, it is conceivable that the function $u(x)$ could be so peculiar in its behavior that Δu vanishes repeatedly as $\Delta x \to 0$. For such an unusual function, the above proof would then break down. It is possible to modify the proof to cover such cases as this, but we shall not do so here.

EXERCISES 2

(1–20) Find the derivatives of the following functions with respect to the independent variable involved.

1. $y = (3x + 5)^7$

2. $y = \sqrt{5 - 2t}$

3. $u = (2x^2 + 1)^{3/2}$

4. $x = (y^3 + 7)^6$

5. $f(x) = \dfrac{1}{(x^2 + 1)^4}$

6. $g(x) = \dfrac{1}{(x^2 + x + 1)^3}$

7. $h(t) = \sqrt{t^2 + a^2}$

8. $F(x) = \sqrt[3]{x^3 + 3x}$

9. $G(u) = (u^2 + 1)^3(2u + 1)$

10. $H(y) = (2y^2 + 3)^6(5y + 2)$

11. $x = \dfrac{1}{\sqrt[3]{t^3 + 1}}$

12. $y = \left(t + \dfrac{1}{t}\right)^{10}$

13. $y = \dfrac{(x^2 + 1)^2}{x + 1}$

14. $y = \left(\dfrac{t}{t + 1}\right)^6$

15. $z = \dfrac{x}{\sqrt{x^2 - 1}}$

16. $u = x^2\sqrt{x^3 + a^3}$

17. $y = (x^2 + 1)^{0.6}$

18. $y = \sqrt{\dfrac{3x + 7}{5 + 2x}}$

19. $x = \dfrac{t^2}{\sqrt{t^2 + 4}}$

20. $Z = \dfrac{\sqrt{2x + 1}}{x + 2}$

21. The distance traveled by a moving object up to time t is given by $y = (3t + 1)\sqrt{t + 1}$. Find the instantaneous velocity at time t.

22. The size of a certain population at time t is
$$\left(\frac{t^2 + 3t + 1}{t + 1}\right)^6.$$
Find the rate of change of the population size.

(23–24) Find the marginal cost for the following cost functions.

23. $C(x) = \sqrt{100 + x^2}$

24. $C(x) = 20 + 2x - \sqrt{x^2 - 1}$

25–26. Calculate the marginal average cost for the cost functions of Exercises 23 and 24.

(27–28) Calculate the marginal revenue for the following demand relations.

27. $p = \sqrt{100 - 0.1x - 10^{-4}x^2}$

28. $x = 1000(8 - p)^{1/3}$

29. A manufacturer's cost function is given by
$$C(x) = 2000 + 10x - 0.1x^2 + 0.002x^3.$$
If the current production level is $x = 100$ and is increasing at the rate of 2 per month, find the rate at which the production costs are increasing.

30. The manufacturer in Exercise 29 has a revenue function given by $R(x) = 65x - 0.05x^2$. Calculate the rate at which the revenue is increasing and the rate at which the profit is increasing.

13-3 DERIVATIVES OF EXPONENTIAL AND LOGARITHMIC FUNCTIONS

Figure 1 shows the graph of the exponential function $f(x) = a^x$ in a typical case when $a > 1$. When $x = 0$, $y = a^0 = 1$, so the graph passes through the point $(0, 1)$ for any value of a. The slope of the graph as it crosses the y-axis at this point varies, depending on a: the bigger the value of a, the greater the slope when $x = 0$.

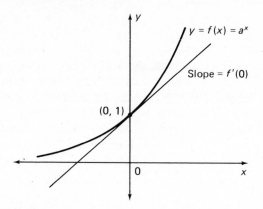

FIGURE 1

Let us select the particular value of a for which the slope of the graph at $x = 0$ is equal to 1. For this value of a, the graph slopes upwards at an angle of $45°$ with the horizontal as it crosses the y-axis. The condition that must be satisfied is that the derivative $f'(0)$ must equal 1. Thus, since in general

$$f'(x) = \lim_{\Delta x \to 0} \frac{f(x + \Delta x) - f(x)}{\Delta x}$$

we have

$$f'(0) = \lim_{\Delta x \to 0} \frac{f(0 + \Delta x) - f(0)}{\Delta x}$$

$$= \lim_{\Delta x \to 0} \frac{f(\Delta x) - f(0)}{\Delta x}$$

$$= \lim_{\Delta x \to 0} \cdot \frac{a^{\Delta x} - a^0}{\Delta x}.$$

Since $a^0 = 1$, the condition $f'(0) = 1$ therefore reduces to

$$\lim_{\Delta x \to 0} \frac{a^{\Delta x} - 1}{\Delta x} = 1. \tag{1}$$

This condition determines the value of a for us. It turns out that the value of a that satisfies this condition is $a = e = 2.71828\ldots$, the base of the natural exponential and logarithmic functions that were introduced in Chapter 6. The proof of this statement is beyond the scope of this book; however Table 1

TABLE 1.

Δx	$\dfrac{(2.7183)^{\Delta x} - 1}{\Delta x}$
1	1.7183
0.1	1.0517
0.01	1.0050
0.001	1.0005
0.0001	1.000057

provides quite convincing evidence of its accuracy. We know that $e = 2.7183$ to four decimal places, and in the table we have computed the values of the quantity $[(2.7183)^{\Delta x} - 1]/\Delta x$ for a series of values of Δx starting with $\Delta x = 1$ and decreasing to $\Delta x = 0.0001$. It is clear that as Δx becomes smaller and smaller, the quantity in question becomes closer and closer to 1. Therefore Equation (1) is satisfied to a very close approximation by taking $a = 2.7183$. A more exact calculation would show that the quantity $[(2.7183)^{\Delta x} - 1]/\Delta x$ does, in fact, approach the limiting value 1.00000668 (to eight decimal places) as $\Delta x \to 0$.

Instead of taking $a = 2.7183$, we could take an even better approximation to the irrational number e—for example we could take $a = 2.718282$, which is correct to seven significant figures. Then by constructing a table similar to the one above, we could convince ourselves that the limiting value of $(a^{\Delta x} - 1)/\Delta x$ as $\Delta x \to 0$ is even closer to 1. (In fact, with $a = 2.718282$, this limiting value is equal to 1.0000000631 to ten decimal places.) We can then be confident that condition (1) is satisfied by choosing the base of the exponential expression to be e.

Let us now evaluate the derivative of the function e^x for a general x. Setting $y = e^x$, we have

$$\frac{dy}{dx} = \lim_{\Delta x \to 0} \frac{e^{x + \Delta x} - e^x}{\Delta x}.$$

But using a basic property of exponents, $e^{x + \Delta x} = e^x \cdot e^{\Delta x}$, and so

$$\frac{dy}{dx} = \lim_{\Delta x \to 0} e^x \frac{e^{\Delta x} - 1}{\Delta x}$$

$$= e^x \lim_{\Delta x \to 0} \frac{e^{\Delta x} - 1}{\Delta x}$$

$$= e^x$$

after using the Equation (1) (with a replaced by e).

Thus we have the important result that the derivative of the function e^x is the function itself.

$$\text{If } y = e^x, \frac{dy}{dx} = e^x.$$

The reason that the natural exponential function is so important rests in this property that its derivative is everywhere equal to the function itself. It is, apart from a constant factor, the only function that possesses this property. It is this fact that accounts for our interest in the number e and in exponential expressions and logarithms that have e as their bases.

EXAMPLE 1   Evaluate dy/dx if $y = xe^x$.

Solution   In order to differentiate the function xe^x, we must use the product rule since we can write $y = uv$ with $u = x$ and $v = e^x$. Then

$$\frac{du}{dx} = 1 \quad \text{and} \quad \frac{dv}{dx} = e^x.$$

Therefore,

$$\frac{dy}{dx} = u\frac{dv}{dx} + v\frac{du}{dx}$$

$$= (x)(e^x) + (e^x)(1)$$

$$= (x + 1)e^x.$$

EXAMPLE 2   A certain item can be manufactured and sold at a profit of $10 each. If the manufacturer spends x dollars on advertising the product, then the number of items that can be sold will be equal to $1000(1 - e^{-kx})$, where $k = 0.001$. If P denotes the net profit from sales, calculate dP/dx and interpret this derivative. Evaluate dP/dx when $x = 1000$ and when $x = 3000$.

Solution   Since each item produces a profit of $10, the total gross profit from sales is obtained by multiplying the number of sales by $10. The net profit is then obtained by subtracting the advertising costs:

$$P = 10,000(1 - e^{-kx}) - x.$$

Therefore

$$\frac{dP}{dx} = -10,000 \frac{d}{dx}(e^{-kx}) - 1.$$

In order to differentiate e^{-kx}, we use the chain rule, since this function can be written as a composite function. Denoting $y = e^{-kx}$, we have $y = e^u$ where $u = -kx$. Therefore

$$\frac{dy}{dx} = \frac{dy}{du} \cdot \frac{du}{dx}$$

$$= (e^u)(-k) = -ke^u = -ke^{-kx}.$$

Consequently,

$$\frac{dP}{dx} = -10,000(-ke^{-kx}) - 1$$

$$= 10,000ke^{-kx} - 1.$$

Since $k = 0.001$,

$$\frac{dP}{dx} = 10e^{-0.001x} - 1.$$

The interpretation of this derivative is that it measures the rate of change of net profit with respect to advertising expenditure. In other words, dP/dx gives the number of dollars increase in net profit produced by an additional dollar spent on advertising.

When $x = 1000$,

$$\frac{dP}{dx} = 10e^{-1} - 1 = 10(0.3679) - 1 = 2.679.$$

So when $1000 is spent on advertising, each additional dollar yields an increase of $2.68 in the net profit.

When $x = 3000$,

$$\frac{dP}{dx} = 10(e^{-3}) - 1 = 10(0.0498) - 1 = -0.502.$$

Thus when $3000 is spent on advertising, an additional dollar spent this way yields a decrease of $0.50 in the net profit. It is clear in this case that the manufacturer should not do more advertising—the cost of extra advertising would outweigh the value of the additional sales that it would generate. (In fact, when $x = 3000$, more is already being spent on advertising than is desirable.)

EXAMPLE 3 A population grows according to the logistic model (see Section 4 of Chapter 6) such that at time t its size y is given by

$$y = y_m[1 + Ce^{-kt}]^{-1}$$

with y_m, C, and k constants. Find the rate of increase of population at time t.

Solution The required rate of increase is dy/dt. We observe that y is a composite function of t of the form

$$y = y_m(inside)^{-1}, \qquad inside = 1 + Ce^{-kt}.$$

Therefore

$$\frac{dy}{dt} = y_m(-1)(inside)^{-2} \frac{d}{dt}(inside)$$

$$= -y_m[1 + Ce^{-kt}]^{-2} \frac{d}{dt}(Ce^{-kt}).$$

This remaining derivative can be evaluated as in the last example by writing e^{-kt} as the composite function e^u, where $u = -kt$. Then

$$\frac{d}{dt}(Ce^{-kt}) = \frac{d}{du}(Ce^u) \frac{du}{dt}$$

$$= Ce^u(-k) = -kCe^{-kt}.$$

Substituting back into dy/dt, we obtain the growth rate of the population.

$$\frac{dy}{dt} = -y_m[1 + Ce^{-kt}]^{-2}(-kCe^{-kt})$$

$$= \frac{ky_m Ce^{-kt}}{(1 + Ce^{-kt})^2}$$

In the previous examples, we have used the chain rule to differentiate functions of the type e^{kx} with respect to x. In fact, we can differentiate composite functions of the type $e^{u(x)}$ where $u(x)$ is any differentiable function of x. We obtain the following.

$$\text{If } y = e^{u(x)}, \text{ then } \frac{dy}{dx} = e^{u(x)}u'(x).$$

In verbal form we can say

$$\frac{d}{dx}e^{inside} = e^{inside}\frac{d}{dx}(inside)$$

where *inside* is any differentiable function of x.

Let us now evaluate the derivative of the function $y = \ln x$, the natural logarithm function.

If $y = \ln x$, then $x = e^y$. Let us differentiate this second equation with respect to x.

$$\frac{d}{dx}(e^y) = \frac{d}{dx}(x) = 1$$

But from the chain rule, we see that

$$\frac{d}{dx}(e^y) = \frac{d}{dy}(e^y) \cdot \frac{dy}{dx} = e^y\frac{dy}{dx},$$

since $(d/dy)(e^y) = e^y$. Therefore $e^y(dy/dx) = 1$, and so

$$\frac{dy}{dx} = \frac{1}{e^y} = \frac{1}{x}.$$

Thus if

$$y = \ln x, \qquad \frac{dy}{dx} = \frac{1}{x}.$$

EXAMPLE 4 Find dy/dx if $y = \ln(x + c)$, where c is a constant.

Solution We have y a composite function, with $y = \ln u$ and $u = x + c$. Therefore, from the chain rule,

$$\frac{dy}{dx} = \frac{dy}{du} \cdot \frac{du}{dx}$$

$$= \frac{d}{du}(\ln u) \cdot \frac{du}{dx}$$

$$= \left(\frac{1}{u}\right) \cdot (1) = \frac{1}{x+c}.$$

In general, the chain rule allows us to differentiate any composite function of the form $y = \ln u(x)$ in the following way:

$$\frac{dy}{dx} = \frac{dy}{du} \cdot \frac{du}{dx} = \frac{d}{du}(\ln u) \cdot u'(x) = \frac{1}{u}u'(x).$$

So, if $y = \ln u(x)$, then $\dfrac{dy}{dx} = \dfrac{u'(x)}{u(x)}$.

Alternatively, in verbal form,

$$\frac{d}{dx}\ln(inside) = \frac{1}{inside}\frac{d}{dx}(inside)$$

where *inside* stands for any differentiable function of x.

EXAMPLE 5 Differentiate $\ln(x^2 + x - 2)$.

Solution Here we take *inside* $= (x^2 + x - 2)$.

$$\frac{d}{dx}\ln(x^2 + x - 2) = \frac{1}{(x^2 + x - 2)}\frac{d}{dx}(x^2 + x - 2)$$

$$= \frac{1}{(x^2 + x - 2)}(2x + 1)$$

$$= \frac{2x + 1}{x^2 + x - 2}$$

When we want to differentiate the logarithm of a product or quotient of various expressions, it is often useful to simplify the given function first by making use of the properties of logarithms.

EXAMPLE 6 Find dy/dx when $y = \ln(e^x/\sqrt{x+1})$.

Solution We first simplify y.

$$y = \ln\left(\frac{e^x}{\sqrt{x+1}}\right) = \ln(e^x) - \ln(\sqrt{x+1})$$

$$= x \ln e - \tfrac{1}{2}\ln(x+1)$$

Therefore (since $\ln e = 1$)

$$\frac{dy}{dx} = 1 - \frac{1}{2}\frac{d}{dx}\ln(x+1) = 1 - \frac{1}{2(x+1)}.$$

EXAMPLE 7   Find dy/dx if $y = \log(x)$.

Solution   In order to differentiate the common logarithm, we express it in terms of the natural logarithm,

$$y = \log(x) = \log_{10} x = \frac{\ln(x)}{\ln(10)}.$$

Therefore

$$\frac{dy}{dx} = \frac{1}{\ln(10)} \frac{d}{dx} \ln(x) = \frac{1}{\ln(10)} \cdot \frac{1}{x}$$

$$= \frac{0.4343\ldots}{x}$$

since $1/\ln(10) = 1/2.3026\ldots = 0.4343\ldots$.

Observe that in this example, the common logarithm had to be expressed in terms of a natural logarithm before it could be differentiated. This is equally true of logarithms with respect to any other base, such as $\log_a x$: Such functions must first be expressed as natural logarithms. Similarly, a general exponential function a^x must be expressed as e^{kx} ($k = \ln a$) before it can be differentiated.

Now that we have introduced the derivatives of the exponential and logarithmic functions, let us summarize the three forms of the chain rule that we shall use most. In Table 2, *inside* represents any differentiable function of x.

TABLE 2

$f(x)$	$f'(x)$
$(inside)^n$ or $[u(x)]^n$	$n(inside)^{n-1} \dfrac{d}{dx}(inside)$ or $n[u(x)]^{n-1}u'(x)$
e^{inside} or $e^{u(x)}$	$e^{inside} \dfrac{d}{dx}(inside)$ or $e^{u(x)}u'(x)$
$\ln(inside)$ or $\ln u(x)$	$\dfrac{1}{inside} \dfrac{d}{dx}(inside)$ or $\dfrac{1}{u(x)}u'(x)$

EXERCISES 3

(1–26) Find dy/dx for each of the following functions.

1. $y = xe^x$

2. $y = \dfrac{e^x}{x}$

3. $y = e^{x^2}$

4. $y = e^{\sqrt{x}}$

5. $y = \dfrac{e^{\sqrt{x}}}{e^x}$

6. $y = e^{ax^3+bx^2+cx+d}$

7. $y = \ln(x^2)$

8. $y = \ln(ax^3 + bx^2 + cx + d)$

9. $y = \dfrac{1}{\ln x}$ 10. $y = (\ln x)^2$ 11. $y = \log(e^x)$

12. $y = \log(e^x - 1)$ 13. $y = x(\ln x - 1)$ 14. $y = x^2 \ln(x^2 + 1)$

15. $y = \dfrac{\ln x}{x}$ 16. $y = \dfrac{x+1}{\ln(x+1)}$ 17. $y = \ln\left(\dfrac{x+2}{\sqrt{x^2+1}}\right)$

18. $y = \ln\left(\dfrac{e^x\sqrt{x-1}}{x^3}\right)$ 19. $y = \sqrt{\ln x}$ 20. $y = \left(\dfrac{\ln x}{e^x}\right)^{1/3}$

(*Hint:* Use the base-change formula for Exercises 21–26.)

21. $y = \log_a x$ 22. $y = \log_3(x+1)$ 23. $y = a^x$

24. $y = xa^{x^2}$ 25. $y = \log_x(x+1)$ 26. $y = \log_x(x^2)$

(27–30) Compute the marginal revenue for the following demand relations.

27. $p = 5 - e^{0.1x}$ 28. $p = 4 + e^{-0.1x}$

29. $x = 1000(2 - e^p)$ 30. $x = 100\ln(16 - p^2)$

(31–32) Calculate the marginal cost and the marginal average cost for the following cost functions.

31. $C(x) = 100 + x + e^{-0.5x}$ 32. $C(x) = \sqrt{25 + x + \ln(x+1)}$

*33. A certain population is growing according to the formula

$$y = y_m(1 - Ce^{-kt})^3$$

where y_m, C, and k are constants. Find the rate of growth at time t and show that

$$\frac{dy}{dt} = 3ky^{2/3}(y_m^{1/3} - y^{1/3}).$$

*34. The proportion p of physicians who have heard of a new drug t months after it has become available satisfies the equation

$$\ln p - \ln(1 - p) = k(t - C)$$

where k and C are constants. Express p as a function of t and calculate dp/dt. Show that

$$\frac{dp}{dt} = kp(1 - p).$$

*35. Prove that $(d/dx)(x^n) = nx^{n-1}$ for n any real number and $x > 0$. (*Hint:* Write $x^n = e^{n \ln x}$.)

13-4 HIGHER DERIVATIVES

If $y = f(t)$ is a function of time t, then, as we have seen, the derivative $dy/dt = f'(t)$ represents the rate at which y changes. For example, if $s = f(t)$ is the distance traveled by a moving object, then $ds/dt = f'(t)$ gives the rate of change of distance or, in other words, the instantaneous *velocity* of the object. Let us denote this velocity by v. Then v is also a function of t, and—as a rule—may be differentiated to give the derivative dv/dt.

When the velocity of an object increases, we say that it *accelerates*. For example, when we press the gas pedal of a car, we cause it to accelerate, that is, to go faster. Let us suppose that over a period of 5 seconds, the car accelerates from a speed of 20 feet/second (which is about 14 miles per hour) to 80 feet/second (55 miles per hour). The increment in velocity is $\Delta v = 60$ feet/second and the time increment $\Delta t = 5$ seconds, so the average acceleration is given by

$$\frac{\Delta v}{\Delta t} = \frac{60}{5} = 12 \text{ feet/second/second (or ft/sec}^2\text{)}.$$

For a moving body, we are often interested in the *instantaneous acceleration*, which is defined as the limit of the average acceleration $\Delta v/\Delta t$ as $\Delta t \rightarrow 0$. In other words, instantaneous acceleration is the derivative dv/dt. It gives the instantaneous rate at which the velocity is increasing.

So, to calculate the acceleration, we must differentiate s and then differentiate the result once more. We have

$$\text{Acceleration} = \frac{dv}{dt} = \frac{d}{dt}\left(\frac{ds}{dt}\right).$$

Acceleration is called the *second derivative* of s w.r.t. t and is usually denoted by $f''(t)$ or by d^2s/dt^2.

We can also differentiate the acceleration with respect to t, since $f''(t)$ is, in general, a function of t that is differentiable. The result is denoted by $f'''(t)$ or by d^3s/dt^3 and is called the *third derivative* of s w.r.t. t. It represents the rate of change of the acceleration of the object. (There is no special name such as velocity or acceleration for this derivative—we simply call it the third derivative of distance with respect to time.)

In problems involving moving objects, the second derivative, acceleration, is a quantity of prime importance. For example, the degree of safety of the braking system of an automobile depends on the maximum deceleration it can give (deceleration is just a negative acceleration). Or the medical effects of rocket launching on an astronaut depend on the level of acceleration to which he is subjected. More fundamentally, it is one of the basic laws of mechanics that when an object is acted on by a force, it is caused to accelerate, and the magnitude of the acceleration is directly proportional to the size of the force. Thus acceleration enters into the basic laws of motion in an essential way.

We shall now examine the higher order derivatives in a more abstract context. Let $y = f(x)$ be a given function of x with derivative $dy/dx = f'(x)$. In full, we call this the **first derivative** of y w.r.t. x. If $f'(x)$ is a differentiable function of x, it may be differentiated and its derivative is called the **second derivative** of y w.r.t. x. If the second derivative is a differentiable function of x, its derivative is called the **third derivative** of y, and so on.

The first and all higher-order derivatives of y w.r.t. x are generally denoted by one of the following types of notation.

$$\frac{dy}{dx}, \quad \frac{d^2y}{dx^2}, \quad \frac{d^3y}{dx^3}, \ldots, \frac{d^ny}{dx^n}.$$

$$y', \quad y'', \quad y''', \ldots, y^{(n)}.$$

$$f'(x), \quad f''(x), \quad f'''(x), \ldots, f^{(n)}(x)$$

From the definition of higher-order derivatives, it is clear that

$$\frac{d^2y}{dx^2} = \frac{d}{dx}\left(\frac{dy}{dx}\right), \qquad \frac{d^3y}{dx^3} = \frac{d}{dx}\left(\frac{d^2y}{dx^2}\right)$$

and so on.

EXAMPLE 1   Find the first and higher-order derivatives of $3x^4 - 5x^3 + 7x^2 - 1$.

Solution   Let $y = 3x^4 - 5x^3 + 7x^2 - 1$. Then

$$\frac{dy}{dx} = \frac{d}{dx}(3x^4 - 5x^3 + 7x^2 - 1)$$

$$= 12x^3 - 15x^2 + 14x.$$

The second derivative of y is obtained by differentiating the first derivative.

$$\frac{d^2y}{dx^2} = \frac{d}{dx}\left(\frac{dy}{dx}\right)$$

$$= \frac{d}{dx}(12x^3 - 15x^2 + 14x)$$

$$= 36x^2 - 30x + 14$$

Differentiating again, we obtain the third derivative.

$$\frac{d^3y}{dx^3} = \frac{d}{dx}\left(\frac{d^2y}{dx^2}\right)$$

$$= \frac{d}{dx}(36x^2 - 30x + 14)$$

$$= 72x - 30$$

Continuing this process,

$$\frac{d^4y}{dx^4} = \frac{d}{dx}\left(\frac{d^3y}{dx^3}\right) = \frac{d}{dx}(72x - 30) = 72$$

$$\frac{d^5y}{dx^5} = \frac{d}{dx}\left(\frac{d^4y}{dx^4}\right) = \frac{d}{dx}(72) = 0$$

$$\frac{d^6y}{dx^6} = \frac{d}{dx}\left(\frac{d^5y}{dx^5}\right) = \frac{d}{dx}(0) = 0$$

and so on.

In this particular example, all derivatives higher than the fourth derivative are zero. This occurs because the fourth derivative is a constant.

EXAMPLE 2   Find the second derivative of $f(t) = e^{t^2+1}$.

Solution   To find the first derivative, we use the chain rule. Thus

$$f'(t) = e^{t^2+1} \cdot \frac{d}{dt}(t^2 + 1)$$

$$= e^{t^2+1} \cdot 2t = 2te^{t^2+1}.$$

Now $f'(t)$ is the product of two functions $u = 2t$ and $v = e^{t^2+1}$. To find $f''(t)$, we shall use the product rule.

$$f''(t) = 2t\frac{d}{dt}(e^{t^2+1}) + e^{t^2+1}\frac{d}{dt}(2t)$$

$$= 2t\left[e^{t^2+1}\frac{d}{dt}(t^2 + 1)\right] + e^{t^2+1}(2)$$

where we have used the chain rule to differentiate $v = e^{t^2+1}$.

Therefore

$$f''(t) = 2t[e^{t^2+1} \cdot 2t] + 2e^{t^2+1}$$
$$= 2e^{t^2+1}(2t^2 + 1).$$

EXAMPLE 3   A body falling under gravity from a position of rest falls a distance $s = 16t^2$ in t seconds. Find its acceleration.

Solution   The velocity after t seconds is

$$\frac{ds}{dt} = \frac{d}{dt}(16t^2) = 32t \text{ feet/second.}$$

We obtain the acceleration by differentiating again.

$$\text{Acceleration} = \frac{d^2s}{dt^2} = \frac{d}{dt}(32t) = 32 \text{ feet/second}^2$$

Note that this is independent of t: A body falling under gravity has a constant acceleration of 32 feet/second².

If $C(x)$ is a manufacturer's cost function—the cost of producing x items—then the first derivative $C'(x)$ gives the marginal cost, that is, the cost per additional item of a small increase in production. The second derivative $C''(x)$ gives the rate of increase of marginal cost with respect to an increase in production. We shall have more to say on the interpretation of this quantity in the next chapter, but meanwhile the following example will illustrate certain aspects of its significance.

EXAMPLE 4   For the cost function

$$C(x) = 0.001x^3 - 0.3x^2 + 40x + 1000,$$

the marginal cost is

$$C'(x) = 0.003x^2 - 0.6x + 40.$$

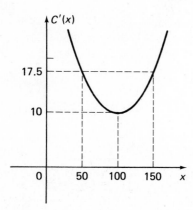

FIGURE 2

The second derivative is

$$C''(x) = 0.006x - 0.6$$
$$= 0.006(x - 100).$$

When $x = 150$, the marginal cost is $C'(150) = 17.5$. Furthermore, $C''(150) = 0.006(150 - 100) = 0.3$. We can interpret this result as signifying that each additional unit produced leads to an increase of 0.3 in the marginal cost.

Observe that in this example, $C''(x) < 0$ when $x < 100$. This means that when $x < 100$, increases in production lead to decreases in marginal cost. The graph of $C'(x)$ as a function of x slopes downwards when $x < 100$. (See Figure 2.) However when $x > 100$, the graph of $C'(x)$ slopes upwards, so its slope, $C''(x)$, is positive. In this case, increases in production lead to increases in the marginal cost.

(1–4) Find the first and higher-order derivatives of the following functions w.r.t. the independent variable involved.

1. $y = 3x^5 + 7x^3 - 4x^2 + 12$ 2. $u = (t^2 + 1)^2$

3. $f(x) = x^3 - 6x^2 + 9x + 16$ 4. $y(u) = (u^2 + 1)(3u - 2)$

5. Find y'' if $y = \dfrac{x^2}{(x^2 + 1)}$.   6. Find $f'''(t)$ if $f(t) = \dfrac{(t-1)}{(t+1)}$.

7. Find $g^{(4)}(u)$ if $g(u) = \dfrac{1}{3u + 1}$.   8. Find $\dfrac{d^2 y}{dt^2}$ if $y = \sqrt{t^2 + 1}$.

9. Find $\dfrac{d^2 u}{dx^2}$ if $u = \dfrac{1}{x^2 + 1}$.   10. Find $\dfrac{d^3 y}{dx^3}$ if $y = \dfrac{x^3 - 1}{x - 1}$, $(x \neq 1)$.

11. Find y''' if $y = \ln x$.   12. Find $y^{(4)}$ if $y = x \ln x$.

13. Find $y^{(4)}$ if $y = xe^x$.   14. Find y'' if $y = e^{x^2}$.

15. Find y'' if $y = \ln[(x + 1)(x + 2)]$.   16. Find y''' if $y = x^3 + e^{2x}$.

17. Find y'' if $y = (x + 1)e^{-x}$.   18. Find y'' if $y = \dfrac{x^2 + 1}{e^x}$.

19. Find the velocity and the acceleration of a moving object for each given distance s traveled in time t.

     a. $s = 9t + 16t^2$ b. $s = 3t^3 + 7t^2 - 5t$

20. Suppose the distance s traveled in time t is given by $s = t(3 - t)$.

     a. At what times is the velocity zero?

     b. What is the value of acceleration when the velocity equals zero?

(21–22) Find the marginal cost and the rate of change of marginal cost with respect to volume of production for the following cost functions.

21. $C(x) = 500 + 30x - 0.1x^2 + 0.002x^3$

22. $C(x) = 500 + 20x - 2x \ln x + 0.01x^2$

23. If $\bar{C}(x)$ is the average cost function, show that

$$\bar{C}''(x) = \frac{C''(x)}{x} - \frac{2C'(x)}{x^2} + \frac{2C(x)}{x^3}.$$

24. If $R(x)$ is the revenue function, show that

$$R''(x) = 2p'(x) + xp''(x)$$

where $p = p(x)$ is the price as a function of demand.

REVIEW EXERCISES FOR CHAPTER 13

1. State whether each of following is true or false. Replace each false statement by a corresponding true statement.

     a. The derivative of the product of two functions is equal to the product of their derivatives.

b. The derivative of the quotient of two functions is equal to the derivative of the numerator divided by the denominator all plus the numerator multiplied by the derivative of one over the denominator.

c. If $y = [u(x)]^n$, then $\dfrac{dy}{dx} = n[u(x)]^{n-1}$.

d. If $y = \ln\left[\dfrac{1}{u(x)}\right]$, then $\dfrac{dy}{dx} = u(x)\dfrac{d}{dx}\left[\dfrac{1}{u(x)}\right]$.

e. If $y = e^{\ln u(x)}$, then $\dfrac{dy}{dx} = u'(x)$.

f. The second derivative of any quadratic function is zero.

g. If the acceleration of a moving object is zero, then its velocity is also zero.

h. If $y = [u(x)]^n$ then $\dfrac{d^2y}{dx^2} = n[u(x)]^{n-1}u''(x)$.

i. $\dfrac{d}{dx}(e^{x^2}) = e^{2x}$

j. $\dfrac{d}{dx}\ln(x^2 + 1) = \dfrac{1}{x^2 + 1}$

k. $\dfrac{d}{dx}\ln 2 = \tfrac{1}{2}$

l. $\dfrac{d}{dx}e^x = xe^{x-1}$

m. $\dfrac{d}{dx}\left(\dfrac{1}{x^3}\right) = \dfrac{1}{3x^2}$

(2–11) Find dy/dx for the following functions.

2. $y = \dfrac{x}{\sqrt{x^2 + 1}}$ ⎯ **3.** $y = x\sqrt{x^2 + 4}$

4. $y = (x + 1)\sqrt{x + 3}$ ⎯ **5.** $y = (2x + 1)^3(3x - 1)^4$

6. $y = \dfrac{(x^2 + 1)^3}{(x - 1)^4}$ ⎯ **7.** $y = \dfrac{\sqrt{x + 1}}{\sqrt[3]{x + 1}}$

8. $y = x^2 e^{x^2}$ ⎯ **9.** $y = x^{\sqrt{2}}\ln x$

10. $y = \ln\dfrac{2^x}{\sqrt{x^3 + 1}}$ ⎯ **11.** $y = x^x$

(12–15) Find d^2y/dx^2 for the following functions.

12. $y = \sqrt[3]{x^3 + a^3}$ ⎯ **13.** $y = (3x - 7)^6(x + 1)^4$

14. $y = x^n \ln x$ ⎯ **15.** $y = \ln(\ln x)$

(16–17) Calculate the marginal revenue for the following demand relations.

16. $p = a - b \ln x$ ⎯ **17.** $x = a - b \ln p$

(18–19) Calculate the marginal cost and marginal average cost for the following cost functions.

18. $C(x) = 600 + 25x - 4(x + 1)\ln(x + 1) + 0.02x^2$

19. $C(x) = 100 + 0.5x + 0.01xe^x$

OPTIMIZATION AND CURVE SKETCHING

CHAPTER

14-1 DERIVATIVES AND GRAPHS OF FUNCTIONS

In this section we shall consider the significance of the first and second derivatives of a function as they relate to its graph. We shall begin with the first derivative.

DEFINITION A function $y = f(x)$ is said to be an **increasing function** over an interval of values of x if y increases with increase of x. That is, if x_1 and x_2 are any two values in the given interval with $x_2 > x_1$, then $f(x_2) > f(x_1)$.

A function $y = f(x)$ is said to be a **decreasing function** over an interval of its domain if y decreases with increase of x. That is, if $x_2 > x_1$ are two values of x in the given interval, then $f(x_2) < f(x_1)$.

Parts (a) and (b) of Figure 1 illustrate the graphs of an increasing and a decreasing function, respectively.

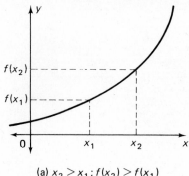 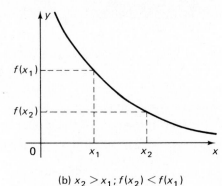

(a) $x_2 > x_1$; $f(x_2) > f(x_1)$

(b) $x_2 > x_1$; $f(x_2) < f(x_1)$

FIGURE 1

THEOREM 1

(a) If $f(x)$ is an increasing function that is differentiable, then $f'(x) \geq 0$.

(b) If $f(x)$ is a decreasing function that is differentiable, then $f'(x) \leq 0$.

PROOF

(a) Let x and $x + \Delta x$ be two values of the independent variable, with $y = f(x)$ and $y + \Delta y = f(x + \Delta x)$ the corresponding values of the dependent variable. Then

$$\Delta y = f(x + \Delta x) - f(x).$$

There are two cases to consider, depending on whether $\Delta x > 0$ or $\Delta x < 0$. They are illustrated in Figures 2 and 3.

If $\Delta x > 0$, then $x + \Delta x > x$. Therefore, since $f(x)$ is an increas-

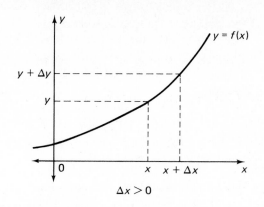

FIGURE 2

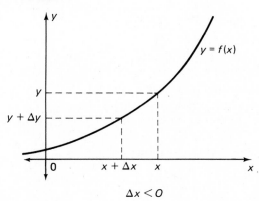

FIGURE 3

ing function, $f(x + \Delta x) > f(x)$, so that $\Delta y > 0$. Consequently, both Δx and Δy are positive, so that $\Delta y/\Delta x > 0$.

The second possibility is that $\Delta x < 0$. Then $x + \Delta x < x$ and so $f(x + \Delta x) < f(x)$. Hence $\Delta y < 0$. In this case, Δx and Δy are both negative, so that again $\Delta y/\Delta x > 0$.

So, in both cases, $\Delta y/\Delta x$ is positive. The derivative $f'(x)$ is the limit of $\Delta y/\Delta x$ as $\Delta x \to 0$, and since $\Delta y/\Delta x$ is always positive, it is clearly impossible for it to approach a negative number as limiting value. Therefore $f'(x) \geq 0$, as stated in the theorem.

The proof of part (b), when $f(x)$ is a decreasing function, is quite similar and is left as an exercise.

This theorem has a converse, which may be stated as follows.

THEOREM 2

(a) If $f'(x) > 0$ for all x in some interval, then $f(x)$ is an increasing function of x over that interval.

(b) If $f'(x) < 0$ for all x in some interval, then $f(x)$ is a decreasing function of x over that interval.

Note: Observe that in Theorem 2, the inequalities are strict.

The proof of this theorem will not be given. However, it is an intuitively obvious result. In part (a), for example, the fact that $f'(x) > 0$ means, geometrically, that the tangent to the graph at any point has positive slope. If the graph of $f(x)$ always slopes upward to the right, then clearly y must increase as x increases. Correspondingly, in part (b), if $f'(x) < 0$, then the graph slopes downward to the right and y decreases as x increases.

These theorems are used to determine the intervals in which a function is increasing or decreasing—that is, where the graph is rising or falling.

EXAMPLE 1   Find the values of x for which the function

$$f(x) = x^2 - 2x + 1$$

is increasing or decreasing.

Solution   Since $f(x) = x^2 - 2x + 1$, we have $f'(x) = 2x - 2$. Now $f'(x) > 0$ implies that $2x - 2 > 0$, that is, $x > 1$. Thus $f(x)$ is increasing for all values of x in the interval $x > 1$. Similarly, $f'(x) < 0$ implies that $2x - 2 < 0$, that is, $x < 1$. The function is decreasing for $x < 1$.

The graph of $y = f(x)$ is shown in Figure 4. (Note that $f(1) = 0$, so the point $(1, 0)$ lies on the graph.) For $x < 1$, the graph slopes negatively and for $x > 1$, it slopes positively. The graph of $f'(x)$ is shown in Figure 5 and we observe that this graph lies below the x-axis for $x < 1$ and above the x-axis for $x > 1$.

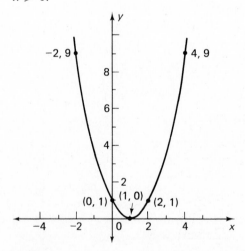

FIGURE 4   FIGURE 5

EXAMPLE 2   Find the values of x for which the function

$$f(x) = x^3 - 3x$$

is increasing or decreasing.

Solution   We have $f'(x) = 3x^2 - 3 = 3(x - 1)(x + 1)$.

To find the intervals of x in which $f'(x)$ is positive or negative, we first find the values of x where $f'(x)$ is zero. These are the points at which $f'(x)$ can change from negative to positive values (or vice versa), and so represent the possible endpoints of the intervals we are seeking.

In the present case, $f'(x) = 0$ when $(x - 1)(x + 1) = 0$, that is, when $x = -1$ or 1. So the possible intervals in which we must examine the sign of $f'(x)$ are $x < -1$, $-1 < x < 1$, and $x > 1$.

When $x > 1$, both $(x - 1)$ and $(x + 1)$ are positive. Therefore $f'(x) = 3(x - 1)(x + 1)$ is the product of positive numbers and is itself positive. So in the region $x > 1$, $f(x)$ is an increasing function.

When $-1 < x < 1$, $(x + 1)$ is still positive, but $(x - 1)$ is negative. Therefore $f'(x)$ is the product of numbers, one of which is negative; hence $f'(x) < 0$. So in the region $-1 < x < 1$, $f(x)$ is a decreasing function.

When $x < -1$, both $(x - 1)$ and $(x + 1)$ are negative, so $f'(x)$ is again positive. For $x < -1$, $f(x)$ is an increasing function.

We note that $f(-1) = 2$ and $f(1) = -2$, so the points $(-1, 2)$ and $(1, -2)$ lie on the graph of $y = f(x)$. The graph is sketched in Figure 6 and shows the regions in which the function is increasing or decreasing. (One further piece of information is given in the figure, namely that the graph crosses the x-axis $(y = 0)$ when $x = 0$ and when $x = \pm\sqrt{3}$. Setting $y = 0$, we get the equation $x^3 - 3x = 0$, or $x(x^2 - 3) = 0$, with roots of 0, $\pm\sqrt{3}$.)

The graph of $f'(x)$ is shown in Figure 7. We note that this graph is above the x-axis in the regions where $f(x)$ is increasing and below the x-axis in the region $-1 < x < 1$, where $f(x)$ is decreasing.

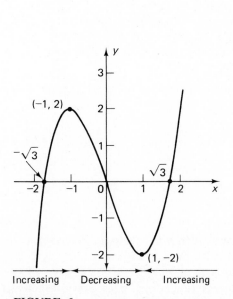

FIGURE 6

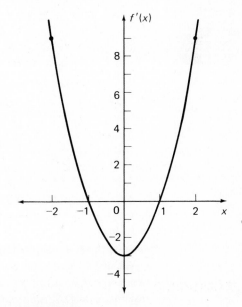

FIGURE 7

EXAMPLE 3   For the cost function $C(x) = 500 + 20x$ and the demand relation $p = 100 - x$, find the regions in which the cost function, revenue function, and profit function are increasing and decreasing functions of x.

Solution   Since $C(x) = 500 + 20x$, $C'(x) = 20$ is always positive. Hence the cost function is an increasing function of x for all values of x. The revenue function is

$$R(x) = xp = x(100 - x) = 100x - x^2.$$

Therefore the marginal revenue is

$$R'(x) = 100 - 2x.$$

So $R'(x) > 0$ when $100 - 2x > 0$, that is, when $x < 50$. When $x > 50$, $R'(x) < 0$. So the revenue function is an increasing function of x for $x < 50$ and a decreasing function of x for $x > 50$.

The profit function is

$$\begin{aligned} P(x) &= R(x) - C(x) \\ &= 100x - x^2 - (500 + 20x) \\ &= 80x - x^2 - 500. \end{aligned}$$

Then $P'(x) = 80 - 2x$ and $P'(x) > 0$ when $80 - 2x > 0$, or $x < 40$; alternatively, $P'(x) < 0$ when $x > 40$. So the profit function is an increasing function of x for $x < 40$, and it is a decreasing function of x for $x > 40$. The graphs of the three functions are shown in Figure 8.

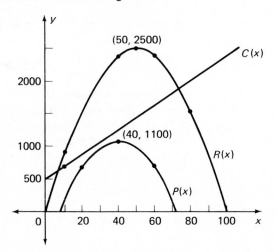

FIGURE 8

The type of behavior found for these three functions is quite typical of general cost, revenue, and profit functions. The cost function is usually an increasing function of the quantity of goods produced (it usually costs more to produce more, although exceptions do occur with certain pricing policies for the raw materials.) Similarly, the revenue function is, in general, an increasing function for small volumes of sales, but usually becomes a decreasing function for large volumes of sales. The profit function commonly has this same qualitative behavior of increasing for small x and decreasing for large x.

We see from the above that the sign of the first derivative has a geometric significance that is extremely useful when we need to obtain a qualitative idea of the graph of a function. We shall now go on to consider the second derivative, which, as we shall see, also has an important geometric interpretation.

Consider a function $f(x)$ whose graph has the general shape indicated in Figure 9. The slope of the graph is positive, $f'(x) > 0$, so y is an increasing function of x. Furthermore, the graph has the property that as we move to the right (that is, as x increases), the slope of the graph becomes steeper. That is, the derivative $f'(x)$ is also an increasing function of x. The graph of $f'(x)$ must have a form indicated qualitatively in Figure 10.

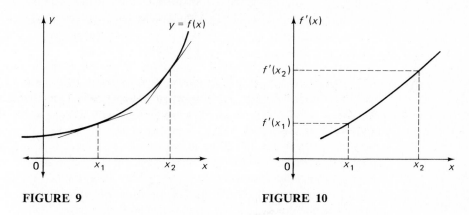

FIGURE 9   **FIGURE 10**

Now, if $f'(x)$ is an increasing function of x, its derivative must be greater than or equal to zero by Theorem 1. That is, $f''(x) \geq 0$.

Conversely, if $f'(x) > 0$ and $f''(x) > 0$, then the graph of $y = f(x)$ must slope upwards to the right, and furthermore the graph must slope more and more steeply as x increases. (By Theorem 2, $f'(x)$ is increasing if $f''(x) > 0$.)

Now consider a function $f(x)$ with a graph of the form shown in Figure 11. Here the graph slopes downwards to the right, with $f'(x) < 0$, but the slope is becoming less steep as x increases. Thus $f'(x)$ is increasing from large negative values towards zero, as indicated in Figure 12. Again $f'(x)$ is an increasing function of x, so that $f''(x) \geq 0$.

Conversely, if $f'(x) < 0$ and $f''(x) > 0$, then the graph of $f(x)$ has the general form of Figure 11. That is, the graph slopes downward to the right but becomes less steep as x increases.

A third type of graph is shown in Figure 13. This type consists essentially of an amalgamation of the two types discussed above. For $x < a$, $f'(x) < 0$, but for $x > a$, $f'(x) > 0$. Furthermore $f'(x)$ increases from negative values to zero at $x = a$, then to positive values for $x > a$. Thus $f'(x)$ is always increasing, so $f''(x) \geq 0$.

The geometric property that characterizes the three types of graphs dis-

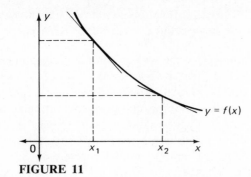

FIGURE 11

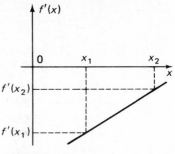

FIGURE 12

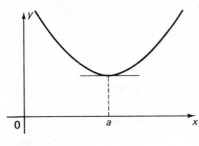

FIGURE 13

cussed above is that they are all **concave upwards** (or convex downwards).* We conclude, therefore, that if the graph of $y = f(x)$ is concave upwards, then $f''(x) \geq 0$. Conversely, if $f''(x) > 0$, then the graph of $y = f(x)$ must be concave upwards.

Now let us consider the alternative possibility, that is, that the graph of $y = f(x)$ is **concave downwards**.* The various cases corresponding to the three types discussed above are shown in Figure 14. Part (a) illustrates the case when $f'(x) > 0$ but the slope is becoming less steep as x increases. Part (b) illustrates the case when $f'(x) < 0$ and the slope becomes steeper as x increases. Part (c) shows the case when $f'(x) > 0$ for $x < a$ and $f'(x) < 0$ for $x > a$.

In each case, $f'(x)$ is a decreasing function of x. Therefore we conclude that when the graph of $y = f(x)$ is concave downwards, $f''(x) \leq 0$. Conversely, when $f''(x) < 0$, the graph of $y = f(x)$ is concave downwards.

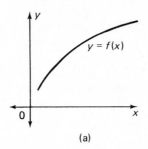

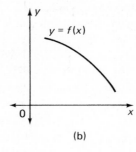

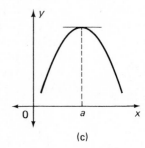

(a)   (b)   (c)

FIGURE 14

EXAMPLE 4   Find the values of x for which the graph of

$$y = \tfrac{1}{6}x^4 - x^3 + 2x^2$$

is concave upwards or concave downwards.

*A function $f(x)$ is *concave upwards* in an interval (a, b) if, given any two points x_1 and x_2 in this interval, the straight line segment connecting $(x_1, f(x_1))$ and $(x_2, f(x_2))$ lies above the graph of $y = f(x)$. The function is *concave downwards* in (a, b) if such a straight line segment always lies entirely below the graph of $y = f(x)$.

Solution

$$y = \tfrac{1}{6}x^4 - x^3 + 2x^2$$
$$y' = \tfrac{4}{6}x^3 - 3x^2 + 4x$$
$$y'' = 2x^2 - 6x + 4$$
$$= 2(x^2 - 3x + 2) = 2(x - 1)(x - 2)$$

In order to find out whether the graph is concave upwards or downwards, we must examine the sign of y''. We note that $y'' = 0$ when $x = 1$ and when $x = 2$, so that we must consider the three regions $x < 1$, $1 < x < 2$, and $x > 2$.

Note that when $x = 1$, $y = \tfrac{7}{6}$, and when $x = 2$, $y = \tfrac{8}{3}$. Thus the two points $(1, \tfrac{7}{6})$ and $(2, \tfrac{8}{3})$ lie in the graph.

When $x > 2$, both $x - 1$ and $x - 2$ are positive, so that $y'' = 2(x - 1)(x - 2)$ is the product of positive factors. Hence $y'' > 0$, so that the graph is concave upwards for $x > 2$.

When $1 < x < 2$, $x - 1$ is positive but $x - 2$ is negative. Hence $y'' = 2(x - 1)(x - 2)$ has one negative factor, so $y'' < 0$. Hence the graph is concave downwards in this region.

When $x < 1$, both $x - 1$ and $x - 2$ are negative, so their product is positive. Hence $y'' > 0$ and the graph is concave upwards.

The graph of $y = f(x)$ is shown in Figure 15. Note the changes in concavity at the points $(1, \tfrac{7}{6})$ and $(2, \tfrac{8}{3})$ on the graph.

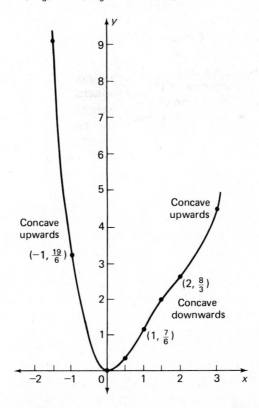

FIGURE 15

EXAMPLE 5   Examine the concavity properties of the cost function

$$C(x) = 2000 + 10x - 0.03x^2 + 10^{-4}x^3.$$

Solution

$$C'(x) = 10 - 0.06x + (3 \times 10^{-4})x^2$$

$$C''(x) = -0.06 + (6 \times 10^{-4})x = (6 \times 10^{-4})(x - 100).$$

We observe that for $x < 100$, $C''(x)$ is negative, which means that the graph of the cost function is concave downwards. For $x > 100$, $C''(x) > 0$ and the graph is therefore concave upwards. The graph of $C(x)$ has the form shown in Figure 16.

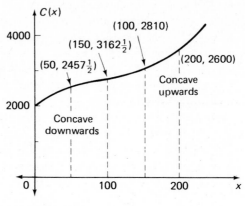

FIGURE 16

The cost function in Example 5 has a qualitative shape that is quite typical of such functions. For small values of x, the cost function is commonly concave downwards. This property is due to the fact that increases of production introduce economies of scale, so the marginal cost $C'(x)$ decreases. Past a certain level of production, however, it becomes more costly to increase production because, for example, new machinery must be purchased and workers paid overtime. At this stage, the marginal cost starts to increase and the cost function becomes concave upwards.

Note that the graph of $C(x)$ always slopes upwards to the right ($C'(x) > 0$).

DEFINITION   A **point of inflection** on a curve is a point where the curve changes from concave upwards to concave downwards, or vice versa.

If $x = x_1$ is a point of inflection of the graph of $y = f(x)$, then on one side of x_1 the graph is concave upwards, that is, $f''(x) > 0$; on the other side of x_1, the graph is concave downwards, that is, $f''(x) < 0$. Thus on passing from one side to the other of $x = x_1$, $f''(x)$ changes sign. At $x = x_1$ itself, it is necessary either that $f''(x_1) = 0$ or that $f''(x_1)$ fails to exist ($f''(x)$ may become infinitely large as $x \longrightarrow x_1$).

In Example 4, the graph of $y = \frac{1}{6}x^4 - x^3 + 2x^2$ has points of inflection at $x = 1$ and $x = 2$. For example, for $x < 1$, the graph is concave upwards, while for x just above 1, the graph is concave downwards. So $x = 1$ is a point where the concavity changes, that is, a point of inflection. This is also true for $x = 2$.

Example 4 corresponds to a point of inflection at which $y'' = 0$. Example 6 illustrates the alternative possibility.

EXAMPLE 6   Find the points of inflection of $y = x^{1/3}$.

Solution   We have $y' = \frac{1}{3}x^{-2/3}.$

$$y'' = \frac{1}{3}(-\frac{2}{3})x^{-5/3} = -\frac{2}{9}x^{-5/3}$$

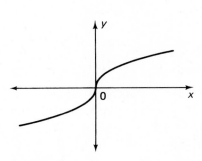

Now for $x > 0$, $x^{5/3}$ is positive, so $y'' < 0$. For $x < 0$, $x^{5/3}$ is negative, so $y'' > 0$. Thus the graph is concave upwards for $x < 0$ and concave downwards for $x > 0$. The value $x = 0$, at which y is also 0, is therefore a point of inflection. (See Figure 17.) In this case, y'' becomes indefinitely large as $x \rightarrow 0$, so we have a point of inflection at which the second derivative fails to exist. (Note also that as $x \rightarrow 0$, y' becomes infinite, so that the slope of the graph becomes vertical at the origin for this particular function.)

FIGURE 17

Observe that the tangent to a graph at a point of inflection always crosses the graph at that point. This is an unusual property for a tangent—as a rule the graph lies entirely on one side of the tangent line in the neighborhood of the point of tangency.

EXERCISES 1

(1–24)   Find the values of x for which the following functions are: (a) increasing; (b) decreasing; (c) concave upwards; (d) concave downwards. Also, find the points of inflection, if any.

1. $y = x^2 - 6x + 7$ 2. $y = x^3 - 12x + 10$
3. $f(x) = x^3 - 3x + 4$ 4. $f(x) = 2x^3 - 9x^2 - 24x + 20$
5. $f(x) = x + \dfrac{1}{x}$ 6. $f(x) = x^2 + \dfrac{1}{x^2}$ 7. $f(x) = \dfrac{x}{x + 1}$
8. $f(x) = \dfrac{x + 1}{x - 1}$ 9. $y = x + \ln x.$ 10. $y = x - e^x$
11. $y = x \ln x$ 12. $y = xe^{-x}$ 13. $y = x^5 - 5x^4 + 1$
14. $y = x^7 - 7x^6$ 15. $y = x^2 - 4x + 5$ 16. $y = x^3 - 3x + 2$
17. $y = 5x^6 - 6x^5 + 1$ 18. $y = x^4 - 2x^2$ 19. $y = x^{2/3}$
20. $y = x^{1/5}$ 21. $y = \ln x$ 22. $y = e^{-2x}$
23. $y = \dfrac{2}{x}$ 24. $y = \dfrac{-1}{x}$

(25–28)   For the following cost functions and demand relations, determine the regions in which (a) the cost function, (b) the revenue function, and (c) the profit function are increasing and decreasing.

25. $C(x) = 2000 + 10x; \quad p = 100 - \frac{1}{2}x$

26. $C(x) = 4000 + x^2$; $p = 300 - 2x$

27. $C(x) = C_0 + kx$; $p = a - bx$ (a, b, k, C_0 are positive constants.)

28. $C(x) = \sqrt{100 + x^2}$; $p = a - (b/x)\sqrt{100 + x^2}$ (Assume $b > a > 0$.)

(29–32) Discuss the concavity of the following cost functions.

29. $C(x) = a + bx$ **30.** $C(x) = \sqrt{100 + x^2}$

31. $C(x) = 1500 + 25x - 0.1x^2 + 0.004x^3$

32. $C(x) = 1000 + 40\sqrt{x} - x + 0.02x^{3/2}$

33. Show that the average cost function $\bar{C}(x)$ is an increasing function when the marginal cost exceeds the average cost.

14-2 CRITICAL POINTS

Many of the important applications of derivatives involve finding the maximum or minimum values of a particular function. For example, the profit a manufacturer makes depends on the price charged for the product, and the manufacturer is interested in knowing the price which makes his profit maximum. This **optimum** price (or **best** price) is obtained by a process called **maximization** or **optimization** of the profit function. In a similar way, a real estate company may be interested in knowing the rent to charge for the offices or apartments it controls to generate the maximum rental income; a railway company may want to know the average speed at which trains should run in order to minimize the cost per mile of operation; or an economist may wish to know the level of taxation in a country that will promote the maximum rate of growth of the economy. Before we look at applications such as these, however, we shall discuss the theory of maxima and minima.

DEFINITIONS

(a) A function $f(x)$ is said to have a **local maximum** at $x = c$ if $f(c) > f(x)$ for all x sufficiently near to c.

Thus the points P and Q in the graphs in Figure 18 correspond to local maxima of the corresponding functions.

(b) A function $f(x)$ is said to have a **local minimum** at $x = c$ if $f(c) < f(x)$ for all x sufficiently close to c.

The points A and B in the graphs in Figure 19 correspond to local minima.

A function may have more than one local maximum and more than one local minimum, as is shown in Figure 20. The points A, C, and E on the graph correspond to points where the function has local maxima, and the points B, D, and F correspond to points where the function has local minima.

A (local) *maximum or minimum value* of a function is the y-coordinate at the point at which the graph has a local maximum or minimum. A local minimum value of a function may be greater than a local maximum value. This can be easily seen from the above graph, where the ordinate of F is greater than the ordinate of A.

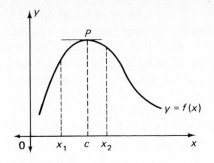

(a)

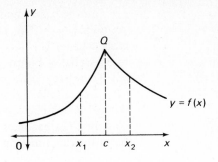

(b)

FIGURE 18

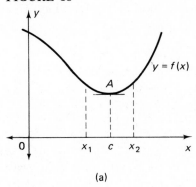

(a)

(b)

FIGURE 19

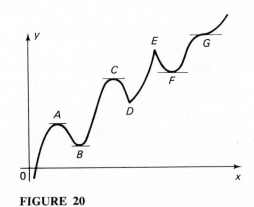

FIGURE 20

   (c) The term **extremum** is used to denote either a local maximum or a local minimum. Extrema is the plural of extremum.

   (d) The value $x = c$ is called a **critical point** for a continuous function f if

   1. either $f'(c) = 0$ or $f'(x)$ fails to exist at $x = c$; and
   2. $f(c)$ is well-defined.

In the case when $f'(c) = 0$, the tangent to the graph of $y = f(x)$ is horizontal at $x = c$. This possibility is illustrated in part (a) of Figure 21. The second case, when $f'(c)$ fails to exist, occurs when the graph has a corner at $x = c$ (see part (b) of Figure 21) or when the tangent to the graph becomes vertical at $x = c$ (so that $f'(x)$ becomes infinitely large as $x \longrightarrow c$). (See part (c) of Figure 21.)

We emphasize the fact that for c to be a critical point, $f(c)$ must be well-defined. Consider for example $f(x) = x^{-1}$, whose derivative is $f'(x) = -x^{-2}$. Clearly $f'(x)$ becomes unbounded as $x \longrightarrow 0$. However $x = 0$ is not a critical point for this function since $f(0)$ does not exist.

It is clear from the graphs discussed above that local extrema correspond to critical points of a function f. But not every critical point of a function corresponds to a local minimum or a local maximum. The point P in part (a) of Figure 22, where the tangent is horizontal, corresponds to a critical point but is neither a local maximum nor a local minimum point. The points Q and R

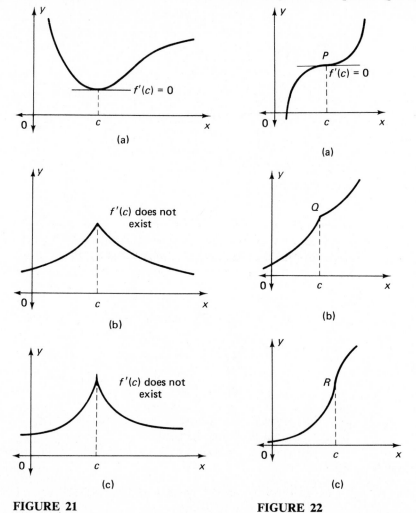

FIGURE 21   FIGURE 22

in parts (b) and (c) correspond to critical points at which $f'(c)$ fails to exist, but which are not extrema of $f(x)$. In fact, P and R are points of inflection.

In the following section, we shall develop certain tests that will enable us to distinguish those critical points which are local extrema from those which are not. First let us examine critical points themselves through some examples.

EXAMPLE 1 Determine the critical points of the function

$$f(x) = x^3(2x^3 - 3x).$$

Solution We have $f(x) = 2x^6 - 3x^4$. Differentiating, we get

$$f'(x) = 12x^5 - 12x^3 = 12x^3(x^2 - 1).$$

It is clear that $f'(x)$ exists for all x, so the only critical points are those at which $f'(x)$ vanishes:

$$f'(x) = 12x^3(x^2 - 1) = 0$$

so

$$x^3 = 0 \quad \text{or} \quad x^2 - 1 = 0.$$

So the critical points are $x = 0, \pm 1$.

EXAMPLE 2 Determine the critical points of the function

$$f(x) = x^4(x - 1)^{4/5}.$$

Solution Differentiating, using the product rule, we get

$$f'(x) = 4x^3(x - 1)^{4/5} + x^4(\tfrac{4}{5})(x - 1)^{-1/5}$$
$$= \tfrac{4}{5}x^3(x - 1)^{-1/5}[5(x - 1) + x]$$
$$= \tfrac{4}{5}x^3(x - 1)^{-1/5}(6x - 5).$$

Now $f'(x) = 0$ when either $x^3 = 0$ or $6x - 5 = 0$, so we have critical points at $x = 0$ and $x = \tfrac{5}{6}$. However, we observe that $f'(x)$ becomes infinitely large as $x \to 1$ because of the negative power. Since $f(1)$ is well-defined (in fact $f(1) = 0$), $x = 1$ must be a critical point of the type at which $f'(x)$ fails to exist.

EXAMPLE 3 Find the critical points of the function

$$f(x) = x^3 e^{-x^2}.$$

Solution We use the product rule.

$$f'(x) = 3x^2 e^{-x^2} + x^3(-2xe^{-x^2})$$
$$= x^2 e^{-x^2}(3 - 2x^2)$$

The factor e^{-x^2} is never zero. Therefore $f'(x) = 0$ either when $x^2 = 0$ or when $3 - 2x^2 = 0$; that is, either when $x = 0$ or when $x = \pm\sqrt{\tfrac{3}{2}}$. So the given function has three critical points: $x = 0, \pm\sqrt{\tfrac{3}{2}}$.

EXERCISES 2

(1–24) Find the critical points for the following functions.

1. x^7　　　　　　2. x^4　　　　　　3. $2x + 3$

4. $2x^2 + 8x + 1$ **5.** $4 - x - 3x^2$ **6.** $x^3 - 3x$

7. $2x^3 - 6x$ **8.** $x^3 + 3x^2 + 1$

9. $2x^3 - 3x^2 - 36x + 1$ **10.** $x^3 - 9x^2 + 24x + 2$

11. $x^4 - 2x^2$ **12.** $x^4 - 4x^3$ **13.** $x + x^{-1}$

14. $3x + \dfrac{1}{3x}$ **15.** $\dfrac{x-1}{x+1}$ **16.** $\dfrac{x^2}{x-1}$

17. $x^{2/3} - x^{1/3}$ **18.** $x^{4/5} - 2x^{2/5}$ **19.** $\dfrac{(x-1)^{1/5}}{x+1}$

20. $x(x-1)^{1/3}$ **21.** xe^{-3x} **22.** x^2e^{-x}

23. $x \ln x$.   **24.** $x^2 \ln x$

14-3 TESTS FOR LOCAL EXTREMA

We have seen that the local extrema of a function are to be found among its critical points. We shall now describe the two tests that are used in order to decide whether or not a given critical point is a local maximum or minimum.

Consider first the case when the local extremum occurs at a critical point given by $f'(x) = 0$, that is, when the tangent line is horizontal at the point on the graph of f corresponding to the extremum. Then if the point is a local maximum, the graph is concave downwards, and if the point is a local minimum, the graph is concave upwards. But we know that whenever $f''(x) < 0$, the graph of f is concave downwards and whenever $f''(x) > 0$, the graph is concave upwards. This leads to the following theorem.

THEOREM 1   (SECOND-DERIVATIVE TEST)
Let $f(x)$ be twice differentiable at $x = c$. Then

1. $x = c$ is a local maximum of f whenever $f'(c) = 0$ and $f''(c) < 0$;

2. $x = c$ is a local minimum of f whenever $f'(c) = 0$ and $f''(c) > 0$.

EXAMPLE 1   Find the local maximum and minimum values of

$$x^3 + 2x^2 - 4x - 8.$$

Solution   Let $f(x) = x^3 + 2x^2 - 4x - 8$.

$$f'(x) = 3x^2 + 4x - 4.$$

To find the critical points, we set $f'(x) = 0$.

$$3x^2 + 4x - 4 = 0$$

$$(3x - 2)(x + 2) = 0$$

This gives $x = \frac{2}{3}$ or -2. Now $f''(x) = 6x + 4$. At $x = \frac{2}{3}$,

$$f''(\tfrac{2}{3}) = 6(\tfrac{2}{3}) + 4 = 8 > 0.$$

Hence, since $f''(x)$ is positive when $x = \frac{2}{3}$, $f(x)$ has a local minimum when $x = \frac{2}{3}$. The local minimum value is given by

$$f(\tfrac{2}{3}) = (\tfrac{2}{3})^3 + 2(\tfrac{2}{3})^2 - 4(\tfrac{2}{3}) - 8 = -\tfrac{256}{27}.$$

When $x = -2$, $f''(-2) = 6(-2) + 4 = -8 < 0$. Hence, since $f''(x)$ is negative when $x = -2$, $f(x)$ has a local maximum when $x = -2$. The local maximum value is given by

$$f(-2) = (-2)^3 + 2(-2)^2 - 4(-2) - 8 = 0.$$

Thus the only local maximum value of $f(x)$ is 0, and it occurs when $x = -2$; the only local minimum value is $-\frac{256}{27}$, and it occurs when $x = \frac{2}{3}$.

Note that in Example 1, $f'(x)$ is well-defined for all values of x, so that the only critical points are those at which $f'(x)$ is zero.

EXAMPLE 2 Determine the local maxima and minima for $f(x) = (\ln x)/x$.

Solution Using the quotient rule, we have

$$f'(x) = \frac{x \cdot \dfrac{1}{x} - \ln x \cdot 1}{x^2}$$

$$= \frac{1 - \ln x}{x^2}.$$

For a critical point, $f'(x) = 0$, or

$$\frac{1 - \ln x}{x^2} = 0.$$

That is, $1 - \ln x = 0$. Thus $\ln x = \ln e = 1$ and so $x = e$.

In this case, we have only one critical point, $x = e$. (Note that $f'(x)$ becomes infinite as $x \to 0$. However, $x = 0$ is not a critical point because $f(0)$ is not defined.)

We use the quotient rule again.

$$f''(x) = \frac{x^2(1 - \ln x)' - (1 - \ln x) \cdot (x^2)'}{(x^2)^2}$$

$$= \frac{x^2(-1/x) - (1 - \ln x)(2x)}{x^4}$$

$$= \frac{2 \ln x - 3}{x^3}$$

When $x = e$,

$$f''(e) = \frac{2 \ln e - 3}{e^3} = \frac{2 - 3}{e^3} = -\frac{1}{e^3} < 0,$$

where we have used the fact that $\ln e = 1$. Hence $f(x)$ has a local maximum when $x = e$. In this case, there are no local minima.

The second-derivative test can be used for all local extrema at which $f'(c) = 0$ and $f''(c)$ is nonzero. When $f''(x) = 0$ at a critical point $x = c$, or when $f''(c)$ fails to exist, then the second-derivative test cannot be used to ascertain whether $x = c$ is a local maximum or minimum point. In such cases, we must resort to a different test, called the *first-derivative* test for local extrema.

The first-derivative test is also used for all critical points of the type at which $f'(c)$ fails to exist. It also happens in some cases that even though the second-derivative test works, the first-derivative test is simpler to use.

THEOREM 2 (First Derivative Test) If $x = c$ is a critical point for $f(x)$, that is, either $f'(c) = 0$ or $f'(x)$ fails to exist as $x \to c$, then:

1. $x = c$ is a local *maximum* of f if $f'(x)$ changes sign from positive to negative as x changes from just below c to just above c. (See Part (a) of Figure 23. The $(+)$, $(-)$, or (0) in brackets in the figure indicate the sign of the slope of the graph at given points.)

2. $x = c$ is a local *minimum* of f if $f'(x)$ changes sign from negative to positive as x changes from just below c to just above c. (See Part (b) of Figure 23.)

3. $x = c$ is not a local extremum if $f'(x)$ does not change sign as x changes from just below $x = c$ to just above $x = c$. (See Part (c) of Figure 23.) In such cases, $x = c$ will be either a point of inflection or a corner on the graph of $f(x)$.

EXAMPLE 3   Find the local extrema for $f(x) = x^4 - 4x^3 + 7$.

Solution   In this case $f'(x) = 4x^3 - 12x^2 = 4x^2(x - 3)$. For a critical point, $f'(x) = 0$ or $4x^2(x - 3) = 0$, that is, $x = 0$ or 3.

Now $f''(x) = 12x^2 - 24x$. At $x = 3$, $f''(3) = 12(9) - 24(3) = 108 - 72 = 36 > 0$. Hence $x = 3$ is a local minimum point for $f(x)$.

At $x = 0$, $f''(0) = 0$. Thus we cannot use the second-derivative test to determine the nature of the critical point $x = 0$. For this, we must resort to the first-derivative test.

First of all, let x be just below the critical point at $x = 0$, that is, let x be negative but small. Then $x^2 > 0$ and $x - 3 < 0$. Therefore $f'(x) = 4x^2(x - 3) < 0$, since it is the product of a postive number ($4x^2$) and a negative number $(x - 3)$. Secondly, take x to be just above the critical point at $x = 0$, that is, take x small and positive. Then $x^2 > 0$ and $x - 3 < 0$, so that $f'(x) = 4x^2(x - 3) < 0$. Thus $f'(x)$ is negative both just below and just above the point $x = 0$, and does not change sign as x increases through the value 0. Hence $x = 0$ is neither a maximum nor a minimum (it is in fact a point of inflection).

EXAMPLE 4   Investigate the local extrema for $f(x) = x^4/(x - 1)$.

Solution   We use the quotient rule (with $u = x^4$ and $v = x - 1$).

$$f'(x) = \frac{(x - 1) \cdot 4x^3 - x^4 \cdot 1}{(x - 1)^2} = \frac{x^3(3x - 4)}{(x - 1)^2}$$

For a critical point, $f'(x) = 0$; thus $x = 0$ or $\frac{4}{3}$. (Note that $x = 1$ is not a critical point since $f(1)$ is not defined.)

We now have the following.

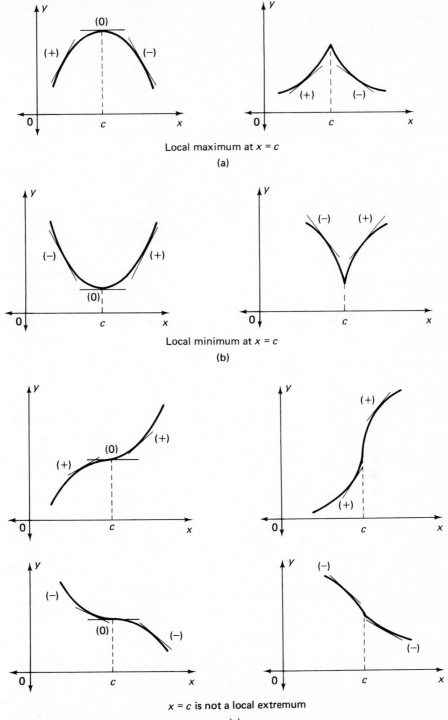

Local maximum at $x = c$

(a)

Local minimum at $x = c$

(b)

$x = c$ is not a local extremum

(c)

FIGURE 23

$$f''(x) = \frac{(x-1)^2(d/dx)(3x^4 - 4x^3) - (3x^4 - 4x^3)(d/dx)(x-1)^2}{(x-1)^4}$$

$$= \frac{(x-1)^2(12x^3 - 12x^2) - (3x^4 - 4x^3) \cdot 2(x-1) \cdot 1}{(x-1)^4}$$

$$= \frac{12x^2(x-1)(x-1) - 2x^3(3x-4)}{(x-1)^3}$$

$$= \frac{2x^2(3x^2 - 8x + 6)}{(x-1)^3}$$

At $x = \frac{4}{3}$,

$$f''(\tfrac{4}{3}) = \frac{2(\tfrac{4}{3})^2(3 \cdot \tfrac{16}{9} - 8 \cdot \tfrac{4}{3} + 6)}{(\tfrac{4}{3} - 1)^3} = 64 > 0.$$

Hence $x = \frac{4}{3}$ is a local minimum point.

At $x = 0$, $f''(0) = 0$ and so we must make use of the first-derivative test in this case. Going back to $f'(x)$, we observe that when x is slightly negative, that is, just below the critical point at $x = 0$, x^3 and $3x - 4$ are both negative, and $(x-1)^2$ is positive. Thus $f'(x) = x^3(3x-4)/(x-1)^2$ involves two negative quantities in the numerator and a positive quantity in the denominator, so it is positive.

When x is slightly positive, that is, just above the critical point at $x = 0$, x^3 and $(x-1)^2$ are positive, whereas $3x - 4$ is negative; thus $f'(x)$ is negative.

Thus $f'(x)$ changes from positive to negative at $x = 0$, and by the first-derivative test $x = 0$ is a local maximum point.

The given function therefore has a local maximum at $x = 0$ and a local minimum at $x = \frac{4}{3}$.

Note that we could, if we like, use the first-derivative test for the point $x = \frac{4}{3}$ even though the second derivative test works there. Since the second differentiation is a bit messy, the first derivative test may even be preferable in this case.

EXAMPLE 5   Investigate the local extrema for $f(x) = (x-1)^{2/3}$.

Solution   We have

$$f'(x) = \frac{2}{3}(x-1)^{-1/3} = \frac{2}{3(x-1)^{1/3}}.$$

There is no value of x for which $f'(x)$ becomes zero. In this case, the critical point occurs where $f'(x)$ becomes infinitely large—that is, for $x = 1$.

Whenever we deal with a critical point at which f' is infinite, we must always resort to the first-derivative test to find out if it is a local maximum or a local minimum point.

When x is slightly less than one, $(x-1) < 0$ and therefore also $(x-1)^{1/3} < 0$. So $f'(x) < 0$.

When x is slightly greater than one, both $x - 1$ and $(x-1)^{1/3}$ are positive, and so $f'(x) > 0$. Thus $f'(x)$ changes sign from negative to positive at $x = 1$ and $x = 1$ is a local minimum point. The graph of $f(x)$ is shown in Figure 24.

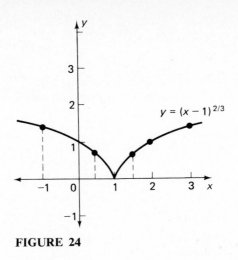

$$y = (x - 1)^{2/3}$$

FIGURE 24

The method of finding the maxima and minima of a function $f(x)$ may be summarized in the following steps.

Step 1   Find $f'(x)$ and solve the equation $f'(x) = 0$ for x.

Step 2   Test the values of x found in Step 1 for local maxima and minima.

(a) Find $f''(x)$ and evaluate this at each value found in Step 1. [*Note:* if $f''(x)$ is complicated to work out, go directly to part (b)]. Let c denote any one of these values of x.

   If $f''(c) < 0$, then $f(x)$ has a local maximum at $x = c$.

   If $f''(c) > 0$, then $f(x)$ has a local minimum at $x = c$.

   If $f''(c) = 0$ or if $f''(x)$ does not exist, the test fails. In this case use the first derivative test as described in part (b).

(b) If $f'(x)$ changes sign from positive to negative at $x = c$, that is, if $f'(x) > 0$ for $x < c$ and $f'(x) < 0$ for $x > c$, then $f(x)$ has a local *maximum* at $x = c$. If $f'(x)$ changes sign from negative to positive at $x = c$, then $f(x)$ has a local *minimum* at $x = c$. If $f'(x)$ does not change sign at $x = c$, then $f(x)$ has a *point of inflection* at $x = c$.

Step 3   If $f'(x)$ fails to exist at some point for which $f(x)$ is defined, then examine this point for a possible local maximum or minimum by using the first-derivative test described in part (b) of Step 2.

EXERCISES 3

(1–16)   Find the values of x at the local maxima and minima of the following functions.

1. $f(x) = x^2 - 12x + 10$
2. $f(x) = 1 + 2x - x^2$
3. $f(x) = x^3 - 6x^2 + 7$
4. $f(x) = x^3 - 3x + 4$
5. $y = 2x^3 - 9x^2 + 12x + 6$
6. $y = 4x^3 + 9x^2 - 12x + 5$
7. $y = x^3 - 18x^2 + 96x$
8. $y = x^3 - 3x^2 - 9x + 7$

9. $y = x^5 - 5x^4 + 5x^3 - 10$

10. $y = x^4 - 4x^3 + 3$

11. $f(x) = x^3(x - 1)^2$

12. $f(x) = x^4(x + 2)^2$

13. $f(x) = x^{4/3}$

14. $f(x) = x^{1/3}$

15. $f(x) = x \ln x$

16. $f(x) = xe^{-x}$

(17–28) Find the local maximum and minimum values of the following functions.

17. $f(x) = 2x^3 + 3x^2 - 12x - 15$

18. $f(x) = \frac{1}{3}x^3 + ax^2 - 3xa^2$

19. $f(x) = xe^x$

20. $f(x) = xe^{-2x}$

21. $f(x) = x^3(x - 1)^{2/3}$

22. $f(x) = x^4(x - 1)^{4/5}$

23. $f(x) = \dfrac{\ln x}{x^2}$

24. $f(x) = \dfrac{(\ln x)^2}{x}$

25. $f(x) = |x - 1|$

26. $f(x) = 2 - |x|$

27. $f(x) = (x - 2)^{4/3}$

28. $f(x) = (x + 1)^{7/5} + 3$

29. Show that $f(x) = x^3 - 3x^2 + 3x + 7$ has neither a local maximum nor a minimum at $x = 1$.

30. Show that $f(x) = x + 1/x$ has a local maximum and a local minimum value, but the maximum value is less than the minimum value.

14-4 APPLICATIONS OF MAXIMA AND MINIMA

Many situations arise in practice when we want to maximize or minimize a certain quantity. The following example represents a typical case in point.

EXAMPLE 1 A conservationist is stocking a lake with fish. The more fish put in, the more competition there will be for the available food supply, and so the fish will gain weight more slowly. In fact, it is known from previous experiments that when there are n fish per unit area of water, the average amount that each fish gains in weight during one season is given by $w = 600 - 30n$ grams. What value of n leads to the maximum total production of weight in the fish?

Solution The gain in weight of each fish is $w = 600 - 30n$. Since there are n fish per unit area, the total production per unit area, P, is equal to nw. Therefore

$$P = n(600 - 30n)$$
$$= 600n - 30n^2.$$

The graph of P against n is shown in Figure 25. P is zero when n is zero since there are then no fish to produce. As n increases, P increases to a maximum value, then decreases to zero again when $n = 20$. When n gets large, P decreases because for large values of n the fish put on very little weight; even though there are lots of them, the total production is small.

To find the value of n at which P is maximum, we differentiate and set the derivative dP/dn equal to zero.

$$\frac{dP}{dn} = 600 - 60n$$

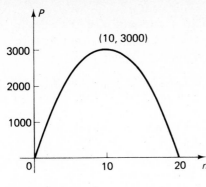

FIGURE 25

and $dP/dn = 0$ when $600 - 60n = 0$, that is, when $n = 10$. Thus the density of 10 fish per unit area gives the maximum total production. The maximum value of P is given by

$$P = 600(10) - 30(10)^2 = 3000$$

that is 3000 grams per unit area. It is obvious from the graph of P as a function of n that the value $n = 10$ corresponds to a maximum of P. However, we can check this by using the second derivative.

$$\frac{d^2P}{dn^2} = -60$$

The second derivative is negative (for all values of n in fact) so that the critical value $n = 10$ corresponds to a maximum of P.

Let us consider another example of a purely mathematical nature.

EXAMPLE 2   Find two numbers whose sum is 16 and whose product is as large as possible.

Solution   Let the two numbers be x and y, so that $x + y = 16$. If $P = xy$ denotes the product of the two numbers, then we are required to find the values of x and y that make P a maximum.

We cannot differentiate P immediately, since it is a function of two variables, x and y. These two variables are not independent, however, but are related through the condition $x + y = 16$. We must use this condition to eliminate one of the variables from P, thus leaving P as a function of a single variable. We have $y = 16 - x$, and so

$$P = xy = x(16 - x) = 16x - x^2.$$

We must find the value of x that makes P a maximum.

$$\frac{dP}{dx} = 16 - 2x$$

Thus $dP/dx = 0$ when $16 - 2x = 0$, that is, when $x = 8$. The second derivative $d^2P/dx^2 = -2 < 0$, and so $x = 8$ corresponds to a maximum of P.

When $x = 8$, $y = 8$ also, so the maximum value of P is then equal to 64.

The solution of optimization problems of the type given above is often found to be one of the most difficult areas of the differential calculus. The main difficulty arises at the level of translating the given word problem into the necessary equations. Once the equations have been constructed, it is usually much more straightforward to complete the solution by using the appropriate bit of calculus. This task of phrasing word problems in terms of mathematical equations is one that occurs repeatedly in all branches of applied mathematics, and it is something which the applied student should master if his or her calculus courses are ever to be useful.

Unfortunately, it is not possible to give hard and fast rules by means of which any word problem can be translated into equations. However there are a few guiding principles that are useful to bear in mind.*

1. Identify all of the variables involved in the problem and denote each by a symbol.

   In Example 1, the variables were n, the number of fish per unit area, w, the average gain in weight per fish, and P, the total production of fish weight per unit area. In Example 2, the variables were the two numbers x and y and P, their product.

2. Identify the variable that is to be maximized or minimized and express it in terms of the other variables in the problem.

   In Example 1, the total production P is maximized, and we wrote $P = nw$, expressing P in terms of n and w. In Example 2, the product P of x and y is maximized, and of course $P = xy$.

3. Identify all of the relationships between the variables. Express these relationships mathematically.

   In the first example, the relationship $w = 600 - 3n$ was given. In the second example, the relationship between x and y is that their sum is equal to 16, so we write the mathematical equation $x + y = 16$.

4. Express the quantity to be maximized or minimized in terms of just one of the other variables. In order to do this, the relationships obtained in Step 3 are used in order to eliminate all but one of the variables.

   In Example 1, we have $P = nw$ and $w = 600 - 3n$, so, eliminating w, we obtain P in terms of n: $P = n(600 - 3n)$. In Example 2, we have $P = xy$ and $x + y = 16$, so, eliminating y, we obtain $P = x(16 - x)$.

5. Having expressed the required quantity as a function of one variable, calculate its critical points and test each for local maximum or minimum.

Let us follow through these steps in another example.

EXAMPLE 3 A tank is to be constructed with a horizontal, square base and vertical, rectangular sides. There is no top. The tank must hold 4 cubic meters of water. The material of which the tank is to be constructed costs $10 per square meter. What dimensions for the tank minimize the cost of material?

Solution *Step 1* The variables in the problem are the dimensions of the tank and the cost of construction materials. The cost depends upon the total area of the base and sides, which determines the amount of material used in the construction. We let x denote the length of one side of the base and y denote the height of the

*Points 1 and 3 apply not only to optimization problems but to word problems in general.

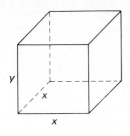

FIGURE 26

tank. (See Figure 26.) The quantity to be minimized is the total cost of materials, which we denote by C.

Step 2 C is equal to the area of the tank multiplied by $10, which is the cost per unit area. The base is a square with side x, so has an area equal to x^2. Each side is a rectangle with dimensions x and y, and has an area xy. The total area of base plus the four sides is therefore $x^2 + 4xy$. Consequently, we can write

$$C = 10(x^2 + 4xy).$$

Step 3 We observe that the quantity to be minimized is expressed as a function of two variables, so we need a relationship between x and y to eliminate one of these variables. This relationship is obtained from the requirement (stated in the problem) that the volume of the tank must be 4 cubic meters. The volume equals the area of the base times the height, that is, x^2y, and so we have the condition

$$x^2y = 4.$$

Step 4 From Step 3, $y = 4/x^2$, and so

$$C = 10[x^2 + 4x(4/x^2)] = 10[x^2 + 16/x].$$

Step 5 We can at last differentiate to find the critical points of C.

$$\frac{dC}{dx} = 10\left(2x - \frac{16}{x^2}\right) = 20\left(x - \frac{8}{x^2}\right) = 0$$

Thus, $x - 8/x^2 = 0$ and so $x^3 = 8$; that is, $x = 2$.

The base of the tank should therefore have a side 2 meters in length. The height of the tank is then given by

$$y = 4/x^2 = 4/(2)^2 = 1.$$

It is easily verified that $d^2C/dx^2 > 0$ when $x = 2$, so this value of x provides a local minimum of C.

One of the most important applications of the theory of maxima and minima is to the operations of business firms. This occurs for a very simple reason, namely that a business firm selects its mode and level of operation in such a way as to maximize its profit. Thus if the management knows how the profit depends on some variable that can be adjusted, then they will choose the value of that variable that makes the profit as large as possible.

Let us consider the case in which the variable to be adjusted is simply the level of production, x (the number of units of the firm's product produced per week or per month). If the units are sold for price p each, then the revenue is $R(x) = px$. The cost of producing x items depends on x and is denoted by $C(x)$, the cost function. Then the profit as a function of x is given by

$$P(x) = R(x) - C(x) = px - C(x).$$

We wish to choose the value of x that makes this a maximum.

Consider first the case of a small firm that is selling its product in a competitive market. In this case, the volume x of sales by this particular firm will not affect the market price for the item in question. We can assume that the price p is constant, independent of x, being determined by market forces outside the control of our small firm. The following example illustrates a problem of this kind.

EXAMPLE 4   A small manufacturing firm can sell all the items it can produce at a price of \$6 each. The cost of producing x items per week (in dollars) is

$$C(x) = 1000 + 6x - 0.003x^2 + 10^{-6}x^3.$$

What value of x should be selected in order to maximize the profits?

Solution   The revenue from selling x items at \$6 each is $R(x) = 6x$ dollars. Therefore the profit per week is

$$\begin{aligned} P(x) &= R(x) - C(x) \\ &= 6x - (1000 + 6x - 0.003x^2 + 10^{-6}x^3) \\ &= -1000 + 0.003x^2 - 10^{-6}x^3. \end{aligned}$$

To find the maximum value of P, we find the critical values in the usual way and then test them for local extrema. Differentiating we get

$$P'(x) = 0.006x - (3 \times 10^{-6})x^2$$

and setting $P'(x) = 0$, we find that either $x = 0$ or $x = 2000$. We can test each of these values using the second-derivative test:

$$P''(x) = 0.006 - (6 \times 10^{-6})x$$

so that

$$P''(0) = 0.006 > 0 \quad \text{and} \quad P''(2000) = -0.006 < 0.$$

So $x = 0$ is a local minimum of $P(x)$, while $x = 2000$ is a local maximum. Clearly this latter value provides us with the level of production at which the profit is greatest. The maximum profit is given by

$$P(2000) = -1000 + 0.003(2000)^2 - 10^{-6}(2000)^3$$

$$= 3000$$

or \$3000 per week.

_____

A different situation occurs in the case of a large business firm that is essentially the only supplier of a particular product. In such a case, the firm controls or monopolizes the market and can choose the price at which it wishes to sell the product. The volume of sales is then determined by the price at which the product is offered (through the demand equation). If the demand equation is written in the form $p = f(x)$, then the revenue function is $R = xp = x f(x)$. The profit function is then

$$P(x) = \text{Revenue} - \text{Cost}$$

$$= x f(x) - C(x)$$

and x must be chosen to maximize this function.

EXAMPLE 5   The cost of producing x items per week is

$$C(x) = 1000 + 6x - 0.003x^2 + 10^{-6}x^3.$$

For the particular item in question, the price at which x items can be sold per week is given by the demand equation

$$p = 12 - 0.0015x.$$

Determine the price and volume of sales at which the profit is maximum.

Solution   The revenue per week is

$$R(x) = px = (12 - 0.0015x)x.$$

The profit is therefore given by

$$
\begin{aligned}
P(x) &= R(x) - C(x) \\
&= (12x - 0.0015x^2) - (1000 + 6x - 0.003x^2 + 10^{-6}x^3) \\
&= -1000 + 6x + 0.0015x^2 - 10^{-6}x^3.
\end{aligned}
$$

To find the maximum value of $P(x)$, we set $P'(x) = 0$.

$$P'(x) = 6 + 0.003x - (3 \times 10^{-6})x^2 = 0$$

We change signs throughout this equation, divide through by 3, and multiply by 10^6 to obtain $x^2 - 1000x - 2 \times 10^6 = 0$. We can factor the left side as

$$(x - 2000)(x + 1000) = 0$$

and so the solutions are $x = 2000$ or -1000. (These solutions could also have been obtained using the quadratic formula.)

The negative root has no practical significance, so we need only consider $x = 2000$. To verify that this does indeed represent a local maximum of the profit function, we can check that $P''(2000) < 0$. This is easily done.

$$P''(x) = 0.003 - (6 \times 10^{-6})x$$
$$P''(2000) = 0.003 - (6 \times 10^{-6})(2000) = -0.009$$

Thus the sales volume of 2000 items per week does give the maximum profit. The price per item corresponding to this value of x is

$$p = 12 - 0.0015x = 12 - 0.0015(2000) = 9.$$

For any firm, the profit is the difference between revenue and costs:

$$P(x) = R(x) - C(x).$$

Therefore, assuming that all functions are differentiable,

$$P'(x) = R'(x) - C'(x).$$

When the profit is maximum, $P'(x) = 0$, and so it follows that $R'(x) = C'(x)$.

This result provides an important general conclusion regarding the operation of any firm: *At the level of production at which the profit is maximum, the marginal revenue equals the marginal cost.*

In a competitive market in which many firms produce similar products at about the same price, the volume of sales can be increased by advertising.

However, if too much money is spent on advertisement, the expenditure will outweigh the gain in revenue through increased sales. Again the criterion that must be used in deciding how much to spend on advertising is that the profit should be maximum.

EXAMPLE 6   A company makes a profit of $5 on each item of its product it sells. If it spends A dollars per week on advertising, then the number of items per week it sells is given by

$$x = 2000(1 - e^{-kA})$$

where $k = 0.001$. Find the value of A that maximizes the net profit.

Solution   The gross profit from selling x items is $5x$ dollars, and from this we must subtract the cost of advertising. This leaves a net profit given by

$$P = 5x - A$$
$$= 10,000(1 - e^{-kA}) - A. \qquad (1)$$

We differentiate to find the maximum value of P.

$$\frac{dP}{dA} = 10,000(ke^{-kA}) - 1 = 10e^{-kA} - 1$$

since $k = 0.001$. Setting this to zero, we get

$$10e^{-kA} = 1 \quad \text{or} \quad e^{kA} = 10$$

and taking natural logarithms, we obtain

$$kA = \ln 10 = 2.30$$

to three significant figures. Therefore

$$A = \frac{2.30}{k} = \frac{2.30}{0.001} = 2300.$$

The optimum amount to be spent on advertising is therefore $2300 per week.

The maximum profit is found by substituting this value of A into Equation (1). Since $e^{-kA} = \frac{1}{10}$, it follows that the maximum weekly profit is

$$P_{\text{max}} = 10,000(1 - \tfrac{1}{10}) - 2300 = 6700 \text{ dollars.}$$

We shall conclude this section by describing the application of maxima and minima to an **inventory cost model**. Let us consider a particular example. Suppose that a manufacturer has to make 50,000 units of a certain item during a year. There is a choice of a number of different production schedules. All the required units could be made at the beginning of the year in one production run. Because of the economies of mass production, this would minimize the cost of production. However, it would mean that large numbers of items would have to be held in storage until they were needed for sale, and so storage costs would be high and could outweigh the advantage of lower productiun costs.

Let us suppose that it costs $400 to prepare the manufacturing plant for each production run, that each item then costs $4 to manufacture, and that it costs 40 cents per year for each item carried in storage. We assume that the same

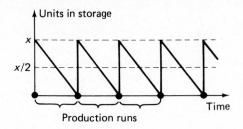

Units in storage

Production runs

Time

FIGURE 27

number of items is produced in each production run, and denote that number by x. We shall assume that after a batch has been made, the x units are placed in storage and are sold at a uniform rate so that the units stored are exactly used up when the next production run is made. Then the number of units in storage as a function of time is illustrated in Figure 27.

At each production run, the number leaps from 0 to x, then steadily decreases at a constant rate to zero. When it reaches zero, the next batch is produced and the number in storage goes up to x again.

It is clear from Figure 27 that the average number of units in storage is $x/2$. Since it costs \$0.40 to store each item per year, the storage costs over the year will be $(0.4)(x/2)$ dollars, or $x/5$ dollars.

Since the necessary 50,000 items are produced in batches of size x, the number of production runs per year must be $50,000/x$. The cost of preparing the plant for these runs is therefore $(400)(50,000/x) = (2 \times 10^7/x)$ dollars. The manufacturing cost of producing 50,000 items at \$4 each is \$200,000. Therefore the total manufacturing and storage costs over one year are given (in dollars) by

$$C = \frac{2 \times 10^7}{x} + 200,000 + \frac{x}{5}.$$

We wish to find the value of x that makes C a minimum. Differentiating gives

$$\frac{dC}{dx} = -\frac{2 \times 10^7}{x^2} + \frac{1}{5}.$$

Setting this derivative equal to zero, we obtain the following result.

$$\frac{2 \times 10^7}{x^2} = \frac{1}{5}$$

$$x^2 = (2 \times 10^7)(5) = 10^8$$

$$x = 10^4 = 10,000$$

(The negative root has no practical significance.) Furthermore, we see that

$$\frac{d^2C}{dx^2} = \frac{4 \times 10^7}{x^3}$$

which is positive when $x = 10,000$. So this value of x provides a local minimum of C.

Consequently, the minimum cost is obtained by making $50,000/10,000 = 5$ production runs per year, each run producing 10,000 units.

This type of inventory cost model also applies to businesses such as warehouses or retail outlets that maintain stocks of items to be sold either to the public or to other businesses. The question is how great a quantity should be ordered each time any item is restocked. If a very large quantity is ordered, the firm will be faced with substantial storage costs, although it will have the advantage of not having to reorder for a long time. On the other hand, if only a small quantity is ordered each time the item is restocked, the storage costs will be low but the costs of placing the orders will be high, since orders must be placed frequently. Somewhere between these extremes we can expect there to be an optimum size for each order that will make the total cost of storage plus ordering a minimum. The method of determining this optimum order size, at least for the simplest model, is similar to the preceding example. (See Exercise 23 in this section and Exercise 27 in the Review Exercises.)

EXERCISES 4

1. Find two numbers with sum 10 and with maximum product.

2. Find two numbers with sum 8, such that the sum of their squares is a minimum.

3. Find two positive numbers with sum 75, such that the product of one times the square of the other is a maximum.

4. Find two positive numbers with sum 12, such that the sum of their cubes is a minimum.

5. Show that among all the rectangles of area 100 square centimeters, the one with the smallest perimeter is the square of side 10 centimeters.

6. What is the area of the largest rectangle that can be drawn inside a circle of radius a?

7. What is the area of the largest rectangle that can be drawn inside a semicircle of radius a?

8. A farmer wishes to enclose a rectangular paddock using only 100 yards of fencing. What is the largest area that can be enclosed?

9. Repeat Exercise 8 for the case in which one side of the paddock makes use of an existing fence and only three new sides need to be constructed using the 100 yards of available fencing.

10. A handbill is to contain 48 square inches of printed matter with 3-inch margins at the top and bottom and 1-inch margins on each side. What dimensions for the handbill will consume the least amount of paper?

11. A cistern is to be constructed to hold 324 cubic feet of water. The cistern has a square base and four vertical sides, all made of concrete, and a square top made of steel. If the steel costs twice as much per unit area as the concrete, determine the dimensions of the cistern which minimize the total cost of construction.

12. Repeat Exercise 11 if the shape of the cistern is a cylinder with circular base and top.

13. The average cost of manufacturing a certain article is given by

$$\bar{C} = 5 + \frac{48}{x} + 3x^2,$$

where x is the number of articles produced. Find the minimum value of $\bar{C}$.

14. The cost of the annual production of an item is

$$C = 5000 + \frac{80,000,000}{x} + \frac{x}{20}$$

where x is the average batch size per production run. Find the value of x which makes C a minimum.

15. The cost of producing x items of a certain product is

$$C(x) = 4000 + 3x + 10^{-3}x^2 \quad \text{(dollars)}.$$

Find the value of x that makes the average cost per item a minimum.

16. Repeat Exercise 15 for the cost function $C(x) = 16,000 + 3x + 10^{-6}x^3$ (dollars).

17. A firm sells all units it produces at \$4 per unit. The firm's total cost C of producing x units is given in dollars by

$$C = (50 + 1.3x + 0.001x^2).$$

   a. Write the expression for total profit P as a function of x.

   b. Find the production volume x so that the profit P is maximum.

   c. What is the value of maximum profit?

18. A company finds that it can sell out a certain product that it produces at the rate of \$2 per unit. It estimates the cost function of the product to be $(1000 + \frac{1}{2}(x/50)^2)$ dollars for x units produced.

   a. Find an expression for the total profit if x units are produced and sold.

   b. Find the number of units produced that will maximize profit.

   c. What is the amount of the maximum profit?

   d. What would be the profit if 6000 units were produced?

19. In Exercise 15, the items in question are sold for \$8 each. Find the value of x that maximizes the profit and calculate the maximum profit.

20. In Exercise 16, the items are sold for \$30 each. Find the value of x that maximizes the profit and calculate the maximum profit.

21. For a certain item, the demand equation is $p = 5 - 0.001x$. What value of x maximizes the revenue? If the cost function is $C = 2800 + x$, find the value of x that maximizes the profit. Calculate the maximum profit.

22. Repeat Exercise 21 for the demand equation $p = 8 - 0.02x$ and the cost function $C = 200 + 2x$.

23. By an *economic order quantity*, we mean the size x of each purchase order that minimizes the total cost (T) incurred in obtaining and storing material for a certain time period to fulfill a given rate of demand for the material during the time period.

    The material demanded is 10,000 units per year; the cost price of the material is \$2 per unit; the cost of replenishing the stock of the material per order, regardless of the size of the order (x), is \$40 per order; and the cost of storing material is 10% per year on the dollar value of the average inventory $(x/2)$ on hand.

   a. Show that $T = 20,000 + 400,000/x + x/10$.

   b. Find the economic order quantity.

24. A factory has to produce 96,000 units of an item per year. The cost of material is \$2 per unit and the cost of replenishing the stock of material per order regardless of the size x of the order is \$25 per order. The cost of storing the material

is 30¢ per item per year on the inventory $(x/2)$ in hand. Show that the total cost C is given by

$$C = 192,000 + \frac{2400000}{x} + \frac{3x}{20}.$$

Also find the economic lot size (that is, the value of x for which C is minimum).

25. A forest company plans to log a certain area of fir trees after a given number of years. The average number of board feet obtained per tree over the given period is known to be equal to $50 - 0.5x$, where x is the number of trees per acre, when x lies between 35 and 80. What density of trees should be maintained in order to maximize the amount of timber per acre?

26. The yield y (bushels per acre) of a certain crop of wheat is given by $y = a(1 - e^{-kx}) + b$, where a, b, and k are constants and x is the number of pounds per acre of fertilizer. The profit from sale of the wheat is given by $P = py - c_o - cx$ where p is the profit per bushel, c is the cost per pound of fertilizer and c_o is an overhead cost. Determine how much fertilizer must be used in order to maximize the profit P.

*27. The quantity of an item x that can be sold per month at price p is given by $x = 100(5 - p)$. The quantity that suppliers will make available at a price p_1 is given by $x = 200(p_1 - 1)$. If there is a tax t on each item (so $p_1 = p - t$), determine the quantity x that is sold per month if the market is in equilibrium. Find the value of t that provides the maximum total tax per month for the government.

*28. Repeat Exercise 27 if the demand equation is $x = 400(15 - p)$ and the supply equation is $x = 400(2p_1 - 3)$. Calculate the monthly tax yield to the government.

29. The cost of erecting a building containing n floors can often be taken to be of the form $a + bn + cn^2$, where a, b, and c are constants. (Here a represents fixed costs such as land costs, b represents a cost that is the same for every floor, such as interior walls, windows, floor covering, and cn^2 represents costs such as structural members, which increase as the square of the number of floors.) Calculate the value of n that makes the average cost per floor a minimum. Show that as land costs increase, this optimum value of n increases.

30. A travel agent provides charter holidays for group travel on the following basis: For groups of size up to 50, the fare is $400 per person, while for larger groups, the fare per person is reduced for the whole group by $2 for each person traveling in excess of 50. Find the group size that maximizes the travel agent's revenue.

*31. A manufacturer prices a product at $10 each for orders less than 200 and offers a reduction in price of 2¢ for each item by which an order exceeds 200, the reduction applying to the whole order. Find the order size that maximizes the manufacturer's revenue. If the items cost $5 each to manufacture, find the order size that maximizes the manufacturer's profit. How is this last result changed if the manufacturing cost rises to $7 per item?

14-5 ABSOLUTE MAXIMA AND MINIMA

In some problems, it happens that the independent variable x is restricted to some interval of values, say $a \leq x \leq b$, and we need to find the largest or smallest value of some function $f(x)$ over this set of values of x. In fact, most of our problems in the last section were of this type, although we did not emphasize the fact there. For example, if x is the level of production by some manufacturing firm, then x is restricted to the interval $x \geq 0$ and we are interested in the maximum value of the profit function in this interval. Any local maximum that might occur for a negative value of x is of no significance. This restriction on x does not affect any of the results we obtained, but cases do arise in which similar restrictions can affect the conclusions regarding the optimum.

EXAMPLE 1   An underground cistern is to be constructed to hold 100 cubic feet of radioactive waste. The cistern is to be a circular cylinder in shape. The circular base and vertical sides, which are all underground, cost \$100 per square foot and the lid, at ground level, costs \$300 per square foot because of the necessary shielding. Furthermore, the depth of the tank cannot exceed 6 feet because of a hard rock layer beneath the surface, which would increase the excavation costs enormously if it were to be penetrated. Finally, the radius of the tank cannot exceed 4 feet because of space limitations. What dimensions for the tank will make its cost a minimum?

Solution   Let the radius be r and the depth be x. (See Figure 28.) Then the volume is $\pi r^2 x$, which must be the required 100 cubic feet.

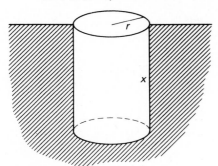

$$\pi r^2 x = 100 \qquad (1)$$

The area of the vertical sides is $2\pi rx$ and of the base is πr^2, and all of these cost \$100 per square foot. So

Cost (in dollars) of Base and Sides
$$= (2\pi rx + \pi r^2)(100).$$

The top costs $(\pi r^2)(300)$ dollars. Therefore the total cost C (in dollars) is

$$C = (2\pi rx + \pi r^2)(100) + (\pi r^2)(300)$$
$$= 200\pi rx + 400\pi r^2.$$

FIGURE 28

But from Equation (1), $x = 100/\pi r^2$, so substituting for x we find that

$$C = \frac{20{,}000}{r} + 400\pi r^2.$$

To find the minimum value of C we set $dC/dr = 0$ and solve for r.

$$\frac{dC}{dr} = -\frac{20{,}000}{r^2} + 800\pi r = 0$$

$$800\pi r = \frac{20{,}000}{r^2}$$

$$r^3 = \frac{20{,}000}{800\pi} = \frac{25}{\pi}$$

Therefore $r = \sqrt[3]{25/\pi} \approx 2.00$.

The corresponding value of x is

$$x = 100/\pi r^2 \approx 100/\pi(2.00)^2 = 7.96.$$

Thus the dimensions that give the cheapest construction are a radius of 2 feet and a depth of 7.96 feet. However we are not allowed to have a value of x in excess of 6 feet. So although the value $x = 7.96$ gives the minimum value of C, it does not provide the solution to the problem as posed.

The graph of C as a function of r is shown in Figure 29. Now the largest allowed value of r is 4. The smallest allowed value occurs when the depth is greatest, that is, $x = 6$. Then $r^2 = (100/\pi x)$, so $r = \sqrt{100/6\pi} \approx 2.30$. So r is restricted to the range $2.30 \leq r \leq 4$. The local minimum of C occurs when $x = 7.96$ and $r = 2.00$, and lies outside this allowed range. It is clear from the graph that within the allowed range of values, the minimum value of C occurs when $r = 2.30$ (that is, when $x = 6$). The minimum cost is given by

$$C_{\min} = 20,000/2.30 + 400\pi(2.30)^2 = 15,400, \text{ or } \$15,400.$$

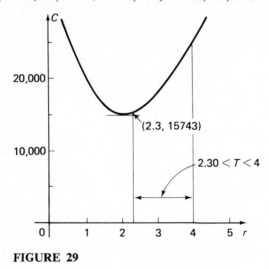

FIGURE 29

We shall continue the discussion at a more abstract level.

DEFINITION The **absolute maximum** value of $f(x)$ over an interval $a \leq x \leq b$ of its domain is the largest value of $f(x)$ as x takes all the values from a to b. Similarly, the **absolute minimum** value of $f(x)$ is the smallest value of $f(x)$ as x increases from a to b.

It is intuitively obvious that if $f(x)$ is continuous in $a \leq x \leq b$, the point at which $f(x)$ attains its absolute maximum must be either a local maximum of $f(x)$ or else one of the endpoints a or b. A similar statement holds for the absolute minimum. Thus to find the absolute maximum and absolute minimum values of $f(x)$ over $a \leq x \leq b$, we simply select the largest and the smallest values from among the values of $f(x)$ at the critical points lying in $a \leq x \leq b$ and at the end points a and b. This is illustrated in Example 2.

EXAMPLE 2   Determine the absolute maximum and minimum values of
$$f(x) = 1 + 12x - x^3 \text{ in } 1 \le x \le 3.$$

Solution   We have $f'(x) = 12 - 3x^2$.

Since $f'(x)$ is defined for all x, the critical points of f are given by $f'(x) = 0$, or $x^2 = 4$; that is, $x = \pm 2$. But $x = -2$ is *not* within the given interval $1 \le x \le 3$. Thus we consider only the critical point $x = 2$, plus the endpoints $x = 1$ and $x = 3$. The values of $f(x)$ at these points are

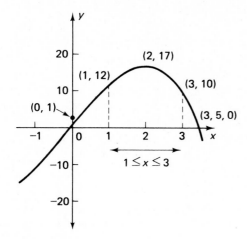

$$f(1) = 1 + 12 - 1 \ = 12$$
$$f(2) = 1 + 24 - 8 \ = 17$$
$$f(3) = 1 + 36 - 27 = 10.$$

Thus the absolute maximum value of $f(x)$ is 17, which occurs at $x = 2$, and the absolute minimum is 10, which occurs at the endpoint $x = 3$. The graph of $y = 1 + 12x - x^3$ is shown in Figure 30. Within the interval $1 \le x \le 3$, the graph has a single local maximum occuring at $x = 2$. The absolute minimum value occurs at the endpoint $x = 3$.

FIGURE 30

EXERCISES 5

(1–8) Find the absolute extrema of the following functions in the indicated intervals.

1. $f(x) = x^2 - 6x + 7;\quad 1 \le x \le 6$

2. $f(x) = 9 + 6x - x^2;\quad 1 \le x \le 5$

3. $f(x) = x^3 - 75x + 1;\quad -1 \le x \le 6$

4. $f(x) = x^3 - 3x + 4;\quad -2 \le x \le 2$

5. $f(x) = x^3 - 18x^2 + 60x;\quad -1 \le x \le 5$

6. $f(x) = \dfrac{(x-1)(x-3)}{x^2};\quad \frac{1}{2} \le x \le 2$

7. $f(x) = \dfrac{(x+1)(x-6)}{x^2};\quad \frac{1}{2} \le x \le 2$

8. $f(x) = x + 1/x;\quad -2 \le x \le \frac{1}{2}$

9. When deposited in a lake, organic waste decreases the oxygen content of the water. If t denotes the time in days after the waste is deposited, then it is found experimentally in one instance that the oxygen content is given by

$$y = t^3 - 30t^2 + 6000$$

for $0 \le t \le 25$. Find the maximum and minimum values of y during the first 25 days following the depositing of the waste.

10. The cost function for a manufacturer is

$$C(x) = 1000 + 5x + 0.1x^2$$

when x items are produced per day. If at most 80 items can be produced per day, determine the value of x that gives the lowest average cost per item.

11. The cost of producing x items per week is

$$C(x) = 1000 + 6x - 0.003x^2 + 10^{-6}x^3$$

but not more than 3000 items can be produced each week. If the demand equation is

$$p = 12 - 0.0015x$$

determine the level of production that maximizes the revenue and the level that maximizes the profit.

14-6 CURVE SKETCHING

Let us suppose that we are given an explicit relationship $y = f(x)$ between two variables x and y. It often happens that we would like to get a rough qualitative picture of what the graph of this relation looks like. Of course, we could do this by actually plotting a large number of points (x, y), which we would calculate in the usual way from the given function $y = f(x)$. In fact, such a procedure would give us the precise graph of the relation. However, if all we need is a qualitative idea of the shape of the graph, it is often much easier to make use of certain properties of derivatives in order to sketch the graph rather than plotting points. The first and second derivatives, $f'(x)$ and $f''(x)$, are effective tools in studying the nature of graphs, and in this chapter we shall study their use for this purpose. Before doing so, however, we shall study the behavior of certain types of functions for very large values of their arguments. Information regarding such behavior is also often an important component for sketching the graph of the function.

The behavior of functions for large values of their arguments is of considerable practical interest. Often, in the application of mathematics, we are concerned with using mathematical equations to describe processes which evolve in time. In such cases, the independent variable x is identified with time (and t is generally used in place of x). The state of the system at any instant of time is described by a certain function of t (in more complex systems, it may be necessary to use several functions of t in order to specify the state of the system). For example, we may be concerned with a mathematical model describing the volume of sales of a certain item as a function of time. Or, on a grander scale, we might be interested in the progress of a national economy with, for example, $f(t)$ being the unemployment rate as a function of time t. (In this latter case, several other functions of t would be involved in a complete model).

When we are investigating systems that evolve in time, one aspect that is often of great interest is the behavior of the system for large values of time. While the behavior of the system may in general be very complex, it often happens that after a while it settles down into some much simpler pattern of behavior. We call this the *asymptotic behavior* of a system.

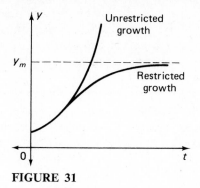

FIGURE 31

As an illustration, consider the population of a certain geographical area. (See Figure 31.) The size of the population, y, is a function of t. The growth of the population may be unrestricted—that is, y may continue to increase indefinitely as time increases. However, if the environment places certain limitations on the continued growth, then the growth of the population will slow down. For large values of t, y approaches a certain limiting value, y_m, which is the maximum population size which can be supported by the given environment. In this case, the asymptotic behavior of the system is that y approaches the constant limiting value y_m. We write $t \longrightarrow \infty$ to indicate the fact that t takes larger and larger values (read t *approaches infinity*). Then, for restricted growth, we write

$$y \longrightarrow y_m \quad \text{as} \quad t \longrightarrow \infty \quad \text{or} \quad \lim_{t \to \infty} y = y_m.$$

With this type of example in mind, we shall now study limits as $x \longrightarrow \infty$ in a more abstract way.

Consider the function f defined by

$$f(x) = \frac{2x + 1}{x}.$$

Let us determine the behavior of f as x gets larger and larger without bound—that is, as x approaches infinity. Let x take the values 1, 10, 100, 1000, and 10 000. The corresponding values of $f(x)$ are given in Table 1.

TABLE 1

x	1	10	100	1000	10,000
$f(x)$	3	2.1	2.01	2.001	2.0001

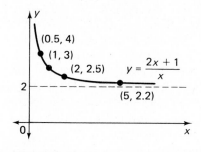

FIGURE 32

We observe from Table 1 that as x gets larger and larger without bound, $f(x)$ gets closer and closer to 2. In other words, the difference between $f(x)$ and 2 can be made as small as we please provided that we choose x sufficiently large. In terms of limits, we say that $f(x) \longrightarrow 2$ as $x \longrightarrow \infty$ and write

$$\lim_{x \to \infty} f(x) = 2.$$

The graph of $y = (2x + 1)/x$ is shown in Figure 32 for $x > 0$. As x gets larger, the graph becomes closer and closer to the horizontal line $y = 2$.

Consider another example, $f(x) = 1/x$. The behavior of $f(x)$ as x gets larger and larger is shown in Table 2.

TABLE 2

x	1	10	100	1000	10000	100000	$\ldots \longrightarrow \infty$
$f(x)$	1	0.1	0.01	0.001	0.0001	0.00001	$\ldots \longrightarrow 0$

It is clear from Table 2 that as x becomes larger and larger, $f(x)$ gets closer and closer to zero. That is, the difference between $f(x)$ and zero can be made as small as we please provided that we take x sufficiently large (see Figure 33). Thus $\lim_{x \to \infty} f(x) = 0$ or

$$\lim_{x \to \infty} \frac{1}{x} = 0.$$

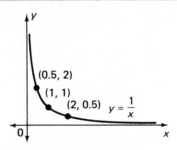

FIGURE 33

DEFINITION   A function $f(x)$ approaches the **limiting value** L as $x \longrightarrow \infty$ if the value of $f(x)$ can be made as close as we like to L simply by taking x large enough. We write

$$\lim_{x \to \infty} f(x) = L.$$

Limits as x approaches $-\infty$ can be defined in a similar way.

DEFINITION   A function $f(x)$ approaches the **limiting value** L as $x \longrightarrow -\infty$ if the value of $f(x)$ can be made as close to L as we like by taking x to be a negative number of sufficiently large absolute value. We write

$$\lim_{x \to -\infty} f(x) = L.$$

As we have seen, the function $1/x$ approaches the limit zero as $x \longrightarrow \infty$. This function also approaches the same limit as $x \longrightarrow -\infty$. These results generalize to inverse powers.

THEOREM 1

$$\lim_{x \to \infty} \frac{1}{x^n} = 0 \text{ for all } n > 0.$$

$$\lim_{x \to -\infty} \frac{1}{x^n} = 0 \text{ for all } n > 0, \text{ provided that } \frac{1}{x^n} \text{ is defined for } x < 0.$$

EXAMPLE 1 $\lim_{x \to \infty} 1/x^2 = 0$, $\lim_{x \to \infty} 1/\sqrt{x} = 0$, and $\lim_{x \to -\infty} x^{-4/3} = 0$.

Note that limits such as $\lim_{x \to -\infty} 1/\sqrt{x}$ do not exist because $\sqrt{x}$ is not defined for $x < 0$.

___

We are interested in the geometric significance of the fact that $f(x)$ approaches some limit L as $x \to +\infty$ or $x \to -\infty$. If $f(x) \to L$ as $x \to \infty$, then the graph of $y = f(x)$ gets closer and closer to the line $y = L$ as x moves further towards the right. We say that the line $y = L$ is a **horizontal asymptote** of the graph at $+\infty$.

If the graph of $y = f(x)$ has $y = L$ as a horizontal asymptote at $+\infty$, the graph may stay entirely on one side of the line $y = L$ or may cross and recross the asymptote repeatedly as x increases. Typical examples are shown in Figure 34.

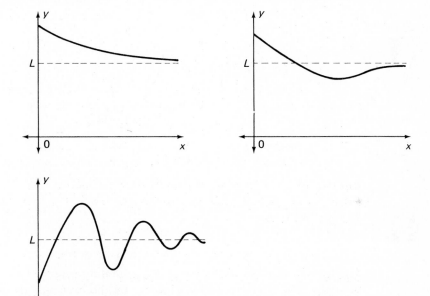

FIGURE 34

Similarly, if $f(x) \to L'$ as $x \to -\infty$, then the graph of $y = f(x)$ gets closer and closer to the horizontal line $y = L'$ as x moves further to the left. This line is a horizontal asymptote of the graph at $-\infty$.

Sometimes a function $f(x)$ grows to arbitrarily large values as x approaches either $+\infty$ or $-\infty$. For example, the simple function $f(x) = x^3$ becomes indefinitely large and positive as $x \to \infty$. On the other hand, as $x \to -\infty$, this function becomes indefinitely large and negative. The graph of $y = x^3$, drawn in Figure 35, shows these two properties.

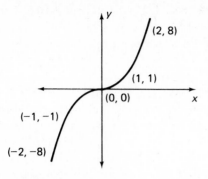

FIGURE 35

More generally, we say that $f(x) \to \infty$ as $x \to \infty$ if $f(x)$ can be made as large as we please simply by ensuring that x is large enough. We say that $f(x) \to -\infty$ as $x \to \infty$ if $f(x)$ can be made as large and negative as we please by ensuring that x is large enough. An alternative way of writing these properties is

$$\lim_{x \to \infty} f(x) = \infty \quad \text{or} \quad -\infty$$

respectively.

In a similar way, we can define corresponding types of behavior as $x \to -\infty$; we write $f(x) \to +\infty$ (or $-\infty$) as $x \to -\infty$ and

$$\lim_{x \to -\infty} f(x) = \infty \quad \text{(or } -\infty\text{)}.$$

EXAMPLE 2   (a) $\lim_{x \to \infty} (x^2) = \infty$ and $\lim_{x \to -\infty} (x^2) = \infty$

(b) $\lim_{x \to \infty} (1 - 2x) = -\infty$ and $\lim_{x \to -\infty} (1 - 2x) = \infty$

(c) $\lim_{x \to \infty} (x^3 - 2x^2) = \infty$ and $\lim_{x \to -\infty} (x^3 - 2x^2) = -\infty$

In this case, the highest power, x^3, determines the behavior of the function for large values of x, since when x is large, the term x^3 is much larger than the term $2x^2$.

———————————

To generalize part (c) of Example 2, we can say that *the behavior of any polynomial function of x as $x \to \pm\infty$ is determined completely by the behavior of the term with the highest power.* For example, the behavior of the function $y = x - 2x^3 - x^4$ as $x \to \pm\infty$ is the same as the behavior of the highest power, namely $y = -x^4$. We can see this by writing the given polynomial in the form

$$y = -x^4\left(1 + \frac{2}{x} - \frac{1}{x^3}\right).$$

The term in the bracket approaches the limiting value 1 as $x \to \pm\infty$, so the behavior of y is determined completely by the term outside the bracket. We conclude that $y \to -\infty$ as $x \to \infty$ and as $x \to -\infty$.

Let us now bring together these results with those in Section 1, showing how they can be used in order to obtain a qualitative sketch of the graph of a given function $f(x)$. First, let us summarize the steps involved in this process. The order in which the steps are carried out can be varied, but the following is a convenient procedure.

1.   Find a few explicit points on the graph. For example, the points of intersection with the coordinate axes are often useful. The intersection with the y-axis is obtained by letting $x = 0$, so that $y = f(0)$. The intersection with the x-axis is obtained by letting $y = 0$. This gives the equation $f(x) = 0$, which must be solved for the corresponding values of x. Sometimes this equation turns out to be too complicated to solve, and in such a case we have to manage without this information.

2. Examine the behavior of $f(x)$ as $x \rightarrow \pm\infty$. If $f(x)$ approaches a finite limit L as x approaches either ∞ or $-\infty$, the graph has the horizontal line $y = L$ as an asymptote. If $f(x)$ takes indefinitely large values, either positive or negative, as $x \rightarrow \pm\infty$, then we have an indication of the direction in which the graph is tending at its extremities.

3. Find $f'(x)$. Find the coordinates of the points where $f'(x) = 0$: at these points the graph has horizontal tangents. Find the values of x for which $f'(x)$ is greater than or less than zero: these provide the regions in which the graph is increasing or decreasing.

4. Find $f''(x)$. Find the regions for which $f''(x)$ is positive or negative: these provide the regions in which the graph is concave upwards or downwards. The points where f'' changes sign are the points of inflection.

EXAMPLE 3   Sketch the graph of $y = 3 + 5x - 2x^2$.

Solution   ***Step 1*** $y = 0$ when $2x^2 - 5x - 3 = 0$. The factors of this quadratic are $(2x + 1)(x - 3)$, so the roots are $x = -\frac{1}{2}$ and $x = 3$. Hence the graph crosses the x-axis at the points $(-\frac{1}{2}, 0)$ and $(3, 0)$. Next, setting $x = 0$, we find $y = 3$, so the graph crosses the y-axis at $(0, 3)$.

Step 2   The largest power of x in the function occurs in the last term. Hence when x is large, y behaves like $-2x^2$. Thus as $x \rightarrow \pm\infty$, y becomes larger and larger in the negative direction.

Step 3 $y' = 5 - 4x$. Thus $y' = 0$ when $x = \frac{5}{4}$. At this value of x,

$$y = 3 + 5(\tfrac{5}{4}) - 2(\tfrac{5}{4})^2 = \tfrac{49}{8}.$$

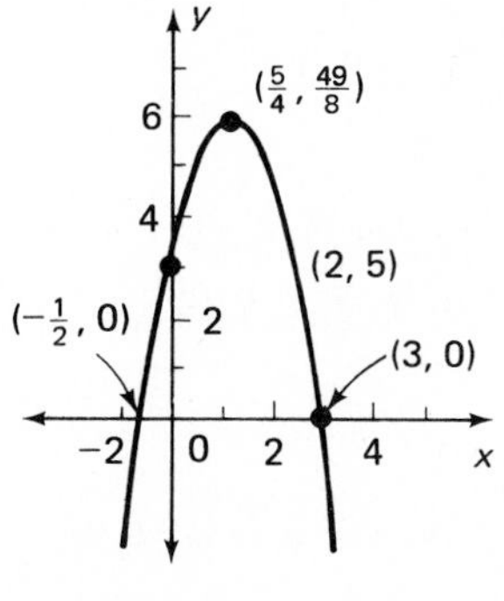

FIGURE 36

So the graph has a horizontal tangent at the point $(\frac{5}{4}, \frac{49}{8})$. When $x < \frac{5}{4}$, $y' > 0$, so the graph is increasing in this region, but for $x > \frac{5}{4}$, $y' < 0$ and the graph is decreasing.

Step 4 $y'' = -4$. Since y'' is negative for all x, the graph is concave down at all points.

Putting all this information together, we can draw a reasonably accurate sketch of the graph, as shown in Figure 36. Of course, in this simple example, we could tell from the beginning that the graph had to be a parabola opening downwards. The point $(\frac{5}{4}, \frac{49}{8})$ is the vertex.

EXAMPLE 4   If the number of items produced per week is x (measured in thousands), a manufacturer's cost function is

$$C = 2 + x - \tfrac{1}{4}x^2 + \tfrac{1}{24}x^3$$

(in thousands of dollars). Sketch the graph of C as a function of x.

Solution   ***Step 1***   For obvious reasons, we are only concerned with the region $x \geq 0$. When $x = 0$, $C = 2$, so the point $(0, 2)$ lies on the graph. If we let $C = 0$ in order to find the intersections with the x-axis, we obtain a cubic equation for x. Since we don't know how to solve such equations, we must abandon it.

Step 2   As $x \to \infty$, C behaves like its term of highest degree, that is, $\frac{1}{24}x^3$. Hence $C \to +\infty$ as $x \to \infty$. (Also $C \to -\infty$ as $x \to -\infty$, but this is of no practical interest.)

Step 3   Differentiating, we obtain

$$C'(x) = 1 - \tfrac{1}{2}x + \tfrac{1}{8}x^2.$$

First of all, we set $C'(x) = 0$ to obtain the points where the graph has horizontal tangents.

$$1 - \tfrac{1}{2}x + \tfrac{1}{8}x^2 = 0$$
$$x^2 - 4x + 8 = 0$$

From the quadratic formula,

$$x = \frac{-(-4) \pm \sqrt{(-4)^2 - 4 \cdot 1 \cdot 8}}{2 \cdot 1} = \frac{4 \pm \sqrt{-16}}{2}.$$

Because of the negative number under the radical, x is not a real number. We conclude that $C'(x)$ is never zero. In fact, $C'(x) > 0$ for all x. This follows since $C'(0) = 1$, which is positive. Since C' never vanishes, and is a continuous function of x, it can never change sign. Since it is positive when $x = 0$, it must remain positive for all x. Hence the graph always slopes upwards to the right.

Step 4   Differentiating again, we find that

$$C''(x) = -\tfrac{1}{2} + \tfrac{1}{4}x$$
$$= \tfrac{1}{4}(x - 2).$$

Therefore, when $x > 2$, $C''(x) > 0$ and the graph is concave upwards. When $x < 2$, $C''(x) < 0$ and the graph is concave downwards. There is a point of inflection at $x = 2$. At the point of inflection,

$$C(2) = 2 + 2 - \tfrac{1}{4}(2)^2 + \tfrac{1}{24}(2)^3 = 10/3$$
$$C'(2) = 1 - \tfrac{1}{2}(2) + \tfrac{1}{8}(2)^2 = \tfrac{1}{2}.$$

So the point of inflection is at $(2, \tfrac{10}{3})$ and the graph has slope $\tfrac{1}{2}$ at that point. Putting these results together, we obtain the graph shown in Figure 37. One other point, $(4, \tfrac{14}{3})$, has been plotted.

EXAMPLE 3   Sketch the graph of the function $y = e^{-x^2}$.

Solution   **Step 1**   When $x = 0$, $y = e^0 = 1$. So the graph crosses the y-axis at $(0, 1)$.

e^{-x^2} is not zero for any value of x, so the graph does not meet the x-axis.

Step 2   As $x \to \pm\infty$, the exponent $-x^2$ becomes increasingly large and negative. Hence $e^{-x^2} \to 0$. So the graph has the x-axis ($y = 0$) as a horizontal asymptote at both $+\infty$ and $-\infty$.

Step 3   We have the following,

$$f(x) = e^{-x^2}$$

$$f'(x) = -2xe^{-x^2}   \text{(from the chain rule)}$$

The factor e^{-x^2} is never zero, so $f'(x) = 0$ only when $x = 0$. That is, the graph has a horizontal tangent at the point $(0, 1)$ where it crosses the y-axis.

Since e^{-x^2} is always positive, we see that when $x < 0$, $f'(x) > 0$, so the

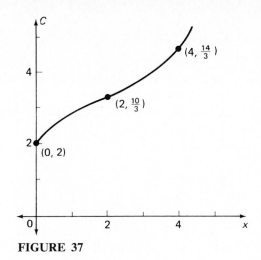

FIGURE 37

graph is increasing for $x < 0$. Correspondingly, when $x > 0$, $f'(x) < 0$ and the graph decreases.

Step 3   We use the product rule and differentiate a second time.

$$f''(x) = -2\frac{d}{dx}(xe^{-x^2}) = 2(2x^2 - 1)e^{-x^2}$$

The points of inflection, where $f''(x) = 0$, are given by $2x^2 - 1 = 0$, that is, $x = \pm 1/\sqrt{2}$.

The corresponding values of y are $y = e^{-(\pm 1/\sqrt{2})^2} = e^{-0.5}$. So the points of inflection are $(\pm 1/\sqrt{2}, e^{-0.5}) \approx (\pm 0.71, 0.61)$. The second derivative changes sign at these points of inflection. The factor e^{-x^2} is always positive, so the sign of $f''(x)$ is the same as the sign of $2x^2 - 1$. When $x < -1/\sqrt{2}$, $x^2 > \frac{1}{2}$ so $2x^2 - 1 > 0$. Thus $f''(x) > 0$ in this region and the graph is concave upwards. When $-1/\sqrt{2} < x < 1/\sqrt{2}$, $x^2 < \frac{1}{2}$, so $2x^2 - 1 < 0$. Thus $f''(x) < 0$ in this region and the graph is concave downwards. When $x > 1/\sqrt{2}$, $x^2 > \frac{1}{2}$ and $2x^2 - 1 > 0$. Thus again $f''(x) > 0$ and the graph is concave upwards.

Bringing this information all together, we are able to provide the sketch of the graph shown in Figure 38. The graph is related to the familiar "bell-shaped curve" of probability theory.

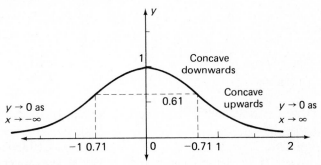

FIGURE 38

(1–14) Sketch the graphs of the functions given in Exercises 1–4 and 13–22 in Section 1.

(15–16) Sketch the graphs of the two cost functions in Exercises 31 and 32 in Section 1 ($x > 0$ only).

17. If an amount A (in thousands of dollars) is spent on advertising per week, a company finds that the weekly sales volume is given by

$$x = 2000(1 - e^{-A}).$$

The items are sold at a profit of \$2 each. If P denotes the net profit (that is, profit from sales minus advertising costs), express P as a function of A and sketch its graph.

*18. Sketch the graph of the logistic function

$$y = \frac{y_m}{1 + ce^{-t}} \qquad (y_m, c > 0).$$

14-7 VERTICAL ASYMPTOTES

Consider the behaviour of the function $y = 1/x$ as x approaches 0. If x becomes smaller and smaller, its reciprocal becomes larger and larger, as illustrated by the succession of values in Table 3.

TABLE 3

x	1	0.1	0.01	0.001
$y = \dfrac{1}{x}$	1	10	100	1000

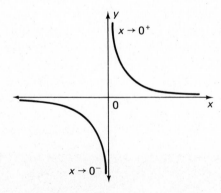

FIGURE 39

This feature is illustrated by the graph of $y = 1/x$ since the graph climbs to arbitrarily high values as x decreases towards 0. (See Figure 39.) We write this as

$$\lim_{x \to 0^+} \frac{1}{x} = +\infty.$$

It should be pointed out that this notation is purely a matter of convention, and does not imply that $\lim_{x \to 0^+} (1/x)$ exists in the ordinary sense of a limit. It simply means that as x approaches zero from above, the function $1/x$ increases without bound.

As x approaches zero from below, the values of $1/x$ become larger and larger in a negative direction, as illustrated by Table 4.

TABLE 4

x	-1	-0.1	-0.01	-0.001
$\dfrac{1}{x}$	-1	-10	-100	-1000

This is written as

$$\lim_{x \to 0^-} \frac{1}{x} = -\infty,$$

indicating that as x approaches 0 from below, the function $1/x$ decreases without bound.

The line $x = 0$ is called a **vertical asymptote** of the graph of $y = 1/x$. The graph approaches the vertical asymptote more and more closely, y becoming indefinitely large, as x approaches 0. This compares with the line $y = 0$ (the x-axis) which is a *horizontal* asymptote of the graph. The *horizontal* asymptote is obtained from the limit as x approaches $\pm \infty$: $\lim_{x \to \pm \infty} 1/x = 0$. The *vertical* asymptote is obtained at the limiting values of x that make y approach $\pm \infty$.

EXAMPLE 1　　　Find the horizontal and vertical asymptotes of the function

$$y = \frac{2x - 9}{x - 2}$$

and sketch its graph.

Solution　　　First of all, we observe that we can divide numerator and denominator by x and write

$$y = \frac{2x - 9}{x - 2} = \frac{2 - 9/x}{1 - 2/x} \to \frac{2 - 0}{1 - 0} = 2 \text{ as } x \to \pm \infty.$$

Therefore the graph of the given function approaches the line $y = 2$ as its horizontal asymptote both as $x \to +\infty$ and as $x \to -\infty$.

The domain of the given function is the set of all real numbers except $x = 2$. As x approaches 2, the denominator $x - 2$ approaches zero and so y becomes very large. The line $x = 2$ must therefore be a vertical asymptote.

In order to complete the sketch of the graph, we must decide on which sides of the asymptotes the graph lies. As $x \to 2^+$ (x approaches 2 from above), the factor $2x - 9$ in the numerator approaches the limit -5. The denominator $x - 2$ approaches zero through positive values. Therefore y becomes very large and negative, since its numerator is negative and its denominator small but positive.

On the other hand, as $x \to 2^-$ (x approaches 2 from below) the numerator still approaches the limit -5, but the denominator is small and negative. Hence y becomes large and positive. We therefore conclude that

$$y \to -\infty \text{ as } x \to 2^+ \quad \text{and} \quad y \to +\infty \text{ as } x \to 2^-.$$

We are thus able to place the graph in relation to the vertical asymptote at $x = 2$. (See Figure 40.) The sections of the graph between the asymptotes can now be filled in. In doing this, it is helpful to find where the graph crosses the two coordinate axes. We note that when $x = 0$, $y = \frac{9}{2}$, so that the graph crosses the y-axis at the point $(0, \frac{9}{2})$. To find where the graph crosses the x-axis, we must set $y = 0$, which means that $2x - 9 = 0$, or $x = \frac{9}{2}$; the crossing occurs at $(\frac{9}{2}, 0)$. These two points are marked on Figure 40.

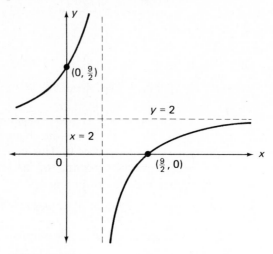

FIGURE 40

EXAMPLE 2   A manufacturer's cost function for producing x thousands of items per week is given in dollars by

$$C = 500\,(4 + 2x + x^2).$$

If $\bar{C}(x)$ denotes the average cost per item, sketch the graph of $\bar{C}$ as a function of x.

Solution   The number of items produced is $1000x$, so their average cost is

$$\bar{C}(x) = \frac{C(x)}{1000x} = \frac{500(4 + 2x + x^2)}{1000x}$$

$$= \frac{2}{x} + 1 + \frac{x}{2}.$$

Of course, we are only concerned with the region $x \geq 0$. As $x \to 0$ from above, the first term, $2/x$, becomes unbounded and positive, so $\bar{C}(x) \to +\infty$ as $x \to 0^+$. The graph therefore has a vertical asymptote at $x = 0$.

As x becomes large, the term $2/x$ becomes small, and $\bar{C}(x) \approx 1 + x/2$. But the function $y = 1 + x/2$ has a straight line with slope $\frac{1}{2}$ and y-intercept 1 as its graph, so the graph of $\bar{C}(x)$ approaches closer and closer to this straight line as $x \to \infty$.

Differentiating, we obtain

$$\bar{C}'(x) = -\frac{2}{x^2} + \frac{1}{2}$$

$$= \frac{1}{2x^2}(x^2 - 4).$$

When $0 < x < 2$, this derivative is negative, so the graph has negative slope. For $x > 2$, the slope is positive. At $x = 2$, therefore, there is a local minimum. The value of $\bar{C}$ at this minimum is

$$\bar{C}(2) = \frac{2}{2} + 1 + \frac{2}{2} = 3.$$

We are now in a position to sketch the graph, as shown in Figure 41. The additional values $\bar{C}(1) = \bar{C}(4) = \frac{7}{2}$ have been used to improve the accuracy of the sketch.

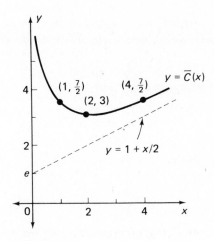

FIGURE 41

EXERCISES 7

(1–10)   Evaluate (a) $\lim\limits_{x \to c^+} f(x)$ and (b) $\lim\limits_{x \to c^-} f(x)$ for the following functions $f(x)$ and points c.

1. $f(x) = \dfrac{1}{x - 2}$, $c = 2$

2. $f(x) = \dfrac{1}{x + 1}$, $c = -1$

3. $f(x) = \dfrac{1}{4 - x^2}$, $c = 2$

4. $f(x) = \dfrac{1}{4 - x^2}$, $c = -2$

5. $f(x) = \dfrac{1}{x^2}$, $c = 0$

6. $f(x) = \dfrac{x}{(x + 1)^2}$, $c = -1$

7. $f(x) = \dfrac{x}{x + 1}$, $c = -1$

8. $f(x) = \dfrac{\sqrt{x}}{x + 1}$, $c = -1$

9. $f(x) = \dfrac{\sqrt{x^2 - 1}}{x - 1}$, $c = 1$

10. $f(x) = \dfrac{\sqrt{4 - x^2}}{x - 2}$, $c = 2$

(11–16)   Find the horizontal and vertical asymptotes of the following functions and sketch their graphs.

11. $y = \dfrac{1}{x - 1}$

12. $y = \dfrac{-2}{x + 2}$

13. $y = \dfrac{2x + 1}{x + 1}$

14. $y = \dfrac{3x - 6}{x - 1}$

*15. $y = \dfrac{x^2 + 1}{x^2 - 1}$

*16. $y = \dfrac{x^2 - 2}{x^2 - 3x + 2}$

(17–20) For the following cost functions $C(x)$, sketch the graphs of the corresponding average cost $\bar{C}(x) = C(x)/x$.

17. $C(x) = 2 + 3x$

18. $C(x) = 3 + x^2$

*19. $C(x) = 2 + x - \frac{1}{4}x^2 + \frac{1}{24}x^3$

20. $C(x) = 3 + 2x + \frac{1}{6}x^2$

REVIEW EXERCISES FOR CHAPTER 14

1. State whether each of the following is true or false. Replace each false statement by a corresponding true statement.

a. The function $f(x)$ is increasing for values of x at which $f(x) > 0$ and is decreasing for values of x at which $f(x) < 0$.

b. If $f(x)$ is increasing for all values of x, then $f'(x)$ is never zero.

c. The graph of $y = [f(x)]^2$ is concave upwards whenever $f(x)f''(x) + [f'(x)]^2 > 0$.

d. If the graph of $y = f(x)$ is increasing at $x = a$, then the graph of $y = -f(x)$ is decreasing at $x = a$.

e. At a point of inflection, $f''(x) = 0$.

f. Every local maximum occurs at a critical point of the function concerned.

g. If a function f has a maximum or a minimum at $x = c$, then $f'(c)$ must be zero.

h. If $f'(c) = 0$, then the function f has either a maximum or a minimum at $x = c$.

i. The tangent to the graph of a function at a point where it is maximum or minimum is either horizontal or vertical.

j. The tangent to the graph of a function at a point of inflection is always horizontal.

k. A local maximum value of a function is always greater than a local minimum value of the same function.

l. Any quadratic function has exactly one local extremum.

m. Any cubic function has two local extrema.

n. A firm is operating optimally if it maximizes its revenues.

o. If $f(x)$ has no local extrema for $a \leq x \leq b$ and is differentiable in that interval, then its absolute maximum value in the interval is either $f(a)$ or $f(b)$.

p. "Advertising always pays, and the more advertising the better."

q. If $f'(x) \leq 0$ for $a \leq x \leq b$, then the absolute maximum value of $f(x)$ in this interval is $f(a)$.

r. If $f(x) \longrightarrow L$ as $x \longrightarrow +\infty$, then $f(x) \longrightarrow L$ as $x \longrightarrow -\infty$.

s. As $x \longrightarrow -\infty$, $x^{-1/2} \longrightarrow 0$.

t. The graph of a function can cross a horizontal asymptote but can never cross a vertical asymptote.

(2–7) Find the values of x for which the following functions are: (a) increasing; (b) decreasing; (c) concave upwards; (d) concave downwards. Sketch their graphs.

2. $y = -2x^2 + 9x - 4$ **3.** $y = x^3 - 9x^2 + 24x - 18$

4. $y = 1 - e^{-x^2/2}$ **5.** $y = \frac{1}{6}x^6 - x^4$

6. $y = x^5 - \frac{5}{3}x^3$ **7.** $y = xe^x$

(8–13) Find the critical points of the following functions and ascertain which of them are local maxima or minima.

8. $3 - 2x - 4x^2$ **9.** $2t^3 - 3t^2 + 1$ **10.** $x^2 e^{3x}$

11. $2x^2 - \ln x$ **12.** $\sqrt{|x|}$ **13.** $x^{2/5}(1 - x)^2$

14. Determine two values of the constant c so that $f(x) = x + c/x$ may have: (a) a local maximum at $x = -1$; (b) a local minimum at $x = 2$.

15. Determine the constant k in such a way that the function $f(x) = x^3 + k/x^2$ may have: (a) a local minimum at $x = 1$; (b) a local maximum at $x = -2$; (c) a point of inflection at $x = 2$.

16. Determine the constants A and B so that the function $f(x) = x^3 + Ax^2 + Bx + C$ may have: (a) a maximum at $x = -2$ and a minimum at $x = 1$; (b) a maximum at $x = -3$ and a point of inflection at $x = -2$.

17. Find the restrictions on the constants A, B, and C in order that $f(x) = Ax^2 + Bx + C$ may have a local minimum.

18. Find the absolute extrema of $g(x) = \sqrt{x^2 - 4}$ in $2 \leq x \leq 3$.

19. Find the absolute extrema of $f(x) = x^2(x - 2)^{2/3}$ in $-2 \leq x \leq \frac{5}{2}$.

20. The value of a certain fruit crop (in dollars) is given by

$$V = A(1 - e^{-KI})$$

where A and K are constants and I is the number of pounds per acre of insecticide with which the crop is sprayed. If the cost of spraying is given by $C = BI$, where B is a constant, find the value of I that makes $V - C$ a maximum. What is the interpretation of your result when $AK < B$?

21. A company has examined its cost structure and its revenue structure and has determined that the total cost C, the total revenue R, and the number of units produced x are related by

$$C = 100 + 0.015x^2 \quad \text{and} \quad R = 3x.$$

Find the production rate x that will maximize the profits of the firm. Find that profit and also the profit when $x = 120$.

22. A company notices that higher sales of a particular item that it produces are achieved only by lowering the price charged. As a result, the total revenue from the sales at first rises as the number of units sold increases, reaches the highest point, and then falls off. This pattern of total revenue is described by the relation

$$R = 4,000,000 - (x - 2000)^2$$

where R is the total revenue and x the number of units sold.

a. Find the number of units sold that maximizes total revenue.

b. What is the amount of this maximum total revenue?

c. What would be the total revenue if 2500 units were sold?

23. The total cost C of producing x units of a commodity is given by $C = 50 + 2x + 0.5x^2$ and the total revenue R received from the sales is $R = 20x - x^2$. Find the production rate x that will maximize the profits.

24. Solve Exercise 23 when

$$C = 300 + 0.075x^2 \quad \text{and} \quad R = 3x.$$

25. A radio manufacturer finds that x instruments per week can be sold at p dollars each, where $5x = 375 - 3p$. The cost of production is $(500 + 13x + \frac{1}{5}x^2)$ dollars. Show that the maximum profit is obtained when the production is 30 instruments per week.

26. A manufacturer has to produce 144,000 units of an item per year. The cost of material is $5 per unit and it costs $160 to make the factory ready for the production run of the item, regardless of the number of units x produced in a run. The cost of storing the material is 50¢ per item per year on the inventory ($x/2$) in hand. Show that the total cost C is given by

$$C = 720,000 + \frac{23,040,000}{x} + \frac{x}{4}.$$

Find also the economic lot size, that is, the value of x for which C is minimum.

27. By an *economic order quantity*, we mean a quantity Q, which (when purchased in each order) minimizes the total cost T incurred in obtaining and storing material for a certain time period to fulfill a given rate of demand for the material during the time period. The material demanded is 10,000 units per year; the cost price of material is $1 per unit; the cost of replenishing the stock of the material per order, regardless of the size Q of the order, is $25; and the cost of storing the material is $12\frac{1}{2}\%$ per year on the dollar value of the average inventory ($Q/2$) on hand.

a. Show that $T = 10,000 + \dfrac{250,000}{Q} + \dfrac{Q}{16}$.

b. Find the economic order quantity and the total cost T corresponding to that value of Q.

c. Find the total cost when each order is placed for 2500 units.

28. The yield of fruit from each tree of an apple orchard decreases as the density of the trees planted increases. When there are n trees per acre, the average number of apples per tree is known to be equal to $900 - 10n$ for a particular variety of apple (when n lies between 30 and 60). What value of n gives the maximum total yield of apples per acre?

29. A shoe manufacturer can use her plant to make either men's or women's shoes. If she makes x and y thousands pairs of each, respectively, per week, then x and

y are related by the product transformation equation

$$2x^2 + y^2 = 25.$$

The manufacturer's profit is \$10 on each pair of men's shoes and \$8 on each pair of women's shoes. Determine how many pairs of each she should make in order to maximize her weekly profit.

(30–31) Sketch the graphs of the following functions.

30. $y = x - \ln x$ **31.** $y = xe^{-2x}$

(32–33) Find the horizontal and vertical asymptotes of the following functions and sketch their graphs.

32. $y = \dfrac{3x + 1}{x - 2}$ **33.** $y = \ln |x|$

MORE ON DERIVATIVES

15-1 DIFFERENTIALS

Let $y = f(x)$ be a differentiable function of the independent variable x. Up to now, we have used dy/dx to denote the derivative of y with respect to x and treated dy/dx as a single symbol, not as a ratio of dy and dx. Now we shall define the new concept of a *differential* so that dx and dy will have separate meanings; this will permit us to think of dy/dx either as the symbol for the derivative of y with respect to x or as the ratio of dy and dx.

DEFINITION   Let $y = f(x)$ be a differentiable function of x. Then

(a) dx, called the **differential of the independent variable x** is simply an arbitrary increment of x; that is

$$dx = \Delta x;$$

(b) dy, the **differential of the dependent variable y** is a function of x and dx given by

$$dy = f'(x)\, dx.$$

The differential dy is also denoted by df.

The following are obvious from the above definition of differentials dx and dy.

1. If $dx = 0$ then $dy = 0$.
2. If $dx \neq 0$, then the ratio of dy divided by dx is given by

$$\frac{dy}{dx} = \frac{f'(x)\, dx}{dx} = f'(x)$$

and so is equal to the derivative of y with respect to x.

There is nothing strange about the last result, because we deliberately defined dy as the product of $f'(x)$ and dx in order that the result in statement (2) would be true.

EXAMPLE 1   If $y = x^3 + 5x + 7$, find dy.

Solution   Let $y = f(x)$ so that $f(x) = x^3 + 5x + 7$. Then $f'(x) = 3x^2 + 5$ and, by definition,

$$dy = f'(x)\, dx = (3x^2 + 5)\, dx.$$

It should be noted that dx (or Δx) is another independent variable and the value of dy depends on the *two* independent variables x and dx.

Geometrically, we know that $f'(x)$ represents the slope of the tangent to the curve $y = f(x)$ at the point x. Thus if P is the point on the curve whose abscissa is x and PT is the tangent at P, then $f'(x)$ is the slope of the tangent line PT. (See Figure 1.)

The slope is the ratio of rise and run. Let us consider a run of PR from the value x of the abscissa to $x + \Delta x$. Then $PR = \Delta x = dx$. In this case, the tangent PT has the rise TR, so that

$$\frac{\text{rise}}{\text{run}} = \frac{TR}{PR} = \text{slope of tangent line } PT = f'(x).$$

In other words, $TR = f'(x) \cdot PR = f'(x)\,dx = dy$. Thus, dy is the length of the line segment TR.

We note also that Δy, the increment in y, is the length of the line segment QR. It is clear that in general, even though $dx = \Delta x$, the differential dy is not the same as the increment in y, that is, $dy \neq \Delta y$.

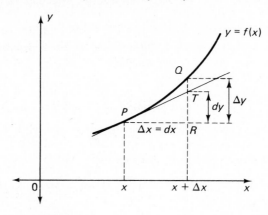

FIGURE 1

EXAMPLE 2   If $y = x^3 + 3x$, find dy and Δy when $x = 2$ and $\Delta x = 0.01$.

Solution   If $y = f(x) = x^3 + 3x$, then

$$f'(x) = 3x^2 + 3.$$

Therefore

$$dy = f'(x)\,dx = (3x^2 + 3)\,dx.$$

When $x = 2$, $\Delta x = 0.01$ then $dy = (12 + 3)(0.01) = 0.15$.

By definition,

$$\Delta y = f(x + \Delta x) - f(x)$$
$$= f(2.01) - f(2)$$
$$= [(2.01)^3 + 3(2.01)] - [2^3 + 3(2)]$$
$$= [8.120601 + 6.03] - 14 = 0.150601.$$

Thus $dy = 0.15$ and $\Delta y = 0.150601$, showing that the differential and increment of y are not quite equal to one another.

Referring back to Figure 1, the difference between Δy and dy is equal to the distance QT between the point Q on the graph of $f(x)$ and the point T on the tangent at P. It is clear that if we allow Δx to become smaller, so that Q moves around the curve towards P, then this distance QT rapidly shrinks to zero. Because of this, we can use dy as an approximation to Δy provided that Δx is sufficiently small:

$$\Delta y \approx dy = f'(x)\, dx.$$

Thus, since $f(x + \Delta x) = y + \Delta y$,

$$f(x + \Delta x) \approx f(x) + f'(x)\, \Delta x.$$

This approximation is useful because it is often easier to calculate the right side than to calculate $f(x + \Delta x)$. The reason for this is that the right side is a *linear* function of Δx, whereas the left side might in general be a complicated function of Δx. The following example illustrates the way in which this formula can be used to replace a complicated function of Δx by a linear function that is approximately equal to it.

EXAMPLE 3   Find an approximation to the value of $\sqrt{16 + h}$ when h is small.

Solution   Let $f(x) = \sqrt{x}$. Then when $x = 16$, $f(16) = \sqrt{16} = 4$. We are interested in the approximate value of $f(16 + h) = \sqrt{16 + h}$. So, taking $x = 16$ and $\Delta x = h$ in the above formula, we have

$$f(16 + h) \approx f(16) + f'(16)h. \tag{1}$$

But if $f(x) = \sqrt{x}$, then $f'(x) = 1/(2\sqrt{x})$. In particular,

$$f'(16) = \frac{1}{2\sqrt{16}} = \frac{1}{8}.$$

Substituting $f(16) = 4$ and $f'(16) = \frac{1}{8}$ into Equation (1), we get

$$f(16 + h) \approx 4 + \tfrac{1}{8}h$$

that is, $\sqrt{16 + h} \approx 4 + \tfrac{1}{8}h$. (For example, taking $h = 0.1$, we find that $\sqrt{16.1} \approx 4 + \tfrac{1}{8}(0.1) = 4.0125$. This compares with the exact value, which is 4.01248 to 5 decimal places.)

The usefulness of this kind of approximation is apparent from this example: It is much easier to calculate with the approximate expression $(4 + \tfrac{1}{8}h)$ then with the expression $\sqrt{16 + h}$, because *the approximation is a linear function* of h.

EXAMPLE 4   A section of land consists of a square with sides of one mile (5280 feet) in length. If a strip of 20 feet is removed along each side for a roadway, how much area is lost from the section?

Solution   If x denotes the length of a side, then the area is

$$A = f(x) = x^2.$$

If the side is changed to $x + \Delta x$, then the change in area ΔA is given approximately by the differential

$$\Delta A \approx f'(x) \, \Delta x = 2x \, \Delta x.$$

In this example, $x = 5280$ feet and $\Delta x = -40$ feet (a strip of 20 feet removed from each side). Therefore

$$\Delta A \approx 2(5280)(-40) = -422{,}400.$$

Thus the loss of area is approximately 422,400 square feet.

In the approximate formula $f(x + \Delta x) \approx f(x) + f'(x)\Delta x$, let us change the notation a bit and write $x = a$:

$$f(a + \Delta x) \approx f(a) + f'(a) \, \Delta x.$$

Now let us replace $a + \Delta x$ by x. Then $\Delta x = x - a$, and we end up with the following formula

$$f(x) \approx f(a) + (x - a)f'(a).$$

But the right side here is a linear function of x. If we define $m = f'(a)$ and $b = f(a) - af'(a)$, then the approximation becomes simply $f(x) \approx mx + b$.

Thus we have established the very important result that, over a short interval of x, any differentiable function $f(x)$ can be approximated by a linear function.

Use is often made of this result in devising mathematical models of complex phenomena. Suppose that x and y are two economic variables that are related in some complex and not very well-understood way. Then, regardless of the degree of complexity of the relationship (as long as it is smooth), we may approximate it by a linear model $y = mx + b$ for certain constants m and b provided that the range of variation of x is sufficiently restricted. Linear models of this kind are frequently used in economics and elsewhere as a starting point in the analysis of complex phenomena.

Differentials are useful in assessing the effects of errors in the measured or estimated values of quantities. Let x be a variable whose value is measured or estimated with a certain possible error and let $y = f(x)$ be some other variable that is calculated from the measured value of x. If the value of x that is used in calculating y is in error, then of course the calculated value of y will also be incorrect.

Let x be the true value of the measured variable and $x + dx$ be the measured value. Then dx is now the **error** in this variable. The true value of the calculated variable is $y = f(x)$, but the actual calculated value is $f(x + dx)$. Thus the error in y is equal to $f(x + dx) - f(x)$. If dx is small, which can usually be presumed to be the case, we can approximate this error in y by the differential dy. Thus we arrive at the result that the error in y is given approximately by $dy = f'(x) \, dx$.

The ratio dx/x is called the **relative error** in x. Correspondingly, the relative error in y is dy/y. If the relative error is multiplied by 100, we obtain what is called the **percentage error** in the variable in question. Often the sign is ignored in stating the percentage error, so we might speak of a percentage error of 2% and mean that the error is either $\pm 2\%$.

EXAMPLE 5   A sales manager estimates that his staff will sell 10,000 units during the next month. He believes his estimate is accurate to within a maximum percentage error of 3%. If the profit function is

$$P(x) = x - (4 \times 10^{-5})x^2 \quad \text{(dollars per month)}$$

(where x = number of units sold per month), find the maximum percentage error in the estimated profit.

Solution   If $x = 10,000$, the profit will be

$$P = 10,000 - (4 \times 10^{-5})(10,000)^2 = 6000.$$

The maximum percentage error in the estimated value of x is 3%, so the maximum error dx is given by

$$100 \frac{dx}{x} = 3$$

and so

$$dx = \frac{3x}{100} = \frac{3(10,000)}{100} = 300.$$

The corresponding error in profit is given approximately by

$$\begin{aligned} dP &= P'(x)\,dx \\ &= (1 - 8 \times 10^{-5}x)\,dx \\ &= [1 - 8 \times 10^{-5}(10,000)](300) \\ &= (0.2)(300) = 60. \end{aligned}$$

So the maximum error in the estimated profit is $60. The percentage error is therefore given by

$$100 \frac{dP}{P} = 100 \frac{60}{6000} = 1.$$

The maximum percentage error in profit is 1%.

We close this section by summarizing a number of formulas for differentials. These are easily obtained from corresponding formulas for the derivatives.

DERIVATIVES	DIFFERENTIALS
1. $\dfrac{d}{dx}(c) = 0$	$d(c) = 0$
2. $\dfrac{d}{dx}(cu) = c\dfrac{du}{dx}$	$d(cu) = c\,du$
3. $\dfrac{d}{dx}(u+v) = \dfrac{du}{dx} + \dfrac{dv}{dx}$	$d(u+v) = du + dv$
4. $\dfrac{d}{dx}(u \cdot v) = u\dfrac{dv}{dx} + v\dfrac{du}{dx}$	$d(u \cdot v) = u\,dv + v\,du$

5. $\dfrac{d}{dx}\left(\dfrac{u}{v}\right) = \dfrac{v(du/dx) - u(dv/dx)}{v^2}$ $\qquad d\left(\dfrac{u}{v}\right) = \dfrac{v\,du - u\,dv}{v^2}$

6. $\dfrac{d}{dx}(u^n) = nu^{n-1}\dfrac{du}{dx}$ $\qquad d(u^n) = nu^{n-1}\,du$

7. $\dfrac{d}{dx}(x^n) = nx^{n-1}$ $\qquad d(x^n) = nx^{n-1}\,dx$

8. $\dfrac{d}{dx}(e^x) = e^x$ $\qquad d(e^x) = e^x\,dx$

9. $\dfrac{d}{dx}(\ln x) = \dfrac{1}{x}$ $\qquad d(\ln x) = \dfrac{1}{x}\,dx$

EXERCISES 1

(1–10) Find dy for the following functions.

1. $y = x^2 + 7x + 1$ $\qquad$ 2. $y = (t^2 + 1)^4$ $\qquad$ 3. $y = t \ln t$

4. $y = ue^{-u}$ $\qquad$ 5. $y = \ln(z^2 + 1)$ $\qquad$ 6. $y = \dfrac{x+1}{x^2+1}$

7. $y = \dfrac{e^u}{u+1}$ $\qquad$ 8. $y = \dfrac{e^u+1}{e^u-1}$ $\qquad$ 9. $y = \sqrt{x^2 - 3x}$

10. $y = \sqrt{\ln x}$

11. Find dy for $y = x^2 - 1$ when $x = 1$.

12. Find dx for $x = \sqrt{t+1}$ when $t = 3$.

13. Find dt for $t = \ln(1 + y^2)$ when $y = 0$.

14. Find du for $u = e^{0.5\ln(1-t^2)}$ when $t = \frac{1}{2}$.

15. Find dy for $y = x^3$ when $x = 2$ and $dx = 0.01$.

16. Find du for $u = t^2 + 3t + 1$ when $t = -1$ and $dt = 0.02$.

17. Find dx for $x = y \ln y$ when $y = 1$ and $dy = 0.003$.

18. Find df for $f(x) = xe^x$ when $x = 0$ and $dx = -0.01$.

(19–22) Find dy and Δy for the following functions.

19. $y = 3x^2 + 5$ when $x = 2$ and $dx = 0.01$.

20. $y = \sqrt{t}$ when $t = 4$ and $dt = 0.41$.

21. $y = \ln u$ when $u = 3$ and $du = 0.06$.

22. $y = \sqrt{x+2}$ when $x = 2$ and $dx = 0.84$.

23. Use differentials to approximate the cube root of 9.

24. Use differentials to approximate the 4th root of 17.

25. Use differentials to approximate the 5th root of 31.

26. Use differentials to approximate the value of $(4.01)^3 + \sqrt{4.01}$.

27. The radius of a sphere is equal to 8 centimeters, with a possible error of ± 0.002 centimeters. The volume is calculated assuming that the radius is exactly 8 centimeters. Use differentials to estimate the maximum error in the calculated volume.

28. If the volume of a sphere is to be determined to within a percentage error that does not exceed 2%, what is the maximum percentage error allowable in the measured value of the radius?

29. A manufacturer estimates that sales will be 400 units per week with a possible percentage error of 5%. If the revenue function is $R(x) = 10x - 0.01x^2$, find the maximum percentage error in the estimated revenue.

30. The cost function for the manufacturer in Exercise 29 is $C(x) = 1000 + x$.

    a. Find the maximum percentage error in the estimated costs.

    b. Find the maximum percentage error in the estimated profit.

31. The demand equation for a certain product is $p = 100/\sqrt{x + 100}$. Use differentials to find the approximate price at which 2500 units are demanded.

32. The cost function for a certain manufacturer is $C(x) = 400 + 2x + 0.1x^{3/2}$. Use differentials to estimate the change in cost if the production level is increased from 100 to 110.

33. For the inventory-cost model (see Section 4 of Chapter 14), let D be the total annual demand, s the storage cost per unit per year, a the setup cost for each production run, and b the production cost per item. Then the optimum batch size per production run is given by $x = \sqrt{2aD/s}$. The minimum cost per year of producing the items is $C = bD + \sqrt{2aDs}$. If $D = 10,000$, $s = 0.2$, $a = 10$, and $b = 0.1$, evaluate x and C. Use differentials to estimate the errors in x and C if the true value of s is 0.22.

15-2 IMPLICIT DIFFERENTIATION

As we discussed in Section 5 of Chapter 5, a relationship between two variables is sometimes expressed through an implicit relation rather than by means of an explicit function. Thus instead of having y given as a function $f(x)$ of the independent variable x, it is possible to have x and y related through an equation of the form $F(x, y) = 0$, in which both variables occur as arguments of some function F. For example, the equation

$$F(x, y) = x^3 + 2x^2y + 3xy^2 + y^3 - 1 = 0$$

expresses a certain relationship between x and y, but y is not given explicitly in terms of x.

The question we wish to consider in this section is how to calculate the derivative dy/dx when x and y are related by an implicit equation. In certain cases, it is possible to solve the implicit equation $F(x, y) = 0$ and to obtain y explicitly in terms of x. In such cases, the standard techniques of differentiation enable the derivative to be calculated in the usual way. However, in many cases it is not possible to solve for the explicit function, and to cope with such situations it is necessary to use a new technique which is called **implicit differentiation**.

When using this technique, we differentiate each term in the given implicit relation with respect to the independent variable. This involves differentiating expressions involving y w.r.t. x, and to do this, we make use of the chain rule. For example, suppose we wish to differentiate y^3 or ln y w.r.t. x. We write the following.

$$\frac{d}{dx}(y^3) = \frac{d}{dy}(y^3) \cdot \frac{dy}{dx} = 3y^2 \frac{dy}{dx}$$

$$\frac{d}{dx}(\ln y) = \frac{d}{dy}(\ln y) \frac{dy}{dx} = \frac{1}{y} \frac{dy}{dx}$$

In general,

$$\frac{d}{dx}(f(y)) = f'(y) \frac{dy}{dx}.$$

EXAMPLE 1   Find dy/dx if $x^2 + y^2 = 4$.

Solution   Differentiate each term w.r.t. x.

$$\frac{d}{dx}(x^2) = 2x, \qquad \frac{d}{dx}(y^2) = \frac{d}{dy}(y^2) \frac{dy}{dx} = 2y \frac{dy}{dx}, \qquad \frac{d}{dx}(4) = 0$$

We differentiate the given relation and solve for dy/dx.

$$2x + 2y \frac{dy}{dx} = 0$$

$$2y \frac{dy}{dx} = -2x$$

$$\frac{dy}{dx} = -\frac{2x}{2y} = -\frac{x}{y}$$

Check   Let us check this result using one of the explicit functions associated with the implicit relation $x^2 + y^2 = 4$, namely

$$y = \sqrt{4 - x^2} = (4 - x^2)^{1/2}.$$

Using the chain rule,

$$\frac{dy}{dx} = \frac{1}{2}(4 - x^2)^{1/2 - 1} \cdot (-2x)$$

$$= -\frac{x}{\sqrt{4 - x^2}} = -\frac{x}{y}$$

which is the same result as in Example 1.

Note: Had we taken the other explicit function, associated with $x^2 + y^2 = 4$, namely $y = -\sqrt{4 - x^2}$, we still would have found that $dy/dx = -x/y$.

EXAMPLE 2   Find dy/dx if $xy + \ln (xy^2) = 7$.

Solution   We first simplify the logarithm: $\ln (xy^2) = \ln x + 2 \ln y$. Then the relation takes the form

$$xy + \ln x + 2 \ln y = 7.$$

Differentiating w.r.t. x, we obtain

$$\frac{d}{dx}(xy) + \frac{d}{dx}(\ln x) + 2 \frac{d}{dx}(\ln y) = \frac{d}{dx}(7) = 0.$$

From the product rule,

$$\frac{d}{dx}(xy) = \frac{d}{dx}(x) \cdot y + x \frac{d}{dx}(y)$$

$$= 1 \cdot y + x \frac{dy}{dx} = y + x \frac{dy}{dx}.$$

Also,

$$\frac{d}{dx}(\ln x) = \frac{1}{x}$$

and

$$\frac{d}{dx}(\ln y) = \frac{d}{dy}(\ln y) \cdot \frac{dy}{dx} = \frac{1}{y} \frac{dy}{dx}.$$

Therefore

$$\left(y + x \frac{dy}{dx} \right) + \frac{1}{x} + \frac{2}{y} \frac{dy}{dx} = 0.$$

We group all the derivative terms on the left and move the other terms to the right and solve for dy/dx.

$$\left(x + \frac{2}{y} \right) \frac{dy}{dx} = -\left(y + \frac{1}{x} \right)$$

$$\frac{dy}{dx} = -\frac{y + 1/x}{x + 2/y} = -\frac{y(xy + 1)}{x(xy + 2)}$$

EXAMPLE 3   Find the equation of the tangent line at the point $(2, -\frac{1}{2})$ on the graph of the implicit relation

$$xy^2 - x^2 y + y - x = 0.$$

Solution   The slope of the tangent line is equal to the derivative dy/dx evaluated at $x = 2$ and $y = -\frac{1}{2}$. Differentiating through the implicit relation w.r.t. x, we obtain

$$\frac{d}{dx}(xy^2) - \frac{d}{dx}(x^2 y) + \frac{dy}{dx} - 1 = 0.$$

The first two terms must be evaluated using the product rule. We obtain

$$\left(y^2 \cdot 1 + x \cdot 2y \frac{dy}{dx} \right) - \left(x^2 \cdot \frac{dy}{dx} + y \cdot 2x \right) + \frac{dy}{dx} - 1 = 0$$

and so $(2xy - x^2 + 1)(dy/dx) = 2xy - y^2 + 1$. Therefore

$$\frac{dy}{dx} = \frac{2xy - y^2 + 1}{2xy - x^2 + 1}.$$

Setting $x = 2$ and $y = -\frac{1}{2}$, we obtain the slope of the tangent line at the required point to be

$$\frac{dy}{dx} = \frac{2(2)(-\frac{1}{2}) - (-\frac{1}{2})^2 + 1}{2(2)(-\frac{1}{2}) -- (2)^2 + 1} = \frac{1}{4}.$$

The equation of the tangent line is obtained from the point-slope formula:

$$y - y_1 = m(x - x_1)$$
$$y - (-\tfrac{1}{2}) = \tfrac{1}{4}(x - 2)$$
$$y = \tfrac{1}{4}x - 1.$$

When we evaluate dy/dx from an implicit relation $F(x, y) = 0$, we are assuming that x is the independent variable and y the dependent variable. However, given the implicit relation $F(x, y) = 0$, we could instead regard y as the independent variable with x a function of y. In that case, we should evaluate the derivative dx/dy.

EXAMPLE 4   Given $x^2 + y^2 = 4xy$, find dx/dy.

Solution   Here x is an implicit function of y. We differentiate both sides w.r.t. y.

$$\frac{d}{dy}(x^2) + \frac{d}{dy}(y^2) = 4\frac{d}{dy}(xy)$$

$$2x\frac{dx}{dy} + 2y = 4\left(x \cdot 1 + y\frac{dx}{dy}\right)$$

$$2\frac{dx}{dy}(x - 2y) = 2(2x - y)$$

$$\frac{dx}{dy} = \frac{2x - y}{x - 2y}$$

An interesting result regarding the derivative of an inverse function can be obtained via implicit differentiation. Let $y = f(x)$ be a relation expressing y as an explicit function of x. When this equation is uniquely solvable for x in terms of y we obtain the inverse function $x = f^{-1}(y)$, and its derivative is the derivative of x w.r.t. y.

$$\frac{dx}{dy} = \frac{d}{dy}f^{-1}(y)$$

But let us differentiate the original equation $y = f(x)$ w.r.t. y. We have

$$\frac{d}{dy}(y) = \frac{d}{dy}f(x) = \frac{d}{dx}[f(x)] \cdot \frac{dx}{dy}$$

or

$$1 = f'(x)\frac{dx}{dy}.$$

Therefore

$$\frac{dx}{dy} = \frac{1}{f'(x)}.$$

Alternatively, we can write this in the form

$$\frac{dx}{dy} = \frac{1}{dy/dx}.$$

Therefore we see that *the derivative of the inverse function is the reciprocal of the derivative of the original function.*

Higher-order derivatives can also be calculated from an implicit relation. The method consists of first finding the first derivative in the manner outlined above and then differentiating the resulting expression with respect to the independent variable.

EXAMPLE 5 Find d^2y/dx^2 when $x^3 + y^3 = 3x + 3y$.

Solution Here x is the independent variable since we are required to find derivatives w.r.t. x. So, differentiating implicity w.r.t. x, we obtain

$$3x^2 + \frac{d}{dx}(y^3) = 3 + 3\frac{dy}{dx}$$

or

$$3x^2 + 3y^2\frac{dy}{dx} = 3 + 3\frac{dy}{dx}.$$

Therefore

$$(1 - y^2)\frac{dy}{dx} = x^2 - 1$$

and so

$$\frac{dy}{dx} = \frac{x^2 - 1}{1 - y^2}.$$

We differentiate again w.r.t. x and use the quotient rule.

$$\frac{d^2y}{dx^2} = \frac{d}{dx}\left(\frac{x^2 - 1}{1 - y^2}\right)$$

$$= \frac{(1 - y^2)(d/dx)(x^2 - 1) - (x^2 - 1)(d/dx)(1 - y^2)}{(1 - y^2)^2}$$

$$= \frac{2x(1 - y^2) + 2y(x^2 - 1)(dy/dx)}{(1 - y^2)^2}$$

At this stage, we observe that the expression for the second derivative still involves the first derivative. Hence, to complete the solution, we must substitute $dy/dx = (x^2 - 1)/(1 - y^2)$.

$$\frac{d^2y}{dx^2} = \frac{2x(1 - y^2) + 2y(x^2 - 1)[(x^2 - 1)/(1 - y^2)]}{(1 - y^2)^2}$$

$$= \frac{2x(1 - y^2)^2 + 2y(x^2 - 1)^2}{(1 - y^2)^3}$$

In the last step, we have multiplied numerator and denominator of the fraction by $1 - y^2$.

EXERCISES 2

(1–14) Find dy/dx in each case.

1. $x^2 + y^2 + 2y = 15$
2. $\sqrt{x} + \sqrt{y} = 1$
3. $x^3 + y^3 = a^3$ (*a* is constant)
4. $x^2 - xy + y^2 = 3$

5. $(y - x)(y + 2x) - 12 = 0$ 6. $x^4 + y^4 = 2x^2y^2 + 3$

7. $xy^2 + yx^2 = 6$ 8. $x^2y^2 + x^2 + y^2 = 3$

9. $x^5 + y^5 = 5xy$ 10. $\dfrac{x^2}{a^2} - \dfrac{y^2}{b^2} = 1$ (a, b are constants)

11. $xy + e^y = 1$ 12. $\dfrac{x}{y} + \ln\left(\dfrac{y}{x}\right) = 6$

13. $xy + \ln(xy) = -1$ 14. $x^2 + y^2 = 4e^{x+y}$

15. Find dx/dt if $3x^2 + 5t^2 = 15$.

16. Find du/dy if $u^2 + y^2 + u - y = 1$.

17. Find dx/dy if $x^3 + y^3 = xy$.

18. Find dt/dx if $x^3 + t^3 + x^3t^3 = 9$.

(19–20)   Find the equation of the tangent to the following curves at the given points.

19. $x^3 + y^3 - 3xy = 3$; $(1, 2)$

20. $x^2 + y^2 = 2x + y + 15$; $(-3, 1)$

21. Find d^2y/dx^2 if $x^2 + y^2 = 4xy$.

22. Find d^2u/dt^2 when $u = 1$ and $t = -1$ if $u^5 + t^5 = 5ut + 5$.

23. Find d^2x/dy^2 when $x = 2$ and $y = 1$ if $x^3 + y^3 - 3xy = 3$.

24. Find d^2y/dx^2 if $(x + 2)(y + 3) = 7$.

25. Find d^2x/dy^2 if $x + y + \ln(xy) = 2$.

26. Find d^2y/dx^2 if $x^2 + y^2 + e^{3y} = 4$.

(27–30)   Find dy for the following implicit relations.

27. $xy + y^2 = 3$ 28. $y^2 + z^2 - 4yz = 1$
29. $\ln(yz) = y + z$ 30. $xe^y + ye^x = 1$

*31. By writing $y = x^{p/q}$ in the form $y^q - x^p = 0$, use implicit differentiation to prove that $(d/dx)(x^n) = nx^{n-1}$ when n is a rational number p/q.

15-3 LOGARITHMIC DIFFERENTIATION AND ELASTICITY

With certain types of functions, a technique known as *logarithmic differentiation* can be used to ease the calculation of the derivative. One situation in which this technique can be used arises when the given function consists of the product or quotient of a number of factors, where each factor may be raised to some power. The method is perhaps best demonstrated through an example.

EXAMPLE 1   Calculate dy/dx if

$$y = \frac{(x + 1)\sqrt{x^2 - 2}}{(x^2 + 1)^{1/3}}.$$

Solution   We could differentiate this function by use of the product and quotient rules. However, let us instead take the natural logarithm of both sides. Then using the properties of logarithms, we proceed as follows.

$$\ln y = \ln\left[\frac{(x+1)\sqrt{x^2-2}}{(x^2+1)^{1/3}}\right]$$

$$= \ln(x+1) + \ln\sqrt{x^2-2} - \ln(x^2+1)^{1/3}$$

$$= \ln(x+1) + \tfrac{1}{2}\ln(x^2-2) - \tfrac{1}{3}\ln(x^2+1)$$

Now, let us differentiate both sides w.r.t. x. We use the chain rule as usual with implicit differentiation.

$$\frac{d}{dx}(\ln y) = \frac{d}{dy}(\ln y)\frac{dy}{dx} = \frac{1}{y}\frac{dy}{dx}$$

After differentiating the terms on the right, we find that

$$\frac{1}{y}\frac{dy}{dx} = \frac{1}{x+1} + \frac{1}{2}\cdot\frac{1}{(x^2-2)}\cdot 2x - \frac{1}{3}\cdot\frac{1}{x^2+1}\cdot 2x.$$

We next simplify and multiply by y.

$$\frac{dy}{dx} = y\left[\frac{1}{x+1} + \frac{x}{x^2-2} - \frac{2x}{3(x^2+1)}\right]$$

We can, if we wish, substitute $y = (x+1)\sqrt{x^2-2}/(x^2+1)^{1/3}$ in this expression in order to obtain dy/dx entirely in terms of x.

Another situation in which logarithmic differentiation is useful arises when we must differentiate one function raised to the power of another function. We shall give two examples, the first an elementary one and the second more complicated.

EXAMPLE 2   Find dy/dx if $y = x^x$ $(x > 0)$.

Solution   First of all, let us observe that this derivative can be found using the ordinary techniques of differentiation if we first write y in the form

$$y = x^x = e^{x\ln x}.$$

The chain rule combined with the product rule then allows us to determine dy/dx. However, the method of logarithmic differentiation can be used as an alternative. Taking logarithms of both sides, we get

$$\ln y = \ln(x^x) = x\ln x.$$

We then differentiate w.r.t. x and use the product rule on the right.

$$\frac{d}{dx}(\ln y) = (1)\ln x + x\left(\frac{1}{x}\right)$$

$$\frac{1}{y}\frac{dy}{dx} = \ln x + 1$$

Therefore

$$\frac{dy}{dx} = y(\ln x + 1) = x^x(\ln x + 1).$$

EXAMPLE 3   Find dy/dx if

$$y = (x^2+1)^{\sqrt{x^3-1}}.$$

Solution   Again the calculation is considerably simplified if we take logarithms before differentiating.

$$\ln y = \ln [(x^2 + 1)^{\sqrt{x^3-1}}] = \sqrt{x^3 - 1} \ln (x^2 + 1)$$

We can now differentiate w.r.t. x (using the product rule on the right).

$$\frac{d}{dx}(\ln y) = \frac{d}{dx}\sqrt{x^3 - 1} \cdot \ln (x^2 + 1) + \sqrt{x^3 - 1}\frac{d}{dx} \ln (x^2 + 1)$$

$$\frac{1}{y}\frac{dy}{dx} = \frac{1}{2}(x^3 - 1)^{-1/2}(3x^2)\cdot\ln (x^2 + 1) + \sqrt{x^3 - 1}\left(\frac{1}{x^2 + 1}\right)2x$$

Simplifying and multiplying by y, we obtain finally

$$\frac{dy}{dx} = y\left[\frac{3x^2}{2\sqrt{x^3 - 1}} \ln (x^2 + 1) + \frac{2x\sqrt{x^3 - 1}}{x^2 + 1}\right].$$

It can be seen from these examples that the essence of this method consists of taking the natural logarithm of y before differentiation. The expression

$$\frac{d}{dx} \ln y = \frac{1}{y}\frac{dy}{dx}$$

that arises with this method is called the **logarithmic derivative** of y w.r.t. x.

EXAMPLE 4   Calculate the logarithmic derivatives of the following functions.
(a) ax^n (b) $[f(x)]^n$ (c) $u(x)v(x)$

Solution   (a) If $y = ax^n$, then $y' = anx^{n-1}$. The logarithmic derivative is therefore

$$\frac{y'}{y} = \frac{anx^{n-1}}{ax^n} = \frac{n}{x}.$$

In the special case when $n = 1$, $y = ax$ and the logarithmic derivative is $1/x$.

(b) If $y = [f(x)]^n$, then $y' = n[f(x)]^{n-1}f'(x)$ by the chain rule. Therefore the logarithmic derivative is

$$\frac{y'}{y} = \frac{n[f(x)]^{n-1}f'(x)}{[f(x)]^n} = \frac{nf'(x)}{f(x)}.$$

(c) If $y = u(x)v(x)$, then from the product rule it follows that
$$y' = u'v + uv'.$$

Therefore the logarithmic derivative is

$$\frac{y'}{y} = \frac{u'v + uv'}{uv} = \frac{u'v}{uv} + \frac{uv'}{uv}$$

$$= \frac{u'}{u} + \frac{v'}{v}.$$

This result can be summarized as follows: the logarithmic derivative of the product uv is the sum of the logarithmic derivatives of u and v.

EXAMPLE 5   Find dy/dx if $y = x^x + (1 + x)^{1+x}$.

Solution   Examples of this type are traps for the unwary student. It is a great temptation to take logarithms immediately and write

$$\ln y = x \ln x + (1 + x) \ln (1 + x).$$

Of course, a moment's thought will reveal the error in doing this. What we must do is to write $y = u + v$ where $u = x^x$ and $v = (1 + x)^{1+x}$. Then

$$\frac{dy}{dx} = \frac{du}{dx} + \frac{dv}{dx}$$

and the two derivatives du/dx and dv/dx can be found by logarithmic differentiation. The first of these can be obtained from Example 2.

$$\frac{du}{dx} = x^x(\ln x + 1)$$

For dv/dx, we have:

$$\ln v = (1 + x) \ln (1 + x)$$

and therefore, after differentiation w.r.t. x,

$$\frac{1}{v} \frac{dv}{dx} = \ln (x + 1) + 1$$

Consequently, $dv/dx = (1 + x)^{1+x}[\ln (1 + x) + 1]$. Adding the values for du/dx and dv/dx, we obtain dy/dx as required.

Note: When logarithmic differentiation is used to differentiate a function of the type $y = [f(x)]^{g(x)}$, it is assumed that $f(x) > 0$.

Elasticity

A concept widely used in economics and closely related to logarithmic differentiation is that of elasticity. We shall introduce this idea via the so-called **elasticity of demand**.

For a given item, let p be the price per unit and x the number of units that will be purchased during a specified time interval at the price p, and let $x = f(p)$. The elasticity of demand is usually represented by the Greek letter η (eta) and is defined as follows.

$$\eta = \frac{p}{x} \frac{dx}{dp} = \frac{pf'(p)}{f(p)}$$

Before doing any examples, let us discuss the significance of η. Suppose that the price is increased from p to $p + \Delta p$. Then, of course, the quantity demanded will change, say to $x + \Delta x$, where $x + \Delta x = f(p + \Delta p)$. Thus $\Delta x = f(p + \Delta p) - f(p)$.

The increment in price is Δp; this increase is a fraction $\Delta p/p$ of the original price. We can also say that the percentage increase in price is $100(\Delta p/p)$. For example, let the original price per unit be $p = \$2$ and let the new price be $\$2.10$. Then $\Delta p = \$0.10$. This increase is a fraction $\Delta p/p = 0.10/2 = 0.05$ of the original price. Multiplying by 100, we see that the percentage increase in price is $100(\Delta p/p) = 100(0.05) = 5\%$.

Similarly, the change Δx in demand is a fraction $(\Delta x/x)$ of the original demand. The percentage change in demand is $100(\Delta x/x)$. (Note that with an increase in price, the demand will actually decrease, so this percentage change in demand will be negative.)

Consider the ratio of these two percentage increases:

$$\frac{\text{Percentage Change in Demand}}{\text{Percentage Change in Price}} = \frac{100(\Delta x/x)}{100(\Delta p/p)}$$

$$= \frac{p}{x}\frac{\Delta x}{\Delta p}.$$

Comparing this with the definition of η, we see that

$$\eta = \frac{p}{x}\frac{dx}{dp} = \lim_{\Delta p \to 0}\frac{p}{x}\frac{\Delta x}{\Delta p}.$$

Thus the elasticity of demand is equal to the limiting value of the ratio of percentage change in demand to percentage change in price in the limit as the change in price approaches zero.

When the change in price is small, the ratio $\Delta x/\Delta p$ of the two increments is approximately equal to the derivative dx/dp. Thus for Δp small,

$$\frac{p}{x}\frac{\Delta x}{\Delta p} \approx \frac{p}{x}\frac{dx}{dp}$$

and so the ratio of percentage change in demand to percentage change in price is approximately equal to η. Alternatively, we can say that, when the price change is small,

> Percentage Change in Demand $\approx \eta$(Percentage Change in Price).

For example, if a 2% increase in price causes the demand to decrease by 3%, then the elasticity of demand is approximately equal to $(-3)/(2) = -1.5$. Or, if the elasticity of demand is -0.5, then a 4% increase in price would lead to a change in demand of approximately $(-0.5)(4\%) = -2\%$.

(Note that η is defined with an extra minus sign in some books.)

EXAMPLE 6   Calculate the elasticity of demand if the demand equation is $x = k/p$, where k is some positive constant.

Solution   Since $x = k/p$, $dx/dp = -k/p^2$. Therefore

$$\eta = \frac{p}{x}\frac{dx}{dp} = \frac{p}{(k/p)}\left(-\frac{k}{p^2}\right) = -1.$$

The elasticity of demand is therefore constant in this case and is equal to -1.

This means that a small percentage increase in price will always lead to an equal percentage decrease in demand.

EXAMPLE 7   Calculate the elasticity of demand if $x = 500(10 - p)$ for each value of p.
    (a) $p = 2$ (b) $p = 5$ (c) $p = 6$

Solution   In this case, $dx/dp = -500$. Therefore

$$\eta = \frac{p}{x}\frac{dx}{dp} = \frac{p}{500(10 - p)}(-500)$$

$$= -\frac{p}{10 - p}.$$

We see that the elasticity of demand varies, depending on the price p.

(a) $p = 2$: $\eta = -2/(10 - 2) = -0.25$

Thus when $p = 2$, the percentage decrease in demand is one-fourth of the percentage increase in price.

(b) $p = 5$: $\eta = -5/(10 - 5) = -1$

When $p = 5$, a small percentage increase in price gives an equal percentage decrease in demand.

(c) $p = 6$: $\eta = -6/(10 - 6) = -1.5$

The percentage decrease in demand is one and one-half times the percentage increase in price when $p = 6$.

DEFINITION   We say that demand is **elastic** if $\eta < -1$ and is **inelastic** if $-1 < \eta < 0$. If $\eta = -1$, we have **unit elasticity**. (In the case of unit elasticity, a small percentage change in price gives an equal percentage change in demand.)

The idea of elasticity can be used for any pair of variables that are functionally related. If $y = f(x)$, then the *elasticity of y w.r.t. x is defined as*

$$\eta = \frac{x}{y}\frac{dy}{dx}$$

(again denoted by η). It is approximately equal to the ratio of the percentage change in y to the percentage change in x, provided that these changes are small. For example, we can talk about the elasticity of supply with respect to price, which is the percentage change in the supply of an item divided by the percentage change in its price (strictly, in the limit as the price change approaches zero).

Elasticity is closely related to logarithmic derivatives. The logarithmic derivative of y w.r.t. x is

$$\frac{d}{dx}(\ln y) = \frac{1}{y}\frac{dy}{dx}.$$

The logarithmic derivative of x itself is similarly given by

$$\frac{d}{dx}(\ln x) = \frac{1}{x}\frac{dx}{dx} = \frac{1}{x}.$$

It follows therefore that *the elasticity of y w.r.t. x is equal to the logarithmic derivative of y divided by the logarithmic derivative of x:*

$$\eta = \frac{(d/dx)(\ln y)}{(d/dx)(\ln x)}.$$

Returning to the case of elasticity of demand, we can establish a close connection between this quantity and marginal revenue. The revenue function is given by

$$R(x) = (\text{quantity sold}) \times (\text{price}) = xp$$

and so the marginal revenue is

$$R'(x) = \frac{d}{dx}(xp) = p + x\frac{dp}{dx}$$

where the product rule has been used. But we saw in Section 2 that the two derivatives dx/dy and dy/dx obtained from the same relation between two variables x and y are reciprocals of one another. In particular, therefore,

$$\frac{dp}{dx} = \left(\frac{dx}{dp}\right)^{-1} = \left(\frac{x\eta}{p}\right)^{-1} = \frac{p}{x\eta}.$$

It follows that

$$R'(x) = p + x\frac{p}{x\eta} = p\left(1 + \frac{1}{\eta}\right).$$

It can be seen from this relation that *marginal revenue is positive when demand is elastic and is negative when demand is inelastic* (that is, $R' > 0$ when $\eta < -1$ and $R' < 0$ when $-1 < \eta < 0$).

EXERCISES 3

(1–16)   Use logarithmic differentiation to evaluate dy/dx for the following functions.

1. $y = (x^2 + 1)(x - 1)^{1/2}$ 　　　　**2.** $y = (3x - 2)(3x^2 + 1)^{1/2}$

3. $y = (x^2 - 2)(2x^2 + 1)(x - 3)^2$ 　**4.** $y = (x^3 - 1)(x + 1)^3(x + 2)^2$

5. $y = \dfrac{(x^2 + 1)^{1/3}}{x^2 + 2}$ 　　　　**6.** $y = \dfrac{(2x^2 - 3)^{1/4}}{x(x + 1)}$

7. $y = \left(\dfrac{2x^2 + 5}{2x + 5}\right)^{1/3}$ 　　　　**8.** $y = \sqrt{\dfrac{(x + 1)(x + 2)}{x^3 - 3}}$

9. $y = x^{x^2}$ 　　　**10.** $y = x^{\sqrt{x}}$ 　　　**11.** $y = e^{e^x}$

12. $y = x^{e^x}$ 　　　**13.** $y = x^{\ln x}$ 　　　**14.** $y = (\ln x)^x$

15. $y = x^x + x^{1/x}$ 　　　　　**16.** $y = (x^2 + 1)^x - x^{x^2+1}$

(17–20)   Find the elasticity of demand for the following demand relations.

17. $x = k/p^n$ 　　$(k, n \text{ constants})$ 　　**18.** $x = 100(5 - p)$

19. $x = 50(4 - \sqrt{p})$ 　　　　　　　　**20.** $x = 200\sqrt{9 - p}$

21. If the demand relation is $x = 400 - 100p$, find the elasticity of demand when:
(a) $p = 1$; (b) $p = 2$; (c) $p = 3$.

22. For the demand relation $x/1000 + p/8 = 1$, find the elasticity of demand when:
(a) $p = 2$; (b) $p = 4$; (c) $p = 6$.

(23–26)   For the following demand relations, determine the values of p for which the demand is: (a) elastic; (b) inelastic.

23. $x = 100(6 - p)$ 　　　　　　　　　**24.** $x = 800 - 100p$

25. $x = 100(2 - \sqrt{p})$

26. $x = k(a - p)$ 　　$(k, a \text{ positive constants})$

1. State whether each of following is true or false. Replace each false statement by a corresponding true statement.

   a. The differential of x^2 is $2x$.

   b. For a linear function f, $df = \Delta f$.

   c. The derivative dy/dx is equal to the ratio of differentials $(dy) \div (dx)$.

   d. In an implicit relation $f(x, y) = 0$, x and y are both independent variables.

   e. $\left(\dfrac{dy}{dx}\right)\left(\dfrac{dx}{dy}\right) = -1$

   f. If y is an increasing function of x, then x is a decreasing function of y.

   g. The logarithmic derivative of y w.r.t. x is the derivative of $\ln y$ w.r.t. x.

   h. The logarithmic derivative of x w.r.t. y is the reciprocal of the logarithmic derivative of y w.r.t. x.

   i. The logarithmic derivative of x^n is nx^{n-1}.

   j. The logarithmic derivative of x^x is $\ln(ex)$.

   k. When the elasticity of demand is -1, the marginal revenue is zero.

   l. When the revenue is maximum, the elasticity of demand is -1.

   m. For the demand relation $x = kp^{-\alpha}$ (k, α constants), the elasticity of demand is constant.

2. Find dy if $y = \sqrt{x^2 - 2}$.

3. Evaluate dy when $x = 1$ and $dx = \frac{1}{4}$ for the function $y = \ln(3 - x^2)$.

4. Find dy and Δy when $t = 7$ and $dt = 1.03$ for the function $y = (t + 1)^{1/3}$.

5. Use differentials to find the approximate value of $(4 \cdot 1)^2 \sqrt{4.1}$.

6. Find dy/dx if $e^{xy} + x + y = 1$.

7. Find dx/dt if $x^2 t + xt^2 + \ln(x + t) = 0$.

8. Find the equation of the tangent to the graph of the relation $x^3 y^2 + xy^3 - x^3 - xy - x^2 - y = 0$ at the point $(\frac{1}{3}, 2)$.

9. Find dy if $x = -1$, $y = 0$, and $dx = \frac{1}{3}$, where x and y satisfy the relation in Exercise 8.

10. Find d^2y/dx^2 at $x = -1$, $y = 1$ if $x^3 + y^3 + xy = -1$.

11. Find d^2x/dy^2 at $x = 1$, $y = 0$ if $e^{xy} + e^x + e^y = 2 + e$.

(12–15) Use logarithmic differentiation to find dy/dx for the following functions.

12. $y = (x + 1)(x^3 - 3)^{1/2}(2 - x^2)^{-1/4}$

13. $y = \left[\dfrac{x^4 - 4}{x(x + 1)^2}\right]^{1/3}$ 14. $y = x^{x^{-2}}$ 15. $y = x^{1/(\ln x)}$

16. If the demand relation is $x = 1000 - 50p$, find the elasticity of demand when: (a) $p = 5$; (b) $p = 10$; (c) $p = 15$.

17. For the demand relation $x/600 + p/12 = 1$, find the values of p for which: (a) $\eta = -1$; (b) $\eta = -2$; (c) $\eta = -\frac{1}{3}$.

18. For the demand relation $x = k(1 - p - p^2)$, find the value of p for which $\eta = -1$. Find the values of p for which demand is: (a) elastic; (b) inelastic.

19. If the demand relation is $x^2 + p^2 = 25$, find the elasticity of demand when (a) $p = 3$; (b) $p = 4$.

20. For the demand relation $x^2 + px + p^2 = 7$, find the elasticity of demand when $p = 2$.

21. Find dy when $x^y = e^x$.

22. Find du if $u^x = x^u$.

INTEGRATION

CHAPTER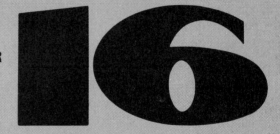

16-1 ANTIDERIVATIVES

So far in our study of calculus, we have been concerned with the process of differentiation—that is, the calculation and use of the derivatives of functions. This part of the subject is called **differential calculus**. We shall now turn to the second area of study within the general area of calculus, called **integral calculus**, in which we are concerned with the process opposite to differentiation.

We have seen before that, if $s(t)$ is the distance traveled in time t by a moving object, then the instantaneous velocity is $v(t) = s'(t)$, the derivative of $s(t)$. In order to calculate v, we simply differentiate $s(t)$. However, it may happen that we already know the velocity function $v(t)$ and wish to calculate the distance s traveled. In such a situation, we know the derivative $s'(t)$ and require the function $s(t)$, a step opposite to that of differentiation. As another example, we may be concerned with a cost model in which the marginal cost is a known function of production level, and we may wish to calculate the total cost of producing x items. Or, we might know the rate of production of an oil well as a function of time and wish to calculate the total production over a certain period of time.

The process of finding the function when its derivative is given is called **integration**, and the function to be found is called the **antiderivative** or the **integral** of the given function.

To evaluate the antiderivative of some given function $f(x)$, we must find a function $F(x)$ whose derivative is equal to $f(x)$. For example, suppose $f(x) = 1/x$. Since we know that $d/dx (\ln x) = 1/x$, we conclude that we can take $F(x) = \ln x$. An antiderivative of $1/x$ is therefore $\ln x$.

However, it should be observed that this answer is not unique, because the functions $(\ln x) + 1$, $(\ln x) - 3$, and $(\ln x) + \frac{1}{2}$ all have derivative $1/x$. In fact, for any constant C, $(\ln x) + C$ has derivative $1/x$, and therefore $(\ln x) + C$ is an antiderivative of $1/x$ for any C. The constant C, which can have any arbitrary value, is called the **constant of integration**.

This aspect, that they are not unique, is common to all antiderivatives. Any constant can be added to them without destroying their property of being the antiderivative of a given function. However, this is the only ambiguity that there is: if $F(x)$ is any antiderivative of $f(x)$, then any other antiderivative of $f(x)$ differs from $F(x)$ only by a constant. Therefore we can say that if $F'(x) = f(x)$, then the general antiderivative of $f(x)$ is given by $F(x) + C$, where C is an arbitrary constant.

Since the constant of integration is arbitrary—that is, it can be any real number—the integral so obtained is given the more complete name **indefinite integral**. Sometimes different methods of evaluating an integral can give different forms for the answer, but it will always be the case that the two answers differ only by a constant.

Let $F(x)$ be an antiderivative of $f(x)$. We write this statement in the form

$$\int f(x)\, dx = F(x) + C$$

which is read as *the integral of* $f(x)$, *dx, is equal to* $F(x) + C$. The function $f(x)$ to be integrated is called the **integrand** and the symbol $\int$ is the **integral sign**. The symbol

$$\int \ldots dx$$

stands for *integral, with respect to x, of* . . . . It is the inverse of the symbol

$$\frac{d}{dx} \cdots$$

which means *derivative, with respect to x, of* . . . . The integral sign and dx go together; the integral sign means the operation of integration and the dx specifies that the *variable of integration* is x. The integrand is always put between the integral sign and the differential of the variable of integration.

For example, we can write

$$\int \frac{1}{x}\, dx = \ln x + C.$$

From the definition of the integral, it is clear that

$$\frac{d}{dx}\left[\int f(x)\, dx\right] = f(x).$$

That is, the process of differentiation neutralizes the result of the process of integration.

We shall establish a number of simple and standard formulas for integration. The first of these is known as the **power formula**; it gives us the rule to integrate any power of x except the inverse of x.

$$\int x^n\, dx = \frac{x^{n+1}}{n+1} + C \qquad (n \neq -1) \qquad \text{(Power Formula)}$$

Thus *to integrate any power of x except the inverse first power, we must increase the power by 1, then divide by the new exponent* and, finally, add the arbitrary constant of integration.

This formula is obtained by reversing the corresponding formula for differentiation. We observe that

$$\frac{d}{dx}\left(\frac{x^{n+1}}{n+1}\right) = \frac{1}{n+1}\frac{d}{dx}(x^{n+1})$$

$$= \frac{1}{n+1}(n+1)x^n = x^n.$$

Therefore, since the derivative of $x^{n+1}/(n+1)$ is x^n, an antiderivative of x^n must be $x^{n+1}/(n+1)$. The general antiderivative is then obtained by adding the constant of integration.

EXAMPLE 1   (a) $\displaystyle\int x^3\,dx = \frac{x^{3+1}}{3+1} + C = \frac{x^4}{4} + C \qquad (n = 3)$

(b) $\displaystyle\int \frac{1}{x^2}\,dx = \int x^{-2}\,dx = \frac{x^{-2+1}}{-2+1} + C = \frac{x^{-1}}{-1} + C$

$\displaystyle\qquad = -\frac{1}{x} + C \qquad (n = -2)$

(c) $\displaystyle\int \frac{1}{\sqrt{t}}\,dt = \int t^{-1/2}\,dt = \frac{t^{-1/2+1}}{(-\frac{1}{2}+1)} + C$

$\displaystyle\qquad = 2\sqrt{t} + C \qquad (n = -\tfrac{1}{2})$

(d) $\displaystyle\int dx = \int 1\,dx = \int x^0\,dx = \frac{x^{0+1}}{0+1} + C = x + C \qquad (n = 0)$

A number of formulas giving antiderivatives of simple functions are given in Table 1. Each formula is stated a second time with the variable changed from x to u.

TABLE 1   Table of Standard Elementary Integrals

1. $\displaystyle\int x^n\,dx = \frac{x^{n+1}}{n+1} + C \quad (n \neq -1)$ or	$\displaystyle\int u^n\,du = \frac{u^{n+1}}{n+1} + C$
2. $\displaystyle\int \frac{1}{x}\,dx = \ln|x| + C$ or	$\displaystyle\int \frac{1}{u}\,du = \ln|u| + C$
3. $\displaystyle\int e^x\,dx = e^x + C$ or	$\displaystyle\int e^u\,du = e^u + C$

All these results are obtained by simply reversing corresponding results for derivatives. Formula 2 requires some comment. For $x > 0$, this formula is straightforward, since then $|x| = x$, and we know that

$$\frac{d}{dx}\ln x = \frac{1}{x}.$$

Since $1/x$ is the derivative of $\ln x$, it follows that the antiderivative of $1/x$ must be $\ln x$, plus the constant of integration.

When $x < 0$, we have $|x| = -x$. Therefore

$$\frac{d}{dx}\ln|x| = \frac{d}{dx}\ln(-x) = \frac{1}{(-x)}(-1) = \frac{1}{x},$$

where the chain rule has been used in carrying out the differentiation. Thus $1/x$ is the derivative of $\ln|x|$ for $x < 0$, as well as for $x > 0$. Therefore the antiderivative of $1/x$ must be $\ln|x| + C$, as given in the table.

Now we shall prove two theorems that will simplify the algebra of integration.

THEOREM 1   The integral of the product of a constant and a function of x is equal to the constant times the integral of the function. That is, if c is a constant,

$$\int c\,f(x)\,dx = c \int f(x)\,dx.$$

EXAMPLE 2   (a) $\displaystyle\int 3\,x^2\,dx = 3 \int x^2\,dx = 3 \cdot \frac{x^3}{3} + C = x^3 + C$

(b) $\displaystyle\int 2\,e^x\,dx = 2 \int e^x\,dx = 2e^x + C$

(c) $\displaystyle\int 5\,dx = 5 \int 1\,dx = 5x + C$

PROOF OF THEOREM 1   We have

$$\frac{d}{dx}\left[c \int f(x)\,dx\right] = c\,\frac{d}{dx}\left[\int f(x)\,dx\right] = c\,f(x).$$

Therefore $c\,f(x)$ is the derivative of $c \int f(x)\,dx$, and so from the definition of the antiderivative, it follows that $c \int f(x)\,dx$ must be the antiderivative of $c\,f(x)$. In other words,

$$\int c\,f(x)\,dx = c \int f(x)\,dx$$

which proves the result.

From this theorem, it follows that we can move any multiplicative constant across the integral sign.

Caution   Variables must not be moved across the integral sign. For example,

$$\int xe^{-x}\,dx \neq x \int e^{-x}\,dx.$$

THEOREM 2   The integral of the sum of two functions is equal to the sum of their integrals.

$$\int [f(x) + g(x)]\,dx = \int f(x)\,dx + \int g(x)\,dx$$

Note   This result may be extended to the difference of two functions or an algebraic sum of any finite number of functions.

EXAMPLE 3   Find the integral of $(x - 3/x)^2$.

Solution   We expand $(x - 3/x)^2$ to express the integrand as a sum of power functions.

$$\int \left(x - \frac{3}{x}\right)^2 dx = \int \left(x^2 - 6 + \frac{9}{x^2}\right) dx$$

$$= \int x^2 \, dx - \int 6 \, dx + \int 9x^{-2} \, dx$$

$$= \int x^2 \, dx - 6 \int 1 \, dx + 9 \int x^{-2} \, dx$$

$$= \frac{x^{2+1}}{2+1} - 6x + 9 \frac{x^{-2+1}}{-2+1} + C$$

$$= \frac{x^3}{3} - 6x - \frac{9}{x} + C$$

EXAMPLE 4 Find the antiderivative of

$$\frac{3 - 5t + 7t^2 + t^3}{t^2}.$$

Solution

$$\int \frac{3 - 5t + 7t^2 + t^3}{t^2} \, dt = \int \left(\frac{3}{t^2} - \frac{5}{t} + 7 + t\right) dt$$

$$= 3 \int t^{-2} \, dt - 5 \int \frac{1}{t} \, dt + 7 \int 1 \, dt + \int t \, dt$$

$$= 3 \frac{t^{-2+1}}{-1} - 5 \ln |t| + 7t + \frac{t^{1+1}}{2} + C$$

$$= -\frac{3}{t} - 5 \ln |t| + 7t + \frac{t^2}{2} + C$$

PROOF OF THEOREM 2

$$\frac{d}{dx}\left[\int f(x) \, dx + \int g(x) \, dx\right] = \frac{d}{dx}\left[\int f(x) \, dx\right] + \frac{d}{dx}\left[\int g(x) \, dx\right]$$

$$= f(x) + g(x)$$

Therefore $f(x) + g(x)$ is the derivative of $\int f(x) \, dx + \int g(x) \, dx$, and so by the definition of the antiderivative,

$$\int [f(x) + g(x)] \, dx = \int f(x) \, dx + \int g(x) \, dx.$$

EXAMPLE 5 A company is at present producing 150 units per week of its product. From its past experience, it is known that the cost of producing the xth unit per week (that is, the marginal cost) is given by

$$C'(x) = 25 - 0.02x.$$

Assuming that this marginal cost continues to apply, find the extra cost per week that would be involved in raising the output from 150 to 200 units per week.

Solution The marginal cost is the derivative of the cost function. Therefore the cost function is obtained by integrating the marginal cost function.

$$C(x) = \int C'(x)\, dx$$

$$= \int (25 - 0.02x)\, dx$$

$$= 25x - (0.02)\frac{x^2}{2} + K = 25x - 0.01x^2 + K$$

where K is the constant of integration. We do not have enough information to determine the value of K. However, we want to calculate the increase in cost resulting from increasing x from 150 to 200—that is, $C(200) - C(150)$.

$$C(200) = 25(200) - 0.01(200)^2 + K = 4600 + K$$
$$C(150) = 25(150) - 0.01(150)^2 + K = 3525 + K$$

and therefore

$$C(200) - C(150) = (4600 + K) - (3525 + K) = 1075.$$

The increase in weekly cost would therefore be $1075. Notice that the unknown constant K is not in the final answer.

EXAMPLE 6 The marginal revenue of a firm is given by

$$R'(x) = 15 - 0.01x.$$

(a) Find the revenue function.
(b) Find the demand relation for the firm's product.

Solution (a) The revenue function $R(x)$ is the integral of the marginal revenue function. Thus

$$R(x) = \int R'(x)\, dx = \int (15 - 0.01x)\, dx$$

$$= 15x - 0.01\frac{x^2}{2} + K = 15x - 0.005x^2 + K$$

where K is the constant of integration. To determine K, we use the fact that the revenue must be zero when no units are sold. That is, when $x = 0$, $R = 0$. Putting $x = 0$ and $R = 0$ into our expression for $R(x)$, we get

$$0 = 15(0) - 0.005(0^2) + K$$

which gives $K = 0$. Therefore the revenue function is

$$R(x) = 15x - 0.005x^2.$$

(b) If each item the firm produces sells at a price p, then the revenue obtained by selling x items is given by $R = px$. Thus

$$px = 15x - 0.005x^2$$

or

$$p = 15 - 0.005x$$

which is the required demand relation.

EXERCISES 1

(1–6) Write the integrals of the following.

1. **a.** x^7 **b.** $\sqrt{x}$ **c.** $\dfrac{1}{\sqrt{x}}$ **d.** 7

2. $7x^2 - 3x + 8 - \dfrac{1}{\sqrt{x}} + \dfrac{1}{x} + \dfrac{1}{x^2}$

3. $x^7 + 7x + \dfrac{x}{7} + \dfrac{7}{x}$ **4.** $e^x + x^e + e + x$

5. $x^2\left(x + \dfrac{2}{\sqrt{x}}\right)$ **6.** $\left(\sqrt{x} + \dfrac{1}{\sqrt{x}}\right)\left(x - \dfrac{2}{x}\right)$

(7–12) Find the antiderivatives of the following functions with respect to the independent variable involved.

7. $4x^3 + 3x^2 + 2x + 1 + \dfrac{1}{x} + \dfrac{1}{x^3}$ **8.** $3e^t - 5t^3 + 7 + \dfrac{3}{t}$

9. $\sqrt{u}\,(u^2 + 3u + 7)$ **10.** $\dfrac{2y^3 + 7y^2 - 6y + 9}{3y}$

11. $\sqrt{x}\,(x + 1)(2x - 1)$ **12.** $\dfrac{(t - t^2)^2}{t\sqrt{t}}$

(13–16) Evaluate the following integrals.

13. $\displaystyle\int \dfrac{1 + 3x + 7x^2 - 2x^3}{x^2}\,dx$ **14.** $\displaystyle\int \dfrac{(2t + 1)^2}{3t}\,dt$

15. $\displaystyle\int \left(30^2 - 60 + \dfrac{9}{\theta} + 4e^\theta\right) d\theta$ **16.** $\displaystyle\int (\sqrt{2}\,y + 1)^2\,dy$

17. The velocity of motion at time t is $(t + \sqrt{t})^2$. Find the distance traveled in time t.

18. The acceleration of a moving object at time t is $3 + 0.5t$.

  a. Find the velocity at any time t if the initial velocity at $t = 0$ is given to be 60 units.

  b. Find the distance traveled by the object at time t if the distance is zero when $t = 0$.

19. The marginal cost function of a firm is $C'(x) = 30 - 0.05x$.

  a. Determine the cost function, $C(x)$, if the firm's fixed costs are $2000 per month.

  b. How much will it cost to produce 150 units in a month?

20. The marginal cost of a certain firm is given by $C'(x) = 24 - 0.03x + 0.006x^2$. If the cost of producing 200 units is $22,700, find:

  a. the cost function;   **b.** the fixed costs of the firm;

  c. the cost of producing 500 units.

21. The marginal cost of ABC Products Limited is $C'(x) = 3 - 0.001x$ and the cost of manufacturing 100 units is $995. What is the cost of producing 200 units?

22. The marginal cost of a certain firm is $C'(x) = 5 + 0.002x$. What are the total variable costs of manufacturing x units?

23. The marginal revenue function of a certain firm is $R'(x) = 4 - 0.01x$.

    a. Determine the revenue obtained by selling x units of its product.

    b. What is the demand function for the firm's product?

24. The marginal revenue function of a certain firm is
$$R'(x) = 20 - 0.02x - 0.003x^2.$$

    a. Find the revenue function.

    b. How much revenue will be obtained by selling 100 units of the firm's product?

    c. What is the demand function for the firm's product?

25. The marginal profit function of a firm is $P'(x) = 5 - 0.002x$ and the firm made a profit of $310 when 100 units were sold. What is the profit function of the firm?

16-2 METHOD OF SUBSTITUTION

Not all integrals can be evaluated directly by the use of the standard integrals discussed in the previous section. Many times, however, the given integral can be reduced to a standard integral already known by a change of the variable of integration. Such a method is called the **method of substitution** and corresponds to the chain rule in differentiation.

First, we shall discuss linear substitutions, in which we replace the original variable by a linear expression. This is explained in the following theorem.

THEOREM 1

> If $\int f(x)\, dx = F(x) + C$, then
>
> $$\int f(ax + b)\, dx = \frac{1}{a} F(ax + b) + C$$

where a and b are any two constants ($a \neq 0$). In other words, in order to integrate $f(ax + b)$, we treat $(ax + b)$ as if it were a single variable, then divide the resulting integral by a, the coefficient of x.

The proof of this theorem will follow as a special case of Theorem 2, to be proved later. Let us illustrate it with some examples. First of all, we saw in the last section that the rule for integrating a power of x is

$$\int x^n\, dx = \frac{x^{n+1}}{n + 1} + C \qquad (n \neq -1).$$

This corresponds to setting $f(x) = x^n$ and $F(x) = x^{n+1}/(n + 1)$ in the statement of the theorem. Then, according to the theorem, we can replace the argument x by $ax + b$:

$$f(ax + b) = (ax + b)^n \quad \text{and} \quad F(ax + b) = \frac{(ax + b)^{n+1}}{(n + 1)}.$$

The theorem then gives the following result:

$$\int (ax + b)^n \, dx = \frac{1}{a} \frac{(ax + b)^{n+1}}{n + 1} + C.$$

For example, when $a = 2$, $b = 3$, and $n = 4$, we obtain the formula

$$\int (2x + 3)^4 \, dx = \frac{1}{2} \frac{(2x + 3)^{4+1}}{4 + 1} + C$$

$$= \frac{(2x + 3)^5}{10} + C. \tag{1}$$

When $f(x) = 1/x$, $F(x) = \ln |x|$, since we have the standard formula

$$\int \frac{1}{x} \, dx = \ln |x| + C.$$

If x is replaced by $ax + b$, the two functions become

$$f(ax + b) = \frac{1}{ax + b} \quad \text{and} \quad F(ax + b) = \ln |ax + b|.$$

Then the theorem provides the following result.

$$\int f(ax + b) \, dx = \frac{1}{a} F(ax + b) + C$$

$$\int \frac{1}{ax + b} \, dx = \frac{1}{a} \ln |ax + b| + C \tag{2}$$

For example, when $a = 3$ and $b = -2$, this formula becomes

$$\int \frac{1}{3x - 2} \, dx = \frac{1}{3} \ln |3x - 2| + C.$$

It is easy enough to verify that the results contained in these examples are correct. For example, in order to prove that the result in Equation (1) is correct, we must show that the derivative of the function $[(2x + 3)^5/10 + C]$ that appears on the right side is the given integrand. But from the chain rule,

$$\frac{d}{dx}\left[\frac{1}{10}(2x + 3)^5 + C\right] = \frac{1}{10} \cdot 5(2x + 3)^4 \frac{d}{dx}(2x + 3) + \frac{d}{dx}(C)$$

$$= \frac{1}{2}(2x + 3)^4(2) + 0 = (2x + 3)^4.$$

So we see that the required integrand is obtained, and hence Equation (1) is correct.

In the same way, we can verify that the result in Equation (2) is correct by showing that the derivative of the right side is the integrand $1/(ax + b)$. Setting $u = ax + b$ and using the chain rule, we find that

$$\frac{d}{dx} \ln |ax + b| = \frac{d}{du} \ln |u| \cdot \frac{du}{dx} = \frac{1}{u}(a) = \frac{a}{ax + b}.$$

Therefore

$$\frac{d}{dx}\left[\frac{1}{a} \ln |ax + b| + C\right] = \frac{1}{ax + b}$$

from which it follows that

$$\int \frac{1}{ax+b} \, dx = \frac{1}{a} \ln|ax+b| + C.$$

Theorem 1 is a powerful tool and can be used to generalize each integral in Table 1 (see Section 1) by replacing x by $ax + b$ $(a \neq 0)$. This leads to the following list of types of integrals that can be evaluated by using this theorem.

TABLE 2

1. $\int x^n \, dx = \frac{x^{n+1}}{n+1} + C \quad (n \neq -1)$	1. $\int (ax+b)^n \, dx = \frac{1}{a} \cdot \frac{(ax+b)^{n+1}}{n+1} + C$ $(a \neq 0, \ n = 1)$
2. $\int \frac{1}{x} \, dx = \ln|x| + C$	2. $\int \frac{1}{ax+b} \, dx = \frac{1}{a} \cdot \ln|ax+b| + C \quad (a \neq 0)$
3. $\int e^x \, dx = e^x + C$	3. $\int e^{ax+b} \, dx = \frac{e^{ax+b}}{a} + C \quad (a \neq 0)$

It can be seen from this table that the integrals of $f(x)$ and $f(ax + b)$ are essentially similar in form.

EXAMPLE 1   Evaluate $\int (3x - 7)^5 \, dx$.

Solution   From the first general result in Table 2,

$$\int (ax+b)^n \, dx = \frac{(ax+b)^{n+1}}{a(n+1)} + C.$$

We must set $a = 3$, $b = -7$, and $n = 5$ in this general formula in order to evaluate the required integral.

$$\int (3x - 7)^5 \, dx = \frac{(3x-7)^{5+1}}{(3)(5+1)} + C = \frac{1}{18}(3x - 7)^6 + C.$$

EXAMPLE 2   Evaluate $\int e^{5-3x} \, dx$.

Solution   Setting $a = -3$ and $b = 5$ in Formula (3) of the table, we obtain

$$\int e^{5-3x} \, dx = \frac{e^{5-3x}}{(-3)} + C = -\frac{1}{3} e^{5-3x} + C.$$

The general substitution method is explained in the following theorem.

THEOREM 2   If $F'(x) = f(x)$, then

$$\int f[g(x)]g'(x) \, dx = F[g(x)] + C$$

for any differentiable function $g(x)$ that is not a constant function.

Let us illustrate this theorem with some examples before proving it. Again, let us start from the power formula,

$$\int x^n \, dx = \frac{x^{n+1}}{n+1} + C \qquad (n \neq -1)$$

which corresponds to setting $f(x) = x^n$ and $F(x) = x^{n+1}/(n+1)$. Then according to Theorem 2, we must replace the argument x in these two functions by the function $g(x)$:

$$f[g(x)] = [g(x)]^n \quad \text{and} \quad F[g(x)] = \frac{[g(x)]^{n+1}}{(n+1)}.$$

In this particular case, the theorem then states that

$$\int [g(x)]^n g'(x) \, dx = \frac{[g(x)]^{n+1}}{n+1} + C \quad (n \neq -1).$$

In this result, $g(x)$ can be any differentiable function that is not constant. For example, let us take $g(x) = x^2 + 1$ and $n = 4$. Then $g'(x) = 2x$ and we obtain

$$\int (x^2 + 1)^4 \cdot 2x \, dx = \frac{(x^2 + 1)^{4+1}}{4 + 1} + C.$$

After division by 2, this becomes

$$\int (x^2 + 1)^4 x \, dx = \frac{(x^2 + 1)^5}{10} + C_1$$

where $C_1 = C/2$. (Note that C_1 can still be any arbitrary constant, since dividing by 2 does not remove the arbitrariness.)

As a further example, let us take $g(x) = \ln x$ and $n = 2$. Since $g'(x)$ then is $1/x$, we get the result

$$\int \frac{(\ln x)^2}{x} \, dx = \frac{(\ln x)^3}{3} + C.$$

It is clear that by choosing different functions $f(x)$ and $g(x)$, a great variety of different integrals can be evaluated. When actually using this substitution method to evaluate a given integral, it is necessary to spot how to choose these functions in such a way that the given integrand is expressed in the form $f[g(x)]g'(x)$ with f a sufficiently simple function. We shall elaborate on this later, but first let us pause to prove the theorem.

PROOF OF THEOREM 2   Set $u = g(x)$. Then from the chain rule,

$$\frac{d}{dx} F[g(x)] = \frac{d}{dx} F(u) = \frac{d}{du} F(u) \cdot \frac{du}{dx}$$

$$= f(u)g'(x)$$

$$= f[g(x)]g'(x).$$

Therefore, from the definition of the antiderivative, it follows that

$$\int f[g(x)]g'(x) \, dx = F[g(x)] + C,$$

as required.

Observe that if we take $g(x) = ax + b \ (a \neq 0)$, the general result of Theorem 2 reduces to the special case of Theorem 1. Consequently, our proof of Theorem 2 provides a proof of Theorem 1 at the same time.

Important Note: When using this theorem, we would get the right answer if we simply substitute $u = g(x)$ into the given integral, pretending that dx can be treated as a differential. For $du = g'(x) \, dx$, and so

$$\int f[g(x)]g'(x) \, dx = \int f(u) \, du = F(u) + C$$
$$= F[g(x)] + C.$$

When using the substitution method in practice, this is usually the easiest way in which to look upon it. You may find it helpful to refer back to the second set of formulas in Table 1 (in Section 1) when using this technique.

EXAMPLE 3   Evaluate $\int (x^2 + 3x - 7)^5(2x + 3) \, dx.$

Solution   We observe that the differential of $x^2 + 3x - 7$ is equal to $(2x + 3) \, dx$, which appears in the integral. Therefore we set $x^2 + 3x - 7 = u$. Then $(2x + 3) \, dx = du$. Using this substitution, the given integral reduces to

$$\int (x^2 + 3x - 7)^5(2x + 3) \, dx = \int u^5 \, du = \frac{u^6}{6} + C$$
$$= \frac{1}{6}(x^2 + 3x - 7)^6 + C$$

where we have substituted the value of u again.

EXAMPLE 4   Evaluate $\int \frac{1}{x \ln x} \, dx.$

Solution   The given integral is

$$\int \frac{1}{x \ln x} \, dx = \int \frac{1}{\ln x} \cdot \frac{1}{x} \, dx.$$

Note that we have separated the integrand in such a way that the combination $(1/x) \, dx$ occurs as a distinct factor. This combination is the differential of $\ln x$, and moreover the rest of the integrand is also a simple function of $\ln x$. So we let $\ln x = u$. Then $(1/x) \, dx = du$. The given integral now reduces to

$$\int \frac{1}{x \ln x} \, dx = \int \frac{1}{\ln x} \cdot \frac{1}{x} \, dx = \int \frac{1}{u} \cdot du$$
$$= \ln |u| + C = \ln |\ln x| + C$$

after substituting $u = \ln x$.

We observe from these examples that the appropriate technique in using the substitution method is to *look for a function $u = g(x)$ with a differential $g'(x) \, dx$ that occurs in the original integral*. The choice of substitution is by nature ambiguous, but you will soon learn from experience to spot the right one to make.

EXAMPLE 5   Evaluate $\int e^{x^2-5x}(2x - 5)\, dx$.

Solution   We observe that $(2x - 5)\, dx$ occurs in the integral, and this quantity is the differential of $x^2 - 5x$. Therefore we set $u = x^2 - 5x$. Then $du = (2x - 5)\, dx$ and the integral becomes

$$\int e^{x^2-5x}(2x - 5)\, dx = \int e^u\, du = e^u + C$$

$$= e^{x^2-5x} + C.$$

Sometimes the appropriate exact differential may not appear in the integral itself, but the function that does appear must be multiplied or divided by a certain constant. This is illustrated by the following examples.

EXAMPLE 6   Evaluate $\int x^2 e^{x^3+1}\, dx$.

Solution   The derivative of $x^3 + 1$ is $3x^2$. Since the combination $x^2\, dx$ occurs in the integrand, this suggests setting $u = x^3 + 1$. Then $du = 3x^2\, dx$, and so $x^2\, dx = \frac{1}{3} du$. Thus

$$\int x^2 e^{x^3+1}\, dx = \int e^u (\tfrac{1}{3} du) = \tfrac{1}{3} \int e^u\, du$$

$$= \tfrac{1}{3} e^u + C = \tfrac{1}{3} e^{x^3+1} + C.$$

We remarked earlier that linear substitutions can be regarded as a special case of general substitutions.

EXAMPLE 7   Evaluate $\int \sqrt{2x + 3}\, dx$.

Solution   Writing $u = 2x + 3$, we find that $du = 2dx$, that is, $dx = \frac{1}{2} du$. Then

$$\int \sqrt{2x + 3}\, dx = \int \sqrt{u} \cdot \tfrac{1}{2}\, du = \tfrac{1}{2} \int u^{1/2}\, du$$

$$= \tfrac{1}{2} \cdot \tfrac{2}{3} u^{3/2} + C = \tfrac{1}{3}(2x + 3)^{3/2} + C.$$

The result could also have been obtained by a direct use of Theorem 1.

EXERCISES 2

(1–14)   Make use of a linear substitution or use of Theorem 1 to evaluate the following integrals.

1. $\int (2x + 1)^7\, dx$ 2. $\int \sqrt{3x - 5}\, dx$ 3. $\int \frac{1}{(2 - 5t)^2}\, dt$

4. $\int \frac{1}{\sqrt{5 - 2x}}\, dx$ 5. $\int \frac{1}{2y - 1}\, dy$ 6. $\int \frac{1}{1 - 3t}\, dt$

7. $\int \frac{2u - 1}{4u^2 - 1}\, du$ 8. $\int \frac{2x + 3}{9 - 4x^2}\, dx$ 9. $\int e^{3x+2}\, dx$

10. $\int e^{5-2x}\, dx$ 11. $\int \frac{e^5}{e^x}\, dx$ 12. $\int \frac{e^{2x}}{e^{5-x}}\, dx$

13. $\int \dfrac{e^{2x+3}}{e^{1-x}} dx$ **14.** $\int \left(\dfrac{e^3}{e^{x-1}}\right)^2 dx$

(15–34) Use an appropriate substitution to evaluate the following antiderivatives.

15. $\int (x^2 + 7x + 3)^4 (2x + 7) \, dx$ **16.** $\int (x + 2)(x^2 + 4x + 2)^{10} \, dx$

17. $\int \dfrac{2x + 3}{(x^2 + 3x + 1)^3} dx$ **18.** $\int \dfrac{4x - 1}{(2x^2 - x + 1)} dx$

19. $\int \dfrac{2x + 3}{x^2 + 3x + 1} dx$ **20.** $\int \dfrac{x + 1}{x^2 + 2x - 1} dx$

21. $\int t e^{t^2} \, dt$ **22.** $\int x^3 e^{x^4} \, dx$

23. $\int \dfrac{e^{x^n}}{x^{1-n}} dx$ **24.** $\int \dfrac{e^{\sqrt{x}}}{\sqrt{x}} dx$

25. $\int \dfrac{e^x}{(e^x + 1)^2} dx$ **26.** $\int \dfrac{e^{x/2}}{1 - e^{x/2}} dx$

27. $\int \dfrac{1}{x} (\ln x)^3 \, dx$ **28.** $\int \dfrac{\ln (x + 1)}{x + 1} dx$

29. $\int \dfrac{1}{x(1 + \ln x)} dx$ **30.** $\int \dfrac{1}{(x + 2) \ln (x + 2)} dx$

31. $\int \dfrac{3t^2 + 1}{t(t^2 + 1)} dt$ **32.** $\int \dfrac{y}{\sqrt{1 + y^2}} dy$

33. $\int (x + 2)\sqrt{x^2 + 4x + 1} \, dx$ **34.** $\int \dfrac{x + 1}{\sqrt{x^2 + 2x + 7}} dx$

35. The marginal cost (in dollars) of a company manufacturing shoes is given by

$$C'(x) = \frac{x}{1000}\sqrt{x^2 + 2500}$$

where x is the number of pairs of shoes produced. If the fixed costs are $100, find the cost function.

36. A fabric manufacturer has a marginal cost (in dollars) per roll of a particular cloth given by $C'(x) = 20xe^{0.01x^2}$, where x is the number of rolls of the cloth produced. If the fixed costs are $1500, find the cost function.

16-3 TABLES OF INTEGRALS

In the previous section, we introduced the method of substitution, by means of which certain complex integrals can be reduced to one of the three standard integrals listed in Section 1. Apart from the substitution method, there are other techniques that are useful when it comes to evaluating integrals, and one of these will be discussed in Section 4.

In general, the evaluation of integrals is a matter that requires considerable skill and often ingenuity. The variety of methods that are available for the purpose is an indication of this fact. Moreover, it is not possible to give hard and fast rules about which method or which substitution will work in a given situation, but it is necessary to develop through experience an intuition for which method is likely to work best.

In face of these difficulties, by far the most convenient way to evaluate integrals is by use of a table of integrals. A table of integrals consists simply of a list of a large number of integrals, together with their values. In order to evaluate a certain integral, it is necessary only to extract the answer from the table, substituting the values of any constants as necessary. A number of such tables exist, some more complete than others; there is a fairly short table of integrals in the Appendix of this book; it will, however, be sufficiently complete to allow the evaluation of all integrals appearing in our examples and exercises. The integrals in this table are classified under certain headings to facilitate the use of the table. For example, all integrands involving a factor of the type $\sqrt{ax + b}$ are listed together and integrands involving $\sqrt{x^2 + a^2}$ are listed together, as are those involving exponential functions, and so on.

EXAMPLE 1   Evaluate $\int \dfrac{1}{(4 - x^2)^{3/2}}\, dx$.

Solution   We must look through the table of integrals until we find an integral of the same form as that given above. The section titled "Integrals Containing $\sqrt{a^2 - x^2}$" is the appropriate place to look, and in Formula 33, we find the result

$$\int \frac{1}{(a^2 - x^2)^{3/2}}\, dx = \frac{1}{a^2}\frac{x}{\sqrt{a^2 - x^2}}.$$

This holds for any nonzero value of the constant a, so if we set $a = 2$, we obtain the required integral.

$$\int \frac{1}{(4 - x^2)^{3/2}}\, dx = \frac{1}{4}\frac{x}{\sqrt{4 - x^2}} + C$$

Observe that we must add the constant of integration.

EXAMPLE 2   Evaluate $\int \dfrac{1}{2x^2 - 7x + 4}\, dx$.

Solution   If we compare this with the standard integral

$$\int \frac{1}{ax^2 + bx + c}\, dx$$

that appears in the table of integrals, we have $a = 2$, $b = -7$, and $c = 4$. Therefore

$$b^2 - 4ac = (-7)^2 - 4(2)(4) = 49 - 32 = 17 > 0.$$

When $b^2 - 4ac > 0$, we have (see Formula 66)

$$\int \frac{1}{ax^2 + bx + c}\, dx = \frac{1}{\sqrt{b^2 - 4ac}} \ln \left| \frac{2ax + b - \sqrt{b^2 - 4ac}}{2ax + b + \sqrt{b^2 - 4ac}} \right|$$

Substituting the values of a, b, and c, we have

$$\int \frac{1}{2x^2 - 7x + 4} dx = \frac{1}{\sqrt{17}} \ln \left| \frac{4x - 7 - \sqrt{17}}{4x - 7 + \sqrt{17}} \right| + C$$

where C is the constant of integration that should always be included.

_____

Sometimes the use of tables is not quite so straightforward, and it may be necessary to use the table two or more times in evaluating an integral. The following example illustrates this point.

EXAMPLE 3 Evaluate $\int \frac{1}{x^2\sqrt{2 - 3x}} dx$.

Solution If we look up the integrals involving $\sqrt{ax + b}$ in the table, then Formula 23 states that

$$\int \frac{1}{x^n\sqrt{ax + b}} dx = -\frac{\sqrt{ax + b}}{(n - 1)bx^{n-1}} - \frac{(2n - 3)a}{(2n - 2)b} \int \frac{1}{x^{n-1}\sqrt{ax + b}} dx; \quad (n \neq 1).$$

In our example, $n = 2$, $a = -3$, and $b = 2$. Therefore

$$\int \frac{1}{x^2\sqrt{2 - 3x}} dx = -\frac{\sqrt{2 - 3x}}{2x} + \frac{3}{4} \int \frac{1}{x\sqrt{2 - 3x}} dx. \tag{1}$$

To evaluate the integral on the right in Equation (1), we again look up the part of the table of integrals that involves $\sqrt{ax + b}$; Formula 22 gives

$$\int \frac{1}{x\sqrt{ax + b}} dx = \frac{1}{\sqrt{b}} \ln \left| \frac{\sqrt{ax + b} - \sqrt{b}}{\sqrt{ax + b} + \sqrt{b}} \right|, \quad \text{if } b > 0.$$

Putting $a = -3$ and $b = 2$ in this, we have

$$\int \frac{1}{x\sqrt{2 - 3x}} dx = \frac{1}{\sqrt{2}} \ln \left| \frac{\sqrt{2 - 3x} - \sqrt{2}}{\sqrt{2 - 3x} + \sqrt{2}} \right|.$$

Using this value on the right side in Equation (1),

$$\int \frac{1}{x^2\sqrt{2 - 3x}} dx = -\frac{\sqrt{2 - 3x}}{2x} + \frac{3}{4\sqrt{2}} \ln \left| \frac{\sqrt{2 - 3x} - \sqrt{2}}{\sqrt{2 - 3x} + \sqrt{2}} \right| + C$$

where we have again added the constant of integration C.

_____

Sometimes, before the table of integrals can be used, it is necessary to make a change of variable by means of substitution to reduce the given integral to one that appears in the table.

EXAMPLE 4 Evaluate $\int \frac{e^x}{(e^x + 2)(3 - e^x)} dx$.

Solution In this case, we do not find the integral in the tables. Let us change the variable of integration first. Clearly $e^x\, dx$, the differential of e^x, appears in the integral, so we let $e^x = y$. Then $e^x\, dx = dy$ and the given integral now becomes

$$\int \frac{e^x}{(e^x + 2)(3 - e^x)} dx = \int \frac{1}{(y + 2)(3 - y)} dy.$$

A general integral of this form is given in the tables (Formula 15):

$$\int \frac{1}{(ax+b)(cx+d)}\,dx = \frac{1}{bc-ad}\ln\left|\frac{cx+d}{ax+b}\right| \qquad (bc-ad \neq 0).$$

In our example, $a = 1$, $b = 2$, $c = -1$, and $d = 3$, and x is replaced by y. Thus

$$\int \frac{1}{(y+2)(3-y)}\,dy = \frac{1}{(2)(-1)-(1)(3)}\ln\left|\frac{-y+3}{y+2}\right| + C$$

$$= -\frac{1}{5}\ln\left|\frac{3-y}{y+2}\right| + C$$

where C is the constant of integration. Substituting the value $y = e^x$, we have

$$\int \frac{e^x}{(e^x+2)(3-e^x)}\,dx = -\frac{1}{5}\ln\left|\frac{3-e^x}{e^x+2}\right| + C.$$

Whenever an integral is evaluated using a table of integrals, we may readily verify that the answer obtained is correct by differentiating it: The result of the differentiation should be the original integrand. For instance, it is readily verified by standard methods of differentiation that

$$\frac{d}{dx}\left(-\frac{1}{5}\ln\left|\frac{3-e^x}{e^x+2}\right|\right) = \frac{e^x}{(e^x+2)(3-e^x)}.$$

This provides a check on the answer to Example 4.

You may wonder how tables of integrals are constructed in the first place. There are, in fact, a number of techniques (apart from the general substitution method) that are useful in evaluating integrals and that are used in constructing tables of the type given in the Appendix. In the following section, we shall provide an introduction to one of the most important of these techniques.

Provided that you have developed sufficient skill at using tables of integrals, the technique to be given in the following section will not be used that frequently. However, it will still be of some use, since sometimes an integral will be encountered that is not listed in your table. In such a case, this technique may be useful in transforming the given integral into one that is listed.

EXERCISES 3

(1–26) Make use of tables of integrals to evaluate the following integrals.

1. $\displaystyle\int \frac{1}{x^2 - 3x + 1}\,dx$

2. $\displaystyle\int \frac{1}{2x^2 + 5x - 3}\,dx$

3. $\displaystyle\int \frac{x}{(2x-3)^2}\,dx$

4. $\displaystyle\int \frac{y}{(3y+7)^5}\,dy$

5. $\displaystyle\int \frac{\sqrt{3x+1}}{x}\,dx$

6. $\displaystyle\int \frac{t}{(2t+3)^{5/2}}\,dt$

7. $\displaystyle\int \frac{1}{t\sqrt{16+t^2}}\,dt$

8. $\displaystyle\int \frac{u^2}{\sqrt{u^2+25}}\,du$

9. $\displaystyle\int \frac{y^2}{\sqrt{y^2-9}}\,dy$

10. $\displaystyle\int \frac{\sqrt{x^2+9}}{x}\,dx$

11. $\displaystyle\int \frac{1}{x\sqrt{3x+4}}\,dx$

12. $\displaystyle\int \frac{1}{x^2\sqrt{25-x^2}}\,dx$

13. $\displaystyle\int \frac{1}{x(2x+3)^2}\,dx$

14. $\displaystyle\int \frac{x^2}{\sqrt{x^2-9}}\,dx$

15. $\displaystyle\int x^2(x^2-1)^{3/2}\,dx$

16. $\displaystyle\int x^3(\ln x)^2\,dx$

17. $\displaystyle\int x^3 e^{2x}\,dx$

18. $\displaystyle\int y^2 e^{-3y}\,dy$

19. $\displaystyle\int \sqrt{\frac{2x+3}{4x-1}}\,dx$

20. $\displaystyle\int \frac{x^2}{3x-1}\,dx$

21. $\displaystyle\int \frac{e^x}{(1-e^x)(2-3e^x)}\,dx$

22. $\displaystyle\int \frac{1}{x\ln x(1+\ln x)}\,dx$

23. $\displaystyle\int \frac{x}{(x^2+1)(2x^2+3)}\,dx$

24. $\displaystyle\int \frac{y}{(2y^2+1)(3y^2+2)}\,dy$

25. $\displaystyle\int \frac{\ln x}{x(3+2\ln x)}\,dx$

26. $\displaystyle\int x^5 e^{-x^2}\,dx$

16-4 INTEGRATION BY PARTS

The method of integration by parts can often be used to evaluate an integral with an integrand that consists of a product of two functions. It is analogous to the product formula of differential calculus, and is in fact derived from it.

From differential calculus, we know that

$$\frac{d}{dx}[u(x)v(x)] = u'(x)v(x) + u(x)v'(x)$$

or

$$u(x)v'(x) = \frac{d}{dx}[u(x)v(x)] - u'(x)v(x).$$

Integrating both sides with respect to x, we get

$$\int u(x)v'(x)\,dx = u(x)v(x) - \int u'(x)v(x)\,dx. \tag{1}$$

This equation is commonly written in the form

$$\int u\,dv = uv - \int v\,du$$

after introducing the differentials $du = u'(x)\,dx$ and $dv = v'(x)\,dx$. An alternative way of writing it, however, is as follows.

Let $u(x) = f(x)$ and $v'(x) = g(x)$. Then we can write $v(x) = G(x)$, where $G(x)$ denotes the integral of $g(x)$, and then Equation (1) becomes

$$\int f(x)g(x)\,dx = f(x)G(x) - \int f'(x)G(x)\,dx.$$

This formula expresses the integral of the product $f(x)g(x)$ in terms of the integral of the product $f'(x)G(x)$. It is useful because in many cases the integral of $f'(x)G(x)$ is easier to evaluate than the integral of the original product $f(x)g(x)$. The following example illustrates this point.

EXAMPLE 1   Evaluate $\int xe^{2x} \, dx$.

Solution   Choose $f(x) = x$ and $g(x) = e^{2x}$, so that the given integral is equal to $\int f(x)g(x) \, dx$. Then $f'(x) = 1$ and $G(x)$, the integral of $g(x)$, is given by $G(x) = \frac{1}{2}e^{2x} + C_1$, where C_1 is a constant of integration. Substituting these values into the formula for integration by parts, we obtain

$$\int f(x)g(x) \, dx = f(x)G(x) - \int f'(x)G(x) \, dx.$$

$$\int xe^{2x} \, dx = x(\tfrac{1}{2}e^{2x} + C_1) - \int (1)(\tfrac{1}{2}e^{2x} + C_1) \, dx$$

$$= \tfrac{1}{2}xe^{2x} + C_1 x - \tfrac{1}{2} \int (e^{2x} + 2C_1) \, dx$$

$$= \tfrac{1}{2}xe^{2x} + C_1 x - \tfrac{1}{4}e^{2x} - C_1 x + C$$

$$= \tfrac{1}{4}(2x - 1)e^{2x} + C$$

where C again is a constant of integration.

The integral in this example could also be found using Formula 69 in Table A.2 (in the Appendix). You should verify that the answer obtained is the same as that in Example 1.

Note: It should be observed that the first constant of integration C_1 in the above example, which arises in integrating $g(x)$ to obtain $G(x)$, cancels from the final answer. This is always the case when integrating by parts. Therefore, in practice, we never bother to include a constant of integration in $G(x)$, but simply take $G(x)$ to be any particular antiderivative of $g(x)$.

When using this method, it is important to make the right selection of $f(x)$ and $g(x)$ in expressing the original integrand as a product. Otherwise, the integral of $f'(x)G(x)$ may turn out to be no easier to evaluate than the integral of $f(x)g(x)$. For example, if we reverse the choices in Example 1, setting $f(x) = e^{2x}$ and $g(x) = x$, then $f'(x) = 2e^{2x}$ and $G(x) = \frac{1}{2}x^2$, so that the formula for integration by parts becomes

$$\int e^{2x}x \, dx = e^{2x} \cdot \tfrac{1}{2}x^2 - \int 2e^{2x} \cdot \tfrac{1}{2}x^2 \, dx.$$

This equation is quite correct, but it is not much help since the integral on the right is more complicated than our original integral.

One obvious criterion in choosing f and g is that we must be able to integrate $g(x)$ in order to find $G(x)$. Usually we should choose $g(x)$ in such a way that its antiderivative $G(x)$ is a fairly simple function. The following guidelines will be helpful in deciding the choice of f and g.

1. If the integrand is the product of a polynomial in x and an exponential function, it is often useful to take $f(x)$ as the given polynomial. The preceding example illustrates this type of choice.

2. If the integrand contains a logarithmic function as a factor, it is often useful to choose this function as $f(x)$. If the integrand consists entirely of a logarithmic function, we can take $g(x) = 1$. The following examples illustrate this.

EXAMPLE 2   Evaluate $\int x^2 \ln x \, dx \quad (x > 0)$.

Solution   Choose $f(x) = \ln x$ and $g(x) = x^2$. Then $f'(x) = 1/x$ and $G(x) = \frac{1}{3}x^3$. Substituting into the formula for integration by parts, we obtain

$$\int f(x)g(x) \, dx = f(x)G(x) - \int f'(x)G(x) \, dx$$

$$\int \ln x \cdot x^2 dx = \ln x \cdot \frac{1}{3}x^3 - \int \frac{1}{x} \cdot \frac{1}{3}x^3 \, dx.$$

Therefore

$$\int x^2 \ln x \, dx = \frac{1}{3}x^3 \ln x - \frac{1}{3}\int x^2 \, dx$$

$$= \frac{1}{3}x^3 \ln x - \frac{1}{9}x^3 + C.$$

EXAMPLE 3   Evaluate $\int \ln (2x - 1) \, dx$.

Solution   In this case, we can express the integrand as a product by writing $f(x) = \ln (2x - 1)$ and $g(x) = 1$. Then

$$f'(x) = \frac{1}{2x - 1} \cdot 2 = \frac{2}{2x - 1} \quad \text{and} \quad G(x) = x.$$

Integration by parts gives

$$\int f(x)g(x) \, dx = f(x)G(x) - \int f'(x)G(x) \, dx$$

or

$$\int \ln (2x - 1) \, dx = \ln (2x - 1) \cdot x - \int \frac{2}{2x - 1} \cdot x \, dx$$

$$= x \ln (2x - 1) - \int \frac{2x}{2x - 1} dx$$

$$= x \ln (2x - 1) - \int \left(1 + \frac{1}{2x - 1}\right) dx$$

$$= x \ln (2x - 1) - x - \frac{\ln |2x - 1|}{2} + C$$

$$= (x - \tfrac{1}{2}) \ln (2x - 1) - x + C.$$

In the last step we have written $\ln |2x - 1| = \ln (2x - 1)$, since the given integral is defined only when $2x - 1 > 0$.

EXAMPLE 4   Evaluate $\int x^2 e^{mx}\, dx \quad (m \neq 0)$.

Solution   Here we choose $f(x) = x^2$ and $g(x) = e^{mx}$. Then $f'(x) = 2x$ and $G(x) = e^{mx}/m$. Using the formula for integration by parts, we have

$$\int f(x)g(x)\, dx = f(x)G(x) - \int f'(x)G(x)\, dx \tag{2}$$

or

$$\int x^2 e^{mx}\, dx = x^2 \cdot \frac{e^{mx}}{m} - \int 2x \cdot \frac{e^{mx}}{m}\, dx$$

$$= \frac{1}{m} x^2 e^{mx} - \frac{2}{m} \int x e^{mx}\, dx. \tag{3}$$

(Compare this with Formula 70 in the table of integrals.) To evaluate the integral on the right, we again use integration by parts, with $f(x) = x$ and $g(x) = e^{mx}$. Then $f'(x) = 1$ and $G(x) = e^{mx}/m$. Using Equation (2), we get

$$\int x e^{mx}\, dx = x \cdot \frac{e^{mx}}{m} - \int 1 \cdot \frac{e^{mx}}{m}\, dx$$

$$= \frac{x}{m} e^{mx} - \frac{1}{m} \cdot \frac{e^{mx}}{m}.$$

Substituting the value of this integral into Equation (3), we get

$$\int x^2 e^{mx}\, dx = \frac{1}{m} x^2 e^{mx} - \frac{2}{m}\left(\frac{x}{m} e^{mx} - \frac{1}{m^2} e^{mx}\right) + C$$

$$= \frac{1}{m^3} e^{mx}(m^2 x^2 - 2mx + 2) + C$$

where we have finally added the constant of integration C.

EXERCISES 4

(1–20)   Evaluate the following integrals.

1. $\int x \ln x\, dx$
2. $\int x^3 \ln x\, dx$
3. $\int x^n \ln x\, dx$

4. $\int \ln (x + 1)\, dx$
5. $\int \ln x\, dx$
6. $\int \frac{\ln (x^2)}{x^2}\, dx$

7. $\int x e^x\, dx$
8. $\int x e^{-x}\, dx$
9. $\int x e^{mx}\, dx$

10. $\int \frac{x}{e^{2x}}\, dx$
11. $\int (2x + 1)e^{3x}\, dx$
12. $\int e^{x + \ln x}\, dx$

13. $\int \ln (x^x)\, dx$
14. $\int \ln (x e^x)\, dx$

15. $\int x^2 e^x\, dx$
16. $\int y^2 e^{3y}\, dy$

17. $\int x^3 e^{x^2}\, dx$ (*Hint:* Let $x^2 = u$.)
18. $\int e^{\sqrt{x}}\, dx$ (*Hint:* Let $\sqrt{x} = u$.)

19. $\displaystyle\int \ln (x^{x^2})\, dx$ **20.** $\displaystyle\int e^{2x} \ln (e^x)\, dx$

21. Use integration by parts to verify Formula 74 in Table A.2. in Appendix.

22. Verify Formula 64 in Table A.2 in Appendix.

23. A firm has a marginal cost per unit of its product given by

$$C'(x) = \frac{5000 \ln (x + 20)}{(x + 20)^2}$$

where x is the level of production. If the fixed costs are \$2000, determine the cost function.

REVIEW EXERCISES FOR CHAPTER 16

1. State whether each of the following is true or false. Replace each false statement by a corresponding true statement.

   a. The antiderivative of an integrable function is unique.

   b. The integral of the sum of two functions is equal to the sum of their integrals.

   c. The integral of the product of two functions is equal to the product of their integrals.

   d. $\displaystyle\int \frac{d}{dx}[f(x)]\, dx = f(x)$

   e. $\displaystyle\frac{d}{dx}\left(\int f(t)\, dt\right) = f(t)$

   f. If $f'(x) = g'(x)$, then $f(x) = g(x)$.

   g. $\displaystyle\int \ln x\, dx = \frac{1}{x} + C$

   h. $\displaystyle\int e^x\, du = e^x + C$

   i. $\displaystyle\int 1/e^t\, dt = 1/e^t + C$

   j. $\displaystyle\int [f(x)]^n\, dx = \frac{[f(x)]^{n+1}}{n+1} + C \quad (n \neq -1)$

   k. $\displaystyle\int x^n\, dx = \frac{x^{n+1}}{n+1} + C \quad \text{for all } n$

   l. $\displaystyle\int x f(x)\, dx = x \int f(x)\, dx$

   m. $\displaystyle\int \frac{1}{x^2}\, dx = \ln x^2 + C$

n. $\int e^{x^2} dx = e^{x^3/3} + C$

o. $\int e^t dt = \dfrac{e^{t+1}}{t+1} + C$

(2–9) Make use of an appropriate substitution to evaluate the following integrals.

2. $\int e^x \sqrt{e^x + 1}\, dx$

3. $\int \dfrac{1}{x(1 + \ln x)}\, dx$

4. $\int \dfrac{e^{1/x}}{x^2}\, dx$

5. $\int \dfrac{e^{1+\sqrt{x}}}{\sqrt{x}}\, dx$

6. $\int \dfrac{x}{\sqrt{1 + x^2}}\, dx$

7. $\int \dfrac{x^2}{\sqrt[3]{1 + x^3}}\, dx$

8. $\int \dfrac{1}{(x + 2)\ln (x + 2)}\, dx$

9. $\int \dfrac{1}{x\sqrt{2 + \ln x}}\, dx$

(10–27) Make use of tables or otherwise to evaluate the following integrals.

10. $\int \dfrac{3x + 2}{(x - 1)(2x + 1)}\, dx$

11. $\int \dfrac{3x - 1}{(x - 1)(x + 2)}\, dx$

12. $\int \dfrac{1}{x(4 - x^2)}\, dx$

13. $\int \dfrac{1}{x^2(9 - x^2)^{3/2}}\, dx$

14. $\int \sqrt{4x^2 - 9}\, dx$

15. $\int \sqrt{25t^2 + 9}\, dt$

16. $\int x^3 e^{2x}\, dx$

17. $\int \dfrac{1}{1 + 2e^{3x}}\, dx$

18. $\int x \ln |x + 1|\, dx$

19. $\int x^5 \log_x x^3\, dx$

20. $\int \log_3 x\, dx$

21. $\int x^2 (\ln x)^2\, dx$

*22. $\int \dfrac{1}{x(x^4 + 1)}\, dx$

*23. $\int \dfrac{1}{x(x^3 - 1)}\, dx$

24. $\int \dfrac{\ln (e^{2x})}{e^x}\, dx$

25. $\int \dfrac{e^x}{(e^x + 1)(e^x - 4)^2}\, dx$

26. $\int \dfrac{e^{\sqrt{x}}}{\sqrt{x}}\, dx$

27. $\int \dfrac{e^{(1/x^2)}}{x^3}\, dx$

28. The marginal cost function of a certain firm at a production level x is $C'(x) = 5 - 2x + 3x^2$ and the cost of manufacturing 30 units is \$29,050. Determine the cost of manufacturing 50 units.

29. The marginal revenue function of a firm is $R'(x) = 12 - 0.2x + 0.03x^2$.

    a. Determine the revenue function.

    b. How much revenue will be obtained when 20 units are sold?

    c. What is the demand function for the firm's product?

    d. How many units will the firm be able to sell it if charges \$3 per unit?

30. A firm finds that a price increase of $1 causes a drop in sales of its product by 4 units. In addition, the firm can sell 50 units at a price of $8 each. Find the firm's demand function. (*Hint:* If x is the demand at a price p, then $dx/dp = -4$.)

31. After an individual has been working for t hours on a particular machine, x units will have been produced, where the rate of production (number of units per hour) is given by

$$\frac{dx}{dt} = 10(1 - e^{-t/50}).$$

How many units are produced during the individual's first 50 hours on the machine? How many are produced during the second 50 hours?

THE DEFINITE INTEGRAL

CHAPTER

17-1 AREAS UNDER CURVES

In this and the following sections, we shall be concerned with the calculation of the areas of regions that have curved boundaries. Such areas can be evaluated by using what are called definite integrals.

DEFINITION   Let $f(x)$ be a function with an antiderivative that we denote by $F(x)$. Let a and b be any two real numbers such that $f(x)$ and $F(x)$ exist for all values of x in the closed interval with endpoints a and b. Then the **definite integral of $f(x)$ from $x = a$ to $x = b$** is denoted by $\int_a^b f(x)dx$ and is defined by

$$\int_a^b f(x)\, dx = F(b) - F(a).$$

The numbers a and b are called the **limits of integration,** a the **lower limit** and b the **upper limit.** Usually $a < b$, but this is not essential.

When evaluating a definite integral, it is usual as a matter of convenience to use large square brackets on the right side in the following way:

$$\int_a^b f(x)\, dx = \left[F(x) \right]_a^b = F(b) - F(a).$$

We read *the definite integral of $f(x)$ from $x = a$ to $x = b$ is $F(x)$ at b minus $F(x)$ at a.* The bracket notation in the middle means that the function inside the bracket must be evaluated at the two values of the argument indicated after the bracket. The difference between these two values of the function is then taken in order, value at the top argument minus the value at the bottom argument.

In evaluating definite integrals, we drop the constant of integration from the antiderivative of $f(x)$ because this constant of integration cancels in the final answer. Let $F(x) + C$ be any antiderivative of $f(x)$, where C is a constant of integration. Then by the above definition

$$\int_a^b f(x)\, dx = \left[F(x) + C \right]_a^b$$
$$= [F(b) + C] - [F(a) + C]$$
$$= F(b) - F(a)$$

and C has disappeared from the answer.

EXAMPLE 1   Evaluate the following definite integrals.

(a) $\displaystyle\int_a^b x^4\, dx$ (b) $\displaystyle\int_1^3 \frac{1}{t}\, dt$ (c) $\displaystyle\int_0^2 e^{3x}\, dx$

Solution   (a) We have, $\int x^4 \, dx = x^5/5$. Thus

$$\int_a^b x^4 \, dx = \left[\frac{x^5}{5}\right]_a^b = \frac{b^5}{5} - \frac{a^5}{5} = \frac{1}{5}(b^5 - a^5).$$

(b) $\int_1^3 \frac{1}{t} \, dt = \left[\ln|t|\right]_1^3 = \ln|3| - \ln|1|$

$$= \ln 3 - \ln 1 = \ln 3$$

(Note that $\ln 1 = 0$.)

(c) $\int_0^2 e^{3x} \, dx = \left[\frac{e^{3x}}{3}\right]_0^2 = \frac{e^6}{3} - \frac{e^0}{3}$

$$= \frac{1}{3}(e^6 - 1)$$

When evaluating definite integrals where the antiderivative is found by the method of substitution, it is important to note that the limits of integration also change when the variable of integration changes. This is illustrated in the following example.

EXAMPLE 2   Evaluate $\int_1^2 x \, e^{x^2} \, dx$.

Solution   Let $I = \int_1^2 xe^{x^2} \, dx$. To find an antiderivative of xe^{x^2}, we can make use of the substitution method. We write the given integral as

$$I = \frac{1}{2} \int_1^2 e^{x^2} \cdot 2x \, dx.$$

Since $2x \, dx$, the differential of x^2, occurs in the integral, we let $x^2 = u$ so that $2x \, dx = du$. When $x = 1$, $u = 1^2 = 1$ and when $x = 2$, $u = 2^2 = 4$. Therefore

$$I = \frac{1}{2} \int_1^4 e^u \, du.$$

Note that in terms of the new variable u, the limits of integration are 1 and 4. Then

$$I = \frac{1}{2}\left[e^u\right]_1^4 = \frac{1}{2}(e^4 - e^1) = \frac{1}{2}e(e^3 - 1).$$

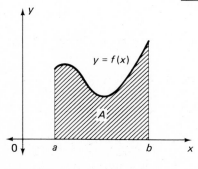

FIGURE 1

Our main concern in this section will be the calculation of areas bounded by curves. Let $f(x)$ be some given function defined and continuous in an interval $a \le x \le b$ and taking nonnegative values in that interval. The graph of $y = f(x)$ then lies entirely above the x-axis, as illustrated in Figure 1. We wish to find a formula for the area A that lies between such a graph and the x-axis and between the vertical lines at $x = a$ and $x = b$. This area is shaded in Figure 1.

There exists a close connection between the area A and the antiderivative of the function $f(x)$. This connection is contained in a theorem called the *fundamental theorem of calculus*, perhaps the most remarkable theorem in the whole of calculus.

THEOREM 1 (FUNDAMENTAL THEOREM OF CALCULUS)
Let $f(x)$ be a continuous nonnegative function in $a \leq x \leq b$ and let $F(x)$ be an antiderivative of $f(x)$. Then A, the area between $y = f(x)$ and the x-axis and the vertical lines $x = a$ and $x = b$, is given by the definite integral

$$A = \int_a^b f(x) \, dx = F(b) - F(a).$$

Before discussing the proof of this theorem, let us illustrate its use with some examples.

EXAMPLE 3   Evaluate the area between the graph $y = x^2$ and the x-axis from $x = 0$ to $x = 2$.

Solution   The required area is shaded in Figure 2. Since $f(x) = x^2$ is nonnegative, this area is given by the definite integral $\int_a^b f(x) \, dx$, where $f(x) = x^2$, $a = 0$, and $b = 2$. Thus the area is

$$\int_0^2 x^2 \, dx = \left[\frac{x^3}{3}\right]_0^2 = \frac{2^3}{3} - \frac{0^3}{3} = \frac{8}{3}.$$

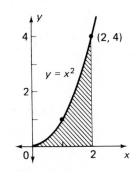

FIGURE 2

EXAMPLE 4   Evaluate the area bounded by the curve $y = 3x^2 + 2x + 5$, the x-axis, and the lines $x = 1$ and $x = 3$.

Solution   Clearly $f(x) = 3x^2 + 2x + 5$ is nonnegative for values of x in $1 \leq x \leq 3$. Thus the required area is given by the following definite integral.

$$\int_1^3 (3x^2 + 2x + 5) \, dx = \left[x^3 + x^2 + 5x\right]_1^3$$
$$= [3^3 + 3^2 + 5(3)] - [1^3 + 1^2 + 5(1)]$$
$$= 51 - 7 = 44 \text{ square units.}$$

If $C(x)$ denotes the total cost of producing x units of a certain commodity, then $C'(x)$ represents the marginal cost function. Now, by the definition of the definite integral,

$$\int_a^b C'(x)\,dx = \left[C(x)\right]_a^b = C(b) - C(a).$$

But $C(b) - C(a)$ represents the change in total cost when the production level is changed from a units to b units. It follows that $\int_a^b C'(x)\,dx$ also represents this same change in total cost.

Thus we have the following important result: The change in production costs in increasing the level of production from a units to b units is equal to the area underneath the graph of the marginal cost function ($y = C'(x)$) between $x = a$ and $x = b$.

Similarly, if $R'(x)$ is the marginal revenue function, then the change in revenue when the sales level changes from a units to b units is given by $\int_a^b R'(x)\,dx$. A similar interpretation may be given to $\int_a^b P'(x)\,dx$ where $P'(x)$ is the marginal profit function; it is the change in profit when x changes from a to b.

EXAMPLE 5   The marginal cost function for a firm at the production level x is given by

$$C'(x) = 23.5 - 0.01x.$$

Find the increase in total cost when the production level is increased from 1000 to 1500 units.

Solution   The increase in total cost is given by

$$\int_{1000}^{1500} C'(x)\,dx = \int_{1000}^{1500} (23.5 - 0.01x)\,dx$$

$$= \left[23.5x - 0.01\left(\frac{x^2}{2}\right)\right]_{1000}^{1500}$$

$$= 23.5(1500) - 0.005(1500^2)$$

$$\quad - [23.5(1000) - 0.005(1000^2)]$$

$$= 35{,}250 - 11{,}250 - (23{,}500 - 5000) = 5500.$$

The cost increase is thus $5500.

———————

Theorems 2 and 3 provide some simple properties of definite integrals.

THEOREM 2   If $f(t)$ is continuous in $a \leq t \leq x$, then

$$\frac{d}{dx}\left(\int_a^x f(t)\,dt\right) = f(x).$$

PROOF   Let $F(t)$ be an antiderivative of $f(t)$; then by the definition of definite integrals,

$$\int_a^x f(t)\, dt = \Big[F(t) \Big]_a^x = F(x) - F(a).$$

This is a function of x and can be differentiated with respect to x. Thus

$$\frac{d}{dx}\left[\int_a^x f(t)\, dt \right] = \frac{d}{dx}[F(x) - F(a)] = F'(x).$$

But since $F(t)$ is an antiderivative of $f(t)$, $F'(t) = f(t)$, and so

$$\frac{d}{dx}\left[\int_a^x f(t)\, dt \right] = f(x).$$

EXAMPLE 6 Evaluate $\dfrac{d}{dx}\left[\displaystyle\int_1^x \dfrac{t}{\ln(t+1)}\, dt \right]$.

Solution By Theorem 2, we have

$$\frac{d}{dx}\left[\int_1^x \frac{t}{\ln(t+1)}\, dt \right] = \frac{x}{\ln(x+1)}.$$

We need not first evaluate the integral and then differentiate.

EXAMPLE 7 Evaluate each of the following.

(a) $\dfrac{d}{dx}\left[\displaystyle\int_1^3 \dfrac{u \ln u}{u^2+1}\, du \right]$ 　　　　(b) $\displaystyle\int_0^1 \dfrac{d}{dx}(x^3 e^{\sqrt{x}})\, dx$

Solution (a) In this case, it is important to note that the definite integral $\displaystyle\int_1^3 \dfrac{u \ln u}{u^2+1}\, du$ has a constant value and does not depend on x. Thus

$$\frac{d}{dx}\left(\int_1^3 \frac{u \ln u}{u^2+1}\, du \right) = 0.$$

(b) From the definition of antiderivatives, if $F'(x) = f(x)$,

$$\int f(x)\, dx = \int F'(x)\, dx = F(x) + C.$$

Thus

$$\int \frac{d}{dx}(x^3 e^{\sqrt{x}})\, dx = x^3 e^{\sqrt{x}} + C$$

and so, disregarding C,

$$\int_0^1 \frac{d}{dx}(x^3 e^{\sqrt{x}})\, dx = \Big[x^3 e^{\sqrt{x}} \Big]_0^1$$
$$= 1^3 e^{\sqrt{1}} - 0 \cdot e^{\sqrt{0}} = e.$$

Note: It is worthwhile to notice the difference between the parts (a) and (b) of Example 7. The positions of the integral sign and the differentiation operator d/dx are reversed.

THEOREM 3

(a) $\displaystyle\int_a^a f(x)\, dx = 0$

(b) $\displaystyle\int_a^b f(x)\,dx = -\int_b^a f(x)\,dx$

(c) $\displaystyle\int_a^b f(x)\,dx = \int_a^c f(x)\,dx + \int_c^b f(x)\,dx$ where c is any other number.

PROOF Let $F(x)$ be any antiderivative of $f(x)$. Then, from the definition of the definite integral, we have the following.

(a) $\displaystyle\int_a^a f(x)\,dx = \left[F(x)\right]_a^a = F(a) - F(a) = 0$

(b) We have

$$\int_a^b f(x)\,dx = \left[F(x)\right]_a^b = F(b) - F(a)$$

and

$$\int_b^a f(x)\,dx = \left[F(x)\right]_b^a = F(a) - F(b)$$

so that

$$\int_a^b f(x)\,dx = -\int_b^a f(x)\,dx.$$

(c) The proof of this part is left as an exercise.

We shall conclude this section by giving a proof of the fundamental theorem of calculus. The proof we shall give will necessarily be nonrigorous since we have not given a proper mathematical definition of the area under a curve. Nevertheless, the proof will be a convincing one, and we can assure the more skeptical readers that rigorous proofs do exist.

PROOF OF THE FUNDAMENTAL THEOREM OF CALCULUS We shall prove the theorem for the particular case when $f(x)$ is a nonnegative *increasing* function in $a \le x \le b$, although the proof can quite easily be extended to all continuous functions.

When $f(x) \ge 0$, we want to find an expression for A, the total area under the curve $y = f(x)$. Let us define the area function $A(x)$, which represents the area under the curve $y = f(x)$ from the value a to the value x of the abscissa, where x is any number such that $a \le x \le b$.

$A(x)$ is the shaded area in Figure 3. Thus $A(a) = 0$, because the area obviously shrinks to zero as x approaches a. Further, $A(b)$ is clearly the area under the curve from a to b, that is, the quantity A that we require: $A(b) = A$.

When x is changed to $x + \Delta x (\Delta x > 0)$, the area $A(x)$ also increases to $A + \Delta A$, where $A + \Delta A$ is the area under the curve between the values a and $x + \Delta x$ of the abscissa. (See Figure 4.) It is reasonable to

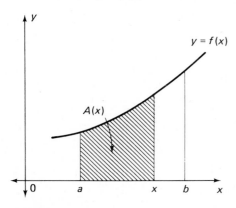

FIGURE 3

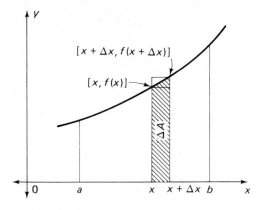

FIGURE 4

expect that ΔA is equal to the area of the strip that is shaded in this figure. (We cannot prove this rigorously here since we do not have a rigorous definition of area.)

The area ΔA is greater than the area of the inscribed rectangle with height $f(x)$ and width Δx; and ΔA is less than the area of the circumscribed rectangle with height $f(x + \Delta x)$ and width Δx. Thus

$$f(x) \cdot \Delta x < \Delta A < f(x + \Delta x) \cdot \Delta x.$$

Dividing throughout by Δx, we obtain

$$f(x) < \frac{\Delta A}{\Delta x} < f(x + \Delta x).$$

Since f is continuous, $f(x + \Delta x) \to f(x)$ as $\Delta x \to 0$. Upon taking the limits of the above inequalities as $\Delta x \to 0$, it follows that $\Delta A / \Delta x$ has a limit, and

$$\lim_{\Delta x \to 0} \frac{\Delta A}{\Delta x} = f(x), \quad \text{or} \quad A'(x) = f(x).$$

Because $F(x)$ is an antiderivative of $f(x)$, it follows also that $F'(x) = f(x)$. Thus $F(x)$ and $A(x)$ are both antiderivatives of $f(x)$ and hence they can differ from each other by at most a constant; that is

$$A(x) = F(x) + C \tag{1}$$

where C is some constant.

Letting $x = a$ and remembering that $A(a) = 0$, we have

$$A(a) = F(a) + C = 0,$$

and so $C = -F(a)$. Replacing C by $-F(a)$ in Equation (1) above, we get

$$A(x) = F(x) - F(a).$$

Finally, putting $x = b$ in this value, we arrive at the result that

$$A(b) = F(b) - F(a).$$

But $A(b) = A$, the required total area under the curve, and we have proved that

$$A = F(b) - F(a) = \int_a^b f(x)\, dx$$

(from the definition of the definite integral).

EXERCISES 1

(1–16)   Evaluate the following definite integrals.

1. $\displaystyle\int_0^1 x^2\, dx$

2. $\displaystyle\int_{-1}^3 t^3\, dt$

3. $\displaystyle\int_1^2 (3x^2 - 5x + 7)\, dx$

4. $\displaystyle\int_0^5 (u^2 + u + 1)\, du$

5. $\displaystyle\int_{-1}^3 (4y - 2e^y)\, dy$

6. $\displaystyle\int_0^1 t^4 \ln(e^t)\, dt$

7. $\displaystyle\int_0^1 x\sqrt{x^2 + 1}\, dx$

8. $\displaystyle\int_0^1 xe^{x^2}\, dx$

9. $\displaystyle\int_e^{e^2} \frac{\ln t}{t}\, dt$

10. $\displaystyle\int_1^e \frac{1}{y(1 + \ln y)}\, dy$

11. $\displaystyle\int_2^2 \frac{x^2 + 2x - 8}{e^x + \ln x}\, dx$

12. $\displaystyle\int_3^3 e^{x^2}\, dx$

13. $\displaystyle\int_1^1 (2x + 1)(x^2 + x - 5)^7\, dx$

14. $\displaystyle\int_5^5 \frac{e^{2x} - (\ln x)^7}{3x + 4}\, dx$

15. $\displaystyle\int_0^1 \frac{d}{dt}\left(\frac{e^t + 2t - 1}{3 + \ln(1 + t)}\right) dt$

16. $\displaystyle\int_0^1 \frac{d}{dx}\left(\frac{1}{e^{2x} + e^x + 1}\right) dx$

(17–22)   Evaluate the areas beneath the graphs of the following functions between the given values of x.

17. $y = 3x + 2, \quad x = 1$ and $x = 3$

18. $y = 5x^2, \quad x = 0$ and $x = 2$

19. $y = 4 - x^2, \quad x = 0$ and $x = 2$

20. $y = 2x^2 + 3x - 1, \quad x = 1$ and $x = 4$

21. $y = x^3, \quad x = 0$ and $x = 3$

22. $y = 1 + x^3, \quad x = 0$ and $x = 2$

(23–30)   Evaluate the following.

23. $\displaystyle\frac{d}{dx}\left(\int_2^x \frac{e^t \ln t}{1 + t^2}\, dt\right)$

24. $\displaystyle\frac{d}{dt}\left(\int_1^t \frac{x^3 \ln x}{e^x - 1}\, dx\right)$

25. $\displaystyle\frac{d}{dx}\left(\int_x^4 \frac{1 + u}{1 - \ln u}\, du\right)$

26. $\displaystyle\frac{d}{du}\left(\int_u^3 \{e^x(\ln x)^4\}\, dx\right)$

27. $\displaystyle\frac{d}{dx}\left(\int_1^2 \frac{e^t \ln(t^2 + 1)}{1 + t^3}\, dt\right)$

28. $\displaystyle\frac{d}{dt}\left(\int_2^5 \frac{e^{x^2}}{x + 1}\, dx\right)$

29. $\displaystyle\int_1^2 \frac{d}{dx}(x^2 e^{\sqrt{x}} \ln x)\, dx$

30. $\displaystyle\int_e^1 \frac{d}{dx}\left(\frac{\ln x}{x^2 + 1}\right) dx$

31.   The marginal revenue function for a firm is given by $R'(x) = 12.5 - 0.02x$. Find the increase in the total revenue of the firm when the sales level increases from 100 units to 200 units.

32. The marginal cost of a certain firm is given by $C'(x) = 15.7 - 0.002x$, whereas its marginal revenue function is $R'(x) = 22 - 0.004x$. Determine the increase in the profits of the firm when the sales are increased from 500 to 600 units.

33. In Exercise 31, the sales level is first decreased from 100 units to 80 units and then is increased to 150 units. Find the overall change in total revenue.

34. In Exercise 32, find the change in profit when the sales decrease from 500 to 400 units.

17-2 MORE ON AREAS

In the last section, we proved that the area under the curve $y = f(x)$ bounded by the lines $x = a$, $x = b$, and $y = 0$ (the x-axis) is given by the definite integral $\int_a^b f(x)\, dx$ in the case when $f(x) \geq 0$ in $a \leq x \leq b$.

Consider now the corresponding area bounded by the curve $y = f(x)$, the lines $x = a$, $x = b$, and the x-axis in the case when $f(x) \leq 0$ for $a \leq x \leq b$. The area in question clearly lies below the x-axis, as shown in Figure 5.

Let us define $g(x) = -f(x)$ so that $g(x) \geq 0$ for $a \leq x \leq b$. The area bounded by $y = g(x)$ (or $y = -f(x)$), the lines $x = a$, $x = b$ and the x-axis lies above the x-axis. (See Figure 6.) This latter area, as in the last section, is given by the definite integral $\int_a^b g(x)\, dx$. Now

$$\int_a^b g(x)\, dx = G(b) - G(a)$$

where $G(x)$ is the antiderivative of $g(x)$. But since $g(x) = -f(x)$, it must follow that $F(x) = -G(x)$ is an antiderivative of $f(x)$. Thus $G(b) - G(a) = -F(b) + F(a)$, or

$$\int_a^b g(x)\, dx = -[F(b) - F(a)] = -\int_a^b f(x)\, dx.$$

Comparing Figures 5 and 6, it is clear that the two shaded areas are equal in magnitude since one area can be obtained simply by reflecting the other about

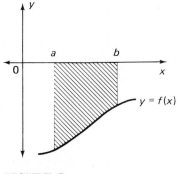

FIGURE 5

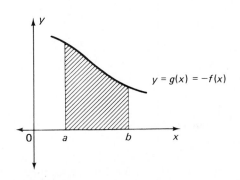

FIGURE 6

the x-axis. Thus the area below the x-axis, bounded by the curve $y = f(x)$ and the lines $x = a$ and $x = b$, is given by the definite integral

$$-\int_a^b f(x)\, dx.$$

EXAMPLE 1   Find the area bounded by $y = x^2 - 9$, $x = 0$, $x = 2$, and the x-axis.

Solution   The graph of $y = x^2 - 9$ lies below the x-axis for $0 \le x \le 2$. The required area (shaded in Figure 7) is given by

$$-\int_0^2 (x^2 - 9)\, dx = \int_0^2 (9 - x^2)\, dx$$

$$= \left[9x - \frac{x^3}{3} \right]_0^2$$

$$= \left(9(2) - \frac{2^3}{3} \right) - \left(9(0) - \frac{0^3}{3} \right) = \tfrac{46}{3} \text{ square units.}$$

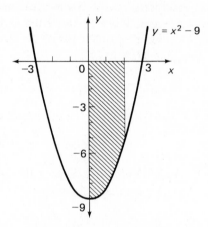

FIGURE 7

Let us now consider the area bounded by the curve $y = f(x)$ and the lines $x = a$, $x = b$, and the x-axis in the case when $f(x)$ is sometimes positive and sometimes negative in the interval $a \le x \le b$. (See Figure 8.) Such an area has parts below the x-axis and parts above the x-axis. We shall assume that we can find the points where the graph of $y = f(x)$ crosses the x-axis, that is, the values of x for which $f(x) = 0$. In Figure 8, we have illustrated the case when there are two such points, denoted by $x = p$ and $x = q$. In this case,

$$f(x) \ge 0 \quad \text{for} \quad a \le x \le p,$$
$$f(x) \le 0 \quad \text{for} \quad p \le x \le q,$$

and

$$f(x) \ge 0 \quad \text{for} \quad q \le x \le r.$$

In a problem of this type, we calculate the area in each subinterval separately; the required area is then the sum of all these areas. In Figure 8, the areas

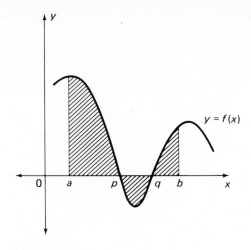

FIGURE 8

between $x = a$ and $x = p$ and between $x = q$ and $x = b$ lie above the x-axis, whereas the area between $x = p$ and $x = q$ lies below the x-axis. Therefore the required area is equal to

$$\int_a^p f(x)\,dx + \left[-\int_p^q f(x)\,dx \right] + \int_q^b f(x)\,dx.$$

EXAMPLE 2   Find the area bounded by the x-axis, the curve $y = x^2 - 9$, and the lines $x = 0$ and $x = 4$.

Solution   The graph of $y = x^2 - 9$ is shown in Figure 7. For $0 \le x < 3$, it lies below the x-axis, while for $3 < x < 4$, it lies above. Therefore the required area is given by

$$\int_0^3 -(x^2 - 9)\,dx + \int_3^4 (x^2 - 9)\,dx$$

$$= \left[-\frac{x^3}{3} + 9x \right]_0^3 + \left[\frac{x^3}{3} - 9x \right]_3^4$$

$$= \left(-\frac{3^3}{3} + 9 \cdot 3 \right) - \left(-\frac{0^3}{3} + 9 \cdot 0 \right) + \left(\frac{4^3}{3} - 9 \cdot 4 \right) - \left(\frac{3^3}{3} - 9 \cdot 3 \right)$$

$$= 18 - 0 + (-\tfrac{44}{3}) - (-18) = \tfrac{64}{3} \text{ square units.}$$

Area Between Two Curves

Let us now consider the area bounded by the two curves $y = f(x)$ and $y = g(x)$ and the lines $x = a$ and $x = b$. We shall suppose initially that $f(x) > g(x) \ge 0$ in $a \le x \le b$ so that both curves lie above the x-axis and the curve $y = f(x)$ lies above the curve $y = g(x)$. The area in question is shaded in Figure 9. Clearly this area is the difference between the area bounded by $y = f(x)$ and the x-axis and the area bounded by $y = g(x)$ and the x-axis; that is, the area of the region $CDEF$ between the two curves is equal to the area of $ABEF$ minus the area of $ABDC$.

Thus the required area is given by

$$\int_a^b f(x)\, dx - \int_a^b g(x)\, dx = \int_a^b [f(x) - g(x)]\, dx.$$

Note that in the integrand $[f(x) - g(x)]$, the first term $f(x)$ relates to the top curve and the second term $g(x)$ relates to the bottom curve. A convenient way of remembering this formula is, therefore,

$$\int_a^b (y_{\text{upper}} - y_{\text{lower}})\, dx.$$

In this form, it can also be used to calculate the area between two curves when one or both of them lie below the x-axis and also when the curves cross one another.

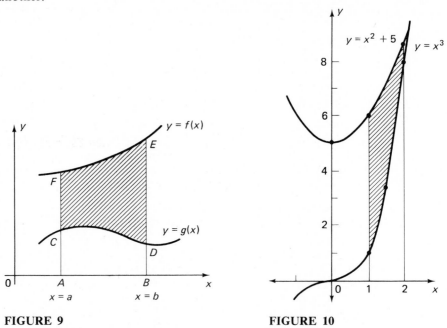

FIGURE 9 **FIGURE 10**

EXAMPLE 3   Find the area between the curves $y = x^2 + 5$ and $y = x^3$ and the lines $x = 1$ and $x = 2$.

Solution   The graph of $y = x^2 + 5$ lies above the curve $y = x^3$ in the interval $1 \le x \le 2$. Thus the required area (shaded in Figure 10) is given by

$$
\begin{aligned}
A &= \int_1^2 (y_{\text{upper}} - y_{\text{lower}})\, dx \\
&= \int_1^2 [(x^2 + 5) - x^3]\, dx \\
&= \left[\frac{x^3}{3} + 5x - \frac{x^4}{4} \right]_1^2 \\
&= (\tfrac{8}{3} + 10 - 4) - (\tfrac{1}{3} + 5 - \tfrac{1}{4}) = 3\tfrac{7}{12}
\end{aligned}
$$

or $3\tfrac{7}{12}$ square units.

EXAMPLE 4   Find the area of the region which is enclosed by the curves $y = -x^2$ and $y = x^2 - 8$.

Solution   In this case, we are not given the limits of integration. The first step is to sketch the graphs of the two curves in order to determine the required area that they enclose and the limits of integration. Sketches of the two curves are shown in Figure 11, in which the enclosed area is shaded.

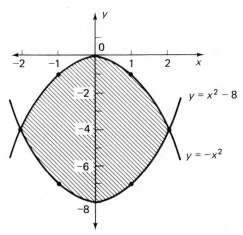

FIGURE 11

To find the points of intersection of two curves, we must treat the two equations of the curves as simultaneous equations and solve them for x and y. In this particular example, equating the two values of y gives:

$$-x^2 = x^2 - 8 \quad \text{or} \quad 2x^2 - 8 = 0.$$

Therefore, $x = \pm 2$. For the area shown in Figure 11, x thus varies from -2 to $+2$. Therefore

$$\text{Area} = \int_{-2}^{2} [(-x^2) - (x^2 - 8)]\, dx$$

$$= \int_{-2}^{2} (8 - 2x^2)\, dx = \left[8x - \tfrac{2}{3}x^3 \right]_{-2}^{2}$$

$$= (16 - \tfrac{16}{3}) - (-16 + \tfrac{16}{3}) = \tfrac{64}{3} \text{ square units.}$$

EXAMPLE 5   Find the area bounded by the curves $y = 1/x$ and $y = x^2$ between $x = \tfrac{1}{2}$ and $x = 2$.

Solution   The two curves $y = 1/x$ and $y = x^2$ intersect where $1/x = x^2$, or $x^3 = 1$; that is, when $x = 1$. (See Figure 12.) In this case, we divide the problem into two parts, because for $\tfrac{1}{2} < x < 1$, $1/x < x^2$, but for $1 < x < 2$, $x^2 > 1/x$.

Thus the required area is given by

$$A = \int_{\frac{1}{2}}^{1} \left(\frac{1}{x} - x^2 \right) dx + \int_{1}^{2} \left(x^2 - \frac{1}{x} \right) dx$$

$$= \left[\ln x - \frac{x^3}{3} \right]_{\frac{1}{2}}^{1} + \left[\frac{x^3}{3} - \ln x \right]_{1}^{2}$$

$$= \tfrac{47}{24} \text{ square units.}$$

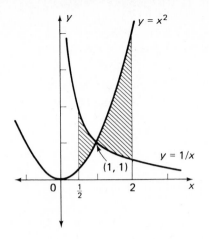

FIGURE 12

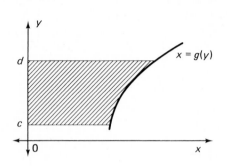

FIGURE 13

We close this section by giving the expression for the area bounded by the curve $x = g(y)$, the y-axis, and the horizontal lines $y = c$ and $y = d$. This area (shaded in Figure 13) is given by

$$\int_c^d g(y)\, dy$$

where $d \geq c \geq 0$. We can see this if we redraw the figure with the y-axis horizontal and the x-axis vertical, as shown in Figure 14. The area in question then becomes the area between the curve and the horizontal axis, and is given by the appropriate definite integral. The names of the variables x and y are simply interchanged.

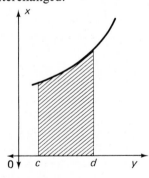

FIGURE 14

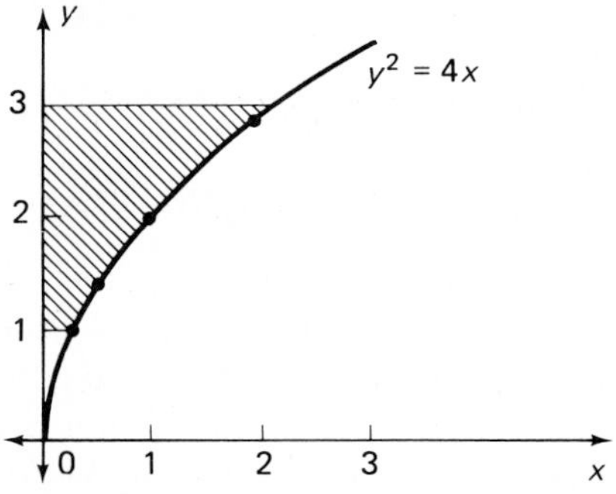

FIGURE 15

EXAMPLE 6   Find the area bounded by the parabola $y^2 = 4x$, the y-axis, and the horizontal lines $y = 1$ and $y = 3$.

Solution   The required area is shown in Figure 15. Here $x = y^2/4$, so that $g(y) = y^2/4$. Thus the required area is

$$\int_1^3 \frac{y^2}{4}\, dy = \left[\frac{1}{4} \cdot \frac{y^3}{3} \right]_{y=1}^3$$

$$= \frac{1}{12}(3^3 - 1^3) = \frac{13}{6} \text{ square units.}$$

(1–8)   In each of the following exercises, find the area bounded by the curve $y = f(x)$, the x-axis, and the lines $x = a$ and $x = b$.

1. $y = -x^2$; $x = 0, x = 3$
2. $y = 1 - \sqrt{x}$; $x = 1, x = 9$
3. $y = -e^x$; $x = \ln 2, x = \ln 5$
4. $y = x^3$; $x = -1, x = 1$
5. $y = x^2 - 4$; $x = 0, x = 3$
6. $y = x^2 - 3x + 2$; $x = 0, x = 3$
7. $y = 1 - x^2$; $x = 0, x = 2$
8. $y = 2x - 1$; $x = 0, x = 1$

(9–14)   Find the area between the following pairs of curves and between the given vertical lines.

9. $y = x^2, y = 3x$; $x = 1, x = 2$
10. $y = x^2, y = 2x - 1$; $x = 0, x = 2$
11. $y = \sqrt{x}, y = x^2$; $x = 0, x = 1$
12. $y = x^2, y = x^3$; $x = 0, x = 2$
13. $y = e^x, y = x^2$; $x = 0, x = 1$
14. $y = x^3, y = 3x - 2$; $x = 0, x = 2$

(15–18)   Determine the area of the region enclosed between the following pairs of curves.

15. $y = x^2, y = 2 - x^2$
16. $y = x^2, y = \sqrt{x}$
17. $y = x^3, y = x^2$
18. $y = x^2, y = 2x$

(19–20)   Find the area bounded by the following curves and lines.

19. $y = x^2, y = 0, y = 4$, and $x = 0$ (y-axis)
20. $y^2 = x, y = 0, y = 2$, and $x = 0$

17-3 APPLICATIONS TO BUSINESS AND ECONOMICS

Coefficient of Inequality for Income Distributions

Let y be the proportion of the total income of a certain population that is received by the proportion x of income recipients whose income is least. For example, suppose that when $x = \frac{1}{2}$ then $y = \frac{1}{4}$. This would mean that the lowest paid 50% of the population receive 25% of the total income. Or if $y = 0.7$ when $x = 0.9$, then the lowest paid 90% of the population receive 70% of the total income. In general, since x and y are fractional parts of a whole, they both lie between 0 and 1 inclusive ($0 \le x \le 1$ and $0 \le y \le 1$) and y is a function of x, that is, $y = f(x)$.

We assume that there is no person who receives zero income, so that $f(0) = 0$. Furthermore, all the income is received by 100% of the recipients, so $f(1) = 1$. The graph of the function $f(x)$ describing the actual income distribution is called a **Lorentz curve**.

Suppose a Lorentz curve is given by the equation $y = \frac{15}{16}x^2 + \frac{1}{16}x$. (See Figure 16.) When $x = 0.2$, we have

$$y = \tfrac{15}{16}(0.2)^2 + \tfrac{1}{16}(0.2) = 0.05.$$

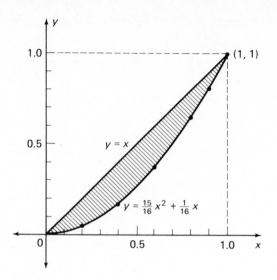

FIGURE 16

This means that the lowest paid 20% of the people receive only 5% of the total income. Similarly, when $x = 0.5$, we have

$$y = \tfrac{15}{16}(0.5)^2 + \tfrac{1}{16}(0.5) = 0.2656$$

that is, the lowest paid 50% of the people receive only 26.56% of the total income.

Perfect equality of income distribution is represented by the line $y = x$. According to this, for example, 10% of the people receive 10% of the total income, 20% of the people receive 20% of the total income, and so on. The deviation of the actual income distribution from perfect equality is measured by the amount by which the actual Lorentz curve departs from the straight line $y = x$. If the Lorentz curve is close to the straight line, income will be distributed approximately uniformly, while a large departure from the line indicates considerable inequality of distribution. We define the **coefficient of inequality** of the Lorentz curve as

$$L = \frac{\text{Area Between the Curve and the Line } y = x}{\text{Area Under the Line } y = x}.$$

Now, the area under the line $y = x$ is the area of $\triangle OAB$, so it is given by

$$\tfrac{1}{2} \cdot OA \cdot OB = \tfrac{1}{2} \cdot 1 \cdot 1 = \tfrac{1}{2}.$$

Therefore the coefficient of inequality of a Lorentz curve is given by

$$L = 2 \cdot \text{Area Between Lorentz Curve and the Line } y = x$$

$$= 2 \int_0^1 [x - f(x)]\, dx$$

where $y = f(x)$ is the equation of the Lorentz curve.

For example, the coefficient of inequality for the Lorentz curve given by $y = f(x) = \frac{15}{16}x^2 + \frac{1}{16}x$ is

$$L = 2\int_0^1 \left[x - \left(\frac{15}{16}x^2 + \frac{1}{16}x \right) \right] dx$$

$$= 2\int_0^1 \left(\frac{15}{16}x - \frac{15}{16}x^2 \right) dx$$

$$= 2 \cdot \frac{15}{16} \int_0^1 (x - x^2)\, dx = \frac{15}{8}\left[\frac{x^2}{2} - \frac{x^3}{3} \right]_0^1$$

$$= \frac{15}{8}\left(\frac{1}{2} - \frac{1}{3} - 0 + 0 \right) = \frac{15}{8} \cdot \frac{1}{6} = \frac{5}{16}.$$

The coefficient of inequality always lies between 0 and 1, as is clear from its geometric definition. When the coefficient is zero, income is distributed perfectly uniformly; the closer the coefficient is to 1, the greater the inequality of distribution of income.

Learning Curves

In production industry, the management often has to estimate in advance the total number of work-hours that will be required to produce a given number of units of its product. This is required, for example, in order to establish the selling price or the delivery date or to bid for a contract. A tool that is often used for such forecasting is called a *learning curve*.

It is found that a person tends to require less time to perform a particular task if he or she has already done it a number of times before. In other words, the more often a person repeats a task, the more efficient he or she becomes and the less time is required to do it again. Thus as more units are produced on a production run, the time needed to produce each unit goes down.

Let $T = F(x)$ denote the time (for example, in work-hours) necessary for the production of the first x units. An increment Δx in production requires an increment ΔT in time, and the ratio $\Delta T / \Delta x$ is the average time per additional unit produced when the number produced changes from x to $x + \Delta x$. In the limit as $\Delta x \longrightarrow 0$, this ratio approaches the derivative $dT/dx = F'(x)$, which is the time required per additional unit when there is a small increase in production. As with other marginal rates, this quantity may be identified to a close approximation with the time necessary to produce the next unit, that is, the $(x + 1)$st unit.

If we set $F'(x) = f(x)$, the function commonly used for such a situation is of the form

$$f(x) = ax^b$$

where a and b are constants with $a > 0$ and $-1 \le b < 0$. The choice of ax^b with $-1 \le b < 0$ assures that the time required per unit declines as more and

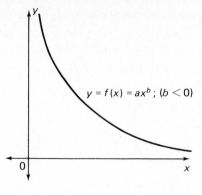

$y = f(x) = ax^b$; $(b < 0)$

FIGURE 17

more units are produced. (See Figure 17.) The graph of $f(x)$ is called a **learning curve**. In practice, the constants a and b would be determined from some preliminary production run or from past experience with similar products.

Provided that the improvement in efficiency or learning is regular enough, the learning curve—once it has been established—can be used to predict the total number of work-hour requirements in advance for future production. *The total number of work-hours ΔT required to produce units numbered $c + 1$ through d is given by $\Delta T = F(d) - F(c)$, that is,*

$$\Delta T = \int_c^d f(x)\, dx = \int_c^d ax^b\, dx.$$

EXAMPLE 1   After producing 1000 television sets, a manufacturing firm determines that its assembly plant is following a learning curve of the form

$$f(x) = 20x^{-0.152}$$

where $f(x)$ is the number of work-hours required to assemble the $(x + 1)$st set. Estimate the total number of work-hours required to assemble an additional 4000 television sets.

Solution   The total number of work-hours required to assemble an additional 4000 sets after the first 1000 sets is given by

$$\Delta T = \int_{1000}^{5000} f(x)\, dx = \int_{1000}^{5000} 20x^{-0.152}\, dx$$

$$= \left[20 \cdot \frac{x^{-0.152+1}}{(-0.152 + 1)} \right]_{1000}^{5000}$$

$$= \frac{20}{0.848}[(5000)^{0.848} - (1000)^{0.848}]$$

$$= 23.59(1370 - 350) = 24,060.$$

Profit Maximizing Over Time

There exist certain business operations such as mining and oil drilling that turn out to be nonprofitable after a certain period of time. In such operations, the rate of revenue $R'(t)$ (say dollars per month) can be very high at the beginning of the operation but can decrease as time passes because of depletion of the resource. That is, $R'(t)$ eventually becomes a decreasing function of time. On the other hand, the cost rate $C'(t)$ of the operation is small at the beginning but often increases as time passes because of increased maintenance, higher cost of extraction, and many other factors. The cost rate $C'(t)$ is therefore often an increasing function of time. In such operations, there comes a time when the cost rate of running the operation becomes more than the rate of revenue and the operation starts to lose money. The management of such an operation is faced with selecting a time at which to close it down that will result in the maximum profit being obtained.

Let $C(t)$, $R(t)$, and $P(t)$ denote the total cost, total revenue, and the total profit up to the time t (measured from the start of operation), respectively. Then

$$P(t) = R(t) - C(t)$$

and

$$P'(t) = R'(t) - C'(t).$$

The maximum total profit occurs when

$$P'(t) = 0 \quad \text{or} \quad R'(t) = C'(t).$$

In other words, the operation should run until the time t_1, at which $R'(t_1) = C'(t_1)$, that is, until the time at which the rate of revenue and the rate of cost are equal. The business operation should be closed down at time t_1. (See Figure 18.)

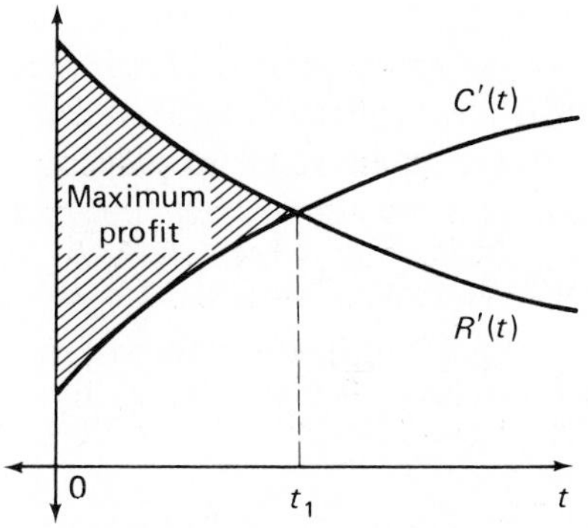

The total profit at time t_1 is given by

$$P(t_1) = \int_0^{t_1} P'(t)\, dt$$

$$= \int_0^{t_1} [R'(t) - C'(t)]\, dt.$$

This is the maximum profit that can be obtained and is clearly the area bounded by the graphs of $R'(t)$ and $C'(t)$ and lying between $t = 0$ and $t = t_1$.

FIGURE 18

Note Since $t = 0$ is the time at which the operation starts production, the total revenue $R(0)$ at that time is zero. In the above analysis, we have also assumed that the total cost $C(0)$ is also zero. This may not be the case in general because of fixed costs (that is, setup costs) which are incurred before production begins. Thus, in practice, we must subtract these fixed costs from the above expression for $P(t_1)$ in order to obtain the actual maximum profit.

EXAMPLE 2   The cost and the revenue rates for a certain mining operation are given by

$$C'(t) = 5 + 2t^{2/3} \quad \text{and} \quad R'(t) = 17 - t^{2/3}$$

where C and R are measured in millions of dollars and t is measured in years. Determine how long the operation should continue and find the total profit that can be earned during this period.

Solution   The optimal time t_1 that will result in maximum profit is the time at which the two rates (of cost and revenue) are equal. That is,

$$C'(t) = R'(t)$$
$$5 + 2t^{2/3} = 17 - t^{2/3}$$
$$3t^{2/3} = 17 - 5 = 12$$
$$t^{2/3} = 4$$
$$t = 4^{3/2} = 8.$$

Thus the operation should continue for $t_1 = 8$ years. The profit that can be earned during this period of 8 years is given by

$$P = \int_0^8 [R'(t) - C'(t)]\, dt$$

$$= \int_0^8 [17 - t^{2/3} - (5 + 2t^{2/3})]\, dt$$

$$= \int_0^8 (12 - 3t^{2/3})\, dt = \left[12t - 3\frac{t^{5/3}}{5/3}\right]_0^8$$

$$= 96 - \tfrac{9}{5}(32) = 38.2 \text{ (millions of dollars).}$$

Consumers' and Producers' Surplus

Let the demand curve be $p = f(x)$ for a certain commodity and let the supply curve for the same commodity be given by $p = g(x)$. Here x denotes the amount of the commodity that can be sold or supplied at a price p per unit. In general, the demand function $f(x)$ is a decreasing function indicating that the consumers will buy less if the price increases. On the other hand, the supply function $g(x)$ in general is an increasing function because the producers are willing to supply more if they get higher prices. The market equilibrium (x_0, p_0) is the point of intersection of the demand and supply curves. This means that at a price of p_0 per unit, the consumers are willing to buy and the producers are willing to sell the same number x_0 of units of the commodity. (See Figure 19.)

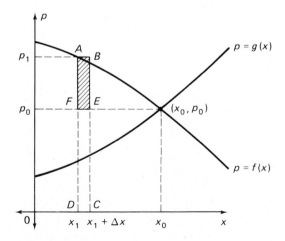

FIGURE 19

From the graph of the demand curve, it is clear that as the price increases, the demand decreases. This implies that there are some consumers who would be willing to buy the commodity at a higher price than the market equilibrium price p_0 that they actually have to pay. These consumers therefore save money as a result of the operation of the free marketplace.

Consider the quantity Δx of units that lie between x_1 and $x_1 + \Delta x$. The area $p_1 \Delta x$ of the rectangle $ABCD$ in the above figure can be interpreted as the total amount of money that the consumers would pay for these Δx units if the price were $p_1 = f(x_1)$ per unit. At the market equilibrium price p_0, the actual amount spent by the consumers on these Δx units is $p_0 \Delta x$. In other words, the consumers save an amount equal to $p_1 \Delta x - p_0 \Delta x = [f(x_1) - p_0] \Delta x$ on these units. This saving is equal to the area of the shaded rectangle $ABEF$ in Figure 19. If we divide the range from $x = 0$ to $x = x_0$ into a large number of intervals of length Δx, we obtain a similar result for each interval: the savings to consumers is equal to the area of a rectangle like $ABEF$ lying between the demand curve and the horizontal line $p = p_0$. Summing up all such savings from $x = 0$ to $x = x_0$, we obtain the total benefit (or savings) to the consumers. This is known as the **consumers' surplus** (C.S.) and is given by the area between the demand curve $p = f(x)$ and the horizontal line $p = p_0$. (See Figure 20.)

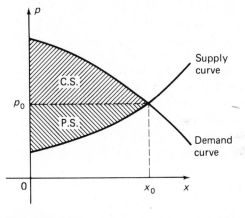

FIGURE 20

The consumers' surplus is given by the definite integral

$$\text{C.S.} = \int_0^{x_0} [f(x) - p_0] \, dx.$$

Similarly, in a free market there are also producers who would be willing to sell the commodity at a price lower than the market price p_0 that the consumers actually pay. In such a situation, the producers also benefit; this benefit to the producers is called the **producers' surplus** (P.S.).

Using similar reasoning to that above, we can show that the total gain to producers, or the producers' surplus (P.S.), is given by

$$\text{P.S.} = \int_0^{x_0} [p_0 - g(x)] \, dx$$

where $p = g(x)$ is the supply curve. Geometrically, the producers' surplus is the area between the supply curve and the line $p = p_0$ (see Figure 20).

EXAMPLE 3 The supply and demand functions for a certain product are given by

$$S: \quad p = g(x) = 52 + 2x \tag{1}$$
$$D: \quad p = f(x) = 100 - x^2. \tag{2}$$

Determine the consumers' and producers' surplus, assuming that market equilibrium has been established.

Solution The equilibrium point (x_0, p_0) is obtained by solving the supply and demand equations simultaneously for x and p. Equating the two values of p in Equations (1) and (2), we have

$$52 + 2x = 100 - x^2$$
$$x^2 + 2x - 48 = 0$$
$$(x - 6)(x + 8) = 0$$

which gives $x = 6$ or $x = -8$. Since the negative value of x is inadmissible, we have $x = 6$. Putting $x = 6$ in Equation (1), we get $p = 52 + 12 = 64$. Thus we have the equilibrium values $x_0 = 6$ and $p_0 = 64$. The consumers' surplus is now given by

$$\text{C.S.} = \int_0^{x_0} [f(x) - p_0] \, dx$$
$$= \int_0^6 [(100 - x^2) - 64] \, dx$$
$$= \left[36x - \frac{x^3}{3} \right]_0^6 = 216 - \frac{216}{3} = 144.$$

The producers' surplus is given by

$$\text{P.S.} = \int_0^{x_0} [p_0 - g(x)] \, dx$$
$$= \int_0^6 [64 - (52 + 2x)] \, dx$$
$$= \left[12x - x^2 \right]_0^6 = 72 - 36 = 36.$$

EXERCISES 3

1. The income distribution of a certain country is given by the Lorentz curve $y = \frac{19}{20}x^2 + \frac{1}{20}x$, where x is the proportion of income recipients and y the proportion of total income received.

   a. What proportion of total income is received by the poorest 20% of the people?

   b. Find the coefficient of inequality for the Lorentz curve.

2. Repeat Exercise 1 for the Lorentz curve $y = 0.94x^2 + 0.06x$.

3. After painting the first 40 cars, an auto painting shop estimates that the learning curve is of the form $f(x) = 10x^{-0.25}$. Find the total number of work-hours that will be required to paint an additional 60 cars.

4. X & Y Sound manufactures radios on an assembly line. It is known that the first 100 radios (1 unit) took a total time of 150 work-hours and for each additional unit of 100 radios, less time was required according to the learning curve $f(x) = 150x^{-0.2}$, where $f(x)$ is the number of work-hours required to assemble the $(x + 1)$st unit. How many work-hours will be required to assemble 5 units (that is, 500 radios) after the first 5 units have been assembled?

5. Murphy Electronics manufactures electronic calculators on its assembly line. The first 50 calculators took 70 hours, and for each additional unit of 50 calculators, less time was required according to the learning curve $f(x) = 70x^{-0.32}$. How much time will be required to assemble 500 calculators after the first 200 calculators have been assembled?

6. Assuming there is 20% improvement, every time the production doubles (for example the sixth unit requires 80% of the time taken by the third unit, the twentieth unit requires 80% of the time taken by the tenth unit and so on) find the value of the constant b for the learning curve $f(x) = ax^b$.

7. The revenue and cost rates for an oil drilling operation are given by

$$R'(t) = 14 - t^{1/2} \quad \text{and} \quad C'(t) = 2 + 3t^{1/2}$$

respectively, where the time t is measured in years and R and C are measured in millions of dollars. How long should the drilling be continued to obtain the maximum profit? What is this maximum profit?

8. The revenue and cost rates for a certain mining operation are given by

$$R'(t) = 10 - 2t^{1/3} \quad \text{and} \quad C'(t) = 2 + 2t^{1/3}$$

respectively, where t is measured in years and R and C are measured in millions of dollars. Find how long the operation can be continued for a maximum profit. What is the amount of maximum profit, assuming that the fixed costs for initial operation are $3 million?

(9–14) Find the consumers' and producers' surplus for a product whose demand and supply functions are given below. (Assume that the market equilibrium has been established.)

9. $D: \quad p = 15 - 2x$
     $S: \quad p = 3 + x$

10. $D: \quad p = 17 - 0.5x$
      $S: \quad p = 5 + 0.3x$

11. $D: \quad p = 1200 - 1.5x^2$
     $S: \quad p = 200 + x^2$

12. $D: \quad p = 120 - x^2$
      $S: \quad p = 32 + 3x$

13. $D: \quad p = \dfrac{280}{x + 2}$
     $S: \quad p = 20 + 2.5x$

14. $D: \quad p = \dfrac{370}{x + 6}$
      $S: \quad p = 3.8 + 0.2x$

*15. If the demand curve is $p = f(x)$, show that $(d/dx_0)(\text{C.S.}) = -x_0 f'(x_0)$. (*Hint:* If $x_0 \rightarrow x_0 + \Delta x_0$, then $\Delta(\text{C.S.}) \approx x_0(-\Delta p_0)$.) If the supply curve is $p = g(x)$, show that

$$(d/dx_0)(\text{P.S.}) = x_0 g'(x_0).$$

Show also that

$$\text{C.S.} = -\int_0^{x_0} xf'(x)\,dx \quad \text{and} \quad \text{P.S.} = \int_0^{x_0} xg'(x)\,dx.$$

Using integration by parts, obtain the expressions for C.S. and P.S. given in the text.

16. Show that

$$\text{P.S.} = \int_0^{p_0} x\,dp \quad \text{and} \quad \text{C.S.} = \int_{p_0}^{p_m} x\,dp$$

where p_m is the price at which the demand falls to zero.

*17. In a business enterprise in which the capital assets are considered fixed, let $P(x)$ be the dollar value of the output when x work-hours of labor are employed per week. The derivate $P'(x)$ is called the **marginal productivity of labor**. If w is the wage rate (dollars per work-hour), the profit function is given by $P(x) - wx$ (ignoring overhead). Show that it makes sense to hire x_0 work-hours where x_0 is the solution of the equation $P'(x_0) = w$. Show that the profit is then given by

$$\int_0^{x_0} [P'(x) - P'(x_0)]\,dx$$

and interpret this as an appropriate area. This quantity is called the **economic rent** of the given capital assets. Determine the economic rent if the marginal productivity is given by $P'(x) = 120(x + 400)^{-1/2}$, when the wage rate is: (a) \$3 per hour; (b) \$4 per hour; (c) \$5 per hour.

18. If $A(t)$ is the amount of capital stock in a business enterprise at time t and $I(t)$ is the rate of investment, then $dA/dt = I$. Determine the increase in capital stock between $t = 4$ and $t = 9$ if the rate of investment is given by $I(t) = 4 + \sqrt{t}$ (thousands of dollars per year).

17-4 DIFFERENTIAL EQUATIONS (OPTIONAL SECTION)

There are many situations in business and economics where the mathematical formulation of a problem results in an equation that involves the derivative of an unknown function. Consider, for example, the following situation.

An amount of capital A_0 is invested at the nominal rate of interest R percent per annum where the investment is subject to a continuous growth at every instant, that is, the interest on the investment is compounded continuously. (See Section 4 of Chapter 6.) Suppose we wish to determine the total value of the investment $A(t)$ at any time t. We choose $t = 0$ to correspond to the time at which the initial investment is made. In other words, $A(0) = A_0$.

To formulate this problem mathematically, we first calculate the value of the investment $A(t)$ when the interest is compounded n times a year. If Δt denotes the length of each interest period and there are n interest periods in each year, then $n \cdot \Delta t = 1$ or $\Delta t = 1/n$ years. If $A(t)$ and $A(t + \Delta t)$ are the values of the investment at times t and $t + \Delta t$, then the interest earned during the interval of time from t to $t + \Delta t$ is given by the difference

$$A(t + \Delta t) - A(t) = \Delta A.$$

This interest ΔA is earned on the principal sum, which was $A(t)$ at the beginning of the given time interval.

But if the nominal annual rate of interest is R percent, with n periods per year, then the percentage interest during one period is R/n. So the interest during the interval Δt is also equal to

$$\text{(Principal)} \times \text{(Percentage Interest)}/100 = A(t)(R/100n) = A(t)r \, \Delta t$$

where $r = R/100$ and $\Delta t = 1/n$. Therefore

$$\Delta A = rA \, \Delta t$$

or

$$\frac{\Delta A}{\Delta t} = rA.$$

If the interest is to be compounded continuously, we must increase the number of interest periods in a year indefinitely, that is, we must take the limit as $n \longrightarrow \infty$. As $n \longrightarrow \infty$, $\Delta t = 1/n \longrightarrow 0$ and $\Delta A/\Delta t \longrightarrow dA/dt$. The above equation then becomes

$$\frac{dA}{dt} = rA. \tag{1}$$

Now dA/dt represents the rate of change in the value of investment at any time t. The above equation therefore states that the *rate of growth of the investment is proportional to the value of the investment at time t when the interest is compounded continuously.*

The value of the investment $A(t)$ at any time t must satisfy Equation (1), which involves the derivative of the unknown function $A(t)$. This equation is an example of what are known as *differential equations.* Let us now give some formal definitions.

DEFINITION Let $y = f(t)$ be a differentiable function of the independent variable t and let y', y'', ..., $y^{(n)}$ denote the derivatives of y with respect to t of orders up to and including n. Then a **differential equation of order n** for the function y is an equation relating the variables $t, y, y', \ldots, y^{(n)}$. The **order** n is the order of the highest derivative that occurs in the differential equation.

EXAMPLE 1 (a) $dy/dt = ry$ is a first-order differential equation. (It is the same as Equation (1).)

(b) $d^2y/dt^2 - e^{ty} = 0$ is a second-order differential equation.

(c) $d^4y/dt^4 - t^2(d^3y/dt^3) = t^2 + 1$ is a fourth-order differential equation.

DEFINITION A differential equation is said to be **linear** if the dependent variable y and all of its derivatives appear linearly in the equation. Otherwise it is said to be a **nonlinear** differential equation.

EXAMPLE 2   (a) In Example 1, the differential equations in parts (a) and (c) are linear. Part (b) is not linear, however, because y appears in the term e^{ty}, which is not a linear function of y.

(b) $d^2y/dt^2 = 3(dy/dt)^2$ is a nonlinear, second-order differential equation.

(c) $d^2y/dt^2 = 3t^2(dy/dt)$ is a linear, second-order differential equation. Note that y and its derivatives appear linearly. The fact that the independent variable t occurs as the factor t^2 does not make the equation nonlinear.

DEFINITION   A function $y(t)$ is said to be a **solution** of a differential equation if, upon substituting $y(t)$ and its derivatives into the differential equation, this equation is satisfied for all values of t.

EXAMPLE 3   (a) The function $y = t^2$ is a solution of the differential equation $t(dy/dt) - 2y = 0$. This is so because $dy/dt = 2t$ and so

$$t\frac{dy}{dt} = t \cdot 2t = 2t^2 = 2y.$$

(b) The function $y = e^{kt}$, where k is a constant, is a solution of the differential equation $d^2y/dt^2 - k^2y = 0$ since

$$\frac{dy}{dt} = ke^{kt} \quad \text{and} \quad \frac{d^2y}{dt^2} = k^2e^{kt} = k^2y.$$

(c) The function $y = 2 \ln t$ is a solution of the differential equation $d^2y/dt^2 + \frac{1}{2}(dy/dt)^2 = 0$.

We have

$$\frac{dy}{dt} = \frac{2}{t} \quad \text{and} \quad \frac{d^2y}{dt^2} = -\frac{2}{t^2},$$

and so

$$\frac{d^2y}{dt^2} + \frac{1}{2}\left(\frac{dy}{dt}\right)^2 = -\frac{2}{t^2} + \frac{1}{2}\left(\frac{2}{t}\right)^2 = 0.$$

In this section, we shall discuss only the solutions of first-order differential equations that are of the *separable variables* type, that is, where the terms containing the dependent variable can be written on one side of the equation and the terms containing the independent variable on the other side.

We begin by solving the differential equation that resulted from the continued growth of an investment.

EXAMPLE 4   Solve the differential equation

$$\frac{dA}{dt} = rA,$$

where r is a constant and $A(0) = A_0$.

Solution   The given equation can be written as

$$\frac{dA}{A} = r \, dt$$

where we have multiplied both sides by the differential dt and divided by A. The purpose of doing this is to put all the A's on one side of the equation and all the t's on the other. Integrating both sides, we get

$$\int \frac{1}{A}\, dA = \int r\, dt.$$

Thus $\ln A = rt + C_1$ (because $A > 0$) where C_1 is the constant of integration. Solving for A, we get

$$A = e^{rt+C_1} = e^{C_1} \cdot e^{rt} = Ce^{rt} \tag{2}$$

where $C = e^{C_1}$ is another constant. The value of C can be determined by making use of the additional fact that $A(0) = A_0$. Thus, putting $t = 0$ in Equation (2),

$$A_0 = A(0) = Ce^{r(0)} = C.$$

Thus from Equation (2),

$$A(t) = A_0 e^{rt}.$$

In other words, when the interest is being compounded continuously, the investment grows exponentially. This result agrees with that found earlier in Section 4 of Chapter 6.

There are also many situations in the natural sciences that result in the same differential equation as that of continuous growth of an investment. For example: The rate of growth of a population at any time is in many cases proportional to the size of the population at that time; the rate of decay of a radioactive substance is proportional to the amount of substance present.

EXAMPLE 5   The population of the United States was 75 million in 1900, and in 1950 it was 150 million. Assuming that the growth rate is at any time proportional to the population size, find the population size at a general time t. (Take 1900 as $t = 0$.) What is the projected population in 1980 on the basis of this solution?

Solution   If $P(t)$ denotes the population size at any time t, then we are given that the growth rate dP/dt is proportional to P. That is,

$$\frac{dP}{dt} = kP$$

where k is the constant of proportionality. As in the previous example, the solution is of the exponential form,

$$P(t) = Ce^{kt} \tag{3}$$

where C is a constant.

At $t = 0$ (that is, in 1900), $P(0) = 75 \times 10^6$. Using this value in Equation (3), we get

$$P(0) = 75 \times 10^6 = Ce^0 = C$$

or

$$C = 75 \times 10^6.$$

Also, when $t = 50$ (in 1950), $P(50) = 150 \times 10^6$. Using this in Equation (3), we find

$$P(50) = Ce^{k(50)}$$

or

$$150 \times 10^6 = 75 \times 10^6 \cdot e^{50k}$$

where we have used the value of C found above. It follows that

$$2 = e^{50k}.$$

We take natural logarithms of both sides, and solve for k.

$$50k = \ln 2$$

$$k = \frac{\ln 2}{50} = \frac{0.6931}{50} = 0.01386$$

Thus the population at time t is given by

$$P(t) = 75 \times 10^6 \cdot e^{(0.01386)t}.$$

The year 1980 corresponds to $t = 80$, and the projected population then is

$$P(80) = 75 \times 10^6 \cdot e^{(0.01386)(80)}$$

$$= 75 \times 10^6 \cdot e^{1.109}$$

$$= 75 \times 10^6 (3.03) = 227 \times 10^6.$$

(As discussed in Chapter 6, such exponential growth models are applicable for populations only over the short term.)

EXAMPLE 6   Solve the differential equation

$$e^x \frac{dy}{dx} = y^2.$$

Solution   Note that the independent variable is denoted by x, not t. The given equation can be written as

$$\frac{1}{y^2}\, dy = \frac{1}{e^x}\, dx$$

where we have separated all the terms containing the dependent variable y on the left and the terms containing the independent variable x on the right. Integrating both sides, we get

$$\int \frac{1}{y^2}\, dy = \int \frac{1}{e^x}\, dx$$

$$\int y^{-2}\, dy = \int e^{-x}\, dx.$$

Therefore

$$\frac{y^{-1}}{-1} = \frac{e^{-x}}{-1} + C$$

or

$$\frac{1}{y} = e^{-x} - C$$

where C is the constant of integration. Solving for y, the solution is

$$y = \frac{1}{e^{-x} - C} = \frac{e^x}{1 - Ce^x}. \tag{4}$$

The solution in Example 6, Equation (4), satisfies the given differential equation for all values of the unknown constant C, and so this solution is called the **general solution**. The general solution of any first-order differential equation (with few exceptions that occur in certain unusual cases) always involves one unknown constant. In order to determine this constant, we require certain additional information over and above the differential equation itself. For example, in Example 4, the growing investment $A(t)$ satisfied the differential equation $dA/dt = rA$, where r was given, and we were told in addition that at $t = 0$, A had some given value A_0. This extra piece of information enabled us to find the value of C, the unknown constant that occurred in the solution, in terms of A_0. The condition that $A(0) = A_0$ is called an **initial condition** on the function $A(t)$.

In Example 6, let us suppose that in addition to the differential equation, we are also given the initial condition that $y = \frac{1}{2}$ when $x = 0$. Using the information in Equation (4), we have

$$\frac{1}{2} = \frac{e^0}{(1 - Ce^0)} = \frac{1}{1 - C}.$$

It follows that $C = -1$. Using this value of C in Equation (4), we get

$$y = \frac{e^x}{(1 + e^x)}$$

This provides the **particular solution** of the given differential equation which satisfies the initial condition.

EXAMPLE 7   If the elasticity of demand for a certain commodity is $-\frac{1}{2}$, determine the demand function $p = f(x)$, where x units are demanded at a price p per unit.

Solution   We know that the elasticity of demand η is given by the formula

$$\eta = \frac{p/x}{dp/dx}.$$

(See Section 3 of Chapter 15.) Since $\eta = -\frac{1}{2}$, the above equation becomes

$$-\frac{1}{2} = \frac{p/x}{dp/dx} \quad \text{or} \quad \frac{dp}{dx} = -\frac{2p}{x}.$$

Separating the variables, we obtain

$$\frac{1}{p} dp = -\frac{2}{x} dx.$$

Integrating both sides, we get

$$\int \frac{1}{p} dp = -\int \frac{2}{x} dx.$$

That is, $\ln p = -2 \ln x + C_1$, where C_1 is the constant of integration (since

$p > 0$, $x > 0$). That is, $\ln(px^2) = C_1$, which gives $px^2 = e^{C_1} = C$ (where C is just another constant). Thus the demand relation is

$$p = C/x^2$$

where C is some positive constant. Without some additional information, C must remain unknown.

EXERCISES 4

(1–4)   Show that the functions given below satisfy the stated differential equations.

1. $y = t^{-4}$; $t\, dy/dt + 4y = 0$

2. $y = te^{-t}$; $t\, dy/dt + ty = y$

3. $y = t \ln t$; $t^2\, d^2y/dt^2 - t\, dy/dt + y = 0$

4. $y = t^3 + 2\sqrt{t}$; $2t^2\, d^2y/dt^2 - 5t\, dy/dt + 3y = 0$

(5–16)   Find the general solution of the following differential equations.

5. $dy/dt = t^2 + 1/t$	6. $dy/dx = xe^x$	7. $dy/dt - 4y = 0$
8. $2\, dy/dt + y = 0$	9. $dy/dt - 2y = 1$	10. $3\, dy/dt + y = 2$
11. $dy/dx = xy$	12. $dy/dx = x + xy$	13. $dy/dt = y(y - 1)$
14. $dy/dt + y^2 = 4$	15. $t\, dy/dt + ty = y$	16. $t\, dy/dt - ty = 2y$

(17–22)   Find the solutions of the following differential equations that satisfy the given initial conditions.

17. $dy/dt + 2y = 0$; $y = 1$ when $t = 1$.

18. $2\, dy/dt - y = 0$; $y = 3$ when $t = \frac{1}{4}$.

19. $dy/dx = 2xy$; $y = 1$ when $x = 0$.

20. $dy/dx = y(y - 1)$, $y > 1$; $y = 2$ when $x = 0$.

21. $dy/dt = te^{t+y}$; $y = 0$ when $t = 0$.

22. $du/dy = e^{u-y}$; $u = 0$ when $y = 0$.

23. The elasticity of demand for a certain commodity is $\eta = -\frac{2}{3}$. Determine the demand relation $p = f(x)$ if $p = 2$ when $x = 4$.

24. The elasticity of demand for a certain commodity is given by $\eta = -2$. Determine the demand function $p = f(x)$ if $p = \frac{1}{2}$ when $x = 4$.

25. The elasticity of demand for a certain commodity is given by $\eta = (x - 200)/x$. Determine the demand function $p = f(x)$ if $0 < x < 200$ and $p = 5$ when $x = 190$.

26. The elasticity of demand is $\eta = p/(p - 10)$. Determine the demand function $p = f(x)$ if $0 < p < 10$ and $p = 7$ when $x = 15$.

27. An initial investment of \$10,000 is growing continuously at a nominal annual rate of interest of 5%.

   a.   Find the value of the investment at any time t.

   b.   What is the value of the investment after 8 years?

   c.   After how many years will the values of the investment be \$20,000?

28. A stock of initial value $2000 is growing continuously at a constant rate of 6% growth per annum.

    a. Determine the value of the stock after t years.

    b. After how long will the stock be worth $3000?

29. Assume that the proportional growth rate $y'(t)/y(t)$ of the human population of the earth is constant. The population in 1930 was 2 billion and in 1975 was 4 billion. Taking 1930 to be $t = 0$, determine the population $y(t)$ of the earth at time t. According to this model, what should the population have been in 1960?

*30. A population is growing according to the differential equation $dy/dt = 0.1y(1 - 10^{-6}y)$ when t is measured in years. How many years does it take the population to increase from an initial size of 10^5 to a size of 5×10^5? (This differential equation is an example of the logistic equation. See also Section 4 of Chapter 6.)

REVIEW EXERCISES FOR CHAPTER 17

1. State whether each of the following is true or false. Replace each false statement by a corresponding true statement.

    a. If $f(x)$ is continuous in $a \le x \le b$, then $\int_a^b f(x)\,dx$ represents the area bounded by the curve $y = f(x)$, the x-axis, and the lines $x = a$ and $x = b$.

    b. If $\int_a^b f(x)\,dx = \int_b^a f(x)\,dx$, then $\int_a^b f(x)\,dx = 0$.

    c. $\dfrac{d}{dx}\left[\displaystyle\int_a^x f(t)\,dt\right] = f'(x).$

    d. $\dfrac{d}{dx}\left[\displaystyle\int_a^b f(x)\,dx\right] = \displaystyle\int_a^b \dfrac{d}{dx}[f(x)]\,dx.$

    e. If $F(x)$ is an antiderivative of $f(x)$, then $\dfrac{d}{dx}\left[\displaystyle\int_a^x f(t)\,dt\right] = F'(x).$

    f. $\int_a^b f(x)\,dx$ is a function of x.

    g. $\int_a^b f(x)\,dx$ and $\int_a^b f(t)\,dt$ are different from one another.

    h. The function $y = e^{kt}$ is a solution of the differential equation $y(d^2y/dt^2) = (dy/dt)^2$ for all values of k.

    i. The differential equation $dy/dt = y + t$ may be solved by separation of variables.

    j. The differential equation $2(dy/dt)^2 = t^2\,dy/dt + 2$ is of second order.

    k. The solution of the differential equation $dy/dt = yt^2$ may be obtained as follows:

$$y = \int yt^2 \, dt = y \int t^2 \, dt = \tfrac{1}{3} yt^3 + C.$$

Therefore $y(1 - \tfrac{1}{3}t^3) = C$ or $y = C(1 - t^3/3)^{-1}$.

2. Prove that $\displaystyle\int_a^{ab} \frac{1}{t} \, dt = \int_1^b \frac{1}{t} \, dt.$

(3–5) Find the area bounded by $y = f(x)$, the x-axis, and the lines $x = a$ and $x = b$ where $f(x)$, a, and b have the given values.

3. $f(x) = \ln x; \quad a = 1, b = 2$ 4. $f(x) = e^x; \quad a = -2, b = 2$

5. $f(x) = 1/x^2; \quad a = 1, b = 3$

6. Find the area bounded by the two curves $y = x^2$ and $y = \sqrt{x}$.

7. Find the area in the first quadrant bounded by $y = x^3$, $y = 2 - x^2$, and $x = 0$.

8. The marginal cost of producing the xth unit of a certain commodity is $6 - 0.02x$. Find the change in the total cost of production if the production level changes from 150 to 200.

9. The marginal price of a commodity is given by $p'(x) = 15 - x$. Find the total change in price per unit if the demand increases from $x = 10$ to $x = 15$.

10. Find the coefficient of inequality for the income distribution given by the Lorentz curve $y = \tfrac{14}{15}x^2 + \tfrac{1}{15}x$, where x is the cumulative proportion of income recipients and y the cumulative proportion of national income.

11. After observing the first 400 units of its product, a firm determined that the labor time required to assemble the $(x + 1)$st unit was $f(x) = 500x^{-1/2}$. Find the total number of hours of labor required to produce an additional 500 units.

12. The marginal cost and marginal revenue functions of a firm are $C'(x) = 5 + (5 - x)^2$ and $R'(x) = 37 - 4x$, respectively, where x denotes the number of units produced. The fixed costs are 25.

     a. Find the level of production which will maximize the profits of the firm.

     b. Find the total profit of the firm at this production level.

     c. Find the profit if the production level is increased by 2 units beyond the maximum profit level output.

13. Find the consumers' surplus and producers' surplus if the demand function is $p = 25 - 3x$ and the supply function is $p = 5 + 0.5x^2$.

(14–19) Solve the following differential equations.

14. $dy/dt = 2y(y - 1), \quad y > 1$ 15. $dy/dx = xe^{x-y}$

16. $dy/dx = x^2/y$

17. $dy/dx = 4x\sqrt{y} + 2\sqrt{y}\, e^x, \quad x = 0$ when $y = 0$

18. $dy/dt = y/(1 - y), \quad y = \tfrac{1}{2}$ when $t = 0$

19. $dy/dt + y(2 - y) = 0, \quad y > 2$

20. The proportional growth rate $y'(t)/y(t)$ of a certain firm's asset value is given by $\tfrac{1}{3}\sqrt[3]{t}$ and its initial net worth at $t = 0$ was \$50,000. (t is measured in years).

     a. Determine the net worth $y(t)$ of the firm at any time t.

     b. After how many years will the firm be worth \$600,000?

21. An initial investment of P dollars is growing continuously at an annual rate of 6%. If the investment is worth \$26,997 after 5 years, find P.

22. The Pacific Dairy Farm finds that its marginal profits are y dollars per liter of milk when the total production is x liters of milk, where

$$y = \frac{5,000,000 \ln (x + 50)}{(x + 50)^3}.$$

The farm breaks even (that is, has zero profit) when $x = 200$. If the farm produces 450 liters of milk each day, calculate the total daily profits of the farm.

23. The cost and revenue rates for an oil drilling operation are given by $C'(t) = 9 + 2t^{1/2}$ and $R'(t) = 19 - 3t^{1/2}$, where t is measured in years and R and C are measured in millions of dollars. How long should the drilling be continued? What will be the maximum profit?

24. Repeat Exercise 23, when $C'(t) = 4 + 3t^{2/3}$ and $R'(t) = 20 - t^{2/3}$.

SEVERAL VARIABLES

 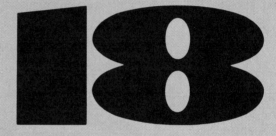

18-1 FUNCTIONS AND DOMAINS

So far, we have restricted our attention to cases in which the dependent variable is a function of a single independent variable, $y = f(x)$. However, in many—perhaps most—applications, we come across situations in which one quantity depends not on just one other variable but on several variables.

EXAMPLE 1 (a) Consider a rectangle of length x and width y. Its area A is given by the product of length and width, or

$$A = xy.$$

The variable A depends on the two variables x and y.

(b) The demand, or total sales volume, for a product depends on the price at which it is offered for sale. However, in many cases the sales volume also depends on additional factors such as the amount spent by the manufacturer on advertising the product and the prices of competing products.

(c) The balance of payments of any nation is a function of a large number of variables. Interest rates in the country will affect the amount of foreign investment that flows in. The exchange rate of the national currency will affect the prices of its goods and hence will determine the volume of exports and also of imports. Average wage rates will also affect the prices of exports and therefore the volume. The amount of existing foreign investment in the nation will affect the profits taken out each year. Even the weather can have a powerful effect on the balance of payments if tourism plays a large role in the economy, or if the economy depends substantially on some agricultural crop.

In cases such as these, we need to study functions of several independent variables. For most of this chapter, we shall consider the case of two independent variables, and usually we shall use x any y to stand for them. The generalization to three or more independent variables is in most (but not all) respects quite straightfoward. The dependent variable will usually be denoted by z, and we use the notation $z = f(x, y)$ to indicate that z is a function of both x and y.

We first give a formal definition of a function of two variables.

DEFINITION Let D be a set of pairs of real numbers (x, y), and let f be a rule that specifies a unique real number for each pair (x, y) in D. Then we say that f is a **function of the two variables** x and y and the set D is the **domain** of f. The value of f at the pair (x, y) is denoted by $f(x, y)$ and the set of all of these values is called the **range** of f.

EXAMPLE 2   If $f(x, y) = 2x + y$, calculate the value of f at the pair $(1, 2)$. Find the domain of f.

Solution   The value of a function of two variables is obtained simply by substituting the given values of x and y into the expression for $f(x, y)$:

$$f(1, 2) = 2(1) + 2 = 4.$$

In this case, the value of f is a well-defined real number for all real values of x and y, so that the domain is the set of all pairs (x, y) of real numbers.

The domain D of a function of two variables can be viewed as a subset of points in the xy-plane. In Example 2 all pairs of real numbers (x, y) belong to the domain, so that from a geometric viewpoint, we can say that the domain consists of the whole xy-plane. The range of a function of two variables is a subset of the real numbers, just as it is for a function of one variable.

EXAMPLE 3   Given $f(x, y) = \sqrt{4 - x^2 - y^2}$, calculate $f(0, 2)$, $f(1, -1)$, and $f(1, 2)$. Find the domain of f and represent it graphically.

Solution   Substituting the given values of x and y, we obtain the following values.

$$f(0, 2) = \sqrt{4 - 0^2 - 2^2} = \sqrt{0} = 0$$

$$f(1, -1) = \sqrt{4 - 1^2 - (-1)^2} = \sqrt{2}$$

$$f(1, 2) = \sqrt{4 - 1^2 - 2^2} = \sqrt{-1} \qquad \text{(not defined)}$$

The pair $(1, 2)$ therefore does not belong to the domain of f.

In order for $f(x, y)$ to be a well-defined real number, the quantity under the radical sign must be nonnegative. Thus

$$4 - x^2 - y^2 \geq 0$$
$$x^2 + y^2 \leq 4.$$

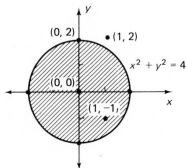

FIGURE 1

The domain of f therefore consists of those points (x, y) such that $x^2 + y^2 \leq 4$.

Geometrically, $x^2 + y^2 = 4$ is the equation of a circle centered at the origin with radius 2, and the inequality $x^2 + y^2 \leq 4$ holds at points inside and on this circle. These points form the domain D. (See Figure 1.) The point $(1, 2)$ lies outside the circle, consistent with our earlier finding that $f(1, 2)$ does not exist.

EXAMPLE 4   A firm produces two products, A and B. The cost of material and labor is $4 for each unit of product A and $7 for each unit of B. The fixed costs are $1500 per week. Express the weekly cost C in terms of the units of A and B produced each week.

Solution   If x units of the product A and y units of product B are produced each week, then the labor and material costs for the two types of products are $4x$ and $7y$ dollars, respectively. Thus the cost C (in dollars) is given by

$$C = \text{Labor and Material Costs} + \text{Fixed Costs}$$
$$= 4x + 7y + 1500.$$

C is a function of x and y.

Now let us consider the generalization of the preceding ideas to functions of more than two variables. When there are three independent variables, it is usual to denote them by x, y, and z, and to denote the dependent variable by w. The function consists of a rule that assigns a real number to each set of three values (x, y, z) of the independent variables. We write the value as $w = f(x, y, z)$.

EXAMPLE 5   If

$$f(x, y, z) = \frac{\sqrt{9 - x^2 - y^2}}{x + z}$$

evaluate $f(1, -1, 4)$ and $f(-1, 2, 1)$. Find the domain of f.

Solution   The value of f at any given (x, y, z) is obtained by substituting the given values of x, y, and z into the algebraic expression that defines f.

$$f(1, -1, 4) = \frac{\sqrt{9 - 1^2 - (-1)^2}}{1 + 4} = \frac{\sqrt{7}}{5}$$

$$f(-1, 2, 1) = \frac{\sqrt{9 - (-1)^2 - 2^2}}{-1 + 1} = \frac{\sqrt{4}}{0} \qquad \text{(not defined)}$$

We see that the point $(-1, 2, 1)$ does not belong to the domain of f.

For $f(x, y, z)$ to be well-defined, it is necessary that the quantity under the radical sign be nonnegative and also that the denominator of f be nonzero. Thus we have the conditions $9 - x^2 - y^2 \geq 0$, or $x^2 + y^2 \leq 9$, and $x + z \neq 0$. Using set notation, we may write the domain as

$$D = \{(x, y, z) \mid x^2 + y^2 \leq 9, \quad x + z \neq 0\}.$$

When more than three independent variables occur, it is common to use subscript notation to denote them rather than to introduce new letters. Thus, if there are n independent variables, we would denote them by $x_1, x_2, x_3, \ldots, x_n$. Using z as the dependent variable, we would denote a function of the n variables by $z = f(x_1, x_2, \ldots, x_n)$. Subscript notation is also frequently used for functions of two or three variables; for example, we might write $w = f(x_1, x_2, x_3)$ instead of $w = f(x, y, z)$.

EXAMPLE 6   If

$$z = x_1^2 + e^{x_1 + x_2} + (2x_1 + x_4)^{-1}\sqrt{x_2^2 + x_3^2},$$

evaluate z at the point $(3, -3, 4, -5)$.

Solution   By substituting $x_1 = 3$, $x_2 = -3$, $x_3 = 4$, and $x_4 = -5$ into the expression for z, we find

$$z = 3^2 + e^{3 + (-3)} + [2(3) + (-5)]^{-1}\sqrt{(-3)^2 + 4^2}$$
$$= 9 + e^0 + (6 - 5)^{-1}\sqrt{9 + 16}$$
$$= 9 + 1 + \tfrac{5}{1} = 15.$$

We have seen how the graph of a function of a single variable helps us to visualize its important features, such as where it is increasing or decreasing, where it is concave up or down, where it is maximum and minimum, and so on. To sketch the graph of $z = f(x, y)$, a function of two variables, we need coordinates in three dimensions, one for each of the variables x, y, and z.

In three dimensions, the x-, y- and z-axes are constructed at right angles to one another, as shown in Figure 2. Each pair of axes determines a plane; for example, the x-axis and y-axis determine the xy-plane, the x-axis and z-axis determine the xz-plane, and so on. On the xy-plane, the third coordinate z is equal to zero, and the coordinates x and y are used in the usual way to plot the positions of points in that plane. In Figure 2, the points (2, 4, 0) and (−3, 2, 0) are plotted in order to demonstrate this procedure.

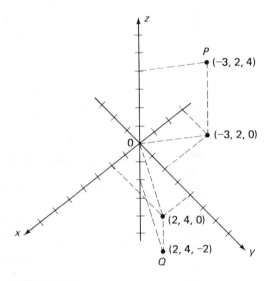

FIGURE 2

In order to plot the position of a general point (x, y, z) for which $z \neq 0$, we first plot the point $(x, y, 0)$ in the xy-plane and then move from this point parallel to the z-axis according to the given value of the z-coordinate. For example, when plotting (−3, 2, 4), we first plot (−3, 2, 0), as in Figure 2 and then move a distance of 4 units in the direction of the positive z-axis to the point P. In plotting the point (2, 4, −2), we first plot (2, 4, 0) in the xy-plane and then move 2 units parallel to the negative z-axis to the point Q.

It is often convenient to think of the xy-plane as being horizontal and the z-axis as pointing vertically upward. The negative z-axis then points downward.

All points in the xy-plane satisfy the condition $z = 0$. Correspondingly, all points in the xz-plane satisfy the condition $y = 0$ and all points in the yz-plane satisfy the condition $x = 0$. On the z-axis, both x and y are zero. Correspondingly, on the x-axis, $y = z = 0$, and on the y-axis, $x = z = 0$.

EXAMPLE 7   Plot the points $(0, 2, 4)$, $(3, 0, -2)$, $(0, 0, 5)$, and $(0, -3, 0)$.

Solution   The points are plotted in Figure 3. Note that the four points lie, respectively, in the yz-plane, in the xz-plane, on the z-axis, and on the y-axis.

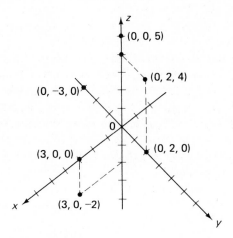

FIGURE 3

Let $z = f(x, y)$ be a function of two variables. Its domain D consists of the set of points in the xy-plane at which the function is defined. For any point (x, y) in D, we can calculate the corresponding value of $z = f(x, y)$ and plot the point (x, y, z) using three-dimensional coordinates. By doing this for every point (x, y) in D, we obtain a set of points (x, y, z) that form a surface in three dimensions. There is one point (x, y, z) on this surface lying above each point of the domain D (or below if $z = f(x, y)$ turns out to be negative). This surface is said to be the **graph** of the function $z = f(x, y)$.

In actual practice, the task of sketching a surface in three-dimensions that is the graph of a function $z = f(x, y)$ is by no means as easy as sketching the graph of a function $y = f(x)$ of a single variable. When faced with this task, it is often helpful to examine what are called **sections** of the graph. These are slices made through the graph by specified planes. For this purpose, we usually use either slices by horizontal planes or slices by vertical planes parallel to the xz- and yz-planes. Any such plane, slicing through the graph of a function $z = f(x, y)$, intersects the graph in a certain curve. By sketching a few such curves, it is often possible to convey a good idea of the general shape of the surface of the graph itself.

Let us consider sections by horizontal planes. A horizontal plane (parallel to the xy-plane) satisfies an equation of the type $z = c$, where c is a constant that gives the height of the plane above the xy-plane (or below, if $c < 0$). So the section of a graph by such a plane consists of points on the graph that lie at a constant height above (or below) the xy-plane. Such a horizontal section can be plotted as a curve in the xy-plane and is called a **contour line** or **level curve**.

Consider, for example, the function, $z = \sqrt{4 - x^2 - y^2}$. The points on the graph of this function that also lie on the horizontal plane $z = c$ satisfy

$$c^2 = 4 - x^2 - y^2.$$

That is,

$$x^2 + y^2 = 4 - c^2.$$

This equation relating x and y is the equation of a circle in the xy-plane centered at $x = y = 0$ and with radius equal to $\sqrt{4 - c^2}$.

For example, let us take $c = 1$, so that we are considering the horizontal slice through the graph by the plane lying 1 unit above the xy-plane. The section is then a circle in the xy-plane with radius $\sqrt{4 - 1^2} = \sqrt{3}$ and center at the point $(0, 0)$. Similarly, if $c = \frac{1}{2}$, the section is a circle of radius $\sqrt{15}/2$, while if $c = \frac{3}{2}$, the section is a circle of radius $\sqrt{7}/2$.

The circles $x^2 + y^2 = 4 - c^2$ corresponding to these three values of c, as well as the outer boundary $x^2 + y^2 = 4$ of the domain, are shown in Figure 4.

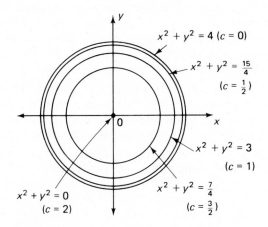

FIGURE 4

The graph of the function $z = \sqrt{4 - x^2 - y^2}$ in three dimensions is a hemisphere centered at the origin, with radius 2 units. The graph is shown in Figure 5, which also shows the contour lines corresponding to $z = 0, \frac{1}{2}, 1$, and $\frac{3}{2}$ in their three-dimensional positions.

We can also use sections of a graph by vertical planes parallel to the xz- and yz-coordinate planes. A plane parallel to the xz-plane is one on which y is a constant, while a plane parallel to the yz-plane is one on which x is a constant. Thus these vertical sections may be found in a way similar to the horizontal sections, that is, by setting x or y equal to a constant. Sections on which x is set equal to a constant can be drawn as curves in the yz-plane and sections on which y is a constant can be drawn as curves in the xz-plane. We shall illustrate the procedure with the following two examples.

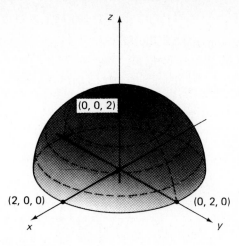

FIGURE 5

EXAMPLE 8   Draw vertical sections of the graph of $z = x^2 - y^2$.

Solution   Let us consider first the section on which $x = c$, c a constant. This is the section by the vertical plane that is parallel to the yz-plane and is at a distance c from it. Substituting $x = c$ into the given function $z = x^2 - y^2$, we obtain $z = c^2 - y^2$. This equation in terms of y and z describes a parabola, opening downward, with vertex at the point $y = 0$ and $z = c^2$. For example, if $c = 1$, the vertex of the parabola is at $(y, z) = (0, 1)$. The parabolas corresponding to the values $c = 0, \pm 1, \pm 2$, drawn in the yz-plane, are shown in Figure 6. Let us consider the section on which $y = c$, c a constant, which is the section by the vertical plane that is parallel to the xz-plane and is at a distance c from it. Substituting $y = c$ in the given equation, we obtain $z = x^2 - c^2$. This equation in terms of x and z represents a parabola with vertex $x = 0$ and $z = -c^2$; this parabola opens upwards. The parabolas corresponding to $c = 0, \pm 1, \pm 2$ are shown in Figure 7.

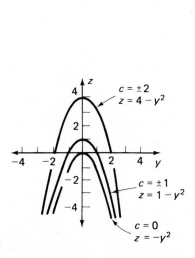

FIGURE 6

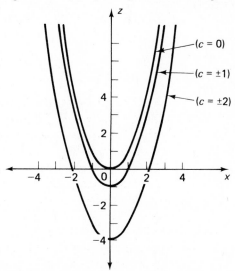

FIGURE 7

The graph of the function $z = x^2 - y^2$ in three dimensions is given in Figure 8, on which are also shown the vertical sections corresponding to $x = 0$, ± 1, and ± 2 and $y = 0$, -1, and -2. From the figure, we can immediately see the dominant feature of this graph, namely its saddle-like shape near the origin.

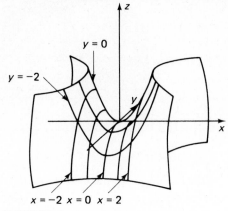

FIGURE 8

EXAMPLE 9   The volume of sales of a particular item depends on its price and also, in many instances, on the amount that the manufacturer spends on promotion and advertising. Let p be the price and A the advertising expenditure per month (both in dollars) and let x be the monthly sales. Then in general, $x = f(p, A)$. Suppose that in a certain case

$$x = 1000(5 - pe^{-kA})$$

where $k = 0.001$. Draw graphs of x versus p for $A = 0$, 500, 1000, and 1500 and draw graphs of x versus A for $p = 1$, 3, 5, and 8.

Solution   The required graphs of x versus p are shown in Figure 9. For example, when $A = 0$, $e^{-kA} = e^{-k(0)} = 1$ and so

$$x = 1000(5 - p).$$

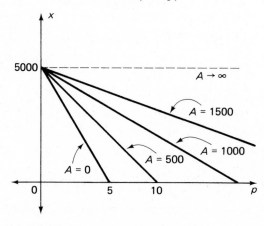

FIGURE 9

The graph of this function is a straight line that intersects the x-axis ($p = 0$) at the value $x = 5000$ and cuts the p-axis ($x = 0$) at $p = 5$. Similarly, when $A = 1000$, $e^{-kA} = e^{-(0.001)(1000)} = e^{-1} = 0.368$ and so $x = 1000(5 - 0.368p)$. This again is a straight line that intersects the x-axis at $x = 5000$ and the p-axis at $p = 5/0.368 \approx 13.6$. This graph represents the demand x as a function of price p when \$1000 per month is spent on advertising.

When p is fixed at the required values, we have the graphs of x versus A shown in Figure 10. For example, when $p = 3$,

$$x = 5000 - 3000e^{-0.001A}.$$

This function provides the volume of sales in terms of the advertising expenditure when the item is priced at \$3.

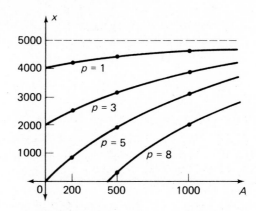

FIGURE 10

EXERCISES 1

(1–8) Calculate the values of the given functions at the indicated points.

1. $f(x, y) = x^2 - 2xy + y^2$; $(x, y) = (3, -2)$ and $(-4, -4)$

2. $f(x, y) = \dfrac{(x - 1)(y - 1)}{(x + y)}$; $(x, y) = (1, -2), (2, -2)$, and $(3, -2)$

3. $f(x, t) = \dfrac{x - t + 1}{x^2 + t^2}$; $(x, t) = (2, 1), (3, \frac{1}{2})$, and $(-\frac{1}{4}, \frac{3}{4})$

4. $f(u, v) = u + \ln|v|$; $(u, v) = (2, 1), (-2, -e)$, and $(0, e^3)$

5. $f(x, y, z) = x^2 + 2y^2 + 3z^2$; $(x, y, z) = (1, 2, 3)$ and $(-2, 1, -4)$

6. $f(x, y, t) = \dfrac{x + y + t}{x + y - t}$; $(x, y, t) = (\frac{1}{2}, -\frac{1}{2}, 1)$ and $(\frac{1}{2}, \frac{1}{2}, -1)$

7. $f(u, v, z) = \dfrac{2u + 3v + 4z}{4u - 3v - z}$; $(u, v, z) = (\frac{1}{2}, 1, 1)$ and $(\frac{1}{4}, -\frac{1}{3}, 2)$

8. $f(a, b, c) = \dfrac{2a^2 + b^2}{\sqrt{c^2 - 4}}$; $(a, b, c) = (1, 2, 3)$ and $(2, 2, -4)$

(9–16) Find the domains of the following functions.

9. $f(x, y) = x^2 + 2xy + y^2$ **10.** $f(x, y) = \dfrac{x^2}{y^2 - 1}$

11. $f(x, y) = \sqrt{x^2 + y^2 - 9}$

12. $f(x, y) = \sqrt{1 - (x + y)^2}$

13. $f(x, t) = \ln(x - t)$

14. $f(x, y) = e^{y-x}$

15. $f(x, y, z) = x + \sqrt{yz}$

16. $f(u, v, w) = \sqrt{e^{u+v+w} - 1}$

(17–22) Sketch the level curves for each of the following functions corresponding to the given values of z.

17. $z = 2x + 3y$; $z = 0, 1, 2, 3$

18. $z = 3x - y$; $z = 0, 1, -2, 3$

19. $z = \sqrt{16 - x^2 - y^2}$; $z = 0, 1, 2, 3$

20. $z = \sqrt{25 - x^2 - y^2}$; $z = 0, 1, 2, 3$

21. $z = x^2 + y^2$; $z = 1, 2, 3, 4$

22. $z = x^2 - y^2$; $z = 0, \pm1, \pm2$

(23–26) Sketch the vertical sections of the graphs of the following functions corresponding to given values of x or y.

23. $z = \sqrt{16 - x^2 - y^2}$; $x = 0, \pm1, \pm2$

24. $z = \sqrt{25 - x^2 + y^2}$; $y = 0, \pm1, \pm2$

25. $z = x^2 + y^2$; $y = 0, \pm1, \pm2, \pm3$

26. $z = 2x^2 - y^2$; $x = 0, \pm1, \pm2, y = 0, \pm1, \pm2$

27. A cylindrical can has radius r and height h. If the material from which it is made costs $2 per unit area, express the cost of the can, C, as a function of r and h.

28. In Exercise 27, find an expression for C that includes the cost of joining the two ends of the can to the curved side. This cost is $0.40 per unit length of perimeter of each end.

29. An open rectangular tank is to be constructed to hold 100 cubic feet of water. The material costs $5 per square foot for the base and for $3 per square foot the vertical walls. If C denotes the total cost (in dollars), determine C as a function of the dimensions of the base.

30. Repeat Exercise 29 if the open tank is of cylindrical shape.

31. A firm produces two products, X and Y. The units costs of labor and material are $5 for product X and $12 for product Y. In addition, the firm also has overhead costs of $3000 per month. Express the monthly cost C (in dollars) as a function of the units of X and Y produced. What is the total cost of producing 200 units of X and 150 units of Y?

32. Western Electronics manufactures two sizes of cassette tapes, 60 minutes and 90 minutes. The unit cost of labor and material for the two sizes are 30¢ and 40¢. In addition, the firm has weekly fixed costs of $1200.

   a. Give the weekly cost C (in dollars) as a function of the units of the two sizes of tapes produced.

   b. Evaluate the total cost of producing 10,000 tapes of 60-minute size and 8000 tapes of 90-minute size.

   c. If the company sells the two kinds of tapes at 60¢ and 75¢ each, respectively, give the weekly profit as a function of the numbers of units produced and sold each week.

33. A pipeline is to be constructed from a point A to a point B that lies 500 miles south and 500 miles east of A. From A, the 200 miles to the south consist of tundra, the next 100 miles consist of swamp, and the last 200 miles consist of a dry rocky terrain. The pipeline costs P dollars per mile over this last terrain, $3P$ dollars per mile over the swamp, and $2P$ dollars per mile over the tundra. Let the pipeline consist of three straight sections, one across each type of terrain, and let it travel x miles to the east across the strip of tundra and a further y miles to the east across the swamp. Express its total cost in terms of x and y.

18-2 PARTIAL DERIVATIVES

We shall now turn to the question of differentiating functions of several variables. In this section, we shall simply concern ourselves with the mechanics of differentiation, but in the following sections, we shall turn to matters of interpretation and use of the resulting derivatives.

Let $z = f(x, y)$ be a function of two independent variables. If the variable y is held fixed at a value $y = y_0$, then the relation $z = f(x, y_0)$ expresses z as a function of the one variable x. This function will have as its graph a curve in the xz-plane, which is in fact the vertical section of the graph of $z = f(x, y)$ by the plane $y = y_0$.

Figure 11 illustrates a typical section by the plane $y = y_0$ of the graph of $z = f(x, y)$. The section is drawn as a curve with respect to xz-coordinates and is described by the equation $z = f(x, y_0)$. At a general point on this curve, the tangent line can be constructed and its slope can be calculated by differentiating z with respect to x from the relation $z = f(x, y_0)$. This derivative is found in the usual way as a limit according to the following formula:

$$\frac{d}{dx} f(x, y_0) = \lim_{\Delta x \to 0} \frac{f(x + \Delta x, y_0) - f(x, y_0)}{\Delta x}.$$

It is called the *partial derivative of z with respect to x*, and is usually denoted by $\partial z/\partial x$. (Note that we use ∂ not d in this situation. The letter d is reserved for the derivative of a function of a single variable).

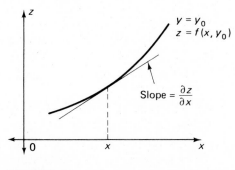

FIGURE 11

DEFINITION   Let $z = f(x, y)$ be a function of x and y. Then the **partial derivative of z with respect to x** is defined to be

$$\frac{\partial z}{\partial x} = \lim_{\Delta x \to 0} \frac{f(x + \Delta x, y) - f(x, y)}{\Delta x}.$$

In writing this definition we have dropped the subscript from y_0; we must remember that *when calculating $\partial z / \partial x$, the variable y is held constant.*

Correspondingly, the **partial derivative of z with respect to y** is defined to be

$$\frac{\partial z}{\partial y} = \lim_{\Delta y \to 0} \frac{f(x, y + \Delta y) - f(x, y)}{\Delta y}.$$

In calculating $\partial z / \partial y$, the variable x is held constant and the differentiation is carried out with respect to y only.

At a point (x_0, y_0) in the domain of the given function $z = f(x, y)$, the partial derivative $\partial z / \partial x$ provides the slope of the vertical section of the graph by the plane $y = y_0$. Correspondingly, the partial derivative $\partial z / \partial y$ provides the slope of the vertical section by the plane $x = x_0$. This latter vertical section has the equation $z = f(x_0, y)$ expressing z as a function of y, and its slope is obtained by differentiating z with respect to y with x set equal to x_0 and held fixed.

These geometric interpretations of partial derivatives are illustrated in Figure 12. Here $A'B'$ represents the vertical section by the plane $y = y_0$ and the tangent to this curve at $x = x_0$ is the straight line AB. The slope of this line is given by the partial derivative $\partial z / \partial x$ evaluated at (x_0, y_0). Similarly, the straight line CD is the tangent to the vertical section by the plane $x = x_0$. Its slope is $\partial z / \partial y$ evaluated at (x_0, y_0).

Partial derivatives can be evaluated using essentially the same techniques as those used for evaluating ordinary derivatives. We must simply remember to treat any variable except the one with respect to which we are differentiating as if it were a constant. Apart from this, the familiar power formula, product and quotient rules, and chain rule can all be used in the usual way.

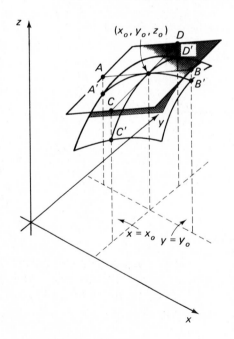

FIGURE 12

EXAMPLE 1   Calculate $\partial z / \partial y$ when $z = x^3 + 5xy^2 + 2y^3$.

Solution   Treating x as a constant and differentiating w.r.t. y, we have

$$\frac{\partial z}{\partial y} = 0 + 5x(2y) + 2(3y^2) = 10xy + 6y^2.$$

EXAMPLE 2   Calculate $\partial z / \partial x$ for $z = \sqrt{x^2 + y^2}$.

Solution   With y held constant, we use the the chain rule.

$$\frac{\partial z}{\partial x} = \frac{\partial}{\partial x}(x^2 + y^2)^{1/2}$$

$$= \frac{1}{2}(x^2 + y^2)^{-1/2}\frac{\partial}{\partial x}(x^2 + y^2)$$

$$= \frac{1}{2}(x^2 + y^2)^{-1/2}(2x + 0)$$

since $\partial(y^2)/\partial x = 0$ as y^2 is held constant. Therefore

$$\frac{\partial z}{\partial x} = x(x^2 + y^2)^{-1/2} = \frac{x}{\sqrt{x^2 + y^2}}.$$

EXAMPLE 3   Calculate $\partial z / \partial x$ and $\partial z / \partial y$ for $z = (x^2 + y^2)/(\ln x)$.

Solution   Using the quotient formula, we obtain

$$\frac{\partial z}{\partial x} = \frac{\ln x\,(\partial/\partial x)(x^2 + y^2) - (x^2 + y^2)(\partial/\partial x)(\ln x)}{(\ln x)^2}$$

$$= \frac{\ln x \cdot (2x) - (x^2 + y^2) \cdot (1/x)}{(\ln x)^2}$$

$$= \frac{2x^2 \ln x - (x^2 + y^2)}{x(\ln x)^2}$$

after multiplying numerator and denominator by x.

We do not need to use the quotient formula in order to evaluate $\partial z / \partial y$, since the denominator of the given quotient is a function of x alone, and so is a constant as far as partial differentiation with respect to y is concerned.

$$\frac{\partial z}{\partial y} = \frac{\partial}{\partial y}\left(\frac{x^2 + y^2}{\ln x}\right) = \frac{1}{\ln x}\frac{\partial}{\partial y}(x^2 + y^2)$$

$$= \frac{1}{\ln x}(0 + 2y) = \frac{2y}{\ln x}$$

It can be seen from these examples that the calculation of partial derivatives of a function of two variables is essentially no different from differentiating a function of just one variable. We must simply remember that *when finding the partial derivative with respect to one of the variables, we treat the other variable as a constant*, then differentiate in the familiar way.

The partial derivative $\partial z / \partial x$ is itself a function of x and y, and therefore we can construct its partial derivatives with respect to both x and y. These are called **second-order partial derivatives** of z, and the following notation is used:

$$\frac{\partial^2 z}{\partial x^2} = \frac{\partial}{\partial x}\left(\frac{\partial z}{\partial x}\right) \quad \text{and} \quad \frac{\partial^2 z}{\partial y \, \partial x} = \frac{\partial}{\partial x}\left(\frac{\partial z}{\partial y}\right).$$

Similarly, $\partial z/\partial y$ may be differentiated with respect to x and y, thus providing two more second-order partial derivatives:

$$\frac{\partial^2 z}{\partial y^2} = \frac{\partial}{\partial y}\left(\frac{\partial z}{\partial y}\right) \quad \text{and} \quad \frac{\partial^2 z}{\partial x \, \partial y} = \frac{\partial}{\partial y}\left(\frac{\partial z}{\partial x}\right).$$

The two derivatives $\partial^2 z/\partial x \, \partial y$ and $\partial^2 z/\partial y \, \partial x$ are often called **mixed partial derivatives** of second order. Provided these mixed partial derivatives are continuous functions of x and y, they are equal to one another:

$$\frac{\partial^2 z}{\partial x \, \partial y} = \frac{\partial^2 z}{\partial y \, \partial x}.$$

EXAMPLE 4　　Calculate all the second-order derivatives of the function $z = \sqrt{x^2 + y^2}$.

Solution　　In Example 2, we showed that

$$\frac{\partial z}{\partial x} = \frac{x}{\sqrt{x^2 + y^2}}$$

for this function. It follows in a similar way that

$$\frac{\partial z}{\partial y} = \frac{y}{\sqrt{x^2 + y^2}}.$$

The two mixed derivatives of second-order are obtained as follows (using the chain rule in the intermediate step).

$$\frac{\partial^2 z}{\partial x \, \partial y} = \frac{\partial}{\partial y}\left(\frac{\partial z}{\partial x}\right) = \frac{\partial}{\partial y}\left(\frac{x}{\sqrt{x^2 + y^2}}\right) = x\frac{\partial}{\partial y}[(x^2 + y^2)^{-1/2}]$$

$$= x(-\tfrac{1}{2})(x^2 + y^2)^{-3/2}(2y)$$

$$= -xy(x^2 + y^2)^{-3/2}$$

$$\frac{\partial^2 z}{\partial y \, \partial x} = \frac{\partial}{\partial x}\left(\frac{\partial z}{\partial y}\right) = \frac{\partial}{\partial x}\left(\frac{y}{\sqrt{x^2 + y^2}}\right) = y\frac{\partial}{\partial x}[(x^2 + y^2)^{-1/2}]$$

$$= -xy(x^2 + y^2)^{-3/2}$$

It can be seen that these two derivatives are equal to one another.

For the remaining two derivatives, the quotient rule must be used.

$$\frac{\partial^2 z}{\partial x^2} = \frac{\partial}{\partial x}\left(\frac{x}{\sqrt{x^2 + y^2}}\right)$$

$$= \frac{\sqrt{x^2 + y^2}\cdot(\partial/\partial x)(x) - x(\partial/\partial x)(\sqrt{x^2 + y^2})}{(\sqrt{x^2 + y^2})^2}$$

$$= \frac{\sqrt{x^2 + y^2}\cdot(1) - x\cdot(x/\sqrt{x^2 + y^2})}{(x^2 + y^2)}$$

$$= \frac{(x^2 + y^2) - x^2}{(x^2 + y^2)\sqrt{x^2 + y^2}} = \frac{y^2}{(x^2 + y^2)^{3/2}}$$

In a similar way, we can show that

$$\frac{\partial^2 z}{\partial y^2} = \frac{x^2}{(x^2 + y^2)^{3/2}}.$$

We may continue this process and calculate partial derivatives of higher orders:

$$\frac{\partial^3 z}{\partial x^3} = \frac{\partial}{\partial x}\left(\frac{\partial^2 z}{\partial x^2}\right), \qquad \frac{\partial^3 z}{\partial x^2\, \partial y} = \frac{\partial}{\partial y}\left(\frac{\partial^2 z}{\partial x^2}\right), \qquad \frac{\partial^3 z}{\partial x\, \partial y\, \partial x} = \frac{\partial}{\partial x}\left(\frac{\partial^2 z}{\partial x\, \partial y}\right)$$

and so on. Provided that all derivatives of the given order are continuous, the order in which the x and y differentiations are carried out is immaterial. Thus, for example, the following mixed derivatives are all equal.

$$\frac{\partial^3 z}{\partial y\, \partial x^2} = \frac{\partial^3 z}{\partial x\, \partial y\, \partial x} = \frac{\partial^3 z}{\partial x\, \partial x\, \partial y}$$

They are denoted by $\partial^3 z/\partial x^2\, \partial y$, indicating two differentiations with respect to x and one with respect to y.

EXAMPLE 5   Calculate $\partial^3 z/\partial y\, \partial x^2$ and $\partial^4 z/\partial x\, \partial y^3$ for $z = x^3 y^4$.

Solution   We have

$$\frac{\partial z}{\partial y} = x^3 \cdot 4y^3 = 4x^3 y^3$$

$$\frac{\partial^2 z}{\partial y\, \partial x} = \frac{\partial}{\partial x}(4x^3 y^3) = 4y^3 \cdot 3x^2 = 12x^2 y^3.$$

Therefore

$$\frac{\partial^3 z}{\partial y\, \partial x^2} = \frac{\partial}{\partial x}\left(\frac{\partial^2 z}{\partial x\, \partial y}\right) = \frac{\partial}{\partial x}(12x^2 y^3) = 24xy^3$$

and,

$$\frac{\partial^3 z}{\partial x\, \partial y^2} = \frac{\partial}{\partial y}\left(\frac{\partial^2 z}{\partial x\, \partial y}\right) = \frac{\partial}{\partial y}(12x^2 y^3) = 36x^2 y^2.$$

Thus

$$\frac{\partial^4 z}{\partial x\, \partial y^3} = \frac{\partial}{\partial y}\left(\frac{\partial^3 z}{\partial x\, \partial y^2}\right) = \frac{\partial}{\partial y}(36x^2 y^2) = 72x^2 y.$$

As with ordinary derivatives, there are several alternative notations that are used for partial derivatives. The most commonly encountered of these is the use of subscripts to indicate partial derivatives, and we shall use this notation ourselves from time to time. According to this notation we have the following.

$\dfrac{\partial z}{\partial x}$ is denoted by z_x or $f_x(x, y)$.

$\dfrac{\partial z}{\partial y}$ is denoted by z_y or $f_y(x, y)$.

$\dfrac{\partial^2 z}{\partial x^2}$ is denoted by z_{xx} or $f_{xx}(x, y)$.

$\dfrac{\partial^2 z}{\partial y\, \partial x}$ is denoted by z_{xy} or $f_{xy}(x, y)$. (Note that $z_{xy} = z_{yx}$ if they are continuous.)

$\dfrac{\partial^4 z}{\partial y^3\, \partial x}$ is denoted by z_{xyyy} or $f_{xyyy}(x, y)$.

Further partial derivatives are denoted in a similar manner.

The notion of partial derivatives extends in a straightforward way to functions $z = f(x_1, x_2, \ldots, x_n)$ of several variables. For example $\partial z/\partial x_1$ is obtained by differentiating z with respect to x_1 keeping $x_2, \ldots, x_n$ all constant, and so on.

EXAMPLE 6   If $z = f(x_1, x_2, x_3) = x_1^2 + x_1\sqrt{x_2^2 - x_3^2}$, find $\partial z/\partial x_1$, $\partial z/\partial x_2$, and $\partial z/\partial x_3$.

Solution

$$\frac{\partial z}{\partial x_1} = 2x_1 + \sqrt{x_2^2 - x_3^2}$$

$$\frac{\partial z}{\partial x_2} = 0 + x_1(\tfrac{1}{2})(x_2^2 - x_3^2)^{-1/2}(2x_2) = \frac{x_1 x_2}{\sqrt{x_2^2 - x_3^2}}$$

$$\frac{\partial z}{\partial x_3} = 0 + x_1(\tfrac{1}{2})(x_2^2 - x_3^2)^{-1/2}(-2x_3) = -\frac{x_1 x_3}{\sqrt{x_2^2 - x_3^2}}$$

EXERCISES 2

(1–16)   Calculate $\partial z/\partial x$ and $\partial z/\partial y$ for the following functions.

1. $z = x^2 y^4$ **2.** $z = \sqrt{xy^5}$ **3.** $z = \sqrt{x - y}$

4. $z = \sqrt{x^2 - y^2}$ **5.** $z = (x + 2y^3)^{1/3}$ **6.** $z = x(y - x)^{-1/2}$

7. $z = e^{x+3y}$ **8.** $z = e^{x^2 y^3}$ **9.** $z = x^2 e^{-y}$

10. $z = \sqrt{e^x - ye^{-x}}$ **11.** $z = (x/y)e^{xy}$ **12.** $z = \ln(x^2 + 2y^2)$

13. $z = (x^2 + y^2)\ln(x + y)$ **14.** $z = \sqrt{x^2 + y^2}\ln(x^2 y^2)$

15. $z = \ln(e^x + xy^3)$ **16.** $z = e^{xy}(\ln(x + y))^{-1}$

(17–20)   Calculate $\partial^2 z/\partial x^2$ and $\partial^2 z/\partial x\, \partial y$ for the following functions.

17. $z = x^{3/2}y^{-4}$ **18.** $z = x^5 y^{-1/2}$

19. $z = \ln(x + 2y)$ **20.** $z = e^{(x^2 + y^2)}$

21. If $z = e^{y/x}$, show that $xz_x + yz_y = 0$.

22. If $z = x^2 e^{-x/y}$, show that $xz_x + yz_y = 2z$.

23. If $z = x^3 + y^3$, show that $xz_x + yz_y = 3z$.

24. If $z = f(ax + by)$ show that $bz_x - az_y = 0$.

25. If $C = ae^{kx+wt}$, show that $\partial C/\partial t = (p/4)(\partial^2 C/\partial x^2)$, provided $w = pk^2/4$.

26. If $f(x, y) = xe^{y/x}$, prove that $xf_{xx} + yf_{xy} = 0$.

18-3 APPLICATIONS TO BUSINESS ANALYSIS

The ordinary derivative dy/dx can be regarded as the rate of change of y w.r.t. x. This interpretation is often useful—for example, the marginal revenue $R'(x)$ gives the rate of change of revenue with respect to the volume of sales, or, approximately, the change in revenue per additional unit sold. Similar interpretations can be made in the case of partial derivatives. For example, if $z = f(x, y)$, then $\partial z/\partial x$ gives the rate of change of z w.r.t. x when y is constant.

EXAMPLE 1 A new product is launched onto the market. The volume of sales x increases as a function of time t and also depends on the amount A spent on the advertising campaign. If, with t measured in months and A in dollars,

$$x = 200(5 - e^{-0.002A})(1 - e^{-t})$$

calculate $\partial x/\partial t$ and $\partial x/\partial A$. Evaluate these derivatives when $t = 1$ and $A = 400$ and interpret them.

Solution We have

$$\frac{\partial x}{\partial t} = 200(5 - e^{-0.002A})e^{-t}$$

$$\frac{\partial x}{\partial A} = 0.4e^{-0.002A}(1 - e^{-t}).$$

Setting $t = 1$ and $A = 400$, we obtain the values

$$\frac{\partial x}{\partial t} = 200(5 - e^{-0.8})e^{-1} = 335$$

$$\frac{\partial x}{\partial A} = 0.4e^{-0.8}(1 - e^{-1}) = 0.11.$$

The partial derivative $\partial x/\partial t$ gives the rate of increase in the sales volume with respect to time when the advertising expenditure is maintained fixed. For example, when this expenditure is fixed at \$400, the volume of sales after one month ($t = 1$) is growing at the instantaneous rate of 335 per month.

Similarly, $\partial x/\partial A$ gives the increase in the sales volume at a fixed time that occurs for each additional dollar spent on advertising. At the time $t = 1$, when \$400 is already spent on advertising, an additional dollar so spent will increase the sales volume by 0.11 units.

Marginal Productivity

The total output of the product of a business firm depends on a number of factors, which the firm often has some flexibility to change. The two most important such factors are usually the amount of labor employed by the firm and the amount of capital invested in buildings, machinery, and so on. Let L denote the number of units of labor employed by the firm (say in work-hours per year or in dollars per year spent in wages) and let K denote the cost of the capital investment in the firm's productive plant. Then the total output P—for example, the number of units of the firm's product produced per month—is some function of L and K, and we write $P = f(L, K)$. This function is known as the firm's **production function** and the variables L and K are examples of **production input factors**—that is, variables that affect the level of production.

In certain cases, changes in K and L are not independent of one another. For example, if the firm buys an extra machine it must also hire extra labor to operate it. On the other hand, K and L are often to some degree independently variables in the context of the firm's basic production strategy. For example, the firm can choose to invest a large amount of capital in a highly automated plant and so make use of relatively little labor or, on the other hand, it can decide to use less sophisticated machinery and more labor. Thus, in general, K and L can be regarded as independent variables.

The partial derivative $\partial P/\partial L$ is called the **marginal productivity of labor** and $\partial P/\partial K$ is called the **marginal productivity of capital**. $\partial P/\partial L$ measures the increase in production per unit increase in the amount of labor employed when the capital input K is held fixed. Correspondingly, $\partial P/\partial K$ measures the increase in production per unit increase in the capital invested when the labor usage is constant.

EXAMPLE 2   The production function of a certain firm is given by

$$P = 5L + 2L^2 + 3LK + 8K + 3K^2$$

where L is the labor input measured in thousands of work-hours per week, K is the cost of capital investment measured in thousands of dollars per week, and P is the weekly production in hundreds of items. Determine the marginal productivities when $L = 5$ and $K = 12$ and interpret the result.

Solution   Given that

$$P = 5L + 2L^2 + 3LK + 8K + 3K^2,$$

the marginal productivities are

$$\frac{\partial P}{\partial L} = 5 + 4L + 3K \quad \text{and} \quad \frac{\partial P}{\partial K} = 3L + 8 + 6K.$$

When $L = 5$ and $K = 12$,

$$\frac{\partial P}{\partial L} = 5 + 4(5) + 3(12) = 61$$

$$\frac{\partial P}{\partial K} = 3(5) + 8 + 6(12) = 95.$$

This means that when $L = 5$ and $K = 12$ (that is, 5000 work-hours per week are used and the cost of capital investment is $12,000 per week), then P increases by 61 for each unit increase in L and P increases by 95 for each unit increase in K. Thus the production increases by 6100 items per week for each additional 1000 work-hours of employed labor when K is held fixed, and the production increases by 9500 items per week for each additional $1000 increase in the weekly cost of capital investment when L is held fixed.

The second derivatives of P w.r.t. K and L also have interpretations as marginal rates of change. The rate at which the marginal productivity $\partial P/\partial K$ increases with respect to changes in the cost of capital is measured by $\partial^2 P/\partial K^2$. Similarly, $\partial^2 P/\partial L^2$ measures the rate at which the marginal productivity $\partial P/\partial L$

increases with respect to changes in the amount of labor employed. Corresponding interpretations can be made for the mixed derivatives $\partial^2 P/\partial K\,\partial L$ and $\partial^2 P/\partial L\,\partial K$.

Demand Relations: Cross Elasticities

Now let us consider a different application—to demand relations. Earlier we supposed that the demand for a commodity depends only on the price per unit of that particular commodity. In practice, this is not always true because the demand for a commodity can be affected by the price of some other related commodity. For example, the demand for beef in the supermarket not only depends on the price per pound of beef but also on the price per pound of pork. Any change in the price of pork will always affect the demand for beef and vice versa, since some customers will be willing to switch from one product to the other.

In general, let A and B be two related commodities such that the change in price of one affects the demand for the other. Let p_A and p_B denote the unit prices for the two commodities. Then, their demands x_A and x_B are assumed to be functions of both the prices p_A and p_B, that is,

$$x_A = f(p_A, p_B) \quad \text{and} \quad x_B = g(p_A, p_B).$$

We can calculate four partial first-order derivatives.

$$\frac{\partial x_A}{\partial p_A}, \quad \frac{\partial x_A}{\partial p_B}, \quad \frac{\partial x_B}{\partial p_A}, \quad \frac{\partial x_B}{\partial p_B}$$

The partial derivative $\partial x_A/\partial p_A$ may be interpreted as the **marginal demand for A with respect to p_A**. Similarly, $\partial x_A/\partial p_B$ is the **marginal demand for A with respect to p_B** and measures the amount by which the demand for A increases per unit increase in the price of B. Similar interpretations can be given to the other two partial derivatives.

If the price of commodity B is held fixed, then, in general, an increase in the price of A results in a decrease in the demand x_A for A. In other words, $\partial x_A/\partial p_A < 0$. Similarly, $\partial x_B/\partial p_B < 0$. The partial derivatives $\partial x_A/\partial p_B$ and $\partial x_B/\partial p_A$ can be positive or negative, depending on the particular interaction between the two products. Suppose, for example, the two commodities are beef (A) and pork (B). An increase in the price of A (beef) in general results in an increase in demand for B (pork) when the price of B remains unchanged, since some consumers will switch from A to B. Thus $\partial x_B/\partial p_A > 0$. Similarly, if the price of A (beef) remains unchanged, an increase in the price of B (pork) will result in an increase in demand for A (beef), that is, $\partial x_A/\partial p_B > 0$.

The two commodities A and B are said to be **competitive** if

$$\frac{\partial x_B}{\partial p_A} > 0 \quad \text{and} \quad \frac{\partial x_A}{\partial p_B} > 0$$

that is, if an increase in the price of either one of them results in an increase in the demand for the other.

Sometimes an increase in the price of either commodity results in a decrease in the demand for the other (assuming its price remains unaltered). In other words, $\partial x_A/\partial p_B$ and $\partial x_B/\partial p_A$ are both negative. In such a case, the two products A and B are said to be **complementary**. For example, film and cameras are two complementary products. If cameras become costlier, there will be a drop in the demand for film.

EXAMPLE 3   The demands x_A and x_B for the two products A and B are given by the functions

$$x_A = 300 + 5p_B - 7p_A^2 \quad \text{and} \quad x_B = 250 - 9p_B + 2p_A$$

where p_A and p_B are the unit prices of A and B, respectively. Determine the four marginal demand functions and find whether the products A and B are competitive or complementary.

Solution   The four marginal demand functions are given by the four partial derivatives.

$$\frac{\partial x_A}{\partial p_A} = -14p_A \qquad\qquad \frac{\partial x_A}{\partial p_B} = 5$$

$$\frac{\partial x_B}{\partial p_A} = 2 \qquad\qquad \frac{\partial x_B}{\partial p_B} = -9$$

Since $\partial x_A/\partial p_B$ and $\partial x_B/\partial p_A$ are both positive, the two products are competitive.

Consider the demand function for the product A: $x_A = f(p_A, p_B)$ where p_A is the price per unit of A and p_B is the unit price for the related product B. Then the **price elasticity of demand for A** is defined to be

$$\eta_{p_A} = \frac{\partial x_A/\partial p_A}{x_A/p_A} = \frac{p_A}{x_A}\frac{\partial x_A}{\partial p_A}.$$

(See Section 3 of Chapter 15.) The **cross elasticity of demand for A with respect to p_B** is defined to be

$$\eta_{p_B} = \frac{\partial x_A/\partial p_B}{x_A/p_B} = \frac{p_B}{x_A}\frac{\partial x_A}{\partial p_B}.$$

Here, η_{p_A} may be interpreted as the ratio of the percentage change in the demand for A to the percentage change in the price of A when the price of B remains fixed. Similarly, η_{p_B} may be thought of as the ratio of the percentage change in the demand for A to the percentage change in the price of B when the price of A is unchanged.

EXAMPLE 4   The demand function for the product of A is given by

$$x_A = 250 + 0.3p_B - 5p_A^2.$$

Determine η_{p_A} and η_{p_B} when $p_A = 6$ and $p_B = 50$.

Solution   In this case, we have

$$\frac{\partial x_A}{\partial p_A} = -10p_A \quad \text{and} \quad \frac{\partial x_A}{\partial p_B} = 0.3.$$

When $p_A = 6$ and $p_B = 50$, we have

$$x_A = 250 + 0.3(50) - 5(6^2) = 85$$

$$\frac{\partial x_A}{\partial p_A} = -10(6) = -60 \quad \text{and} \quad \frac{\partial x_A}{\partial p_B} = 0.3.$$

Therefore

$$\eta_{p_A} = \frac{\partial x_A / \partial p_A}{x_A / p_A} = \frac{-60}{(85/6)} \approx -4.24$$

and

$$\eta_{p_B} = \frac{\partial x_A / \partial p_A}{x_A / p_B} = \frac{0.3}{(85/50)} \approx 0.176.$$

Thus we can say that an approximate increase of 1% in the price of A will result in a 4.24% drop in the demand for this product, while a 1% increase in the price of B will result in a 0.176% increase in the demand for A.

Approximations

In the case of a function $y = f(x)$, we saw in Section 1 of Chapter 15 how the derivative can be used to calculate approximate values of the function at points $x_0 + \Delta x$ when $f(x_0)$ is known, provided that Δx is sufficiently small. The approximation is given by

$$f(x_0 + \Delta x) \approx f(x_0) + f'(x_0)\, \Delta x.$$

This approximation formula extends in quite a straightforward way to functions of several variables.

Let $z = f(x, y)$ be a function of two variables that is suitably differentiable. Then, provided that Δx and Δy are small enough,

$$f(x_0 + \Delta x, y_0 + \Delta y) \approx f(x_0, y_0) + f_x(x_0, y_0)\, \Delta x + f_y(x_0, y_0)\, \Delta y.$$

EXAMPLE 5   For $f(x, y) = \sqrt{x + y} + \sqrt{x - y}$, it is readily seen that $f(10, 6) = 6$. Find an approximate expression for $f(10 + h, 6 + k)$ valid for small values of h and k.

Solution   After partial differentiation, we obtain

$$f_x(x, y) = \tfrac{1}{2}(x + y)^{-1/2} + \tfrac{1}{2}(x - y)^{-1/2}$$
$$f_y(x, y) = \tfrac{1}{2}(x + y)^{-1/2} - \tfrac{1}{2}(x - y)^{-1/2}.$$

At the point $(x_0, y_0) = (10, 6)$, these partial derivatives have the values

$$f_x(10, 6) = \tfrac{1}{2}(10 + 6)^{-1/2} + \tfrac{1}{2}(10 - 6)^{-1/2} = \tfrac{3}{8}$$
$$f_y(10, 6) = \tfrac{1}{2}(10 + 6)^{-1/2} - \tfrac{1}{2}(10 - 6)^{-1/2} = -\tfrac{1}{8}.$$

In this example, $x_0 = 10$ and $x_0 + \Delta x = 10 + h$, so $\Delta x = h$; also, $y_0 = 6$ and $y_0 + \Delta y = 6 + k$, so $\Delta y = k$. Therefore

$$f(10 + h, 6 + k) \approx f(x_0, y_0) + f_x(x_0, y_0)\, \Delta x + f_y(x_0, y_0)\, \Delta y$$
$$= 6 + \tfrac{3}{8}(h) + (-\tfrac{1}{8})(k)$$
$$= 6 + \frac{3h - k}{8}. \tag{1}$$

For example, take $h = 0.1$ and $k = -0.2$. Then we get

$$f(10.1, 5.8) \approx 6 + \frac{0.3 + 0.2}{8} = 6.0625.$$

For comparison, the exact value of $f(10.1, 5.8)$ is

$$\sqrt{10.1 + 5.8} + \sqrt{10.1 - 5.8} = \sqrt{15.9} + \sqrt{4.3} = 6.0611 \ldots .$$

The approximate formula in Equation (1) is a *linear* function of h and k, and consequently it is much easier to work with than the complete expression for $f(10 + h, 6 + k)$. This illustrates the general advantage of this approximation technique in replacing a complicated function by a linear one.

EXAMPLE 6   By using L units of labor and K units of capital, a firm can produce P units of its product, where $P = f(L, K)$. The firm does not know the precise form of this production function, but it does have the following information.

1. When $L = 64$ and $K = 20$, P is equal to 25,000.
2. When $L = 64$ and $K = 20$, the marginal productivities of labor and capital are $P_L = 270$ and $P_K = 350$.

The firm is contemplating an expansion in its plant that would change L to 69 and K to 24. Find the approximate increase in output which would result.

Solution   Taking $L_0 = 64$ and $K_0 = 20$, then for small ΔL and ΔK

$$P = f(L_0 + \Delta L, K_0 + \Delta K) \approx f(L_0, K_0) + f_L(L_0, K_0)\, \Delta L + f_K(L_0, K_0)\, \Delta K$$
$$= 25{,}000 + 270\, \Delta L + 350\, \Delta K.$$

In the new operation, we would have $\Delta L = 69 - 64 = 5$ and $\Delta K = 24 - 20 = 4$. Therefore

$$P \approx 25{,}000 + 270(5) + 350(4) = 27{,}750.$$

The increase in output is therefore 2750.

EXERCISES 3

(1–6) For the following production functions $P(L, K)$, find the marginal productivities for the given values of L and K.

1. $P(L, K) = 7L + 5K + 2LK - L^2 - 2K^2; \quad L = 3, K = 10$
2. $P(L, K) = 18L - 5L^2 + 3LK + 7K - K^2; \quad L = 4, K = 8$
3. $P(L, K) = 50L + 3L^2 - 4L^3 + 2LK^2 - 3L^2K - 2K^3; \quad L = 2, K = 5$
4. $P(L, K) = 25L + 2L^2 - 3L^3 + 5LK^2 - 7L^2K + 2K^2 - K^3; \quad L = 3, K = 10$
5. $P(L, K) = 100L^{0.3}K^{0.7}$
6. $P(L, K) = 250L^{0.6}K^{0.4}$

7. A production function of the form $P(L, K) = cL^aK^b$, where c, a, and b are positive constants and $a + b = 1$, is called a *Cobb-Douglass production function*. Prove that for this production function,

$$L\, \partial P/\partial L + K\, \partial P/\partial K = P.$$

8. A production function $P(L, K)$ is said to be homogeneous of degree n if $L\, \partial P/\partial L + K\, \partial P/\partial K = nP$ for some constant n. Determine whether the production function given by

$$P(L, K) = 5LK + L^2 - 3K^2 + a(L + K)$$

is homogeneous or not. If it is homogeneous, what is the degree of its homogeneity?

(9–12) For the following demand functions for the two products A and B, find the four marginal demand functions and determine whether the products A and B are competitive or complementary.

9. $x_A = 20 - 3p_A + p_B$; $x_B = 30 + 2p_A - 5p_B$

10. $x_A = 150 - 0.3p_B^2 - 2p_A^2$; $x_B = 200 - 0.2p_A^2 - 3p_B^2$

11. $x_A = 30\sqrt{p_B}/\sqrt[3]{p_A^2}$; $x_B = 50p_A/\sqrt[3]{p_B}$

12. $x_A = 200p_B/p_A^2$; $x_B = 300\sqrt{p_A}/p_B^3$

(13–16) For the following demand functions for the product A, determine η_{p_A} and η_{p_B} at the given price levels for the two related products A and B.

13. $x_A = 250 + 0.3p_B - 2p_A^2$; $p_A = 5, p_B = 40$

14. $x_A = 127 - 0.2p_B - p_A^2$; $p_A = 6, p_B = 30$

15. $x_A = 60p_B/\sqrt{p_A}$; $p_A = 9, p_B = 2$

16. $x_A = 250/(p_A\sqrt{p_B})$; $p_A = 5, p_B = 4$

17. The demand function for the product A is given by

$$Q = 327 + 0.2I + 0.5p_B - 2p_A^2$$

where Q is the quantity demanded, I is the consumers' personal disposable income, and p_A and p_B are the unit price of A and the unit price of the related product B, respectively.

   a. Compute the price elasticity of demand η_{p_A} when $p_A = 3$, $p_B = 20$, and $I = 200$.

   b. Compute the cross elasticity of demand η_{p_B} for A when $p_A = 3$, $p_B = 20$, and $I = 200$.

   c. Compute the income elasticity of demand for A,

$$\eta_I = \frac{\partial Q/\partial I}{Q/I} = \frac{I}{Q}\frac{\partial Q}{\partial I}$$

   when $p_A = 3$, $p_B = 20$, and $I = 200$.

18. Repeat Exercise 17 for a product A if the demand is given by the formula

$$Q = 250 + 0.1I + 0.3p_B - 1.5p_A^2.$$

*19. The demand for a certain commodity is given by the function $x = ap^{-b}I^c$, where a, b, and c are constants, p is the price, and I is the consumers' disposable income. Calculate the price elasticity and the income elasticity of demand. (See Exercise

17.) If the supply function for the commodity is $x = rp^s$, where r and s are constants, find the value of p at which market equilibrium is achieved. From this p calculate dp/dI and interpret this derivative.

20. The profit per acre from a certain crop of wheat is found to be

$$P = 40L + 5S + 20F - 3L^2 - S^2 - 2F^2 - 4SF$$

where L is the cost of labor, S the cost of seed, and F the cost of fertilizer. Find $\partial P/\partial L$, $\partial P/\partial S$, and $\partial P/\partial F$ and evaluate them when $L = 10$, $S = 3$, and $F = 4$. Interpret these derivatives.

(21–22) If $f(x, y) = \sqrt{x^2 + y^2}$, find the approximate value of each of the following.

21. $f(3.1, 4.1)$ **22.** $f(5.1, 11.8)$

(23–24) If $f(x, y) = \sqrt{x^2 - y^2}$, find the approximate value of each of the following.

23. $f(5.2, 2.9)$ **24.** $f(25.1, 23.9)$

(25–26) If $f(x, y) = (x - y)/\sqrt{x + y}$, find the approximate value of each of the following.

25. $f(2.1, 1.95)$ **26.** $f(4.0, 5.1)$

27. A firm can produce P units of its product when it uses L units of labor and K units of capital, where

$$P(L, K) = 100L^{3/4}K^{1/4}.$$

a. Calculate the total output when $L = 81$ and $K = 16$.

b. Approximate the effect of reducing L to 80 and increasing K to 17.

28. A firm's production function is given by

$$P(L, K) = 450L^{3/5}K^{2/5}$$

where P represents the output when L units of labor and K units of capital are used.

a. Determine firm's output when $L = 243$ and $K = 32$.

b. Approximate the effect of increasing the labor to 248 units and decreasing the capital to 31 units.

29. The production function of a firm is given by

$$P(L, K) = 9L^{2/3}K^{1/3}$$

where P represents the total output when L units of labor and K units of capital are used. Approximate the total output when $L = 1003$ and $K = 28$.

18-4 OPTIMIZATION

We saw in Chapter 14 that one of the most important and widely applicable uses of the calculus of functions of a single variable is to calculate maximum and minimum values of functions. The corresponding problem, calculating maxima and minima of functions of several variables, is equally important, and in this section we shall discuss it in the case of functions of two variables.

DEFINITION The function $f(x, y)$ has a **local maximum** at the point (x_0, y_0) if $f(x, y) < f(x_0, y_0)$ for all points (x, y) sufficiently close to (x_0, y_0), except for (x_0, y_0) itself.

The function $f(x, y)$ has a **local minimum** at the point (x_0, y_0) if $f(x, y) > f(x_0, y_0)$ for all points (x, y) sufficiently close to (x_0, y_0), except for (x_0, y_0) itself.

The corresponding value $f(x_0, y_0)$ is called the **local maximum value** (or **local minimum value,** as the case may be) of the function f. The term **extremum** is used to cover both maxima and minima.

In the case of functions of one variable, we discussed two types of extrema, one for which the derivative vanished and the other for which the derivative failed to exist, corresponding to a corner or a spike on the graph of the function. In this section, for the sake of simplicity we shall restrict ourselves to the first type. That is, we shall only consider functions whose graphs are smooth surfaces in three dimensions; the possibility that the graph has corners, for example, will not be considered. This restriction is not too serious since the vast majority of applications concern functions with smooth graphs.

Let the function $z = f(x, y)$ have a local maximum at (x_0, y_0). Let us construct the vertical section of the graph on which $y = y_0$, that is, the section through the maximum point. This has the equation $z = f(x, y_0)$ and can be represented by a graph in the xz-plane. (See Figure 13.) Since the surface $z = f(x, y)$ has a local maximum when $x = x_0$ and $y = y_0$, this section must have a local maximum at $x = x_0$. Therefore the slope of the section, which is given by the derivative $\partial z/\partial x = f_x(x, y_0)$, must be zero when $x = x_0$.

In a similar way, we can consider the section on which $x = x_0$, which consists of a curve in the yz-plane with equation $z = f(x_0, y)$. This curve has a maximum when $y = y_0$, and so the slope $\partial z/\partial y = f_y(x_0, y)$ must be zero when $y = y_0$. (See Figure 14.)

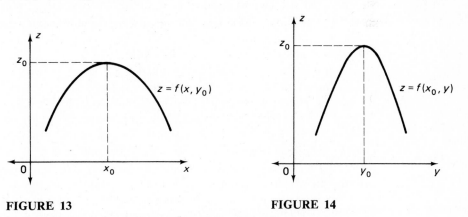

FIGURE 13   **FIGURE 14**

Thus we are led to the following theorem.

THEOREM 1 If $f(x, y)$ has a local maximum or a local minimum at the point (x_0, y_0), then it is necessary that

$$f_x(x_0, y_0) = 0 \quad \text{and} \quad f_y(x_0, y_0) = 0.$$

(The discussion for a local minimum is parallel to that given above for a local maximum).

DEFINITION A **critical point** of a smooth function $f(x, y)$ is a point (x_0, y_0) at which $f_x(x_0, y_0) = f_y(x_0, y_0) = 0$.

It is clear from the preceding discussion that every local extremum of a smooth function must be a critical point. However, not every critical point is an extremum, just as for functions of a single variable. We shall return to this question in a moment.

EXAMPLE 1 Find the critical points of the function

$$f(x, y) = x^3 + x^2y + x - y.$$

Solution We must set the two partial derivatives f_x and f_y equal to zero:

$$f_x(x, y) = 3x^2 + 2xy + 1 = 0$$
$$f_y(x, y) = x^2 - 1 = 0.$$

From the second of these equations, it follows that $x^2 = 1$, or $x = \pm 1$. From the first equation, we then have $2xy = -3x^2 - 1 = -3(1) - 1 = -4$, that is, $y = -4/2x = -2/x$. Thus, $y = -2$ when $x = 1$; and when $x = -1$, $y = +2$. There are therefore two critical points, $(1, -2)$ and $(-1, 2)$.

In the case of a function $f(x)$ of one variable, we saw in Chapter 14 that not every critical point is necessarily a local extremum. A critical point for which $f'(x) = 0$ can be either a local maximum or a local minimum or else a point of inflection, and in Chapter 14 we developed tests to distinguish between these possibilities. Similar tests are necessary in the case of a function $f(x, y)$ of two variables, since it is again true that not every critical point need be an extremum. This is illustrated by the function $z = x^2 - y^2$, which was considered in Example 8 of Section 1. This function has a critical point at the origin which is neither a local maximum nor a local minimum. The vertical section of its graph by the plane $y = 0$ has a local minimum at the origin, while the vertical section by the plane $x = 0$ has a local maximum at the origin. (See Figures 6, 7 and 8.) A critical point of this type is called a **saddle-point**.

If $f(x, y)$ has a local maximum at (x_0, y_0), then it is necessary that the section on which $y = y_0$ should also have a local maximum at $x = x_0$. (This is clear from Figure 13.) Thus it is necessary that $f_x(x, y_0)$ should vanish at $x = x_0$, as we have seen; it is also necessary that the second partial derivative $f_{xx}(x, y_0)$ should be nonpositive at $x = x_0$ since the section $y = y_0$ must be concave downwards at the local maximum point. Conversely, if $f_{xx}(x_0, y_0) < 0$, then the section by the plane $y = y_0$ has a local maximum at (x_0, y_0).

Similarly, we can see that if $f_{yy}(x_0, y_0) < 0$, then the section of the graph on which $x = x_0$ is constant must be concave downwards and so has a local maximum at (x_0, y_0).

The two conditions $f_{xx} < 0$ and $f_{yy} < 0$ at (x_0, y_0) are, however, not sufficient to guarantee that the surface itself has a local maximum at (x_0, y_0). They guarantee only that the vertical sections by the two coordinate planes $x = x_0$ and $y = y_0$ have local maxima at the point (x_0, y_0). It is quite possible for the sections of the graph to have local maxima on these vertical planes, yet to have a local minimum on some other vertical plane through (x_0, y_0).

It is clear, therefore, that some extra condition is required in order to complete the test for a local maximum or minimum. This is provided by the following theorem, which we shall not prove.

THEOREM 2 Let (x_0, y_0) be a critical point of the function $f(x, y)$ for which $f_x(x_0, y_0) = f_y(x_0, y_0) = 0$. Let

$$\Delta(x, y) = f_{xx}(x, y)f_{yy}(x, y) - [f_{xy}(x, y)]^2.$$

(a) If $f_{xx}(x_0, y_0) < 0$, $f_{yy}(x_0, y_0) < 0$, and $\Delta(x_0, y_0) > 0$, then $f(x, y)$ has a local maximum at (x_0, y_0).

(b) If $f_{xx}(x_0, y_0) > 0$, $f_{yy}(x_0, y_0) > 0$, and $\Delta(x_0, y_0) > 0$, then $f(x, y)$ has a local minimum at (x_0, y_0).

(c) If $\Delta(x_0, y_0) < 0$, then (x_0, y_0) is not a local extremum of $f(x, y)$, but is a saddle-point.

Notes: 1. If $\Delta(x_0, y_0) = 0$, then this theorem cannot be used to test for a maximum or minimum.

2. If $\Delta(x_0, y_0) > 0$, then f_{xx} and f_{yy} necessarily have the same sign at (x_0, y_0). Therefore in cases (a) and (b) of Theorem 2, the sign of only one of these second derivatives needs to be checked.

EXAMPLE 2   Find the local extrema of the function

$$f(x, y) = x^2 + 2xy + 2y^2 + 2x - 2y.$$

Solution   First, let us find the critical points.

$$f_x = 2x + 2y + 2 = 0$$
$$f_y = 2x + 4y - 2 = 0$$

Solving these two simultaneous equations, we obtain $x = -3$ and $y = 2$. Thus $(-3, 2)$ is the only critical point.

Now let us apply Theorem 2 in order to test whether this critical point is a local maximum or a local minimum. We find upon differentiating a second time that

$$f_{xx} = 2, \quad f_{yy} = 4, \quad \text{and} \quad f_{xy} = 2.$$

Therefore $\Delta = f_{xx}f_{yy} - f_{xy}^2 = (2)(4) - 2^2 = 8 - 4 = 4$. So we see that $f_{xx} > 0$, $f_{yy} > 0$, and $\Delta > 0$, and thus the point $x = -3$, $y = 2$ is a local minimum of f. The local minimum value of f is

$$f(-3, 2) = (-3)^2 + 2(-3)(2) + 2(2)^2 + 2(-3) - 2(2) = -5.$$

EXAMPLE 3   The Organic Toothpastes Corporation produces toothpaste in two sizes, 100 milliliter and 150 milliliter. The costs of production for each size tube are 60¢ and 90¢, respectively. The weekly demands x_1 and x_2 (in thousands) for the two sizes are

$$x_1 = 3(p_2 - p_1)$$
$$x_2 = 320 + 3p_1 - 5p_2$$

where p_1 and p_2 are the prices in cents per tube. Determine the prices p_1 and p_2 that will maximize the company's profits.

Solution   The profit obtained from each 100-milliliter tube of toothpaste is $(p_1 - 60)$ cents and the profit from each 150-milliliter tube is $(p_2 - 90)$ cents. Therefore the profit P (in thousands of cents, because the demands are in thousands) obtained by selling x_1 tubes of 100-milliliter size and x_2 of 150-milliliter size is given by

$$P = (p_1 - 60)x_1 + (p_2 - 90)x_2$$
$$= 3(p_1 - 60)(p_2 - p_1) + (p_2 - 90)(320 + 3p_1 - 5p_2)$$
$$= -3p_1^2 - 5p_2^2 + 6p_1 p_2 - 90p_1 + 590p_2 - 28{,}800.$$

Therefore,

$$\frac{\partial P}{\partial p_1} = 6p_2 - 6p_1 - 90$$

and

$$\frac{\partial P}{\partial p_2} = 6p_1 - 10p_2 + 590.$$

For maximum profit, $\partial P/\partial p_1 = \partial P/\partial p_2 = 0$. That is,

$$6p_2 - 6p_1 - 90 = 0 \quad \text{and} \quad 6p_1 - 10p_2 + 590 = 0.$$

Solving these two equations, we get $p_1 = 110$ and $p_2 = 125$. Also $\partial^2 P/\partial p_1^2 = -6$, $\partial^2 P/\partial p_2^2 = -10$, and $\partial^2 P/\partial p_1 \partial p_2 = 6$. Consequently,

$$\Delta = \frac{\partial^2 P}{\partial p_1^2} \cdot \frac{\partial^2 P}{\partial p_2^2} - \left(\frac{\partial^2 P}{\partial p_1 \partial p_2}\right)^2$$
$$= (-6)(-10) - 6^2 > 0.$$

Since $\Delta > 0$ and $\partial^2 P/\partial p_1^2$, $\partial^2 P/\partial p_2^2$ are negative, the prices $p_1 = 110$¢ and $p_2 = 125$¢ will yield a maximum profit for the company. At these values of p_1 and p_2, the demands are $x_1 = 75$ and $x_2 = 25$ (thousands per week).

Problems also arise in which we are required to find the maximum and minimum values of a function $f(x_1, x_2, \ldots, x_n)$ of several variables. We again solve such problems by setting all of the first partial derivatives equal to zero:

$$\frac{\partial f}{\partial x_1} = \frac{\partial f}{\partial x_2} = \cdots = \frac{\partial f}{\partial x_n} = 0.$$

This provides n equations that must be solved for the variables $x_1, \ldots, x_n$. The resulting point is a critical point of f.

The test that must be applied in order to verify whether the critical point is a local maximum or local minimum or a saddle-point is more complicated than for functions of two variables, and we shall not give it here.*

EXERCISES 4

(1–10) Find the critical values of the following functions and test whether each is a local maximum or a local minimum.

1. $f(x, y) = 2x^2 + xy + 2y^2$ 2. $f(x, y) = x^2 + 4xy + y^2$

3. $f(x, y) = 2xy - x^2 - 3y^2 - x - 3y$

4. $f(x, y) = x^2 + 2y^2 - 2x - 2y + 1$

5. $f(x, y) = x^3 + 3x^2y + y^3 - y$

6. $f(u, v) = u^3 + v^3 - 3uv^2 - 3u + 7$

7. $f(x, y) = 2xy(x + y) + x^2 + 2x$

8. $f(p, q) = 25q(1 - e^{-p}) - 50p - q^2$

9. $f(x, y) = xy + \ln x + y^2$

10. $f(x, y) = x^2 + y^2 - \ln (xy^2)$

11. A firm produces two types of products, A and B. The total daily cost (in dollars) of producing x units of A and y units of B is given by $C(x, y) = 250 - 4x - 7y + 0.2x^2 + 0.1y^2$. Determine the number of units of A and B that the firm must produce each day to minimize its total cost.

12. If the firm in Exercise 11 above can sell each unit of A for \$20 and each unit of B for \$16, find the levels of production of A and B that will maximize the profits for the firm. What is this maximum daily profit?

13. Repeat Exercise 11 above if
$$C(x, y) = 1500 - 7.5x - 15y - 0.3xy + 0.3x^2 + 0.2y^2.$$

14. If x denotes the firm's output (in hundreds) and y the amount spent (in thousands of dollars) on the promotional efforts to sell the product, then the firm's profit P (in thousands of dollars) is given by $P(x, y) = 16x + 12y + 2xy - x^2 - 2y^2 - 7$. What values of x and y will yield the maximum profit? What is this maximum profit?

15. The total cost C per production run (in thousands of dollars) of a certain industry is given by $C(x, y) = 3x^2 + 4y^2 - 5xy + 3x - 14y + 20$, where x denotes the number of work-hours (in hundreds) and y the number of units (in thousands) of the product produced per run. What values of x and y will result in the minimum total cost per production run?

16. By using L units of labor and K units of capital, the total weekly output of a firm is given by $P(L, K) = 20K + 32L + 3LK - 2L^2 - 2.5K^2$. Find the number of units of labor and capital that the firm must use to maximize its output.

17. A manufacturing firm uses two types of raw materials, X and Y, in its product. By using x units of X and y units of Y, the firm can produce P units of the product, where $P = 0.52x + 0.48y + 0.12xy - 0.07x^2 - 0.06y^2$. It costs \$5.10 for each unit of X and \$1.80 for each unit of Y used, and the firm can sell

*See, for example, A. E. Taylor and W. R. Mann, *Advanced Calculus*, 2nd ed. (Lexington, Mass.: Xerox College Publishing), p. 230.

all the units it produces at \$15 each. What amounts of X and Y should be used by the firm to maximize its profits?

18. By using L units of labor input and K units of capital input, a firm produces certain output of its product whose total cost T (in millions of dollars) is given by $T = 40 - 5K - 3L - 2KL + 1.5K^2 + L^2$. Find the amount of each input that will make the total cost minimum for the firm. What is this minimum cost?

19. The Western Sweets Candy Company makes candy bars in two sizes at unit costs of 10¢ and 20¢, respectively. The weekly demands (in thousands) x_1 and x_2 for the two sizes are

$$x_1 = p_2 - p_1 \quad \text{and} \quad x_2 = 60 + p_1 - 3p_2$$

where p_1 and p_2 denote the prices of the candy bars of the two sizes. Determine the prices p_1 and p_2 that will maximize the company's weekly profits.

20. Mack-Oh Toys produces two different types of plastic cars at the cost of 10¢ and 30¢ each. The annual demands x_1 and x_2 (in thousands) are given by

$$x_1 = 30 + 2p_2 - 5p_1 \quad \text{and} \quad x_2 = 100 + p_1 - 2p_2$$

where p_1 and p_2 are the unit prices (in cents) of the two types of cars. Determine the prices p_1 and p_2 that the company must charge to maximize its profits.

21. It costs a company \$2 per unit to manufacture its product. If A dollars per month are spent on advertising, then the number of units per month which will be sold is given by $x = 30(1 - e^{-0.001A})(22 - p)$ where p is the selling price. Find the values of A and p that will maximize the firm's net monthly profit, and calculate the value of the maximum profit.

*22. In order to manufacture x items of its product per week, a company's weekly cost function is $C(x) = 50 + \frac{20}{3}x + \frac{1}{60}x^2$. If A dollars per week are spent on advertising, the price p (in dollars) at which the demand will be x items per week is given by

$$p = 20 - \frac{x}{60(1 - e^{-0.001A})}.$$

Find the values of x and A that maximize the weekly profit and calculate this maximum profit.

23. The dollar value of a crop of tomatoes produced under artificial heat is given by $V = 25T(1 - e^{-x})$ per unit area of ground. Here T is the maintained temperature in degrees Celsius above 10°C and x the amount per unit area of fertilizer used. The cost of the fertilizer is $50x$ per unit area and the cost of heating is equal to T^2 per unit area. Find the values of x and T that maximize the profit from the crop. Calculate the maximum profit per unit area.

24. The average number of apples produced per tree in an orchard in which there are n trees per acre is given by $(A - \alpha n + \beta \sqrt{x})$ where A, α, and β are constants and x is the amount of fertilizer used per acre. The value of each apple is V and the cost per unit of fertilizer is F. Find the values of x and n that make the profit (that is, value of crop of apples less the cost of fertilizer) a maximum.

25. A lake is to be stocked with two species of fish. When there are x fish of the first species and y fish of the second species in the lake, the average weights of the fish in the two species at the end of the season are $(3 - \alpha x - \beta y)$ pounds and $(4 - \beta x - 2\alpha y)$ pounds, respectively. Find the values of x and y that make the total weight of fish a maximum.

26. Repeat Exercise 25 for the case when the average weights of the two species of fish are $(5 - 2\alpha x - \beta y)$ pounds and $(3 - 2\beta x - \alpha y)$ pounds, respectively.

27. A tank is to be built with width x, length y, and depth z, and it is to be large enough to hold 256 cubic feet of liquid. If the top is open, what dimensions will minimize the total area of the remaining five sides of the tank (and hence minimize the amount of material used in its construction)?

18-5 LAGRANGE MULTIPLIERS (OPTIONAL SECTION)

Sometimes we are faced with minimizing or maximizing a certain function subject to some constraint on the variables involved. Consider the following example.

EXAMPLE 1 A firm wants to construct a rectangular tank to hold 1500 cubic feet of water. The base and the vertical walls have to be made with concrete and the top with steel. If the steel costs twice as much per unit area as the concrete, determine the dimensions of the tank that will minimize the total cost of construction.

Solution Let x, y, and z (in feet) be the length, width, and height of the rectangular tank, respectively (See Figure 15.) Then,

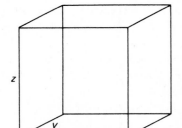

Area of Base = Area of Top = xy

and

Area of Four Walls = $2xz + 2yz$.

Let the cost of concrete per square foot be p. Then the cost of steel per square foot is $2p$. The cost of constructing the base and four vertical walls with concrete at p per unit area is

$$p(xy + 2xz + 2yz).$$

FIGURE 15

The cost of constructing the top with steel at $2p$ per unit area is $2pxy$. The total cost C is therefore

$$C = p(xy + 2xz + 2yz) + 2pxy$$
$$= p(3xy + 2xz + 2yz). \tag{1}$$

The volume of the box should be 1500 cubic feet. That is,

$$xyz = 1500. \tag{2}$$

Notice that we have to minimize the function of Equation (1) subject to the condition in Equation (2). We can solve this problem by using the constraint in Equation (2) to remove one of the variables. From Equation (2), $z = 1500/xy$, and substituting this value of z into Equation (1), we get

$$C = p\left(3xy + \frac{3000}{x} + \frac{3000}{y}\right).$$

Now C is a function of two variables that are independent and we can find its minima in the usual way. For a maximum or minimum,

$$C_x = p\left(3y - \frac{3000}{x^2}\right) = 0 \quad \text{or} \quad x^2 y = 1000$$

$$C_y = p\left(3x - \frac{3000}{y^2}\right) = 0 \quad \text{or} \quad xy^2 = 1000.$$

It follows, therefore, that $x^2 y = xy^2$. Dividing both sides by xy (note that x and y are nonzero), we get $x = y$.

Using $y = x$ in $x^2 y = 1000$, we get $x^3 = 1000$ or $x = 10$. Therefore $y = x = 10$.

It is readily verified that when $x = y = 10$, C_{xx}, C_{yy}, and $\Delta = C_{xx}C_{yy} - C_{xy}^2$ are all positive. Therefore the cost C is minimum. When $x = 10$ and $y = 10$, Equation (2) gives $z = 15$. Thus for minimum cost, the dimensions of the tank should be 10 feet by 10 feet by 15 feet.

In Example 1, we eliminated one of the variables (z in this case) from the function C with the help of the constraint equation and then found the critical points of C. But it might happen that we cannot solve the constraint equation for any one of the variables, so that none of them can be eliminated. For example, if the constraint equation is $x^5 - 5x^3 y^3 + z^3 + z^5 + 2y^5 + 16 = 0$, we cannot solve for x, y, or z in terms of the other two variables. On the other hand, even if we are able to eliminate one variable by the use of the constraint equation, it may happen that the resulting function to be maximized or minimized is very complicated to handle.

An alternative method—one that avoids the use of elimination—was devised by the French mathematician J. L. Lagrange (1736–1813) and is known as the method of *Lagrange multipliers*. Suppose we are interested in finding the extreme value of the function $f(x, y, z)$ subject to the constraint $g(x, y, z) = 0$. Then we construct an auxiliary function $F(x, y, z, \lambda)$, defined by

$$F(x, y, z, \lambda) = f(x, y, z) - \lambda g(x, y, z).$$

The new variable λ (lambda) is called the **Lagrange multiplier**.

According to the method of Lagrange multipliers, if $(x_0, y_0, z_0, \lambda_0)$ is a critical point of $F(x, y, z, \lambda)$, then (x_0, y_0, z_0) is a critical point of $f(x, y, z)$ subject to the constraint $g(x, y, z) = 0$, and conversely. Thus, in order to find the critical points of $f(x, y, z)$ subject to the constraint $g(x, y, z) = 0$, we can instead find the critical points of the auxiliary function $F(x, y, z, \lambda)$. These are given by the conditions

$$F_x = f_x - \lambda g_x = 0$$
$$F_y = f_y - \lambda g_y = 0$$
$$F_z = f_z - \lambda g_z = 0$$

and

$$F_\lambda = \qquad - g = 0.$$

The last of these equations is nothing but the given constraint equation $g(x, y, z) = 0$. The method of Lagrange multipliers does not indicate directly whether $f(x, y, z)$ will have a maximum, a minimum, or a saddle-point at the critical point. In practical problems, we often rely on intuitive reasoning to decide that the critical point gives a maximum or a minimum. There is a test that can be applied, but it is rather a complicated one.

EXAMPLE 2   Let us solve Example 1 again, this time by the method of Lagrange multipliers. We had the function

$$f(x, y, z) = C = p(3xy + 2yz + 2zx)$$

and the constraint $xyz = 1500$. This constraint can be written in the form

$$g(x, y, z) = xyz - 1500 = 0.$$

The auxiliary function in this case is

$$F(x, y, z, \lambda) = f(x, y, z) - \lambda g(x, y, z)$$
$$= p(3xy + 2yz + 2zx) - \lambda(xyz - 1500).$$

The critical points of F are given by the following conditions

$$F_x = p(3y + 2z) - \lambda yz = 0$$
$$F_y = p(3x + 2z) - \lambda xz = 0$$
$$F_z = p(2x + 2y) - \lambda xy = 0$$

and

$$F_\lambda = -xyz + 1500 \qquad = 0.$$

From the first three equations, we have

$$\frac{\lambda}{p} = \frac{3y + 2z}{yz} = \frac{3}{z} + \frac{2}{y}$$

$$\frac{\lambda}{p} = \frac{3x + 2z}{xz} = \frac{3}{z} + \frac{2}{x}$$

$$\frac{\lambda}{p} = \frac{2x + 2y}{xy} = \frac{2}{x} + \frac{2}{y}.$$

From the first and second values of λ/p, we have

$$\frac{3}{z} + \frac{2}{y} = \frac{3}{z} + \frac{2}{x} \quad \text{or} \quad \frac{2}{y} = \frac{2}{x}$$

from which it follows that $x = y$. From the second and third values of λ/p,

$$\frac{3}{z} + \frac{2}{x} = \frac{2}{x} + \frac{2}{y} \quad \text{or} \quad \frac{3}{z} = \frac{2}{y}.$$

Therefore $z = 3y/2$. Substituting expressions $x = y$ and $z = 3y/2$ into the expression for F_λ, we have

$$-y \cdot y \cdot \tfrac{3}{2} y + 1500 = 0 \quad \text{or} \quad y^3 = 1000.$$

Hence $y = 10$. Therefore $x = y = 10$ and $z = \tfrac{3}{2} y = 15$.

The critical point of $C(x, y, z)$ subject to constraint $xyz = 1500$ is thus given by $x = 10$, $y = 10$, and $z = 15$, as before.

EXAMPLE 3   By using L units of labor and K units of capital, a firm can produce P units of its product, where

$$P(L, K) = 50L^{2/3}K^{1/3}.$$

It costs the firm $100 for each unit of labor and $300 for each unit of capital used. The firm has a sum of $45,000 available for production purposes.

(a) Use the method of Lagrange multipliers to determine the units of labor and capital that the firm should use to maximize its production.

(b) Show that at this maximum level of output, the ratio of the marginal costs of labor and capital is equal to the ratio of their unit costs.

(c) Show that if $1 additional is available for production at this maximum level of production, the firm can produce approximately λ extra units of its product, where λ is the Lagrange multiplier. In other words, λ can be interpreted as the *marginal productivity of money.*

Solution   (a) Here the function to be maximized is

$$P(L, K) = 50L^{2/3}K^{1/3}.$$

The cost of using L units of labour at $100 each and K units of capital at $300 each is $(100L + 300K)$ dollars. Since we want to make use of the whole available sum of $45,000, we must have

$$100L + 300K = 45,000.$$

We wish to maximize $P(L, K)$ subject to this constraint.

The auxiliary function is

$$F(L, K, \lambda) = 50L^{2/3}K^{1/3} - \lambda(100L + 300K - 45,000).$$

To obtain a maximum of $P(L, K)$, we must have

$$F_L = \tfrac{100}{3}L^{-1/3}K^{1/3} - 100\lambda = 0$$

$$F_K = \tfrac{50}{3}L^{2/3}K^{-2/3} - 300\lambda = 0$$

$$F_\lambda = -(100L + 300K - 45,000) = 0.$$

Solving the first two equations for λ, we get

$$\lambda = \tfrac{1}{3}L^{-1/3}K^{1/3} \quad \text{and} \quad \lambda = \tfrac{1}{18}L^{2/3}K^{-2/3}. \tag{3}$$

We then equate the two values of λ.

$$\tfrac{1}{3}L^{-1/3}K^{1/3} = \tfrac{1}{18}L^{2/3}K^{-2/3}$$

Multiplying both sides by $L^{1/3}K^{2/3}$, we get

$$\tfrac{1}{3}K = \tfrac{1}{18}L \quad \text{or} \quad L = 6K.$$

Using this in the value of F_λ we get

$$600K + 300K - 45,000 = 0 \quad \text{or} \quad K = 50.$$

Therefore $L = 6K = 300$ and the firm can maximize its output if it uses 300 units of labor and 50 units of capital.

(b) The marginal productivities of labor and capital are given by

$$P_L = \tfrac{100}{3}L^{-1/3}K^{1/3}, \qquad P_K = \tfrac{50}{3}L^{2/3}K^{-2/3}.$$

At the maximum level of output, that is, when $L = 300$ and $K = 50$, we have
$$P_L = \tfrac{100}{3}(300)^{-1/3}(50)^{1/3} \quad \text{and} \quad P_K = \tfrac{50}{3}(300)^{2/3}(50)^{-2/3}.$$
Therefore
$$\frac{\text{Marginal Productivity of Labor}}{\text{Marginal Productivity of Capital}} = \frac{P_L}{P_K}$$
$$= \frac{\tfrac{100}{3}(300)^{-1/3}(50)^{1/3}}{\tfrac{50}{3}(300)^{2/3}(50)^{-2/3}} = \frac{1}{3}.$$
Also,
$$\frac{\text{Unit Cost of Labor}}{\text{Unit Cost of Capital}} = \frac{100}{300} = \frac{1}{3}.$$

Thus, at the maximum level of output, the ratio of the marginal productivities of labor and capital is equal to the ratio of the unit costs of labor and capital.

(c) At the maximum level of production, when $L = 300$ and $K = 50$, we have two ways of calculating λ [from Equations (3)]:
$$\lambda = \tfrac{1}{3}(300)^{-1/3}(50)^{1/3} = 0.1835$$
$$\lambda = \tfrac{1}{18}(300)^{2/3}(50)^{-2/3} = 0.1835.$$

Suppose we can buy ΔL units of labor and ΔK units of capital with the extra \$1 available. Then
$$100\,\Delta L + 300\,\Delta K = 1. \tag{4}$$
The increase in production when labor is increased from 300 to $300 + \Delta L$ and capital is increased from 50 to $50 + \Delta K$ is given by
$$\Delta P = P(300 + \Delta L, 50 + \Delta K) - P(300, 50)$$
$$\approx P_L(300, 50) \cdot \Delta L + P_K(300, 50) \cdot \Delta K.$$

Now from the equations for F_L and F_K in part (a), it follows that at the maximum, $P_L - 100\lambda = 0$ and $P_K - 300\lambda = 0$; thus $P_L(300, 50) = 100\lambda$ and $P_K(300, 50) = 300\lambda$. Therefore the increase in production is approximately given by
$$\Delta P \approx 100\lambda\,\Delta L + 300\lambda\,\Delta K$$
$$= \lambda(100\,\Delta L + 300\,\Delta K) = \lambda$$
where we used Equation (4). Thus an extra dollar available for production will increase the production by an approximate amount $\lambda = 0.1835$ units. In other words, λ represents the marginal productivity of money.

EXAMPLE 4   A company can use its plant to produce two types of products, A and B. It makes a profit of \$4 per unit of A and \$6 per unit of B. The numbers of units of the two types that can be produced by the plant are restricted by the product transformation equation, which is
$$x^2 + y^2 + 2x + 4y - 4 = 0$$
where x and y are the numbers of units (in thousands) of A and B, respectively, produced per week. Find the amounts of each type that should be produced in order to maximize the profit.

Solution   We wish to maximize the profit P, which is given by
$$P(x, y) = 4x + 6y$$
(in thousands of dollars per week). Here x and y are subject to the constraint
$$g(x, y) = x^2 + y^2 + 2x + 4y - 4 = 0. \qquad (5)$$
Using the method of Lagrange multipliers, we construct the function
$$F(x, y, \lambda) = P(x, y) - \lambda g(x, y).$$
Then the critical points are given by
$$F_x = P_x - \lambda g_x = 4 - \lambda(2x + 2) = 0$$
$$F_y = P_y - \lambda g_y = 6 - \lambda(2y + 4) = 0$$
$$F_\lambda = -g = 0.$$
This value of F_λ duplicates the given constraint equation. From the values of F_x and F_y,
$$\lambda = \frac{2}{x + 1} = \frac{3}{y + 2}.$$
Therefore $2(y + 2) = 3(x + 1)$ or $y = (3x - 1)/2$. Substituting this into Equation (5), we obtain an equation for x alone.
$$x^2 + \left(\frac{3x - 1}{2}\right)^2 + 2x + 4\left(\frac{3x - 1}{2}\right) - 4 = 0$$
After simplification, this reduces to $13x^2 + 26x - 23 = 0$. From the quadratic formula, we find the roots
$$x = 1 \pm \frac{6\sqrt{13}}{13} = 0.664 \quad \text{or} \quad -2.664.$$
Of course, only the positive root $x = 0.664$ is meaningful. With this value of x, we have
$$y = \frac{3x - 1}{2} = \frac{3(0.664) - 1}{2} = 0.496.$$

Thus the optimum production levels are 664 units of A and 496 units of B per week. The maximum profit is
$$P = 4(0.664) + 6(0.496) = 5.63,$$
that is, \$5630 per week.

The method of Lagrange multipliers can also be used when there are more than one constraint. If $f(x, y, z)$ is to be maximized or minimized subject to two constraints $g_1(x, y, z) = 0$ and $g_2(x, y, z) = 0$, then we construct the auxiliary function F as follows.
$$F(x, y, z, \lambda_1, \lambda_2) = f(x, y, z) - \lambda_1 g_1(x, y, z) - \lambda_2 g_2(x, y, z)$$
The critical points are then obtained by solving the equations
$$F_x = F_y = F_z = F_{\lambda_1} = F_{\lambda_2} = 0.$$

EXERCISES 5

(1–10) Use the method of Lagrange multipliers to determine the critical points of f subject to the given constraints.

1. $f(x, y) = x^2 + y^2;\quad 2x + 3y = 7$

2. $f(x, y) = x^2 + y^2 - 3xy;\quad 2x + 3y = 31$

3. $f(x, y) = 3x + 2y;\quad x^2 + y^2 = 13$

4. $f(x, y) = 2x^2 + 3y^2;\quad xy = \sqrt{6}$

5. $f(x, y, z) = x^2 + y^2 + z^2;\quad 2x + 3y + 4z = 29$

6. $f(x, y, z) = xyz;\quad xy + yz + 2zx = 24\quad (xyz \neq 0)$

7. $f(x, y, z, u) = x^2 + 2y^2 - 3z^2 + 4u^2;\quad 2x - 3y + 4z + 6u = 73$

8. $f(u, v, w, x) = 3u^2 - v^2 + 2w^2 + x^2;\quad 3u + v - 2w + 4x = 20$

9. $f(x, y, z) = x^2 + 2y^2 - 3z^2;\quad x + 2y - 3z = 5, 2x - 3y + 6z = -1$

10. $f(u, v, w) = uv + vw + wu;\quad 3u - v + 2w + 13 = 0, 2u + 3v - w = 0$

11. The cost of producing x regular models and y deluxe models of a firm's product is given by the joint cost function $C(x, y) = x^2 + 1.5y^2 + 300$. How many units of each type should be produced to minimize total costs if the firm decides to produce a total of 200 units?

12. A firm can manufacture its product at two of its plants. The cost of manufacturing x units at the first plant and y units at the second plant is given by the joint cost function $C(x, y) = x^2 + 2y^2 + 5xy + 700$. If the firm has a supply order of 500 units, how many should be manufactured at each plant to minimize the total cost?

13. The production function for a firm is $P(L, K) = 80L^{3/4}K^{1/4}$ where L and K represent the numbers of units of labor and capital used and P the number of units of the product produced. Each unit of labor costs \$60 and each unit of capital costs \$200, and the firm has \$40,000 available for production purposes.

   a. Use the method of Lagrange multipliers to determine the number of labor and capital units that the firm must use to obtain a maximum output.

   b. Show that when the labor and capital are at their maximum levels, the ratio of their marginal productivities is equal to the ratio of their unit costs.

   c. At this maximum level of output, determine the increase in production if \$1 extra is available for production. Show that it is approximately equal to the Lagrange multiplier.

14. Repeat Exercise 13 for $P(L, K) = 800\sqrt{3L^2 + 1.5K^2}$. The unit costs of labor and capital are \$250 and \$50, and the firm has \$6750 to spend for production.

15. Repeat Exercise 13 if $P(L, K) = 113L + 15K + 3LK - L^2 - 2K^2$ and the unit costs for labor and capital are \$60 and \$100, respectively. The firm has a budget constraint of \$7200 for production.

16. Repeat Exercise 13 for $P(L, K) = 72L + 30K + 5LK - 2L^2 - 3K^2$. The unit costs for labor and capital are \$80 and \$150, respectively. The budget constraint is \$5640.

17. By using L units of labor and K units of capital, a firm can produce P units of

its product, where $P(L, K) = 60L^{2/3}K^{1/3}$. The costs for labor and capital are $64 and $108 per unit. Suppose the firm decides to produce 2160 units of its product.

a. Use the method of Lagrange multipliers to find the number of labor and capital inputs that must be used to minimize the total cost.

b. Show that at this level of production, the ratio of marginal costs of labor and capital is equal to the ratio of their unit costs.

18. Repeat Exercise 17, if $P(L, K) = 60\sqrt{5(L^2 + K^2)}$ and the unit costs for labor and capital are $200 and $100, respectively. The firm decides to produce 4500 units.

19. An investment of p dollars in the four investments A, B, C, and D results in an annual return of $\sqrt{p}$, $\sqrt{1.2p}$, $\sqrt{1.3p}$, and $\sqrt{1.5p}$ dollars, respectively. A person has $12,000 to invest in these four enterprises. How much should be invested in each to maximize the annual return?

20. If a firm spends x thousand dollars on advertising in city A, its potential sales (in thousands of dollars) in that city are given by $300x/(x + 10)$. If it spends x thousand dollars advertising in city B, its potential sales (in thousands of dollars) in that city are given by $500x/(x + 13.5)$. If the profit is 25% of its sales and the firm has $16,500 for advertising budget in the two cities, how much should be spent on each city to maximize the firm's net profit?

18-6 METHOD OF LEAST SQUARES

On many occasions in the course of this book, we have quoted formulas for such things as the demand relation for a particular product, the cost of manufacturing x items of a product, the sales volume as a function of advertising expenditure, production functions, and so on. In writing a textbook, we are in the fortunate position of being able to invent our own examples of these functions. However, in real situations, a firm is not able to invent its own cost function, for example, but instead must determine this function from observation of its operations.

In these real cases, we usually do not have a mathematical formula expressing the relationship in question; what we do have are certain data collected from measurements made in the past. Sometimes these data arise in the course of the normal operations of the firm and sometimes they arise as a result of deliberate experimentation. For example, in order to test the effectiveness of its advertising, a company might conduct comparative tests in different towns, varying the advertising expenditure from one town to another.

The measured data can be plotted as a series of points on a graph. In order to obtain an approximation to the complete graph of the relationship, a smooth curve is drawn passing as close as possible to these data points. Usually the curve which is drawn will not pass through every one of the data points, because to make it do so would reduce its smoothness. In fact, we often approximate the relationship by drawing the graph as a straight line passing as closely as possible to the plotted points. Consider the following example.

Suppose the management of the Pacific Rubber Company is faced with the problem of forecasting its tire sales in the coming years. From past experience, it is known that tire sales increase with the number of cars on the road. The firm has the following data, collected in the past, available.

TABLE 1

Number of Cars (in millions)	18	18.3	18.9	19.4	19.8	20.3
Tire Sales (in thousands)	40	44	52	59	67	77

If we plot the number of cars along the x-axis and the tire sales along the y-axis, we obtain the set of points shown in Figure 16.

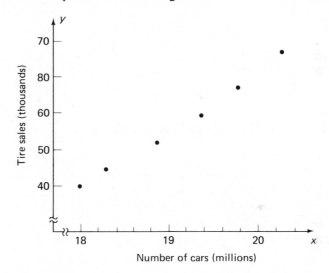

FIGURE 16

Looking at the points, we can reasonably conclude that the relationship between x and y is approximately linear, and on this basis we can draw the straight line that lies closest to the set of points. (See Figure 17.) Even though all the points do not lie precisely on the straight line, the line does approximate the observed data quite well. This line can be used to predict future tire sales if the management of the firm has some estimation of the number of cars that will be on the road in future years.

Drawing such a line by eye is not objective in the sense that it may be possible to draw another line that appears to fit the set of data points just as well or even better than the one drawn. What is needed is some objective criterion for deciding on the particular straight line that provides the best fit to the observed points. Such a criterion is provided by the **method of least squares**.

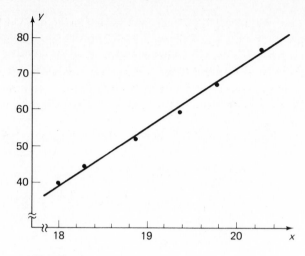

FIGURE 17

Let us suppose that there are n observed data that are plotted as a sequence of points $(x_1, y_1), (x_2, y_2), \ldots, (x_n, y_n)$ on the xy-plane. We shall seek the straight line that in a certain sense lies closest to these points.

Let the equation of the straight line of best fit through the given n points be

$$y = ax + b \tag{1}$$

where a and b are constants. Our purpose is to determine a and b, which will then fix the straight line. When $x = x_i$, the observed value of y is y_i; however, the "correct" value is $ax_i + b$, obtained by replacing $x = x_i$ in Equation (1).

The **error** in the value y_i is equal to the difference $y_i - (ax_i + b)$ between the observed value and the theoretical value of y. (See Figure 18.) The **square error** is defined to be simply $(y_i - ax_i - b)^2$. Then the **mean square error**, E, is defined as the average of all the square errors. That is,

$$E = \frac{1}{n}[(y_1 - ax_1 - b)^2 + (y_2 - ax_2 - b)^2 + \cdots + (y_n - ax_n - b)^2].$$

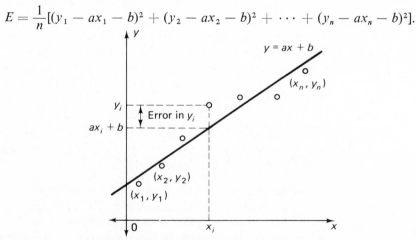

FIGURE 18

Thus, in calculating E, we determine the square error from each individual data point, add these together for all n data points, and then divide by n.

Of course, we cannot calculate E yet, since we do not know the values of the constants a and b. According to the method of least squares, what we must do is to choose a and b in such a way that E is minimized. Necessary conditions for this are that the two partial derivatives $\partial E/\partial a$ and $\partial E/\partial b$ be zero.

$$\frac{\partial E}{\partial a} = \frac{\partial}{\partial a} \frac{1}{n}[(y_1 - ax_1 - b)^2 + \cdots + (y_n - ax_n - b)^2]$$

$$= \frac{1}{n}[2(y_1 - ax_1 - b)(-x_1) + \cdots + 2(y_n - ax_n - b)(-x_n)]$$

$$= \frac{2}{n}[(-x_1y_1 + ax_1^2 + bx_1) + \cdots + (-x_ny_n + ax_n^2 + bx_n)]$$

$$= \frac{2}{n}[a(x_1^2 + x_2^2 + \cdots + x_n^2) + b(x_1 + x_2 + \cdots + x_n)$$

$$- (x_1y_1 + x_2y_2 + \cdots + x_ny_n)]$$

and

$$\frac{\partial E}{\partial b} = \frac{\partial}{\partial b} \frac{1}{n}[(y_1 - ax_1 - b)^2 + \cdots + (y_n - ax_n - b)^2]$$

$$= \frac{1}{n}[2(y_1 - ax_1 - b)(-1) + \cdots + 2(y_n - ax_n - b)(-1)]$$

$$= \frac{2}{n}[a(x_1 + x_2 + \cdots + x_n) + nb - (y_1 + y_2 + \cdots + y_n)]$$

Therefore, setting these two derivatives equal to zero, we obtain the following two equations.

$$a(x_1^2 + x_2^2 + \cdots + x_n^2) + b(x_1 + x_2 + \cdots + x_n)$$
$$= (x_1y_1 + x_2y_2 + \cdots + x_ny_n)$$
$$a(x_1 + x_2 + \cdots + x_n) + nb = (y_1 + y_2 + \cdots + y_n)$$

These equations form a pair of simultaneous linear equations for the unknown constants a and b, and they may be solved in the usual way. Having calculated a and b, the best straight line through the given data points has equation $y = ax + b$.

Let us find the equation of the best straight line through the data points given for the Pacific Rubber Company. If x denotes the number of cars (in millions) on the road and y the number of tire sales (in thousands) of the company, then we have the data given in Table 2.

TABLE 2

x	18.0	18.3	18.9	19.4	19.8	20.3
y	40	44	52	59	67	77

When using the method of least squares, it is convenient to show the calculations as illustrated in Table 3. In the four columns of the table, the values of x_i, y_i,

TABLE 3

x_i	y_i	x_i^2	$x_i y_i$
18.0	40	324.00	720.0
18.3	44	334.89	805.2
18.9	52	357.21	982.8
19.4	59	376.36	1144.6
19.8	67	392.04	1326.6
20.3	77	412.09	1563.1
114.7	339	2196.59	6542.3

x_i^2, and $x_i y_i$ are listed for each data point. Then the columns are summed. In this case, we have

$$x_1 + x_2 + \cdots = 114.7$$
$$y_1 + y_2 + \cdots = 339$$
$$x_1^2 + x_2^2 + \cdots = 2196.59$$
$$x_1 y_1 + x_2 y_2 + \cdots = 6542.3.$$

In addition, we have six data points and so $n = 6$. The constants a and b are now given by

$$a(x_1^2 + x_2^2 + \cdots) + b(x_1 + x_2 + \cdots) = x_1 y_1 + x_2 y_2 + \cdots$$
$$a(x_1 + x_2 + \cdots) + nb = y_1 + y_2 + \cdots.$$

That is,

$$2196.59a + 114.7b = 6542.3$$
$$114.7a + 6b = 339.$$

Solving these two equations, we obtain

$$a = 15.8 \quad \text{and} \quad b = -246.$$

Thus the best straight line through the given data points has the equation

$$y = 15.8x - 246.$$

As an example of the way in which this result could be used, let us suppose that the government forecast that the number of cars on the road next year would be 22.3 million. Then the Pacific Rubber Company can estimate that its tire sales will be (in thousands)

$$(15.8)(22.3) - 246 = 106.$$

It can be shown without too much difficulty that $\partial^2 E / \partial a^2 > 0$, $\partial^2 E / \partial b^2 > 0$, and (with a little more difficulty) that

$$\Delta = \frac{\partial^2 E}{\partial a^2} \cdot \frac{\partial^2 E}{\partial b^2} - \left(\frac{\partial^2 E}{\partial a\, \partial b} \right)^2 > 0$$

so that the values of a and b found by setting $\partial E/\partial a = \partial E/\partial b = 0$ do correspond to a minimum of E.

It is worth mentioning that the method of least squares is not limited to fitting best straight lines but can be extended to many types of curves. For example, it is often used to fit the best polynomial function to a set of data points. (See Exercise 29 in the Review Exercises for an illustration.)

EXERCISES 6

(1–4) Using the method of least squares find the best straight line through the following sets of data points.

1.

x	2	3	5	6	9	12
y	3	4	6	5	7	8

2.

x	3	4	5	6	7	8
y	0.7	1.9	2.1	2.5	3.4	4.5

3.

x	0	1	2	3
y	1	1.5	2.5	3

4.

x	2	3	4	5	6
y	2	4	3.5	5	6.5

5. A department store finds that the trend of sales of a new electric razor is as follows.

Week Number (x)	1	2	3	4	5	6
Units Sold (y)	20	24	28	33	35	39

Find the equation of the straight line that best fits the data.

6. A firm finds that its net profit increases with increase in the amount spent on advertising the product. The firm has the following data available from its past records.

Advertising Expenditure (x) (in thousands of dollars)	10	11	12.3	13.5	15
Net Profits (y) (in thousands of dollars)	50	63	68	73	75

a. Find the equation of the straight line that best fits the data.

b. Estimate the money that should be spent on advertising to obtain a net profit of $80,000.

7. A firm is trying to determine the demand curve for its product. It sells the product in different cities at different prices and determines the volume of sales. After one month, the following data are obtained.

Price (in dollars) (p)	2	2.25	2.50	2.75	2.90
Volume Sales (x)	300	290	270	230	200

   a. Determine the straight line that best fits the data.

   b. Use the demand curve of part (a) to determine the volume of sales if the price is $3.

   c. Use the result of part (a) to determine the price that maximizes the monthly revenue.

8. The production level and the profits of a certain firm for the past few years are shown in this table.

Production (x) (in thousands of units)	40	47	55	70	90	100
Profits (y) (in thousands of dollars)	32	34	43	54	72	85

   a. Determine the equation of the straight line that best fits the data.

   b. Estimate the profits when the production level is increased to 120 thousand units.

9. A marketing firm wishes to determine the effect of television commercials on the sales of a certain product. The firm has the following feedback from six large cities.

City	A	B	C	D	E	F
No. of commercials (x)	10	12	15	20	18	21
Sales (in hundreds) (y)	40	45	56	68	67	70

Determine the equation of the straight line that best fits the data. Estimate the volume of sales that would result from 24 commercials.

10. The sales commissions paid and the sales volume at seven branches of a large chain store for the last year were as follows.

Store	1	2	3	4	5	6	7
Commissions (x) (in thousands of dollars)	37.2	45.3	80.5	56.4	67.2	74.6	62.7
Sales (y) (in hundred thousands of dollars)	4.3	5.1	7.9	5.4	7.1	7.2	6.5

Determine the equation of the straight line that best fits the data.

11. Four-year averages for the gross national product (GNP) of a certain country are given in billions of dollars by the following table.

YEAR (x)	1956	1960	1964	1968	1972	1976
G.N.P. (y)	453	562	691	862	1054	1310

Determine the equation of the straight line that best fits the data. Estimate the GNP for 1980.

12. The average yield y in bushels of corn per acre in the United States varies from one year to another. The values for the period 1960–1971 are given in the following table, in which t denotes the date starting with $t = 0$ in 1960 and increasing to $t = 11$ in 1971.

t	0	1	2	3	4	5	6	7	8	9	10	11
y	54	63	65	67	70	73	72	80	79	87	83	88

Show that during this period, a linear equation of the form $y = at + b$ fits this data quite well, and determine the values of a and b.

REVIEW EXERCISES FOR CHAPTER 18

1. State whether each of the following is true or false. Replace each false statement by a corresponding true statement.

a. The range of a function $z = f(x, y)$ is the region in the xy-plane where the function takes its values.

b. The domain of $f(x, y) = (x + y)/(x^2 + y^2 + 1)$ is the set of all real numbers.

c. In three-dimensions, the x-coordinate is zero on the x-axis.

d. In three-dimensions, $y = 0$ and $z = 0$ on the yz-plane.

e. If $z = f(x + y)$ is any function in which x and y occur only in the combination $(x + y)$, such as $z = (x + y)^2 \ln (x + y)$, then $\partial z/\partial x = \partial z/\partial y$.

f. If $z = f(x, y)$ and if $\partial z/\partial x = 0$, then z is independent of x, and we can write $z = g(y)$, a function of y only.

g. If the second-order partial derivatives of $f(x, y)$ are all continuous, then

$$\frac{\partial^3 f}{\partial x^2 \, \partial y} = \frac{\partial^3 f}{\partial y \, \partial x^2}.$$

h. $\dfrac{\partial}{\partial x}(x^3 y^2) = \dfrac{x^4}{4} y^2$

i. $\dfrac{\partial}{\partial y}\left(\dfrac{x^2}{y}\right) = x^2 \ln y$

j. If $f(x, y)$ has a local maximum at (a, b), then $f_x(a, b) = f_y(a, b) = 0$.

k. If (a, b) is a critical point of $f(x, y)$ and f_{xx}, f_{yy} are negative at (a, b), then (a, b) is a local maximum point for $f(x, y)$.

l. If f_{xx} and f_{yy} are of opposite sign at a critical point (a, b) of $f(x, y)$, then f has a saddle-point at (a, b).

m. If $f_x(a, b) = 0$ and $f_y(a, b) = 0$, then $f(x, y)$ has a local extremum at (a, b).

n. If f_{xx} and f_{yy} are positive at the point (a, b), then (a, b) is a local minimum point for $f(x, y)$.

o. The straight line that best fits a given set of data points must pass through at least two of the data points.

p. Given only two data points, the straight line obtained by the method of least squares passes through both points.

q. The critical points of $x^2 + y^2$ subject to the condition $x - y = \ln(x + y)$ can be obtained by finding the critical points of the function $F(x, y, \lambda) = x^2 + y^2 - \lambda(y + \ln(x + y) - x)$.

(2–5) Give the domains of the following functions.

2. $z = \sqrt{x(y + 1)}$

3. $z = y^{-1} \ln(x + y)$

4. $z = \sqrt{1 - x_1^2 - x_2^2 - x_3^2}$

5. $z = \dfrac{\ln(x_1 + x_2 + x_3)}{\sqrt{x_1 - x_2}}$

(6–9) Evaluate $\partial z/\partial x$, $\partial z/\partial y$, $\partial^2 z/\partial x\,\partial y$, and $\partial^2 z/\partial y^2$ for the following functions.

6. $z = \sqrt{x}/y$

7. $z = xy(x + y)$

8. $z = xe^{x+y}$

9. $z = \ln(x^2 + y^2) + e^{y\sqrt{x}}$

10. If $z = f(ax + by) + g(ax - by)$, show that $a^2 z_{yy} - b^2 z_{xx} = 0$.

11. Burnaby Mountain Service Station has total annual profits P given by

$$P(x, y, z) = 3xy + 5yz + zx - x^2 - 2y^2 - 1.5z^2$$

where x is the number of employees, y is the number of gas pumps, and z is the value of other supplies (such as oil or tires) carried in inventory. Calculate P_x, P_y, and P_z and interpret P_y.

12. A company's production function is

$$P(L, K, T) = 30L + 25K + 4T - \tfrac{1}{2}L^2 - \tfrac{1}{3}K^2 - \tfrac{1}{20}T^2$$

where P represents the total output and L, K, and T are production input factors. Find the marginal productivity function for each of the factors of production.

13. The demand x_A for a product A is given by

$$x_A = 100\sqrt{p_A p_B}$$

where p_A is the price per unit of A and p_B the price per unit of a related product B.

a. Show that $p_A \dfrac{\partial x_A}{\partial p_A} + p_B \dfrac{\partial x_A}{\partial p_B} = x_A$.

b. Calculate the elasticities of demand η_{p_A} and η_{p_B} and evaluate their sum.

14. If L units of labour and K units of capital are used to produce P items of a certain product, the firm's total cost of producing P units is given by

$$C = 2L^2 + 3K^2 - 5K - 4L \qquad \text{(in millions of dollars).}$$

Find $\partial C/\partial L$ and $\partial C/\partial K$. Interpret $\partial C/\partial L$.

15. A monopolist faces the demand functions for its two products A and B given by

$$x_A = 3 - p_A + 0.2p_B, \qquad x_B = 5 + 0.3p_A - 2p_B.$$

The joint cost function is given by

$$C = x_A^2 + x_B^2 - x_A x_B.$$

Find $\partial C/\partial p_A$ and $\partial C/\partial p_B$. What is the meaning of these derivatives.

(16–19) Determine the local maxima and minima of the following functions?

16. $f(x, y) = 7 + 2xy + 5x - x^2 - 2y^2$

17. $g(u, v) = uv + \dfrac{1}{u} - \dfrac{8}{v} + 7$

18. $F(x, y) = 2xy - \sqrt{x^2 + 4y^2 - 31}$

19. $G(x, y) = \dfrac{x}{y} - 2y^2 + \dfrac{8}{3}x^3$

20. The Fresh Meats Company can sell x pounds of pork at p cents per pound and y pounds of beef at q cents per pound, where

$$x = 600 + 4q - 10p \quad \text{and} \quad y = 120 + 5p - 3q.$$

What prices per pound for pork and beef should the company charge to maximize its revenue?

21. A meat company can sell x pounds of beef at a price of p cents per pound and y pounds of pork at a price of q cents per pound, where

$$p = 40.5 - 0.03x - 0.004y \quad \text{and} \quad q = 25.4 - 0.005x - 0.02y.$$

How much of each kind of meat should the company sell to maximize its revenue?

22. By using L units of labor and M units of material, a firm can produce T units of its product, where

$$T = 180L + 150M + 3LM - L^2 - 4M^2.$$

a. Determine the number of units of labor and material that must be used to maximize the firm's output.

b. Suppose the firm can sell all it produces at $5 per unit. It costs the firm $40 per unit of labor and $10 for each unit of material. How many units of each should be used to maximize the profits? What is this maximum profit?

c. The unit costs of labor and material are as in part (b). The firm has $12,660 available for both labor and material. Determine the optimal allocation of these funds.

23. The monthly profits (in dollars) of a service organization are given by

$$P(x, y) = 448x + 233y + xy - 2x^2 - 3y^2 - 15,000$$

where x denotes the number of workers and y the number of times the firm advertises.

a. Determine x and y that will maximize the organization's monthly profits. What are these maximum profits?

b. The workers get a wage of $500 per month and the advertising costs $100 each time. The working capital is such that an expenditure of $53,100 is to be made on labor and advertisement. Determine the values of x and y that make the profit a maximum.

24. A firm uses two types of raw materials A and B to manufacture its product. By using x units of A and y units of B, the firm can produce T units of its product, where $\qquad\qquad T = 70x + 240y + 3xy - 4x^2 - 5y^2$.

a. How many units of each raw material should the firm use in order to maximize its output? What is this maximum output?

b. If it costs the firm $5 for each unit of A and $7 for each unit of B and the firm can sell all it produces at $10 per unit, what amounts of A and B will maximize the firm's profits?

c. The costs for raw materials are as in part (b). If the firm has $250 available for raw materials, what amounts of each will maximize the firm's production?

d. In part (c), when the amounts of the two raw materials used are at the optimum levels, show that the ratio of their marginal productivities is equal to the ratio of their unit costs.

e. Approximate the increase in production when the amount available for raw materials in part (c) is increased by $1.

*25. By using L units of labor and K units of capital, a firm can produce $P(L, K)$ units of its product. The unit costs of labor and capital are p and q dollars, respectively. The firm has a budget constraint of C dollars.

a. Use the method of Lagrange multipliers to show that at the maximum level of production, the ratio of the marginal productivities of labor and capital is equal to the ratio of their unit costs.

b. Show that the firm can produce approximately λ extra units of its product if $1 extra is available at this maximum level of output, where λ is the Lagrange multiplier.

*26. When L units of labor and K units of capital are used, a firm's output is given by $P(L, K)$. The unit costs of labor and capital are a and b dollars, respectively. Suppose the firm decides to produce P_o units of its product and the combination of labor and capital is used that produces these units at minimum cost. Show that the ratio of the marginal productivities of labor and capital is equal to the ratio of their unit costs.

27. The annual advertising expenditures and sales of six brand-name soaps for a particular year were given by the following data.

Advertising Expenditure (x) (in hundreds of thousands of dollars)	9	7	11	8	4	6
Sales (y) (in millions of dollars)	13	10	15	11	5	8

Determine the equation of the straight line that best fits this data.

28. A study made on the median income in thousands of dollars of families in seven large cities and the percentage of families who own at least one car gave the following results (obtained from census data).

Median Income (x)	7.1	4.3	6.5	3.7	5.2	7.8	5.9
Percentage of Car Owners (y)	67	48	62	49	54	72	60

Determine the equation of the straight line that best fits this data.

*29. It is desired to fit a set of experimental data $\{(x_i, y_i)\}$ with a quadratic function $y = ax^2 + bx + c$. We define the mean square error to be

$$E = \frac{1}{n}[(y_1 - ax_1^2 - bx_1 - c)^2 + (y_2 - ax_2^2 - bx_2 - c)^2 + \cdots$$
$$+ (y_n - ax_n^2 - bx_n - c)^2].$$

By setting $\partial E/\partial a$, $\partial E/\partial b$, and $\partial E/\partial c$ equal to zero, find three equations for $a, b,$ and c.

Evaluate $a, b,$ and c from these equations for the data given below.

x	0	1	2	3	4
y	9.9	8.2	6.1	3.7	2.4

TABLE OF STANDARD DERIVATIVES

I. BASIC FORMULAS

1. The derivative of a constant is zero.

2. For any constant c, $\dfrac{d}{dx}[cf(x)] = cf'(x)$.

3. $\dfrac{d}{dx}[f(x) \cdot g(x)] = f(x)g'(x) + g(x)f'(x)$.   —Product Formula

4. $\dfrac{d}{dx}\left(\dfrac{f(x)}{g(x)}\right) = \dfrac{g(x)f'(x) - f(x)g'(x)}{[g(x)]^2}$.   —Quotient Formula

5. If $y = f(u)$ and $u = g(x)$ then

$$\frac{dy}{dx} = \frac{dy}{du} \cdot \frac{du}{dx},$$ —Chain Rule

or

$$\frac{d}{dx}(f[g(x)]) = f'[g(x)] \cdot g'(x)$$ —Chain Rule

6. $\dfrac{d}{dx}(x^n) = nx^{n-1}$.   —Power Formula

7. If $x = f(t)$, $y = g(t)$ then $\dfrac{dy}{dx} = \dfrac{g'(t)}{f'(t)}$ or $\dfrac{dy}{dx} = \dfrac{dy/dt}{dx/dt}$.

II. EXPONENTIAL AND LOGARITHMIC FUNCTIONS

$\dfrac{d}{dx}(e^x) = e^x$.

$\dfrac{d}{dx}(a^x) = a^x \ln a$.

$\dfrac{d}{dx}(\ln x) = \dfrac{1}{x}$.

$\dfrac{d}{dx}(\log_a x) = \dfrac{1}{x} \log_a e = \dfrac{1}{x \ln a}$.

TABLE OF INTEGRALS

NOTE. In every integral the constant of integration is omitted and should be supplied by the reader.

SOME FUNDAMENTAL FORMULAS

1. $\int [f(x) \pm g(x)] \, dx = \int f(x) \, dx \pm \int g(x) \, dx.$

2. $\int cf(x) \, dx = c \int f(x) \, dx.$

3. $\int f[g(x)]g'(x) \, dx = \int f(u) \, du \quad$ where $\quad u = g(x).$

4. $\int f(x)g(x) \, dx = f(x) \int g(x) \, dx - \int f'(x) \left\{ \int g(x) \, dx \right\} dx.$

RATIONAL INTEGRANDS INVOLVING $(ax + b)$

5. $\int (ax + b)^n \, dx = \dfrac{(ax + b)^{n+1}}{a(n + 1)} \quad (n \neq -1).$

6. $\int (ax + b)^{-1} \, dx = \dfrac{1}{a} \ln |ax + b|.$

7. $\int x(ax + b)^n \, dx = \dfrac{1}{a^2}(ax + b)^{n+1} \left[\dfrac{ax + b}{n + 2} - \dfrac{b}{n + 1} \right] \quad (n \neq -1, -2).$

8. $\int x(ax + b)^{-1} \, dx = \dfrac{x}{a} - \dfrac{b}{a^2} \ln |ax + b|.$

9. $\int x(ax + b)^{-2} \, dx = \dfrac{1}{a^2} \left[\ln |ax + b| + \dfrac{b}{ax + b} \right].$

10. $\int \dfrac{x^2}{ax + b} \, dx = \dfrac{1}{a^3} \left[\dfrac{1}{2}(ax + b)^2 - 2b(ax + b) + b^2 \ln |ax + b| \right].$

11. $\int \dfrac{x^2}{(ax + b)^2} \, dx = \dfrac{1}{a^3} \left[ax + b - \dfrac{b^2}{ax + b} - 2b \ln |ax + b| \right].$

12. $\int \dfrac{1}{x(ax + b)} \, dx = \dfrac{1}{b} \ln \left| \dfrac{x}{ax + b} \right| \quad (b \neq 0).$

13. $\int \dfrac{1}{x^2(ax + b)} \, dx = -\dfrac{1}{bx} + \dfrac{a}{b^2} \ln \left| \dfrac{ax + b}{x} \right| \quad (b \neq 0).$

14. $\int \dfrac{1}{x(ax + b)^2} \, dx = \dfrac{1}{b(ax + b)} - \dfrac{1}{b^2} \ln \left| \dfrac{ax + b}{x} \right| \quad (b \neq 0).$

15. $\int \dfrac{1}{(ax + b)(cx + d)} \, dx = \dfrac{1}{bc - ad} \ln \left| \dfrac{cx + d}{ax + b} \right| \quad (bc - ad \neq 0).$

16. $\displaystyle \int \frac{x}{(ax+b)(cx+d)}\,dx = \frac{1}{bc-ad}\left\{\frac{b}{a}\ln|ax+b| - \frac{d}{c}\ln|cx+d|\right\}$

$(bc-ad \neq 0)$.

17. $\displaystyle \int \frac{1}{(ax+b)^2(cx+d)}\,dx = \frac{1}{bc-ad}\left\{\frac{1}{ax+b} + \frac{c}{bc-ad}\ln\left|\frac{cx+d}{ax+b}\right|\right\}$

$(bc-ad \neq 0)$.

18. $\displaystyle \int \frac{x}{(ax+b)^2(cx+d)}\,dx = -\frac{1}{bc-ad}\left\{\frac{b}{a(ax+b)} + \frac{d}{bc-ad}\ln\left|\frac{cx+d}{ax+b}\right|\right\}$

$(bc-ad \neq 0)$.

INTEGRALS CONTAINING $\sqrt{ax+b}$

19. $\displaystyle \int x\sqrt{ax+b}\,dx = \frac{2}{a^2}\left[\frac{(ax+b)^{5/2}}{5} - \frac{b(ax+b)^{3/2}}{3}\right].$

20. $\displaystyle \int x^2\sqrt{ax+b}\,dx = \frac{2}{a^3}\left[\frac{(ax+b)^{7/2}}{7} - \frac{2b(ax+b)^{5/2}}{5} + \frac{b^2(ax+b)^{3/2}}{3}\right].$

21. $\displaystyle \int \frac{x}{\sqrt{ax+b}}\,dx = \frac{2ax-4b}{3a^2}\sqrt{ax+b}.$

22. $\displaystyle \int \frac{1}{x\sqrt{ax+b}}\,dx = \frac{1}{\sqrt{b}}\ln\left|\frac{\sqrt{ax+b}-\sqrt{b}}{\sqrt{ax+b}+\sqrt{b}}\right| \quad (b>0).$

23. $\displaystyle \int \frac{1}{x^n\sqrt{ax+b}}\,dx = -\frac{1}{b(n-1)}\frac{\sqrt{ax+b}}{x^{n-1}} - \frac{(2n-3)a}{(2n-2)b}\int \frac{1}{x^{n-1}\sqrt{ax+b}}\,dx \quad (n\neq 1).$

24. $\displaystyle \int \frac{\sqrt{ax+b}}{x}\,dx = 2\sqrt{ax+b} + b\int \frac{1}{x\sqrt{ax+b}}\,dx \quad \text{(see 22)}.$

25. $\displaystyle \int \frac{\sqrt{ax+b}}{x^2}\,dx = -\frac{\sqrt{ax+b}}{x} + \frac{a}{2}\int \frac{1}{x\sqrt{ax+b}}\,dx \quad \text{(see 22)}.$

INTEGRALS CONTAINING $a^2 \pm x^2$

26. $\displaystyle \int \frac{1}{a^2-x^2}\,dx = \frac{1}{2a}\ln\left|\frac{x+a}{x-a}\right|.$

27. $\displaystyle \int \frac{1}{(a^2-x^2)^2}\,dx = \frac{x}{2a^2(a^2-x^2)} + \frac{1}{4a^3}\ln\left|\frac{x+a}{x-a}\right|.$

28. $\displaystyle \int \frac{x}{(a^2 \pm x^2)}\,dx = \pm\frac{1}{2}\ln|a^2 \pm x^2|.$

29. $\displaystyle \int \frac{1}{x(a^2 \pm x^2)}\,dx = \frac{1}{2a^2}\ln\left|\frac{x^2}{a^2 \pm x^2}\right|.$

INTEGRALS CONTAINING $\sqrt{a^2 - x^2}$

30. $\int \dfrac{x}{\sqrt{a^2 - x^2}}\, dx = -\sqrt{a^2 - x^2}.$

31. $\int \dfrac{1}{x\sqrt{a^2 - x^2}}\, dx = -\dfrac{1}{a} \ln\left|\dfrac{a + \sqrt{a^2 - x^2}}{x}\right|.$

32. $\int \dfrac{1}{x^2\sqrt{a^2 - x^2}}\, dx = -\dfrac{\sqrt{a^2 - x^2}}{a^2 x}.$

33. $\int \dfrac{1}{(a^2 - x^2)^{3/2}}\, dx = \dfrac{1}{a^2}\dfrac{x}{\sqrt{a^2 - x^2}}.$

34. $\int \dfrac{x}{(a^2 - x^2)^{3/2}}\, dx = \dfrac{1}{\sqrt{a^2 - x^2}}.$

35. $\int \dfrac{1}{x(a^2 - x^2)^{3/2}}\, dx = \dfrac{1}{a^2\sqrt{a^2 - x^2}} - \dfrac{1}{a^3} \ln\left|\dfrac{a + \sqrt{a^2 - x^2}}{x}\right|.$

36. $\int \dfrac{1}{x^2(a^2 - x^2)^{3/2}}\, dx = \dfrac{1}{a^4}\left[-\dfrac{\sqrt{a^2 - x^2}}{x} + \dfrac{x}{\sqrt{a^2 - x^2}}\right].$

37. $\int x\sqrt{a^2 - x^2}\, dx = -\tfrac{1}{3}(a^2 - x^2)^{3/2}.$

38. $\int \dfrac{\sqrt{a^2 - x^2}}{x}\, dx = \sqrt{a^2 - x^2} - a \ln\left|\dfrac{a + \sqrt{a^2 - x^2}}{x}\right|.$

39. $\int x(a^2 - x^2)^{3/2}\, dx = -\tfrac{1}{5}(a^2 - x^2)^{5/2}.$

40. $\int \dfrac{(a^2 - x^2)^{3/2}}{x}\, dx = \dfrac{(a^2 - x^2)^{3/2}}{3} + a^2\sqrt{a^2 - x^2} - a^3 \ln\left|\dfrac{a + \sqrt{a^2 - x^2}}{x}\right|.$

41. $\int x^n(a^2 - x^2)^{3/2}\, dx = \dfrac{1}{n + 1}x^{n+1}(a^2 - x^2)^{3/2} + \dfrac{3}{n + 1}\int x^{n+2}\sqrt{a^2 - x^2}\, dx$

$\qquad\qquad\qquad\qquad\qquad\qquad\qquad\qquad\qquad\qquad (n \neq -1).$

42. $\int x^n\sqrt{a^2 - x^2}\, dx = -\dfrac{1}{n + 2}x^{n-1}(a^2 - x^2)^{3/2} + \dfrac{a^2(n - 1)}{n + 2}\int x^{n-2}\sqrt{a^2 - x^2}\, dx$

$\qquad\qquad\qquad\qquad\qquad\qquad\qquad\qquad\qquad\qquad (n \neq -2).$

INTEGRALS CONTAINING $\sqrt{x^2 \pm a^2}$

43. $\int \dfrac{1}{\sqrt{x^2 \pm a^2}}\, dx = \ln|x + \sqrt{x^2 \pm a^2}|.$

44. $\int \dfrac{x}{\sqrt{x^2 \pm a^2}}\, dx = \sqrt{x^2 \pm a^2}.$

45. $\int \dfrac{x^2}{\sqrt{x^2 \pm a^2}}\, dx = \tfrac{1}{2}x\sqrt{x^2 \pm a^2} \mp \tfrac{1}{2}a^2 \ln|x + \sqrt{x^2 \pm a^2}|.$

46. $\int \dfrac{1}{x\sqrt{x^2 + a^2}}\, dx = -\dfrac{1}{a} \ln\left|\dfrac{a + \sqrt{x^2 + a^2}}{x}\right|.$

47. $\int \dfrac{1}{x^2\sqrt{x^2 \pm a^2}}\, dx = \mp\dfrac{\sqrt{x^2 \pm a^2}}{a^2 x}.$

48. $\displaystyle\int \frac{1}{(x^2 \pm a^2)^{3/2}}\, dx = \pm \frac{1}{a^2}\, \frac{x}{\sqrt{x^2 \pm a^2}}.$

49. $\displaystyle\int \frac{x}{(x^2 \pm a^2)^{3/2}}\, dx = -\frac{1}{\sqrt{x^2 \pm a^2}}.$

50. $\displaystyle\int \frac{x^2}{(x^2 \pm a^2)^{3/2}}\, dx = -\frac{x}{\sqrt{x^2 \pm a^2}} + \ln|x + \sqrt{x^2 \pm a^2}|.$

51. $\displaystyle\int \frac{1}{x(x^2 + a^2)^{3/2}}\, dx = \pm \frac{1}{a^2}\left\{\frac{1}{\sqrt{x^2 + a^2}} + \int \frac{1}{x\sqrt{x^2 + a^2}}\, dx\right\}$ (see 46).

52. $\displaystyle\int \frac{1}{x^2(x^2 \pm a^2)^{3/2}}\, dx = -\frac{1}{a^4}\left\{\frac{\sqrt{x^2 \pm a^2}}{x} + \frac{x}{\sqrt{x^2 \pm a^2}}\right\}.$

53. $\displaystyle\int \frac{1}{(x^2 \pm a^2)^{5/2}}\, dx = \frac{1}{a^4}\left\{\frac{x}{\sqrt{x^2 \pm a^2}} - \frac{1}{3}\frac{x^3}{(x^2 \pm a^2)^{3/2}}\right\}.$

54. $\displaystyle\int \frac{x}{(x^2 \pm a^2)^{5/2}}\, dx = -\frac{1}{3}\frac{1}{(x^2 \pm a^2)^{3/2}}.$

55. $\displaystyle\int \frac{x^2}{(x^2 \pm a^2)^{5/2}}\, dx = \pm \frac{1}{3a^2}\frac{x^3}{(x^2 \pm a^2)^{3/2}}.$

56. $\displaystyle\int \sqrt{x^2 \pm a^2}\, dx = \tfrac{1}{2}x\sqrt{x^2 \pm a^2} \pm \tfrac{1}{2}a^2 \ln|x + \sqrt{x^2 \pm a^2}|.$

57. $\displaystyle\int x\sqrt{x^2 \pm a^2}\, dx = \tfrac{1}{3}(x^2 \pm a^2)^{3/2}.$

58. $\displaystyle\int x^2\sqrt{x^2 \pm a^2}\, dx = \frac{x}{4}(x^2 \pm a^2)^{3/2} \pm \frac{1}{8}a^2x\sqrt{x^2 \pm a^2} - \frac{1}{8}a^4 \ln|x + \sqrt{x^2 \pm a^2}|.$

59. $\displaystyle\int \frac{\sqrt{x^2 + a^2}}{x}\, dx = \sqrt{x^2 + a^2} - a \ln\left|\frac{a + \sqrt{x^2 + a^2}}{x}\right|.$

60. $\displaystyle\int \frac{\sqrt{x^2 \pm a^2}}{x^2}\, dx = -\frac{\sqrt{x^2 \pm a^2}}{x} + \ln|x + \sqrt{x^2 \pm a^2}|.$

61. $\displaystyle\int (x^2 \pm a^2)^{3/2}\, dx = \frac{x}{4}(x^2 \pm a^2)^{3/2} \pm \frac{3}{8}a^2x\sqrt{x^2 \pm a^2} + \frac{3}{8}a^4 \ln|x + \sqrt{x^2 \pm a^2}|.$

62. $\displaystyle\int x(x^2 \pm a^2)^{3/2}\, dx = \tfrac{1}{5}(x^2 \pm a^2)^{5/2}.$

63. $\displaystyle\int \frac{(x^2 \pm a^2)^{3/2}}{x}\, dx = \frac{1}{3}(x^2 \pm a^2)^{3/2} \pm a^2 \int \frac{\sqrt{x^2 \pm a^2}}{x}\, dx.$

64. $\displaystyle\int x^n(x^2 \pm a^2)^{3/2}\, dx = \frac{1}{n+1}x^{n+1}(x^2 \pm a^2)^{3/2} - \frac{3}{n+1}\int x^{n+2}\sqrt{x^2 \pm a^2}\, dx$
$(n \neq -1).$

65. $\displaystyle\int x^n\sqrt{x^2 \pm a^2}\, dx = \frac{1}{n+2}x^{n-1}(x^2 \pm a^2)^{3/2} \pm \frac{a^2(n-1)}{n+2}\int x^{n-2}\sqrt{x^2 \pm a^2}\, dx$
$(n \neq -2).$

INTEGRALS CONTAINING $ax^2 + bx + c$

66. $\displaystyle\int \frac{1}{ax^2 + bx + c}\, dx = \frac{1}{\sqrt{b^2 - 4ac}} \ln\left|\frac{2ax + b - \sqrt{b^2 - 4ac}}{2ax + b + \sqrt{b^2 - 4ac}}\right|$ $(b^2 - 4ac > 0)$

INTEGRALS CONTAINING EXPONENTIALS AND LOGARITHMS

67. $\int e^{ax}\,dx = \dfrac{1}{a}e^{ax}.$

68. $\int a^x\,dx = \dfrac{1}{\ln a}a^x.$

69. $\int xe^{ax}\,dx = \dfrac{1}{a^2}(ax - 1)e^{ax}.$

70. $\int x^n e^{ax}\,dx = \dfrac{1}{a}x^n e^{ax} - \dfrac{n}{a}\int x^{n-1}e^{ax}\,dx.$

71. $\int \dfrac{1}{b + ce^{ax}}\,dx = \dfrac{1}{ab}[ax - \ln(b + ce^{ax})] \quad (ab \neq 0).$

72. $\int \ln|x|\,dx = x\ln|x| - x.$

73. $\int x\ln|x|\,dx = \tfrac{1}{2}x^2\ln|x| - \tfrac{1}{4}x^2.$

74. $\int x^n \ln|x|\,dx = \dfrac{1}{n+1}x^{n+1}\left[\ln|x| - \dfrac{1}{n+1}\right] \quad (n \neq -1).$

75. $\int \dfrac{\ln|x|}{x}\,dx = \ln|\ln|x||.$

76. $\int \ln^n|x|\,dx = x\ln^n|x| - x\int \ln^{n-1}|x|\,dx.$

77. $\int x^m \ln^n|x|\,dx = \dfrac{1}{m+1}\left\{x^{m+1}\ln^n|x| - n\int x^m \ln^{n-1}|x|\,dx\right\} \quad (m \neq -1).$

78. $\int \dfrac{\ln^n|x|}{x}\,dx = \dfrac{1}{n+1}\ln^{n+1}|x|.$

MISCELLANEOUS INTEGRALS

79. $\int \dfrac{1}{x(ax^n + b)}\,dx = \dfrac{1}{nb}\ln\left|\dfrac{x^n}{ax^n + b}\right| \quad (n \neq 0,\ b \neq 0).$

80. $\int \dfrac{1}{x\sqrt{ax^n + b}}\,dx = \dfrac{1}{n\sqrt{b}}\ln\left|\dfrac{\sqrt{ax^n + b} - \sqrt{b}}{\sqrt{ax^n + b} + \sqrt{b}}\right| \quad (b > 0).$

81. $\int \sqrt{\dfrac{x + a}{x + b}}\,dx = \sqrt{x + b}\sqrt{x + a} + (a - b)\ln|\sqrt{x + b} + \sqrt{x + a}|.$

NUMERICAL TABLES

TABLE A.3.1 Four Place Common Logarithms.

N	0	1	2	3	4	5	6	7	8	9
1.0	.0000	.0043	.0086	.0128	.0170	.0212	.0253	.0294	.0334	.0374
1.1	.0414	.0453	.0492	.0531	.0569	.0607	.0645	.0682	.0719	.0755
1.2	.0792	.0828	.0864	.0899	.0934	.0969	.1004	.1038	.1072	.1106
1.3	.1139	.1173	.1206	.1239	.1271	.1303	.1335	.1367	.1399	.1430
1.4	.1461	.1492	.1523	.1553	.1584	.1614	.1644	.1673	.1703	.1732
1.5	.1761	.1790	.1818	.1847	.1875	.1903	.1931	.1959	.1987	.2014
1.6	.2041	.2068	.2095	.2122	.2148	.2175	.2201	.2227	.2253	.2279
1.7	.2304	.2330	.2355	.2380	.2405	.2430	.2455	.2480	.2504	.2529
1.8	.2553	.2577	.2601	.2625	.2648	.2672	.2695	.2718	.2742	.2765
1.9	.2788	.2810	.2833	.2856	.2878	.2900	.2923	.2945	.2967	.2989
2.0	.3010	.3032	.3054	.3075	.3096	.3118	.3139	.3160	.3181	.3201
2.1	.3222	.3243	.3263	.3284	.3304	.3324	.3345	.3365	.3385	.3404
2.2	.3424	.3444	.3464	.3483	.3502	.3522	.3541	.3560	.3579	.3598
2.3	.3617	.3636	.3655	.3674	.3692	.3711	.3729	.3747	.3766	.3784
2.4	.3802	.3820	.3838	.3856	.3874	.3892	.3909	.3927	.3945	.3962
2.5	.3979	.3997	.4014	.4031	.4048	.4065	.4082	.4099	.4116	.4133
2.6	.4150	.4166	.4183	.4200	.4216	.4232	.4249	.4265	.4281	.4298
2.7	.4314	.4330	.4346	.4362	.4378	.4393	.4409	.4425	.4440	.4456
2.8	.4472	.4487	.4502	.4518	.4533	.4548	.4564	.4579	.4594	.4609
2.9	.4624	.4639	.4654	.4669	.4683	.4698	.4713	.4728	.4742	.4757
3.0	.4771	.4786	.4800	.4814	.4829	.4843	.4857	.4871	.4886	.4900
3.1	.4914	.4928	.4942	.4955	.4969	.4983	.4997	.5011	.5024	.5038
3.2	.5051	.5065	.5079	.5092	.5105	.5119	.5132	.5145	.5159	.5172
3.3	.5185	.5198	.5211	.5224	.5237	.5250	.5263	.5276	.5289	.5302
3.4	.5315	.5328	.5340	.5353	.5366	.5378	.5391	.5403	.5416	.5428
3.5	.5441	.5453	.5465	.5478	.5490	.5502	.5514	.5527	.5539	.5551
3.6	.5563	.5575	.5587	.5599	.5611	.5623	.5635	.5647	.5658	.5670
3.7	.5682	.5694	.5705	.5717	.5729	.5740	.5752	.5763	.5775	.5786
3.8	.5798	.5809	.5821	.5832	.5843	.5855	.5866	.5877	.5888	.5899
3.9	.5911	.5922	.5933	.5944	.5955	.5966	.5977	.5988	.5999	.6010
4.0	.6021	.6031	.6042	.6053	.6064	.6075	.6085	.6096	.6107	.6117
4.1	.6128	.6138	.6149	.6160	.6170	.6180	.6191	.6201	.6212	.6222
4.2	.6232	.6243	.6253	.6263	.6274	.6284	.6294	.6304	.6314	.6325
4.3	.6335	.6345	.6355	.6365	.6375	.6385	.6395	.6405	.6415	.6425
4.4	.6435	.6444	.6454	.6464	.6474	.6484	.6493	.6503	.6513	.6522
4.5	.6532	.6542	.6551	.6561	.6571	.6580	.6590	.6599	.6609	.6618
4.6	.6628	.6637	.6646	.6656	.6665	.6675	.6684	.6693	.6702	.6712
4.7	.6721	.6730	.6739	.6749	.6758	.6767	.6776	.6785	.6794	.6803
4.8	.6812	.6821	.6830	.6839	.6848	.6857	.6866	.6875	.6884	.6893
4.9	.6902	.6911	.6920	.6928	.6937	.6946	.6955	.6964	.6972	.6981
5.0	.6990	.6998	.7007	.7016	.7024	.7033	.7042	.7050	.7059	.7067
5.1	.7076	.7084	.7093	.7101	.7110	.7118	.7126	.7135	.7143	.7152
5.2	.7160	.7168	.7177	.7185	.7193	.7202	.7210	.7218	.7226	.7235
5.3	.7243	.7251	.7259	.7267	.7275	.7284	.7292	.7300	.7308	.7316
5.4	.7324	.7332	.7340	.7348	.7356	.7364	.7372	.7380	.7388	.7396
N	0	1	2	3	4	5	6	7	8	9

TABLE A.3.1 Four Place Logarithms (*Continued*).

N	0	1	2	3	4	5	6	7	8	9
5.5	.7404	.7412	.7419	.7427	.7435	.7443	.7451	.7459	.7466	.7474
5.6	.7482	.7490	.7497	.7505	.7513	.7520	.7528	.7536	.7543	.7551
5.7	.7559	.7566	.7574	.7582	.7589	.7597	.7604	.7612	.7619	.7627
5.8	.7634	.7642	.7649	.7657	.7664	.7672	.7679	.7686	.7694	.7701
5.9	.7709	.7716	.7723	.7731	.7738	.7745	.7752	.7760	.7767	.7774
6.0	.7782	.7789	.7796	.7803	.7810	.7818	.7825	.7832	.7839	.7846
6.1	.7853	.7860	.7868	.7875	.7882	.7889	.7896	.7903	.7910	.7917
6.2	.7924	.7931	.7938	.7945	.7952	.7959	.7966	.7973	.7980	.7987
6.3	.7993	.8000	.8007	.8014	.8021	.8028	.8035	.8041	.8048	.8055
6.4	.8062	.8069	.8075	.8082	.8089	.8096	.8102	.8109	.8116	.8122
6.5	.8129	.8136	.8142	.8149	.8156	.8162	.8169	.8176	.8182	.8189
6.6	.8195	.8202	.8209	.8215	.8222	.8228	.8235	.8241	.8248	.8254
6.7	.8261	.8267	.8274	.8280	.8287	.8293	.8299	.8306	.8312	.8319
6.8	.8325	.8331	.8338	.8344	.8351	.8357	.8363	.8370	.8376	.8382
6.9	.8388	.8395	.8401	.8407	.8414	.8420	.8426	.8432	.8439	.8445
7.0	.8451	.8457	.8463	.8470	.8476	.8482	.8488	.8494	.8500	.8506
7.1	.8513	.8519	.8525	.8531	.8537	.8543	.8549	.8555	.8561	.8567
7.2	.8573	.8579	.8585	.8591	.8597	.8603	.8609	.8615	.8621	.8627
7.3	.8633	.8639	.8645	.8651	.8657	.8663	.8669	.8675	.8681	.8686
7.4	.8692	.8698	.8704	.8710	.8716	.8722	.8727	.8733	.8739	.8745
7.5	.8751	.8756	.8762	.8768	.8774	.8779	.8785	.8791	.8797	.8802
7.6	.8808	.8814	.8820	.8825	.8831	.8837	.8842	.8848	.8854	.8859
7.7	.8865	.8871	.8876	.8882	.8887	.8893	.8899	.8904	.8910	.8915
7.8	.8921	.8927	.8932	.8938	.8943	.8949	.8954	.8960	.8965	.8971
7.9	.8976	.8982	.8987	.8993	.8998	.9004	.9009	.9015	.9020	.9025
8.0	.9031	.9036	.9042	.9047	.9053	.9058	.9063	.9069	.9074	.9079
8.1	.9085	.9090	.9096	.9101	.9106	.9112	.9117	.9122	.9128	.9133
8.2	.9138	.9143	.9149	.9154	.9159	.9165	.9170	.9175	.9180	.9186
8.3	.9191	.9196	.9201	.9206	.9212	.9217	.9222	.9227	.9232	.9238
8.4	.9243	.9248	.9253	.9258	.9263	.9269	.9274	.9279	.9284	.9289
8.5	.9294	.9299	.9304	.9309	.9315	.9320	.9325	.9330	.9335	.9340
8.6	.9345	.9350	.9355	.9360	.9365	.9370	.9375	.9380	.9385	.9390
8.7	.9395	.9400	.9405	.9410	.9415	.9420	.9425	.9430	.9435	.9440
8.8	.9445	.9450	.9455	.9460	.9465	.9469	.9474	.9479	.9484	.9489
8.9	.9494	.9499	.9504	.9509	.9513	.9518	.9523	.9528	.9533	.9538
9.0	.9542	.9547	.9552	.9557	.9562	.9566	.9571	.9576	.9581	.9586
9.1	.9590	.9595	.9600	.9605	.9609	.9614	.9619	.9624	.9628	.9633
9.2	.9638	.9643	.9647	.9652	.9657	.9661	.9666	.9671	.9675	.9680
9.3	.9685	.9689	.9694	.9699	.9703	.9708	.97:3	.9717	.9722	.9727
9.4	.9731	.9736	.9741	.9745	.9750	.9754	.9759	.9763	.9768	.9773
9.5	.9777	.9782	.9786	.9791	.9795	.9800	.9805	.9809	.9814	.9818
9.6	.9823	.9827	.9832	.9836	.9841	.9845	.9850	.9854	.9859	.9863
9.7	.9868	.9872	.9877	.9881	.9886	.9890	.9894	.9899	.9903	.9908
9.8	.9912	.9917	.9921	.9926	.9930	.9934	.9939	.9943	.9948	.9952
9.9	.9956	.9961	.9965	.9969	.9974	.9978	.9983	.9987	.9991	.9996
N	0	1	2	3	4	5	6	7	8	9

TABLE A.3.2 Natural Logarithms.

	0.00	0.01	0.02	0.03	0.04	0.05	0.06	0.07	0.08	0.09
1.0	0.0000	0.0100	0.0198	0.0296	0.0392	0.0488	0.0583	0.0677	0.0770	0.0862
1.1	0.0953	0.1044	0.1133	0.1222	0.1310	0.1398	0.1484	0.1570	0.1655	0.1740
1.2	0.1823	0.1906	0.1989	0.2070	0.2151	0.2231	0.2311	0.2390	0.2469	0.2546
1.3	0.2624	0.2700	0.2776	0.2852	0.2927	0.3001	0.3075	0.3148	0.3221	0.3293
1.4	0.3365	0.3436	0.3507	0.3577	0.3646	0.3716	0.3784	0.3853	0.3920	0.3988
1.5	0.4055	0.4121	0.4187	0.4253	0.4318	0.4383	0.4447	0.4511	0.4574	0.4637
1.6	0.4700	0.4762	0.4824	0.4886	0.4947	0.5008	0.5068	0.5128	0.5188	0.5247
1.7	0.5306	0.5365	0.5423	0.5481	0.5539	0.5596	0.5653	0.5710	0.5766	0.5822
1.8	0.5878	0.5933	0.5988	0.6043	0.6098	0.6152	0.6206	0.6259	0.6313	0.6366
1.9	0.6419	0.6471	0.6523	0.6575	0.6627	0.6678	0.6729	0.6780	0.6831	0.6881
2.0	0.6931	0.6981	0.7031	0.7080	0.7130	0.7178	0.7227	0.7275	0.7324	0.7372
2.1	0.7419	0.7467	0.7514	0.7561	0.7608	0.7655	0.7701	0.7747	0.7793	0.7839
2.2	0.7885	0.7930	0.7975	0.8020	0.8065	0.8109	0.8154	0.8198	0.8242	0.8286
2.3	0.8329	0.8372	0.8416	0.8459	0.8502	0.8544	0.8587	0.8629	0.8671	0.8713
2.4	0.8755	0.8796	0.8838	0.8879	0.8920	0.8961	0.9002	0.9042	0.9083	0.9123
2.5	0.9163	0.9203	0.9243	0.9282	0.9322	0.9361	0.9400	0.9439	0.9478	0.9517
2.6	0.9555	0.9594	0.9632	0.9670	0.9708	0.9746	0.9783	0.9821	0.9858	0.9895
2.7	0.9933	0.9969	1.0006	1.0043	1.0080	1.0116	1.0152	1.0188	1.0225	1.0260
2.8	1.0296	1.0332	1.0367	1.0403	1.0438	1.0473	1.0508	1.0543	1.0578	1.0613
2.9	1.0647	1.0682	1.0716	1.0750	1.0784	1.0818	1.0852	1.0886	1.0919	1.0953
3.0	1.0986	1.1019	1.1053	1.1086	1.1119	1.1151	1.1184	1.1217	1.1249	1.1282
3.1	1.1314	1.1346	1.1378	1.1410	1.1442	1.1474	1.1506	1.1537	1.1569	1.1600
3.2	1.1632	1.1663	1.1694	1.1725	1.1756	1.1787	1.1817	1.1848	1.1878	1.1909
3.3	1.1939	1.1970	1.2000	1.2030	1.2060	1.2090	1.2119	1.2149	1.2179	1.2208
3.4	1.2238	1.2267	1.2296	1.2326	1.2355	1.2384	1.2413	1.2442	1.2470	1.2499
3.5	1.2528	1.2556	1.2585	1.2613	1.2641	1.2669	1.2698	1.2726	1.2754	1.2782
3.6	1.2809	1.2837	1.2865	1.2892	1.2920	1.2947	1.2975	1.3002	1.3029	1.3056
3.7	1.3083	1.3110	1.3137	1.3164	1.3191	1.3218	1.3244	1.3271	1.3297	1.3324
3.8	1.3350	1.3376	1.3403	1.3429	1.3455	1.3481	1.3507	1.3533	1.3558	1.3584
3.9	1.3610	1.3635	1.3661	1.3686	1.3712	1.3737	1.3762	1.3788	1.3813	1.3838
4.0	1.3863	1.3888	1.3913	1.3938	1.3962	1.3987	1.4012	1.4036	1.4061	1.4085
4.1	1.4110	1.4134	1.4159	1.4183	1.4207	1.4231	1.4255	1.4279	1.4303	1.4327
4.2	1.4351	1.4375	1.4398	1.4422	1.4446	1.4469	1.4493	1.4516	1.4540	1.4563
4.3	1.4586	1.4609	1.4633	1.4656	1.4679	1.4702	1.4725	1.4748	1.4770	1.4793
4.4	1.4816	1.4839	1.4861	1.4884	1.4907	1.4929	1.4952	1.4974	1.4996	1.5019
4.5	1.5041	1.5063	1.5085	1.5107	1.5129	1.5151	1.5173	1.5195	1.5217	1.5239
4.6	1.5261	1.5282	1.5304	1.5326	1.5347	1.5369	1.5390	1.5412	1.5433	1.5454
4.7	1.5476	1.5497	1.5518	1.5539	1.5560	1.5581	1.5602	1.5623	1.5644	1.5665
4.8	1.5686	1.5707	1.5728	1.5748	1.5769	1.5790	1.5810	1.5831	1.5851	1.5872
4.9	1.5892	1.5913	1.5933	1.5953	1.5974	1.5994	1.6014	1.6034	1.6054	1.6074
5.0	1.6094	1.6114	1.6134	1.6154	1.6174	1.6194	1.6214	1.6233	1.6253	1.6273
5.1	1.6292	1.6312	1.6332	1.6351	1.6371	1.6390	1.6409	1.6429	1.6448	1.6467
5.2	1.6487	1.6506	1.6525	1.6544	1.6563	1.6582	1.6601	1.6620	1.6639	1.6658
5.3	1.6677	1.6696	1.6715	1.6734	1.6752	1.6771	1.6790	1.6808	1.6827	1.6845
5.4	1.6864	1.6882	1.6901	1.6919	1.6938	1.6956	1.6974	1.6993	1.7011	1.7029

$$\ln (N \cdot 10^m) = \ln N + m \ln 10, \qquad \ln 10 = 2.3026$$

TABLE A.3.2 Natural Logarithms (*Continued*).

	0.00	0.01	0.02	0.03	0.04	0.05	0.06	0.07	0.08	0.09
5.5	1.7047	1.7066	1.7084	1.7102	1.7120	1.7138	1.7156	1.7174	1.7192	1.7210
5.6	1.7228	1.7246	1.7263	1.7281	1.7299	1.7317	1.7334	1.7352	1.7370	1.7387
5.7	1.7405	1.7422	1.7440	1.7457	1.7475	1.7492	1.7509	1.7527	1.7544	1.7561
5.8	1.7579	1.7596	1.7613	1.7630	1.7647	1.7664	1.7682	1.7699	1.7716	1.7733
5.9	1.7750	1.7766	1.7783	1.7800	1.7817	1.7834	1.7851	1.7867	1.7884	1.7901
6.0	1.7918	1.7934	1.7951	1.7967	1.7984	1.8001	1.8017	1.8034	1.8050	1.8066
6.1	1.8083	1.8099	1.8116	1.8132	1.8148	1.8165	1.8181	1.8197	1.8213	1.8229
6.2	1.8245	1.8262	1.8278	1.8294	1.8310	1.8326	1.8342	1.8358	1.8374	1.8390
6.3	1.8406	1.8421	1.8437	1.8453	1.8469	1.8485	1.8500	1.8516	1.8532	1.8547
6.4	1.8563	1.8579	1.8594	1.8610	1.8625	1.8641	1.8656	1.8672	1.8687	1.8703
6.5	1.8718	1.8733	1.8749	1.8764	1.8779	1.8795	1.8810	1.8825	1.8840	1.8856
6.6	1.8871	1.8886	1.8901	1.8916	1.8931	1.8946	1.8961	1.8976	1.8991	1.9006
6.7	1.9021	1.9036	1.9051	1.9066	1.9081	1.9095	1.9110	1.9125	1.9140	1.9155
6.8	1.9169	1.9184	1.9199	1.9213	1.9228	1.9242	1.9257	1.9272	1.9286	1.9301
6.9	1.9315	1.9330	1.9344	1.9359	1.9373	1.9387	1.9402	1.9416	1.9430	1.9445
7.0	1.9459	1.9473	1.9488	1.9502	1.9516	1.9530	1.9544	1.9559	1.9573	1.9587
7.1	1.9601	1.9615	1.9629	1.9643	1.9657	1.9671	1.9685	1.9699	1.9713	1.9727
7.2	1.9741	1.9755	1.9769	1.9782	1.9796	1.9810	1.9824	1.9838	1.9851	1.9865
7.3	1.9879	1.9892	1.9906	1.9920	1.9933	1.9947	1.9961	1.9974	1.9988	2.0001
7.4	2.0015	2.0028	2.0042	2.0055	2.0069	2.0082	2.0096	2.0109	2.0122	2.0136
7.5	2.0149	2.0162	2.0176	2.0189	2.0202	2.0215	2.0229	2.0242	2.0255	2.0268
7.6	2.0282	2.0295	2.0308	2.0321	2.0334	2.0347	2.0360	2.0373	2.0386	2.0399
7.7	2.0412	2.0425	2.0438	2.0451	2.0464	2.0477	2.0490	2.0503	2.0516	2.0528
7.8	2.0541	2.0554	2.0567	2.0580	2.0592	2.0605	2.0618	2.0631	2.0643	2.0656
7.9	2.0669	2.0681	2.0694	2.0707	2.0719	2.0732	2.0744	2.0757	2.0769	2.0782
8.0	2.0794	2.0807	2.0819	2.0832	2.0844	2.0857	2.0869	2.0882	2.0894	2.0906
8.1	2.0919	2.0931	2.0943	2.0956	2.0968	2.0980	2.0992	2.1005	2.1017	2.1029
8.2	2.1041	2.1054	2.1066	2.1078	2.1090	2.1102	2.1114	2.1126	2.1138	2.1150
8.3	2.1163	2.1175	2.1187	2.1190	2.1211	2.1223	2.1235	2.1247	2.1258	2.1270
8.4	2.1282	2.1294	2.1306	2.1318	2.1330	2.1342	2.1353	2.1365	2.1377	2.1389
8.5	2.1401	2.1412	2.1424	2.1436	2.1448	2.1459	2.1471	2.1483	2.1494	2.1506
8.6	2.1518	2.1529	2.1541	2.1552	2.1564	2.1576	2.1587	2.1599	2.1610	2.1622
8.7	2.1633	2.1645	2.1656	2.1668	2.1679	2.1691	2.1702	2.1713	2.1725	2.1736
8.8	2.1748	2.1759	2.1770	2.1782	2.1793	2.!804	2.1815	2.1827	2.1838	2.1849
8.9	2.1861	2.1872	2.1883	2.1894	2.1905	2.1917	2.1928	2.1939	2.1950	2.1961
9.0	2.1972	2.1983	2.1994	2.2006	2.2017	2.2028	2.2039	2.2050	2.2061	2.2072
9.1	2.2083	2.2094	2.2105	2.2116	2.2127	2.2138	2.2148	2.2159	2.2170	2.2181
9.2	2.2192	2.2203	2.2214	2.2225	2.2235	2.2246	2.2257	2.2268	2.2279	2.2289
9.3	2.2300	2.2311	2.2322	2.2332	2.2343	2.2354	2.2364	2.2375	2.2386	2.2396
9.4	2.2407	2.2418	2.2428	2.2439	2.2450	2.2460	2.2471	2.2481	2.2492	2.2502
9.5	2.2513	2.2523	2.2534	2.2544	2.2555	2.2565	2.2576	2.2586	2.2597	2.2607
9.6	2.2618	2.2628	2.2638	2.2649	2.2659	2.2670	2.2680	2.2690	2.2701	2.2711
9.7	2.2721	2.2732	2.2742	2.2752	2.2762	2.2773	2.2783	2.2793	2.2803	2.2814
9.8	2.2824	2.2834	2.2844	2.2854	2.2865	2.2875	2.2885	2.2895	2.2905	2.2915
9.9	2.2925	2.2935	2.2946	2.2956	2.2966	2.2976	2.2986	2.2996	2.3006	2.3016

TABLE A.3.3 Exponential Functions.

x	e^x	e^{-x}	x	e^x	e^{-x}
0.00	1.0000	1.0000	0.45	1.5683	0.6376
0.01	1.0101	0.9900	0.46	1.5841	0.6313
0.02	1.0202	0.9802	0.47	1.6000	0.6250
0.03	1.0305	0.9704	0.48	1.6161	0.6188
0.04	1.0408	0.9608	0.49	1.6323	0.6126
0.05	1.0513	0.9512	0.50	1.6487	0.6065
0.06	1.0618	0.9418	0.51	1.6653	0.6005
0.07	1.0725	0.9324	0.52	1.6820	0.5945
0.08	1.0833	0.9231	0.53	1.6989	0.5886
0.09	1.0942	0.9139	0.54	1.7160	0.5827
0.10	1.1052	0.9048	0.55	1.7333	0.5769
0.11	1.1163	0.8958	0.56	1.7507	0.5712
0.12	1.1275	0.8869	0.57	1.7683	0.5655
0.13	1.1388	0.8781	0.58	1.7860	0.5599
0.14	1.1503	0.9694	0.59	1.8040	0.5543
0.15	1.1618	0.8607	0.60	1.8221	0.5488
0.16	1.1735	0.8521	0.61	1.8044	0.5434
0.17	1.1853	0.8437	0.62	1.8589	0.5379
0.18	1.1972	0.8353	0.63	1.8776	0.5326
0.19	1.2092	0.8270	0.64	1.8965	0.5273
0.2(	1.2214	0.8187	0.65	1.9155	0.5220
0.21	1.2337	0.8106	0.66	1.9348	0.5169
0.22	1.2461	0.8025	0.67	1.9542	0.5117
0.23	1.2586	0.7945	0.68	1.9739	0.5066
0.24	1.2712	0.7866	0.69	1.9937	0.5016
0.25	1.2840	0.7788	0.70	2.0138	0.4966
0.26	1.2969	0.7711	0.71	2.0340	0.4916
0.27	1.3100	0.7634	0.72	2.0544	0.4868
0.28	1.3231	0.7558	0.73	2.0751	0.4819
0.29	1.3364	0.7483	0.74	2.0959	0.4771
0.30	1.3499	0.7408	0.75	2.1170	0.4724
0.31	1.3634	0.7334	0.76	2.1383	0.4677
0.32	1.3771	0.7261	0.77	2.1598	0.4630
0.33	1.3910	0.7189	0.78	2.1815	0.4584
0.34	1.4049	0.7118	0.79	2.2034	0.4538
0.35	1.4191	0.7047	0.80	2.2255	0.4493
0.36	1.4333	0.6977	0.81	2.2479	0.4449
0.37	1.4477	0.6907	0.82	2.2705	0.4404
0.38	1.4623	0.6839	0.83	2.2933	0.4360
0.39	1.4770	0.6771	0.84	2.3164	0.4317
0.40	1.4918	0.6703	0.85	2.3396	0.4274
0.41	1.5068	0.6637	0.86	2.3632	0.4232
0.42	1.5220	0.6570	0.87	2.3869	0.4190
0.43	1.5373	0.6505	0.88	2.4109	0.4148
0.44	1.5527	0.6440	0.89	2.4351	0.4107

TABLE A.3.3 Exponential Functions (*Continued*).

x	e^x	e^{-x}	x	e^x	e^{-x}
0.90	2.4596	0.4066	2.75	15.643	0.0639
0.91	2.4843	0.4025	2.80	16.445	0.0608
0.92	2.5093	0.3985	2.85	17.288	0.0578
0.93	2.5345	0.3946	2.90	18.174	0.0550
0.94	2.5600	0.3906	2.95	19.106	0.0523
0.95	2.5857	0.3867	3.00	20.086	0.0498
0.96	2.6117	0.3829	3.05	21.115	0.0474
0.97	2.6379	0.3791	3.10	22.198	0.0450
0.98	2.6645	0.3753	3.15	23.336	0.0429
0.99	2.6912	0.3716	3.20	24.533	0.0408
1.00	2.7183	0.3679	3.25	25.790	0.0388
1.05	2.8577	0.3499	3.30	27.113	0.0369
1.10	3.0042	0.3329	3.35	28.503	0.0351
1.15	3.1582	0.3166	3.40	29.964	0.0334
1.20	3.3201	0.3012	3.45	31.500	0.0317
1.25	3.4903	0.2865	3.50	33.115	0.0302
1.30	3.6693	0.2725	3.55	34.813	0.0287
1.35	3.8574	0.2592	3.60	36.598	0.0273
1.40	4.0552	0.2466	3.65	38.475	0.0260
1.45	4.2631	0.2346	3.70	40.447	0.0247
1.50	4.4817	0.2231	3.75	42.521	0.0235
1.55	4.7115	0.2122	3.80	44.701	0.0224
1.60	4.9530	0.2019	3.85	46.993	0.0213
1.65	5.2070	0.1920	3.90	49.402	0.0202
1.70	5.4739	0.1827	3.95	51.935	0.0193
1.75	5.7546	0.1738	4.00	54.598	0.0183
1.80	6.0496	0.1653	4.10	60.340	0.0166
1.85	6.3598	0.1572	4.20	66.686	0.0150
1.90	6.6859	0.1496	4.30	73.700	0.0136
1.95	7.0287	0.1423	4.40	81.451	0.0123
2.00	7.3891	0.1353	4.50	90.017	0.0111
2.05	7.7679	0.1287	4.60	99.484	0.0101
2.10	8.1662	0.1225	4.70	109.95	0.0091
2.15	8.5849	0.1165	4.80	121.51	0.0082
2.20	9.0250	0.1108	4.90	134.29	0.0074
2.25	9.4877	0.1054	5.00	148.41	0.0067
2.30	9.9742	0.1003	5.20	181.27	0.0055
2.35	10.486	0.0954	5.40	221.41	0.0045
2.40	11.023	0.0907	5.60	270.43	0.0037
2.45	11.588	0.0863	5.80	330.30	0.0030
2.50	12.182	0.0821	6.00	403.43	0.0025
2.55	12.807	0.0781	7.00	1096.6	0.0009
2.60	13.464	0.0743	8.00	2981.0	0.0003
2.65	14.154	0.0707	9.00	8103.1	0.0001
2.70	14.880	0.0672	10.00	22026.	0.00005

ANSWERS TO ODD-NUMBERED QUESTIONS

CHAPTER 1

Exercises 1

1. **a.** True   **b.** False; $(3x)(4x) = 12x^2$ **c.** False; $2(5 - 4y) = 10 - 8y$
   d. False; $-(x + y) = -x - y$ **e.** False; $5x - (2 - 3x) = 5x - 2 + 3x = 8x - 2$
   f. False; $5 - 2x \neq 3x$, $5 - 2x$ cannot be simplified.
   g. False; $-3(x - 2y) = -3x + 6y$ **h.** False; $(-a)(-b)(-c) \div (-d) = abc \div d$
   i. True   **j.** True   **k.** False; $(-x)(-y) = xy$ **l.** True ·
3. -4 5. 21 7. 3 9. 7 11. -30 13. -10 15. 12
17. $x + 3$ 19. $-2x - 6$ 21. $-4x + 24$ 23. $xy + 6x$ 25. $-xyz$
27. $2xy - 3xyz$ 29. $-6pq^2 + 6p^2q$ 31. $-6xy - 24x$ 33. $x + t$
35. $3x^2 + 4xy$ 37. $x^2 - 5x$ 39. $4x - 8$ 41. $2 - 1/x$ 43. $-2/x - \frac{2}{3}$
45. $-2/y + 3/x$

Exercises 2

1. **a.** True   **b.** False; $x/3 + x/4 = 7x/12$
   c. False; $a/b + c/d = (ad + bc)/bd$ **d.** True   **e.** True
   f. False; $(a/b) \div [(c/d) \div (e/f)] = ade/bcf$ **g.** False; $1/a + 1/b = (b + a)/ab$
   h. False; $x/(x + y) = 1/(1 + yx^{-1})$ **i.** False; $(\frac{6}{7})(\frac{8}{9}) = 6 \cdot 8/7 \cdot 9 = \frac{48}{63}$ **j.** True
3. 10 5. $\frac{2}{7}$ 7. $35x/36$ 9. $10x^2/3$ 11. $\frac{35}{3}$ 13. $\frac{9}{25}$ 15. $10/3y$
17. $45/32x^2$ 19. $\frac{1}{6}$ 21. $3/2x$ 23. $(3y + 2)/6x$ 25. $7a/18b$
27. $(9y - 5x)/30x^2$ 29. $\frac{119}{135}$ 31. $23a/31b$

Exercises 3

1. 2^{10} 3. $32/x$ 5. $x^{10}y^7z^3$ 7. x^4/y^2 9. x^2y 11. $2^4 = 16$
13. 3^6 15. $1/x^8y^5$ 17. $-8y^2$ 19. -3 21. $x^6 - 2x^3$ 23. $2x^6 + 6$
25. $2x^6 - x^5 - 3x^2$ 27. $2x/(x + 2)$ 29. $1/(x + y)$ 31. $15/4x^2$
33. $(9y^2 + 4x^2)/30x^3y$

Exercises 4

1. $\frac{10}{3}$ **3.** $-\frac{2}{3}$ **5.** $\frac{1}{8}$ **7.** 9 **9.** $\frac{5}{4}$ **11.** -2 **13.** 3 **15.** $\frac{1}{27}$
17. 2.5 **19.** $9x^2/16$ **21.** $2a/(3b)$ **23.** $\frac{2}{3}$ **25.** a^2/b^2 **27.** $x^3 b y^{3b}$
29. 1 **31.** $2\sqrt{2}$ **33.** 0
35. a. False **b.** True **c.** True **d.** True **e.** False **f.** False **g.** False
h. False **i.** False **j.** False **k.** True

Exercises 5

1. $3a + 10b + 6$ **3.** $5\sqrt{a} + 3\sqrt{b}$ **5.** $t^3 + 12t^2 + 3t - 5$
7. $\sqrt{x} + 3\sqrt{2y}$ **9.** $2x^3 - 2x^2 y + 3xy^2 - y^3$ **11.** $3a^2 + 2a - 8$
13. $2x^3 + x^2 - 8x + 21$ **15.** $a - b$ **17.** $x^2 + y^2 + 2xy - z^2$
19. $4x^2 + 12xy + 9y^2$ **21.** $2x^2 - 2x\sqrt{6y} + 3y$ **23.** $x^5 - x^3 + 2x^2 - 2$
25. $3x^2 + 135x - 90$ **27.** $2a^3 + 8a$ **29.** $x + 7 - 5/x + 4/x^2$
31. $t^{3/2} - 2\sqrt{t} + 7/\sqrt{t}$ **33.** $x - 3$ **35.** $t + 1 + 2/(t - 1)$
37. $x^2 - 2x + 3 + 3/(2x + 1)$

Exercises 6

1. $3(a + 2b)$ **3.** $2y(2x - 3z)$ **5.** $(2 - a)(u - v)$ **7.** $2(3x + 2y)(z - 4)$
9. $(x - 4)(x + 4)$ **11.** $3(t - 6a)(t + 6a)$ **13.** $(x + 2)(x + 3)$
15. $5y^2(y + 7)(y - 2)$ **17.** $(2x + 3)(x + 1)$ **19.** $t(2t - 5)(3t + 4)$
21. $xy(x - 5y)(x + 5y)$ **23.** $(3t - 2)^2$ **25.** $(x - 3)(x^2 + 3x + 9)$
27. $(3u + 2v)(9u^2 - 6uv + 4v^2)$ **29.** $2xy(x - 1)(3x + 5)$
31. $(x - 3)(x + 3)(y - 2)(y + 2)$ **33.** $(x - 2)(x + 2)(x^2 + z^2)$
35. $(a + b + 2)(a^2 - ab - 2a + b^2 + 4b + 4)$
37. $(x - \sqrt{2}\,y)(x + \sqrt{2}\,y)(x^2 - \sqrt{2}\,xy + 2y^2)(x^2 + \sqrt{2}\,xy + 2y^2)$
39. $(x + a)(a + 1)$ **41.** $(x^2 - 2xy + 2y^2)(x^2 + 2xy + 2y^2)$
43. $(x - 2y)(x + 2y)(x^2 + 4y^2)$

Exercises 7

1. 2 **3.** $x - 2$ **5.** $(5x + 7)/(x + 2)$ **7.** $2(x^2 + x + 3)/(x + 2)(2x - 1)$
9. $2/(x - 1)(x - 2)(x - 3)$ **11.** $(x^2 + 3)/(x - 1)^2(x + 3)$
13. $(10 + 4x - 2x^2)/(x + 3)(x + 1)(x - 1)$ **15.** $-\frac{2}{3}(x + 1)$ **17.** 3
19. $(x - 1)(2x - 1)/(x + 1)^2$ **21.** $(x^2 - 1)/(x - 2)$
23. $(x - 1)(x + 2)/(x - 2)(x - 5)$ **25.** $\frac{1}{3}(3 - \sqrt{7})$
27. $\frac{1}{2}(\sqrt{5} + \sqrt{10} - \sqrt{3} - \sqrt{6})$ **29.** $\frac{1}{3}(3 - \sqrt{3})$

Review Exercises for Chapter 1

1. a. False; $a^m b^n$ cannot be simplified by the laws of exponents.
b. False; $a^m + b^m \neq (a + b)^m$. For example, $(a + b)^2 = a^2 + 2ab + b^2$ and not
$a^2 + b^2$.
c. True **d.** False; $(a - b)^2 = a^2 - 2ab + b^2$ **e.** False; $-2(a + b) = -2a - 2b$
f. False; $(x + y)^2 = x^2 + 2xy + y^2$
g. False; $\sqrt{a - b} \neq \sqrt{a} - \sqrt{b}$. For example, if $a = 25$, $b = 9$, then
$\sqrt{a - b} = \sqrt{25 - 9} = 4$ and $\sqrt{a} - \sqrt{b} = 5 - 3 = 2$; clearly $4 \neq 2$.
h. False; $(a + 2b)/a = 1 + 2b/a$ **i.** True **j.** False; $(1/a) - (1/b) = (b - a)/ab$
k. False; $\dfrac{a/b}{c} = \dfrac{a}{b} \cdot \dfrac{1}{c}$ **l.** False; $(2a)^5 = 2^5 a^5 = 32a^5$ **m.** True **n.** True
o. True **p.** True **q.** True
r. False; A rational number can be expressed either as a terminating decimal or a
repeating decimal.

3. $3/2^{10}$ **5.** $x^{2ab-2bc}$ **7.** $(3 + 2x^2)/(x^2 + 1)$
9. $(4x^2 + 15x - 1)/(x + 1)^2(x + 3)(x - 2)$ **11.** $(x + 2)(y + 2)/(x + 3)(y + 3)$
13. $(a + b)(x - 3)/(a - b)(x + 3)$ **15.** $(a + 2)(a + 1)(a - 3)/a$
17. $3(x - 5y)(x + 5y)$ **19.** $(3x - 5)(2x + 3)$ **21.** $3(a + 3)(a - 1)$
23. $-3(4x + 7)$ **25.** $(x + 2/x)(x^2 - 2 + 4/x^2)$

CHAPTER 2

Exercises 1

1. Yes **3.** No **5.** 2 is a solution and 5 is not. **7.** No **9.** No
11. $10x^2 - x - 7 = 0$; degree 2. **13.** $y - 6 = 0$; degree 1. **15.** 4 **17.** $\frac{17}{5}$
19. -1 **21.** $-\frac{19}{7}$ **23.** $-\frac{13}{50}$ **25.** -2 **27.** 3 **29.** $\frac{4}{3}$ **31.** 2

Exercises 2

1. $-2, -3$ **3.** $-2, -7$ **5.** -2 **7.** $3, 4$ **9.** $1, -1$ **11.** $0, 8$
13. $-\frac{1}{4}, -\frac{1}{6}$ **15.** $\frac{1}{2}(-3 \pm \sqrt{5})$ **17.** $\frac{1}{4}(-3 \pm \sqrt{41})$ **19.** $\frac{1}{2}(-1 \pm \sqrt{13})$
21. $-\frac{5}{2}$ **23.** $\frac{1}{5}(-5 \pm \sqrt{10})$ **25.** $-3 \pm \sqrt{10}$ **27.** $\frac{1}{2}(3 \pm \sqrt{13})$
29. $\frac{1}{2}(2 \pm \sqrt{7})$ **31.** $-1 \pm \sqrt{5}$ **33.** $\pm\sqrt{\frac{11}{6}}$ **35.** $0, \frac{11}{6}$ **37.** $4, -\frac{4}{3}$
39. $\frac{3}{2}, \frac{1}{3}$ **41.** $-1 \pm \sqrt{5}$ **43.** $\frac{1}{2}(4 \pm \sqrt{10})$ **45.** $6, -\frac{1}{2}$

Exercises 3

1. $x + 4$ **3.** $3 + x/2$ **5.** $x - 1$ **7.** 18 **9.** 15 **11.** 25 yr
13. 10 dimes and 5 quarters **15.** \$52,000 at 8\% and \$8,000 at 10.5\% **17.** 10,000
19. \$2200 and \$700 **21.** \$50 **23.** 5\% **25.** \$165 or \$195
27. $\$(38 \pm 2\sqrt{21})$ per copy **29.** 4\% and 8\%

Review Exercises for Chapter 2

1. **a.** True; provided the constant is nonzero.
    b. True; provided the expression is well-defined for all values of x.
    c. False; Multiplying both sides of an equation by an expression containing the variable may result in new roots that are not the roots of the original equation.
    d. False; For example, if we square $x = 2$, we get $x^2 = 4$ whose roots are 2 and -2 which are not the same as the roots of $x = 2$.
    e. False; if $px = q$, then $x = q/p$.
    f. False; $ax^2 + bx + c = 0$ is a quadratic equation, provided $a \neq 0$.
    g. False; The solution of $x^2 = 4$ is given by $x = 2$ or -2.
    h. False; The roots of the equation $ax^2 + bx + c = 0$ $(a \neq 0)$ are given by $x = (-b \pm \sqrt{b^2 - 4ac})/2a$.
    i. True
    j. False; A quadratic equation may have two identical roots or no real roots at all.
    k. False; A linear equation will always have exactly one root. **l.** True
3. $\frac{1}{3}$ **5.** $2, \frac{2}{3}$ **7.** abc (provided $a + b + c \neq 0$) **9.** -1 **11.** 5
13. $1, -4$ **15.** $3, 3/2$ **17.** 4 **19.** 2 **21.** $\frac{9}{5}$
23. **a.** $r = (a - S)/(l - S)$ **b.** $l = (a - S + rS)/r$
25. \$75,000 at 8\% and \$25,000 at 10\% **27.** 1600 **29.** $p = \$4$ or \$5

CHAPTER 3

Exercises 1

1. $\{-1, 0, 1, 2, 3, 4\}$ 3. $\{2, 3, 5, 7, 11, 13, 17, 19\}$ 5. $\{2, 3\}$
7. $\{x \mid x \text{ is an even number, } 0 < x < 100\}$ or $\{x \mid x = 2n, n \text{ is a natural number } 1 < n < 49\}$
9. $\{x \mid x \text{ is an odd number, } 0 < x < 20\}$ or $\{x \mid x = 2n + 1, n \text{ is an integer and } 0 < n \le 9\}$
11. $\{x \mid x \text{ is a natural number divisible by 3}\}$ or $\{x \mid x = 3n, n \text{ is a natural number}\}$
13. **a.** True   **b.** False; $3 \in \{1, 2, 3, 4\}$.   **c.** False; $4 \notin \{1, 2, 5, 7\}$.
     d. True
     e. False; $\varnothing$ is a set, whereas 0 is a number. A set cannot be equal to a number.
     f. False; $\varnothing$ is an empty set with no element, whereas the set $\{0\}$ contains the element 0.
     g. False; $\varnothing$ does not contain any element, so 0 cannot be in $\varnothing$.
     h. False; The empty set $\varnothing$ is not a member of $\{0\}$.   **i.** True   **j.** True
     k. False; $2 \notin \{x \mid (x - 2)^2/(x - 2) = 0\}$, whereas $2 \in \{x \mid x - 2 = 0\}$.   **l.** True
     m. True
     n. False; The set of all squares in a plane is a subset of the set of all rectangles in a plane.
     o. True   **p.** True   **q.** False; $\{x \mid 2 \le x \le 3\} \subset \{y \mid 1 \le y \le 5\}$.

Exercises 2

1. $x < 2$ 3. $u \ge -\frac{17}{3}$ 5. $x > 2$ 7. $x > \frac{1}{8}$ 9. $-\frac{2}{3} < x < \frac{2}{3}$
11. $x \ge 2$ 13. No solution   15. More than 1500   17. More than 1875
19. 112,000 or more

Exercises 3

1. $2 < x < 5$ 3. $x \le -3$ or $x \ge \frac{5}{3}$ 5. $3 \le x \le 4$ 7. $y < -2$ or $y > \frac{3}{2}$
9. all x 11. $x \le -2$ or $x \ge 2$ 13. $x = 3$ 15. 60 units
17. More than 150
19. If x yards is the length of one side of the field, then $30 \le x \le 70$.   21. $R \ge 4$

Exercises 4

1. $1, -\frac{1}{7}$ 3. $\frac{1}{2}$ 5. $-1, \frac{3}{2}$ 7. No solution   9. $\frac{27}{17}; \frac{33}{19}$
11. $-\frac{11}{3} < x < -1; (-\frac{11}{3}, -1)$ 13. $x \le -\frac{1}{5}$ or $x \ge 1; (-\infty, -\frac{1}{5}]$ and $[1, \infty)$
15. No solution   17. all $x; (-\infty, \infty)$
19. **a.** $|x - 3| < 5; x \in (-2, 8)$ **b.** $|y - 7| \le 4; y \in [3, 11]$
    c. $|t - 5| = 3; t \in \{2, 8\}$ **d.** $|z - \mu| < \sigma, z \in (\mu - \sigma, \mu + \sigma)$

Review Exercises for Chapter 3

1. **a.** True
    b. False; When two sides of an inequality are multiplied by a *positive* constant, the direction of inequality is preserved.
    c. False; A quadratic inequality has either no solution or one solution or an *infinite* number of solutions.
    d. False; If a negative number is subtracted from both sides of an inequality, the direction of inequality must be preserved.
    e. False; The statement is true only if $a \ge 0$.   **f.** True   **g.** True   **h.** True
    i. True
    j. False; For example, if $x = 2$ and $y = -7$, then $x > y$, whereas $|x| < |y|$ because $2 < 7$.
    k. True   **l.** True
3. $x \ge \frac{2}{3}$ 5. $-1 < x < \frac{5}{3}$ 7. $2 < x < 6$ 9. $x \le -\frac{1}{2}$ or $x \ge 2$
11. $x \le -2$ or $x \ge 5$ 13. 7/2 or 3/4.

15. a. At least 120,000   **b.** At least 220,000
17. $p = \$5$ or $\$7$; $6 \le p \le 8$

CHAPTER 4

Exercises 1

1.

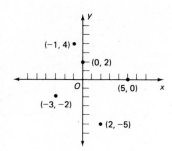

3. $\sqrt{5}$ **5.** $\frac{1}{2}\sqrt{29}$
7. 0 or -6 **9.** 19 or -5
11. $y = -3$ or 1
13. $x^2 + y^2 + 2x - 6y + 1 = 0$
15. $2(x^2 + y^2 + x - y) = 1$

17.

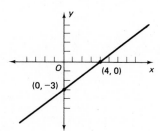

19.

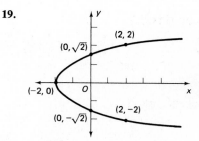

21.

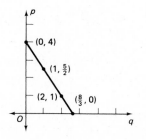

23.

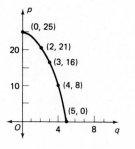

Exercises 2

1. 2   **3.** 0   **5.** No slope   **7.** $y = 5x - 9$ **9.** $y = 4$ **11.** $y = 6x - 19$
13. $x = 3$ **15.** $y = \frac{1}{3}x - 4$ **17.** $\frac{3}{2}$; -3 **19.** 2; -3 **21.** 0; $\frac{3}{2}$
23. a. $2x + 5y = 280$
    b. $m = -\frac{2}{5}$; It indicates that every increase of 5 units of the first type will be at the cost of 2 units of the second type.
    c. 40
25. a. $y = 650 - 25t$ **b.** 26 days   **c.** At the end of the 21st day.

Exercises 3

1. $x = -1, y = -2$ **3.** $x = 1, y = 6$ **5.** $x = -1, t = 3$ **7.** $x = 4, y = 3$
9. $x = 40, y = 60$ **11.** No solution

13. Coordinates of any point on the line $x + 2y = 4$.　15.　$x = 3, y = -2, z = 1$
17. $x = 5, y = -2$ or $x = -2, y = 5$　19.　1600 lb of I and 600 lb of II.
21. 100 units of X and 40 units of Y.
23. 60 gal of 25% acid solution and 140 gal of 15% acid solution.　25.　18 and 35

Exercises 4

1. $y_c = 7x + 150$; $850　3. a. $y_c = 3x + 45$　b. $105　c. $3 and $45
5. $y_c = 5.5x + 300$; $465　7. $y_c = 10x + 150$　9.　800
11. a. 500　b. $4.14
13. Yes, because he will have to sell fewer items to break even.　15.　$x = 40$ or 20
17. $x = 100$

Exercises 5

1. $p = 1.7 - 0.00005x$　3. $p = 0.00025x + 0.5$　5.　$x = 30, p = 5$
7. $x = 10, p = 10$　9.　$x = 3, p = 4$
11. a. $p = 42 - 0.06x$　b. $x = 150, p = 33$
　　c. $p_1 = $33.90, x_1 = 135$; Price increases by $0.90 and the demand decreases by
　　　15 units.
　　d. $5.44　e. $4.08
13. $x = -\frac{3}{7}, p = \frac{32}{7}$; Since x cannot be negative, market equilibrium occurs at $x = 0$
　　(that is, no goods are being produced and sold).

Review Exercises for Chapter 4

1. a. False; If a point lies on x-axis, its *ordinate* is zero.
　b. False; Each point on the y-axis has its x-coordinate zero.
　c. False; If a point is in the first quadrant, then $x > 0, y > 0$.
　d. False; The origin (0, 0) does not lie in any quadrant.
　e. False; A horizontal line has *zero* slope.　f. True
　g. False; A vertical line has *no* slope.
　h. False; The distance of the point (a, b) from the origin is $\sqrt{a^2 + b^2}$.
　i. False; Slope $= (y_2 - y_1)/(x_2 - x_1)$, provided $x_2 \neq x_1$.
　j. False; The equation $Ax + By + C = 0$ represents a straight line, provided the
　　constants A and B are not both zero.
　k. False; The slope of the line given by $x = my + b$ is $1/m$, provided $m \neq 0$.
　l. True　m. True　n. True　o. True　p. True
3. $y = 2$　5.　$x = 2$　7.　$x = 3, y = -1$　9.　$x = 3, y = -2, z = 1$
11. $x = 6, y = 3$ or $x = 3, y = 6$
13. If x units of A and y units of B are produced, then $5x + 8y = 640$.
15. The cost y_c of producing x units is given by $y_c = 25x + 3000$; $5500.
17. $2.50 and $3.00　19.　$15,000; 6%
21. a. S: $90p = x + 1200$; D: $10p + x = 5000$　b. $x = 4380, p = $62
　　c. $1.80; 18 tons;　d. $6.11
23. a. $y_c = 4x + 2500$　b. 2000 units　c. 2160 units　25.　Over 5000 belts

CHAPTER 5

Exercises 1

1. a. 7　b. 9　c. 49　d. $\frac{21}{4}$　e. 19　f. $3c^2 - 5c + 7$
　g. $3(c + h)^2 - 5(c + h) + 7$　h. $6c + 3h - 5$
3. a. 6　b. 11　c. 12　d. $f(5 + h) = 7 + 2h$; $f(5 - h) = 3h - 9$
7. 10　9. Set of all real numbers.　11. Set of all real numbers except 2.
13. $\{x \mid x \geq 2\}$　15.　$\{t \mid t > \frac{3}{2}\}$

17. $C(x) = 15x + 3000$; $R(x) = 25x$; $P(x) = 10x - 3000$
19. If x denotes one of the sides, then $A = x(100 - x)$.
21. x = side of square base; $C(x) = 5.5x^2 + 1800/x$.
23. $C(x) = \begin{cases} 25x \text{ if } x \leq 50 \\ 20x \text{ if } x > 50 \end{cases}$

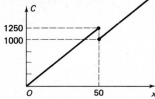

25. No **27.** No **29.** Yes

Exercises 2

1.

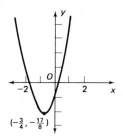

3.

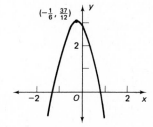

5. 600; $R_{max} = \$3600$
7. a. $C(x) = 25x + 2000$ **b.** 3000; $R_{max} = \$90,000$ **c.** 1750; $P_{max} = \$28,625$
9. 15,625 sq. yd **11.** $x = 10$ **13.** \$22.50; $R_{max} = \$202,500$
15. \$175; $R_{max} = \$6125$

Exercises 3

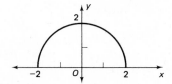

1. $D_f = \{x \mid -2 \leq x \leq 2\}$

3. $D_f = \{x \mid x \leq 3\}$

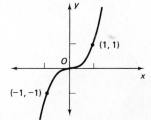

5. $D_f = \{x \mid x \neq 0\}$

7. $D_f = \{\text{all real numbers}\}$
$= \{x \mid x \text{ is real}\}$

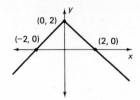

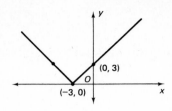

9. $D_f = \{x \mid x \text{ is real}\}$

11. $D_f = \{x \mid x \text{ is real}\}$

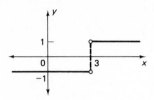

13. $D_f = \{x \mid x \neq 3\}$

15. a. Yes; $y = \sqrt{9 - x^2}$.   **b. No**
    c. No   **d.** Yes; $y = -\sqrt{4 - x^2}$.

17. $x^2 + y^2 - 4x - 10y + 20 = 0$

19. $x^2 + y^2 = 49$

21. $x^2 + y^2 + 4x - 2y - 8 = 0$

23.

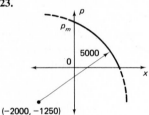

$P_m = \$3332.57$

25.

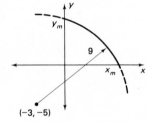

Max. Coronado $(x_m) = 4.48$
Max. Eastern Star $(y_m) = 3.49$

Exercises 4

1. $(f \pm g)(x) = x^2 \pm 1/(x - 1)$; $(fg)(x) = x^2/(x - 1)$; $(f/g)(x) = x^2(x - 1)$;
$(g/f)(x) = 1/x^2(x - 1)$; $D_{f+g} = D_{f-g} = D_{fg} = D_{f/g} = \{x \mid x \neq 1\}$; $D_{g/f} = \{x \mid x \neq 0, 1\}$

3. $(f \pm g)(x) = \sqrt{x - 1} \pm 1/(x + 2)$; $(fg)(x) = \sqrt{x - 1}/(x + 2)$;
$(f/g)(x) = \sqrt{x - 1}(x + 2)$; $(g/f)(x) = 1/\sqrt{x - 1}(x + 2)$;
$D_{f+g} = D_{f-g} = D_{fg} = D_{f/g} = \{x \mid x \geq 1\}$; $D_{g/f} = \{x \mid x > 1\}$

5. $(f \pm g)(x) = (x + 1)^2 \pm 1/(x^2 - 1)$; $(fg)(x) = (x + 1)/(x - 1)$;
$(f/g)(x) = (x + 1)^3(x - 1)$; $(g/f)(x) = 1/(x + 1)^3(x - 1)$;
$D_{f+g} = D_{f-g} = D_{fg} = D_{f/g} = D_{g/f} = \{x \mid x \neq \pm 1\}$

7. $\sqrt{8}$ **9.** $\sqrt{3}$ **11.** Not defined   **13.** 0

15. $f \circ g(x) = |x| + 1$; $g \circ f(x) = (\sqrt{x} + 1)^2$

17. $f \circ g(x) = 2 + |x - 2|$; $g \circ f(x) = x$

19. $f(x) = x^3$, $g(x) = x^2 + 1$ is the simplest answer.

21. $f(x) = 1/x$, $g(x) = x^2 + 7$ is the simplest answer.   **23.** $R = x(2000 - x)/15$

Exercises 5

1. $y = 3 - 3x/4$ **3.** $y = x/(1 - x)$ **5.** $y = -x$ or $y = x + 1$

7. $y = -x + 2$ or $y = -x - 2$ **9.** $y = \frac{2}{3}\sqrt{9 - x^2}$, $y = -\frac{2}{3}\sqrt{9 - x^2}$

11. $y = (1 - \sqrt{x})^2$ **13.** $y = -x, y = 1/x$

15. $x = f^{-1}(y) = -(y + 4)/3$

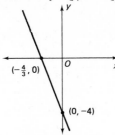

$$y = -3x - 4$$

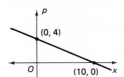

$$x = -\tfrac{1}{3}(y + 4)$$

17. $x = f^{-1}(p) = 10 - 5p/2$

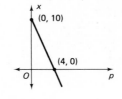

$$p = 4 - \tfrac{2}{5}x$$

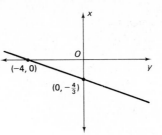

$$x = 10 - \tfrac{5}{2}p$$

19. $x = f^{-1}(y) = (y^2 + 4)/3, \quad (y \geq 0)$

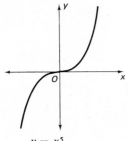

$$y = \sqrt{3x - 4}$$

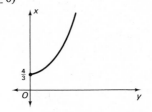

$$x = \tfrac{1}{3}(y^2 + 4)$$

21. $x = f^{-1}(y) = y^{1/5}$

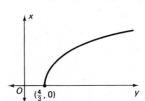

$$y = x^5$$

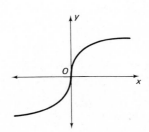

$$x = y^{1/5}$$

23. $x = f^{-1}(y) = 4 - y^2$

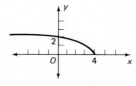

$$y = \sqrt{4 - x}$$

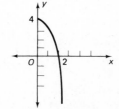

$$x = 4 - y^2, \quad (y \geq 0)$$

25. $x = f^{-1}(y) = -1 + \sqrt{y}, \quad x \geq -1; x = f^{-1}(y) = -1 - \sqrt{y}, \quad x \leq -1$
27. $x = f^{-1}(y) = y^{3/2}, \quad \text{if } x \geq 0; x = f^{-1}(y) = -y^{3/2}, \quad \text{if } x \leq 0$

Review Exercises for Chapter 5

1. **a.** False; The domain is the set of all real numbers. **b.** True **c.** True
   d. False; $|x^2 - 9|/(x - 3) = x + 3$ if $x^2 > 9$, that is, if $x < -3$ or $x > 3$;
   $|x^2 - 9|/(x - 3) = -(x + 3)$ if $x^2 < 9$, that is, if $-3 < x < 3$
   e. False; A curve is the graph of a function if any vertical line meets the graph in *at most* one point.
   f. False; A function is a rule which assigns to each value in the domain *only* one value in the range.
   g. True **h.** False; True only if $a \neq 0$.
   i. False; The domain of a polynomial function is the set of all *real numbers*.
   j. False; The domain of f/g may differ from that of $f + g, f - g$, and fg.
   k. False; In general, $f \circ g \neq g \circ f$. **l.** False; The vertex need not be at the origin.
   m. False; In $F(x, y) = 0$, x, and y are not both independent variables; either one can be the independent variable, but not both.
   n. True
   o. False; The graph of f^{-1} is the reflection of the graph of f in the line $y = x$.
3. $F(x)$ and $G(x)$ are equal to $f(x)$; $g(x)$ and $h(x)$ are not. 5. $p = -3$ or 5
7. D_f = set of all real numbers 9. $f \circ g(x) = g \circ f(x) = x^2$

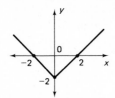

11. $g(x) = \sqrt{x}, f(x) = x/(x + 1)$ is the simplest answer.

13. **a.** $R(p) = 108p - 0.4p^2, p$ = rent in dollars per suite.
    b. $R(x) = 270x - 2.5x^2, x$ = number of suites occupied.
    A rent of \$135 per suite will yield the max. revenue.

15.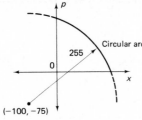

    highest price = \$159.57

17. $y = \pm\sqrt{x - 1}$ 19. $x = f^{-1}(y) = 4 - y^2$

CHAPTER 6

Exercises 1

1.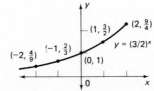

3.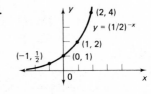

5. 1.5068 **7.** 2981.0 **9.** 0.5066 **11.** \$2524.95 **13.** \$146.93 **15.** 7.18%
17. 14.61% **19.** 28.98 billions **21.** 409,400; 274,400
23. 1.98%; It is constant and does not depend on time. **25. a.** \$2019 **b.** 18.1%

Exercises 2

1. $\log_{27}\left(\frac{1}{81}\right) = -\frac{4}{3}$ **3.** $\log_{125} 25 = \frac{2}{3}$ **5.** $\log_{8/27}\left(\frac{3}{2}\right) = -\frac{1}{3}$ **7.** $3^3 = 27$
9. $4^{-1/2} = \frac{1}{2}$ **11.** 9 **13.** 8 **15.** -3 **17.** 100 **19.** $p/2$ **21.** $\frac{1}{3}$
23. 0.3010 **25.** 1.0791 **27.** 1.4771 **29.** $-\frac{13}{8}$ **31.** $\frac{3}{2}$ **35.** 1.2267
37. 4.4332 **39.** -1.0759

Exercises 3

1. 1.3979 **3.** 0.4362 **5.** 0.7737 **7.** 2.155 **9.** $\log c(\log a - \log b)^{-1}$
11. 46.3 yr after 1976. **13.** 38.4 yr after 1976. **15.** After 23.2 months.
17. 14.27 yr **19.** 3.92% semiannually **21.** \$2577.10 **23.** $y = e^{(0.6931)t}$
25. $y = 5e^{(0.0392)t}$ **27.** $y = 4e^{(0.0198)t}$ billion
29. a. 10.13% **b.** $I = 121e^{(0.0965)t}$ **c.** $t = 7.52$
31. $100(e^k - 1)$ percent; $(1/k) \ln 2$; $(1/k) \ln 3$

Exercises 4

1. 8.66 yr **3.** $R = 6.93$ **5.** 4.6% **7.** 6.93% **9.** \$3935; \$6321; 75.8%
11. 5×10^6; 4×10^7; 2×10^8 **13.** $c = 49$; $k = 0.973$; 6.26 yr

Review Exercises for Chapter 6

1. a. False; The logarithm of any number greater than zero to the same base is equal to 1.
b. False; If $a^x = y$, then $\log_a y = x$ holds only if $a > 0$. **c.** True
d. False; $\log(78) = \log(7.8) + 1$ **e.** True **f.** True
g. False; $\log_a (xy) = \log_a x + \log_a y$ **h.** False; If $\ln x > 1$, then $x > e$.
i. True **j.** True.
k. False; The logistic model is only one of the various models for restricted growth.
3. $-\frac{1}{4}$ **5.** $(3 - 4x)/2$ **7.** $x = 1$ **9.** 0.5204 **11.** \$802.89 **13.** \$576.19
15. 7.18% **17.** 1.86% **19.** 10.99%
21. a. 4.14% **b.** $e^{0.04055t}$ **c.** 18.1 yr from 1970

CHAPTER 7

Exercises 1

1. 39; 59 **3.** $74 - 2r$ **5.** 54 **7.** 27th **9.** 1335 **11.** $n(5n - 1)/2$
13. 414 **15.** 12 **17.** \$120 **19.** \$201 **21. a.** 30 **b.** \$241
23. \$1275 **25.** \$1122 **27.** 9

Exercises 2

1. 768 **3.** $\left(\frac{2}{9}\right)\left(-\frac{3}{2}\right)^{n-1}$ **5.** 10th **7.** 16, 24, 36, 54, 81, ...; 19,683/32
9. $(3^{12} - 1) = 531,440$ **11.** $(2^n - 1)$ **13.** 2 **15.** $2\sqrt{2}/3$ **19.** $\sqrt{2}$
21. 6 yr **23.** \$4502.02 **25. a.** \$4246.71 **b.** \$5081.96 **27.** \$49,045.42

Exercises 3

1. a. \$625.38 **b.** $(20,000/3)[(1.0075)^n - 1]$ **3.** \$114.66 **5.** \$77,698.00
7. a. \$79,426.86 **b.** \$71,607.25 **9.** \$1358.68 **11.** \$50,053.40 **13.** \$304.91
15. \$335.68 **17. a.** \$37,308.98 **b.** \$26,499.03

Review Exercises for Chapter 7

1. **a.** False; $T_n = a + (n-1)d$ is the nth term only if the sequence is in A.P.
   b. False; The given formula is the sum to n terms of a G.P.
   c. False; The formula only applies when $-1 < r < 1$.
   d. False; The pth term of a G.P. is ar^{p-1}.   **e.** True   **f.** True   **g.** True
   h. True; Unless $r = 1$.   **i.** True   **j.** True
   k. False; The sequence $1, x, x^2, x^3, \ldots$ is in G.P.
3. $\frac{2}{3}, \frac{6}{3}, \frac{10}{3}, \frac{14}{3}, \frac{18}{3}, \frac{22}{3}$ 5. $8, 4, 2, 1, 0.5, 0.25$ 7. 820 9. $3(2^n - 1)$
11. 10.8 13. $\$155; \$5$ 15. nth payment $= (242 - 2n)$; $\$420$
17. **a.** $\$137,639.05$ **b.** $\$117,817.77$ 19. $\$131.67$

CHAPTER 8

Exercises 1

1. $\{A, B, C, D, E\}$ where $A, \ldots, E$ are the names of the five candidates.
3. $\{H1, H2, H3, H4, H5, H6, T1, T2, T3, T4, T5, T6\}$
5. $\{ABC, ACB, BCA, BAC, CAB, CBA\}$ where A, B, C are the names of the salespeople.
7. $\{BBB, BBW, BWW\}$ where B = brown, W = white, and the order of B's and W's is of no significance.
9. The sample space consists of 13 points, one for each spade card in the deck.
11. $\{(6, 4), (5, 5), (4, 6)\}$ 13. $\{(6, 1), (5, 2), (4, 3), (3, 4), (2, 5), (1, 6)\}$
15. $E_1 \cup E_2 = \{x \mid x$ is a black card or a heart$\}$ is the event that the card drawn is either a black card or a heart.
17. $E_1 \cup E_3 = \{x \mid x$ is a heart or is of denomination less than 7, or both$\}$ is the event that the drawn card is either a heart or is of denomination less than 7.
19. $E_3 \cap E_4 = \{x \mid x$ is an ace$\} = E_4$ is the event that the drawn card is an ace and is of denomination less than 7.
21. $E_2' = \{x \mid x$ is a red card$\}$ is the event that the drawn card is not black.
23. The following pairs are mutually exclusive: E_1 and E_4; E_3 and E_4; E_3 and E_5; E_6 and E_k where $k = 1, 2, 3, 4, 5$.
25. The given events are *not* mutually exclusive.
27. The given two events *are* mutually exclusive.
29. **a.** $F' \cap U$ **b.** $U' \cap E'$ **c.** $(U \cap E') \cap F$ **d.** $(U' \cap E) \cap F'$
31. **a.** The applicant has experience and no degree and is over forty.
   b. The applicant has experience, has a degree, and is over forty.
   c. The applicant has no degree and is under forty.
   d. The applicant has a degree but no experience.
   e. The applicant has no experience and in addition either has a degree and is over forty or else has no degree and is under forty.

Exercises 2

1. $\frac{1}{4}$ 3. $\frac{3}{4}$ 5. $\frac{19}{52}$ 7. $\frac{3}{8}$ 9. $\frac{7}{8}$ 11. 1 13. $\frac{5}{18}$ 15. $\frac{11}{36}$
17. **a.** 0.55 **b.** 0.75 **c.** 0 **d.** 0.3 **e.** 0.25 **f.** 1
19. **a.** $E_2' =$ individual earns less than 20,000; $P(E_2') = 0.65$.
   b. $E_2' \cup E_1 =$ either individual earns less than 20,000 or has been employee for 10 yr or more, or both; $P(E_2' \cup E_1) = 0.85$.
   c. $E_1' \cap E_2 =$ individual has been employed for less than 10 yr and earns 20,000 or more; $P(E_1' \cap E_2) = 0.15$.
   d. $(E_1' \cap E_2')' = E_1 \cup E_2 =$ the individual is not in the category of being both an employee for less than 10 yr and earning less than 20,000; $P[(E_1' \cap E_2')'] = 0.4$
21. $\frac{5}{18} + (\frac{13}{18})(\frac{5}{18}) = \frac{155}{324}$ 23. **a.** $\frac{4}{25}$ **b.** $\frac{16}{25}$ **c.** $\frac{61}{125}$
25. **a.** 0.6 **b.** 0.3 **c.** 0.1 **d.** Insufficient information to calculate $P(7)$.

27. $\frac{14}{60}$ **29. a.** 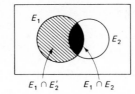   **b.**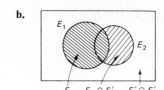

Exercises 3

1. $\frac{1}{2}$ **3.** No, $P(A) = \frac{3}{4}$, $P(B) = \frac{1}{2}$, $P(A \cap B) = \frac{1}{4} \neq P(A)\,P(B)$.   **5.** $\frac{1}{2}$ **7.** $\frac{2}{6}$
9. $\frac{20}{26}$ **11.** $\frac{3}{6}$ **13.** $\frac{3}{4}$ **15.** 0.1   **17. a.** $\left(\frac{150}{500}\right)\left(\frac{149}{499}\right)$ **b.** $\left(\frac{350}{500}\right)\left(\frac{349}{499}\right)$
19. 3%   **a.** 0.065   **b.** $\frac{7}{13}$ **21.** $\frac{3}{7}$ **23.** $\frac{6}{13}$

Exercises 4

1. 90   **3.** 120   **5.** 435   **7.** 380   **9.** 7   **11.** $1/13^3 = 1/2197$
13. a. $\frac{2}{21}$ **b.** $\frac{10}{21}$ **15.** $\frac{969}{2639} = 0.37$ **17.** 20 outcomes
19. 40 (assuming no distinction between which driver drives which cab).   **21.** 72
23. $\frac{28}{33}$ **25.** $2^{10} = 1024$ **27.** 26^{-11} **29.** $\frac{5}{12}$

Exercises 5

1. $\frac{1}{4}$ **3.** $10(5^3/6^5) = 625/3888$ **5.** $\frac{128}{625}$ **7.** $1 - (\frac{4}{5})^6 = 11529/15{,}625$
9. $1 - 61(3^6/4^8) = 0.32$ **11. a.** $\frac{135}{4096}$ **b.** $\frac{1}{4096}$ **13.** $\frac{63}{256} = 0.25$
15. $252(4^5/5^{10}) = 0.026$ **17. a.** $(\frac{4}{5})^8$ **b.** $1 - 3(\frac{4}{5})^8$
19. $1 - 90(4^6/5^8) = 0.056$ **21.** $\frac{25}{36}$; $\frac{171}{1296}$
23. a. 0.251   **b.** 0.215   **c.** 0.201

Review Exercises for Chapter 8

1. a. False; If A and B are mutually exclusive, then $P(A \mid B) = P(B \mid A) = 0$.
  b. True   **c.** False; If E_1 and E_2 are independent then $P(E_1 \cap E_2) = P(E_1)P(E_2)$.
  d. True
  e. False; In general, the outcomes have unequal probabilities, though in many cases they are equally likely.
  f. False; The sum of the probabilities of complementary events is 1.
  g. False; If E_1 and E_2 are independent, $P(E_1 \cap E_2) = P(E_1)P(E_2)$. If they are mutually exclusive, $P(E_1 \cap E_2) = 0$.
  h. True   **i.** True   **j.** False; $P(A \mid B) = P(B \mid A)[P(A)/P(B)]$ **k.** True
  l. True   **m.** False; $P(A \mid A') = 0$.   **n.** False; If $E_2 \subseteq E_1$ then $P(E_1 \mid E_2) = 1$.
  o. False; $P(E_1 \mid E_2) = P(E_2 \mid E_1)[P(E_1)/P(E_2)]$.
  p. False; If E_1 and E_2 are independent, then $P(E_1 \mid E_2) = P(E_1)$.
  q. True   **r.** True
  s. False; For example, take $B = C$. Then B and C are certainly not independent. Alternatively, let A be the event that a coin lands heads, B be the event that a card drawn from a deck is a spade, and C the event that this same card is a red card.
3. 56   **5.** n/r **7. a.** $\frac{2}{15}$ **b.** $\frac{1}{3}$ **c.** $\frac{2}{3}$
9. No; $P(\text{Cancer} \cap \text{Smokes}) \neq P(\text{Cancer})P(\text{Smokes})$.   **11.** 12%   **15.** $\frac{93}{256}$
17. $\frac{5}{12}$; 10.5%   **19.** $\frac{16}{31}$ **21.** $\frac{3}{5}$; $\frac{9}{20}$ **23.** $_{36}P_{30}$; $_{30}P_{26}$ **25.** $\frac{2}{3}$, $\frac{8}{15}$
27. $\frac{8}{81}$ **29.** $\frac{1}{17}$

CHAPTER 9

Exercises 1

1. $A: 2 \times 2$; $B: 2 \times 3$; $C: 3 \times 1$; $D: 3 \times 3$; $E: 2 \times 3$; $F: 2 \times 2$; $G: 1 \times 3$; $H: 1 \times 1$

3. $A = \begin{bmatrix} 0 & 1 \\ 1 & 2 \end{bmatrix}$

5. Any matrix of the form $\begin{bmatrix} 0 & x & y \\ -x & 0 & z \\ -y & -z & 0 \end{bmatrix}$

7. $\begin{bmatrix} 6 & 12 \\ 3 & 9 \end{bmatrix}$

9. $\begin{bmatrix} 2 & 0 & 5 \\ 0 & 6 & -1 \end{bmatrix}$

11. $\begin{bmatrix} -4 & 13 \\ 1 & 6 \end{bmatrix}$

13. $\begin{bmatrix} 2 & 1 & 12 \\ 13 & 4 & -12 \\ 5 & 10 & 21 \end{bmatrix}$

15. $x = 1, y = 4$

17. $x = 1, y = 5, z = -2$

19. $x = 6, y = 5, z = 2, t = -2, u = 2, v = 3$

21. $x = 1, y = 2, z = 3, t = 4, u = -1, v = 2, w = 5$

23. $x = 0, y = 1, z = 2, t = -1, u = -2, v = 3, w = 0$

25. a. $\begin{bmatrix} 11 & 13 & 16 \\ 14 & 11 & 13 \\ 9 & 16 & 7 \\ 17 & 10 & 11 \end{bmatrix}$ b. $\begin{bmatrix} 12 & 14.4 & 18 \\ 15.6 & 12 & 14.4 \\ 9.6 & 18 & 7.2 \\ 19.2 & 10.8 & 12 \end{bmatrix}$

27. a. $\begin{bmatrix} 0 & 33 & 39 \\ 35 & 0 & 38 \\ 45 & 30 & 0 \end{bmatrix}$ b. $\begin{bmatrix} 0 & 165 & 195 \\ 175 & 0 & 190 \\ 225 & 150 & 0 \end{bmatrix}$

29. a. $\begin{bmatrix} 65 & 64 & 46 \\ 97 & 45 & 34 \\ 37 & 50 & 57 \end{bmatrix}$ b. $\begin{bmatrix} 88.75 & 88.5 & 62.5 \\ 132.5 & 61.25 & 46.5 \\ 49.75 & 69 & 77.5 \end{bmatrix}$

Exercises 2

1. 3×3

3. 2×4

5. 2×5

7. $[23]$

9. $\begin{bmatrix} 18 \\ 28 \end{bmatrix}$

11. $\begin{bmatrix} 1 & 4 \\ 5 & -1 \\ -4 & 5 \end{bmatrix}$

13. $\begin{bmatrix} 11 \\ -6 \\ 32 \end{bmatrix}$

15. $\begin{bmatrix} -25 & 14 \\ -58 & 32 \end{bmatrix}$

17. $\begin{bmatrix} 8 & 33 \\ 5 & -22 \end{bmatrix}$

19. $\begin{bmatrix} 4 & 12 \\ 12 & 16 \end{bmatrix}$

21. a. $\begin{bmatrix} 9 & 5 \\ 0 & 4 \end{bmatrix}$ b. $\begin{bmatrix} 6 & 0 \\ 3 & 7 \end{bmatrix}$ c. $(A + B)^2 \neq A^2 + 2AB + B^2$

23. $A = [3, -1]$

25. $A = \begin{bmatrix} 3 & 0 \\ 0 & 1 \end{bmatrix}$

27. $\begin{bmatrix} 2 & 3 \\ 1 & 4 \end{bmatrix} \begin{bmatrix} x \\ y \end{bmatrix} = \begin{bmatrix} 7 \\ 5 \end{bmatrix}$

29. $\begin{bmatrix} 1 & 2 & 3 \\ 2 & -1 & 4 \\ 0 & 3 & -2 \end{bmatrix} \begin{bmatrix} x \\ y \\ z \end{bmatrix} = \begin{bmatrix} 8 \\ 13 \\ 5 \end{bmatrix}$

31. $\begin{bmatrix} 2 & 1 & 0 & -1 \\ 0 & 3 & 2 & 4 \\ 1 & -2 & 4 & 1 \end{bmatrix} \begin{bmatrix} x \\ y \\ z \\ u \end{bmatrix} = \begin{bmatrix} 0 \\ 5 \\ 12 \end{bmatrix}$

33. $\begin{bmatrix} -2x & -2y \\ x & y \end{bmatrix}$, $(x, y$ arbitrary$)$

35. $A^n = \begin{bmatrix} 1 & 0 \\ 0 & 1 \end{bmatrix}$ for all n

37. $A^n = \begin{bmatrix} 1 & 0 \\ 1 - 2^{-n} & 2^{-n} \end{bmatrix}$

39. $[5 \quad 8 \quad 4 \quad 10] \begin{bmatrix} 650 \\ 550 \\ 500 \\ 300 \end{bmatrix} = 12{,}650$

41.

Let $A = \begin{bmatrix} 3 & 2 & 4 \\ 4 & 1 & 3 \end{bmatrix}$, $B = [20 \quad 30]$, $C = \begin{bmatrix} 6 \\ 10 \\ 12 \end{bmatrix}$.

a. $BA = [180 \quad 70 \quad 170]$ **b.** $AC = \begin{bmatrix} 86 \\ 70 \end{bmatrix}$ **c.** $BAC = [3820]$

Exercises 3

1. $x = 2, y = 1$ **3.** $u = 4, v = -1$ **5.** $x = 1, y = 2, z = 3$
7. $x_1 = 1, x_2 = 2, x_3 = -1$ **9.** $p = -1, q = 2, r = 2$
11. $x = -1, y = 3, z = -3, t = 2$ **13.** $x = y = 1, z = -1, w = 2$
15. $x = 2, y = 1, z = 3$ **17.** $x = 4, p = 17$ **19.** $x = \frac{91}{4}, p_1 = \frac{115}{4}$
21. 100, 150, and 200, units of A, B, and C
23. \$6000 at 6%, \$7200 at 10%, \$6800 at 8%

Exercises 4

1. $x = 2 + z, y = 3 - 2z$ **3.** No solution   **5.** No solution
7. $x = -4 + 6z, y = 10 - 11z$ **9.** No solution   **11.** $u = 1, v = 2, w = -1$
13. No solution   **15.** No solution   **17.** $x = (3 - z)/5, y = (7 + 6z)/5$

Review Exercises for Chapter 9

1. **a.** False; The array is not rectangular.
   b. False; A and B have different sizes, so $A + B$ cannot be formed.
   c. True   **d.** True
   e. False; The number of *columns* in A must equal the number of *rows* in B.
   f. False; Unless A and B are both *square* matrices of the same size.
   g. False; Usually $AB \ne BA$ but not always. For example, take A to be square and $B = I$, then $BA = AB$.
   h. False; AB and BA are both defined if A is $m \times n$ and B is $n \times m$. Then AB is of size $m \times m$ and BA is $n \times n$.
   i. True; (Note that if A is $m \times n$, then I is of size $n \times n$ in the product AI and is of size $m \times m$ in the product IA.)
   j. True   **k.** True
   l. False; For example, take $A = [1 \quad 0]$ and $B = \begin{bmatrix} 0 \\ 1 \end{bmatrix}$.
   m. False; The system may have no solutions, one unique solution, or an infinite number of solutions.
   n. False; If a system with more variables than equations is *consistent* then it must have infinitely many solutions.
   o. False; A system is consistent if it has one or more solutions.

3. $\begin{bmatrix} 1 & -11 \\ 20 & 10 \end{bmatrix}$ **5.** $\begin{bmatrix} 7 & 1 \\ 11 & 9 \end{bmatrix}$ **7.** $\begin{bmatrix} 9 & 1 \\ -5 & -9 \end{bmatrix}$ **9.** $x = 1, y = 2$

11. $x = 1, y = -1$ **13.** $x = -1, y = 2$ **15.** No solution   **17.** $X = \begin{bmatrix} 1 & -1 \\ 0 & 1 \end{bmatrix}$

19. $X = \begin{bmatrix} 2 & -1 \\ 1 & 2 \end{bmatrix}$ **21.** $\begin{bmatrix} 517 & 345 & 189 \\ 257 & 284 & 408 \end{bmatrix}$ or $\begin{bmatrix} 517 & 257 \\ 345 & 284 \\ 189 & 408 \end{bmatrix}$

23. **a.** $\begin{bmatrix} 33 & 59 & 33 \\ 47 & 38 & 54 \end{bmatrix}$ **b.** $\begin{bmatrix} 35.6 & 61.4 & 36 \\ 49.4 & 40.8 & 58.8 \end{bmatrix}$

25. $[3 \quad 5 \quad 2 \quad 3] \begin{bmatrix} 12 \\ 5 \\ 3 \\ 20 \end{bmatrix} = [127]$

27. $PA = [114 \quad 84.5 \quad 92 \quad 84]$; Elements are the earnings in weeks I–IV.

CHAPTER 10

Exercises 1

1. $\begin{bmatrix} -\frac{4}{7} & \frac{5}{7} \\ \frac{3}{7} & -\frac{2}{7} \end{bmatrix}$ 3. $\begin{bmatrix} -2 & -1 \\ -\frac{3}{2} & -\frac{1}{2} \end{bmatrix}$ 5. No inverse

7. $\frac{1}{11}\begin{bmatrix} -1 & 2 & 6 \\ -2 & 4 & 1 \\ 6 & -1 & -3 \end{bmatrix}$ 9. $\begin{bmatrix} -2 & -\frac{1}{3} & \frac{4}{3} \\ 1 & \frac{2}{3} & -\frac{2}{3} \\ \frac{1}{2} & -\frac{1}{6} & -\frac{1}{6} \end{bmatrix}$ 11. No inverse

13. $\begin{bmatrix} \frac{3}{14} & \frac{1}{2} & \frac{1}{14} \\ \frac{1}{14} & -\frac{1}{2} & \frac{5}{14} \\ -\frac{5}{14} & -\frac{1}{2} & \frac{3}{14} \end{bmatrix}$ 15. $\begin{bmatrix} -6 & \frac{7}{2} & \frac{9}{2} & -\frac{3}{2} \\ 3 & -2 & -2 & 1 \\ -4 & \frac{5}{2} & \frac{7}{2} & -\frac{3}{2} \\ 7 & -4 & -5 & 2 \end{bmatrix}$ 17. $x = 2, y = 1$

19. $u = 1, v = 2$ 21. $x = 1, y = 2, z = -1$ 23. $u = 1, v = 0, w = 3$
25. 1600 lb of P and 600 lb of Q

Exercises 2

1. a. $\begin{bmatrix} 0.2 & 0.7 \\ 0.5 & 0.1 \end{bmatrix}$ b. 250 and 180 units for I and II, respectively.
   c. 75 and 36 units for I and II, respectively.
3. a. $\begin{bmatrix} 0.3 & 0.5 \\ 0.4 & 0.2 \end{bmatrix}$ b. $\begin{bmatrix} 470 \\ 450 \end{bmatrix}$ c. 141 and 135 units for P and Q, respectively.
5. Final demands: 80 units for P, 70 for Q. [Total outputs: 275 and 225 units.]

Exercises 3

1. $(an - c)$ 3. $-(am - b)$ 5. 25   7. -38 9. $3a + 2b$ 11. 32
13. -192 15. $(ac - b^2)$ 17. -21 19. 35   21. 0   23. 6
25. adf 27. 10   29. $x = 3$ 31. $x = 6; -1$ 33. $x = 1, y = -1$
35. $x = 1, y = 2$ 37. $x = 6, y = 10$ 39. No solution
41. $x = 1, y = -1, z = -1$ 43. $x = -1, y = -1, z = 3$
45. $x = 3, y = 1, z = 2$ 47. No solution   49. $x = -1, y = 2, z = 1$

Exercises 4

1. $\begin{bmatrix} 2 & 3 \\ 5 & -7 \end{bmatrix}$ 3. $\begin{bmatrix} a_1 & b_1 \\ a_2 & b_2 \\ a_3 & b_3 \end{bmatrix}$ 5. $\begin{bmatrix} 1 & 0 \\ 0 & 1 \end{bmatrix}$ 7. $\begin{bmatrix} \frac{1}{5} & -\frac{2}{5} \\ \frac{1}{5} & \frac{3}{5} \end{bmatrix}$ 9. $\begin{bmatrix} 2 & 3 \\ 4 & 5 \end{bmatrix}$

11. $\begin{bmatrix} -\frac{1}{6} & \frac{1}{2} & -\frac{5}{6} \\ \frac{5}{6} & -\frac{1}{2} & \frac{7}{6} \\ -\frac{1}{2} & \frac{1}{2} & -\frac{1}{2} \end{bmatrix}$ 13. $\frac{1}{9}\begin{bmatrix} 1 & -2 & 4 \\ -2 & 4 & 1 \\ 4 & 1 & -2 \end{bmatrix}$ 15. No inverse exists

17. a. $\begin{bmatrix} 0.2 & 0.2 & 0.1 \\ 0.3 & 0.1 & 0.3 \\ 0.4 & 0.5 & 0.2 \end{bmatrix}$ b. 623, 1007, and 1466 units for I, II, and III, respectively.
   c. 62.3, 201.4, and 586.4 units, respectively.

19. a. $\begin{bmatrix} 0.3 & 0.1 & 0.4 \\ 0.3 & 0.3 & 0.1 \\ 0.2 & 0.2 & 0.3 \end{bmatrix}$ b. 246, 227 and 250 units for A, B and C, respectively.

Review Exercises for Chapter 10

1. a. True   b. True
   c. False; The zero matrix is *not* invertible.
   d. False; The statement is true if **A** is invertible but not for a general **A**.

e. False; For example the identity matrix is invertible.

f. False; For example $\begin{bmatrix} 1 & 1 \\ 1 & 1 \end{bmatrix}$ is not invertible.   **g.** True   **h.** True

i. False; The determinant of $k\mathbf{A}$ is equal to $k^n |\mathbf{A}|$.   **j.** True

k. False; The quantity defined is the minor, not the cofactor.

l. False; The cofactor and minor are equal in absolute value. They sometimes have the same sign, sometimes opposite signs.

m. False; $(\mathbf{AB})^{-1} = \mathbf{B}^{-1}\mathbf{A}^{-1}$ **n.** True

3. $\frac{1}{11}\begin{bmatrix} 5 & 3 \\ -2 & 1 \end{bmatrix}$ **5.** $[1/(a^2 + b^2)]\begin{bmatrix} a & -b \\ b & a \end{bmatrix}$ **7.** $\begin{bmatrix} 1 & 0 & 0 \\ 0 & \frac{1}{2} & 0 \\ 0 & 0 & \frac{1}{3} \end{bmatrix}$

9. $\frac{1}{3}\begin{bmatrix} -2 & 1 & 1 \\ -8 & 7 & -2 \\ 7 & -5 & 1 \end{bmatrix}$ **11.** Not invertible   **13.** Not invertible (not a square matrix).

15. $x = 1, y = 1$ **17.** $x = 1, y = 1, z = -1$ **19.** $x = -\frac{1}{2}, y = \frac{1}{2}$

21. $x = 1, y = 2, z = 3$ **23.** No solution   **25.** $(a + 4)(a - 4)$

27. $(x + 8)(x - 5)$ **29.** $x(1 - x)$

31. **a.** $\begin{bmatrix} 0.1 & 0.4 \\ 0.7 & 0.2 \end{bmatrix}$ **b.** 177.27 and 253.86 units for I and II, respectively.   **c.** 35.45 and 101.54 units, respectively.

CHAPTER 11

Exercises 1

1. 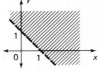   **3.** 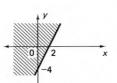   **5.**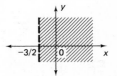

7. 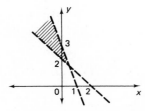   **9.** 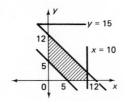   **11.**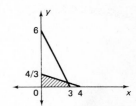

13. $0 \leq x \leq 70, 0 \leq y \leq 90;$
$40 \leq x + y \leq 100$

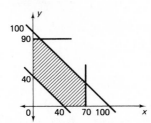

15. $x - 2y \leq 40$

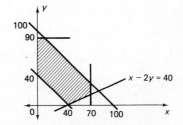

17.

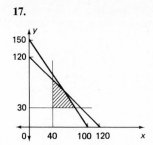

19. $2x + 3y \geq 110$

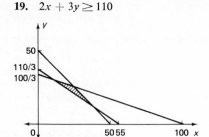

21. $15x + 8y \leq 100; 110x + 83y < 900; 7x + 7y \geq 60; x, y \geq 0$

Exercises 2

1. $Z = 15$ at $(5, 0)$ **3.** $Z = 7$ at $(1, 2)$ **5.** $Z = \frac{35}{3}$ at $(\frac{7}{3}, 0)$ **7.** $Z = 4$ at $(3, 1)$
9. $Z = 8$ at $(4, 1)$ **11.** $Z = 5$ at $(3, 1)$ **13.** $x = 2000, y = 3000, Z = \$28,000$
15. $x = 10, y = 20, Z = \$1700$ **17.** 50 of A, 20 of B; $Z = \$18,500$
19. $(500/3)$ dollars per unit of B
21. $\frac{130}{3}$ and $\frac{170}{3}$ acres in crops I & II; $Z = (64,000/3)$ dollars
23. 2.7 oz of A and 2.2 oz of B   **25.** $x = 3000, y = 0$; Min. Cost is 225,000.

Exercises 3

1.
$$\begin{array}{cccc} & x & y & t \\ t & [1 & 1 & 1 \,|\, 5] \end{array}$$

3.
$$\begin{array}{ccccc} & x & y & t & u \\ t & \begin{bmatrix} 2 & 1 & 1 & 0 \,|\, 4 \\ u & 1 & 2 & 0 & 1 \,|\, 5 \end{bmatrix} \end{array}$$

5.
$$\begin{array}{cccccc} & x & y & t & u & v \\ t & \begin{bmatrix} 3 & 1 & 1 & 0 & 0 \,|\, 7 \\ u & 1 & 1 & 0 & 1 & 0 \,|\, 3 \\ v & 1 & 2 & 0 & 0 & 1 \,|\, 5 \end{bmatrix} \end{array}$$

7.
$$\begin{array}{ccccc} & x & y & t & u \\ t & \begin{bmatrix} 3 & 2 & 1 & 0 \,|\, 12,000 \\ u & 3 & 4 & 0 & 1 \,|\, 18,000 \end{bmatrix} \end{array}$$

9.
$$\begin{array}{ccccc} & x & y & t & u \\ t & \begin{bmatrix} 2 & 4 & 1 & 0 \,|\, 100 \\ u & 5 & 3 & 0 & 1 \,|\, 110 \end{bmatrix} \end{array}$$

11.
$$\begin{array}{cccccc} & x & y & t & u & v \\ t & \begin{bmatrix} 2 & 5 & 1 & 0 & 0 \,|\, 200 \\ u & 4 & 1 & 0 & 1 & 0 \,|\, 240 \\ v & 3 & 2 & 0 & 0 & 1 \,|\, 190 \end{bmatrix} \end{array}$$

13.
$$\begin{array}{cccccc} & x & y & z & t & u \\ t & \begin{bmatrix} 2 & 1 & 1 & 1 & 0 \,|\, 5 \\ u & 1 & 2 & 1 & 0 & 1 \,|\, 4 \end{bmatrix} \end{array}$$

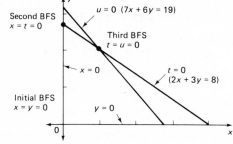

15.
$$\begin{array}{ccccc} & x & y & t & u \\ y & \begin{bmatrix} \frac{2}{3} & 1 & \frac{1}{3} & 0 \,|\, \frac{8}{3} \\ u & 3 & 0 & -2 & 1 \,|\, 3 \end{bmatrix} \end{array} \longrightarrow \begin{array}{ccccc} & x & y & t & u \\ y & \begin{bmatrix} 0 & 1 & \frac{7}{9} & -\frac{2}{9} \,|\, 2 \\ x & 1 & 0 & -\frac{2}{3} & \frac{1}{3} \,|\, 1 \end{bmatrix} \end{array}$$

17.
$$\begin{array}{cccccc} & x & y & z & t & u \\ y & \begin{bmatrix} \frac{1}{2} & 1 & \frac{1}{2} & \frac{1}{2} & 0 \,|\, \frac{5}{2} \\ u & 2 & 0 & 3 & -1 & 1 \,|\, 11 \end{bmatrix} \end{array} \longrightarrow \begin{array}{cccccc} & x & y & z & t & u \\ y & \begin{bmatrix} 0 & 1 & -\frac{1}{4} & \frac{3}{4} & -\frac{1}{4} \,|\, -\frac{1}{4} \\ x & 1 & 0 & \frac{3}{2} & -\frac{1}{2} & \frac{1}{2} \,|\, \frac{11}{2} \end{bmatrix} \end{array}$$
The second solution here is infeasible.

19.

$$
\begin{array}{c}
 & \begin{array}{ccccc} x & y & s & t & u \end{array} \\
\begin{array}{c} s \\ x \\ u \end{array} &
\left[\begin{array}{ccccc|c}
0 & -\frac{17}{2} & 1 & -\frac{3}{2} & 0 & -\frac{17}{2} \\
1 & \frac{9}{4} & 0 & \frac{1}{4} & 0 & \frac{17}{4} \\
0 & -\frac{3}{2} & 0 & -\frac{1}{2} & 1 & -\frac{5}{2}
\end{array}\right] \\[2em]
\begin{array}{c} s \\ x \\ y \end{array} &
\left[\begin{array}{ccccc|c}
0 & 0 & 1 & \frac{4}{3} & -\frac{17}{3} & \frac{17}{3} \\
1 & 0 & 0 & -\frac{1}{2} & \frac{3}{2} & \frac{1}{2} \\
0 & 1 & 0 & \frac{1}{3} & -\frac{2}{3} & \frac{5}{3}
\end{array}\right] \\[2em]
\begin{array}{c} u \\ x \\ y \end{array} &
\left[\begin{array}{ccccc|c}
0 & 0 & -\frac{3}{17} & -\frac{4}{17} & 1 & -1 \\
1 & 0 & \frac{9}{34} & -\frac{5}{34} & 0 & 2 \\
0 & 1 & -\frac{2}{17} & \frac{3}{17} & 0 & 1
\end{array}\right]
\end{array}
$$

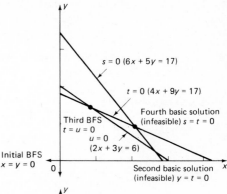

s = 0 (6x + 5y = 17)

t = 0 (4x + 9y = 17)

Fourth basic solution (infeasible) s = t = 0

Third BFS
t = u = 0

u = 0
(2x + 3y = 6)

Initial BFS
x = y = 0

Second basic solution (infeasible) y = t = 0

21.

$$
\begin{array}{c}
 & \begin{array}{ccccc} x & y & p & q & r \end{array} \\
\begin{array}{c} x \\ q \\ r \end{array} &
\left[\begin{array}{ccccc|c}
1 & \frac{2}{3} & \frac{1}{3} & 0 & 0 & \frac{5}{3} \\
0 & \frac{4}{3} & -\frac{1}{3} & 1 & 0 & \frac{4}{3} \\
0 & \frac{13}{3} & -\frac{1}{3} & 0 & 1 & \frac{13}{3}
\end{array}\right] \\[2em]
\begin{array}{c} x \\ y \\ r \end{array} &
\left[\begin{array}{ccccc|c}
1 & 0 & \frac{1}{2} & -\frac{1}{2} & 0 & 1 \\
0 & 1 & -\frac{1}{4} & \frac{3}{4} & 0 & 1 \\
0 & 0 & -\frac{3}{13} & -\frac{4}{13} & 1 & 0
\end{array}\right] \\[2em]
\begin{array}{c} x \\ y \\ q \end{array} &
\left[\begin{array}{ccccc|c}
1 & 0 & \frac{7}{8} & 0 & -\frac{13}{8} & 1 \\
0 & 1 & -\frac{13}{16} & 0 & \frac{39}{16} & 1 \\
0 & 0 & \frac{3}{4} & 1 & -\frac{13}{4} & 0
\end{array}\right]
\end{array}
$$

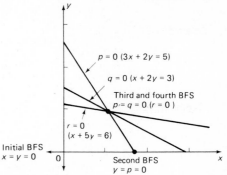

p = 0 (3x + 2y = 5)

q = 0 (x + 2y = 3)

Third and fourth BFS
p = q = 0 (r = 0)

r = 0
(x + 5y = 6)

Initial BFS
x = y = 0

Second BFS
y = p = 0

Exercises 4

Answers to Exercises 1–13 are given in the answers to Exercises 2 above.

15. $Z_{\max} = 4$ at $(0, 0, 4)$

17. 2000, 3000 and 4000 lb of regular, super and delux per day.

19. $x = \frac{11}{7}, y = \frac{6}{7}, z = 0; Z = \frac{23}{7}$

21. Maximum $Z = 4$ is attained at the two vertices $x = 1, y = 1, z = 2$ and $x = 3,$ $y = 1, z = 0$ and therefore at all points on the edge joining them.

Review Exercises for Chapter 11

1. **a.** False; The graph of a linear inequality in two variables is a *region* in the xy-plane that is bounded by a dashed line if the inequality is *strict* and by a solid line if it is weak.

b. False; If $y - 2x \geq 1$, then $2x - y \leq -1$.

c. False; If $y - 3x \leq 2$, then $3x - y \geq -2$.

d. False; If $y > a$ and $x > b$, then $y + x > a + b$. **e.** True

f. False; We cannot conclude separate inequalities for x and y from the single joint inequality $y - x > a - b$.

g. True **h.** False; $4x - 2y > 6$ is equivalent to $-2x + y < -3$.

3.

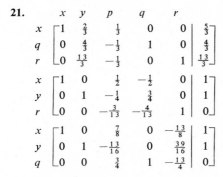

3x + 2y = 20

5. $Z_{\max} = 19$ when $x = 1, y = 2$.

7. $Z_{\max} = \frac{7}{3}$ when $x = \frac{7}{3}, y = 0$.
$Z_{\min} = -\frac{12}{5}$ when $x = 0, y = \frac{12}{5}$.

9. $Z_{\max} = 15$ when $x = 5, y = 0$.

11. $Z_{\min} = 0$ when $x = y = 0$.

13. $Z_{max} = 14$ when $x = 0$, $y = 2$, $z = 2$.   **15.** $Z_{max} = 13$ when $x = 0$, $y = 7$, $z = 1$.
17. $x = 0$, $y = 90$; Min. cost is $1600.
19. Number of S is $\frac{300}{7}$, number of T is $\frac{1200}{7}$, max. weight is $\frac{3300}{7}$ lb.

CHAPTER 12

Exercises 1

1. 0.40   **3.** $g(x)$ is not defined over the whole interval from x to $x + \Delta x$.
5. -50 **7.** $\Delta x - 2\Delta x/x(x + \Delta x)$ **9.** -7 **11.** 1   **13.** 0.1613
15. $3a^2 + 3ah + h^2 + 1$
17. **a.** 40   **b.** 160   **c.** 220   **d.** 250   **e.** $1000 - 240t - 120\Delta t$ **19.** 10.1
21. \$452.38, \$201.06   **23.** $\Delta p = e^{-0.3} - e^{-0.6} = 0.1920$; $\Delta p/\Delta t = 0.064$
25. **a.** 20   **b.** -28 (descending)   **c.** $100 - 32t - 16\Delta t$

Exercises 2

1. 25   **3.** 4   **5.** 0   **7.** 4   **9.** 1   **11.** Limit does not exist.   **13.** $\frac{1}{4}$
15. $\frac{1}{8}$ **17.** 2   **19.** 2   **21.** 7   **23.** 0   **25.** $4x + 5$
27. **a.** 8 ft/sec   **b.** -24 ft/sec

Exercises 3

1. 2   **3.** $6u$ **5.** $-(t + 1)^{-2}$ **7.** $-2/y^3$ **9.** **a.** $-4x$ **b.** 3
11. **a.** $1/2\sqrt{y}$ **b.** $-(y + 2)/y^3$ **13.** -2 **15.** 3   **17.** 7
19. Slope $= -1$; $y = 3 - x$ **21.** Slope $= -2$; $y = 7 - 2x$
23. **a.** 2000   **b.** 400   **c.** -1200

Exercises 4

1. $12x^2 - 6x$ **3.** $12x^3 - 21x^2 + 10x$ **5.** $6u - 6u^{-3}$ **7.** $1/t^2$
9. $(1/2\sqrt{y}) - (1/2y^{3/2})$ **11.** $12x^3 + 8x - 4$ **13.** $4x - 23$ **15.** $4u + 3$
17. $27t^2 + 6t - 5$ **19.** $-3 + 8t + 7/t^2$ **21.** $2 + 7/y^2$
23. $\frac{3}{2}\sqrt{x} - (3/2\sqrt{x}) - (1/2x\sqrt{x})$ **25.** $-4/u^3 - 6/u^4$ **27.** $(1/\sqrt{2y}) - (1/3y^2)$
29. $-(\ln 2)/x^2$ **31.** $1.2x^{0.2} - 0.6x^{-1.6}$ **33.** $-1.48x^{-1.4} - x^{-2}$
35. $(\log 2)x^{\log 2 - 1}$ **37.** $3x^2 - 3/x^4$ **39.** $3u^2 - 10u - 14/3u^3$
43. **a.** $6t^2 - 1/2\sqrt{t}$ **b.** 95.75   **45.** **a.** 0.1   **b.** 0.3   **c.** 0.5

Exercises 5

1. 2   **3.** $0.0003x^2 - 0.18x + 20$ **5.** $1 - 0.02x$
7. $0.1 - (2 \times 10^{-3})x - (2.5 \times 10^{-5})x^{3/2}$ **9.** $R'(x) = 25 - 0.5x$ **11.** 10
13. $20 - 0.5x$ **15.** **a.** 1.23   **b.** 6.25
17. $x = 40$; $P(40) = 300$, $p = 15$ **19.** $R'(x) = 9 - 0.1x$; $p = \$4.50$

Exercises 6

1. 0   **3.** Limit does not exist.   **5.** 1   **7.** $\frac{1}{6}$ **9.** $+\infty$ **11.** $+\infty$
13.   **15.**

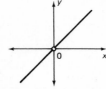

Discontinuous at $x = 0$

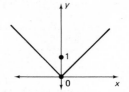

Discontinuous at $x = 0$

17.

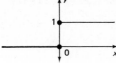

Discontinuous at $x = 0$

19.

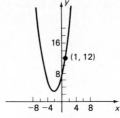

Continuous at $x = 1$

21.

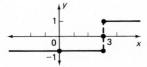

Discontinuous at $x = 3$

23.

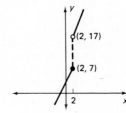

Discontinuous at $x = 2$

25. $h = 2$ **27.** $x = 0$ **29.** No x

31. $C(x) = \begin{cases} 10x & \text{if } 0 \le x \le 50; \\ 3x + 350 & \text{if } x > 50 \end{cases}$

$C(x)$ is continuous for all x and is differentiable at all x except $x = 0$ and $x = 50$.

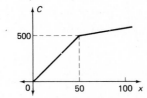

33.

$f(x) = \begin{cases} 12 & \text{if } 0 < x \le 1 \\ 24 & \text{if } 1 < x \le 2 \\ 36 & \text{if } 2 < x \le 3 \\ \quad \cdot & \qquad \cdot \\ \quad \cdot & \qquad \cdot \\ \quad \cdot & \qquad \cdot \\ 96 & \text{if } 7 < x \le 8 \end{cases}$

$f(x)$ is discontinuous and nondifferentiable at $x = 0$, 1, 2, 3, 4, 5, 6, 7, 8.

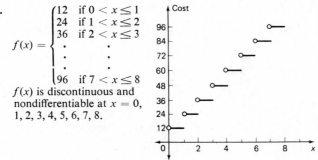

Review Exercises for Chapter 12

1. **a.** False; Increment in the independent variable can be positive or negative.
  b. True
  c. False; For example, $f(x) = (x^2 - 4)/(x - 2)$ is *not* defined at $x = 2$ but $\lim_{x \to 2} f(x)$ exists and is equal to 4.
  d. False; $x/x = 1$ only if $x \ne 0$. **e.** True **f.** True
  g. False; The derivative of y w.r.t. x represents the *instantaneous* rate of change of y w.r.t. x.

h. False; $f(x)$ is continuous at $x = c$ if $\lim\limits_{x \to c} f(x) = f(c)$.

i. False; For example, $f(x) = |x|$ is continuous at $x = 0$ but is *not* differentiable at $x = 0$.

j. True   **k.** False; If $f(x) = |x|$, then $f'(0)$ does not exist.

3. 640; 32   **5.** 0   **7.** $1/2\sqrt{x}$ **9.** $-2(x + 1)^{-3}$ **11.** $\frac{3}{2}x^{1/2} + 3x^{-5/2}$

13. $(e + 1/2)xe^{-1/2}$ **15.** $20x$ **17.** $R'(x) = 50 - 0.1x$ **19.** $40 - 0.1x$

21. No   **23.** $h = 2$

CHAPTER 13

Exercises 1

1. $4x^3 + 3x^2 + 3$ **3.** $11 - 42x$ **5.** $6x^2 - 14x - 13$

7. $24x^3 - 33x^2 + 18x - 11$ **9.** $R'(x) = 500 - x$

11. $R'(x) = 160,000 - 160x + 0.03x^2$ **13.** $6200 + 520t + 21t^2 + 0.4t^3$

15. $-3(x - 1)^{-2}$ **17.** $(t^2 - 10t + 35)(t - 5)^{-2}$ **19.** $-u^{-1/2}(\sqrt{u} - 1)^{-2}$

21. $-2x(x^2 + 1)^{-2}$ **23.** $\bar{C}'(x) = -a/x^2$

25. $(0.6 - 0.12t - 0.003t^2)(4 + 0.1t + 0.01t^2)^{-2}$

Exercises 2

1. $21(3x + 5)^6$ **3.** $6x(2x^2 + 1)^{1/2}$ **5.** $-8x(x^2 + 1)^{-5}$ **7.** $t(t^2 + a^2)^{-1/2}$

9. $2(u^2 + 1)^2(7u^2 + 3u + 1)$ **11.** $-t^2(t^3 + 1)^{-4/3}$

13. $(x^2 + 1)(3x^2 + 4x - 1)(x + 1)^{-2}$ **15.** $-(x^2 - 1)^{-3/2}$

17. $1.2x(x^2 + 1)^{-0.4}$ **19.** $(t^3 + 8t)(t^2 + 4)^{-3/2}$ **21.** $(9t + 7)/2\sqrt{t + 1}$

23. $x/\sqrt{100 + x^2}$ **25.** $-100x^{-2}(x^2 + 100)^{-1/2}$

27. $(100 - 0.15x - (2 \times 10^{-4})x^2)(100 - 0.1x - 10^{-4}x^2)^{-1/2}$

29. $dC/dt = 100$ per month

Exercises 3

1. $(x + 1)e^x$ **3.** $2xe^{x^2}$ **5.** $(1/2\sqrt{x} - 1)e^{\sqrt{x} - x}$ **7.** $2/x$ **9.** $-x^{-1}(\ln x)^{-2}$

11. $\log e$ **13.** $\ln x$ **15.** $(1 - \ln x)x^{-2}$ **17.** $1/(x + 2) - x/(x^2 + 1)$

19. $1/2x\sqrt{\ln x}$ **21.** $(x \ln a)^{-1}$ **23.** $a^x \ln a$

25. $[x \ln x - (x + 1) \ln (x + 1)]/[x(x + 1)(\ln x)^2]$ **27.** $5 - (1 + 0.1x)e^{0.1x}$

29. $\ln (2 - 0.001x) - 0.001x/(2 - 0.001x)$

31. $C'(x) = 1 - 0.5e^{-0.5x}$; $\bar{C}'(x) = -100x^{-2} - (1 + 0.5x)x^{-2}e^{-0.5x}$

33. $dy/dt = 3Cky_me^{-kt}(1 - Ce^{-kt})^2$

Exercises 4

1. $dy/dx = 15x^4 + 21x^2 - 8x$; $d^2y/dx^2 = 60x^3 + 42x - 8$; $d^3y/dx^3 = 180x^2 + 42$; $d^4y/dx^4 = 360x$; $d^5y/dx^5 = 360$; $d^ny/dx^n = 0$ for $n \geq 6$.

3. $f'(x) = 3x^2 - 12x + 9$; $f''(x) = 6x - 12$; $f'''(x) = 6$; $f^{(n)}(x) = 0$ for $n \geq 4$.

5. $y'' = 2(1 - 3x^2)/(1 + x^2)^3$ **7.** $g^{(4)}(u) = 1944(3u + 1)^{-5}$

9. $2(3x^2 - 1)(x^2 + 1)^{-3}$ **11.** $2x^{-3}$ **13.** $(x + 4)e^x$

15. $-(x + 1)^{-2} - (x + 2)^{-2}$ **17.** $(x - 1)e^{-x}$

19. **a.** vel. $= 9 + 32t$; acc. $= 32$ **b.** vel. $= 9t^2 + 14t - 5$; acc. $= 18t + 14$

21. $C'(x) = 30 - 0.2x + 0.006x^2$; $C''(x) = -0.2 + 0.012x$

Review Exerises for Chapter 13

1. **a.** False; $(d/dx)(uv) = uv' + vu'$.

b. True; $(u/v)' = (u \cdot 1/v)' = u'(1/v) + u(1/v)'$ (product rule).

c. False; $(d/dx)[u(x)]^n = n[u(x)]^{n-1}u'(x)$ **d.** True   **e.** True

f. False; The second derivative of any quadratic function is a *constant*.

g. False; If acceleration is zero, then velocity is constant, not necessarily zero.

h. False; $(d^2/dx^2)[u(x)]^n = nu^{n-2}[(n-1)(u')^2 + uu'']$.

i. False; $(d/dx)(e^{x^2}) = 2xe^{x^2}$.   **j.** False; $d/dx \ln(x^2 + 1) = 2x/(x^2 + 1)$.

k. False; $(d/dx)(\ln 2) = 0$, because $\ln 2$ is a constant.

l. False; $(d/dx)(e^x) = e^x$.   **m.** False; $(d/dx)(1/x^3) = (d/dx)(x^{-3}) = -3x^{-4}$.

3. $(2x^2 + 4)/\sqrt{x^2 + 4}$ **5.** $6(2x + 1)^2(3x - 1)^3(7x + 1)$ **7.** $(1/6)(x + 1)^{-5/6}$

9. $x^{\sqrt{2}-1}(1 + \sqrt{2}\ln x)$ **11.** $x^x(1 + \ln x)$

13. $30(3x - 7)^4(x + 1)^2(27x^2 - 18x - 5)$ **15.** $-(1 + \ln x)(x \ln x)^{-2}$

17. $R'(x) = (1 - x/b)e^{(a-x)/b}$

19. $C'(x) = 0.5 + 0.01(x + 1)e^x$; $\bar{C}'(x) = -100/x^2 + 0.01e^x$

CHAPTER 14

Exercises 1

1. a. $x > 3$ **b.** $x < 3$ **c.** All x **d.** No x; No point of inflection.

3. a. $x > 1$ or $x < -1$ **b.** $-1 < x < 1$ **c.** $x > 0$
   d. $x < 0$; $x = 0$ is the point of inflection.

5. a. $x > 1$ or $x < -1$ **b.** $-1 < x < 1$ **c.** $x > 0$
   d. $x < 0$; No point of inflection.

7. a. All $x \neq -1$ **b.** No x **c.** $x < -1$ **d.** $x > -1$; No point of inflection.

9. a. $x > 0$ **b.** No x **c.** No x
   d. All $x > 0$ (Note that y is not defined for $x < 0$); No point of inflection.

11. a. $x > 1/e$ **b.** $0 < x < 1/e$ **c.** $x > 0$ **d.** No x; No point of inflection.

13. a. $x < 0$ or $x > 4$ **b.** $0 < x < 4$ **c.** $x > 3$
   d. $x < 3$; Point of inflection at $x = 3$.

15. a. $x > 2$ **b.** $x < 2$ **c.** All x **d.** No x; No point of inflection.

17. a. $x > 1$ **b.** $x < 1$ **c.** $x < 0$ or $x > \frac{4}{3}$
   d. $0 < x < \frac{4}{3}$; Points of inflection at $x = 0$ and $x = \frac{4}{3}$.

19. a. $x > 0$ **b.** $x < 0$ **c.** No x **d.** $x < 0$ and $x > 0$; No point of inflection.

21. a. $x > 0$ **b.** No x **c.** No x **d.** All $x > 0$; No point of inflection.

23. a. No x **b.** All $x \neq 0$ **c.** $x > 0$ **d.** $x < 0$; No point of inflection.

25. a. Increasing for all $x > 0$.   **b.** Increasing for $0 < x < 100$; decreasing for $x > 100$.
   c. Increasing for $0 < x < 90$; decreasing for $x > 90$.

27. a. Always increasing.   **b.** Increasing for $0 < x < a/2b$; decreasing for $x > a/2b$.
   c. Increasing for $0 < x < (a - k)/2b$; decreasing for $x > (a - k)/2b$.

29. No concavity up or down.

31. Concave up for $x > 25/3$; concave down for $x < 25/3$.

Exercises 2

1. 0 **3.** No critical point   **5.** $-\frac{1}{6}$ **7.** $1; -1$ **9.** $-2; 3$

11. $0; 1; -1$ **13.** $1; -1$ **15.** No critical point   **17.** $0; \frac{1}{8}$ **19.** $\frac{3}{2}; 1$

21. $\frac{1}{3}$ **23.** $1/e$

Exercises 3

1. Minimum at $x = 6$.   **3.** Minimum at $x = 4$; maximum at $x = 0$.

5. Maximum at $x = 1$; minimum at $x = 2$.

7. Maximum at $x = 4$; minimum at $x = 8$.

9. Maximum at $x = 1$; minimum at $x = 3$; point of inflection at $x = 0$.

11. Maximum at $x = \frac{3}{5}$; minimum at $x = 1$; point of inflection at $x = 0$.

13. Minimum at $x = 0$.   **15.** Minimum at $x = 1/e$.

17. Maximum value 5 when $x = -2$; minimum value -22 when $x = 1$.

19. Minimum value $-1/e$ when $x = -1$.

21. Minimum value 0 when $x = 1$; maximum value $(9/11)^3(2/11)^{2/3}$ when $x = 9/11$; point of inflection at $x = 0$.

23. Maximum value $1/2e$ when $x = \sqrt{e}$.   **25.** Minimum value 0 when $x = 1$.

27. Minimum value 0 when $x = 2$.

Exercises 4

1. $5; 5$ **3.** $50; 25$

7. Maximum area a^2 occurs when the length of rectangle is twice the width $(a/\sqrt{2})$.

9. 1250 yd^2 **11.** $6 \text{ ft} \times 6 \text{ ft} \times 9 \text{ ft}$

13. Minimum value of $\bar{C}$ is 41 when $x = 2$.   **15.** $x = 2000$

17. **a.** $P(x) = 2.7x - 0.001x^2 - 50$ **b.** 1350   **c.** 1772.50

19. $x = 2500; \$2250$ **21.** $x = 2500; x = 2000$; max. profit is $\$1200$.   **23.** 2000

25. $x = 50$ **27.** $x = 200(4 - t)/3; t = 2$ **29.** $n = \sqrt{a/c}$

31. $R_{\max}$ when $x = 350; P_{\max}$ when $x = 225; x = 200$

Exercises 5

1. Absolute maximum 7 at $x = 6$; absolute minimum -2 at $x = 3$.

3. Absolute maximum 75 at $x = -1$; absolute minimum -249 at $x = 5$.

5. Absolute maximum 56 at $x = 2$; absolute minimum -79 at $x = -1$.

7. Absolute maximum -3 at $x = 2$; absolute minimum -33 at $x = \frac{1}{2}$.

9. $y_{\max} = 6000$ at $t = 0; y_{\min} = 2000$ at $t = 20$.   **11.** $3000; 2000$

Exercises 6

1.

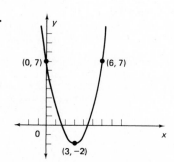

3.

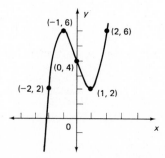

5.

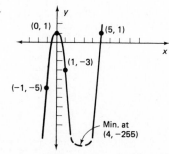

7.

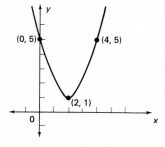

9.

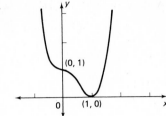

(0, 1)

0 (1, 0) x

11.

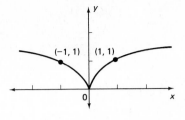

(−1, 1) (1, 1)

0 x

13.

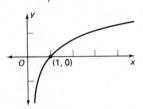

O (1, 0) x

15.

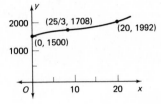

2000 (25/3, 1708) (20, 1992)

(0, 1500)

1000

O 10 20 x

17.

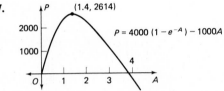

P (1.4, 2614)

2000

$P = 4000\,(1 - e^{-A}) - 1000A$

1000

4

O 1 2 3 A

Exercises 7

1. a. $+\infty$ **b.** $-\infty$ **3. a.** $-\infty$ **b.** $+\infty$ **5. a.** $+\infty$ **b.** $+\infty$
7. a. $-\infty$ **b.** $+\infty$ **9. a.** $+\infty$ **b.** Does not exist
11.

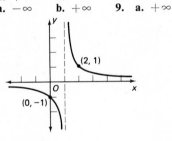

(2, 1)

O x

(0, −1)

Horizontal asymptote: $y = 0$
Vertical asymptote: $x = 1$

13.

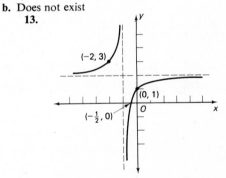

(−2, 3)

(0, 1)

$(-\frac{1}{2}, 0)$ O x

Horizontal asymptote: $y = 2$
Vertical asymptote: $x = -1$

15.

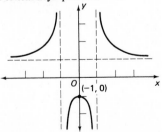

O (−1, 0) x

Horizontal asymptote: $y = 1$
Vertical asymptote: $x = \pm 1$

17.

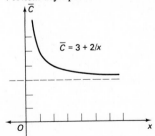

$\overline{C}$

$\overline{C} = 3 + 2/x$

O x

19.

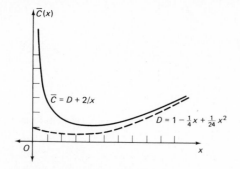

$\bar{C}(x)$

$\bar{C} = D + 2/x$

$D = 1 - \frac{1}{4}x + \frac{1}{24}x^2$

Review Exercises for Chapter 14

1. **a.** False; $f(x)$ is increasing for values of x at which $f'(x) > 0$ and is decreasing for values of x at which $f'(x) < 0$.
b. False; For example $f(x) = x^3$ is increasing for all x, but $f'(0) = 0$.
c. True **d.** True
e. False; At a point of inflection, $f''(x)$ may be undefined. **f.** True
g. False; If $f(x)$ has an extremum at $x = c$, then either $f'(c) = 0$ or $f'(c)$ fails to exist.
h. False; If $f'(c) = 0$, then $f(x)$ could have a point of inflection at $x = c$.
i. False; For example $f(x) = |x|$ has a local minimum at $x = 0$, but the tangent cannot be drawn at this point on the graph.
j. False; The tangent at the point of inflection need not be horizontal.
k. False; A local maximum value of a function can be *less* than a local minimum value. This is the case for $f(x) = x + 1/x$ for example.
l. True **m.** False; A cubic function may have two or no local extrema.
n. False; Maximum revenue need not lead to a maximum profit. **o.** True
p. False; Above a certain level, the cost of further advertising outweighs the extra revenue it generates.
q. True
r. False; For example, $\lim\limits_{x \to +\infty} \dfrac{x + 2}{\sqrt{x^2 + 4}} = 1$, whereas $\lim\limits_{x \to -\infty} \dfrac{x + 2}{\sqrt{x^2 + 4}} = -1$.
s. False; $\lim\limits_{x \to -\infty} \dfrac{1}{\sqrt{x}}$ does not exist, because $\sqrt{x}$ is not defined for *negative* values of x.
t. True; A vertical line cannot cross the graph of a function more than once.
3. **a.** $x < 2$ or $x > 4$
b. $2 < x < 4$
c. $x > 3$
d. $x < 3$

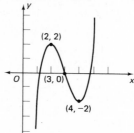

(2, 2)

(3, 0)

(4, −2)

5. **a.** $-2 < x < 0$ or $x > 2$
b. $x < -2$ or $0 < x < 2$
c. $x < -\sqrt{\frac{12}{5}}$ or $x > \sqrt{\frac{12}{5}}$
d. $-\sqrt{\frac{12}{5}} < x < \sqrt{\frac{12}{5}}$

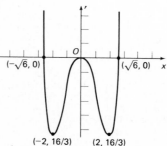

$(-\sqrt{6}, 0)$ $(\sqrt{6}, 0)$ x

$(-2, 16/3)$ $(2, 16/3)$

7. a. $x > -1$
b. $x < -1$
c. $x > -2$
d. $x < -2$

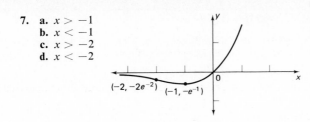

$(-2, -2e^{-2})$ $(-1, -e^{-1})$

9. Local max. at $t = 0$, local min. at $t = 1$.　　**11.** Local min. at $x = \frac{1}{2}$.
13. Local max. at $x = \frac{1}{6}$; local min. at $x = 0$, $x = 1$.
15. a. $k = \frac{3}{2}$　　b. $k = -48$　　c. $k = -32$　　**17.** $A > 0$
19. Absolute min. value 0 at $x = 0$, 2 and absolute max. $8\sqrt[3]{2}$ at $x = -2$.
21. $x = 100$; $P_{max} = 50$; $P(120) = 44$　　**23.** $x = 6$
27. b. $Q = 2000$; $T_{min} = \$10,250$　　c. \$10,256.25
29. 2341 pairs of men's shoes; 3746 pairs of women's shoes.
31.

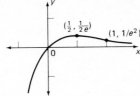

$(\frac{1}{2}, \frac{1}{2e})$ $(1, 1/e^2)$

33.

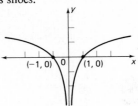

$(-1, 0)$ $(1, 0)$

No horizontal asymptote;
Vertical asymptote: $y = 0$.

CHAPTER 15

Exercises 1

1. $(2x + 7)dx$　　**3.** $(1 + \ln t)dt$　　**5.** $2z(z^2 + 1)^{-1} dz$　　**7.** $ue^u(u + 1)^{-2} du$
9. $[(2x - 3)/2\sqrt{x^2 - 3x}] dx$　　**11.** $2 dx$　　**13.** 0　　**15.** 0.12　　**17.** 0.003
19. $dy = 0.12$, $\Delta y = 0.1203$　　**21.** $dy = 0.02$, $\Delta y = \ln(1.02) = 0.0198$
23. 2.0833　　**25.** 1.9875　　**27.** $\pm 0.512\pi$ cm^3　　**29.** $\frac{5}{3}\%$　　**31.** $p = 1.96$
33. $x = 1000$; $C = 1200$; error in $x = -50$; error in $C = 10$.

Exercises 2

1. $-x/(y + 1)$　　**3.** $-x^2/y^2$　　**5.** $(4x - y)/(x + 2y)$
7. $-y(2x + y)/x(2y + x)$　　**9.** $(x^4 - y)/(x - y^4)$　　**11.** $-y/(e^y + x)$
13. $-y/x$　　**15.** $-5t/3x$　　**17.** $(x - 3y^2)/(3x^2 - y)$　　**19.** $3y = x + 5$　　**21.** 0
23. $-\frac{16}{27}$　　**25.** $x[(y + 1)^2 + (x + 1)^2]/y^2(x + 1)^3$　　**27.** $[-y/(x + 2y)] dx$
29. $[y(z - 1)/z(1 - y)] dz$

Exercises 3

1. $(x^2 + 1)(x - 1)^{1/2}[2x/(x^2 + 1) + 1/2(x - 1)]$
3. $(x^2 - 2)(2x^2 + 1)(x - 3)^2[2x/(x^2 - 2) + 4x/(2x^2 + 1) + 2/(x - 3)]$
5. $(x^2 + 1)^{1/3}(x^2 + 2)^{-1}[2x/3(x^2 + 1) - 2x/(x^2 + 2)]$
7. $[(2x^2 + 5)/(2x + 5)]^{1/3}[4x/3(2x^2 + 5) - 2/3(2x + 5)]$　　**9.** $x^x[x + 2x \ln x]$
11. $e^{(x + e^x)}$　　**13.** $x^{\ln x}(2 \ln x)/x$　　**15.** $x^x(1 + \ln x) + x^{-2 + 1/x}(1 - \ln x)$　　**17.** $-n$
19. $\sqrt{p}/(2\sqrt{p} - 8)$　　**21.** a. $-\frac{1}{3}$　　b. -1　　c. -3
23. a. $3 < p < 6$　　b. $0 < p < 3$　　**25.** a. $\frac{16}{9} < p < 4$　　b. $0 < p < \frac{16}{9}$

Review Exercises for Chapter 15

1. **a.** False; The differential of x^2 is $2xdx$. **b.** True **c.** True (provided $dx \neq 0$).
   d. False; In $f(x, y) = 0$, one of the variables is independent and the other is a dependent variable.
   e. False; $(dy/dx)(dx/dy) = 1$ provided both derivatives are defined.
   f. False; If y is an increasing function of x, then x is also an increasing function of y.
   g. True
   h. False; The logarithmic derivative of x w.r.t. y is $(1/x)(dx/dy)$ and the logarithmic derivative of y w.r.t. x is $(1/y)(dy/dx)$. If the statement is to be true, then we must have $(1/x)\, dx/dy = [(1/y)(dy/dx)]^{-1}$, that is, $(dx/dy)(dy/dx) = yx$, or $xy = 1$, which is not, in general, true.
   i. False; The logarithmic derivative of x^n is n/x. **j.** True **k.** True **l.** True
   m. True
3. $-\frac{1}{4}$ 5. 34 7. $-[1 + x(2t + x)(x + t)][1 + t(2x + t)(x + t)]^{-1}$
9. dy is undefined, because at $x = -1$, $y = 0$, dy/dx does not exist.
11. $-2/e$ 13. $[(x^2 - 4)/x(x + 1)^2]^{1/3}[4x^3/3(x^4 - 4) - 1/3x - 2/3(x + 1)]$
15. 0 17. **a.** $p = 6$ **b.** $p = 8$ **c.** $p = 3$
19. (a) $-9/16$ (b) $-16/9$
21. $(\ln x - 1)\, dx/(\ln x)^2$ or $(y/x - y^2/x^2)\, dx$

CHAPTER 16

Exercises 1

1. **a.** $x^8/8 + C$ **b.** $\frac{2}{3}x^{3/2} + C$ **c.** $2\sqrt{x} + C$ **d.** $7x + C$
3. $x^8/8 + \frac{25}{7}x^2 + 7 \ln|x| + C$ 5. $x^4/4 + \frac{4}{3}x^{5/2} + C$
7. $x^4 + x^3 + x^2 + x + \ln|x| - \frac{1}{2}x^{-2} + C$ 9. $\frac{2}{7}u^{7/2} + \frac{6}{5}u^{5/2} + \frac{14}{3}u^{3/2} + C$
11. $\frac{4}{7}x^{7/2} + \frac{2}{5}x^{5/2} - \frac{2}{3}x^{3/2} + C$ 13. $-1/x + 3 \ln|x| + 7x - x^2 + C$
15. $\theta^3 - 3\theta + 9 \ln|\theta| + 4e^\theta + C$ 17. $s = t^3/3 + 4t^{5/2}/5 + t^2/2$
19. **a.** $C(x) = 2000 + 30x - 0.025x^2$ **b.** \$5937.50 21. \$1280
23. **a.** $R(x) = 4x - 0.005x^2$ **b.** $p = 4 - 0.005x$
25. $P(x) = 5x - 0.001x^2 - 180$

Exercises 2

1. $\frac{1}{16}(2x + 1)^8 + C$ 3. $\frac{1}{5}(2 - 5t)^{-1} + C$ 5. $\frac{1}{2} \ln|2y - 1| + C$
7. $\frac{1}{2} \ln|2u + 1| + C$ 9. $\frac{1}{3}e^{3x+2} + C$ 11. $-e^{5-x} + C$ 13. $\frac{1}{3}e^{3x+2} + C$
15. $\frac{1}{5}(x^2 + 7x + 3)^5 + C$ 17. $-\frac{1}{2}(x^2 + 3x + 1)^{-2} + C$
19. $\ln|x^2 + 3x + 1| + C$ 21. $\frac{1}{2}e^{t^2} + C$ 23. $(1/n)e^{x^n} + C$
25. $-1/(e^x + 1) + C$ 27. $\frac{1}{4}(\ln x)^4 + C$ 29. $\ln|1 + \ln x| + C$
31. $\ln|t^3 + t| + C$ 33. $\frac{1}{3}(x^2 + 4x + 1)^{3/2} + C$
35. $C(x) = \frac{1}{3000}(x^2 + 2500)^{3/2} + \frac{175}{3}$

Exercises 3

1. $(1/\sqrt{5}) \ln|(2x - 3 - \sqrt{5})/(2x - 3 + \sqrt{5})| + C$ (Formula 66)
3. $\frac{1}{4}[\ln|2x - 3| - 3/(2x - 3)] + C$ (Formula 9)
5. $2\sqrt{3x + 1} + \ln|(\sqrt{3x + 1} - 1)/(\sqrt{3x + 1} + 1)| + C$ (Formula 22, 24)
7. $-\frac{1}{4} \ln|(4 + \sqrt{t^2 + 16})/t| + C$ (Formula 46)
9. $\frac{1}{2}y\sqrt{y^2 - 9} + \frac{9}{2} \ln|y + \sqrt{y^2 - 9}| + C$ (Formula 45)
11. $\frac{1}{2} \ln|(\sqrt{3x + 4} - 2)/(\sqrt{3x + 4} + 2)| + C$ (Formula 22)
13. $1/3(2x + 3) - \frac{1}{9} \ln|(2x + 3)/x| + C$ (Formula 14)
15. $(x^3/6 - x/8)(x^2 - 1)^{3/2} - \frac{1}{16}x(x^2 - 1)^{1/2} + \frac{1}{16} \ln|x + (x^2 - 1)^{1/2}| + C$
$\qquad$ (Formulas 58, 64, 65)
17. $\frac{1}{8}(4x^3 - 6x^2 + 6x - 3)e^{2x} + C$ (Formulas 70, 69)

19. $\frac{1}{4}\sqrt{2x+3}\sqrt{4x-1} + (7/4\sqrt{2}) \ln|\sqrt{4x-1} + \sqrt{4x+6}| + C$ (Formula 81)
21. $\ln|(1-e^x)/(2-3e^x)| + C$ (Formula 15)
23. $-\frac{1}{2}\ln|(2x^2+3)/(x^2+1)| + C$ (Formula 15)
25. $\frac{1}{2}\ln x - \frac{3}{4}\ln|3 + 2\ln x| + C$ (Formula 8)

Exercises 4

1. $(x^2/2)\ln x - x^2/4 + C$ 3. $[x^{n+1}/(n+1)]\ln x - x^{n+1}/(n+1)^2 + C$
5. $x \ln x - x + C$ 7. $xe^x - e^x + C$ 9. $(x/m)e^{mx} - (1/m^2)e^{mx} + C$
11. $\frac{1}{3}(2x+1)e^{3x} - \frac{2}{9}e^{3x} + C$ 13. $(x^2/2)\ln x - x^2/4 + C$
15. $(x^2 - 2x + 2)e^x + C$ 17. $\frac{1}{2}(x^2 - 1)e^{x^2} + C$ 19. $(x^3/3)(\ln x - \frac{1}{3}) + C$
23. $C(x) = 2250 + 250 \ln 20 - 5000(x + 20)^{-1}[1 + \ln(x + 20)]$

Review Exercises for Chapter 16

1. a. False; The antiderivative contains an arbitrary constant.   b. True
    c. False; The integral of the product of two functions can often be obtained by integration by parts.
    d. False; $\int (d/dx)[f(x)]\, dx = f(x) + C$.   e. False; $(d/dt)[\int f(t)\, dt] = f(t)$.
    f. False; If $f'(x) = g'(x)$, then $f(x) - g(x)$ is constant, not necessarily zero.
    g. False; $\int (1/x)\, dx = \ln|x| + C$.   h. False; $\int e^x\, dx = e^x + C$.
    i. False; $\int (1/e^t)\, dt = \int e^{-t}\, dt = -e^{-t} + C$.
    j. False; $\int [f(x)]^n f'(x)\, dx = [f(x)]^{n+1}/(n+1) + C, n \neq -1$.
    k. False; $\int x^n\, dx = x^{n+1}/(n+1) + C$ only if $n \neq -1$.
    l. False; Integration by parts gives: $\int xf(x)\, dx = x\int f(x)\, dx - \int (\int f(x)\, dx)\, dx$.
    m. False; $\int (1/x^2)\, dx = (-1/x) + C$.
    n. False; $\int e^{x^2}\, dx$ cannot be expressed in terms of elementary functions.
    o. False; $\int e^t\, dt = e^t + C$.
3. $\ln|1 + \ln x| + C$ 5. $2e^{\sqrt{x}+1} + C$ 7. $\frac{1}{2}(1 + x^3)^{2/3} + C$
9. $2\sqrt{2 + \ln x} + C$
11. $\frac{2}{3}\ln|x - 1| + \frac{7}{3}\ln|x + 2| + C$ (Formula 15, 16)
13. $\frac{1}{81}[-\sqrt{9 - x^2}/x + x/\sqrt{9 - x^2}] + C$ (Formula 36)
15. $\frac{1}{4}t\sqrt{25t^2 + 9} + \frac{9}{10}\ln|5t + \sqrt{25t^2 + 9}| + C$ (Formula 56).
17. $\frac{1}{4}[3x - \ln(1 + 2e^{3x})] + C$ (Formula 71)
19. $\frac{1}{6}x^6 + C$ (Note: $\log_x x^3 = 3\log_x x = 3.1 = 3$.)
21. $\frac{1}{27}x^3[9(\ln x)^2 - 6\ln x + 2] + C$ (Formula 77, 74)
23. $\frac{1}{3}\ln|(x^3 - 1)/x^3| + C$ (Multiply and divide the integrand by x^2 and then use the substitution $x^3 = y$).   (Formula 12)
25. $\frac{1}{25}\ln|(e^x + 1)/(e^x - 4)| - \frac{1}{5}(e^x - 4)^{-1} + C$ (Formula 17; set $e^x = t$).
27. $-\frac{1}{2}e^{(1/x^2)} + C$
29. a. $R(x) = 12x - 0.1x^2 - 0.01x^3$ b. 120   c. $p = 12 - 0.1x - 0.01x^2$
    d. $5(\sqrt{37} - 1) = 25.4$
31. 184; 384

CHAPTER 17

Exercises 1

1. $\frac{1}{3}$ 3. $\frac{13}{2}$ 5. $16 - 2(e^3 - e^{-1})$ 7. $\frac{1}{3}(2\sqrt{2} - 1)$ 9. $\frac{3}{2}$ 11. 0
13. 0   15. $(e + 1)/(3 + \ln 2)$ 17. 16   19. $\frac{16}{3}$ 21. $\frac{81}{4}$
23. $(e^x \ln x)/(1 + x^2)$ 25. $-(1 + x)/(1 - \ln x)$ 27. 0   29. $4e^{\sqrt{2}}\ln 2$
31. 950   33. 500

Exercises 2

1. 9   3. 3   5. $\frac{23}{3}$ 7. 2   9. $\frac{13}{6}$ 11. $\frac{1}{3}$ 13. $e - \frac{4}{3}$ 15. $\frac{8}{3}$
17. $\frac{1}{12}$ 19. $\frac{16}{3}$

Exercises 3

1. a. 4.8% b. $\frac{19}{60}$ 3. 210 5. 356 7. 9 years; $36 million
9. C.S. $= 16$; P.S. $= 8$ 11. C.S. $= 8000$; P.S. $= 16{,}000/3$
13. C.S. $= 178.16$; P.S. $= 45$ 17. a. $1200   b. $400   c. $80

Exercises 4

5. $y = t^3/3 + \ln|t| + C$ 7. $y = ce^{4t}$ 9. $y = -\frac{1}{2} + ce^{2t}$ 11. $y = ce^{x^2/2}$
13. $y = (1 - ce^t)^{-1}$ 15. $y = cte^{-t}$ 17. $y = e^{2-2t}$ 19. $y = e^{x^2}$
21. $y = -t - \ln(1-t)$ 23. $p = 16x^{-3/2}$ 25. $p = 100 - 0.5x$
27. a. $10{,}000e^{0.05t}$ b. $14918.25   c. 13.86 yr
29. $y = 2e^{kt}$ billion, where $k = (\ln 2)/45 = 0.01540$; In 1960, $y = 2e^{30k} = 3.17$ billion.

Review Exercises for Chapter 17

1. a. False; The statement is true only if $f(x) \geq 0$ in $a \leq x \leq b$.   b. True
   c. False; $\left(\dfrac{d}{dx}\right)\left[\displaystyle\int_a^x f(t)\,dt\right] = f(x)$.
   d. False; $\left(\dfrac{d}{dx}\right)\left[\displaystyle\int_a^b f(x)\,dx\right] = 0$ and $\displaystyle\int_a^b \left(\dfrac{d}{dx}\right)[f(x)]\,dx = f(b) - f(a)$ e. True
   f. False; $\displaystyle\int_a^b f(x)\,dx$ is always some real number.
   g. False; $\displaystyle\int_a^b f(x)\,dx = \int_a^b f(t)\,dt$.   h. True
   i. False; The given equation cannot be expressed in the form $f(y)\,dy = g(t)\,dt$.
   j. False; The given equation is of *first* order as it involves derivatives only of first order.
   k. False; It is incorrect to write $\int yt^2\,dt = y\int t^2\,dt$ since y is a function of t and may not be taken outside the integral.
3. $2\ln 2 - 1$ 5. $\frac{2}{3}$ 7. $\frac{17}{12}$ 9. $12.50   11. $10{,}000$
13. C.S. $= 24$, P.S. $= \frac{64}{3}$ 15. $y = \ln[c + (x-1)e^x]$ 17. $y = (x^2 + e^x - 1)^2$
19. $y = 2(1 - ce^{2t})^{-1}$ 21. $20{,}000   23. $t = 4$ yr; $\frac{40}{3}$ million

CHAPTER 18

Exercises 1

1. $f(3, -2) = 25$; $f(-4, -4) = 0$ 3. $f(2, 1) = \frac{2}{5}$; $f(3, \frac{1}{2}) = \frac{14}{37}$; $f(-\frac{1}{4}, \frac{3}{4}) = 0$
5. $f(1, 2, 3) = 36$; $f(-2, 1, -4) = 54$ 7. $f(\frac{1}{2}, 1, 1) = -4$; $f(\frac{1}{4}, -\frac{1}{3}, 2)$ is undefined.
9. $D = $ whole xy-plane   11. $D = \{(x, y) \mid x^2 + y^2 \geq 9\}$
13. $D = \{(x, t) \mid x - t > 0\}$ 15. $D = \{(x, y, z) \mid yz \geq 0\}$
17.   19.

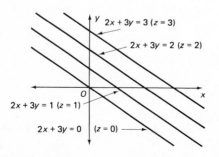

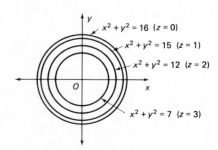

21.

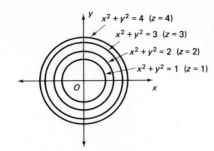

$x^2 + y^2 = 4$ $(z = 4)$
$x^2 + y^2 = 3$ $(z = 3)$
$x^2 + y^2 = 2$ $(z = 2)$
$x^2 + y^2 = 1$ $(z = 1)$

23.

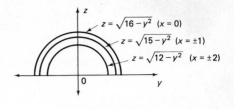

$z = \sqrt{16 - y^2}$ $(x = 0)$
$z = \sqrt{15 - y^2}$ $(x = \pm 1)$
$z = \sqrt{12 - y^2}$ $(x = \pm 2)$

25.

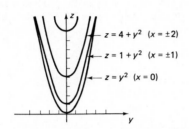

$z = 4 + y^2$ $(x = \pm 2)$
$z = 1 + y^2$ $(x = \pm 1)$
$z = y^2$ $(x = 0)$

27. $C = 4\pi r(r + h)$

29. Let x and y denote the dimensions of the base (in feet). Then
$C = 5xy + 600(1/x + 1/y)$.

31. If x units of X and y units of Y are produced, then $C = 3000 + 5x + 12y$;
$C(200, 150) = \$5800$.

33. $C(x, y) = P[2\sqrt{200^2 + x^2} + 3\sqrt{100^2 + y^2} + \sqrt{200^2 + (500 - x - y)^2}]$

Exercises 2

1. $2xy^4$; $4x^2y^3$ **3.** $\frac{1}{2}(x - y)^{-1/2}$; $-\frac{1}{2}(x - y)^{-1/2}$
5. $\frac{1}{3}(x + 2y^3)^{-2/3}$; $2y^2(x + 2y^3)^{-2/3}$ **7.** e^{x+3y}; $3e^{x+3y}$ **9.** $2xe^{-y}$; $-x^2e^{-y}$
11. $(xy + 1)y^{-1}e^{x+y}$; $x(xy - 1)y^{-2}e^{x+y}$
13. $2x \ln (x + y) + (x^2 + y^2)/(x + y)$; $2y \ln (x + y) + (x^2 + y^2)/(x + y)$
15. $(e^x + y^3)/(e^x + xy^3)$; $3xy^2/(e^x + xy^3)$ **17.** $\frac{3}{4}x^{-1/2}y^{-4}$; $-6x^{1/2}y^{-5}$
19. $-(x + 2y)^{-2}$; $-2(x + 2y)^{-2}$

Exercises 3

1. $P_L(3, 10) = 21$; $P_K(3, 10) = -29$ **3.** $P_L(2, 5) = 4$; $P_K(2, 5) = -122$
5. $P_L = 30(K/L)^{0.7}$; $P_K = 70(L/K)^{0.3}$
9. $\partial x_A/\partial p_A = -3$, $\partial x_A/\partial p_B = 1$; $\partial x_B/\partial p_A = 2$, $\partial x_B/\partial p_B = -5$; Competitive.
11. $\partial x_A/\partial p_A = -20p_B^{1/2}p_A^{-5/3}$; $\partial x_A/\partial p_B = 15p_B^{-1/2}p_A^{-2/3}$; $\partial x_B/\partial p_A = 50p_B^{-1/3}$;
$\partial x_B/\partial p_B = (-50/3)p_A p_B^{-4/3}$; Competitive.
13. $-\frac{25}{53}$; $\frac{3}{53}$ **15.** $-\frac{1}{2}$; 1 **17. a.** $-\frac{36}{359}$ **b.** $\frac{10}{359}$ **c.** $\frac{40}{359}$
19. $\eta_p = -b$, $\eta_I = c$; $p = (aI^c/r)^{1/(b+s)}$; $dp/dI = [c/(s + b)I](aI^c/r)^{1/(b+s)}$; This provides
the rate at which the equilibrium price increases w.r.t. increase in consumers' income.
21. 5.14 **23.** 4.325 **25.** 0.075 **27. a.** 5400 **b.** 5434.375 **29.** 2738.73

Exercises 4

1. Local minimum at $(0, 0)$. **3.** Local maximum at $(-\frac{2}{3}, -1)$.
5. Local minimum at $(0, 1/\sqrt{3})$; local maximum at $(0, -1/\sqrt{3})$; saddle points at
$(\pm 2/\sqrt{15}, \mp 1/\sqrt{15})$.
7. Saddle points at $(2, -1)$ and $(-\frac{2}{3}, \frac{1}{3})$.
9. Saddle points at $(\sqrt{2}, -1/\sqrt{2})$; no extrema. (Note that f is defined only for $x > 0$.)
11. $x = 10$, $y = 35$ **13.** $x = 50$, $y = 75$ **15.** $x = 2$, $y = 3$

17. 27 units of X and 30 units of Y.　　**19.** $p_1 = 20¢, p_2 = 25¢$

21. $p = 12$, $A = 1000 \ln 3$, $P_{max} = 1000(2 - \ln 3)$.

23. $x = \ln 5$, $T = 10$; $P_{max} = \$50\,(2 - \ln 5) = \$19.53$

25. Total weight is maximum when $x = (3\alpha - 2\beta)/(2\alpha^2 - \beta^2)$, $y = (4\alpha - 3\beta)/(4\alpha^2 - 2\beta^2)$, provided that $4\alpha \geq 3\beta$. (We need $\Delta = 2\alpha^2 - \beta^2 > 0$ and $x, y \geq 0$.)

27. $x = y = 8$ ft, $z = 4$ ft

Exercises 5

1. $(\frac{14}{3}, \frac{21}{13})$　　**3.** $(3, 2), (-3, -2)$　　**5.** $(2, 3, 4)$　　**7.** $(12, -9, -8, 9)$

9. $(\frac{5}{2}, -1, -\frac{3}{2})$　　**11.** $x = 120$, $y = 80$　　**13. a.** $L = 500$, $K = 50$　　**c.** $\lambda = 0.5623$

15. a. $L = 70$, $K = 30$　　**c.** $\lambda = 1.05$　　**17.** $L = 54$, $K = 16$

19. $\$2400$, $\$2880$, $\$3120$, and $\$3600$

Exercises 6

1. $y = 0.47x + 2.58$　　**3.** $y = 0.7x + 0.95$　　**5.** $y = 3.8x + 16.53$

7. a. $x = 533.45 - 111.07p$　　**b.** 200　　**c.** \$2.40

9. a. $y = 2.86x + 11.95$　　**b.** 80.6

11. $y = 42.37x + 398.3$; 14.15 ($x = 0$ corresponds to year 1956).

Review Exercises for Chapter 18

1. a. False; The range of a function $f(x, y)$ is the set of values that the function takes. It is a subset of the real numbers, not of the xy-plane.

b. False; The domain is the whole xy-plane.　　**c.** False; On x-axis, $y = z = 0$.

d. False; On yz-plane, $x = 0$.　　**e.** True　　**f.** True

g. False; If the *third* order partial derivatives of f are continuous, then it follows that $\partial^3 f / \partial x^2 \, \partial y = \partial^3 f / \partial y \partial x^2$.

h. False; $\partial/\partial x\ (x^3 y^2) = 3x^2 y^2$.　　**i.** False; $\partial/\partial y(x^2/y) = -x^2/y^2$.

j. True; Provided f is differentiable at (a, b).

k. False; The conditions stated are necessary in order that $f(x, y)$ have a local maximum, but are not sufficient. Sufficient conditions are obtained by adding the condition $f_{xx}f_{yy} - f_{xy}^2 > 0$.

l. True

m. False; If $f_x(a, b) = f_y(a, b) = 0$, then (a, b) could be a saddle point for $f(x, y)$.

n. False; For (a, b) to be a local minimum point for $f(x, y)$, we should have at (a, b), $f_x = f_y = 0, f_{xx} > 0, f_{yy} > 0$, and $f_{xx}f_{yy} - f_{xy}^2 > 0$.

o. False; The line of best fit need not pass through any data points.

p. True　　**q.** True

3. $D = \{(x, y) \mid x + y > 0 \text{ and } y \neq 0\}$

5. $D = \{(x_1, x_2, x_3) \mid x_1 + x_2 + x_3 > 0 \text{ and } x_1 > x_2\}$

7. $2xy + y^2$; $x^2 + 2xy$; $2x + 2y$; $2x$

9. $2x/(x^2 + y^2) + (y/2\sqrt{x})e^{y\sqrt{x}}$; $2y/(x^2 + y^2) + \sqrt{x}\,e^{y\sqrt{x}}$; $-4xy/(x^2 + y^2)^2 + [(1 + y\sqrt{x})/2\sqrt{x}]\,e^{y\sqrt{x}}$; $2(x^2 - y^2)/(x^2 + y^2)^2 + xe^{y\sqrt{x}}$

11. $P_x = 3y + z - 2x$; $P_y = 3x + 5z - 4y$; $P_z = 5y + x - 3z$; P_y represents the increase in profits when an additional gas pump is installed without changing the number of employees or inventory.

13. b. $\eta_{P_A} = \eta_{P_B} = \frac{1}{2}$; sum $= 1$

15. $\partial C/\partial p_A = 1.1 + 2.78p_A - 3.66p_B$; $\partial C/\partial p_B = 13.8 - 3.66p_A + 8.88p_B$; These derivatives represent the rate of change of manufacturing costs w.r.t. increases in the prices of the two products.

17. Local maximum at $(-\frac{1}{2}, 4)$.　　**19.** Saddle point at $(\frac{1}{2}, -\frac{1}{2})$.

21. 600 lb of beef and 500 lb of pork.

23. a. $x = 127$, $y = 60$; maximum profits $= \$20,438$　　**b.** $x = 96$, $y = 51$

27. $y = 1.46x - 0.60$

29. $a(x_1^4 + x_2^4 + \cdots + x_n^4) + b(x_1^3 + x_2^3 + \cdots + x_n^3) + c(x_1^2 + \cdots + x_n^2)$
$\quad = (x_1^2 y_1 + x_2^2 y_2 + \cdots + x_n^2 y_n)$
$a(x_1^3 + x_2^3 + \cdots + x_n^3) + b(x_1^2 + x_2^2 + \cdots + x_n^2) + c(x_1 + x_2 + \cdots + x_n)$
$\quad = (x_1 y_1 + x_2 y_2 + \cdots + x_n y_n)$
$a(x_1^2 + x_2^2 + \cdots + x_n^2) + b(x_1 + x_2 + \cdots + x_n) + nc = (y_1 + y_2 + \cdots + y_n)$
For the given data, these equations reduce to
$354a + 100b + 30c = 104.3$
$100a + 30b + 10c = 41.1$
$30a + 10b + 5c = 30.3$
Then $a = 0.0357$, $b = -2.09$, $c = 10.03$.

INDEX